Fodor's 2023

PARIS

Welcome to Paris

Paris is one of the most beautiful cities on earth, a truth easily appreciated on a stroll that could yield one stunning vista after another, from the epic Eiffel Tower to the regal Jardin des Tuileries to the petite cafés bursting onto the sidewalks. Beyond the city's visual appeal, the cultural riches of the French capital are unsurpassed. Whether you opt to explore the historic, fashion-conscious, bourgeois, or bohemian and arty sides of Paris, one thing is certain: the City of Light will always enthrall. As you plan your upcoming travels to Paris, please confirm that places are still open and let us know when we need to make updates by writing to us at: editors@fodors.com.

TOP REASONS TO GO

★ **Iconic Landmarks:** From the Eiffel Tower to the Arc de Triomphe, Paris dazzles.

★ **Chic Shopping:** The Champs-Élysées and Rue St-Honoré are the ultimate shopaholic high.

★ **Heavenly Food:** Whether it's haute cuisine or baguettes, locals know how to eat.

★ **The Seine:** The river's bridges and islands reward exploration by foot or boat.

★ **Grand Museums:** From the mammoth Louvre to the petite Musée Rodin, art abounds.

★ **Majestic Churches:** Notre-Dame and Sacré-Coeur boldly mark the city's skyline.

Contents

Chapter 1

EXPERIENCE PARIS

20 ULTIMATE EXPERIENCES

Paris offers terrific experiences that should be on every traveler's list. Here are Fodor's top picks for a memorable trip.

1 Luxembourg Gardens

Bordered by St-Germain-des-Prés and the Latin Quarter, these charming gardens are the definition of a true Parisian park. Here, you can relax on a lawn chair in the sunshine or enjoy an impromptu picnic. *(Ch. 12)*

2 Eiffel Tower

Whether you head to the top or pose for a photo in front, the breathtaking Eiffel Tower is the ultimate symbol of Paris for most visitors. *(Ch. 4)*

3 Parisian Cuisine

From pastries and macarons to baguettes and crêpes, food in Paris is nothing short of sublime. *(Ch. 3–14)*

5 Marché aux Puces St-Ouen

The 150-year-old market is the world's largest and maybe most famous flea market, selling everything from vintage couture to gilded mirrors and burnished silver. *(Ch. 8)*

4 Notre-Dame

Despite the 2019 fire, this cathedral is the symbolic heart of Paris and, for many, of France itself. *(Ch. 3)*

6 The Seine

There's nothing like seeing Paris via a walk or boat trip on its main waterway. Along the tranquil Seine, historic bridges connect the city's most famous landmarks. *(Ch. 3)*

7 Champs-Élysées

A mecca for shoppers (both locals and visitors alike), the Champs-Élysées remains the most famous avenue in Paris—and, perhaps, the world. *(Ch. 5)*

8 Parisian Cafés

Still the center of social life for many Parisians, neighborhood cafés offer great food and coffee, and better people-watching. *(Ch. 3–14)*

9 Montmartre

Montmartre, and other neighborhoods like Canal St-Martin and the Latin Quarter, are more like charming villages filled with shops, eateries, and cobblestone streets. *(Ch. 8)*

10 Arc de Triomphe

This colossal monument to military victory is a major landmark of the city, with excellent views from the top of all of Paris. *(Ch. 5)*

11 Opéra Garnier

Home of the Phantom of the Opera and the inspiration for Edgar Degas's dancer paintings, the dazzling Palais Garnier is one location of the National Opera of Paris. *(Ch. 7)*

12 Centre Pompidou

One of modern Paris's more controversial buildings when it was built in 1977, this art complex now houses the city's modern art museum. *(Ch. 9)*

13 Cimetière du Père-Lachaise

Perhaps the world's most famous cemetery, this oasis is the final resting place for notable figures like Marcel Proust, Oscar Wilde, Jim Morrison, and Gertrude Stein. *(Ch. 10)*

14 Musée Rodin

Once the sculptor's studio, this stately 18th-century mansion contains more than 6,000 sculptures, including Rodin's masterpieces *The Thinker* and *The Kiss*. (Ch. 4)

15 Versailles

The famous château was home to Louis XIV and Marie-Antoinette and remains the grandest palace in France, from its dazzling Hall of Mirrors to its landscaped gardens. (Ch. 15)

16 Musée D'Orsay

Under the soaring roof of one of Paris's grand Beaux-Arts railway stations, the Musée d'Orsay contains the world's largest collection of Impressionist masterpieces. (Ch. 12)

17 Musée Picasso

Home to the world's largest public collection of Pablo Picasso works, the paintings, sculptures, and drawings here span the artist's entire career. (Ch. 9)

18 Jardin des Tuileries

This quintessential French garden was once where Paris's wealthiest came to stroll, and today is still one of the city's best walks. *(Ch. 6)*

19 The Louvre

The world's greatest art museum—and the largest, with works from almost every civilization on earth—houses masterpieces like the *Mona Lisa* and the *Venus de Milo*. (Ch. 6)

20 Basilique du Sacré-Coeur

It's hard not to feel as though you're climbing up to heaven when you visit Sacred Heart Basilica, the white castle in the sky perched atop the city. *(Ch. 8)*

WHAT'S WHERE

1 Île de la Cité and Île St-Louis. Just a few steps from the "mainland," these small islands in the Seine are the heart of Paris.

2 Around the Eiffel Tower. With the Champ de Mars, Les Invalides, and the Seine nearby, many lovely strolls give you camera-ready views of Paris's ultimate monument.

3 Champs-Élysées. The Champs-Élysées and Arc de Triomphe are obvious stops for visitors, but several excellent museums here are also well worth checking out.

4 Around the Louvre. This neighborhood is paved with chic streets and *passages couverts* that attract shoppers as well as art lovers.

5 Les Grands Boulevards. Use the Palais Garnier as your landmark as you set out to do some power shopping.

6 Montmartre. Montmartre feels separate from the rest of Paris—but it's prime tourist territory, with Sacré-Coeur as its main attraction.

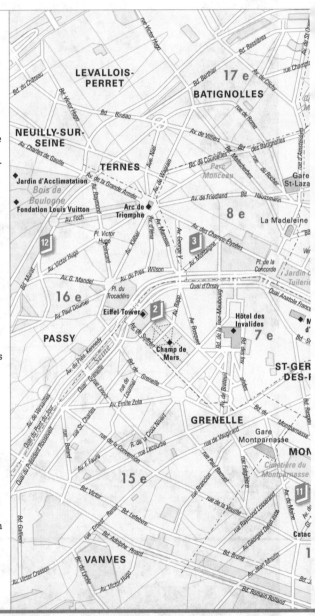

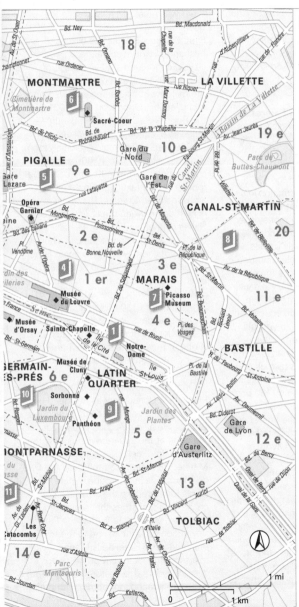

7 Le Marais. Paris's old Jewish neighborhood is now one of the city's hippest hoods. While here, visit the Musée Picasso and linger at Place des Vosges.

8 Eastern Paris. If it's new and happening, you'll find it out here. Neighborhoods like Canal St-Martin overflow with trendy eateries, funky galleries, and edgy boutiques.

9 The Latin Quarter. Built around the fabled Sorbonne, the Latin Quarter has been the center of student life since 1257. It's also home to the Panthéon and Musée de Cluny.

10 St-Germain-des-Prés. The Musée d'Orsay is a must-see, but make sure you leave time to amble through the Jardin du Luxembourg.

11 Montparnasse. Once the haunt of creative souls, Montparnasse is now known for its contemporary-art scene, as well as the Catacombs.

12 Western Paris. The Bois de Boulogne is one great reason to trek here. The popular park contains the kid-friendly Jardin d'Acclimatation and art-filled Fondation Louis Vuitton.

Paris Today

Bienvenue à Paris! Or, welcome to Paris! Although it may seem as if time stands still in this city—with its romantic buildings, elegant parks, and sublime squares—there's an undercurrent of small but significant changes happening here that might not be immediately obvious.

THE 2024 OLYMPICS

Paris is in the final stages of preparing for the 2024 Summer Olympic Games, but don't expect traffic delays or many inconveniences in the lead-up. The city will be using 95% of existing or temporary venues, making the €3.35 billion earmarked for construction lower than the €3.9 billion budget for the event itself. Compare that to the money spent on the Rio (€12.2 billion) or London (€13.5 billion) games, and the Paris games are looking downright affordable. Competitions will be scattered across the city: fencing in the Grand Palais, breakdancing at Place de la Concorde, wrestling in front of the Eiffel Tower, and equestrian matches at Versailles. The 25-year-old Stade de France will be center stage, but for the first time in Olympic history, the opening ceremony will not take place in the main stadium. Instead, national delegations will be paraded by 160 boats for 4 miles along the Seine, ending in front of the Trocadéro for the final show. In fact, the Seine may turn out to be the biggest winner at the Paris Olympics. Officials are determined to resurrect the river—"the most beautiful avenue of the capital"—to make it swimmable after nearly a hundred years. Swimming in the Seine has been banned since 1923, and the river was declared biologically dead in the 1960s. But it will be used as a venue for open-water marathons and triathlons during the 2024 Olympics, and Paris hopes that post-Games it will be open to everyone who wants to swim there.

MUSEUM RENOVATIONS

While Paris aims for a low-cost Games, there was no expense spared in the opening of two museums in spring 2021. First, François Pinault, the billionaire husband of Hollywood actress Selma Hayek, negotiated a 50-year lease of the former stock exchange to display the majority of his personal $1.45 billion art collection. Opened in May 2021, the Bourse de Commerce Museum—Pinault Collection, which includes a 75,000-square-feet main exhibition room, is home to more than 10,000 works of contemporary art by 400 artists that the founder of the luxury group Kering has amassed over 40 years. The museum is nestled between the Louvre and Les Halles district, and its on-site Halle aux Grains is already one of the city's hottest restaurants, led by award-winning father and son chefs Michel and Sébastien Bras. The second big-ticket museum, the Hôtel de la Marine, opened in June 2021 to the tune of €130 million and is one of the most expensive undertakings by the Centre des Monuments Nationaux. This is one of those Paris stories where the classic 18th century-building's history is as fascinating as the artifacts that fill it. Originally known as Place Louis XV, Place de la Concorde was designed by the king's chief architect, Ange-Jacques Gabriel. He also designed two palaces on the edge of the square: what is now the five-star Hôtel de Crillon and Hôtel de la Marine. The latter used to house the Garde-Meuble de la Couronne, where the king's furniture, like the armchairs, sofas, chairs, and tapestries that decorated the châteaux, were stored. After the French Revolution brought an end to the royal era, it became Hôtel de la Marine, headquarters of France's navy ministry for over 200 years. The restored apartments and stately reception rooms, with their furniture of silk, brocade, and damask fabrics painstakingly reupholstered as close to the original as possible, have made the Hôtel de la Marine one of the city's most prestigious monuments to visit. The loggia next to the VIP lounges offers a spectacular view of the Place de la Concorde, the Jardin des Tuileries, the Musée d'Orsay, the Grand Palais, and the Eiffel Tower. Take advantage of the headset for the full historic tour or you might miss the room in which a navy minister signed the execution warrant for Louis XVI and where he later watched the spectacle take place.

LGBTQ+ PRIDE

A study by My Dating Adviser ranked France as the fourth-best country in the world for LGBTQ+ travel. Factors ranged from societal acceptance toward homosexuality and sexual activity rights to anti-discrimination and gender identity laws. France followed Sweden, the Netherlands, and Spain as a gay-friendly destination and scored big points for its civil union (PACS) rights, same-sex marriage rights since 2013, and adoption and military service rights, which include transgender people. City Hall now organizes an annual "14th Pride" (a reference to its location in the 14th arrondissement), a two-week festival to raise public awareness of the fight against LGBTQ+ discrimination with 20 events and cultural activities, most of which are free.

In 2022, France sent a strong message to those who "consider a change of sex or identity as an illness." The National Assembly unanimously passed a law to criminalize conversion therapy, including penalties for people who are convicted of trying to "convert" LGBTQ people to heterosexuality or traditional gender expectations using scientifically discredited practices. This followed legislation in 2021 to allow lesbian couples and single women in France access to medically assisted fertility treatments for the first time.

NIGHTLIFE

Although Paris was once described by Hemingway as being "full of nocturnal pleasure-seekers," the newspaper *Le Monde* named it the "European capital of boredom" a few years ago. To help prevent the City of Light from turning into the City of Lights Out, Paris enlisted a "Nightlife Mayor" to liven things up. Clément Léon promised a revived after-dark scene to rival such Continental hot spots as Berlin, London, and Barcelona. So has Paris turned the beat around? Its exploding cocktail scene, with bitters, lime cordials, and syrups made à la maison, has certainly livened things up. And a veritable invasion of innovative chefs has helped steal the limelight from Berlin and other European culinary capitals. But with all that revelry came noise, and the city then deployed Les Pierrots de la Nuit, or night mimes, whose mission is to silently inform revelers they need to quiet down. Sadly, there may soon be no partiers to hush. After the first year of COVID, 152 of France's 1,600 nightclubs had closed down permanently and the ones that managed to stay open were subjected to on-and-off closures the following 12 months.

What to Eat and Drink in Paris

MACARONS

The French luxe variation of an Oreo cookie consists of flavored buttercream or ganache sandwiched between two gravity-defying soft-meringue shells. This is France's most popular cookie, but they tend to be expensive thanks to the ingredients and the persnickety prep required.

BAGUETTES

Biting off the end of a baguette as you leave a bakery is one of the rare times it's acceptable to eat and walk at the same time in this country. Seriously though, is there anything better than oven-fresh French bread, especially when you can buy it for an average of just one euro? *Une baguette traditionnelle* is more expensive and, by law, can only be made from flour, water, leaven, and salt. If you prefer a softer baguette, order *pas trop cuite* or if you like it crunchy, *trop cuite*. It's hard for any true French bakery to make a bad baguette, but every Parisian has their favorite.

COCKTAILS

Paris nightlife can mean a lot of different things, but if you want to get a taste of how Parisians party, you need to check out the city's cocktail scene. Over the last few years, bars here have seen a surge of mixologists take over drink menus, creating unique and impressive concoctions from a wide range of ingredients. Some of the city's most famed bars have gotten in on the action, too.

CROISSANTS

There might not be any French food more iconic than a simple croissant. Originally shaped to symbolize the Ottoman flag ensign, these days a moon-shaped croissant means it's made with margarine and, by law, must be tucked in on the ends. But between the price of butter and flour skyrocketing and industrial-made croissants with loads of preservatives finding their way into local bakeries, the buttery Gallic icon is currently in crisis. Fortunately, this is Paris, where baked-on-the-premises goods are usually available by 9 am.

WINE

From Bordeaux and Burgundy to Alsace and Beaujolais, tasting wine in Paris is a given, but *vin naturel* is de rigueur. Natural wines are considered a step up from organic, usually with low or no sulfites added. The supply of wine bars here is endless, so be sure to spend some time at one (or several) to discover how to drink like a Parisian.

COFFEE

This is how every Parisian morning should be spent: tasting glorious coffee roasts at a classic café. Coffee culture is pretty serious business in Paris, and it involves sitting or standing—not walking or driving. Most French drink *un petit café* (an espresso), but if that's too strong, order a diluted version: *un café allongé* (or *un café serré* if you need a jolt). A *café crème* is made with steamed milk, and you can sprinkle a little chocolate to make a cappuccino. A *noisette* is an espresso-sized café crème. And, an "American" is a larger cup of brewed coffee (*café dilute*).

Crêpes

PASTRIES

While you're here, throw away the Fitbit and focus on the task at hand: enjoying melt-in-your-mouth traditional pastries that you can find only in Paris. Nearly any pastry shop or bakery you visit will include typical French classics, like madeleines, *pain au chocolat*, éclairs, and profiteroles. But more unique options include *puits d'amour* ("well of love"), a puff pastry with bourbon-vanilla cream glazed with caramel, or Paris-Brest, circular cream puffs filled with praline cream and topped with hazelnuts.

HAUTE GASTRONOMY

While eating in Paris on a budget is possible, it's also very, very easy to spend a small (or large) fortune on dining here, thanks to some of the world's most extravagant, well-reviewed, and yes, expensive restaurants. Before you head off all Michelin-starry-eyed to indulge in haute cuisine, remember that the "best" restaurants in Paris can be uncomfortably ceremonious—think ornate purse stools, price-less menus, and waiters hovering to decrumb the table at every bite. There are currently 10 three-Michelin-starred restaurants in Paris, none of which could be called affordable, but all offer a level of fine dining that is hard to match anywhere else in the world.

CRÊPES

Crêpes are an essential part of French culture. You've probably heard of Pancake Tuesday, but what about Crêpe Chandeleur? A Groundhog Day–esque holiday, La Chandeleur takes place on February 2 each year; if it rains, expect another 40 days of winter. The French are superstitious about La Chandeleur; they hold a coin in their writing hand while flipping crêpes with the other. But of course, you can enjoy crêpes at any time of the year here. The golden *sucré* crêpe is wheat based and topped with sweet ingredients, while the darker galette crêpe is made from gluten-free buckwheat and is a base for savory combinations.

STEAK FRITES

Dig into a French brasserie classic dish: steak and fries. On a menu, it could be entrecôte (rib eye) or *faux filet* (strip steak), and restaurants will even list where the beef is sourced. There's usually a choice of accompanying sauce (which sometimes costs extra) like béarnaise, Roquefort, or peppercorn—or just go for au naturel. Americans have a tendency to overcook meat (*bien cuit*), but if you can't stomach *saignant* (rare), go for *moyen* (medium).

What to Buy in Paris

TEA AND COFFEE

With 800 varieties from 36 countries, French tea, including the famed Mariage Frères haute couture loose-leaf tea, has been exported globally. For coffee lovers, Café Verlet has been roasting since 1880, and large sacks of coffee beans greet you as you enter.

BERET

The one question on all our minds: can you pull off a beret if you're not actually French? The only thing we know for sure is that you should definitely try. The French couture designer Laulhère has been making the iconic disc-shaped hats since 1840. Stop by the boutique to pick up a unisex merino wool Genuine Beret (*Béret Véritable*), a steal at €79.

MARINIÈRE BRETON SWEATER

You can thank Coco Chanel for this French fashion staple (and for making the suntan "a new precedent of beauty" in the 1920s). The *marinière* striped pullover can be credited to 19th-century sailors in Brittany (aka Bretagne) who wore a layer of wool as protection from the harsh weather. But it didn't truly become part of French DNA until 1858, when the wool-knit striped *chandail* became the official naval uniform by decree: 21 white stripes (20 millimeters wide) and 21 blue stripes (10 millimeters wide), 15 white stripes and 14 or 15 blue stripes on the sleeve. According to boutique shop Saint James, which has been making marinières for 130 years, the number 21 was meant to represent the naval victories of Napoléon's fleet against the British.

FRENCH WINE

French wine is sold throughout the world, and while there's nothing like actually visiting the vineyards in Bordeaux and Burgundy, the truth is that in Paris, you're going to see a lot of what you can find at home, unless you know where to look. A good place to stock up on unique wines and rosé is Lavinia, the city's largest wine shop.

ARTWORK

Buying art in Paris requires confidence on two fronts: to get past the judgmental looks when you walk into a gallery and to not be bullied into buying something that's not a *coup de coeur*. Located atop Paris's tallest hill, Place du Tertre has attracted local artists for a century, although for Picasso, Renoir, and Van Gogh, it may have been due to Montmartre's tax-exempt wine laws. Tertre may be touristy, but what a great backdrop for your street-art caricature. Marché de la Création is an open-air art market that takes place every Sunday (10 am to 7 pm) where you can meet the artists in person. For French vintage posters, head to Marché aux Puces de St-Ouen. La Reine Margot is the oldest archaeology gallery in Paris and sells some unique pieces that will fit easily into suitcases.

MACARONS

Take a bite of this chewy soft-meringue cookie and you'll understand why it's France's best-selling biscuit. Its origins date back to 1533 Italy, but it didn't become a sandwich—two shells with flavored ganache in between—until a century ago. Not to be confused with coconut macaroons, these delicacies made of sugar, egg white, and almond flour can be sweet (salted caramel), savory (foie gras), fruity (raspberry rose), nutty (pistachio), or exotic (wasabi).

JEWELRY

Go big or go home sums up the Paris jewelry scene these days. That's not to say you need to over-accessorize—"less is more," as the fashion advice says. Named as one of the coolest jewelers by *Vogue*, Ana Khouri creates responsibly sourced rings and ear pieces to be "worn in an un-black-tie kind of way"; you can find her creations in the boutique shop White Bird. Nearby, Marie Montaud's boutique Medecine Douce lets you stock up on layered pendant necklaces in delicate gold. At the concept store Passage Doré, each collection by Louise Damas is named after a woman, because "wearing jewelry, each woman has her own story." Her exquisite bracelets, earrings, and necklaces are super-feminine and affordable.

PERFUME

Many of the perfumes you'll find in Paris have "Grasse roots." That means they're from the microclimate town of Grasse, located north of Cannes and known as the perfume capital of the world. This status is thanks to Jean de Galimard, who first invented fashionable perfumed gloves to cover the nauseating smell of tanners (workers who

used to tan leather and hides). Some 250 years later, the global perfume industry is a $39.4 billion business, with shops like Kilian selling perfume that goes for $4,200 per ounce (that would be Chanel's Grand Extrait).

ANTIQUES AND VINTAGE CLOTHING

Three words get French shoppers' hearts beating: *Grande Braderie*, which means "giant sale," and *brocante*, a secondhand market (not to be confused with *Dépôts-ventes*, or consignment stores). Marché aux Puces de St-Ouen is the mother of all flea markets with 1,500 high-end antiques dealers and 15 markets sprawling across almost 750,000 square feet. As the only market in central Paris, Marché aux Puce de la Porte de Vanves has 400 stalls with furniture, paintings, and jewelry. For the thrift-hearted, Les Puces de Montreuil is all about vintage clothes, toys, LPs, comics, and furniture. The Marché du Livre Ancien et d'Occasion at Parc de Georges Brassens attracts a European crowd for its books, old documents, vinyl records, and photos.

DESIGNER CLOTHING

Rule number one for dressing like a Parisian: learn to mix casual and dressy, and it doesn't have to be haute couture expensive. Cuisse de Grenouille is a great place to start because the collegiate but feminine cuts are very French without straying too far from an American comfort level. The moderately priced

Beret

Sessùn requires a little more confidence to pull off the eclectic and flowing designs, but you'll be complimented back home for your unique style. And, of course, if you really want to break the bank, you'll have plenty of flagship stores from world-famous designers to browse. Create your own Paris Fashion Week by checking out the haute couture at stores like Chanel, Dior, Saint Laurent, and Hermès. If you prefer one-stop shopping, the department store La Samaritaine finally reopened in June 2021 after a billion-dollar, 16-year renovation. Owned by LVMH and home to 600 brands, there's little chance you will leave without purchases in hand.

LINGERIE

The French are known for being a little more liberal than Americans when it comes to all things sex, so it makes sense that lingerie shops abound in Paris. And we're not talking Victoria's Secret; these are high-fashion, custom-made pieces that are nothing short of works of art. And there are options if you're looking for something provocative and seductive but a little more affordable.

Best Museums in Paris

MUSÉE JACQUEMART-ANDRÉ

This museum was created from the private home—and private collections—of 19th-century Parisians Edouard André and Nélie Jacquemart and is as much a reflection of the lifestyle of the 19th-century Parisian bourgeoisie as it is of the art housed within it.

CENTRE POMPIDOU

Home to the largest modern art museum in Europe, the Pompidou Center is known for its extensive temporary exhibits, often devoted entirely to the work of just one artist. The center itself is a true work of art as well.

CITÉ DES SCIENCES ET DE L'INDUSTRIE

The City of Science and Industry is the largest science museum in Europe, located within the expansive Villette Park in Paris's 19e arrondissement. Particularly popular among children, the Cité des Sciences is home to a planetarium, IMAX Theater, and greenhouse spaces.

THE LOUVRE

Housed within the former royal palace of France's royalty is the Louvre Museum, a collection of more than 380,000 works of art from all over the world. Its most famous pieces include Leonardo da Vinci's *Mona Lisa* and the Venus de Milo.

MUSÉE RODIN

Auguste Rodin is one of France's most well-known sculptors, and this museum, located in the artist's former home not far from Les Invalides, contains one of the most extensive collections of his work. The museum's collections are displayed both within the house and in the expansive private garden outside; there is also a room devoted to the work of Camille Claudel, Rodin's lover and coworker.

PICASSO MUSEUM

Housed within a former private mansion, the collection here includes more than 5,000 of Picasso's works, including many of his larger sculptures. The museum also features pieces from Picasso's own art collection, including works by Cézanne, Degas, and Matisse.

The Louvre

MUSÉE DE L'ORANGERIE

This small museum within the Tuileries Gardens is a former orangery—or citrus greenhouse—transformed into an art gallery devoted to Impressionist and Postimpressionist paintings. The jewel of these collections is the series of eight water lily paintings by Claude Monet: the massive paintings have been permanently glued to the walls of the oval rooms specifically designed to house them.

MUSÉE DE CLUNY

The Musée de Cluny, also known as the Musée National du Moyen Age, is a museum devoted to medieval history and art. Housed within the medieval Hôtel de Cluny and sitting atop the remnants of third-century Gallo-Roman baths, the building itself is as historic as its collections.

MEMORIAL DE LA SHOAH

Paris's Marais has long been the Jewish quarter of Paris, so it's only appropriate that it be home to this memorial and museum to Jewish life during World War II. Opened by President Jacques Chirac, the first French president to publicly apologize for the acts of the French government contributing to the Holocaust; the memorial notably features a wall listing the names of the approximately 76,000 French Jews who were deported and murdered during the Shoah.

MUSÉE D'ORSAY

The Musée d'Orsay houses mostly French works dating from 1848 to 1914 within a former railway station, the Gare d'Orsay. The most famous works here are the pieces that make up the extensive Impressionist collections.

Best Churches in Paris

ST-DENIS BASILICA AND ROYAL NECROPOLIS

From 987 to 1789, the kings and queens of France knew where they would end up: a distinguished burial at St-Denis Basilica. The birthplace of Gothic art, the basilica, 5 km (3 miles) north of Paris, now boasts the first cross-ribbed vault ever built in France.

SACRÉ-COEUR BASILICA

Some 10 million tourists trek up to Montmartre every year (either via the 222 stairs or by funicular) to visit the Sacred Heart of Paris. Unlike other churches in Paris, the basilica features Romanesque-Byzantine architecture, similar to San Marco in Venice.

LA SAINTE-CHAPELLE

You are here for the magnificent medieval stained glass, all 1,113 panes depicting stories from both the New and Old Testaments. La Saint-Chapelle was built between 1242 and 1248 to accommodate the Passion relics that were purchased by King Louis IX in 1239.

ÉGLISE DE LA MADELEINE

Built between 1754 and 1842 and surrounded by 52 Corinthian columns standing 65 feet tall, Église de la Madeleine was intended to be a temple of glory to honor Napoléon's Great Army. In 1806, Napoléon brought architect Pierre-Alexandre Vignon onboard, who drew inspiration from the Temple of Olympian Zeus in Athens to create the Madeleine we know today. After Napoléon's fall, King Louis XVIII ordered the neoclassical building to serve as a functioning church.

SAINT-EUSTACHE PARISH

At 346 feet in length, the dimensionally impressive Saint-Eustache in Les Halles features a range of architectural styles due to being built in 1532 (Louis XIV received communion here) and then restored in 1840. Saint-Eustache's central Chapel of the Blessed Virgin, with its marble Pigalle statue, was inaugurated by Pope Pius VII when he was in town for Napoléon's coronation. Music is a key element of the church's history. Mozart attended his mother's funeral at Saint-Eustace, and in 1855, Berlioz first conducted "Te Deum" with some 900 performers.

SAINT-ÉTIENNE-DU-MONT

Behind the Panthéon in the Latin Quarter, you'll find Saint-Étienne-du-Mont and within it, Paris's last Renaissance rood screen. The finely carved stone structure spans the entire

Église Saint-Sulpice

width of the nave between the north and south walls. Built in the 1530s, the church contains a mix of Gothic and Renaissance artwork and houses the remains of Genevieve, a patron saint of Paris.

ÉGLISE SAINT-SULPICE

Steps from Église St-Germain-des-Prés, the second-tallest church in Paris is famous for its gnomon, which played a role (although factually inaccurate) in the book and film *The Da Vinci Code*. The Église Saint-Sulpice was also where writer Victor Hugo was married. Building started on the Baroque church and its two distinctive mismatched towers in 1646, but it would take almost 100 years to complete. Today it features three paintings by Delacroix in the Chapelle des Anges to the right of the entrance.

CHAPELLE EXPIATOIRE

Built at the request of Louis XVIII to expiate his brother, this neoclassical chapel is where Louis XVI and Marie-Antoinette were buried after their 1793 execution (eventually their remains were moved to the Basilica of St-Denis). Constructed between 1816 and 1826, the Chapelle Expiatoire is a small historic monument with not much to see besides the crypt and a marble sculpture of Louis XVI and Marie-Antoinette. What makes it fascinating is the 2018 discovery that this was the site of the cemetery where 3,000 bodies were thrown after being guillotined at the Place de la Concorde.

ÉGLISE ST-GERMAIN-DES-PRÉS

Originally an abbey founded in 543 dating back to the first kings of France, the oldest church in Paris is one of the city's first examples of Gothic architecture. Église St-Germain-des-Prés has witnessed everything from Viking ransacks to the manslaughter of monks.

Best Parks and Gardens in Paris

PALAIS-ROYAL
Across from the Louvre, the Palais-Royal, with its three magnificent arcades, is the only garden in Paris with the distinction of "Remarkable Garden" by the French Ministry of Culture. Not solely a favorite spot for locals and tourists to hang out, many movies have been filmed here too, including *The Da Vinci Code* and *Interview with the Vampire*.

BOIS DE BOULOGNE
Paris's second largest park used to be a hunting ground for kings of France, but now it mostly attracts art lovers (courtesy of the acclaimed Fondation Louis Vuitton located in the northern part of the park) and nature lovers (thanks to the bridle paths and cycling routes throughout).

JARDIN DES TUILERIES
Nestled between the Louvre and Place de la Concorde, the Tuileries Garden was actually the site of an old tile (*tuile*) factory before the Palais des Tuileries was built in 1564. A century later, King Louis XIV's gardener designed it in the style of a formal French garden, but it wouldn't be until after the French Revolution that it became a public park.

PARC DE LA VILLETTE
At 135 acres, Parc de la Villette is the largest in Paris. It boasts not only 35 green spaces, including several themed gardens like the bamboo garden, the garden of mirrors, and the dragon's garden, but also several art spaces, like the Geode cinema, the Zenith concert hall, and the Paris Philharmonic.

LUXEMBOURG GARDENS

Once upon a time, this 62-acre garden on the Left Bank was the pride of Luxembourg Palace. A central pond divides the space into the geometrically correct French garden and the charming English garden with its 106 statues, apple orchard, and apiary.

JARDIN DES PLANTES

This 400-year-old botanical garden dedicated to scientific research is located in front of the Grande Galerie de l'Evolution, one of three buildings that make up the National Museum of Natural History in the heart of the city.

PARC DES BUTTES-CHAUMONT

The typical *guinguette* of the Camargue in Southern France has been transported to Paris with Rosa Bonheur, a café and wine bar located within the Parc des Buttes-Chaumont. This 19e arrondissement park, a local favorite, is home to one of the highest hills in the city.

COULÉE VERTE

The former railroad line taking well-to-do Parisians to the Vincennes woods has been closed to trains and open to pedestrians: bit by bit, the city is turning these former tracks into parks, one of the most beautiful of which is located near Bastille.

CHAMP DE MARS

Forget the long lines at the Eiffel Tower and head to nearby Champ de Mars, one of the largest outdoor green spaces in Paris. Picnic on the vast lawns or stroll in the gardens and enjoy the Iron Lady like a Parisian. Even better, come after sunset and watch from a perfect perch as the tower's 20,000 lights sparkle for five minutes, every hour on the hour.

PARC MONCEAU

Dating back to the 17th century, this could well be the most elegant garden in Paris. Wrought-iron gates adorned in gold, a Renaissance archway, gorgeous statues, and magnificent trees are all here.

Under-the-Radar Paris

École de Cuisine Alain Ducasse

GO SWIMMING

Opened in 1924, all three pools of the picturesque indoor-outdoor Butte-aux-Cailles complex are fed by an underground spring. Care to swim in the Seine? Afloat on the river (but not in it, whew!), the popular Piscine Joséphine Baker is the next best thing, with a retractable roof that keeps sunbathers happy. The Piscine Molitor is open to guests at the MGallery Hotel only, but it may be worth the splurge for a dip in Paris's most glamorous pool.

WATCH A FILM AT A HISTORIC MOVIE THEATER

The Louxor cinema, a masterpiece of Egyptian-inspired Art Deco architecture, is a designated historic monument situated in the scruffy but up-and-coming Pigalle neighborhood. Dating from 1932, the illustrious Grand Rex on Grands Boulevards boasts Europe's largest screening room with 2,800 seats and Baroque-inspired decor. For strictly-English speakers, the company Lost in Frenchlation holds screenings of the latest French films with English subtitles at independent cinemas in Paris.

The Louxor

TAKE A COOKING CLASS

Whether it's a feather-weight *macaron* or buttery croissant, after a few hours at Le Foodist, you'll be ready to impress your friends with culinary skills acquired firsthand in Paris. At the École de Cuisine Alain Ducasse you can learn to make a baguette or the secrets of bistro or haute cuisine. Though pricier, the classes are also taught in English and are backed by a name synonymous with French cooking.

DANCE THE NIGHT AWAY

To celebrate Bastille Day, two nights a year—on either July 13 or 14—every city hall in Paris and its suburbs hosts a *bal des pompiers* (firemen's ball), starting at 9 pm and lasting into the wee hours of the morning. Once a month at the marvelous 104 Centquatre-Paris, one of the city's reigning contemporary arts centers, locals gather under garlands of lights to dance to live music. The *bals pop* are free and have a different theme each month, listed on the Centquatre website.

EXPLORE AN ABANDONED RAILWAY

Part of a huge, many-year restoration project spearheaded by Paris City Hall, La Petite Ceinture (Little Belt), a 30-km-long (19-mile-long) abandoned railway that rings the city, is Paris's final green frontier. The newest portion of the park, referred to as the "green lung," is located in the 20e arrondissement from Rue de la Mare and Rue Ménilmontant. Adventurers can hop in anywhere along the line to find the favorite lairs of Paris graffiti artists and hidden entrances to the Catacombs.

VISIT A VILLAGE WITHIN THE CITY

On any sunny day in the Mouzaïa (also known as the Quartier d'Amérique), the sound of birdsong fills the air as residents tend their luxuriant gardens. A slice of the countryside in Paris, this is one of the city's last hidden neighborhoods, where nearly 300 unique cottages, dating from the late 19th and early 20th centuries, were built over Paris's old gypsum quarries.

An Art Lover's Guide to Paris

59 Rivoli

LE 104

Centquatre–Paris is a cultural arts center in the 19e arrondissement that was converted from a former municipal morgue around 1905. The monumental, open steel-and-glass space covers 420,000 square feet, more than enough for its countless events.

STREET ART ON RUE ST-MAUR

The 2½-km (1½-mile) stretch along Rue St-Maur in the 10e and 11e arrondissements offers an insider's view of Parisian street art. The street is lined by a variety of art, from popular female artist Kashink to portraits by Shepard Fairey, the graphic designer behind former President Obama's now-iconic "Hope" campaign posters.

59 RIVOLI

For years, artists were illegally squatting in an abandoned bank building located at 59 rue de Rivoli, but their work attracted 40,000 visitors in 2001 alone, which made the space the third most visited center for contemporary art in Paris. The city bought the building in 2006 and reopened it three years later, renting 30 studios to artists who pay minimal rent.

Musée d'Orsay

THE BIG FOUR OF MUSEUMS
No art lover should miss the usual suspects for art in Paris—the Louvre, Musée d'Orsay, Centre Pompidou, and Musée de l'Orangerie—but you should recognize that they come at a cost: crowds. Look for temporary exhibits and book tickets online in advance.

HAUT MARAIS
The tiny streets that run from the Musée Picasso to the Place de la République make up the golden triangle of Paris's coolest designer district, Haut Marais. For a long time, the area was an unexceptional working-class neighborhood. But that changed in 2009 when Marie-France Cohen converted an old wallpaper factory into her fashion and decor shop, Merci. Since then the NoMa, as Haut Marais is called, has exploded with sophisticated bistros, Made in Paris designer shops, and contemporary art galleries.

ARTIST-FOCUSED MUSEUMS
At Musée Rodin, Dalí Paris, Musée Gustave Moreau, and Musée Marmottan Monet, you'll get a deep dive into one particular artist. In many cases, the mansions they're housed in are as intriguing as the art collections themselves.

FONDATION LE CORBUSIER
The apartment-studio where this Swiss-French designer lived with his wife for more than three decades makes for a fascinating visit for art lovers. The modern building, "Immeuble Molitor," was designed by Le Corbusier himself in the 1930s and today is an UNESCO World Heritage site.

L'ATELIER DES LUMIÈRES
Paris's first digital art museum, the Atelier des Lumières uses 140 laser video projectors to create an immersive, three-dimensional, floor-to-ceiling art experience across 30-foot-high walls.

PALAIS DE TOKYO
Steps from the Eiffel Tower, the Palais de Tokyo is the largest center of contemporary art in Europe. The original Palais de Tokyo was built for the 1937 International Exposition of Art and Technology in Modern Life.

Paris with Kids

Paris may be an adult playground, but there's no shortage of children's activities to keep the young ones busy—many of the city's top attractions have carousels parked outside them in summer.

MUSEUMS

Paris has a number of museums that cater to the young and young at heart. They're great places to occupy restless minds, especially if the weather is unfavorable. The Parc de la Villette's **Cité des Sciences et de l'Industrie** is an enormous science center with a kids' area that's divided into two main sections: one for 2- to 7-year-olds, another for the 5-to-12 set. Interactive exhibits let inquisitive young visitors do everything from building a house to learning about communications through the ages. The **Cité de la Musique,** also in the Parc de la Villette, will appeal to more arts-minded children, while the **Palais de la Découverte** has high-definition, 3-D exhibits covering subjects like chemistry, biology, meteorology, and physics. Many of the displays are in French, but that doesn't stop most kids from having a blast—the choice between this and the Louvre is a no-brainer. The **Musée de l'Homme** was previously an anthropological museum but now it's supremely kid-friendly, where little ones can shake hands with a Neanderthal man, sample some of 7,000 languages, and enjoy plenty of interactive exhibits. For more interactive fun, the privately owned museum **Choco Story de Paris** is a crowd-pleaser with 600 pounds of chocolate monuments; visits include tastings, of course.

ZOOS

Visiting a zoo is usually a good way to get kids' attention, although you might want to keep in mind that most European ones aren't as spacious as their American counterparts. As part of the **Muséum National d'Histoire Naturelle** (with its own exceptional butterfly collection and Gallery of Paleontology and Comparative Anatomy with too many bones on display to count), the **Ménagerie** at the Jardin des Plantes is an urban zoo dating from 1794 and is home to more than 200 mammals, nearly 300 birds, 200 reptiles, and 300 insects. The **Parc Zoologique** in the city's largest park, Bois de Vincennes, lets you observe animals in realistic habitats. The **Musée de la Chasse et de la Nature** in the Marais is another place to get up close and personal with ferocious lions, tigers, and one in-your-face polar bear—the only catch being that these aren't alive. The impressive collection of taxidermy trophies takes children on a safari to discover man's relationship with animals.

SHOWS

What child could pass up the circus? There are several in the city, including perennial favorites **Espace Chapiteaux** at the Parc de la Villette and **Cirque d'Hiver de Bouglione** near Place de la République. For traditional entertainment, try **L es Guignols,** French puppet shows. The original Guignol was a marionette character created by Laurent Mourguet, supposedly in his own likeness, celebrating life, love, and wine. Today, shows are primarily aimed at children and are found in open-air theaters throughout the city in the warmer months. Check out the Marionettes des Champs-Élysées, Champ de Mars, Parc Montsouris, Parc des Buttes-Chaumont, Jardin du Luxembourg, and the Parc Floral in the Bois de Vincennes. Even if they don't understand French, kids are usually riveted.

UNDERGROUND PARIS

There's something about exploring underground that seems to fascinate kids, at least the older ones. **Les Égouts** allows a peek into the storied Paris sewer tunnels that harbored revolutionaries on the run throughout the ages. At the redesigned **Catacombs,** in Montparnasse, dark tunnels filled with skulls and skeletons of 6 million Parisians are spookily titillating—provided you're not prone to nightmares. For some cheap underground entertainment without the ick factor, the **métro** itself can be its own sort of adventure, complete with fascinating station art such as the submarine decor at Arts-et-Métiers, the colorful Parisian timeline murals at Tuileries, or the Egyptian statues of the Louvre–Rivoli station. A good tip: *métro* lines 1, 4, and 14 feature driverless trains that let you sit at the very front, and kids love the sensation that they're the conductor.

ACTIVE OPTIONS

Many kids are oddly thrilled at the prospect of climbing countless stairs just to get a cool view. The **Eiffel Tower** is the quintessential Paris climb (especially now that the first level boasts a dizzying glass floor), and the **Arc de Triomphe** is a good bet, since it's at the end of the Champs-Élysées. Parks offer other opportunities for expending energy. In summer, kids can work off steam on trampolines or ride ponies at the **Jardin des Tuileries**; the **Jardin du Luxembourg** has a playground and a pond where they

can rent miniature boats; and the **Bois de Boulogne** has real rowboats, bumper cars, and lots of wide-open spaces. For rainy-day rescues, La Galerie des Enfants at the **Pompidou Centre** has a children's play gallery, with activities tied to the current exhibitions. In winter, consider ice-skating. From mid-December through January several outdoor sites (including one in front of the Eiffel Tower) transform into spectacular rinks with twinkling lights, music, and rental skates available.

SWEET TREATS

All that activity will no doubt make kids hungry, and luckily there's no shortage of special places to stop for a snack. Crêperies always aim to please, and you'll find plenty along the main tourist streets. Also be on the lookout for hot chocolate—the French puddinglike version is deliciously rich and thick, unlike what American children are usually used to. You'll also find plenty of places offering decadent ice cream. French children adore the pastel clouds of meringue that decorate almost every pâtisserie window—and, when in need, a chocolate croissant is never hard to find. After filling up, you can cap the day with perhaps the best treat of all, a **boat ride on the Seine.** It's the perfect way to see the sights while resting weary feet.

What to Read and Watch

AMÉLIE

Nominated for five Academy Awards, this 2001 French romantic comedy is perhaps the best-known cinematic export to many Americans. The film tells the story of a shy waitress, played by Audrey Tautou, who decides to make the lives of those around her better while trying to cope with her own isolation. The movie spotlights the colorful Montmartre neighborhood where Amélie lives; her place of work, Cafe de 2 Moulins, is a real place, too, but don't expect any of the waitresses there to change your life.

A MOVEABLE FEAST BY ERNEST HEMINGWAY

This memoir was first published in 1964, three years after Hemingway died by suicide. His series of vignettes set in Paris in the early 1920s is so perfect, many consider it one of the best books about Paris ever written. With specific addresses of cafés, bars, and places he lived, you can retrace the journey of one of the most prolific writers of the 20th century, who captured the directionless wanderings of the lost generation so well.

THE AUTOBIOGRAPHY OF ALICE B. TOKLAS BY GERTRUDE STEIN

Gertrude Stein admitted to writing this book in six weeks to make a quick buck, and Alice B. Toklas, Stein's life partner, didn't think the story would be a success. Nevertheless, Modern Library has ranked it as one of the 20 greatest nonfiction books of the 20th century. Narrated by Toklas, the book describes the couple's life together in Paris at 27 rue de Fleurus as they rub elbows with some of Paris's great artistic elites and live through WWI while volunteering for the war effort.

THE ELEGANCE OF THE HEDGEHOG BY MURIEL BARBERY

First released in 2006, Muriel Barbery's book became an instant success in France and has been translated into more than 40 languages. It's the story of a concierge at 7 rue de Grenelle in Paris who keeps her intelligence concealed until the 12-year-old daughter of rich upper-class tenants uncovers her aptitude. The events and ideas of the novel touch on philosophy, personal conflict, and class-consciousness through the thoughts and reactions of the two main characters.

EMILY IN PARIS

This 2020 Netflix series starring Lily Collins (daughter of rocker dad Phil) had Parisians up in arms over its portrayal of French stereotypes. Created by Darren Star of Sex and the City fame, the show follows Chicagoan Emily Cooper, who lands her dream job at a French luxury marketing company in the City of Light. The questionably fashioned millennial believes that her American work ethic and can-do smile will win over the office.

GIOVANNI'S ROOM BY JAMES BALDWIN

Baldwin moved to Paris in 1948 and eight years later, at age 32, he published this controversial second novel, a fictional story with what many called explicit homoerotic content. Narrated by an American expat living in Paris, the main character, David, struggles with his sexuality and his internalized shame. He succumbs to social pressure and proposes to Hella, but when she goes away on a trip, David starts a tormented affair with Giovanni, an Italian bartender. Repressing his homosexuality, he leaves Giovanni for Hella until she discovers his secret. Baldwin always maintained a connection to France. In 1970, he moved to the artistic enclave Saint-Paul-de-Vence in the south of France.

GIGI

Remember "Thank Heaven for Little Girls"? This is the movie that song comes from. Perhaps Maurice Chevalier's most celebrated song, this musical follows the story of Gigi, who is sent to live with her aunt to learn the ways of high French society. Although the title song does not stand the test of time and seems quite creepy now, watch the movie if only to see the sparkling charm of Maurice Chevalier and what the Paris of the elites would have looked like at the turn of the century.

GIRLHOOD

This 2014 drama shows a side of Paris far from the Arc de Triomphe and Louvre. Directed by Celine Sciamma, *Girlhood* is a coming-of-age film that tells the story of Marieme, a young Black girl who lives in a rough suburb of Paris. It discusses the perceptions of race, gender, and class that all of France and Europe at large are experiencing now.

LA VIE EN ROSE

It's hard to think of any unofficial anthem for Paris other than the song "La Vie en Rose." The opening notes from the accordion are as emblematic of the city as a beret and baguette. In 2007, Olivier Dahan wrote and directed this stunning biopic on one of France's iconic singers, Edith Piaf. Piaf did not live a charmed life: she grew up a street urchin in Paris, lived through the Nazi occupation, and her love life was heartbreaking, as was her eventual death. Marion Cotillard won an Oscar for her performance in the title role.

LES MISÉRABLES BY VICTOR HUGO

Victor Hugo's novel is widely considered one of the greatest novels of the 19th century, a love story that has been adapted to stage, television, and film. Forget reality TV, this storyline includes lies, theft, pregnancy, justice, and lots of secrets. Set against the backdrop of the June Rebellion of 1832, this is the story of Jean Valjean, who agrees to care for a factory worker's daughter while being hunted down by a policeman named Javert over the course of several decades.

MOULIN ROUGE!

Paris's most famous nightclub and its racy cancan dancers have symbolized a frenzied vision of turn-of-the-century Paris that endures to this day. Baz Luhrmann's 2001 splashy and colorful jukebox musical brings the decadence of the club back to life. Starring Ewan McGregor as a young English poet who falls for cabaret performer and courtesan Nicole Kidman, the film is a whirlwind of boy meets girl and then desperately tries to hold on to that girl.

PARIS STORIES BY MAVIS GALLANT

Celebrated Canadian writer and *New Yorker* contributor Mavis Gallant, who died in 2014 at age 91, spent most of her life in Paris. This series of short stories, selected by Michael Ondaatje, another feted Canadian author, are her most memorable and run the gamut from mysterious to funny as they weave together a tale of the city through the eyes of expats, exiles, children, and wayward saints. The stories form a literary mosaic of a dynamic city in modern times.

PARISIANS: AN ADVENTURE HISTORY OF PARIS BY GRAHAM ROBB

You could spend a lifetime trying to study the history of Paris, but Graham Robb tries to do it through a series of engaging factual stories of various characters who lived in the city. Adulterers, policemen, murderers, prostitutes, and revolution- aries all get a turn as Robb spans the centuries, from 1750 to the present day. The end result not only shows the varied personalities of the City of Light, but also the many events that shaped the city, from the Terror to the May '68 revolt, which took the country to the brink of civil war.

PARIS JE T'AIME

A city like Paris has a thousand stories. The 2006 movie *Paris, je t'aime* contains 18 of them. This anthology film was originally meant to have 20 stories, one for each arrondissement in Paris, but the 15e and 11e arrondissement shorts could not be integrated into the final film. The plots are as eclectic as the different writ- ers and directors who were selected for each vignette. From the Cohen brothers to Japanese director Nobuhiro Suwa, each little film within this big film paints a distinct portrait of Paris.

THE PARIS WIFE BY PAULA MCLAIN

While a great writer, Ernest Hemingway was a poor boxer and an even worse husband. Paula McLain's 2011 best seller is a fictionalized account of Hemingway's first marriage to Hadley Richardson. The narrator is Richardson, who describes her marriage and life in Paris in the early 1920s. Eventually their nuptials fall apart when Hemingway has an affair with her friend, but along the way, they meet famous expats like Gertrude Stein, F. Scott Fitzgerald, and James Joyce.

RATATOUILLE

This 2007 Pixar animated film tells the story of a gastronomically talented rat who stumbles into the path of Linguini, a young man working in one of Paris's fanciest restaurants. While hiding under Linguini's hat, Remy the rat pulls the strings leading to eventual haute cuisine success. Prior to filming, the director and several crew members spent a week in Paris eating at several top restaurants. Sadly, they did not interview any Parisian rats while there.

THE RED BALLOON

If you've taken a high school French class then you have seen *The Red Balloon*. This 1956 French fantasy/comedy/drama follows the adventures of a young boy who one day finds a sentient, mute red balloon. Writer and director Albert Lam- orisse cast his own children as the two main protagonists. It was filmed in the Belleville area of Paris, but much of what you see no longer exists thanks to the city's effort to rebuild the once-decaying neighborhood.

Chapter 2

TRAVEL SMART

2

Updated by
Nancy Heslin

★ **CAPITAL:**
Paris

POPULATION:
2.17 million

LANGUAGE:
French

$ **CURRENCY:**
Euro

☎ **COUNTRY CODE:**
33

⚠ **EMERGENCIES:**
112

🚗 **DRIVING:**
On the right side of the road

⚡ **ELECTRICITY:**
220 v/50 cycles; Continental-type plugs, with two round prongs

⏲ **TIME:**
6 hours ahead of New York

🌐 **WEB RESOURCES:**
en.parisinfo.com;
www.visitparisregion.com;
www.paris.fr

Know Before You Go

As one of the biggest, most fabulous cities in the world, it's easy to feel like you know Paris without ever having been there. And while the capital of France will do its best to welcome you with open arms, it's always helpful to come equipped with some tips and tricks for fitting in like a Parisian.

SAVING MONEY

Buy tickets online when you can; most cultural centers, museums, and tour companies offer reduced ticket sales in advance, and the small service fee you'll pay will probably be worth the time saved waiting in line. Look for alternative entrances at popular sights, and check when rates are reduced, often during once-a-week evening openings. National museums are free the first Sunday of each month (this includes the Louvre, Musée d'Orsay, and Centre Pompidou). The Paris Museum Pass lets you bypass lines at major attractions; the two-, four-, and six-day passes cost €52, €66, and €78, respectively. The Paris Pass offers the perks of the Museum Pass plus a Travelcard for free unlimited travel across Central Paris on the métro, RER, and buses. Adult rates start at €109 and are valid for two years with a 90-day money-back guarantee.

NAVIGATION

Thanks to Baron Haussmann's mid-19th-century redesign, Paris is a compact wonder of wide boulevards, gracious parks, and leafy squares. And without question, the best way to explore it is on foot. The city is divided into 20 arrondissements (neighborhoods) spiraling out from the center of the city. The numbers reveal the neighborhood's location and its age, with the 1er arrondissement at the city's heart being the oldest and where you'll find the Palais Royal and Place Vendôme. The arrondissements in central Paris—the 1er to 8e—are the most visited. Keep in mind that the city is more walkable than you think: the entire length of the Champs-Élysées (8e) is only 2 km (1 mile), and to go from Notre-Dame (4e) to the Louvre (1er) is even less than that, although walking to the Eiffel Tower from Notre-Dame would take longer (about 2½ km [1½ miles]).

LANGUAGE

The French are big on ceremony, whether it's a kiss on each cheek as a greeting or saying "Mesdames, Messieurs" (ladies and gentlemen) when walking into a store or a doctor's office. As a tourist, you'll be fine with the basics. Stick with "bonjour" when you enter a shop or boulangerie. Say "merci" every time someone serves you a coffee or brings you change. This gesture of solidarity can really go a long way here. But be prepared, because no matter how nice you are or how often you try to speak French un peu, the French can be notoriously surly, especially those you come across working in retail and restaurants (customer service does not exist in France).

DINING RULES

Forget about formal table manners (although those are always invaluable); there are more pressing issues to learn when it comes to eating out in Paris. Let's start with baby steps: when to eat. Most restaurants are open for lunch (noon to 2) and dinner (starting at 8 pm). That means many places will be closed entirely from 2 until 8. But if dinner at 6 pm is a must for you, don't fret—eateries in touristy areas tend to serve nonstop throughout the day. For Parisians, a predinner apéro—drinks and snacks with friends—starts at 7. Secondly, leave the picky-eating culture at home; yes, that means abandoning your no wheat, no dairy, no fat diet, and forget ordering off menu. You can ask for dairy-free sauce, but regardless what the server says, you'll most likely be served the same sauce from the same saucepan as everyone else. This can be a serious issue for those with severe food allergies; even if you're able to articulate your issue in French, not all places take allergies as seriously as they do in the United States. People with severe food allergies are better off preparing their meals at their lodging or eating at vegan or organic shops and bakeries; these eateries tend to be more upfront with their ingredients, and their staff are more in tune with health concerns.

Also, eat slowly—there are only two services for dinner so there's lots of time—and don't be embarrassed to order tap water (*une carafe d'eau*) instead of forking out for the bottled stuff. Also, and this is a biggie, don't do work or touch documents when you're eating a meal or you'll be the recipients of many gasps. And to really blend in, make sure you order your tea or coffee after your dessert. Earn brownie points by ordering the plat du jour and break off an extra piece of bread to wipe the plate clean (but never butter your bread!). Typically, tipping is included with a meal's price and is not an incentive for better service. Feel free to leave 5%–10% if the service is excellent. But here's the biggest tip: dress nicely, and if you are with your kids, don't let them run wild.

CLOSURES
Paris is by no means a 24/7 city, so planning your days beforehand can save you some aggravation. Museums are closed one day a week (usually Monday or Tuesday), and most stay open late at least one night each week, which is also the least crowded time to visit. Store hours are generally 9:30 or 10 am to 7 or 8 pm, Monday through Saturday, although post offices, banks, and smaller shops may close for several hours during the afternoon. Department stores—including Galeries Lafayette and Printemps—are open on Sundays, and along the Champs-Élysées, the Marais, Montmartre, and the Latin Quarter, you'll find shops that usually open around 2 pm on Sunday.

In France, summertime (particularly August) is when many businesses shut down for their month-long *fermeture annuelle*, or annual holiday, and residents escape to the countryside. Museums, monuments, and attractions operate as usual, but if there's a certain restaurant you've been dying to try, it's best to confirm in advance it's open in August. There are also 11 national holidays throughout the year. In May there's a holiday nearly every week, so be prepared for stores, banks, and post offices to shut their doors for days at a time. If a holiday falls on a Tuesday or Thursday, many businesses close on that Monday or Friday as well. Bastille Day (July 14) is still observed in true French form. Celebrations begin on the evening of the 13th, when some city firefighters open the doors to their stations, often classed as historical monuments, to host their much-acclaimed all-night balls and finish the next day with the annual military parade and air show.

THE MÉTRO
Taxis in France are ridiculously expensive (and there's a fierce war against Uber), so the *métro* is a practical and often economical way to travel around the city. The walking distance to the next métro is never more than a quarter mile, and it will get you just about anywhere you want to go for €1.90 a ride (the famed carnet, or "pack" of 10 paper tickets, was phased out in 2022 and replaced with contactless tickets, 10 for €14.90); tickets also work on buses, trams, and the RER train line within Paris. Trains start running at 5:30 am with the last train pulling into the station at around 1:15 am weekdays (and 2:15 am on weekends). Tickets can be purchased at the green machines in stations with cash and chip-based credit cards. Remember to validate your ticket at the turnstile and hold on to it in case an inspector asks to see it; otherwise you could be fined. Except for new trains, you'll have to open the doors by button or handle. Use the train number as your guide, not the color. And no matter how you choose to get around Paris, the airports, SNCF train service, métro, and most taxis and boat rides all have apps to give you real-time schedules and traffic info.

Getting Here and Around

Addresses in Paris are fairly straightforward: there's the number, the street name, and the zip code designating one of Paris's 20 *arrondissements* (districts); for instance, in Paris 75010, the last two digits ("10") indicate that the address is in the 10e. The large 16e arrondissement has two numbers assigned to it: 75016 and 75116.

The arrondissements are laid out in a spiral, beginning from the area around the Louvre (1er arrondissement), then moving clockwise through the Marais, the Latin Quarter, St-Germain, and then out from the city center to the outskirts to Ménilmontant/Père Lachaise (20e arrondissement). Occasionally you may see an address with a number plus *bis*—for instance, 20 bis, rue Vavin. This indicates the next entrance or door down from 20 rue Vavin. Note that in France you enter a building on the ground floor, or *rez-de-chaussée* (RC or 0), and go up one floor to the first floor, or *premier étage*. General address terms used in this book are *av.* (avenue), *bd.* (boulevard), *carrefour* (crossway), *cours* (promenade), *passage* (passageway), *pl.* (place), *quai* (quay/wharf/pier), *rue* (street), and *sq.* (square).

Air

Flying time to Paris is about 7 hours from New York, 8 hours from Chicago, and 11 hours from Los Angeles. Flying time from London to Paris is 1½ hours.

The French are notoriously stringent about security, particularly for international flights. Don't be surprised by the armed security officers and military patrolling the airports, and be prepared for very long check-in lines. Peak travel times in France are between mid-July and September, during the

Christmas–New Year's holidays in late December and early January, and during the February school break. Through these periods airports are especially crowded, so allow plenty of extra time. Never leave your luggage unattended, even for a moment, as it will be considered a security risk and may be destroyed.

AIRPORTS

The major airports are Charles de Gaulle (CDG, also known as Roissy), 26 km (16 miles) northeast of Paris, and Orly (ORY), 16 km (10 miles) south of Paris. Both are easily accessible from the city. Whether you take a car, bus, or rideshare to travel from Paris to the airport on your departure, always allot an extra hour because of the often horrendous traffic tie-ups in the airports themselves (especially in peak seasons and at peak times). Free light-rail connections (Orlyval and CDGval), available between the major terminals, are one option for avoiding some of the traffic mess, but still give yourself enough time to navigate these busy airports.

GROUND TRANSPORTATION

By bus from CDG/Roissy: Roissybus, operated by the RATP (Paris Transit Authority), runs between Charles de Gaulle (all terminals) and the Opéra every 15 minutes (though the wait can be far longer) from 6 am to 8:45 pm and then every 20 minutes until 12:30 am; the cost is €13.70, and tickets can be purchased directly from the driver. The trip takes about 60 minutes in regular traffic, about 90 minutes at rush hour.

By taxi from CDG/Roissy: Taxis are the most convenient way into Paris but certainly not the fastest during peak times. At best, the ride takes 30 minutes, but it can hit 90 minutes during rush hour. At least the once-unpredictable fares are now fixed in either direction; count on a flat rate of €53 (Left Bank) and €58

(Right Bank). Taxis G7 has a great app to track your taxi arrival in real time, and it also offers Familycabs with a free baby car seat and two boosters. Only take an official taxi from designated areas outside the terminal; they will have an illuminated roof sign and a meter. Uber, Marcel, and other ride-hailing apps service CDG and are marginally cheaper.

By train from CDG/Roissy: The cheapest—and often the fastest—way into Paris from CDG is via the RER-B Line, the hybrid rapid transit–suburban train, which runs from 5 am to 11 pm daily. The free CDGVal light-rail connects each airport terminal (except 2G) to the Roissypôle RER station in six minutes. For Terminal 2G, take the free N2 "navette" shuttle bus outside Terminal 2F. Trains to central Paris (Les Halles, Gare du Nord, St-Michel, Luxembourg) depart every 10 to 20 minutes. The fare (including métro connection) is €10.30, and journey time is about 35 minutes to Les Halles. If you're catching a flight, be sure to check www.ratp.fr or a transport app for delays (they can be frequent).

By bus from Orly: RATP's Orlybus leaves every 10 to 15 minutes for the Denfert–Rochereau métro station in Montparnasse from Exit L in Orly South and Exit D in Orly West. The cost is €9.50. The cheapest bus is the RATP city bus 183, which shuttles you from métro Porte de Choisy (Line 7) to Orly South (Exit L, stop 4) for just €2. It departs every 15 minutes from 5 am to 12:30 am (frequency may be reduced on Sunday and holidays); travel time is about 45 to 60 minutes.

By taxi from Orly: You'll find taxi stands at Orly South at Exit L and at Orly West at Exit B (look for signs). A cab to Paris costs a flat rate in either direction of €32 (Left Bank) and €37 (Right Bank); plan on 25–40 minutes in normal traffic. Uber and other ride-hailing apps service Orly.

By train from Orly: Bus 183 has replaced the Go C Paris shuttle bus ("*Paris par le train*") to the train station RER-C Pont de Rungis–Aéroport d'Orly. Trains to Paris leave every 15 minutes. Buy tickets at the automatic machines; the combined fare is €6.45 and journey time is about 35 minutes. Another slightly faster option is to take the Orlyval monorail, which runs from both Orly terminals to the Antony RER-B daily every four to seven minutes from 6 am to 11:35 pm. Passengers arriving in the South Terminal should use the automatic machines or Orlyval counter at Exit K; take Exit A if you've arrived in the West Terminal. The fare to Paris is €12.10 including the RER transfer.

■TIP➜ **A Paris-Visite travel pass allows you unlimited public transportation over one, two, three, or five consecutive days. Prices start at €25.25 with airport travel. See en.parisinfo.com/what-to-see-in-paris/paris-pass.**

TRANSFERS BETWEEN AIRPORTS

To travel between Paris's airports, there are several options. The RER-B goes from CDG to Paris St-Michel–Notre-Dame (€10.30) where you transfer to the RER-C to Orly West. Travel time is about 60 to 80 minutes, and tickets cost €21.80. Taxis are available but expensive: from €70 to €110, depending on traffic.

■TIP➜ **The Next Stop Paris app is made specifically for tourists visiting the City of Light. Available in English and nine other languages, you can use it to sort out airport transfers and get help using public transport.**

🚲 Bicycle

Cycling is a terrific way to see the city—and work off the extra calories from all those rich pastries you've sampled. With an extensive system of dedicated

Getting Here and Around

bike lanes, cycling in Paris has never been easier. There are many bike-rental services and tours available, including Vélib' Métropole city bikes. For those too tired to pedal, 40% of the bikes have an electric option (they are aqua blue; regular bikes are light green) clocking a top speed of 25 kph (15 mph). While you may occasionally see a Vélib' with a deliberately punctured tire or a seat twisted off, city cyclists and visitors alike have embraced this service, copied in many cities worldwide, as a hassle-free alternative to public transportation. There are two ways to rent a Vélib': sign up on the website or buy a ticket from a machine at each docking station (major credit cards accepted). First, select the amount of time you wish to rent (the €3 Ticket-V, 24-hour pass Classic €5 or Electric €10 pass, or €20 3-Day Pass), then tap the code you're given on the bike's keypad to unlock it. The idea is to take short rides; depending on the Pass and whether you chose an electric bike, the first 30 to 60 minutes are free, then it's €1 or €2 for every 30 minutes. If you're staying in Paris for more than a week, check out the subscription options on the website.

🚢 Boat

Ferries linking France and the United Kingdom cross the Channel in about 90 minutes; popular routes connect Boulogne and Folkestone, Le Havre, and Portsmouth, and—the most booked passage—Calais and Dover. P&O European Ferries alone has 23 sailings a day between Calais and Dover. A company called Direct Ferries groups the websites for several operators to make reservations more streamlined.

The driving distance from Calais to Paris is 290 km (180 miles). The fastest routes to Paris from each port are via N43, A26, and A1 from Calais and the Channel Tunnel; and via N1 from Boulogne.

Several boat-tour companies operate Seine cruises that include sightseeing and, in some cases, dining. Batobus offers a convenient way to travel between all major sites along the river, including Notre-Dame, the Louvre, and the Eiffel Tower. A ticket for one day of unlimited hop-on/hop-off travel costs €17. One-hour Bateaux Parisiens sightseeing cruises cost €17 and depart from the Eiffel Tower every 60 minutes from 10 am to 10:30 pm (times may vary in high season); themed dinner and'lunch cruises start from €69. Canauxrama organizes leisurely tours year-round in flat-bottom barges along the Seine and the Canal St-Martin in eastern Paris. There are three daily departures from April to October (less during the rest of the year); trips cost €18 and last about 2½ hours, with commentary in French and English. Bateaux-Mouches runs a tight ship 12 months of the year. Tickets for the 70-minute Seine tour cost €14; brunch cruises from €55, and dinner cruises start at €79. Other year-round operators include Paris Canal, which offers 2½-hour trips with live bilingual commentary between the Musée d'Orsay and the Parc de La Villette (€22; €77 dinner cruise).

Bus

ARRIVING AND DEPARTING PARIS

The excellent national train service in France means that long-distance bus transportation in the country is practically nonexistent; regional buses are found where train service is spotty. Local bus information to the rare rural areas where trains do not go can be obtained from the SNCF.

The largest international bus operator here is Flixbus, whose main terminal is in the Parisian suburb of Bagnolet (a ½-hour métro ride from central Paris, at the end of métro Line 3). It runs to more than 2,500 cities in Europe with fares as cheap as €5, so if you have the time and the energy, this is a good way to cut the cost of travel.

IN PARIS

With dedicated bus lanes now in place throughout the city—allowing buses and taxis to whiz past other traffic mired in tedious jams—taking the bus is an appealing option. Although nothing can beat the métro for speed, buses—eco-friendly electric and diesel-electric hybrids—offer great city views, and air-conditioning is a nice perk on sweltering August days.

Paris buses are green and white; the route number and destination are marked in front, and major stopping places are noted along the sides. Glass-covered bus shelters contain timetables and route maps, and most have electronic boards telling you how long you'll wait for your ride; note that buses at stops servicing multiple lines must be hailed. Less frequented stops are designated simply by a pole bearing bus numbers. Today 64 bus lines thread throughout Paris, reaching virtually every nook and cranny of the city. On weekdays and Saturday, buses run every 5 to 10 minutes, but you'll have to wait 15 to 20 minutes on Sunday and holidays. One ticket will take you anywhere within the city and is valid for one bus transfer within 90 minutes. Remember to validate the ticket when you board.

Most routes operate from 7 am to 8:30 pm, with some running in the evening from 8:30 pm until 12:30 am. After 12:30 am you must take either the métro, which begins shutting down at 12:45 am

Sunday through Thursday and 1:45 am on Friday, Saturday, and on major holidays, or one of the Noctilien lines (indicated by a separate signal at bus stops). Using the same tickets as the métro and regular buses, 47 Noctilien buses operate every 15 to 60 minutes (12:30 am–5:30 am) between Châtelet, major train stations, and various nearby suburbs; you can hail them at any point on their route. The N01 and N02 loop around the city's main train stations in opposite directions and are particularly popular with tourists. You can buy a ticket onboard for €2.

A map of the bus system is on the flip side of every métro map, in all métro stations, and at all bus stops. Maps are also found in each bus; a free map is available at RER stations and tourist offices, or download the Bonjour RATP app on iTunes, GooglePlay, or www. ratp.fr. An onboard electronic display announces the name of the next stop. To get off, press one of the red buttons mounted on the silver poles that run the length of the bus, and the *arrêt demandé* (stop requested) light directly behind the driver will light up. Use the middle or rear door to exit.

The Balabus—an orange-and-white public bus that runs on Sunday and holidays from 1:30 pm to 8:30 pm, April through September—gives an eye-catching 50-minute tour around the major sights. You can use your Paris-Visite or Mobilis pass, or one to three bus tickets, depending on how far you ride. The route runs from La Défense to the Gare de Lyon. The city has expanded its modern tram system with several lines linking the city with its outer suburbs; Line T3 (with extensions 3a and 3b) ring Paris from the southern edge at Pont du Garigliano to Porte de la Chapelle in the north. One ticket is good for the entire line.

Getting Here and Around

Trams and buses take the same tickets as the métro. A single ticket can be bought on board for €2 (exact change appreciated) or for €1.90 in advance. Contactless ticket packs of 10 (€14.90) have replaced the paper 10-ticket *carnet*. If you have individual tickets or Paris-Visite passes, you should be prepared to validate your ticket in the gray machines at the entrance of the vehicle. You can also buy tickets in some newsstands and bar-tabac cafés, but this is being phased out in favor of purchasing directly from the Bonjour RATP app.

Car

It can't be said too many times: unless you have a special, compelling reason, do yourself a favor and **avoid driving in Paris.** But if you've decided to do it anyway, there are some things to know. France's roads are classified into five types; they are numbered and have letter prefixes: *A* (*autoroute,* expressways), *N* (*route nationale*), *D* (*route départmentale*), and the smaller *C* or *V.* There are excellent links between Paris and most French cities. When trying to get around Île-de-France, it's often difficult to avoid Paris—just try to steer clear of rush hours (7–9:30 and 4:30–7:30). A *péage* (toll) must be paid on most expressways outside Île-de-France: the rate varies but can be steep. Certain booths allow you to pay with a credit card.

The major ring road encircling Paris is called the *périphérique,* with the *périphérique intérieur* going counterclockwise around the city, and the *périphérique extérieur,* or the outside ring, going clockwise; maximum speed, for the time being, is still 70 kph (43 mph). Up to five lanes wide, the périphérique is a major highway from which 30 *portes* (gates) connect Paris to the major highways of France. The names of these highways function on the same principle as the métro, with the final destination as the determining point in the direction you must take.

Heading north, look for Porte de la Chapelle (direction Lille and Charles de Gaulle Airport); east, for Porte de Bagnolet (direction Metz and Nancy); south, for Porte d'Orléans (direction Lyon and Bordeaux); and west, for Porte d'Auteuil (direction Rouen and Chartres) or Porte de St-Cloud (Boulogne-Billancourt).

PARKING

Finding parking in Paris is tough. If you must have a car, at least paying to park it is easy, if expensive. You have to pay for metered parking from Monday to Saturday from 9 am to 8 pm. Luckily, you no longer have to keep an eye on the two-hour meter. As a *visiteur*, you can park for up to six consecutive hours, which in the capital costs €4 to €6 an hour, depending on whether you're in arrondissements 1e–11e or 12e–20e. Look for the nearest dark green ticket machine *horodateur* and choose English. Enter your license plate number to begin, then choose the amount of time you want, and insert your card (no cash or coins). Place the green receipt on the passenger side of the dashboard. The OPnGO app (www.opngo.com) not only lets you book a parking spot in advance and extend the meter remotely, but also pay in actual time. You can also download the PayByPhone, ParkNow, and Flowbird apps, all verified by City Hall, and pay on your phone. Parking tickets are expensive, and there's no shortage of blue-uniformed parking police doling them out. An often cheaper alternative is finding a lot or underground garage—look for the blue signs with a white "P"; rates in the city center start at about €3.50 an hour, or €20 per day, while outside of the center you'll pay €10 to €15 per day. Parkings de Paris (www.parclick.fr) lets you reserve and prepay a spot in around 150 city car parks. Happily, you can park for free on Sunday and national holidays; sadly, the city stopped the popular practice of free street parking in August.

ROAD CONDITIONS

Chaotic traffic is a way of life in Paris. Some streets in the city center can seem impossibly narrow; street signs are often hard to spot; jaded city drivers often make erratic, last-minute maneuvers without signaling; and motorcycles weave around traffic, often in the oncoming traffic lane. Priority is given to drivers coming from the right, so watch for drivers barreling out of small streets on your right. A move by City Hall cutting the speed limit in much of the capital to 30 kph (18.6 mph) drew scoffs from annoyed drivers, but since 2020 some 85% of city streets have been subject to the lower limit. Watch out for cyclists in 30 kph zones; they are permitted to pedal against traffic on one-way streets. Traffic lights are placed to the left and right of crosswalks, not above, so they may be blocked from view by vehicles ahead of you. And remember, you cannot turn right on a red light.

There are a few major roundabouts at the most congested intersections, notably at L'Étoile (around the Arc de Triomphe), Place de la Bastille, and Place de la Concorde; stick to the outer lane to make your exit. The périphériques (ring roads) are generally easier to use. Quays that parallel the Seine are no longer open to cars, causing even more traffic jams on the roads above. Electronic signs on the périphériques and highways post traffic conditions: *fluide* (clear) or *bouchon* (jammed). And to further complicate matters, many roads, including the Champs-Élysées, are designated car-free the first

Sunday of every month from midmorning to early evening, depending on the time of year.

Some important traffic terms and signs to note: *sortie* (exit), *sens unique* (one way), *stationnement interdit* (no parking), *impasse* (dead end). Blue rectangular signs indicate a highway; triangles carry illustrations of a particular traffic hazard; speed limits are indicated in a circle, with the maximum speed circled in red.

Métro

Taking the métro is the most efficient way to get around Paris: Métro stations are recognizable either by a large yellow "M" within a circle or by the distinctive curly green Art Nouveau railings and archway bearing the full title (*Métropolitain*).

Sixteen métro and five RER (Réseau Express Régional, or the Regional Express Network) lines crisscross Paris and the suburbs, and you are seldom more than 500 yards from the nearest station. The métro network, which is divided into five pricing zones, connects at several points in Paris with the RER, the commuter trains that go from the city center to the suburbs. RER trains crossing Paris on their way from suburb to suburb can be great time-savers because they make only a few stops in the city (you can use the same tickets for the métro and the RER within Paris).

It's essential to know the name of the last station on the line you take, as this name appears on all signs. A connection (you can make as many as you like on one ticket) is called a *correspondance*. At junction stations, illuminated orange signs bearing the name of the line terminus appear over the correct corridors for each correspondence. Illuminated blue signs marked *sortie* indicate the station

Getting Here and Around

exit. Note that tickets are valid only inside the gates, or *limites*. Access to métro and RER platforms is through an automatic ticket barrier. Slide your ticket in and pick it up as it pops out. Keep your ticket during your journey; you'll need it to leave the RER system and in case you run into any green-clad ticket inspectors, who will impose a hefty fine if you can't produce your ticket (they even accept credit cards!).

Métro service starts at 5:30 am and continues until the last trains reach their terminus at 1:15 am Sunday through Thursday, and until 2:15 am on Friday, Saturday, and some national holidays. Some lines and stations in Paris can be dodgy late at night, in particular Lines 2 and 13, and the mazelike stations at Les Halles and République, so don't travel alone. But in general, the biggest risk on the métro is posed by the nimble Parisian pickpockets, so keep an eye on your wallet and pricey gadgets.

All métro tickets and passes are valid not only for the métro but also for all RER, tram, and bus travel within Paris. Métro tickets cost €1.90 each; 10 paperless tickets for €14.90 is a better value. The *Carte Navigo* system is the daily, monthly, and weekly subscription plan, with reusable cards available at automatic ticket machines and ticket windows. (Note that at many stations your only option is to use the machines; they accept bills or cards with electronic chips). Get a Forfait Navigo card for €5 plus the subscription you choose: unlimited travel for one day (€7.50), for one week (€22.80) or one month (€75.20, beginning the first of the month). Be sure to sign your name and immediately attach a passport-size photo (there are photo booths in larger métro stations). The card allows you to swipe through the turnstiles and can be kept for years; just recharge it at any purple

Ticket/Pass	Price
Single Fare	€1.90
Daily Mobilis Pass	From €7.50
Paris-Visite One-Day Pass	€12
10 Paperless Tickets	€14.90
Paris-Visite Two-Day Pass	€19.50
Paris-Visite Three-Day Pass	€26.65
Paris-Visite Five-Day Pass	€38.35
Pass Navigo Découverte Weekly	€22.80
Pass Navigo Découverte Monthly	€75.20

kiosk in the métro stations. If that seems like too much hassle, buy a Mobilis (one day) or Paris-Visite (up to five days) pass for unlimited travel across the regional RATP network; both are valid starting any day of the week. The cost of a Mobilis pass starts at €7.50. Paris-Visite—which also gives you discounts on a few museums and attractions like the Arc de Triomphe—costs €12 (one day) to €38.35 (five days) for Paris Centre, Zones 1–3.

■ TIP→ **For itineraries, maps, and real-time tips on delays and closings, download the RATP transit system's Vianavigo, Moovit, or Citymapper for a trove of handy info like which end of the métro platform gets you closest to your exit on the other end of your journey.**

 ## Taxi

Taxi rates are based on location and time. Monday to Saturday, daytime rates (10 am–5 pm) within Paris are €1.09 per km (½ mile); nighttime rates (7 pm–midnight) are €1.38 per km. On Sunday, you'll pay

€1.61 per km from midnight to 7 am and €1.38 from 7 am to midnight within Paris. Thanks to competition from ride-hailing services like Uber, the once unpredictable rates that official taxis charged to and from the airports into Paris are now fixed, and drivers are obligated to accept credit cards—and most cab companies now have an app. Pay a flat €53 to and from Charles de Gaulle/Roissy for the Right Bank, €58 for the Left Bank; to and from Orly, pay €32 for Left Bank and €37 for Right Bank. There's a basic hire charge of €2.60 for all rides (excluding flat fares and taxis reserved in advance), and a minimum fare of €7.30. It's customary, but not obligatory, to tip up to 5%. Waiting time is charged at €35 per hour. The easiest way to get a taxi is to ask your hotel or a restaurant to call one for you (a reservation supplement of €4–€7 will apply). Order one yourself with the handy app by Taxi G7, or find a taxi stand, which is marked by a square, dark-blue sign with a white "T" in the middle.

 # Train

The SNCF, France's rail system, is fast, reasonably punctual, comfortable, and comprehensive—when it's not on strike. There are various options: local trains, overnight trains with sleeping accommodations, and the high-speed TGVs (or Trains à Grande Vitesse), which average 320 kph.

The TGVs, the fastest way to get around the country, operate between Paris and Lille/Calais, Paris and Lyon/Switzerland/Provence, Paris and Angers/Nantes, Paris and Tours/Poitiers/Bordeaux, Paris and Brussels, and Paris and Amsterdam. TGVs also go direct to Avignon, Marseille, and Nice.

Paris has six international rail stations: Gare du Nord (northern France, northern Europe, and England via Calais or Boulogne); Gare St-Lazare (Normandy, and England via Dieppe); Gare de l'Est (Strasbourg, Luxembourg, Basel, southern Germany, and central Europe); Gare de Lyon (Lyon, Marseille, Provence, Geneva, and Italy); Gare d'Austerlitz (Loire Valley, central France, and overnight to Nice and Spain); and Gare Montparnasse (Brittany, Aquitaine, TGV-Atlantique service to the west and southwest of France, Spain). Smoking is prohibited on all trains in France.

The country has two classes of train service: *première* (first class) or *deuxième* (second). First-class seats have 50% more legroom and nicer upholstery than those in second class, and the first-class cars tend to be quieter. First-class seats on the TGV also have the all-important power sockets for computer connections and individual reading lights, but fares can cost nearly twice as much as those for second-class seats. As part of first-class, Business Premier passengers have access to a lounge, fast-track boarding, and a free newspaper and beverage.

Fares are cheaper if you avoid traveling at peak times of day (and around holidays and weekends) and purchase tickets at least 15 days to three months in advance; for the best prices check the SNCF website for deals. Reserving online is the easiest way to book your trip, but you can call for train information or reserve tickets in any Paris station, irrespective of destination, and you can access the multilingual computerized schedule information network at any Paris station, and buy your tickets there. Go to the Grandes Lignes counter for travel within France and to the Billets Internationaux desk if you're heading out of the country.

Getting Here and Around

France is one of 33 European countries where you can use Eurail passes, which provide unlimited train travel for a set amount of time. If you plan to travel outside Paris by train, consider purchasing a Eurail One Country Pass; it allows for one, two, three, four, five, six, seven, or eight days of unlimited train travel in one country within a one-month period. If you travel solo in France for up to eight days in one month, it will cost between $117 and $392 in second class. If you plan to rack up the miles, get a Eurail Global Pass; it's valid for rail travel in first or second class in two or more of the participating nations. Costs range from $429 (first class) for five days to $1,370 (first class) for three months.

■TIP→ A select few European train stations sell a limited number of Eurail passes, but they cost more—so buy yours at home before you leave for France; purchase through the Eurail website or through travel agents. Remember that a rail pass does not guarantee you a seat on the train. You need to book seats ahead even if you have a pass; this fee can range from €3 to €68— sometimes even €124 for an overnight. If you are comfortable traveling paperless, the Interrail Mobile Pass is delivered immediately and replaced for free should you lose your phone.

Seat reservations are required on TGVs but not on the regional TER network. So if you're traveling by TER, be sure to board early during busy travel periods, especially in July and August, to ensure you get a seat, otherwise it is standing-room only. The trains are notoriously overbooked, and even a first-class ticket may not guarantee you a seat. Fortunately, the Seatmap tool by SNCF allows you to view and select your seat when you book online. Note that you need a reservation for sleeping accommodations.

THE CHANNEL TUNNEL

Short of flying, taking the Channel Tunnel is the fastest way to cross the English Channel: 35 minutes from Folkestone to Calais, 60 minutes from motorway to motorway, or two hours and 15 minutes from London's St. Pancras Station to Paris's Gare du Nord, with stops in Ebbsfleet (UK), Ashford (UK), Calais, and Lille. The Belgian border is just a short drive northeast of Calais. High-speed Eurostar trains use the same tunnels to connect London's St. Pancras Station directly with Midi Station in Brussels in around two hours.

There are three categories of travel and a vast range of prices for Eurostar—round-trip tickets range from €281.75 for business class (with access to the Philippe Starck–designed Première Class lounge, free cancellations, unlimited ticket exchanges, and a three-course Raymond Blanc meal) to €56 for the most basic return ticket. Booking early can save you a bundle. Last-minute tickets can cost more than flying.

It's a good idea to make a reservation with Eurotunnel's Le Shuttle if you're traveling with your car on a Chunnel train; vehicles without reservations, if they can get on at all, are charged a higher fare.

Essentials

🍴 Dining

HOURS

Paris restaurants generally serve food from noon to 2 pm and from 7:30 or 8 pm to about 11 pm. Brasseries have longer hours and often serve all day and late into the evening; some are open 24 hours. Surprisingly, many restaurants close on Sunday and Monday, while annual *fermetures* are typically several weeks in July and August, as well as a week in February, around Easter, or at Christmas.

RESERVATIONS

Restaurant staff will nearly always greet you with the phrase "*Avez-vous réservé?*" (Have you reserved?), and a confident "*Oui*" is the best answer, even in a neighborhood bistro. Although some wine bars do not take reservations—or take them online only—many do, so call and check.

Price per person for a main course at dinner, or if dinner is not served, at lunch, including tax (10%) and service.

What It Costs in Euros			
$	$$	$$$	$$$$
AT DINNER			
under €18	€18–€24	€25–€32	over €32

A new wave of culinary confidence has been running through one of the world's great food cities and spilling over both banks of the Seine. Whether cooking up *grand-mère's* roast chicken and *riz au lait* or placing a whimsical hat of cotton candy atop wild-strawberry-and-rose ice cream, Paris chefs—established and up-and-coming, native and foreign—have been breaking free from the tyranny of tradition and following their passion.

Emblematic of the "bistronomy" movement is the proliferation of "gastrobistros"—often in far-flung or newly chic neighborhoods—steered by established chefs fleeing the constraints of the star system or passionate young chefs unfettered by overblown expectations. But self-expression is not the only driving force behind the current trend. A traditional high-end restaurant can be prohibitively expensive to operate. As a result, more casual bistros and cafés, which reflect the growing allure of less formal dining and often have lower operating costs and higher profit margins, have become attractive opportunities for even top chefs.

For tourists, this development opens up a vast range of possibilities to sample the cooking of the likes of Guy Savoy, Eric Frechon, and Pierre Gagnaire, even if these star chefs rarely cook in their lower-price restaurants.

Like the chefs themselves, Paris diners are breaking away from tradition with renewed enthusiasm. New restaurants, wine bars, and rapidly multiplying *épiceries* (gourmet grocers) and sandwich shops recognize that not everyone wants a three-course blowout every time they dine out. And because Parisians are more widely traveled than in the past, many international restaurants—notably the best North African, Vietnamese–Laotian, Chinese, Spanish, and Japanese spots—are making fewer concessions to French tastes, resulting in far better food.

All establishments must post menus outside so they're available to look over before you enter. Most have two basic types of menu: à la carte and fixed price (*prix fixe, le menu,* or *la formule*). Although it limits your choices, the prix fixe is usually the best value. If you feel like indulging, the *menu dégustation* (tasting menu), consisting of numerous

Essentials

small courses, lets you sample the chef's offerings.

According to French law, prices must include tax and tip (*service compris* or *prix nets*), but pocket change left on the table in cafés, or an additional 5% in better restaurants, is always appreciated. Beware of bills stamped "Service Not Included" in English or restaurants slyly using American-style credit-card slips, hoping that you'll be confused and add the habitual 15% tip.

🛏 Lodging

If your Parisian fantasy involves romantic evenings in a historic grand-dame or a chic boutique hotel that pampers you in high style, here's some good news: you don't have to be wealthy to make your dreams come true. With 1,600 hotels, the City of Light gives visitors swanky options in all price ranges, and a place with plenty of charm is practically a given, especially with the new generation of hotels popping up in the Right Bank (in neighborhoods like Pigalle, Ménilmontant, République, and Bastille) catering to style and affordability.

In terms of location and price, there are more hotels on the *Rive Droite* (the Right Bank) offering formal luxury with premium service than on the *Rive Gauche* (the Left Bank), where the hotels are frequently smaller though richer in charm. The Rive Droite's 1er, 8e, and 16e arrondissements are still the most exclusive, and their prices reflect that. Paris's famed palace hotels—12 hotels in the city that are considered better than a five-star—charge more than €1,000 a night for a standard room, and the high-end competition is heating up. On both sides of the Seine, Paris is in the throes of a lodging renaissance in both established and up-and-coming neighborhoods, with everything from chic new boutique hotels to deluxe five-star dwellings.

But those on a budget should fear not, because less expensive alternatives can be found in the fashionable Marais (the 3e and 4e arrondissements), as well as the Latin Quarter (5e arrondissement), along with a slew of newcomers that have laid their cornerstones in the newly chic 2e (Sentier). The Rive Gauche's 6e arrondissement (St-Germain) is another hotbed for stylish hotels, and choices on all budgets are available in the 5e and 7e. Everything from excellent budget deals to splendid designer spaces can also be found slightly off-the-beaten track in the 10e, 13e, and 20e arrondissements. Wherever possible, in the more expensive neighborhoods we've located budget hotels—check out the handful of budget-priced sleeps in the shadow of Notre-Dame, St-Germain-des-Prés, and the Louvre.

These days, nearly every hotel offers free Wi-Fi (although reception in an 18th-century building is another story), international TV channels (meaning CNN and BBC News in English), high-definition screens, free coffee and tea, minibars, and in-room safes. Another recent change is the increasing availability of air-conditioning in both hotels and restaurants—a godsend in the *canicules* (dog days) of July and August. One thing that hasn't changed, however, is the lack of elbow room. Indoor spaces—from bed- and bathrooms to elevators—may feel cramped to those not used to life on a European scale. If you're flush and looking for enough room to spread out multiple suitcases, be sure to book a suite; they can be found in virtually any hotel, from the most modest boutique to the palaces.

Where Should I Stay?

	NEIGHBORHOOD VIBE	PROS	CONS
St-Germain and Montparnasse (6e, 14e, 15e)	The center of café culture and the emblem of the Rive Gauche.	A safe, historic area with boutiques, famous cafés and brasseries, and lovely side streets; always lively.	Overdeveloped. Noisy along main streets; the busy commercial area is devoid of charm.
The Latin Quarter (5e, 6e)	The historic student quarter of the Rive Gauche. Full of narrow, winding streets, major parks, and sights.	Plenty of cheap eats and sleeps; safe area for walks day and night.	Lacking in métro stations around the Panthéon; can be noisy in summer; hotel rooms tend to be smaller.
Marais and Bastille (3e, 4e, 11e)	Museums, chic shops, and bustling cafés line the narrow streets. Farther east are stylish bars and boutiques.	Excellent shopping, museum-going, and café culture in the active Marais; bargains aplenty at Bastille hotels.	Overcrowded. Rooms don't always come cheap; always noisy around the boulevards of Place de la Bastille.
Montmartre and northeast Paris (18e, 19e, 20e)	The Rive Droite's hilltop district is known for winding streets leading up to the stark-white Sacré-Coeur.	Amazing views of Paris; romantic cobblestone streets; easy access to Roissy-Charles de Gaulle airport.	Inconvenient. Steep staircases can be challenging; few métro stations; Pigalle and Barbès area can be unsafe.
Champs-Élysées and Western Paris (8e, 16e, 17e)	The Triangle D'Or (Golden Triangle) and famous avenues are lively 24/7 with nightclubs, cinemas, and shops.	Home to many of the city's famous palace and five-star hotels, with no shortage of luxury and designer goods.	Expensive. Sky-high prices and commercial, touristy tendencies.
Around the Eiffel Tower (7e, 15e)	The impressive Eiffel Tower and sweeping Champs de Mars sit next to the Seine River.	Safe and quiet, this Rive Gauche area of Paris has picture-perfect views at every turn.	Residential. With fewer shops and restaurants, this district is quiet at night; longer distances between métro stations.
Louvre, Les Halles, Île de la Cité (1er, 2e, 8e)	This central district is known for sightseeing and shopping; Les Halles is a buzzing commercial hub.	Excellent for getting around Paris on foot, bus, or métro. Safe district close to the Seine and major museums.	Noisy. The main artery of Rue de Rivoli can be loud with traffic; restaurants cater to tourists.
Grands Boulevards (9e, 10e)	The newly chic historic district is popular for its lively streets and important sites.	Perfect for walking tours, the area has unique finds and distinct neighborhoods.	Crowded. Tourists and locals keep districts full of cars, buses, trucks, taxis, and scooters.

Essentials

Almost all Parisian hotels charge extra for breakfast, with per-person prices ranging from €12 to more than €50. If you decide to eat elsewhere (and with so many cafés around that's often a better value), inform the staff so breakfast won't be charged to your bill. Occasionally, a continental breakfast—coffee, baguette, croissant, jam, and butter—will be included in the hotel rate, especially with an online booking directly from the hotel.

In France, the "first floor" is the floor above the ground floor (rez-de-chaussée). The number of rooms listed at the end of each review reflects those with private bathroom (which means they have a shower or a tub, but not necessarily both). In budget hotels, cube-sized "tubs" don't always have fixed curtains or shower heads; how the French rinse themselves with the handheld nozzle without flooding the entire bathroom remains a cultural mystery. Moderately priced places that expect guests to share toilets or bathrooms are pretty much extinct, but be sure you know what facilities you are getting when you book an economy hotel.

Prices in the reviews are the lowest cost of a double standard room in high season.

What It Costs in Euros			
$	$$	$$$	$$$$
FOR TWO PEOPLE			
under €125	€125–€225	€226–€350	over €350

🍸 Nightlife

You haven't seen the City of Light until you've seen the city at night. Crowds pour into popular streets, on weekends and weeknights, late and early, filling the air with the melody of engaged conversation and clinking glasses. This is when locals let down their hair and reveal their true bonhomie, laughing and dancing, flirting and talking. Parisians love to savor life together: they dine out, sip red wine, offer innumerable toasts, and are often so reluctant to separate that they party all night.

Paris bars include everything from the toniest hotel lounge to the tiniest neighborhood troquet, where old-timers gather for a chat over their morning petit blanc. Hotel bars were once considered the aristocrats of the genre, but these days even the palaces are seeking a more modern edge. A few still represent the chicest spots for high-roller visitors to Paris, but breathtaking prices and stiff competition from the rival cocktail bar scene means a hotel bar had better be special to be worth the price (and many are: the Hemingway Bar at the Ritz and Les Ambassadeurs at Hôtel de Crillon are two of the city's best).

Parisian cocktail bars focus on mixed drinks—although most offer everything from locally crafted beer to small-producer Champagnes—and run the gamut from dauntingly elegant hotel lounges to designer dives, attracting a diverse crowd willing to shell out anywhere from €7 to €25 a libation. Once called barmen, the new curators of cocktails are "mixologists" whose drinks are crafted, ingredients are sourced, booze is barrel-aged or infused, syrups are house-made, and ice is artisanal.

Wine bars (caves à manger) are different from regular bars in that they also serve food, from simple snacks like cheese and charcuterie to full meals, plus handpicked wines that are often "natural" or biodynamique. Wine bars keep mealtime hours and close earlier than proper bars—somewhere between 11 and midnight. Be warned, though: many establishments calling themselves wine bars or *bars à vins* are in fact full-fledged restaurants, with no bar to speak of.

Paris's cabarets range from vintage venues once haunted by Picasso and Piaf to those sinful showplaces where *tableaux vivants* offer acres of bare flesh. Some of these places, like the Lido, are more Vegas than the petticoat vision re-created by Hollywood in Baz Luhrmann's *Moulin Rouge*—but the rebirth of burlesque is making some of the old-school venues and racier versions like the lascivious Crazy Horse more popular. Although you can dine at many cabarets, food isn't the attraction. Prices range from about €90 (admission only) to more than €250 (dinner plus a show) and can go as high as €450 for the works. At all but a handful of specific cabarets on specific nights, the clientele tends overwhelmingly to be visitors, middle-aged and older, from either the French countryside or abroad.

Paris's hyped *boîtes de nuit*—more often referred to as simply *boîtes* (nightclubs)—tend to be expensive and exclusive. If you're friends with a regular or relatively famous (or if you're a group of women), you'll have an easier time getting through the door. Cover charges at some can be upwards of €25, with drinks at the bar starting at €10 for a beer. Others are free to enter, but you'll pay a fortune inside. Locals looking to dance generally stick to the more laid-back clubs, where the cover ranges from free (usually on slower weekdays) to €20, and the emphasis is on the dancing, music, and offbeat atmosphere (think on a barge or under a bridge). Club popularity depends on the night or event, as Parisians are more loyal to certain DJs than venues and often hit two or three spots before ending up at one of the many after-parties, which can last until noon the next day. No matter where you decide, avoid the overpriced Champs-Élysées neighborhood.

The LGBTQ nightlife scene is mostly concentrated in the Marais and Les Halles, but, unlike the legendary La Mutinerie on Rue Saint-Martin, many of these spots fall in and out of favor at lightning speed. Pick up a copy of the leading LGBTQ magazine *Têtu* (available at newsstands and online at tetu.com), or visit ParisGayVillage (www.parisgayvillage.com) for visits of the city or to get a free copy of their gay and lesbian city guide. The Pride en France site (www.gaypride.fr) is also super informative.

Wherever you end up, know that most bars stay open until between midnight and 2 am, with no specific last call; however, wine bars and hotel bars tend to close earlier. Clubs usually stay open until 5 am, although more dance clubs are staying open until dawn or beyond (some even serve breakfast). Many drinking establishments are closed Sunday night, so check before heading out on the town. If you want to hit bars at a relatively quiet hour, go for an *apéro* around 6 pm, and take advantage of the terrace if weather permits.

The métro runs until 1:15 am Sunday through Thursday; however, there is service on Friday night, Saturday night, and nights before holidays until 2:15 am, when the last train on each line reaches its terminus. After that, you can try a cab, but it can be extremely difficult to find one after midnight (or anytime when there's a chance of rain) or Uber. Another alternative is the Noctilien, the sometimes rowdy night-bus system. And if you're having a lot of fun, you can always wait until the métro starts running again at 5:30 am.

Essentials

🎭 Performing Arts

The performing arts scene in Paris runs the gamut from highbrow to lowbrow, cheap (or even free) to break-the-bank expensive. Venues are indoors and outdoors, opulent or spartan, and dress codes vary accordingly. Regardless of the performance you choose, it's probably unlike anything you've seen before. Parisians have an audacious sense of artistic adventure and a stunning eye for scene and staging. An added bonus in this city of classic beauty is that many of the venues themselves—from the opulent interiors of the Opéra Garnier and the Opéra Royal de Versailles to the Art Deco splendor of the Théâtre des Champs-Élysées—are a feast for the eyes.

One thing that sets Paris apart in the arts world is the active participation of the Ministry of Culture, which sponsors numerous concert halls and theaters, like the Comédie Française, that tend to present less commercial, though artistically captivating, productions. Other venues with broader appeal are known for sold-out shows and decade-long runs. Most performances are in French, although you can find English theater productions. English-language movies are often presented in *version original*, with subtitles and Lost in Frenchlation (www.lostinfrenchlation.com) regularly shows French films with English subtitles. Of course, you don't need to speak the language to enjoy opera, classical music, dance, or the circus.

Detailed entertainment listings can be found online in English at www.sortiraparis.com or in French from the weekly magazine *L'Officiel des Spectacles*, in the Wednesday entertainment insert *Figaroscope* in the *Figaro* newspaper (evene.lefigaro.fr), and in the weekly *À Nous Paris*, distributed free in the métro.

The webzine *Paris Voice* (parisvoice.com) offers superb highlights in English. Most performing arts venues also have their own websites, and many include listings as well as other helpful information in English. The website of the Paris Tourist Office (en.parisinfo.com) has theater and music listings in English.

➕ Safety

Paris is as safe as any big city can be, but you should always be streetwise and alert. Certain neighborhoods are more seedy than dangerous, thanks to the night trade that goes on around Les Halles and St-Denis and on Boulevard de Clichy in Pigalle. Some off-the-beaten-path neighborhoods (particularly the outlying suburban communities) may warrant extra precaution. And, as elsewhere, you could be subjected to bag checks when entering public buildings.

The métro is quite safe overall, though some lines and stations, in particular Lines 2 and 13, get dodgy late at night, so try not to travel alone, memorize the time of the last métro train to your station, ride in the first car by the conductor, and just use common sense. If you're worried, spend the money on a taxi or Uber. Pickpocketing is the main problem, day or night. And it goes without saying, it's best not to put your phone or iPad on a café table.

Scarcely a week goes by without some kind of demonstration or public gathering in Paris, and although most are peaceful, it's usually best for tourists to avoid them. The CRS (French riot police) carefully guard all major protests, directing traffic and preventing violence as they are armed and use tear gas when and if they see fit.

COVID-19

COVID 19 has disrupted travel since March 2020, and travelers should expect sporadic ongoing issues. Always travel with a mask in case it's required, and keep up to date on the most recent testing and vaccination guidelines for Paris.

🛍 Shopping

Nothing, but nothing, can push you into the current of Parisian life faster than a few hours of shopping. Follow the lead of locals, who slow to a crawl as their eyes lock on a tempting display. Window-shopping is one of this city's greatest spectator sports; the French call it *lèche-vitrine*—literally, "licking the windows"—which is fitting because many of the displays look good enough to eat.

Store owners here play to sophisticated audiences with voracious appetites for everything from spangly flagship stores to minimalist boutiques to under-the-radar spots in 19th-century glass-roofed *passages*. Parisians know that shopping isn't about the kill, it's about the chase: walking down cobblestone streets looking for items they didn't know they wanted, they're casual yet quick to pounce. Watching them shop can be almost as much fun as shopping yourself, but remember that here, they ain't charging it: the French do not have credit cards like most Western countries; they might have cards that say Visa or Mastercard, but they are actually debit cards.

As for what to buy, the sky's the limit in terms of choices, but if you shop in January or July, you'll likely come across the six-week official sales periods—aka *les soldes d'hiver* and *les soldes d'été*— as designated by the government. If your funds aren't limitless, take comfort in

knowing that treasures can be found on a budget.

Store hours can be tricky in Paris. Aside from department stores, which keep slightly longer hours and usually shut their doors late on Thursday, shops tend to open around 10 am and close around 7 pm. It's not unusual to find a "back at 3" sign taped on the doors of smaller boutiques at lunchtime. Plan to do most of your foraging between Tuesday and Saturday, as the majority of shops, excluding the two major department stores, Printemps and Galeries Lafayette, are closed Sunday and some on Monday as well. You can find areas—particularly the Marais and tourist-oriented Champs-Élysées—where stores are open on Sunday. However, if you're making a special trip somewhere, it's wise to check hours online or call ahead because in France, Sundays are still cherished days off.

💲 Tipping

In France, tipping is not a cultural norm. Bills in bars and restaurants must by law include service (despite what entrepreneurial servers may tell you), so tipping isn't required. Waiters are paid well; it is polite, however, to round your bill with small change unless you're dissatisfied. The amount varies—from €0.20 for a beer to €1–€3 after a meal. In expensive restaurants, it's common to leave an additional 5%–10% on the table.

In some theaters and hotels cloakroom attendants may expect nothing (watch for signs that say *pourboire interdit*—tipping forbidden; otherwise, give them €1). If you stay more than two or three days in a hotel, leave something for the housekeeper—about €1–€2 per day. Expect to pay €2 (€1 in a moderately priced hotel) to the person who carries your bags or

Essentials

hails a taxi for you. In hotels providing room service, give €1–€2 to the waiter (unless breakfast is routinely served in your room). If the concierge has been helpful, leave a tip of €5–€20 depending on the service. Museum guides should get €1–€1.50 after a tour. For other kinds of tours, tip the guide or leader 10% of the tour cost. It's standard practice to tip long-distance bus drivers about €2 after an excursion, too. Taxi drivers usually aren't tipped, but if you're paying cash, round up to the nearest euro.

📅 When to Go

Although the City of Light is magical all year round, summer is the most popular (and priciest) time to go. It used to be that Paris was largely deserted in August when locals fled to the coast or countryside, leaving a wake of closed shops and restaurants. But today it remains very much alive throughout the summer, with outdoor music festivals, open-air movie screenings, and convivial activities available at the popular Paris Plages, the "beaches" on the Right Bank of the Seine and along the upper Canal St-Martin.

Nevertheless, the city is perhaps most appealing in late spring and early fall. June, when long, warm days translate into extended hours of sightseeing (the sun doesn't set until 10 pm), is particularly gorgeous. Ditto for September, which promises temperate weather, saner rates, and cultural events timed for the *rentrée* (or return), signifying the end of summer vacation. In the third weekend in September, scores of national buildings that are normally closed to the public open for visits during the annual Journées du Patrimoine (Patrimony Days).

Tipping Guidelines for Paris	
Bellhop	€1–€2, depending on the level of the hotel
Hotel Concierge	€5–€20 if he or she performs a service for you
Hotel Doorman	€1–€2 if he helps you get a cab
Hotel Maid	€1–€2 a day (either daily or at the end of your stay, in cash)
Hotel Room-Service Waiter	€1–€2 per delivery, even if a service charge has been added
Tour Guide	10% of the cost of the tour (but museum guides, €1–€1.50 after a tour)
Valet Parking Attendant	€1–€2, but only when you get your car
Waiter	Round up for small bills, €1–€3 for meals, 5%–10% in expensive restaurants
Restroom Attendant	Restroom attendants in more expensive restaurants expect small change or €1

Winter can be dark and cold, but it's also the best time to find cheap airfares and hotel deals. Spring tends to remain damp and chilly into May, when prices start rising in sync with the mercury in local thermometers.

Best Tours in Paris

Sometimes a guided tour is the way to go, even if you usually prefer to fly solo while traveling. Tours can be a great way to explore out-of-the-way neighborhoods, to get an insider's perspective on where locals eat and play, and to learn about interesting aspects of the city's history, inhabitants, or architecture. Whether you want a boat tour along the Seine or a more personal, interest-specific walk, you'll find it here.

BOAT TOURS

Batobus. Hop on and off at one of Batobus's nine stops, which include the Eiffel Tower, Musée d'Orsay, and the Champs-Élysées. A one-day pass for unlimited travel—boats are heated and have panoramic views but offer no commentary—is €17; a two-day pass is only €19. ☒ Port de la Bourdonnais, Eiffel Tower 🕾 01–76–64–79–12 ⊕ www.batobus.com 🖅 From €17.

Green River Cruises. Whether it's an hour-long Sunday cruise or a three-hour candlelight stroll along the Seine, the boat outings offered by Green River Cruises are limited to 12 people maximum, providing a more intimate tour of the city. Champagne is included in some options, but you are welcome to bring your own wine and snacks. ☒ Bateau Play Time, 66 Quai d'Austerlitz, Montparnasse 🕾 06–50–22–90–65 ⊕ www.greenriver-paris.fr/en 🖅 From €34 per person.

WALKING TOURS

Sight Seeker's Delight. This company's unique two- or three-hour walking tours, from "Pièce De Résistance" to "Tickling Your Tastebuds," bring the city's various quarters to life with engaging information and personal insight from English-speaking guides. ☒ Paris 🕾 06–22–52–57–90 ⊕ www.sightseekersdelight.com 🖅 From €35.

Wego Walking Paris. These 3½-hour walking tours in English begin next to Notre-Dame and end at the Eiffel Tower, covering 25 attractions with lots of history and fun anecdotes in between. Often called the most entertaining tour in Paris, it's pay what you wish, or more accurately, you pay your guide what you think they deserve. Due to popularity, it's best to reserve by credit card beforehand, but remember that if you're a no-show or cancel less than 48 hours before the tour, there's a charge of €20. ☒ 1 Pont au Double, Ile de la Cité ⊕ www.wegowalking.com.

SPECIALTY TOURS

Culinary Tours of Paris. Spend more than three hours discovering French food, wine, and culture with a French-American tour guide who has lived in Paris for nearly a decade. During the English-speaking Montmartre tour, you'll dine at three different restaurants, with digestive walks of the neighborhoods in between destinations. ☒ Paris ⊕ www.culinarytoursofparis.com 🖅 From €100.

Midnight In Paris On Wheels. Take in the city's main monuments on a two- or three-hour nocturnal escapade in a classic 2CV car. The tour guide will tailor the ride to your tastes, whether it be history or a desire to discover new areas. A bottle of bubbly is provided, too. ☒ Paris 🕾 33/06–51–19–24–88 ⊕ www.midnightinparisonwheels.com 🖅 From €120.

On the Calendar

January

Paris Fashion Week. The first Paris Fashion Week (PFW) in November 1973 was a fundraiser at Versailles to help cover the palace's $60 million renovation. Its success launched a catwalk rivalry for industry insiders, but the French public would have to wait until 1984 when Thierry Mugler became the first fashion designer to offer paid access to one of his fashion shows. Since then, PFW has become one of the world's leading fashion events, after New York, London, and Milan Weeks. Men and Haute Couture shows are typically in January and June/July, while women's ready-to-wear are in March and September/October. ⊕ fhcm.paris/en/paris-fashion-week-en

The Grand Prix d'Amérique. Held every year on the last Sunday of January since 1920, the Grand Prix d'Amérique at the Vincennes hippodrome is the most prestigious harness race in the world. ⊕ www.prixdameriqueraces.com

February

Carnaval de Paris. The Paris Carnival takes place every year on the Sunday before Mardi Gras. A parade with musical performances starts at 2 pm at Place Gambetta (20e) and ends at the Place de la République around 5 pm, followed by a party. A month later the Carnaval des Femmes (Women's Carnival) kicks off in Place du Châtelet (4e). Both events are free. ⊕ www.carnaval-paris.org

April

Goût de France/Good France. In 2010, the "gastronomic meal of the French" was officially acknowledged as part of humanity's intangible cultural heritage by UNESCO. The organization said the meal "emphasizes togetherness, the pleasure of taste, and the balance between human beings and the products of nature." Over four days in April, food lovers can take part in the Goût de France/Good France (formerly the Fête de la Gastronomie) with events across Paris, including a *dîner à la française* at one of 2,000 restaurants around the world celebrating French gastronomy. ⊕ www.france.fr/fr/campagne/gout-france-good-france

Paris Marathon. What better way to see all the city's major landmarks than running 42.195 km with a Marathon de Paris souvenir T-shirt at the finish? On a Sunday in April, some 57,000 runners from 140 countries depart from the Champs-Elysées, and pass by the Louvre, the Bastille, Notre-Dame Cathedral, and the Eiffel Tower before a photo finish on Avenue Foch near the Arc de Triomphe. If you're not up for running the marathon yourself, join the crowds along the route cheering on the runners. ⊕ www.schneiderelectricparismarathon.com

May

Nuit des Musées. You won't see Ben Stiller, but this cultural event gives the public free access to Paris museums on the third Saturday of May, from 7 pm to 1 am. ⊕ nuitdesmusees.culture.gouv.fr

The French Open. Held over two weeks at the end of May through early June, the French Open, or Roland Garros as it's also known, is one of the four Grand Slam tennis tournaments. The big-name matches are played on the Philippe Chatrier court, and while tickets for the public go on sale in early March, Experience Packages are available two weeks earlier. And in case you're wondering, Roland Garros was not a famous French tennis player but a fighter pilot during WWI. ⊕ www.rolandgarros.com/en-us

June

Orangerie du Parc de Bagatelle Festivals.
The Chopin Festival and the Solistes Festival strike musical high notes in the Orangerie du Parc de Bagatelle, one of Paris's most beautiful gardens. The former runs from mid-June through mid-July, while the latter is held on three consecutive weekends in September. Tickets will set you back €21 to €35. ⊕ ars-mobilis.fr

Fête de la Musique. Also known as World Music Day, Fête de la Musique is an international festival founded in 1981 by French minister of culture Jack Lang. On June 21 (the summer solstice), free concerts by amateurs and professionals alike are performed on city streets and in village squares throughout France. In Paris, it's an all-night party (literally, noise regulations are overlooked) and a great opportunity to hear some music and blend in like a Parisian. ⊕ fetedelamusique.culture.gouv.fr

Paris Pride March. Pride parades in France have taken place on a national level since 1993. Every June, Paris Pride—or the Marche des Fiertés LGBTQ—brings together some 60 LGBTQ+ associations to fight against sexual orientation and gender identity discrimination. The carnival procession unites hundreds of thousands of supporters and ends usually at Place de la Bastille or Place de la République followed by a free concert. Celebrations eventually spill over to nightclubs and bars around the city. ⊕ www.inter-lgbt.org

July

Days Off Festival. Held over 10 days in early July at the Philharmonie de Paris, this festival focuses on pop-rock, with some jazz and electro thrown in for good measure. Headliners like Rufus Wainwright and Blur frontman Damon Albarn lure Parisians away from their offices. Tickets are modestly priced between €18 to €38. ⊕ www.daysoff.fr

Bastille Day. You won't want to miss France's national holiday celebrations on July 14, especially the military parade along the Champs-Élysées in the morning. There is a free symphony Concert de Paris outside the Eiffel Tower followed by fireworks at 11 pm. In between, the Louvre gives you something to smile about as its permanent collection, which includes the Mona Lisa, is free to visit on Bastille Day.

Tour de France. If Lycra is your thing, head to the Champs-Élysées on the final day of the Tour de France. Cyclists, who have just completed some 3,500 kilometers over 23 days (with two days off for rest), arrive in central Paris and follow the Rue de Rivoli on to the Place de la Concorde before entering the Champs-Élysées to the Finish. ⊕ www.letour.fr/en

Paris Summer Festival. The three-week Paris Festival l'Eté offers artistic events, from theater and dance to circus and plastic installations, with the goal of making art and culture available to all. Free and paid performances draw 100,000 spectators to 30 (mostly) outdoor venues across Paris, including national monuments, gardens, swimming pools, and churches. ⊕ www.parislete.fr

Paris Plages. You might not think of Paris as a beach destination, yet for six weeks every summer the Seine riverbanks and Villette canal basin offer everything

On the Calendar

you need to beat the summer heat—free sun umbrellas, deck chairs, palm trees, sports activities, and swimming. ⊕ en.parisinfo.com/discovering-paris/major-events/paris-plages

August

Cinéma en Plein Air. The free open-air summer cinema at the Parc de la Villette is the largest in Paris, showing around 30 new and old releases—both French and *version originale* (VO) foreign films with subtitles. Screenings start at 9:30 or 10:30 pm, and some are accessible for those who are hard of hearing. ⊕ lavillette.com/programmation

Classique au Vert Festival. For free outdoor classical concerts, the Classique au Vert Festival is staged on weekends at 4 pm from August to mid-September, drawing fans to the Parc Floral in Bois de Vincennes (entrance to the park is €2.50). This is also the spot that hosts the Paris Jazz Festival each weekend in June and July. ⊕ festivalsduparcfloral.paris/programmation/classique-au-vert

Rock en Seine. This rock music festival on the outskirts of Paris is one of the largest of its kind in France. Past headliners include the Cure, Lana Del Rey, Arcade Fire, Cypress Hill, and the Foo Fighters. A four-day pass is €199. ⊕ www.rockenseine.com

September

Paris Beer Festival. France is home to more than 1,500 microbreweries, the most in Europe, according to Statista. And although wine is still the favorite drink, beer is the most consumed alcoholic beverage per capita. Paris Beer Week brings together 40 craft microbreweries with beer enthusiasts in various locations in Paris over four days in September. ⊕ parisbeerfestival.fr/en

Jazz à la Villette. The annual Jazz à la Villette Festival is held at various Parc de La Villette venues, including the Philharmonie de Paris and Trabendo, over 10 days in early September. Tickets range from €22 to €32. ⊕ www.jazzalavillette.com/fr

Festival d'Automne à Paris. Since 1972, the Paris Autumn Festival has featured a packed program that includes contemporary dance, theater, music, visual arts, and film. From September to December, 100,000 fans attend 50 productions from more than a dozen countries at various venues in and around the city. ⊕ www.festival-automne.com

October

Nuit Blanche. Don't expect to get too much sleep the first Saturday in October. A contemporary all-night art festival, the Nuit Blanche lets you attend installations, concerts, and artistic performances at museums, cultural institutions, and other public and private spots across the city. And it is all free. ⊕ www.facebook.com/NBParis

Fête des Vendanges de Montmartre. Picasso, Renoir, and van Gogh were inspired by Montmartre's hilltop and its tax-exempt wine laws. That is no longer the case, but locals have been celebrating the Grape Harvest Festival and the arrival of cuvées from Clos Montmartre since 1934 with wine tastings, a wine auction, and lots of live music over a weekend in early October. ⊕ www.fetedesvendangesdemontmartre.com

Salon du Chocolat. Chocoholics will want to head to Porte de Versailles for the world's largest event dedicated to everything chocolate and cocoa. Over five days in October, you can take part in tastings, workshops, and exhibits with the planet's biggest names in chocolate and pastries. There's also a dedicated area for kids. ⊕ www.salon-du-chocolat.com

November

Paris Cheese and Wine Week. Uncorked in 2021, some 80 eclectic cheesemakers, wine merchants, restaurants, bistros, hotels, and bakers offer tastings and events across the city each November. ⊕ parischeeseandwineweek.com

Fête du Beaujolais Nouveau. The third Thursday of November is all about this popular *vin primeur*. While the small Beaujolais wine region in eastern France produces reds, whites, and rosés, it's well known around the globe for its red Beaujolais Nouveau that untypically needs to be consumed within weeks of harvest. The taste can vary from year to year, and wine bars, bistros, and restaurants across Paris wait, corkscrew in hand, for its annual arrival.

December

Christmas Markets. It would not be Christmas in Paris without the Marchés de Noël. Around 15 Christmas markets pop up around the city four Sundays before Christmas. The most popular can be found in Tuileries Garden, next to the Louvre. The amusement park rides and traditional chalets attract about 13 million visitors every season.

Helpful French Phrases

BASICS

Yes/no	wee/nohn	Oui/non
Please	seel voo play	S'il vous plaît
Thank you	mair-**see**	Merci
You're welcome	deh ree-**ehn**	De rien
Excuse me, sorry	pahr-**don**	Pardon
Good morning/ afternoon	bohn-**zhoor**	Bonjour
Good evening	bohn-**swahr**	Bonsoir
Good-bye	o ruh-**vwahr**	Au revoir
Mr. (Sir)	muh-**syuh**	Monsieur
Mrs. (Ma'am)	ma-**dam**	Madame
Miss	mad-mwa-**zel**	Mademoiselle
Pleased to meet you	ohn-shahn-**tay**	Enchanté(e)
How are you?	kuh-mahn-tahl-ay **voo**	Comment allez-vous?
Very well, thanks	tray bee-ehn, mair-**see**	Très bien, merci
And you?	ay voo?	Et vous?

NUMBERS

one	uhn	un
two	deuh	deux
three	twah	trois
four	**kaht**-ruh	quatre
five	sank	cinq
six	seess	six
seven	set	sept
eight	wheat	huit
nine	nuf	neuf
ten	deess	dix
eleven	ohnz	onze
twelve	dooz	douze
thirteen	trehz	treize
fourteen	kah-**torz**	quatorze
fifteen	kanz	quinze
sixteen	sez	seize
seventeen	deez-**set**	dix-sept
eighteen	deez-**wheat**	dix-huit
nineteen	deez-**nuf**	dix-neuf
twenty	vehn	vingt
twenty-one	vehnt-ay-**uhn**	vingt-et-un
thirty	trahnt	trente
forty	ka-**rahnt**	quarante
fifty	sang-**kahnt**	cinquante
sixty	swa-**sahnt**	soixante
seventy	swa-sahnt-**deess**	soixante-dix
eighty	kaht-ruh-**vehn**	quatre-vingts
ninety	kaht-ruh-vehn-**deess**	quatre-vingt-dix
one hundred	sahn	cent
one thousand	meel	mille

COLORS

black	nwahr	noir
blue	bleuh	bleu
brown	bruhn/mar-**rohn**	brun/marron
green	vair	vert
orange	o-**rahnj**	orange
pink	rose	rose
red	rouge	rouge
violet	vee-o-**let**	violette
white	blahnk	blanc
yellow	zhone	jaune

DAYS OF THE WEEK

Sunday	dee-**mahnsh**	dimanche
Monday	luhn-**dee**	lundi
Tuesday	mahr-**dee**	mardi
Wednesday	mair-kruh-**dee**	mercredi
Thursday	zhuh-**dee**	jeudi
Friday	vawn-druh-**dee**	vendredi
Saturday	sahm-**dee**	samedi

MONTHS

January	zhahn-vee-**ay**	janvier
February	feh-vree-**ay**	février
March	marce	mars
April	a-**vreel**	avril
May	meh	mai
June	zhwehn	juin
July	zhwee-**ay**	juillet
August	ah-**oo**	août
September	sep-**tahm**-bruh	septembre
October	awk-**to**-bruh	octobre
November	no-**vahm**-bruh	novembre
December	day-**sahm**-bruh	décembre

USEFUL PHRASES

Do you speak English?	par-lay **voo** ahn-**glay**	Parlez-vous anglais?
I don't speak ...	zhuh nuh parl pah ...	Je ne parle pas ...
French	frahn-**say**	français
I don't understand	zhuh nuh kohm-**prahn** pah	Je ne comprends pas
I understand	zhuh kohm-**prahn**	Je comprends
I don't know	zhuh nuh say **pah**	Je ne sais pas
I'm American/ British	zhuh sweez a-may-ree-**kehn** / ahn-**glay**	Je suis américain/ anglais
What's your name?	ko-mahn vooz a-pell-ay-**voo**	Comment vous appelez-vous?
My name is ...	zhuh ma-**pell** ...	Je m'appelle ...
What time is it?	kel air eh-**teel**	Quelle heure est-il?
How?	ko-**mahn**	Comment?
When?	kahn	Quand?
Yesterday	yair	Hier
Today	o-zhoor-**dwee**	Aujourd'hui

Tomorrow	duh- **mehn**	Demain
Tonight	suh **swahr**	Ce soir
What?	kwah	Quoi?
What is it?	kess-kuh- **say**	Qu'est-ce que c'est?
Why?	poor- **kwa**	Pourquoi?
Who?	kee	Qui?
Where is ...	oo ay	Où est ...
the train station?	la gar	la gare?
the subway station?	la sta- **syon** duh may- **tro**	la station de métro?
the bus stop?	la-ray duh booss	l'arrêt de bus?
the post office?	la post	la poste?
the bank?	la bahnk	la banque?
the ... hotel?	lo- **tel**	l'hôtel ...?
the store?	luh ma-ga- **zehn**	le magasin?
the cashier?	la **kess**	la caisse?
the ... museum?	luh mew- **zay**	le musée ...?
the hospital?	lo-pee- **tahl**	l'hôpital?
the elevator?	la-sahn- **seuhr**	l'ascenseur?
the telephone?	luh tay-lay- **phone**	le téléphone?
Where are the ...	oo sohn lay	Où sont les ...
restrooms?	twah- **let**	toilettes?
(men/women)	(**oh**-mm/ **fah**-mm)	(hommes/femmes)
Here/there	ee- **see** /la	Ici/là
Left/right	a goash/a draht	A gauche/à droite
Straight ahead	too drwah	Tout droit
Is it near/far?	say pray/lwehn	C'est près/loin?
I'd like ...	zhuh voo- **dray**	Je voudrais ...
a room	ewn **shahm**-bruh	une chambre
the key	la clay	la clé
a newspaper	uhn zhoor- **nahl**	un journal
a stamp	uhn **tam**-bruh	un timbre
I'd like to buy ...	zhuh voo- **dray** **ahsh**-tay	Je voudrais acheter ...
cigarettes	day see-ga- **ret**	des cigarettes
matches	days a-loo- **met**	des allumettes
soap	dew sah- **vohn**	du savon
city map	uhn plahn de **veel**	un plan de ville
road map	ewn cart roo-tee- **air**	une carte routière
magazine	ewn reh- **vu**	une revue
envelopes	dayz ahn-veh- **lope**	des enveloppes
writing paper	dew pa-pee- **ay** a **let**-ruh	du papier à lettres
postcard	ewn cart pos- **tal**	une carte postale
How much is it?	say comb-bee- **ehn**	C'est combien?
A little/a lot	uhn peuh/bo- **koo**	Un peu/beaucoup
More/less	plu/mwehn	Plus/moins
Enough/too (much)	a-say/tro	Assez/trop
I am ill/sick	zhuh swee ma- **lahd**	Je suis malade
Call a ...	a-play uhn ...	Appelez un ...
doctor	dohk- **tehr**	docteur
Help!	o suh- **koor**	Au secours!

Stop!	a-reh- **tay**	Arrêtez!
Fire!	o fuh	Au feu!
Caution!/Look out!	a-tahn-see- **ohn**	Attention!

DINING OUT

A bottle of ...	ewn boo- **tay** duh	une bouteille de ...
A cup of ...	ewn tass duh	une tasse de ...
A glass of ...	uhn vair duh	un verre de ...
Bill/check	la-dee-see- **ohn**	l'addition
Bread	dew panh	du pain
Breakfast	luh puh- **tee** day-zhuh- **nay**	le petit-déjeuner
Butter	dew burr	du beurre
Cheers!	ah **vo**-truh sahn- **tay**	A votre santé!
Cocktail/aperitif	uhn ah-pay-ree- **teef**	un apéritif
Dinner	luh dee- **nay**	le dîner
Dish of the day	luh plah dew **zhoor**	le plat du jour
Enjoy!	bohn a-pay- **tee**	Bon appétit!
Fixed-price menu	luh may- **new**	le menu
Fork	ewn four- **shet**	une fourchette
I am diabetic	zhuh swee dee-ah-bay- **teek**	Je suis diabétique
I am vegetarian	zhuh swee vay-zhay-ta-ree- **en**	Je suis végétarien(ne)
I cannot eat ...	zhuh nuh puh pah mahn- **jay** deh	Je ne peux pas manger de ...
I'd like to order	zhuh voo- **dray** ko-mahn- **day**	Je voudrais commander
Is service/the tip included?	ess kuh luh sair- **veess** ay comb- **pree**	Est-ce que le service est compris?
It's good/bad	say bohn/mo- **vay**	C'est bon/mauvais
It's hot/cold	say sho/frwah	C'est chaud/froid
Knife	uhn koo- **toe**	un couteau
Lunch	luh day-zhuh- **nay**	le déjeuner
Menu	la cart	la carte
Napkin	ewn sair-vee- **et**	une serviette
Pepper	dew **pwah**-vruh	du poivre
Plate	ewn a-see- **et**	une assiette
Please give me ...	doe-nay- **mwah**	Donnez-moi ...
Salt	dew sell	du sel
Spoon	ewn kwee- **air**	une cuillère
Sugar	dew **sook**-ruh	du sucre
Waiter!/Waitress!	muh- **syuh** / mad-mwa- **zel**	Monsieur!/ Mademoiselle!
Wine list	la cart day vehn	la carte des vins

Great Itineraries

Paris is a treasure of neighborhoods and history, and a visit to this glorious city is never quite as simple as a quick look at a few landmarks. But if you have only a day to take it all in, there are some icons that you just can't miss. Over five days, you'll have the luxury to truly take in the sights and museums while leaving time for random exploring, including sampling the foods and beverages that have put the capital on the gastronomic world map.

Paris in 1 Day

Begin your day at the Trocadéro métro, where you can get the best views of the **Eiffel Tower** from the esplanade of the Palais de Chaillot. If you want to ride to the top, now is the best time to get in line (it opens at 9:30 am year-round). Afterward, take a walk along the Seine, stopping to visit the sculpture gardens of the **Musée Rodin** (be sure to stop at the café L'Augustine for a coffee), and continuing on to the **Musée d'Orsay** to tackle the late-19th-century works of art and admire the gorgeous former train station.

If your feet are still happy, cross the gilded Pont Tsar Alexandre III to the **Champs-Élysées,** passing the Belle Époque art palaces known as the **Grand Palais** and **Petit Palais.** You can take Bus 73 (€1.90) from the **Assemblée Nationale** across the bridge to **Place de la Concorde** and all the way up **Avenue des Champs-Élysées** to the **Arc de Triomphe.** Open until 10:30 pm, its panoramic viewing platform is ideal for admiring the City of Light.

Next, head to the most famous art museum in the world, the **Louvre.** With just one day in the city, you'll have to limit your time here, but grab a museum guide and hit up the Big Three: the *Mona Lisa, Venus de Milo,* and *Winged Victory*

of Samothrace. There should still be time to get a glimpse of the exterior of **Notre-Dame Cathedral,** which still stands proud and mighty after the 2019 fire that almost destroyed the interior. Renovations are expected to be complete for the 2024 Summer Olympic Games in Paris.

Paris in 5 Days

DAY 1: NOTRE-DAME AND THE LATIN QUARTER

Start your day at Pont Neuf for excellent views off the western tip of Île de la Cité, then explore the island's magnificent architectural heritage, including the **Conciergerie, Sainte-Chapelle,** and **Notre-Dame.**

Take a detour to neighboring Île St-Louis for lunch before heading into the medieval labyrinth of the **Latin Quarter**; its most valuable treasures are preserved in the **Musée de Cluny,** including the reconstructed ruins of 2nd-century Gallo-Roman steam baths. At the summit of the hill above the Sorbonne University is the imposing **Panthéon,** a monument (and mausoleum) of French heroes. Follow Rue Descartes to Rue Mouffetard for a café crème on one of the oldest market streets in Paris.

DAY 2: JARDIN DES TUILERIES, THE LOUVRE, AND THE MUSÉE D'ORSAY

Begin at **Place de la Concorde,** where an Egyptian obelisk replaces the guillotine where Louis XVI and Marie-Antoinette met their bloody fate during the French Revolution, then escape the traffic in the formal **Jardin des Tuileries,** which once belonged to the 16th-century Tuileries Palace, destroyed during the Paris Commune of 1871. Pass through the small Arc du Carrousel to the modern glass pyramid that serves as the main entrance to the **Louvre,** the world's grandest museum, once a 12th-century fortress. You'll never be able to see it all, but take a few hours to explore and make sure you hit up all the essentials.

The **Musée d'Orsay** merits an afternoon gander. The short post-Louvre stroll to this museum on the Left Bank is just long enough to get some fresh air before feasting your eyes on the world's biggest collection of Impressionist and Postimpressionist masterpieces, housed in a building that's equally magnificent visually.

DAY 3: EIFFEL TOWER, CHAMPS-ÉLYSÉES, AND ARC DE TRIOMPHE
Begin your day at the Trocadéro métro, where you can get the best views of the **Eiffel Tower** from the esplanade of the Palais de Chaillot. Visit the **Musée de l'Homme,** with 63 mummies and 700,000 prehistoric artifacts and fossils, and take advantage of the spectacular selfie ops of both the Tour Eiffel and the Seine.

Then meander over to Quai d'Orsay, near Invalides, stopping for a *plat du jour* along the way before crossing the Alexandre III bridge to the Grand Palais, where you can now sneak some rooftop peeks, and then visit its sister, the Petit Palais. From here, you can walk all the way up **Avenue des Champs-Élysées** (focus on the prize and not the chain stores that line the avenue) to the **Arc de Triomphe.** Open until 10:30 pm, its panoramic viewing platform is ideal for admiring the City of Light.

DAY 4: THE MARAIS
In the 4e arrondissement, the hip Marais district just keeps getting hipper and is the perfect neighborhood to spend a relaxing day filled with culture, food, and fashion. To the south you can find the **Hôtel de Sens,** home to King Henry IV's feisty ex-wife Queen Marguerite, and one of the few surviving examples of late-medieval architecture. Around the corner on Rue Charlemagne is a preserved section of the city's 12th-century fortifications built by King Philippe-Augustus. Cross busy Rue St-Antoine to Le Marais and enter the **Hôtel de Sully,** a fine example of the elegant private mansions built here by aristocrats in the early 17th century. Stop by any of the old aristocratic mansions in Le Marais that have been turned into museums, including the **Musée Picasso** and the offbeat **Musée de la Chasse et de la Nature**.

DAY 5: VERSAILLES
On Day 5, head 20 km (12½ miles) southwest of Paris to the gilded palace and reminder of pre-Revolution indulgence that is **Versailles.** The estate is divided into four sections: the Palace with the King's Grand Apartments and the famous Hall of Mirrors, the Grand Trianon, Marie-Antoinette's Estate, and, of, course, the spectacular gardens. Book an English tour, which includes the King's Apartments, Royal Chapel, and Opera, and make sure you get there by 9 am so you can be sure to see everything. The easiest (and least expensive) way to visit Versailles is by the 40-minute Paris RER train serviced from St-Michel–Notre-Dame, Musée d'Orsay, Invalides, and Tour Eiffel stations. Buy tickets (destination: Versailles Rive G) directly from the automatic ticket machines or from the booth.

Contacts

Air

**AIRPORT INFORMA-
TION Charles de Gaulle/
Roissy and Orly.** ☎ *3950
(press "0" for service in
English) €0.35 per minute,
0033/1–70–36–39–50
outside of France* ⊕ *www.
parisaeroport.fr.*

Bicycle

Vélib'. ☎ *01–76–49–12–34*
⊕ *www.velib-metropole.fr.*

🅞 Boat and Ferry

BOAT Bateaux Parisiens.
✉ *Port de la Bourdon-
nais, 7e, Paris* ☎ *08–
25–01–01–01 €0.15/min*
⊕ *www.bateauxparisiens.
com.* **Batobus.** ✉ *Port
de la Bourdonnais, 7e,
Paris* ☎ *01–76–64–79–12*
⊕ *www.batobus.com.*
Canauxrama. ✉ *Bas-
sin de la Villette, 13
quai de la Loire, 19e,*
Paris ☎ *01–42–39–15–00*
⊕ *www.canauxrama.
com.* **Compagnie des
Bateaux-Mouches.** ✉ *Port
de la Conférence, 8e,
Paris* ☎ *01–42–25–96–10*
⊕ *www.bateaux-mouches.
fr.* **Paris Canal.** ✉ *Paris
Canal, Bassin de la Villette,
21 quai de la Loire, 19e,
Paris* ☎ *01–42–40–29–00*
⊕ *www.pariscanal.com.*

FERRY Direct Ferries.
⊕ *www.directferries.fr.*
P&O European Ferries.
☎ *03–66–74–03–25*
⊕ *www.poferries.com.*

🅑 Bus

BUS INFORMATION
Flixbus. ⊕ *global.flixbus.
com/eurolines.* **RATP.**
☎ *3424* ⊕ *www.ratp.fr.*

🅜 Metro

MÉTRO INFORMATION
RATP. ☎ *3424* ⊕ *www.
ratp.fr.*

🚗 Taxi

COMPANIES Alpha Taxis.
☎ *01-45-85-85-85* ⊕ *www.
alphataxis.fr.* **Taxis G7.**
☎ *3607 €0.45/min, 01-41-
27-66-99 for service in
English* ⊕ *www.g7.fr.*

🚆 Train

TRAIN INFORMATION
Eurail. ⊕ *www.eurail.com.*
SNCF. ☎ *3635* ⊕ *www.
sncf.com/en.* **TGV.** ☎ *3635*
⊕ *www.sncf.com/en.*

**CHANNEL TUNNEL
INFORMATION Eurostar.**
☎ *646/934–6454 in U.S.,
01–70–70–60–88 in France*
⊕ *www.eurostar.com.*
Eurotunnel. ☎ *08–10–63–
03–04 €0.06/min* ⊕ *www.
eurotunnel.com.*

Chapter 3

ÎLE DE LA CITÉ AND ÎLE ST-LOUIS

3

Updated by
Jack Vermee

⊙ Sights	🍴 Restaurants	🛏 Hotels	🛍 Shopping	🍸 Nightlife
★★★★☆	★★☆☆☆	★★★☆☆	★★☆☆☆	★☆☆☆☆

NEIGHBORHOOD SNAPSHOT

MAKING THE MOST OF YOUR TIME

This little area of Paris is easily walkable and packed with sights and stunning views, so give yourself as much time as possible to explore. With Notre-Dame, the Conciergerie, and Sainte-Chapelle, you could spend a day wandering, but the islands are easily combined with the St-Germain quarter. On warmer days, Rue de Buci is an ideal place to pick up a picnic lunch to enjoy in leafy Square du Vert-Galant at the tip of Île de la Cité. If you have limited time in the area, survey the ongoing reconstruction of Notre-Dame and go for a stroll.

GETTING HERE

Île de la Cité and Île St-Louis are in the 1er and 4e arrondissements (Boulevard du Palais is the dividing line between the 1er and 4e arrondissements on Île de la Cité). If you're too far away to get here on foot, take the *métro* to St-Michel station or Cité.

PAUSE HERE

At the western tip of the Île de la Cité, the Square Vert-Galant is a favorite spot for local picnickers. The garden is a peaceful oasis in the very heart of the city. Take métro Line 7 to Pont Neuf, cross the famous bridge, nod to the statue of Henri IV on horseback, and then relax.

TOP REASONS TO GO

■ **Notre-Dame.** This gorgeous Gothic cathedral has welcomed visitors to Paris for centuries. While you currently cannot visit inside due to the tragic 2019 fire that nearly destroyed the entire church, the imposing edifice and famed towers still remain a must-see from the outside.

■ **Sainte-Chapelle.** Visit on a sunny day to best appreciate the exquisite stained glass in this 13th-century chapel built for King Louis IX.

■ **Strolling the Islands.** Île de la Cité is where Paris began. Start with the city's oldest bridge, the Pont Neuf (incongruously called the "new bridge") and give a nod to the statue of Henry IV, who once proudly said, "I make love, I make war, and I build." From here, cross to Place Dauphine and make your way to Île St-Louis, one of the city's most exclusive enclaves.

At the heart of Paris, linked to the banks of the Seine by a series of bridges, are two small islands: Île St-Louis and Île de la Cité. They're the perfect places to begin your visit, with postcard-worthy views all around. The Île de la Cité is anchored by mighty Notre-Dame, badly damaged by the 2019 fire but still standing; farther east, the atmospheric Île St-Louis is dotted with charming hotels, cozy restaurants, and small specialty shops.

Île de la Cité

At the western tip of Île de la Cité is regal **Place Dauphine**, one of Paris's oldest squares. The impressive **Palais de Justice** (courthouse) sits between **Sainte-Chapelle**, the exquisite medieval chapel of saintly King Louis IX, and the **Concier-gerie**, the prison where Marie-Antoinette and other bluebloods awaited their slice of history at the guillotine.

The Gothic powerhouse that is **Notre-Dame** originally loomed over a medieval huddle of buildings that were later ordered razed by Baron Georges-Eugène Haussmann, the 19th-century urban planner who transformed Paris into the city we see today. In front of the cathedral is **Place du Parvis**, the point from which all roads in France are measured. On the north side of the square is the **Hôtel-Dieu** (roughly translated as "general hospital");

it was immortalized by 19th-century author Honoré de Balzac as the squalid last stop for the city's most unfortunate, but today it houses a modern hospital. Just behind the cathedral lies Rue du Cloître-Notre-Dame, which cuts through the **Ancien Cloître Quartier**, on whose narrow streets you can imagine the medieval quarter as it once was, densely packed and teeming with activity. At 9–11 quai aux Fleurs, a plaque commemorates the abode that was the setting of the tragic 12th-century love affair between the philosopher Peter Abélard and his young student, Héloïse.

At the eastern tip of Île de la Cité is the **Mémorial des Martyrs de la Déportation**, all but hidden in a pocket-size park. A set of stairs leads down to this impressive and moving memorial, which commemorates the French citizens who died in Nazi concentration camps.

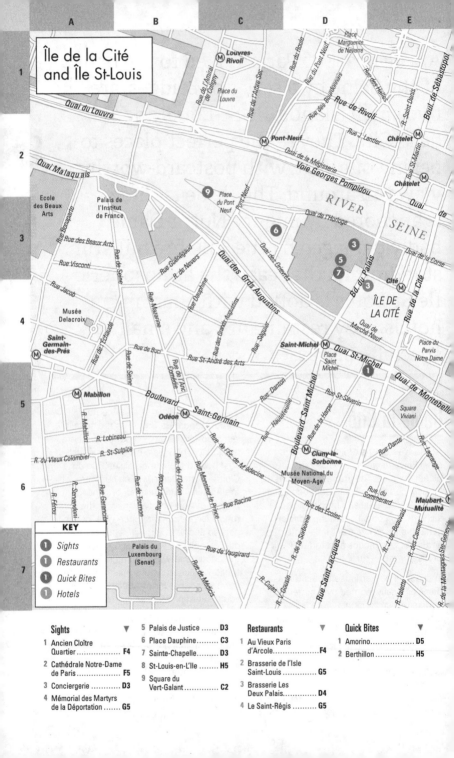

Île de la Cité
and Île St-Louis

RIVER

SEINE

ÎLE DE
LA CITÉ

KEY
- Sights
- Restaurants
- Quick Bites
- Hotels

Sights ▼
1 Ancien Cloître
  Quartier **F4**
2 Cathédrale Notre-Dame
  de Paris **F5**
3 Conciergerie **D3**
4 Mémorial des Martyrs
  de la Déportation **G5**
5 Palais de Justice **D3**
6 Place Dauphine **C3**
7 Sainte-Chapelle **D3**
8 St-Louis-en-L'Ile **H5**
9 Square du
  Vert-Galant **C2**

Restaurants ▼
1 Au Vieux Paris
  d'Arcole **F4**
2 Brasserie de l'Isle
  Saint-Louis **G5**
3 Brasserie Les
  Deux Palais **D4**
4 Le Saint-Régis **G5**

Quick Bites ▼
1 Amorino **D5**
2 Berthillon **H5**

Hotels ▼

Sights

Ancien Cloître Quartier

NEIGHBORHOOD | Hidden in the shadows of Notre-Dame is an evocative, often-overlooked tangle of medieval streets. Through the years lucky folks, including Ludwig Bemelmans (who created the beloved *Madeleine* books) and the Aga Khan have called this area home, but back in the Middle Ages it was the domain of cathedral seminary students. One of them was the celebrated Peter Abélard (1079–1142)—philosopher, questioner of the faith, and renowned declaimer of love poems. Abélard boarded with Notre-Dame's clergyman, Fulbert, whose 17-year-old niece, Héloïse, was seduced by the compelling Abélard, 39 years her senior. She became pregnant, and the vengeful clergyman had Abélard castrated; amazingly, he survived and fled to a monastery, while Héloïse took refuge in a nunnery. The poetic, passionate letters between the two cemented their fame as thwarted lovers, and their story inspired a devoted following during the romantic 19th century. They still draw admirers to the Père-Lachaise Cemetery, where they're interred *ensemble*. The clergyman's house at 10 rue Chanoinesse was redone in 1849; a plaque at the back of the building at 9–11 quai aux Fleurs commemorates the lovers. ⊠ *Rue du Cloître-Notre-Dame north to Quai des Fleurs, Île de la Cité* Ⓜ *Cité.*

★ Cathédrale Notre-Dame de Paris

CHURCH | Looming above Place du Parvis, this Gothic sanctuary is the symbolic heart of Paris and, for many, of France itself, now more than ever. A heartbreaking 2019 fire almost destroyed the entire cathedral. The roof was devastated, and the 300-foot spire collapsed, but after the fire was extinguished, the building was deemed structurally sound, and most of its priceless relics and items survived, including the famed rose windows, the crown of thorns said to have been worn by Jesus Christ, the 800-year-old organ, and numerous pieces of classic artwork. Many of these items sustained some damage, and restoration work for these and for the whole of the cathedral is expected to last several years—the projected reopening is around 2024. While visitors will not be able to go inside until then, the towers outside still stand as testaments to the power, history, and meaning of Notre-Dame. Napoléon was crowned here, and kings and queens exchanged marriage vows before its altar. Begun in 1163, completed in 1345, badly damaged during the Revolution, and restored in the 19th century by Eugène Viollet-le-Duc, Notre-Dame may not be the country's oldest or largest cathedral, but in beauty and architectural harmony it has few peers. ⊠ *6 parvis Notre-Dame– Pl. Jean-Paul II, Île de la Cité* ☎ *01–42– 34–56–10* ⊕ *www.notredamedeparis.fr* Ⓜ *Cité.*

Conciergerie

NOTABLE BUILDING | **FAMILY** | Most of the Île de la Cité's medieval structures fell victim to wunderkind urban planner Baron Haussmann's ambitious rebuilding program of the 1860s. Among the rare survivors are the jewel-like Sainte-Chapelle, a vision of shimmering stained glass, and the Conciergerie, the cavernous former prison where Marie-Antoinette and other victims of the French Revolution spent their final days.

Constructed by Philip IV in the late 13th and early 14th centuries, the Conciergerie—which takes its name from the building's concierge or keeper—was part of the original palace of the kings of France before the royals moved into the Louvre around 1364. In 1391, it became a prison. During the French Revolution, Marie-Antoinette languished 76 days here awaiting her date with the guillotine. There is a re-creation of the doomed queen's sad little cell—plus others that are far smaller—complete with wax figures behind bars. In the chapel, stained glass, commissioned after the queen's

The Île de la Cité is perhaps most charming at night, when its embankments along the Seine are illuminated by street and bridge lights.

death by her daughter, is emblazoned with the initials *M.A.* Outside you can see the small courtyard where women prisoners took meals and washed their clothes in the fountain (men enjoyed no similar respite). Well-done temporary exhibitions on the ground floor aim to please kids and adults alike; themes have included enchanted forests and Gothic castles. There are free guided tours (in French only) most days at 11 and 3. Download a free English guide from the website and pick up a "Histopad" (also free), an "augmented reality" tablet that allows you to go back in time and view 30 reconstructions. ⊠ *2 bd. du Palais, Île de la Cité* ☎ *01–53–40–60–80* ⊕ *www.paris-conciergerie.fr* 🎟 *€11.50; €18.50 with joint ticket to Sainte-Chapelle* Ⓜ *Cité.*

Mémorial des Martyrs de la Déportation
(*Memorial of the Deportation*)
MONUMENT | On the east end of Île de la Cité lies this stark monument to the more than 200,000 French men, women, and children who died in Nazi concentration camps during World War II. The evocative memorial, inaugurated by Charles de Gaulle in 1962, was intentionally designed to be claustrophobic. Concrete blocks mark the narrow entrance to the crypt, which contains the tomb of an unknown deportee killed at the Neustadt camp. A dimly lit narrow gallery studded with 200,000 pieces of glass symbolizes the lives lost, while urns at the lateral ends contain ashes from the camps. ⊠ *Square de l'Île-de-France, 7 quai de l'Archevêché, Île de la Cité* ☎ *01–46–33–87–56* ⊕ *www.onac-vg.fr/ hauts-lieux-memoire-necropoles* 🎟 *Free* 🕑 *Closed Mon.* Ⓜ *Cité, St-Michel.*

Palais de Justice
NOTABLE BUILDING | This 19th-century, neoclassical courthouse complex occupies the site of the former royal palace of St-Louis that later housed Parliament until the French Revolution. It is recognizable from afar with the tower of Sainte-Chapelle, tucked inside the courtyard, peeking out. Although the new Renzo Piano–designed Palais de Justice in the

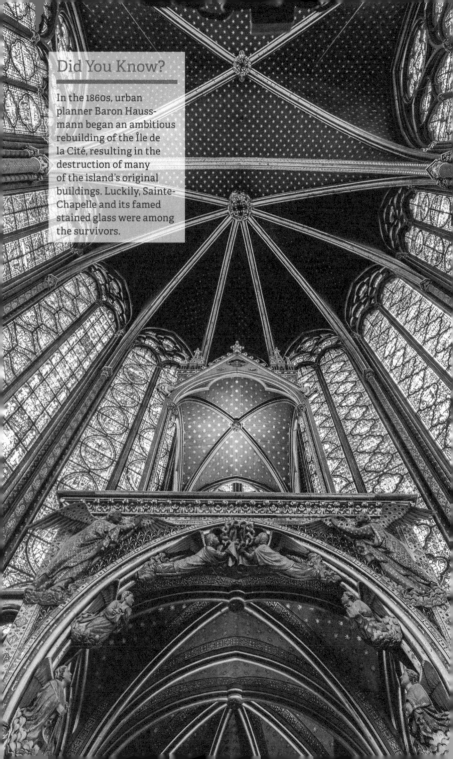

17e arrondissement handles the bulk of the caseload, this venerable edifice is now the court of appeals. Black-frocked judges can often be spotted taking a cigarette break on the majestic rear staircase facing Rue du Harlay. ✉ *4 bd. du Palais, Île de la Cité* ☎ *01–44–32–52–52* ⊕ *www.cours-appel.justice.fr/paris* 🎫 *Free* ◔ *Closed Sun.* Ⓜ *Cité.*

Place Dauphine

PLAZA/SQUARE | The Surrealists called Place Dauphine "le sexe de Paris" because of its suggestive V shape; however, its origins were much more proper. The pretty square on the western side of Pont Neuf was built by Henry IV, who named it in homage to his son the crown prince (or *dauphin*) who became Louis XIII when Henry was assassinated. In warm weather, treat yourself to a romantic meal on a restaurant terrace here—the square is one of the best places in Paris to dine *en plein air*. ✉ *Île de la Cité* Ⓜ *Cité.*

★ Sainte-Chapelle

CHURCH | Built by the obsessively pious Louis IX (1214–70), this Gothic jewel is home to the oldest stained-glass windows in Paris. The chapel was constructed over seven years, at phenomenal expense, to house the king's collection of relics acquired from the impoverished emperor of Constantinople. These included Christ's crown of thorns, fragments of the Cross, and drops of Christ's blood—though even in Louis's time these were considered of questionable authenticity.

The narrow spiral staircase by the entrance takes you to the upper chapel where the famed beauty of Sainte-Chapelle comes alive: 6,458 square feet of stained glass are delicately supported by painted stonework that seems to disappear in the colorful light streaming through the windows. Deep reds and blues dominate the background, noticeably different from later, lighter medieval styles such as those of Notre-Dame's rose windows.

The chapel is essentially an enormous magic lantern illuminating 1,130 biblical figures. Besides the dazzling glass, observe the detailed carvings on the columns and the statues of the apostles. The lower chapel is gloomy and plain, but take note of the low, vaulted ceiling decorated with fleurs-de-lis and cleverly arranged *L*s for "Louis." Audioguides (€3) are available, or you can download a free PDF guide from the website.

Sunset is the optimal time to see the rose window; however, to avoid waiting in killer lines, plan your visit for a weekday morning, the earlier the better. Come on a sunny day to appreciate the full effect of the light filtering through all that glorious stained glass. You can buy a joint ticket with the Conciergerie: lines are shorter if you purchase it there or online. The chapel makes a divine setting for classical concerts; check the schedule at ⊕ *www.classictic.com.* ✉ *4 bd. du Palais, Île de la Cité* ☎ *01–53–40–60–80* ⊕ *www.sainte-chapelle.fr* 🎫 *€11.50; €18.50 with joint ticket to Conciergerie* Ⓜ *Cité.*

Square du Vert-Galant

PLAZA/SQUARE | The equestrian statue of the Vert Galant himself—amorous adventurer Henry IV—keeps a vigilant watch over this leafy square at the western end of the Île de la Cité. The dashing but ruthless Henry, king of France from 1589 until his assassination in 1610, was a stern upholder of the absolute rights of monarchy and a notorious womanizer. He is probably best remembered for his cynical remark that *"Paris vaut bien une messe"* ("Paris is worth a Mass"), a reference to his readiness to renounce Protestantism to gain the throne of predominantly Catholic France. To ease his conscience, he issued the Edict of Nantes in 1598, according French Protestants (almost) equal rights with their Catholic countrymen. The square is a great place for a quai-side picnic. It's also the departure point for Vedette Pont Neuf tour boats (at the bottom of the steps to the right). ✉ *Ile de la Cité* [M] *Pont Neuf.*

🍴 Restaurants

Île de la Cité and Île St-Louis are great for sightseeing, which is why much of the dining scene on these islands revolves around fast food and tourist traps. Luckily, a few long-established brasseries and inspired bistros on elegant Île St-Louis—not to mention the legendary Berthillon, the city's great *glacier* (ice-cream maker)—more than compensate. Among the shops, épiceries, and ancient bookstores of Rue St-Louis-en-l'Île, the island's central spine, you'll find enough quality dining to keep you satisfied at any time of the day.

Au Vieux Paris d'Arcole
$$ | **FRENCH** | Built in 1512 as a residence for the Canon of Notre-Dame, Au Vieux Paris d'Arcole was converted into a wine bar in 1723, making it one of the city's oldest restaurants. It specializes in dishes from the Aveyron region in the southwest (try the *coufidou d'Aubrac*, a rich beef stew made with Marcillac wine) and serves everything in plush red-velvet-and-antiques dining areas that are a treat for the eyes. **Known for:** lovely terrace; quiet setting; quirky antique decor. [$] *Average main: €21* ✉ *24 rue Chanoinesse, Île de la Cité* ☎ *01–40–51–78–52* 🌐 *www.restaurantauvieuxparis.fr* [M] *Cité.*

Brasserie Les Deux Palais
$$ | **BRASSERIE** | Set in the shadow of Sainte-Chapelle's spire, this bright and friendly brasserie has been serving classic fare—*tartare de boeuf, cuisse du canard confit*—to the lawyers and judges of the Palais du Justice across the street since 1930. Take some time to admire the 19th-century lighting fixtures and lovely tiled floor. **Known for:** good value; friendly service; striking historical decor. [$] *Average main: €19* ✉ *3 bd. du Palais, Île de la Cité* ☎ *01–43–54–20–86* 🌐 *www.brasserielesdeuxpalais.fr* [M] *Cité.*

Monsieur Guillotin

Beheading by means of an axe or sword was a popular form of punishment long before the French Revolution, but it was Dr. Joseph-Ignace Guillotin who suggested there was a more humane way of decapitating prisoners. Not surprisingly, Dr. Guillotin's descendants changed their surname.

Île St-Louis

Nearby Pont St-Louis, which always seems to be occupied by street performers, leads to the Île St-Louis, one of the city's best places to wander. There are no cultural hot spots, just a few narrow streets that comprise one of the most privileged areas in Paris. Small hotels, eateries, art galleries, and shops selling everything from chocolate and cheese to silk scarves line the main street, Rue St-Louis-en-L'Île. There were once two islands here, Île Notre-Dame and Île aux Vaches ("Cow Island," an erstwhile grazing pasture), both owned by the Church. Speculators bought the islands, joined them, and sold the plots to builders who created what is today some of the city's most elegant and expensive real estate. Baroque architect Louis Le Vau (who later worked on Versailles) designed fabulous private mansions for aristocrats, including the majestic Hôtel de Lauzun on lovely Quai d'Anjou.

👁 Sights

St-Louis-en-L'Île
CHURCH | You can't miss the unusual lacy spire of this church as you approach the Île St-Louis; it's the only church on the island and there are no other steeples to compete with it. It was built from

1664 to 1726 according to the Baroque designs of architect François Le Vau, brother of the more famous Louis, who designed several mansions nearby—as well as the Palace of Versailles. St-Louis's interior was essentially stripped during the Revolution, as were so many French churches, but look for the odd outdoor iron clock, which dates from 1741. Check the church website for upcoming classical music events. ✉ *19 bis, rue St-Louis-en-L'Île, Île Saint-Louis* ☎ *01–46–34–11–60* 🌐 *www.saintlouisenlile.catholique.fr* [M] *Pont Marie.*

🍴 Restaurants

Brasserie de l'Isle Saint-Louis

$$$ | **BRASSERIE** | With its dream location on the tip of Île St-Louis overlooking the Seine and Notre-Dame, you'd think this charming brasserie, like so many before it, would have succumbed to its own success. Yet it remains exactly what a decent neighborhood brasserie should be, with authentic decor, efficiently friendly service, and reliably good food. **Known for:** decent prices, considering the location; coveted outdoor terrace by the Seine; fantastic views of Notre-Dame. [$] *Average main: €25* ✉ *55 quai de Bourbon, 4e, Île Saint-Louis* ☎ *01–43–54–02–59* 🌐 *www.labrasserie-isl.fr* 🕒 *Closed Wed.* [M] *Pont Marie, Maubert-Mutualité, Sully-Morland.*

Le Saint-Régis

$$ | **BISTRO** | Wondering where locals take their coffee on touristy Île St-Louis? Try this old-time cafe that also features a menu of classic French dishes—it's open until 2 am daily. **Known for:** colorful people-watching; eggs Benedict; brioche French toast with salted caramel ice cream. [$] *Average main: €23* ✉ *6 rue Jean du Bellay, Île Saint-Louis* ☎ *01–43–54–59–41* 🌐 *www.lesaintregis-paris.com* [M] *Pont Marie.*

The Flower Market

Every day of the week, you can find the Marché aux Fleurs (flower market) facing the entrance to the imposing Palais de Justice on Boulevard du Palais. It's a fragrant detour from the Île de la Cité, and the Guimard-designed entrance to the Cité métro station seems to blend beautifully with the potted plants on display in open-air and covered pavilions. On Sunday, the place is chirping with birds and other small pets for sale.

☕ Coffee and Quick Bites

Amorino

$ | **ICE CREAM** | **FAMILY** | Popping up all over—and winning converts faster than you can finish a double scoop—is the Amorino chain of gelaterias, which serves inventive frozen concoctions in the shape of flower blossoms. Popular flavors include rich *bacio* (dark chocolate with hazelnuts) and mascarpone with figs. **Known for:** Italian coffee, tea, and hot chocolate; sweet crêpes and macarons; Italian gelato with a French twist. [$] *Average main: €9* ✉ *47 rue St-Louis-en-l'Île, Île Saint-Louis* ☎ *09–51–83–30–18* 🌐 *www.amorino.com* [M] *Pont-Marie.*

★ **Berthillon**

$ | **ICE CREAM** | Parisian ice cream is served at cafés all over town, but it's worth making the pilgrimage to this mecca of artisanal *crèmes glacées* to understand what all the fuss is about. The family-owned Berthillon shop features more than 30 flavors that change with the seasons, from mouth-puckering *cassis* (black currant) in summer to nutty *marron* (candied chestnut) in winter. **Known for:** classic tearoom atmosphere; long lines; delicious ice cream with natural ingredients. $ *Average main: €8* ✉ *31 rue St-Louis-en-l'Île, Île Saint-Louis* ☎ *01–43–54–31–61* ⊕ *www.berthillon.fr* ⊘ *Closed Mon. and Tues.* Ⓜ *Pont-Marie.*

Hotels

Hôtel Saint-Louis en l'Isle

$$ | HOTEL | The location on the exceptionally charming Île St-Louis is the real draw of this five-story hotel, which retains many of its original 17th-century stone walls and wooden beams. **Pros:** romantic location; friendly staff; ancient architectural details. **Cons:** small rooms; métro stations are not so convenient; location is a bit far from the sights. $ *Rooms from: €205* ✉ *75 rue St-Louis-en-l'Île, Île Saint-Louis* ☎ *01–46–34–04–80* ⊕ *www. saintlouisenlisle.com* 🔁 *20 rooms* ⦿ *No Meals* Ⓜ *Pont Marie.*

Shopping

Although Île de la Cité is so dominated by Notre-Dame, the Palais du Justice, and the Conciergerie that shopping for anything other than tourist trinkets is impossible, Île St-Louis offers visitors a small collection of designer shops and art galleries, nearly all of which are located on Rue St-Louis-en-l'Île, the main street that bisects the island.

Bamyan

WOMEN'S CLOTHING | A shopping destination since 1986, this stylish purveyor of "ethnic chic" showcases the work of talented young Indian and Middle Eastern designers whose multicolored creations range from silk-brocaded saris and stunningly embroidered coats to pashmina scarves and leather handbags. ✉ *72 rue St-Louis-en-l'Île, 4e, Île Saint-Louis* ☎ *01–43–29–39–50* ⊕ *www.bamyanparis. com* Ⓜ *Pont Marie.*

Céline Wright

HOUSEWARES | Poetically binding thousands of strips of *washi* (Japanese paper) into handcrafted, one-of-a-kind lighting fixtures has made Céline Wright a familiar name in Paris's art and design community. Her famous "cocoon" lamps reflect artisanal, eco-friendly traditions while evincing a thoroughly modern sensibility. ✉ *56 rue St-Louis-en-l'Île, 4e, Île Saint-Louis* ☎ *01–43–29–33–93* ⊕ *www. celinewright.com* Ⓜ *Pont Marie.*

Clair de Rêve

TOYS | Stepping into the pleasantly cluttered shop of this maker of marionettes and restorer of automata is like time-traveling to the Belle Époque. Music boxes and wind-up toys are also for sale. ✉ *35 rue St-Louis-en-l'Île, 4e, Île Saint-Louis* ☎ *01–43–81–11–37* ⊕ *www.clairdereve. com* Ⓜ *Pont Marie.*

Les sacs de Louise

HANDBAGS | A warm welcome is guaranteed at this appealing little boutique, which specializes in a well-curated selection of designer handbags and other leather goods. ✉ *56 rue St-Louis-en-l'Île, 4e, Île Saint-Louis* ☎ *06–19–51–47–31* Ⓜ *Pont Marie.*

Chapter 4

AROUND THE
EIFFEL TOWER

4

Updated by
Jennifer Ladonne

⊙ **Sights**
★★★★★

🍴 **Restaurants**
★★★☆☆

🛏 **Hotels**
★★★★★

🛍 **Shopping**
★★★★☆

🍸 **Nightlife**
★★★☆☆

NEIGHBORHOOD SNAPSHOT

GETTING HERE

This neighborhood includes the 7e, 15e, and 16e arrondissements. The most romantic way to reach the Eiffel Tower is by a Bateau Mouche boat or the Batobus, which stops at the foot of the tower. Alternatively, you can head for RER C: Champs de Mars/Tour Eiffel. But for the best views, you have some options: get off at the marvelous Bir-Hakeim métro stop, one of the few elevated stations left in Paris, then take the Allée de Cygnes walkway to get a glimpse of those spectacular views and a replica of the Statue of Liberty (Line 6); the métro stop Alma Marceau (Line 9) for views from the Pont (bridge) de l'Alma; or the Trocadéro station (métro Line 9 or 6) and make the short walk over the Pont d'Iéna to the tower. For the Musée Rodin, get off at Varenne (Line 13). Use this stop, or La Tour-Maubourg (Line 8), for Hôtel des Invalides, home to Napoléon's Tomb.

MAKING THE MOST OF YOUR TIME

This neighborhood is home to one of the world's most iconic sites, the Eiffel Tower. Depending on the time of year, you can wait hours to ascend La Tour (it helps to buy your ticket online, come at night when lines are shorter, join a tour that skirts the line, or, best of all, reserve a spot at the Jules Verne restaurant or the tower's Champagne Bar for access to the VIP elevator). But even if you stay firmly on the ground, it's worth a trip to see the landmark up close. Afterward, explore Rue St-Dominique's shops, bakeries, and cafés. If you have an afternoon to spare, don't miss the Musée Rodin. From here, it's a short walk to Napoléon's over-the-top tomb at the Hôtel des Invalides, which also houses the Musée de l'Armée devoted to military history. To appreciate art from Asia, Africa, and Oceania, spend an hour or two in the Musée du Quai Branly and Asian art at the stellar Musée Guimet.

TOP REASONS TO GO

■ **Eiffel Tower.** No question, the ultimate symbol of France is worth a visit at least once in your life.

■ **Musée Rodin.** A must-see for fans of the master sculptor or really any art lover, this magnificent 18th-century *hôtel particulier* (private mansion) was Rodin's former workshop. The stunning garden (and lake) is a perfect setting for his timeless works, and the indoor-outdoor garden café is a lovely spot for refreshment.

■ **Napoléon's Tomb.** The golden-domed Hôtel des Invalides is a fitting place for Napoléon's remains. Military history buffs will appreciate the impressive display of weaponry and armor in the adjoining Musée de l'Armée.

■ **Palais de Chaillot.** A favorite of fashion photographers, this statue-lined plaza-terrace at Place du Trocadéro has the city's best view of the Eiffel Tower.

■ **A boat ride.** Whether you choose a guided Bateaux Mouches tour or a Batobus (water bus) trip, cruising the Seine is a relaxing way to see city highlights without traffic or crowds. Book a ride after dark when all of Paris is aglow.

The posh 7e arrondissement (where nearly every block affords a view of La Tour Eiffel) is home to the French *bourgeoisie* and well-heeled expats. Commanding the southwestern end of Paris, the Eiffel Tower was considered an iron-latticed monstrosity when it opened in 1889. Today, it's a beloved icon, especially at night, when thousands of twinkling lights sparkle at the top of every hour.

There are other monumental sights here, too, notably the **Hôtel des Invalides,** a sprawling Baroque complex with a towering golden dome under which lies the enormous tomb of Napoléon. Along the river, the **Palais Bourbon,** seat of the French Parliament, is an 18th-century homage to ancient Greek architecture. Nearby is the modern **Musée du Quai Branly,** built by star architect Jean Nouvel. Don't miss the **Musée Rodin,** where the master's sculptures ooze sensuality both outside in the garden and inside the elegant Hôtel Biron. Around Trocadéro, north of the Eiffel Tower, the **Palais de Chaillot complex** includes the Cité de l'Architecture et du Patrimoine, a must for architecture buffs, along with the anthropology-oriented Musée de l'Homme.

From the Eiffel Tower east, the walkway along the Seine will take you past **Les Égouts** (where you can embark on a subterranean tour of actual working sewers) and the **American Church.** For one of the best views in Paris, cross **Pont Alexandre III,** the city's most ornate bridge spanning the Seine, from Invalides to the Grand Palais. Named for the Russian czar to celebrate Franco–Russian friendship, it was built between 1896 and 1900 and is bedecked with gilded sculptures, cherubs, and Art Nouveau lamps.

Sights

American Church
CHURCH | Not to be confused with the American Cathedral across the river at 23 avenue George V, this pretty, neo-Gothic, Protestant church was built between 1927 and 1931. It features a pair of Tiffany stained-glass windows—a rare find in Europe. Besides ecumenical services, the church hosts architectural tours, free classical and acoustic concerts, and lectures and workshops on well-being and topics of current interest. You can check event listings and download a self-guided PDF tour at the church website. ⊠ *65 quai d'Orsay, 7e, Eiffel Tower* ☎ *01–40–62–05–00* ⊕ *www.acparis.org* Ⓜ *Alma-Marceau; RER: Pont de l'Alma.*

Aquarium de Paris

AQUARIUM | FAMILY | An aquarium and cinema may seem like a strange combination, but the two coexist nicely in this attractive space beneath the Trocadéro gardens. In addition to 10,000 fish and a giant tank of small sharks, it promises puppet and magic shows, along with workshops for children in animation, art, and dance (these are offered in French, but the staff speaks English). There are also kid-oriented films showing on one big screen and, for the grown-ups, feature films playing on a second. Book tickets online to avoid lines. ⊠ 5 av. Albert De Mun, 16e, Eiffel Tower 🕾 01–40–69–23–23 ⊕ www.cineaqua. com 🎟 €22.50 ☞ Last entry 1 hr before closing Ⓜ Trocadéro.

Cathédrale de la Sainte-Trinité de Paris

CHURCH | At first glance, the blazing silvery onion domes of this Russian Orthodox cathedral, an easy walk from the Eiffel Tower and the Quay Branly, appear like a mirage of Moscow on the Seine. The ultramodern edifice, designed by French architect Jean-Michel Wilmotte, is worth a quick peek for its graceful icons, mosaics, and colorful frescoes against pristine marble walls. ⊠ 1 Quai Branly, 7e, Eiffel Tower 🕾 07–67–09–81–01 ⊕ www.cathedrale-sainte-trinite.fr Ⓜ Alma-Marceau.

Champ de Mars

CITY PARK | FAMILY | Big changes are afoot for the tree-lined paths and long expanse of grass between the Eiffel Tower and École Militaire. It was previously used as a parade ground and was the site of the world exhibitions in 1867, 1889 (when the tower was built), and 1900. Landscaped at the start of the 20th century, the park has become a centerpiece of current mayor Anne Hildago's plan to reduce pollution and increase Paris's pedestrian and green spaces. The new plans by American architect Kathryn Gustafson call for a total overhaul of the esplanade to be completed in time for the 2024 Paris Olympics. The ambitious project will involve creating a mile-long green space, closing the entire expanse to traffic, planting thousands of trees, and adding fountains and pedestrian walkways under a "unifying axis" that connects the Place du Trocadéro, the Palais de Chaillot, the Champ de Mars, and the École Militaire. At the southern end of the park, Jean-Michel Wilmotte's Grand Palais Ephemère will host the Grand Palais's art exhibits, fashion shows, and sporting events during its four-year restoration and for some of the Olympic games. ⊠ 7e, Eiffel Tower Ⓜ École Militaire; RER: Champ de Mars–Tour Eiffel.

Cité de l'Architecture et du Patrimoine

OTHER MUSEUM | The greatest gems of French architecture are represented at the City of Architecture and Heritage, which occupies the east wing of the Palais de Chaillot. The former French Monuments Museum contains some 350 plaster-cast reproductions spread out over 86,000 square feet. Although it may seem odd to see a collection comprised entirely of copies, these are no ordinary ones: they include partial facades from some of the most important Gothic churches, a gallery of frescoes and windows (among them a stained-glass stunner from the famous Chartres cathedral), plus an assembly of gargoyles practically leaping off the back wall of the soaring first-floor gallery. Video monitors with joysticks allow a 360-degree view of some of the grandest cathedrals. The upper-floor gallery is devoted to architecture since 1851, with a life-size replica of a postwar apartment in Marseille designed by the urban-planning pioneer Le Corbusier. It's well worth picking up the free English audiovisual guide. When you're ready for a break, the museum's small café offers a great view of the Eiffel Tower. ⊠ Palais de Chaillot, 1 pl. du Trocadéro, 16e, Eiffel Tower 🕾 01–58–51–52–00 ⊕ www.citedelarchitecture. fr 🎟 €9; €12 with temporary exhibits ⊙ Closed Tues. Ⓜ Trocadéro.

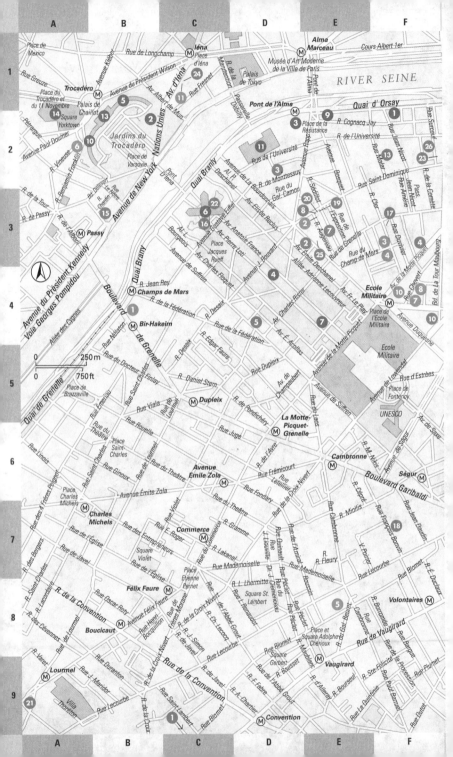

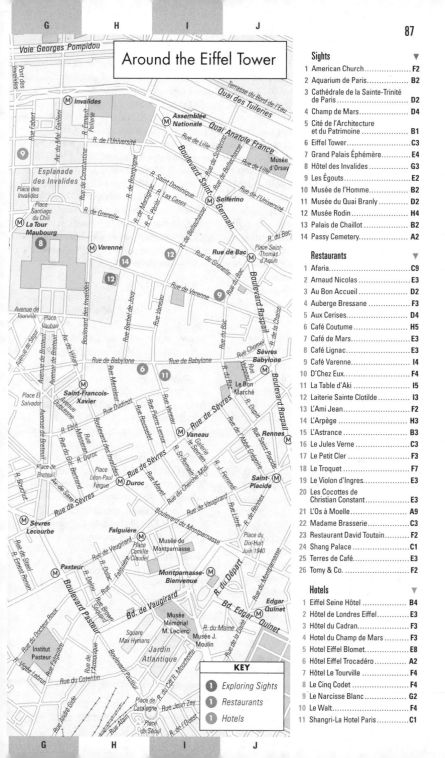

Around the Eiffel Tower

Sights ▼

1. American Church.................... **F2**
2. Aquarium de Paris................. **B2**
3. Cathédrale de la Sainte-Trinité de Paris **D2**
4. Champ de Mars.................... **D4**
5. Cité de l'Architecture et du Patrimoine **B1**
6. Eiffel Tower......................... **C3**
7. Grand Palais Éphémère....... **E4**
8. Hôtel des Invalides **G3**
9. Les Égouts.......................... **E2**
10. Musée de l'Homme.............. **B2**
11. Musée du Quai Branly **D2**
12. Musée Rodin........................ **H4**
13. Palais de Chaillot................ **B2**
14. Passy Cemetery................... **A2**

Restaurants ▼

1. Afaria................................... **C9**
2. Arnaud Nicolas **E3**
3. Au Bon Accueil **D2**
4. Auberge Bressane **F3**
5. Aux Cerises.......................... **D4**
6. Café Coutume **H5**
7. Café de Mars........................ **E3**
8. Café Lignac.......................... **E3**
9. Café Varenne........................ **I4**
10. D'Chez Eux........................... **F4**
11. La Table d'Aki **I5**
12. Laiterie Sainte Clotilde **I3**
13. L'Ami Jean........................... **F2**
14. L'Arpège.............................. **H3**
15. L'Astrance............................ **B3**
16. Le Jules Verne **C3**
17. Le Petit Cler **F3**
18. Le Troquet **F7**
19. Le Violon d'Ingres................. **E3**
20. Les Cocottes de Christian Constant.................. **E3**
21. L'Os à Moelle....................... **A9**
22. Madame Brasserie................. **C3**
23. Restaurant David Toutain....... **F2**
24. Shang Palace....................... **C1**
25. Terres de Café...................... **E3**
26. Tomy & Co. **F2**

Hotels ▼

1. Eiffel Seine Hôtel **B4**
2. Hôtel de Londres Eiffel.......... **E3**
3. Hôtel du Cadran................... **F3**
4. Hotel du Champ de Mars **F3**
5. Hotel Eiffel Blomet............... **E8**
6. Hôtel Eiffel Trocadéro............ **A2**
7. Hôtel Le Tourville **F4**
8. Le Cinq Codet **F4**
9. Le Narcisse Blanc **G2**
10. Le Walt................................ **F4**
11. Shangri-La Hotel Paris............ **C1**

KEY

1 Exploring Sights
1 Restaurants
1 Hotels

★ Eiffel Tower (*Tour Eiffel*)

NOTABLE BUILDING | FAMILY | The Eiffel Tower is to Paris what the Statue of Liberty is to New York and what Big Ben is to London: the ultimate civic emblem. French engineer Gustave Eiffel spent two years working to erect this iconic monument for the World Exhibition of 1889. Because its colossal bulk exudes such a feeling of permanence, it's hard to believe that the tower nearly became 7,000 tons of scrap when the concession expired in 1909. Only its potential use as a radio antenna saved the day. Though many prominent Parisians derided it at first, the tower gradually became part of the city's topography. It's most breathtaking at night, when every girder is highlighted in a glittering show of 20,000 golden lights for five minutes every hour on the hour from nightfall until 1 am.

More recent enhancements include a two-year, €30 million renovation of the first level that added a vertigo-inducing "transparent" floor 187 feet above the esplanade and a mini-turbine plant, four vertical turbine windmills, and eco-friendly solar panels to minimize the tower's carbon footprint over time. You can stride up 704 steps as far as the second level, but only the elevator goes to the top. The view of the flat sweep of Paris at 1,000 feet is sublime—especially if you come in the late evening, after the crowds have dispersed. Beat the crushing lines by reserving your ticket online, or book a skip-the-line guided tour offered by many companies (from €37). On the tower's second floor, the Jules Verne restaurant—with its Michelin star—is about as dramatic a lunch or dinner spot as you'll find. Or you can watch the glimmering lights from the top of the tower over bubbly, or a nonalcoholic drink, at the Bar à Champagne (there's also a sit-down bistro from Jules Verne chef Thierry Marx on the first floor and small "Buffet" snack shops on the esplanade and the first and second floors).

At the tower's tippy top, you'll also find Gustave Eiffel's "secret apartment," which he used as his office, including wax mannequins of Eiffel, Thomas Edison, and a blonde woman in the background who represents Claire, Eiffel's oldest daughter, with whom he was very close. ⊠ *Quai Branly, 7e, Eiffel Tower* ☎ *08–92–70–12–39 €0.35 per min* ⊕ *www.toureiffel.paris* 🎫 *By elevator from €17.10; by stairs from €10.70* ⊗ *Stairs close at 6 pm in off-season (Oct.–June). Closed last 2 wks in Jan. for annual maintenance* Ⓜ *Trocadéro, Bir-Hakeim, École Militaire; RER: Champ de Mars–Tour Eiffel.*

Grand Palais Éphémère

ARTS CENTER | This soaring 2½-acre structure—a stand-in for the original across the Seine while it undergoes massive renovations—was designed by Paris über-architect Jean-Michel Wilmotte as a contemporary, and temporary, rendering of its namesake. Taking pride of place at the foot of the Eiffel Tower's Champs de Mars, the wood-and-transparent-plastic edifice is home to everything from blockbuster art exhibitions and art fairs to concerts, fashion shows, and sporting events. It will also host some of the 2024 Paris Olympic and Paralympic Games. ⊠ *Av. Pierre Loti, 7e, Eiffel Tower* ☎ *01–40–13–48–00* ⊕ *www.grandpalais.fr/en/lieu/grand-palais-ephemere* 🎫 *€14.50* ⊗ *Closed Tues.* Ⓜ *Franklin D. Roosevelt, Champs-Élysées–Clemenceau.*

★ Hôtel des Invalides

HISTORIC SIGHT | The Baroque complex known as Les Invalides (pronounced "lehz-ahn-vah-*leed*") is the eternal home of Napoléon Bonaparte (1769–1821) or, more precisely, his remains, which lie entombed under the golden dome. Louis XIV ordered the facility built in 1670 to house disabled soldiers (hence the name), and, at one time, 4,000 military men lived here. Today, a portion still serves as a veterans' residence and hospital. The Musée de l'Armée, containing an exhaustive collection of military artifacts from antique armor to weapons, is also here.

If you see only a single sight, make it the Église du Dome (one of Les Invalides's two churches) at the back of the complex. Napoléon's tomb was moved here in 1840 from the island of Saint Helena, where he died in forced exile. The emperor's body is protected by no fewer than six coffins—one set inside the next, sort of like a Russian nesting doll—which are then encased in a sarcophagus of red quartzite. The bombastic tribute is ringed by statues symbolizing Napoléon's campaigns of conquest. To see more Napoléoniana, check out the collection in the Musée de l'Armée featuring his trademark gray frock coat and huge bicorne hat. Look for the figurines reenacting the famous coronation scene when Napoléon crowns his empress, Josephine. You can see a grander version of this scene by the painter David hanging in the Louvre.

The best entrance is at the southern end, on Place Vauban (Avenue de Tourville); the ticket office is here, as is Napoléon's Tomb. There are automatic ticket machines at the main entrance on Place des Invalides. ⊠ *Pl. des Invalides, 7e, Eiffel Tower* 🕾 *01–44–42–38–77* ⊕ *www. musee-armee.fr* 🖘 *€14 with temporary exhibitions* ⟲ *Last admission 30 mins before closing* Ⓜ *La Tour–Maubourg, Varenne.*

Les Égouts (The Sewers)

HISTORIC SIGHT | FAMILY | Leave it to the French to make even sewers seem romantic. Part exhibit but mostly, well, sewer, the 1,640-foot stretch of tunnels provides a fascinating—and not too smelly—look at the underbelly of Paris. You can stroll the so-called galleries of this city beneath the city, which comes complete with street signs mirroring those aboveground. Walkways flank tunnels of whooshing wastewater wide enough to allow narrow barges to dredge sand and sediment. Lighted panels, photos, and explanations in English detail the workings of the system. Immortalized as the escape routes of the Phantom of the Opera and Jean Valjean in *Les Misérables*, the 19th-century sewers have a florid real-life history. Since Napoléon ordered the underground network built to clean up the squalid streets, they have played a role in every war, secreting revolutionaries and spies and their stockpiles of weapons. Grenades from World War II were recovered not far from where the gift shop now sits. The display cases of stuffed toy rats and "Eau de Paris" glass carafes fold into the walls when the water rises after heavy rains. Buy your ticket at the kiosk on the Left Bank side of the Pont de l'Alma. Guided one-hour tours by friendly *égoutiers* (sewer workers) are available in French only; call or email ahead for details. ⊠ *Opposite 93 quai d'Orsay, Eiffel Tower* 🕾 *01–53–68–27–81* ⊕ *musee-egouts.paris.fr/en* 🖘 *€9* ⟲ *Closed Mon.* Ⓜ *Alma-Marceau; RER: Pont de l'Alma.*

Musée de l'Homme

HISTORY MUSEUM | FAMILY | When President Jacques Chirac's legacy project (the Musée du Quai Branly, dedicated to the world's indigenous arts and cultures) pilfered half of this museum's pieces, few thought the rest of Paris's storied anthropology museum would survive, but luckily it has come roaring back to life. Focused now on "science and human societies," the Musée de l'Homme has 33,368 square feet of sparkling exhibition space in the west wing of the Palais de Chaillot, where it displays more than 700,000 prehistoric artifacts and art objects. And it now does so using the most modern of museum tricks—including interactive displays, 3-D projections, and educational games—to help visitors understand the history of the human species. While you're admiring the 25,000-year-old Venus of Lespugue or comparing the skull of Cro-Magnon man with that of René Descartes, don't forget to look out the window: the view from the upper floors across to the Eiffel Tower and southern Paris is spectacular. ✉ *Palais de Chaillot, 17 Pl. du Trocadéro, 16e, Eiffel Tower* ☎ *01–44–05–72–72* ⊕ *www.museedelhomme.fr* 🎫 *€7 (€9 with temporary exhibitions)* ⊗ *Closed Tues.* Ⓜ *Trocadéro.*

Musée du Quai Branly

ART MUSEUM | FAMILY | This eye-catching museum overlooking the Seine was built by architect Jean Nouvel to house the state-owned collection of "non-Western" art, culled from the Musée National des Arts d'Afrique et d'Océanie and the Musée de l'Homme. Exhibits mix artifacts from antiquity to the modern age, such as funeral masks from Melanesia, Siberian shaman drums, Indonesian textiles, and African statuary. A corkscrew ramp leads from the lobby to a cavernous exhibition space, which is color coded to designate sections from Asia, Africa, and Oceania. The lighting is dim—sometimes too dim to read the information panels (which makes investing in the €5 audioguide a good idea).

Renowned for his bold modern designs, Nouvel has said he wanted the museum to follow no rules; however, many critics gave his vision a thumbs-down when it was unveiled in 2006. The exterior resembles a massive, rust-color rectangle suspended on stilts, with geometric shapes cantilevered to the facade facing the Seine and louvered panels on the opposite side. The colors (dark reds, oranges, and yellows) are meant to evoke the tribal art within. A "living wall" composed of some 150 species of exotic plants grows on the exterior, which is surrounded by a wild jungle garden with swampy patches—an impressive sight after dark when scores of cylindrical colored lights are illuminated. The trendy Les Ombres restaurant on the museum's fifth floor (separate entrance) has prime views of the Tour Eiffel—and prices to match. The budget-conscious can enjoy the garden at Le Café Branly on the ground floor. ✉ *37 quai Branly, 7e, Eiffel Tower* ☎ *01–56–61–70–00* ⊕ *www.quai-branly.fr* 🎫 *From €12 (free 1st Sun. of month)* ⊗ *Ticket office closes 1 hr before museum. Closed Mon.* Ⓜ *Alma-Marceau.*

★ Musée Rodin

ART MUSEUM | FAMILY | Auguste Rodin (1840–1917) briefly made his home and studio in the Hôtel Biron, a grand 18th-century mansion that now houses this museum dedicated to his work. He died rich and famous, but many of the sculptures that earned him a place in art history were originally greeted with contempt by the general public, which was unprepared for his powerful brand of sexuality and raw physicality.

Most of Rodin's best-known sculptures are in the gardens. The front one is dominated by *The Gates of Hell* (circa 1880), illustrating stories from Dante's *Divine Comedy*. Rodin worked on the sculpture for more than 30 years, and it served as a "sketch pad" for many of his later works: you can see miniature versions of *The Kiss* (bottom right), *The Thinker* (top center), and *The Three Shades* (top center). The museum now showcases long-neglected models, plasters, and paintings, which offer insight into Rodin's creative process. Pieces by other artists from his personal collection are on display as well—including paintings by Van Gogh, Renoir, and Monet. There's also a room devoted to works by Camille Claudel (1864–1943), his student and longtime mistress, who was a remarkable sculptor in her own right. An English audioguide (€6) is available for the permanent collection and for temporary exhibitions. Tickets can be purchased online for priority access. If you wish to linger, L'Augustine serves meals and snacks in the shade of the garden's linden trees. ✉ *77 rue de Varenne, 7e, Eiffel Tower* ☎ *01–44–18–61–10* ⊕ *www.musee-rodin.fr* 🎫 *€13 (free 1st Sun. of month)* ⊗ *Closed Mon.* Ⓜ *Varenne.*

Palais de Chaillot

NOTABLE BUILDING | FAMILY | This honey-colored Art Deco cultural center on Place du Trocadéro was built in the 1930s to replace a Moorish-style building constructed for the 1878 World's Fair. Its esplanade is a top draw for camera-toting visitors intent on snapping the perfect shot of the Eiffel Tower. In the building to the left is the Cité de l'Architecture et du Patrimoine—billed as the largest architectural museum in the world—and the Théâtre National de Chaillot, which occasionally stages plays in English. Also here is the Institut Français d'Architecture, an organization and school. The twin building to the right contains the Musée de l'Homme, a thoroughly modern anthropology museum. Sculptures and fountains adorn the garden leading to the Seine. ⊠ *Pl. du Trocadéro, 16e, Eiffel Tower* Ⓜ *Trocadéro.*

Passy Cemetery

CEMETERY | Visiting graveyards in Paris can become addictive. The Passy Cemetery dates from 1821 and sits in the shadows of Trocadéro. Here you'll find the tombstones of famous aristocrats and artists, such as composer Claude Debussy and Impressionist painters Édouard Manet and Berthe Morisot. ⊠ *2 rue du Commandant Schlœsing, 16e, Eiffel Tower* ☎ *01–47–27–51–42* Ⓜ *Trocadéro.*

🍴 Restaurants

Lively bistros and daring contemporary restaurants bring exuberance to the otherwise sedate streets around the Eiffel Tower. Because money is rarely an object in this area and because it's the home of the Assemblée Nationale, you can find everything from elegant tables favored by politicians to innovative restaurants that draw foodies to nostalgic bistros catering to aristocratic residents with comfort-food cravings.

Afaria

$$ | BISTRO | The otherwise unexciting 15e arrondissement is home to much-lauded chef Ludivine Merlin and her Basque-inspired recipes. Basque cooking is known for its bold flavors and generosity, and the choices at Afaria are no exception. **Known for:** hazelnut soufflé with homemade dark-chocolate sorbet for dessert; artichoke terrine with smoked bacon and aged Comté cheese; laid-back, classic bistro atmosphere. Ⓢ *Average main: €22* ⊠ *15 rue Desnouettes, 15e, Eiffel Tower* ☎ *01–48–42–95–90* ⊕ *www.restaurant-afaria.fr* ♥ *Closed Sun., Mon., and 2 wks at Christmas.* Ⓜ *Convention.*

Arnaud Nicolas

$$ | FRENCH | This "best craftsman of France" revives the gastronomic art of French charcuterie in dishes like dreamy foie gras and succulent slabs of country terrine enrobed in a golden buttery crust. The small-but-choice menu also highlights specialties from the sea: shellfish soufflé or delicate fish quenelles (a specialty of Lyon, France's charcuterie capital). **Known for:** smallish menu; shop on premises; high-quality meats. Ⓢ *Average main: €22* ⊠ *46 Av. de la Bourdonnais, 7e, Eiffel Tower* ☎ *01–45–55–59–59* ⊕ *arnaudnicolas.paris* ♥ *Closed Sun. and Mon.* Ⓜ *École Militaire.*

Auberge Bressane

$$ | FRENCH | Parisian gastronomic extravagance has largely disappeared in favor of leaner fare. Not so at this beloved stalwart, where you can revel in such Gallic classics as towering soufflés, buttery frogs' legs, or a hearty steak smothered in sauce béarnaise. **Known for:** cozy spot; traditional Parisian charm; classics done right. Ⓢ *Average main: €23* ⊠ *16 av. de la Motte-Picquet, 7e, Eiffel Tower* ☎ *01–47–05–98–37* ⊕ *www.auberge-bressane.com* Ⓜ *La Tour-Maubourg, École Militaire.*

Au Bon Accueil

$$$ | BISTRO | To see what well-heeled Parisians eat these days, book a table at this chic little bistro run by Jacques Lacipière as soon as you get to town. The contemporary dining room is unusually comfortable, and the sidewalk tables have an Eiffel Tower view, but it's the excellent, well-priced *cuisine du marché* that has made this spot a hit. **Known for:** scintillating views of the Eiffel Tower from the charming sidewalk terrace; excellent price-to-quality ratio; good value, three-course menus. [$] *Average main: €25* ✉ *14 rue de Monttessuy, 7e, Eiffel Tower* ☎ *01–47–05–46–11* 🌐 *www.aubonaccueilparis.com* 🕓 *Closed Sat., Sun., and 3 wks in Aug.* [M] *Métro or RER: Pont de l'Alma.*

★ **Aux Cerises**

$ | CAFÉ | Don't expect to be mobbed by tourists at this bright café two minutes from the Champs de Mars; locals love it for the sidewalk terrace and garden seating in the back—not to mention the good coffee, tea, and stellar brunch. Even if you don't snag a seat outside, the charming interior is a cheerful spot to tuck into a heaping plate of eggs Benedict, smoked salmon tartine, or avocado toast. **Known for:** minutes from the Eiffel Tower; reservations a good idea on weekends; superb brunch or lunch served seven days a week. [$] *Average main: €15* ✉ *47 av. de Suffren, 7e, Eiffel Tower* ☎ *01–42–73–92–97* 🌐 *www.auxcerises.fr/en.*

Café Coutume

$ | CAFÉ | FAMILY | A lofty space between the Musée Rodin and the Bon Marché makes this the perfect pit stop. Look for healthy salads, sandwiches, snacks, desserts, and a delicious cup of any kind of coffee drink that takes your fancy. **Known for:** prime location near major museums; healthy salads for lunch; some of the finest coffee in town. [$] *Average main: €8* ✉ *47 rue de Babylone, 7e, Eiffel Tower* ☎ *01–45–51–50–47* 🌐 *www.coutumecafe.com* 🕓 *No dinner* [M] *St-François-Xavier, Sèvres–Babylone.*

★ **Café de Mars**

$ | BISTRO | California-born chef Gina McLintock's elegant-cozy interiors perfectly echo her scrumptious gourmet bistro fare with an Asian twist. Crowd-pleasers include dishes like delicate pumpkin beignets, rib-eye steak, and a juicy bacon burger. **Known for:** live jazz on Saturdays; located near Eiffel Tower; great value. [$] *Average main: €17* ✉ *11 rue Augereau, 7e, Eiffel Tower* ☎ *01–45–50–10–90* 🕓 *Closed Sun. and Mon.* [M] *École Militaire.*

Café Lignac

$$ | BISTRO | It doesn't come as a surprise that when beloved Parisian chef Christian Constant left this equally loved café in 2022, superstar-chef-about-town Cyril Lignac swooped in. But don't despair, Lignac has largely kept the down-to-earth, relatively humble bistro's classic red banquettes, wooden tables, and menu of classic French dishes it was justly famous for. **Known for:** neighborhood favorite; classic bistro fare with a gourmet twist; excellent prices, especially at lunch. [$] *Average main: €22* ✉ *139 rue St-Dominique, 7e, Eiffel Tower* ☎ *01–47–53–73–34* 🌐 *www.cafelignac.com* [M] *École Militaire; Métro or RER: Pont de l'Alma.*

Café Varenne

$$ | BISTRO | FAMILY | Giant mirrors, red leatherette banquettes, vintage posters, and checker-tile floors add up to a '60s movie set of a Parisian bistro. But the menu of delicious comfort food—made with top-quality artisanal ingredients and the best produce from throughout France—is delightfully real. **Known for:** charm galore; open all afternoon and until late; reliably good. [$] *Average main: €22* ✉ *36 rue de Varenne, 7e, Eiffel Tower* ☎ *01–45–48–62–72* 🕓 *Closed Sun.* [M] *Frankin D. Roosevelt.*

D'Chez Eux

$$$ | **BISTRO** | The red-checked tablecloths and jovial maître d' at this authentic southwestern French bistro near the Invalides might seem like a tourist trap until you realize that it's just as popular with food-loving locals and top French politicians as it is with foreigners. Everything on the menu is hearty and delicious, if not especially refined—don't miss the gooey help-yourself chocolate mousse. **Known for:** extremely generous portions; famous "house-made" charcuterie; spacious sidewalk terrace. [$] *Average main: €32 ✉ 2 av. de Lowendal, 7e, Eiffel Tower ☎ 01–47–05–52–55 🌐 www.chezeux.com* [M] *Varenne, École Militaire.*

La Laiterie Sainte Clotilde

$$$ | **FRENCH** | It's not just this contemporarary bistro's chic black storefront and floor-to-ceiling windows that stand out among the elegant neighborhood's pale sandstone buildings and pricey dining. A frisson of excitement in fresh, imaginative, and unfussy dishes paired with small-producer wines brings a breath of fresh air, and the €30 lunch menu is especially enticing. **Known for:** quality ingredients; lively atmosphere; chic crowd. [$] *Average main: €26 ✉ 64 rue de Bellechasse, 7e, Eiffel Tower ☎ 01–45–51–74–61 🌐 www.lalaiteriesainteclotilde.fr 🕒 Closed Sun.* [M] *Varenne, Rue du Bac.*

L'Ami Jean

$$$$ | **BASQUE** | If you love Yves Camdeborde's southwestern France–inflected cooking at Le Comptoir but can't get a table for dinner, head to this tavernlike Basque restaurant run by his longtime second-in-command, Stéphane Jégo. Jégo's style is remarkably similar to Camdeborde's because he uses the same suppliers and shares his knack for injecting basic ingredients with sophistication reminiscent of haute cuisine. You can go hearty with Spanish *piquillo* peppers stuffed with salt-cod paste or *poulet basquaise* (chicken stewed with peppers), or lighter with seasonal dishes that change weekly. **Known for:** seasonal, market-driven menu; popularity with locals; convivial atmosphere (especially when rugby is on). [$] *Average main: €39 ✉ 27 rue Malar, 7e, Eiffel Tower ☎ 01–47–05–86–89 🌐 www.lamijean.fr 🕒 Closed Sun., Mon., and Aug.* [M] *Invalides.*

★ L'Arpège

$$$$ | **MODERN FRENCH** | Breton-born Alain Passard, one of the most respected chefs in Paris, famously shocked the French culinary world by declaring that he was bored with meat. Though his vegetarianism is more lofty than practical—L'Arpège still caters to fish and poultry eaters—he does cultivate his own vegetables outside Paris, and his dishes elevate the humblest produce to sublime heights. **Known for:** redefining what a cook can do with simple vegetables; one of Paris's rare three-star restaurants; legendary Paris chef. [$] *Average main: €100 ✉ 84 rue de Varenne, 7e, Eiffel Tower ☎ 01–47–05–09–06 🌐 www.alain-passard.com 🕒 Closed weekends* [M] *Varenne.*

★ L'Astrance

$$$$ | **MODERN FRENCH** | Pascal Barbot rose to fame thanks to his restaurant's reasonable prices and casual atmosphere, but after the passage of several years, L'Astrance has become resolutely haute. His dishes often draw on Asian ingredients, as in grilled lamb with miso-lacquered eggplant and a palate-cleansing white sorbet spiked with chili pepper and lemongrass. **Known for:** extraordinary wine list; space that seats only 25 lucky diners a night; set menus that change daily. [$] *Average main: €120 ✉ 4 rue Beethoven, 16e, Eiffel Tower ☎ 01–40–50–84–40 🌐 www.astrancerestaurant.com 🕒 Closed Sat.–Mon. and Aug.* [M] *Passy.*

La Table d'Aki

$$$$ | **MODERN FRENCH** | Set in a quiet, aristocratic *quartier* near the Musée Rodin, postage stamp–size La Table d'Aki features cuisine centered on the sea. Chef

Eating Vegetarian in Paris 🍴

Vegetarianism was once so uncommon in Paris that star chef Alain Passard caused a sensation when he declared in the early 2000s that he was bored with red meat and would be focusing on vegetables and fish. True to his word, Passard established a small farm outside Paris where he grows heirloom vegetables that are whizzed to his restaurant **L'Arpège** (✉ *84 rue de Varenne 01–45–51–47–33*) by high-speed train. Customers pay the price: a simple yet sensational beet dish costs €45.

Though Paris is hardly a vegetarian paradise today, Passard's initiative seems to have rubbed off on other chefs in the 7e. **Le Violon d'Ingres** (✉ *135 rue St-Dominique 01–45–55–15–05*) and **Restaurant David Toutain** (✉ *29 rue Surcouf 01–45–50–11–10*) both imaginatively cater to vegetarians.

Akihiro Horikoshi works all alone in an open kitchen while 16 lucky diners await the next course: lush, simple dishes like plump langoustine shimmering in a silky shallot-fennel sauce or delicate medallions of sole in a mellow red-wine-and-leek reduction. **Known for:** open kitchen serving just 16 diners at a time; perfectly prepared fish; small, cozy space. [$] *Average main: €45* ✉ *49 rue Vaneau, 7e, Eiffel Tower* ☎ *01–45–44–43–48* ⏲ *Closed Sun., Mon., 2 wks in Feb., and Aug.* [M] *Saint-François-Xavier.*

★ Le Jules Verne

$$$$ | **MODERN FRENCH** | In a highly publicized battle, the prestigious helm of Paris's most *haute* (literally) restaurant was wrested from Alain Ducasse by three-star chef Fréderic Anton of the prestigious Le Pré Catalan in the Bois de Boulogne, with Anton's "zero waste" approach and his idea to serve less complicated fare, focusing on French meats and vegetables produced by smaller French artisanal farms and regional delicacies, winning out. Though not cheap (tasting menus are more than €200), winning a Michelin star in 2020 clinched the restaurant's standing as one of Paris's top splurge-worthy dining rooms. **Known for:** advance reservations a must; lavishly priced dishes; famous Eiffel Tower dining (with accompanying views). [$] *Average main: €100* ✉ *Tour Eiffel, south pillar, Av. Gustave Eiffel, 7e, Eiffel Tower* ☎ *01–45–55–61–44* 🌐 *www.lejulesverne-paris.com* 👔 *Jacket and tie* [M] *Bir-Hakeim.*

Le Petit Cler

$ | **CAFÉ** | From a wine-soaked boeuf bourguignon and garlicky snails to tasty slabs of homemade country paté served with cornichons and a hearty red, this Art Nouveau–era bistro offers all the classics of southwestern France. Check the blackboard menu for the daily specials, delivered in generous portions at breakfast, lunch, and dinner. **Known for:** open all day; open Sunday; generous portions of all the French classics. [$] *Average main: €14* ✉ *29 rue Cler, 7e, Eiffel Tower* ☎ *01–45–50–17–50* [M] *La Tour-Maubourg, École Militaire.*

Les Cocottes de Christian Constant

$$ | **MODERN FRENCH** | Chef Christian Constant has an unfailing sense of how Parisians want to eat these days, as proved by this third addition to his mini restaurant empire near the Eiffel Tower. At Les Cocottes, he's shifted the normally leisurely bistro experience into high gear, which allows him to keep prices moderate. **Known for:** cozy spot

for elevated French comfort food; casual, child-friendly atmosphere; dishes served in cast-iron pots. [$] *Average main: €20* ✉ *135 rue St-Dominique, 7e, Eiffel Tower* ☎ *01–45–50–10–28* 🌐 *lescocottes.paris* [M] *École Militaire; Métro or RER: Pont de l'Alma.*

Le Troquet

$$ | **MODERN FRENCH** | **FAMILY** | A quiet residential street shelters one of Paris's great neighborhood bistros and among the last of the city's authentic ones, which retains its moleskin banquettes, blackboard menus, and small wooden tables where you'll touch elbows with your neighbors. Expect fresh market ingredients in a gastronomic menu that's liberal with deluxe details. **Known for:** dessert soufflé du jour; sampling of the French classics; proximity to the Eiffel Tower. [$] *Average main: €21* ✉ *21 rue François-Bonvin, 15e, Eiffel Tower* ☎ *01–45–66–89–00* 🌐 *www.restaurantletroquet.fr* 🕑 *Closed Sun., Mon., 3 wks in Aug., and 1 wk at Christmas* [M] *Ségur.*

★ **Le Violon d'Ingres**

$$$$ | **MODERN FRENCH** | With chef Alain Solivérès (formerly of Taillevent) now at the helm, this much-beloved outpost has taken on a new shine—and a Michelin star. The food is sophisticated, and the atmosphere is lively and chic. **Known for:** open seven days a week, a rarity in this quartier; famous chef that actually cooks here; few minutes' walk to the Eiffel Tower. [$] *Average main: €40* ✉ *135 rue St-Dominique, 7e, Eiffel Tower* ☎ *01–45–55–15–05* 🌐 *leviolondingres.paris* [M] *École Militaire.*

L'Os à Moelle

$$ | **BISTRO** | **FAMILY** | Come for the early sitting at this little bistro specializing in classic French fare and you'll often discover the dining room filled with more than a few tourists (the waiters speak English perfectly). The reasonably priced (€56) five-course tasting menu may account for the restaurant's popularity—there are two seatings each night. **Known for:** well-priced wines and Champagne by the glass; classic Parisian "blackboard" menu; large portions at good prices. [$] *Average main: €19* ✉ *3 rue Vasco de Gama, 15e, Eiffel Tower* ☎ *01–45–57–27–27* 🌐 *www.facebook.com/losamoelleet-lacave* 🕑 *Closed Sun. and Mon.* [M] *Balard.*

Madame Brasserie

$$$$ | **FRENCH** | There's not a brasserie in Paris with a view to match the one at this eatery set on the second floor of the Eiffel Tower. Chef Thierry Marx—the starred chef headlining at the tower's gastronomic Jules Verne restaurant—also presides over this chic dining room, done up in blonde wood and earth tones, where everything is "stylish, sustainable, and cozy" (and we might add, expensive), with special attention to local and regional products whenever possible. **Known for:** attentive service; unbeatable views; good, if astronomically priced, food. [$] *Average main: €95* ✉ *Eiffel Tower, 7e, Eiffel Tower* ☎ *01–83–77–77–78* 🌐 *www.restaurants-toureiffel.com/en/madame-brasserie/restaurant.html* [M] *Bir Hakeim, Trocadéro.*

★ **Restaurant David Toutain**

$$$$ | **FRENCH FUSION** | Although chef David Toutain's approach may be exasperatingly conceptual for some, others find his earthy, surprising, and inspired concoctions utterly thrilling. Each dish is a lesson in contrasts—of temperature, texture, and flavor—as well as a feat of composition: briny oysters, brussels sprouts, and foie gras in a warm potato consommé; creamy raw oysters with tart kiwi and yuzu; crispy pork chips alongside velvety smoked potato puree. **Known for:** plenty of avant-garde thrills; epitome of "seasonal" cuisine; equally wonderful choices for vegetarians and carnivores. [$] *Average main: €48* ✉ *29 rue Surcouf, 7e, Eiffel Tower* ☎ *01–45–50–11–10* 🌐 *www.davidtoutain.com* 🕑 *Closed weekends* [M] *Invalides, La Tour-Maubourg.*

A Cheese Primer

Their cuisine might be getting lighter, but the French aren't ready to relinquish their cheese. Some restaurants present a single, lovingly selected slice, whereas the more prestigious restaurants wheel in a trolley of specimens aged on the premises. Cheese always comes after the main course and before—or instead of—dessert.

Among the best bistros for cheese are **Astier**, where a giant basket of oozy wonders is brought to the table; **La Brasserie Le Comptoir**, where a dazzling cheese platter is part of the five-course prix-fixe dinner; and **Le Bistrot Paul Bert**, where an overflowing cheese board is left on your table for you to help yourself. A few *bars à fromages* are springing up, too: devoted to cheese the way *bars à vins* are dedicated to wine. **Fromagerie Cantin** is a terrific example.

Armed with these phrases, you can wow the waiter and work your way through the most generous platter.

Avez-vous le Beaufort d'été? Do you have summer Beaufort?

Beaufort is similar to Gruyère, and the best Beaufort is made with milk produced in summer, when cows eat fresh grass. Aged Beaufort is even more reminiscent of a mountain hike.

Je voudrais un chèvre bien frais/bien sec. I'd like a goat cheese that's nice and fresh/nice and dry.

France produces many goat cheeses, some so fresh they can be scooped with a spoon, some tough enough to use as doorstops. It's a matter of taste, but hard-core cheese eaters favor drier specimens, which stick to the roof of the mouth and have a frankly goaty aroma.

C'est un St-Marcellin de vache ou de chèvre? Is this St-Marcellin made with cow's or goat's milk?

St-Marcellin is a more original choice than the ubiquitous *crottin de chèvre* (poetically named after goats' turds). Originally a goat cheese, today it's more often made with cow's milk. The best have an oozy center, though some like it dry as a hockey puck.

C'est un Brie de Meaux ou de Melun? Is this Brie from Meaux or Melun?

There are many kinds of Brie. Brie de Meaux is the best known, with a smooth flavor and runny center; the much rarer Brie de Melun is more pungent and saltier.

Je n'aime pas le Camembert industriel! I don't like industrial Camembert!

Camembert might be a national treasure, but most of it is industrial. Real Camembert has a white rind with rust-color streaks and a yellow center.

Avez-vous de la confiture pour accompagner ce brebis? Do you have any jam to go with this sheep's cheese?

In the Basque region berry jam is the traditional accompaniment for sharp sheep's-milk cheeses like Ossau-Iraty.

C'est la saison du Mont d'Or. It's Mont d'Or season.

This potent mountain cheese, also known as Vacherin, is produced only from September to March. It's so runny, it's eaten with a spoon.

★ Shang Palace

$$$$ | **CHINESE** | The premiere restaurant at the beautiful Shangri-La Hotel is Paris's only Michelin-starred Chinese restaurant. Set in a jewel-box of a dining room, featuring giant Chinese porcelains and inlaid jade paneling, you'll dine on lacquered Peking duck, sliced at your table and delivered with a flourish, and all manner of delicacies from one of the world's great cuisines. **Known for:** gorgeous setting; superb wine list; best Peking duck in Paris. [$] *Average main: €55* ✉ *10 av. d'Iéna, 16e, Eiffel Tower* ☎ *01–53–67–19–92* 🌐 *www.shangri-la.com/paris/shangrila/dining/restaurants/shang-palace* ⏲ *Closed Tues. and Wed.* [M] *Iéna, Trocadéro, Pont de l'Alma.*

★ Terres de Café

$ | **CAFÉ** | A five-minute walk from the Eiffel Tower, Terre de Café is a boon to coffee lovers. It also serves gluten-free pastries, healthy fruit smoothies, and gourmet brunch options. **Known for:** fresh and healthy salads and sandwiches; delicious homemade pastries; great coffee. [$] *Average main: €5* ✉ *67 av. de la Bourdonnais, 7e, Eiffel Tower* ☎ *01–45–50–37–39* 🌐 *www.terresdecafe.com* [M] *École Militaire, Pont-de-l'Alma.*

★ Tomy & Co.

$$$$ | **BISTRO** | Chef Tomy Gousset, who learned his skills in some of the city's most prestigious kitchens, flies solo at this wildly popular bistro, which won its first Michelin star in 2019. The appealingly spare dining room is an excellent backdrop for some truly dazzling dishes that taste every bit as sublime as they look. **Known for:** great wine pairings; inventive dishes; gourmet bistro fare. [$] *Average main: €34* ✉ *22 rue Surcouf, 7e, Eiffel Tower* ☎ *01–45–51–46–93* 🌐 *www.tomygousset.com/tomy-and-co* ⏲ *Closed weekends* [M] *La Tour–Maubourg.*

Hotels

Hotel rooms with views of Paris's reigning icon come at a premium, but your chances of finding a room with a view are best in this quiet, primarily residential neighborhood. If you don't find one, no worries: there are gorgeous vistas to be had from every street corner.

Eiffel Seine Hôtel

$$$ | **HOTEL** | **FAMILY** | This tiny boutique hotel minutes from the Eiffel Tower mixes contemporary amenities and designer furnishings with Art Nouveau flourishes. **Pros:** very close to the Eiffel Tower and Champs de Mars; reasonable rates; easy métro access. **Cons:** street noise in some rooms facing river; minimal space in standard rooms; breakfast not included. [$] *Rooms from: €250* ✉ *3 bd. de Grenelle, Eiffel Tower* ☎ *01–45–78–14–81* 🌐 *www.hoteleiffelseineparis.com* 🛏 *45 rooms* 🍴 *No Meals* [M] *Bir-Hakeim.*

★ Hôtel de Londres Eiffel

$$ | **HOTEL** | Prices at this small boutique hotel in an upscale neighborhood are fairly reasonable considering all you get—top-notch service, stylish homey decor, a lively neighborhood, and some spectacular views. **Pros:** excellent service; quaint setting; just steps from the Eiffel Tower. **Cons:** not super close to métro; food not permitted in rooms; rooms on the small side. [$] *Rooms from: €185* ✉ *1 rue Augereau, 7e, Eiffel Tower* ☎ *01–45–51–63–02* 🌐 *www.hotel-paris-londres-eiffel.com* 🛏 *30 rooms* 🍴 *No Meals* [M] *La Tour–Maubourg, École Militaire.*

Hôtel du Cadran

$$$ | **HOTEL** | A well-located convenience hotel—actually two buildings run by the same management—Hôtel du Cadran's contemporary design appeals as much to business travelers as to urban creative types on a budget. **Pros:** bright, whimsical rooms; convenient to Rue Cler, Eiffel Tower, and Les Invalides; large closets and windows. **Cons:** petite bathrooms; lacks traditional Parisian charm; two separate

buildings means you have to cross the street. $ *Rooms from: €285* ⊠ *16 rue Valadon, Eiffel Tower* ☎ *01–47–53–89–85* ⊕ *www.cadranhotel.com* ⇌ *53 rooms* ᵀ⊙ᴵ *No Meals* Ⓜ *École Militaire.*

Hôtel du Champ de Mars
$$ | HOTEL | Around the corner from picturesque Rue Cler, this charming, affordable hotel welcomes guests with a Provence-inspired lobby and huge picture windows overlooking a quiet street. **Pros:** good value; free Wi-Fi; walking distance to Eiffel Tower, Les Invalides, and Musée Rodin. **Cons:** inconsistent service; no air-conditioning; small rooms compared to larger hotels. $ *Rooms from: €150* ⊠ *7 rue du Champ de Mars, Eiffel Tower* ☎ *01–45–51–52–30* ⊕ *www.hoteldu-champdemars.com* ⇌ *25 rooms* ᵀ⊙ᴵ *No Meals* Ⓜ *École Militaire.*

★ Hotel Eiffel Blomet
$$ | HOTEL | FAMILY | Named for the cabaret a few doors down where Josephine Baker once sang, this handsome Art Deco hotel comes with a luxurious pool, hammam, and sauna. **Pros:** great pool, steam room, and sauna; good value; chic rooms. **Cons:** average breakfast; not that close to the Eiffel Tower; off-the-radar neighborhood. $ *Rooms from: €200* ⊠ *78 rue Blomet, Eiffel Tower* ☎ *01–53–68–70–00* ⊕ *www.hoteleiffelblomet.com* ⇌ *87 rooms* ᵀ⊙ᴵ *No Meals* Ⓜ *Vaugirard, Volontaires.*

Hôtel Eiffel Trocadéro
$$$ | HOTEL | A curious blend of Second Empire and rococo styling awaits guests in this hotel on a quiet corner just off Place Trocadéro. **Pros:** views of Eiffel Tower from upper floors; organic breakfast buffet; upscale residential district convenient to métro. **Cons:** basic rooms feel cramped; long walk to city center; no full-service restaurant. $ *Rooms from: €270* ⊠ *35 rue Benjamin-Franklin, Eiffel Tower* ☎ *01–53–70–17–70* ⊕ *www.hotel-eiffeltrocadero.com* ⇌ *17 rooms* ᵀ⊙ᴵ *No Meals* Ⓜ *Trocadéro.*

Hôtel Le Tourville
$$$ | HOTEL | This cozy, contemporary haven near the Eiffel Tower, Champs de Mars, and Les Invalides is a comfortable base for exploring Paris. **Pros:** convenient location near métro; free Wi-Fi in all rooms; friendly service. **Cons:** no restaurant; air-conditioning only in summer; small standard rooms. $ *Rooms from: €280* ⊠ *16 av. de Tourville, Eiffel Tower* ☎ *01–47–05–62–62* ⊕ *www.hoteltour-ville.com* ⇌ *30 rooms* ᵀ⊙ᴵ *No Meals* Ⓜ *École Militaire.*

★ Le Cinq Codet
$$$ | HOTEL | Set in a 1930s former France Telecom exchange, the Art Deco–era building's streamlined contours create the ideal setting for spaces that mix modern elegance with high-tech advances, while making the most of some very Parisian views of nearby Les Invalides and the Eiffel Tower a few blocks away. **Pros:** fabulous courtyard cocktail bar; some of the chicest rooms in Paris; exceptional terraces with views. **Cons:** not all rooms have terraces; not a lot of nearby nightlife; in a quiet part of the 7e. $ *Rooms from: €350* ⊠ *5 rue Louis Codet, Eiffel Tower* ☎ *01–53–85–15–60* ⊕ *lecinqcodet.com* ⇌ *57 rooms* ᵀ⊙ᴵ *No Meals* Ⓜ *École Militaire, Varenne.*

★ Le Narcisse Blanc
$$$$ | HOTEL | Set in a 19th-century Haussmannian mansion, Le Narcisse Blanc covers all the bases in luxury accommodations with a top-notch gastronomic restaurant (Cléo), stylish common areas, including a pretty garden terrace, a full-service Clarins spa with fitness, sauna, and steam rooms, and a swimming pool. **Pros:** Art Deco–inspired pool, sauna, and steam room; lots of luxury for the price; Eiffel Tower views. **Cons:** 15-minute walk to the Eiffel Tower; neighborhood quiet at night; hard to book during Fashion Weeks. $ *Rooms from: €425* ⊠ *19 bd. de la Tour-Maubourg, Eiffel Tower* ☎ *01–40–60–44–32* ⊕ *www.lenarcisseblanc.com* ⇌ *37 rooms* ᵀ⊙ᴵ *No*

4

Around the Eiffel Tower

Staying in Paris Like a Local

For those willing to forego the services of a hotel, there are plenty of advantages to renting your own Paris apartment, especially in the elegant seventh arrondissement. **Paris Perfect** (www.parisperfect. com) assures meticulously clean, spacious, well-appointed, and beautifully decorated apartments (sleeping from four to eight people), all with fully equipped kitchens and elevators in quiet areas. What's more, some have terraces and Eiffel Tower views. Staffed with friendly, English-speaking representatives, the company's Paris office is helpful with all your needs on the ground. Prices vary, but are often comparable to hotels in the area, especially when you compare the locations and sizes.

Meals Ⓜ *La Tour-Maubourg, Assemblée Nationale.*

Le Walt

$$$ | HOTEL | The convenient location stands out at this boutique hotel in the chic district between the Eiffel Tower and Les Invalides. **Pros:** great location; free Wi-Fi; friendly staff. **Cons:** some complaints about noisy doors in hallways; no hotel restaurant; on a busy street. Ⓢ *Rooms from: €305* ⊠ *37 av. de la Motte Picquet, Eiffel Tower* ☎ *01–45– 51–55–83* ⊕ *www.lewaltparis.com* ⤏ *25 rooms* ❖ *No Meals* Ⓜ *École Militaire.*

★ Shangri-La Hotel Paris

$$$$ | HOTEL | Displaying French elegance at its best, this impressively restored 19th-century mansion gazing across the Seine at the Eiffel Tower was once the stately home of Prince Roland Bonaparte, grandnephew of the emperor himself, and his gilded private apartments have been transformed into La Suite Impériale. **Pros:** some of the best views in Paris; fabulous pool; excellent dining. **Cons:** expensive breakfast; pool open only until 9 pm; astronomical rates. Ⓢ *Rooms from: €1200* ⊠ *10 av. Iéna, Eiffel Tower* ☎ *01–53–67–19–98* ⊕ *www.shangri-la. com* ⤏ *101 rooms* ❖ *No Meals* Ⓜ *Iéna.*

Ⓨ Nightlife

★ Bar Botaniste

BARS | This most opulent of bars offers 15 scintillating cocktails crafted with herbal elixirs, fresh fruits, flower essences, and exotic nectars in honor of Prince Roland Bonaparte, a passionate botanist and the first owner of the mansion that became the Shangri-La Hotel. The cocktail menu changes every two months—all the better to keep ingredients fresh and seasonal. ⊠ *10 av. d'Iéna, 16e, Eiffel Tower* ☎ *01–53–67–19–98* ⊕ *www.shangri-la. com* Ⓜ *Iéna.*

Fitzgerald

BARS | The popularity of this intimate restaurant-cocktail bar could be due to the upscale neighborhood's distinct lack of nightlife, but there's no denying its dusky allure. At cocktail hour, the bar attracts a mix of businesspeople and chic locals; at night, good music, tasty food, and plentiful drinks animate the crowd. ⊠ *54 bd. de la Tour-Maubourg, 7e, Eiffel Tower* ☎ *01–45–50–38–63* ⊕ *www.fitzgerald. paris* Ⓜ *La Tour-Maubourg, Varenne.*

Gatsby

BARS | A chic cocktail bar steps from the Champs de Mars is a rare find indeed, but this one is steeped in a cosmopolitan speakeasy mystique, with wood paneling and 1920s touches (leather chairs, gramophone, old Underwood typewriter) evoking the New York of its namesake. A covered sidewalk terrace and a dance floor in the cellar add to the clubby fun, along with a small menu of tasty morsels and some very good cocktails. ⊠ *64 av. Bosquet, 7e, Eiffel Tower* ☎ *01–45–51– 56–24* ⊕ *www.legatsby.fr* Ⓜ *École-Militaire, La Tour-Maubourg.*

L'Éclair

BARS | Tucked among the cafés on the Rue Cler, this all-purpose bistro-cum-cocktail bar's all-day and night hours (it's open until 2 am), welcoming atmosphere, and tasty cocktail concoctions make it an ideal option in a neighborhood decidedly short on late-night watering spots. ⊠ *32 rue Cler, 7e, Eiffel Tower* ☎ *01–44–18–09–04* ⊕ *l-eclair.paris* Ⓜ *École-Militaire.*

Performing Arts

Théâtre National de Chaillot

THEATER | Housed in an imposing neoclassical building overlooking the Eiffel Tower, Théâtre National de Chaillot has a trio of venues and a total of 1,600 seats. It's dedicated to experimental, world, and avant-garde drama, dance, and music, or a mix of all three. Major names in dance—like the Ballet Royal de Suède and William Forsythe's company—visit regularly. There are programs for children, too. ⊠ *1 pl. du Trocadéro, 16e, Eiffel Tower* ☎ *01–53–65–30–00* ⊕ *theatre-chaillot. fr* Ⓜ *Trocadéro.*

Shopping

Though this is not the neighborhood that springs to mind for a Paris shopping spree, there is plenty to engage both inveterate shoppers and those who love to just stroll and discover along the way.

One of Paris's great market streets, **Rue Cler** is a feast for the eyes and the senses, overflowing with every imaginable

gourmet delight interspersed with florists, chocolatiers, organic cosmetics, wine shops, and scores of lively cafés and bistros. If you have time for only one street in this neighborhood, make this the one.

Rue Saint-Dominique is, hands down, the neighborhood's best street for shopping and browsing. Stretching from Invalides to the Champs des Mars, this lively thoroughfare is jam-packed with enticing one-off boutiques and high-end French clothing chains like Berenice, The Kooples, Des Petits Hauts, and ba&sh, not to mention fabulous cafés and restaurants. Here you'll find everything from decor, housewares, and jewelry to clothing for women, men, and kids.

Rue de Grenelle, parallel to Rue Saint-Dominique, is also a vibrant shopping street, especially as it crosses St-Germain. **Rue du Commerce**, just steps from the Eiffel Tower, is one of those fabulous stretches that no one knows about, lined with an eye-popping range of popular, attractively priced fashion chains and fun shops for everyone. **Rue de Passy**, a well-known shopping street, is elbow to elbow with French fashion chains and high-end boutiques, plus the popular Passy Plaza mall.

Berenice

WOMEN'S CLOTHING | One of the more creative French chains, Berenice has made an international splash for its of-the-moment styles, quality fabrics, and the kind of classic tailoring Parisians adore. Separates run the gamut from bold and bright to streamlined and understated, but they're always versatile and suitable for a wide range of ages. Accessories include shoes, belts, and bags in fun materials, like python-print or studded leather. ⊠ *91 rue Saint-Dominique, 7e, Eiffel Tower* ☎ *01–77–36–03–47* ⊕ *www.berenice.net* Ⓜ *La Tour-Maubourg.*

★ Comptoirs Bourdonnais

WOMEN'S CLOTHING | A stone's throw from the Eiffel Tower, this boutique does all the work for you, with a handpicked collection of standout clothing and accessories from the best smaller French and European labels, like Diega, Pomandere, Absolut Cashmere, Chloë Stora, Apuntob, luscious knitwear from C.T. Plage, and much more. It's an excellent one-stop shop for immediate Parisian chic. ⊠ *41 av. de la Bourdonnais, 7e, Eiffel Tower* ☎ *01–45–56–01–94* ⊕ *www. comptoirs-bourdonnais.com* Ⓜ *École Militaire.*

Cornerluxe

WOMEN'S CLOTHING | If new Parisian designer duds are a bit out of your price range you might consider this classy *depot-vente* (consignment shop), where chic neighborhood ladies deposit last year's barely worn loot. Its clean and artfully displayed stash of A-list designer clothing, accessories, jewelry, scarves, watches, and shoes can be had for half or less than retail, plus some stellar vintage is also for sale. Standouts have included a crocodile Hermès Birkin bag, Cartier watches, and a superb Chanel leather coat. ⊠ *45 av. Bosquet, 7e, Eiffel Tower* ☎ *01–44–18–31–50* ⊕ *www. cornerluxe.com/fr/content/22-de- pot-vente-paris-07* Ⓜ *Les Invalides, École Militaire.*

★ Maison Chaudun

CHOCOLATE | Maverick chocolatier Michel Chaudun was a legend around Paris. Trained at the Maison du Chocolat, the master confectioner was the very first to strike out on his own, long before Paris became a chocolate mecca. He was also the first to introduce granules of cocoa bean into his chocolates to achieve a rich intensity. In 2015, Chaudun passed the baton to Gilles Marchal, who has more than upheld the standard. Specializing in chocolate sculpture, pastries, and other sinful delights, this enchanting boutique is any chocolate lover's dream. ⊠ *149 rue de l'Université, 7e, Eiffel Tower* ☎ *01–47– 53–74–40* ⊕ *www.chaudun.com* Ⓜ *La Tour-Maubourg.*

THE CHAMPS-ÉLYSÉES

Updated by
Jennifer Ladonne

 Sights
★★★★★

 Restaurants
★★★☆☆

 Hotels
★★★★★

 Shopping
★★★★☆

 Nightlife
★★★★★

NEIGHBORHOOD SNAPSHOT

GETTING HERE

This neighborhood includes the 8e and 16e arrondissements. For the top of the Champs-Élysées/Arc de Triomphe, take Métro Line 1, 2, or 6, or the RER A, to Charles-de-Gaulle–Étoile and look for the exit marked "Champs-Élysées." For the bottom of the avenue, near the Grand Palais, go to the Champs-Élysées–Clémenceau or Concord Métro station on Line 1.

MAKING THE MOST OF YOUR TIME

This neighborhood is an essential stop for every first-time visitor to Paris, and returning travelers will find plenty to do, too. The Champs-Élysées is worth a walk from end to end (start at the Arc de Triomphe if you prefer walking downhill). You can stop for (a pricey) lunch or dessert at one of the cafés or tea salons en route (Ladurée is a favorite); then detour down Avenue Montaigne, Paris's answer to Rodeo Drive.

If your time is limited, you can come for just a stroll at night, when the Champs is alight: there are bars and nightclubs for all tastes, plus movie houses showing French films and English-language block-busters (look for V.O., meaning *version originale,* if you prefer to see an undubbed one). At Christmastime the avenue is decked out top-to-toe in glittering lights, creating a magical atmosphere.

VIEWFINDER

The vistas up and down the Champs-Élysées are legendary. From the top of the Arc de Triomphe, you'll truly understand why this is historically called Place de l'Étoile, or "square of the star," as no fewer than 12 broad Haussmannian avenues radiate from the arc at its center. The monument's eye-popping panoramas of Paris are hands down the city's best. But the views of the arc from the bottom of the avenue heading up aren't so shabby either, especially at Christmastime when the avenue is lit up like, well, a star.

TOP REASONS TO GO

■ **Avenue des Champs-Élysées.** Take a walk from the Arc de Triomphe down this splendid avenue and splurge in the upscale boutiques on and around the fabled thoroughfare. Or simply practice the fine art of window-shopping.

■ **Grand Palais and Petit Palais.** This pair of magnificent Beaux-Arts structures, centerpieces of the 1900 World's Fair, host blockbuster art exhibitions. Though the Grand Palais is currently closed until 2024, the Petit Palais—Paris's fine-arts museum—is a gem and well worth a visit.

■ **Palais de Tokyo.** A major arts center, this impos-ing building is home to the city's largest exhibi-tion space, also called the Palais de Tokyo, dedicated to experimental and con-temporary art (hint: kids love it) as well as the superb Musée d'Art Moderne de la Ville de Paris.

■ **Macarons from Ladurée.** Is it worth lining up for 30 minutes to get a little taste of heaven? You decide. But rest assured: the macarons, round meringue cook-ies made by this famous pâtissier since 1862, are as scrumptious as ever.

Make no mistake: the Champs-Élysées, while ceding some of its elegance in recent times, remains the most famous avenue in Paris—and, perhaps, the world. Like New York's Times Square or London's Piccadilly Circus, it is a mecca for travelers and locals alike.

Some Parisians complain that fast-food joints and chain stores have cheapened Avenue des Champs-Élysées, but others are more philosophical, noting that there is something here for everyone. If lunch at Ladurée is out of your budget, there's always McDonald's (and the view from its second floor is terrific).

Anchoring the Champs is the **Arc de Triomphe,** Napoléon's monument to himself. Though the soaring **Grand Palais** is under renovation until 2024, you can still hop across the street to enjoy the **Petit Palais's** permanent art collection (free admission), superb temporary exhibitions, and charming garden café. Between here and **Place du Trocadéro,** a busy traffic circle, you can find several museums housed in some of Paris's most impressive buildings. The **Musée Guimet** has a superlative Asian art collection, while the **Musée Yves Saint Laurent** contains 13 rooms dedicated to the master couturier's groundbreaking designs. The **Musée d'Art Moderne de la Ville de Paris,** on Avenue du Président Wilson, contains a free permanent collection of 20th-century pieces. Contemporary-art lovers should also check out what's showing next door at the trendy **Palais de Tokyo.** These twin Art Nouveau buildings, constructed for the 1937 World's Fair, are notable for their monumental facades. Across the street is the elegant

Palais Galliera, Paris's fashion museum, boasting newly expanded exhibition spaces and a lovely garden with Eiffel Tower views.

Paris's ambitious plan to "green" and pedestrianize the Place Charles de Gaulle—encircling the Arc de Triomphe—the Champs-Élysées, and Place du Trocadéro, all the way across the Seine to the Eiffel Tower, has already begun and is slated for completion by the 2024 Paris Olympics.

 ## Sights

★ Arc de Triomphe
MONUMENT | Inspired by Rome's Arch of Titus, this colossal, 164-foot triumphal arch was ordered by Napoléon—who liked to consider himself the heir to Roman emperors—to celebrate his military successes. Unfortunately, Napoléon's strategic and architectural visions were not entirely on the same plane, and the Arc de Triomphe proved something of an embarrassment. Although the emperor wanted the monument completed in time for an 1810 parade in honor of his new bride, Marie-Louise, it was still only a few feet high, and a dummy arch of painted canvas was strung up to save face. Empires come and go, but Napoléon's had been gone for more than 20 years before the

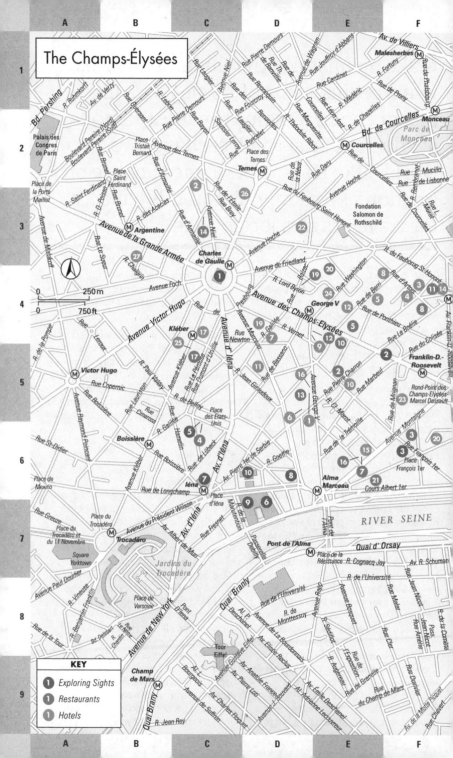

Sights ▼

1 Arc de Triomphe **C4**
2 Avenue des Champs-Élysées **E5**
3 Galerie Dior.............. **F6**
4 Grand Palais............. **G6**
5 La Maison Baccarat.....**C6**
6 Musée d'Art Moderne de la Ville de Paris **D7**
7 Musée Guimet............**C6**
8 Musée Yves Saint Laurent Paris........... **D6**
9 Palais de Tokyo **D7**
10 Palais Galliera, Musée de la Mode **D6**
11 Petit Palais, Musée des Beaux-Arts de la Ville de Paris **H6**

Restaurants ▼

1 Alléno Paris au Pavillon Ledoyen........ **H6**
2 Café La Belle Férronnière.............. **E5**
3 Chez Savy................. **F6**
4 Cristal Room..............**C6**
5 86 Champs................ **E4**
6 Epicure................... **G4**
7 Jean Imbert au Plaza Athénée........... **E6**
8 Komatsubaki **F4**
9 La Scène................. **G4**
10 Ladurée **E4**
11 L'Arôme **F4**
12 Le Café Fouquet's....... **E4**
13 Le Cinq **D5**
14 Le Hide................... **C3**
15 Le Mermoz................ **G4**
16 Le Relais Plaza **E6**
17 LiLi........................**C5**
18 Pavyllon.................. **H6**
19 Pierre Gagnaire **D4**
20 Taillevent................. **E3**
21 Trente-Trois **E6**

Hotels ▼

1 Four Seasons Hôtel George V Paris.......... **D5**
2 Hidden Hotel **C2**
3 Hôtel Bradford Élysées.................... **F4**
4 Hôtel Daniel **F4**
5 Hôtel de Berri **E4**
6 Hôtel de Sers............ **D5**
7 Hôtel Ekta **D4**
8 Hôtel Elysia **F4**
9 Hôtel Fouquet's Barrière................... **E4**
10 Hôtel Grand Powers..... **E5**
11 Hôtel Keppler............ **D5**
12 Hôtel Lancaster.......... **E4**
13 Hôtel Le Bristol.......... **G4**
14 Hôtel Le 123 Elysées..... **F4**
15 Hôtel Plaza Athénée.....**E6**
16 Hôtel Prince des Galles **D5**
17 Hôtel Raphael............**C4**
18 Hôtel Rond Point Champs-Élysées......... **G5**
19 Hotel Vernet............. **D4**
20 La Maison Champs Elysées.................. **F6**
21 La Réserve............... **G5**
22 Le Royal Monceau Raffles Paris............. **D3**
23 Marignan **F5**
24 Monsieur George........ **E4**
25 The Peninsula Paris.......................**C5**
26 Renaissance Paris Arc de Triomphe **D3**
27 Room Mate Alain Champs-Élysées........ **B3**

Arc was finally finished in 1836. A small museum halfway up recounts its history.

The Arc de Triomphe is notable for magnificent sculptures by François Rude, including the *Departure of the Volunteers in 1792,* better known as *La Marseillaise,* to the right of the arch when viewed from the Champs-Élysées. Names of Napoléon's generals are inscribed on the stone facades—the underlined names identify the hallowed figures who fell in battle.

The traffic circle around the Arc is named for Charles de Gaulle, but it's known to Parisians as L'Étoile, or "the Star"—a reference to the streets that fan out from it. Climb the stairs to the top of the arch and you can see the star effect of the 12 radiating avenues and the vista down the Champs-Élysées toward Place de la Concorde and the distant Musée du Louvre.

Paris mayor Anne Hildago's ambitious plans to "green" the city include a total makeover for the Place d'Étoile to make visiting the Arc de Triomphe a safer and more pleasant experience. By 2024, traffic will be limited in favor of enlarged pedestrian areas and a wide expanse of trees extending all the way down the Champs-Élysées.

■ TIP→ **France's Unknown Soldier is buried beneath the arch, and a commemorative flame is rekindled every evening at 6:30. That's the most atmospheric time to visit, but, to beat the crowds, come early in the morning or buy your ticket online.**

⚠ **Be wary of the traffic circle that surrounds the arch. It's infamous for accidents—including one several years ago that involved the French transport minister. Always use the underground passage from the northeast corner of the Avenue des Champs-Élysées.** ✉ *Pl. Charles-de-Gaulle, Champs-Élysées* ☎ *01–55–37–73–77* ⊕ *www.paris-arc-de-triomphe.fr* ✒ *€13* ↻ *Last admission 45 mins before closing* Ⓜ *Métro or RER: Charles de Gaulle–Étoile.*

Remembering Princess Diana

The monument at Place de l'Alma, at the bottom of Avenues Montaigne and George V, along the Seine and just next to the Bateaux Mouches boarding dock, has become Princess Diana's unofficial shrine. Bouquets and messages are still placed here by her admirers—city workers regularly clean up flowers, graffiti, and photographs. The replica of the Statue of Liberty's flame predates Diana's car accident though: it was donated by Paris-based American companies in 1989 in honor of the bicentennial of the French Revolution.

Avenue des Champs-Élysées

STREET | FAMILY | Marcel Proust lovingly described the genteel elegance of the storied Champs-Élysées (pronounced "chahnz- *eleezay,*" with an "n" sound instead of "m," and no "p") during its Belle Époque heyday, when its cobblestones resounded with the clatter of horses and carriages. Today, despite unrelenting traffic and the intrusion of chain stores and fast-food franchises, the avenue still sparkles. There's always something happening here: stores are open late (and many are open on Sunday, a rarity in Paris); nightclubs remain top destinations; and cafés offer prime people-watching, though you'll pay for the privilege—after all, this is Europe's most expensive piece of real estate. Along the 2-km (1¼-mile) stretch, you can find marquee names in French luxury, like Cartier, Guerlain, and Louis Vuitton. Car manufacturers lure international visitors with space-age showrooms. Old stalwarts, meanwhile, are still going strong—including the Lido cabaret and Fouquet's, whose celebrity clientele extends back to James Joyce. The avenue is also the setting for the last leg of the Tour de France bicycle race (the third or fourth Sunday in July), as well as Bastille Day (July 14) and Armistice Day (November 11) ceremonies. The Champs-Élysées, which translates to "Elysian Fields" (the resting place of the blessed in Greek mythology), began life as a cow pasture and in 1666 was transformed into a park by the royal landscape architect André Le Nôtre. Traces of its green origins are visible toward the Concorde, where elegant 19th-century park pavilions house the historic restaurants Ledoyen and Laurent. Soon, the celebrated avenue will once again live up to its name. By 2024, Paris plans to transform the avenue, drastically reducing automobile traffic in favor of expanded pedestrian walkways and hundreds of new trees. ✉ Champs-Élysées Ⓜ Champs-Élysées–Clemenceau, Franklin D. Roosevelt, George V, Charles de Gaulle–Étoile.

★ **Galerie Dior**

OTHER MUSEUM | Following on the heels of the Musée Yves Saint Laurent Paris (and helmed by its former director) this drop-dead gorgeous exhibition space, housed in the same building as the Dior flagship boutique store and restaurant, inaugurates a new direction for Dior, fusing fashion and culture. No doubt inspired by the blockbuster Dior show at Paris's Musée des Arts Décoratif in 2017, the permanent exhibition assembles all of the house's great designers along with iconic pieces from the master himself. This primer on the history of Paris fashion is an absolute must-see for fashion buffs, and afterward, you may be inspired to pop into the Avenue Montaigne boutique next door for some shopping or a quick pick-me-up at the super-chic café. ✉ 11 rue François 1er, 8e, Champs-Élysées ☎ 01–82–20–22–00 ⊕ www.galeriedior. com 🎫 €12 ⊗ Closed Tues. Ⓜ Franklin D. Roosevelt.

Grand Palais

NOTABLE BUILDING | With its curved-glass roof and gorgeous Belle Époque ornamentation, you can't miss the Grand Palais whether you're approaching from the Seine or the Champs-Élysées. It forms an elegant duo with the Petit Palais across Avenue Winston Churchill. Both stone buildings, adorned with mosaics and sculpted friezes, were built for the 1900 World's Fair and, like the Eiffel Tower, were not intended to be permanent. That's why, after 120 years of wear and tear, the graceful yet delicate structure is currently closed for renovation, with plans to fully reopen in time for the 2024 Paris Olympics. The good news is you'll still be able to enjoy the Palais's world-class cultural, fashion, and sporting events—as well as some Olympic events—at the Grand Palais Éphémère, a soaring temporary structure set on the Champs de Mars, the long grassy park that fronts the Eiffel Tower. ✉ Av. Winston Churchill, Champs-Élysées ☎ 01–40–13–48–00 ⊕ www.grandpalais. fr Ⓜ Champs-Élysées–Clemenceau.

La Maison Baccarat

ART MUSEUM | Playing on the building's Surrealist legacy, designer Philippe Starck brought an irreverent Alice in Wonderland approach to the HQ and museum of the venerable Baccarat crystal firm: Cocteau, Dalí, Buñuel, and Man Ray were all frequent guests of the mansion's one-time owner, Countess Marie-Laure de Noailles. At the entrance, talking heads are projected onto giant crystal urns, and a lighted chandelier is submerged in an aquarium. Upstairs, the museum features masterworks created by Baccarat since 1764, including soaring candlesticks made for Czar Nicholas II and the perfume flacon Dalí designed for Schiaparelli. Don't miss the rotunda's "Alchemy" section by Gérard Garouste, showcasing the technical history of cutting, wheel engraving, enameling, and gilding. If you're in the mood for shopping, contemporary crystal by top-name designers as well as stemware, vases, tableware, jewelry, chandeliers, and even furniture are sold in the on-site shop. Set aside a few moments to enjoy the little park just outside in the Place des États-Unis with impressive statues of Washington and Lafayette. The spectacular Crystal Room restaurant, decked out with the house's colorful crystal vases and dinnerware and crowned by a majestic 157-light Baccarat chandelier, is a lovely place for lunch, dinner, teatime, or a drink in the outdoor Garden Lounge. ⊠ 11 pl. des États-Unis, Champs-Élysées ☎ 01–40–22–11–00 ⊕ www.baccarat.fr ☜ €10 ⊘ Closed Sun. and Mon. Ⓜ Iéna.

Musée d'Art Moderne de la Ville de Paris
(*Paris Museum of Modern Art*)
ART MUSEUM | Although the city's modern art museum hasn't generated a buzz comparable to that of the Centre Georges Pompidou, visiting can be a more pleasant experience because it draws fewer crowds. The Art Deco building's vast, white-walled galleries make an ideal backdrop for temporary exhibitions of 20th-century art and postmodern installation projects. The permanent collection on the lower floor takes over where the Musée d'Orsay leaves off, chronologically speaking: among the earliest works are Fauve paintings by Maurice de Vlaminck and André Derain, followed by Pablo Picasso's early experiments in Cubism. Other highlights include works by Robert and Sonia Delaunay, Chagall, Matisse, Rothko, and Modigliani. The museum also organizes excellent temporary exhibitions that rarely come with crowds. The museum's restaurant, Forest, is a lovely choice for lunch or dinner, and in warm weather, it's a prime spot for Eiffel Tower views on the Palais de Tokyo's sprawling terrace. ⊠ 11 av. du Président Wilson, Champs-Élysées ☎ 01–53–67–40–00 ⊕ www.mam.paris.fr ☜ Free; from €7 for temporary exhibitions ⊘ Closed Mon. Ⓜ Alma-Marceau, Iéna.

★ Musée Guimet
ART MUSEUM | The outstanding Musée Guimet boasts the Western world's biggest collection of Asian art, thanks to the 19th-century wanderings of Lyonnaise industrialist Émile Guimet. Exhibits, enriched by the state's vast holdings, are laid out geographically in airy, light-filled rooms. Just past the entry, you can find the largest assemblage of Khmer sculpture outside Cambodia. The second floor has statuary and masks from Nepal, ritual funerary art from Tibet, and jewelry and fabrics from India. Peek into the library rotunda, where Monsieur Guimet once entertained the city's notables under the gaze of eight caryatids atop Ionic columns; Mata Hari danced here in 1905, and the museum still hosts an impressive series of musical events. The much-heralded Chinese collection, made up of 20,000-odd objects, covers seven millennia. At the Hôtel d'Heidelbach next door (19 Avenue d'Iéna), you'll find Asian furniture and implements for tea ceremonies, which are performed on special dates during the year in the garden's authentic Japanese tea pavilion. Grab a free English-language audioguide and brochure at the museum entrance. If you need a pick-me-up, stop at the Salon des Porcelaines café on the lower level for a ginger milkshake or an Asian-influenced meal. Don't miss the Guimet's spectacular offshoot, the Musée d'Ennery, housed in a Belle Époque mansion on Avenue Foch and noted for its exquisite collection of Japanese *netsuke*, as well as 3,000 works of Chinese and Japanese art (open Saturday by appointment only via the Musée Guimet website). ⊠ 6 pl. d'Iéna, Champs-Élysées ☎ 01–56–52–54–33 ⊕ www.guimet.fr ☜ €11.50 ⊘ Closed Tues. Ⓜ Iéna, Boissiére.

Musée Yves Saint Laurent Paris
OTHER MUSEUM | As elegant and stylish as the master couturier's groundbreaking designs, this museum is housed in the very mansion where Yves Saint Laurent did his work and entertained celebrity

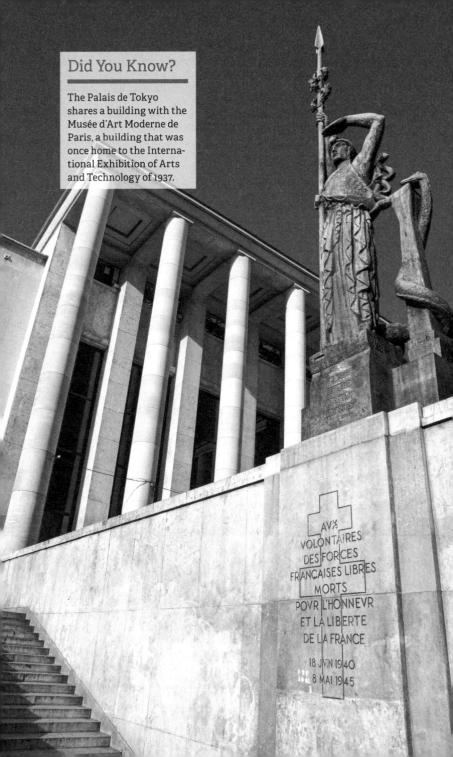

clients. More than 50 prototypes—including such landmarks as the Mondrian dress, the original pantsuit, and the woman's tuxedo—are on display at any one time, as are dozens of design drawings and a glittering array of jewelry. Thanks to its huge windows, the light-bathed upstairs atelier, stuffed with books and fabrics, offers an intimate glimpse into YSL's world. Be sure not to miss the touching short film detailing the relationship between Saint Laurent and his longtime partner Pierre Bergé. All of the exhibits have detailed English labeling, and there is a free English guide available at reception. ✉ 5 av. Marceau, Champs-Élysées ☎ 01–44–31–64–00 ⊕ www.museeyslparis.com ✍ €10 ⊗ Closed Mon. ☞ Last entry 45 mins before closing Ⓜ Alma-Marceau.

Palais de Tokyo

ARTS CENTER | The go-to address for some of the city's liveliest exhibitions, the Palais de Tokyo is a stripped-down venue that spotlights provocative, ambitious contemporary art. There is no permanent collection: instead, cutting-edge temporary shows are staged in a cavernous space reminiscent of a light-filled industrial loft. The programming extends to performance art, concerts, readings, and fashion shows. Night owls will appreciate the midnight closing. The museum's chic Bambini trattoria and cocktail bar—serving delicious authentic Italian cuisine and Neapolitan-style pizzas—is a regular haunt for locals, especially for cocktails, dinner, and late-night cravings thanks to its wraparound terrace and Eiffel Tower views. But there's also a small café area at the restaurant entrance for a quick bite and glass of wine or cup of coffee if you don't feel like a sit-down meal. Visit the offbeat bookshop for colorful souvenirs that are as edgy and subversive as the exhibits. ✉ 13 av. du Président Wilson, Champs-Élysées ☎ 01–81–97–35–88 ⊕ www.palaisdetokyo.com ✍ €12 ⊗ Closed Tues. Ⓜ léna.

★ Palais Galliera, Musée de la Mode

OTHER MUSEUM | The city's Museum of Fashion occupies a suitably fashionable mansion—the 19th-century residence of Marie Brignole-Sale, Duchess of Galliera. Inside, the exhibition spaces, now on two floors, focus on costume and clothing design (a recent retrospective, for instance, honored the visionary Coco Chanel). Covering key moments in fashion history and showcasing iconic French designers, the museum's collection includes 200,000 articles of clothing and accessories that run the gamut from basic streetwear to haute couture. Galleries at the garden level focus on fashion history from the 18th century to the present via pieces from the permanent collection. Details on shows are available on the museum website. Don't miss the lovely 19th-century garden that encircles the palace, a favorite spot for neighborhood Parisians to take a coffee and a book. ✉ 10 av. Pierre-1er-de-Serbie, Champs-Élysées ☎ 01–56–52–86–00 ⊕ www.palaisgalliera.paris.fr ✍ From €8 ⊗ Closed Mon. and between exhibitions Ⓜ léna.

Petit Palais, Musée des Beaux-Arts de la Ville de Paris

ART MUSEUM | The "little" palace has a small overlooked collection of excellent paintings, sculpture, and objets d'art, with works by Monet, Gauguin, and Courbet, among others. Temporary exhibitions, beefed up in recent years (and occasionally free), are particularly good. The building, like the Grand Palais across the street, is an architectural marvel of marble, glass, and gilt built for the 1900 World's Fair, with impressive entry doors and huge windows overlooking the river. Search directly above the main galleries for 16 plaster busts set into the wall representing famous artists. Outside, note two eye-catching sculptures: French World War I hero Georges Clemenceau faces the Champs-Élysées, while a resolute Winston Churchill faces the Seine. In warmer weather, head to

Not far from the Champs-Élysées, the Musée Guimet has one of the world's best collections of Asian art outside of Asia.

the garden café with terrace seating. ✉ *Av. Winston Churchill, Champs-Élysées* ☎ *01–53–43–40–00* 🌐 *www.petitpalais.paris.fr* 🎟 *Free; €11–€14 for temporary exhibitions* 🕓 *Closed Mon.* [M] *Champs-Élysées–Clemenceau.*

🍴 Restaurants

As befits this quintessentially upscale part of town, you'll find some of the city's priciest and most elegant dining around the Champs-Élysées. A handful of Paris's famous and ambitious chefs have settled here, whose restaurants—many located in palatial hotels—are surrounded by bourgeois apartments, embassies, and luxury boutiques. Some, such as Eric Frechon at Le Bristol's Epicure, offer sophisticated updates of French classics, whereas others, like Stéphanie de Quellec's La Scène, Pierre Gagnaire's eponymous dining room, and Yannick Alléno at the historic stunner Le Pavillon Ledoyen, constantly push culinary boundaries to deliver new adventures in fine dining. A few solid bistros survive here, notably the Art Deco stalwart Chez Savy.

★ Alléno Paris au Pavillon Ledoyen

$$$$ | MODERN FRENCH | Tucked away in a quiet garden across from the Petit Palais, Ledoyen—open since 1779—is a study in Empire-style elegance. Star chef Yannick Alléno injects the three-star dining room with a frisson of modernity by putting fresh farmhouse ingredients front and center in his €380, 10-course tasting extravaganza. **Known for:** langoustine tart with caviar; lots of cool history (Napoléon and Joséphine met here); one of the most romantic settings in Paris. [$] *Average main: €120* ✉ *1 av. Dutuit, on Carré des Champs-Élysées, 8e, Champs-Élysées* ☎ *01–53–05–10–01* 🌐 *www.yannick-alleno.com/restaurant/le-pavillon-ledoyen* 🕓 *Closed Sun. and Aug.* 👔 *Jacket required* [M] *Concorde, Champs-Élysées–Clemenceau.*

Café La Belle Férronnière

$$ | BRASSERIE | A favorite of Parisians for business lunches and after-work *apéros*, this traditional brasserie prides itself on using quality ingredients from top French producers (and the family farm) for its homemade fare, along with all the joys of an authentic Parisian brasserie: a daily blackboard menu, brisk service, a generous sidewalk terrace, and convenient all-day hours (open 6:30 am until midnight). Its location a short walk from the Champs-Élysées does mean higher prices, but not as high as the more touristy cafés on the avenue. **Known for:** good selection of reasonable wines by the glass; great location; copious steak tartare. $ *Average main: €23* ⊠ *53 rue Pierre Charron, 8e, Champs-Élysées* ☎ *01–42–25–03–82* ⊕ *www.labelleferronniere.fr* Ⓜ *George V.*

Chez Savy

$$$ | **BISTRO** | Just off glitzy Avenue Montaigne, Chez Savy's Art Deco cream-and-burgundy interior is blissfully intact, occupying its own circa-1930s microcosm. Fill up on rib-sticking specialties from the Aveyron region of central France—lentil salad with bacon, foie gras (prepared on the premises), perfectly charred lamb with feather-light shoestring *frites,* and pedigreed Charolais beef. **Known for:** competent, unpretentious service; authentic brasserie experience; good prices in a pricey neighborhood. $ *Average main: €25* ⊠ *23 rue Bayard, 8e, Champs-Élysées* ☎ *01–47–23–46–98* ⊕ *www.chezsavy. com* ⊙ *Closed weekends and Aug.* Ⓜ *Franklin D. Roosevelt.*

Cristal Room

$$$$ | **MODERN FRENCH** | Though there are more outstanding restaurants in terms of cuisine, this gorgeous dining room in the Baccarat museum certainly ranks among the most beautiful in Paris. Its towering mirrors, gilded moldings, and stunning crystal chandeliers are enhanced by attentive service. **Known for:** affordable lunch menu; fabulous bar with cocktail menu; opulent dining room in a famous Paris mansion. $ *Average main: €42* ⊠ *11 pl. des États-Unis, 16e, Champs-Élysées*

☎ *01–40–22–11–10* ⊕ *www.baccarat.fr* ⊙ *Closed Sun. and Mon.* Ⓜ *Kléber.*

86 Champs

$ | **MODERN FRENCH** | The closest thing the pastry world has to a rock star, Pierre Hermé and his wildly imaginative flavor pairings (think raspberry, rose, and lychee; chestnut and black wheat; or jasmine and *fraise des bois*) are renewed every season and are never humdrum. At 86 Champs, Hermé has teamed up with fragrance and cosmetics giant L'Occitane for a colorful carousel ride of a café, with a half-moon pastry-and-chocolates counter and bar, where you can enjoy breakfast, lunch, or a quick bite. **Known for:** nice terrace with Arc de Triomphe views; good coffee; imaginative and delicious (but expensive) pastries. $ *Average main: €12* ⊠ *86 av. des Champs-Élysées, 8e, Champs-Élysées* ☎ *01–70–38–77–38* ⊕ *www.86champs.com* Ⓜ *George V.*

Epicure

$$$$ | **MODERN FRENCH** | One of the most admired chefs in Paris, Éric Fréchon recently celebrated 23 years at the helm of Le Bristol Hotel's revered restaurant, 13 of them with Michelin's top three-star award, which he's retained since 2009. Fréchon creates masterworks—say, farmer's pork cooked "from head to foot" with truffle-enhanced crushed potatoes and his famous truffle lasagna—that are both deeply satisfying yet unpretentious. **Known for:** relatively affordable lunch menu; superb French provincial dining room; alfresco dining in a beautiful French garden in warm weather. $ *Average main: €175* ⊠ *Hôtel Bristol, 112 rue du Faubourg St-Honoré, 8e, Champs-Élysées* ☎ *01–53–43–43–00* ⊕ *www.lebristolparis.com* 🍴 *Jacket and tie* Ⓜ *Miromesnil.*

★ Jean Imbert au Plaza Athénée

$$$$ | **FRENCH** | In one of the most anticipated announcements in the Parisian food world, the Plaza Athénée named talented young chef Jean Imbert, a protégé of his predecessor Alain Ducasse,

as head of their new temple to gastronomy. A long marble table is the centerpiece of this opulently refurbished dining room (which seems to take Versailles as its model), and the menu is no less splendid, with options like Casparian imperial caviar, Bellevue lobster in a foie gras broth flecked with black truffle, and whole turbot masterfully boned tableside. **Known for:** exemplary service; rising star chef; gorgeous, über-opulent dining room. $ *Average main: €75* ✉ *Hôtel Plaza Athénée, 25 av. Montaigne, 8e, Champs-Élysées* ☎ *01–53–67–65–00* ⊕ *www.dorchestercollection.com/en/paris/hotel-plaza-athenee* ⊗ *Closed Sun. and Mon.* Ⓜ *Alma-Marceau.*

Komatsubaki

$$$$ | **JAPANESE** | Run by Yoichi Kino, a 30-year master sushi chef whose family has specialized in smoked eel for generations, and Ryuma Takubo, who earned a Michelin star in Japan, Komatsubaki specializes in the exquisite vegetarian cuisine favored by Japanese monks. Choose from three sophisticated menus, including a stunning vegetarian version, all served on delicate dishes and accompanied by rare selection of white Burgundies, sakes, and teas. **Known for:** wine list includes white Burgundies and sake selections; authentic dining experience on tatami mats; high-end take-out sushi. $ *Average main: €50* ✉ *3 rue d'Artois, 8e, Champs-Élysées* ☎ *01–42–25–26–78* ⊕ *www.komatsubaki-paris.com* ⊗ *Closed Mon. No lunch* Ⓜ *St-Philippe-du-Roule.*

★ Ladurée

$$$ | **CAFÉ** | With 100-plus locations worldwide, the largest branch of the Ladurée tea salon empire is worth the splurge, thanks to the sumptuous pastries, which steal the show. In addition to more than a dozen flavors of *macarons*, it has assorted cakes, ice cream, pastries, and beautifully boxed treats ideal for gift-giving. **Known for:** beautiful and elegant decor; pricey lunch menu; world-famous macarons. $ *Average main: €27* ✉ *75 av. des Champs-Élysées, 8e, Champs-Élysées* ☎ *01–40–75–08–75* ⊕ *www.laduree.com* Ⓜ *George V.*

L'Arôme

$$$$ | **MODERN FRENCH** | Eric Martins ran a popular bistro in the far reaches of the 15e arrondissement before opening this contemporary restaurant off the Champs-Élysées, and his background in haute cuisine makes this ambitious dining room an easy transition. The spot turns out seasonal dishes with a touch of finesse from the open kitchen. **Known for:** pricey prix-fixe menus (no à la carte); Breton crab with avocado, Japanese rice, and tomato gelée with smoked pepper; masterful wine pairings. $ *Average main: €50* ✉ *3 rue St-Philippe du Roule, 8e, Champs-Élysées* ☎ *01–42–25–55–98* ⊕ *www.larome-paris.com/en* ⊗ *Closed weekends and Aug.* Ⓜ *St-Philippe du Roule.*

★ La Scène

$$$$ | **FRENCH** | Shortly after earning a second Michelin star from the chic open kitchen at the Hôtel Prince des Galles, Stéphanie le Quellec left to strike out on her own. Now she's regained her two stars at this gleaming dining room on the elegant Avenue Matignon, the perfect setting for the refined, scintillating cuisine that earned the former *Top Chef* winner a loyal following among Paris gastronomes. **Known for:** handpicked small-producer wines; famous foie gras tart; beautiful atmosphere. $ *Average main: €100* ✉ *32 av. Matignon, 8e, Champs-Élysées* ☎ *01–42–65–05–61* ⊕ *www.la-scene.paris* ⊗ *Closed weekends* Ⓜ *Miromesnil, St-Philippe-du-Roule.*

Le Café Fouquet's

$$$ | **BRASSERIE** | A Champs-Élysées institution, Le Fouquet's brasserie has served steak tartare and lobster ravioli to the French royalty of stage and screen since 1899 (Edith Piaf and Charles Aznavour were regulars, and the César Awards dinner is still served here every year). The brasserie's two glassed-in terraces overlook Avenue George V and the

Champs-Élysées and provide an excellent spot for watching the Parisian world go by. **Known for:** historic dining room that's a prime people-watching spot; classic French brasserie fare with a luxurious touch; hot spot for Parisian politicians and stars. [$] *Average main: €25* ✉ *99 av. des Champs-Élysées, 8e, Champs-Élysées* ☎ *01–40–69–60–50* 🌐 *www.fouquets-paris.com* [M] *George V.*

★ Le Cinq

$$$$ | MODERN FRENCH | Christian Le Squer is among the most famous and most respected chefs in Paris, as proved by his turn here at one of the city's most deluxe dining rooms. You'll find all the luxury products you might expect—caviar, truffles, game in season—along with a masterful touch that often transforms homey Breton ingredients such as oysters or lamb into imaginative tours de force. **Known for:** unfailingly accommodating service; famous flowery outdoor terrace; Michelin-starred French fine dining. [$] *Average main: €120* ✉ *Hôtel Four Seasons George V, 31 av. George V, 8e, Champs-Élysées* ☎ *01–49–52–70–00* 🌐 *www.fourseasons.com/paris/dining/restaurants/le_cinq* ⏲ *Closed Sun. and Mon. No lunch* 👔 *Jacket and tie* [M] *George V.*

★ Le Hide

$$$ | BISTRO | Hide Kobayashi, known as "Koba," is one of several Japanese chefs in Paris who trained with some of the biggest names in French cuisine before opening their own restaurants. Not surprisingly, this great-value bistro near the Arc de Triomphe became instantly popular with locals as well as visiting Japanese and Americans who follow the food scene. **Known for:** one of Paris's best prix-fixe menus; stellar prices for this pricey neighborhood; chic, unpretentious dining room. [$] *Average main: €26* ✉ *10 rue du Général Lanzerac, 8e, Champs-Élysées* ☎ *01–45–74–15–81* 🌐 *www.lehide.fr* ⏲ *Closed Sun., 2 wks in May, and 2 wks in Aug. No lunch* [M] *Charles de Gaulle–Étoile.*

Le Mermoz

$ | BISTRO | When the opulence of the neighborhood begins to overwhelm, this refreshing island of unpretentious pleasures is a good place to restore both body and budget. In addition to the charm of its bright, cheerful interiors—complete with mirrors, fresh flowers, globe chandeliers, and a zinc bar—you'll find a sophisticated daily menu of market-fresh dishes and small plates. **Known for:** affordable wines by the glass; well-priced small plates; foodie hideaway. [$] *Average main: €15* ✉ *16 rue Jean Mermoz, 8e, Champs-Élysées* ☎ *01–45–63–65–26* 🌐 *www.facebook.com/restaurantlemermoz* ⏲ *Closed weekends* [M] *Saint-Philippe-du-Roule, Champs-Élysées–Clémenceau.*

Le Relais Plaza

$$$$ | FRENCH | Parisian to its core, the Hotel Plaza Athénée's Art Deco dining room—including a mural that's a registered historic landmark—is a cherished neighborhood stalwart. Masterful updates of French classics include dishes like warm salad of delicate greens, thinly sliced artichokes, and Parmesan, flecked with shaved black truffles, and house-made foie gras with slices of fresh figs and a rich dried-fruit chutney. **Known for:** a favorite with the locals; exceptional dining room with historic Art Deco murals; throwback jazz nights every last Wednesday of the month. [$] *Average main: €55* ✉ *Plaza Athénée, 21 av. Montaigne, 8e, Champs-Élysées* ☎ *01–53–67–64–00* 🌐 *www.ducasse-paris.com/en/addresses/relais-plaza* [M] *Alma-Marceau, Franklin D. Roosevelt.*

LiLi

$$$$ | CANTONESE | The operatically beautiful LiLi, in the Peninsula Hotel, puts sophisticated Cantonese cuisine in its rightful place—the gastronomic center of the world. The menu features all the classics, raised to the status of haute cuisine: small plates of dim sum (seafood, vegetable, or pork dumplings) alongside more substantial fare like fried rice studded with market-fresh vegetables, succulent Sichuan shrimp, and barbecued suckling pig. **Known for:** cocktails at the Bar Kléber; gourmet dim sum; authentic Peking duck. $ *Average main: €38 ⊠ The Peninsula Paris, 19 rue Kléber, 16e, Champs-Élysées* ☎ *01–58–12–67–50* ⊕ *www.liliparis.fr* ⊗ *Closed Sun. and Mon.* Ⓜ *Kléber, Charles de Gaulle–Étoile.*

Pavyllon

$$$$ | FRENCH | This is a great opportunity to sample chef Yannick Alléno's cooking for a (slightly) less lofty price tag than at his three-star Pavillon Ledoyen on the same premises. Make no mistake, though guests are seated around a bar, this is as sophisticated an eatery as they come. **Known for:** open seven days; 15 staff to serve 20 diners; outdoor dining. $ *Average main: €55 ⊠ 8 av. Dutuit, 8e, Champs-Élysées* ☎ *01–53–05–10–00* ⊕ *www.yannick-alleno.com/en/restaurants-reservation/pavyllon.html* Ⓜ *Concorde, Madeleine.*

★ Pierre Gagnaire

$$$$ | MODERN FRENCH | If you want to venture to the frontier of contemporary cooking—and if money is no object—dinner here is a must. Chef Pierre Gagnaire's work is at once intellectual and poetic, often blending three or four unexpected tastes and textures in a single dish. Just taking in the menu requires concentration (ask the waiters for help), so complex are the multiline descriptions about each dish's six or seven ingredients. **Known for:** complicated menu descriptions; combines French technical mastery with cutting-edge techniques; consistently ranked among the world's best (and most expensive) restaurants. $ *Average main: €150 ⊠ 6 rue de Balzac, 8e, Champs-Élysées* ☎ *01–58–36–12–50* ⊕ *pierregagnaire.com* ⊗ *Closed weekends and Aug.* Ⓜ *Charles de Gaulle–Étoile.*

★ Taillevent

$$$$ | MODERN FRENCH | Perhaps the most traditional of all Paris luxury restaurants, this two-star grande dame basks in renewed freshness under chef Giuliano Sperandio, who brings a welcome contemporary spirit that translates to daring on the plate. Dishes such as scallops meunière (with butter and lemon) are matched with contemporary choices like a splendid spelt risotto with truffles and frogs' legs or panfried duck liver with caramelized fruits and vegetables. **Known for:** 19th-century salon turned winter garden; discreet hangout for Paris politicians; one of the oldest names in Paris for fine French dining. $ *Average main: €100 ⊠ 15 rue Lamennais, 8e, Champs-Élysées* ☎ *01–44–95–15–01* ⊕ *www.taillevent.com* ⊗ *Closed weekends and Aug.* ⌂ *Jacket and tie* Ⓜ *Charles de Gaulle–Étoile.*

Trente-Trois

$$$$ | FRENCH | Despite opening in the midst of a pandemic, in September 2021, this sumptuous contemporary dining room—tucked away in a stunner of a Belle Époque town house—achieved a Michelin star within five months. Chef Sébastien Sanjou's ingredients all have pedigrees (listed on the menu) for exceptional seasonal fare that's both refined and robust. **Known for:** accommodates all palates and preferences; up-and-coming chef; beautiful atmosphere. $ *Average main: €38 ⊠ 33 rue Jean Goujon, 8e, Champs-Élysées* ☎ *01–45–05–68–00* ⊕ *www.restaurant-trente-trois.com* ⊗ *Closed Sun. and Mon.* Ⓜ *Alma-Marceau.*

🛏 Hotels

The land of the palace hotel, the elegant area around the Golden Triangle is catnip for hedge-fund millionaires and international royalty. More than half of Paris's 13 palace hotels are clustered here, starting with Le Bristol—a Paris legend—and including the Plaza Athénée, the George

V, the Peninsula, and one of Paris's newer palaces, the gemlike La Réserve.

★ Four Seasons Hôtel George V Paris
$$$$ | **HOTEL** | **FAMILY** | As poised and polished as the day it opened in 1928, this superb hotel's original plaster detailing and 17th-century tapestries have been restored, the bas-reliefs regilded, and the marble-floor mosaics rebuilt tile by tile, adding up to an opulence rarely equaled in the city. **Pros:** some of the best dining in the city; indoor swimming pool; courtyard dining in summer. **Cons:** lacks the intimacy of smaller boutique hotels; definitely for the 1%; several blocks from the nearest métro. [$] *Rooms from: €1100* ✉ *31 av. George V, Champs-Élysées* ☎ *01–49–52–70–00* 🌐 *www.fourseasons.com/paris* 🛏 *244 rooms* 🍴 *No Meals* [M] *George V.*

Hidden Hotel
$$$ | **HOTEL** | The rough-hewn wood facade heralds the eco-friendly theme of this under-the-radar boutique hotel a block from the Arc de Triomphe, and the interior follows through with handcrafted glass, wood, stone, and ceramic decor. **Pros:** a block from main métro line and Champs-Élysées; healthy breakfasts; organic toiletries in recycled packaging. **Cons:** separate entrance and breakfast area for some rooms isn't intimate; open-plan bathrooms offer little privacy; rooms on the small side. [$] *Rooms from: €284* ✉ *28 rue de l'Arc de Triomphe, Champs-Élysées* ☎ *01–40–55–03–57* 🌐 *www.hidden-hotel.com* 🛏 *35 rooms* 🍴 *No Meals* [M] *Ternes.*

★ Hôtel Bradford Élysées
$$ | **HOTEL** | **FAMILY** | One of the Astotel group's popular Paris lodgings, this welcoming hotel follows a winning formula: annex a historic building, create attractive spaces in cheerful colors, and offer plenty of perks (free drinks, snacks, and newspapers) and service that go the whole nine yards, all for a reasonable price. **Pros:** lots of freebies, including lobby snacks and complimentary minibar; bargain prices; some rooms have period details. **Cons:** a métro ride to many sights; decor not to all tastes; not in a central neighborhood. [$] *Rooms from: €171* ✉ *10 rue Saint-Philippe du Roule, Champs-Élysées* ☎ *01–45–63–20–20* 🌐 *www.astotel.com/hotel/bradford-elysees* 🛏 *50 rooms* 🍴 *No Meals* [M] *St-Philippe-du-Roule, Franklin D. Roosevelt.*

Hôtel Daniel
$$$$ | **HOTEL** | A contemporary antidote to the minimalist trend, the Daniel is decorated in rich fabrics and antique furnishings from France, North Africa, and the Far East. **Pros:** intimate atmosphere; close to the Champs-Élysées; luxurious decor. **Cons:** inconsistent customer service; expensive rates; across from a noisy bar. [$] *Rooms from: €468* ✉ *8 rue Frédéric Bastiat, Champs-Élysées* ☎ *01–42–56–17–00* 🌐 *www.hoteldanielparis.com* 🛏 *26 rooms* 🍴 *No Meals* [M] *St-Philippe-du-Roule.*

Hôtel de Berri
$$$$ | **HOTEL** | Set back on a quiet side street off the bustling Champs-Élysées, this opulent hotel's glass facade reveals a private garden and extravagant jewel-toned rooms filled with stylish furnishings favoring splashes of leopard. **Pros:** some rooms with garden views; chic decor; iPad-controlled rooms. **Cons:** breakfasts could be better; no spa; pricey. [$] *Rooms from: €500* ✉ *18–22 rue de Berri, Champs-Élysées* ☎ *01–76–53–77–70* 🌐 *www.marriott.fr/hotels/travel/parbe-hotel-de-berri-a-luxury-collection-hotel-paris* 🛏 *75 rooms* 🍴 *No Meals* [M] *George V, St-Philippe-du-Roule.*

Hôtel de Sers
$$$$ | **HOTEL** | Built for the Marquis de Sers with a horse-drawn-carriage entrance, inner courtyard, expansive salons, and monumental staircase, this beautiful structure was transformed into a hotel in 1935. **Pros:** convenient central location in the Golden Triangle; soothing Turkish bath and fitness room; many dining options nearby. **Cons:** on

the expensive side; no formal spa; basic rooms a bit small. [$] *Rooms from: €450* ✉ *41 av. Pierre 1er de Serbie, Champs-Élysées* ☎ *01–53–23–75–75* 🌐 *www.hoteldesers-paris.fr* 🛏 *52 rooms* 🍴 *No Meals* [M] *Alma-Marceau, George V.*

Hôtel Ekta

$$ | **HOTEL** | Two top-tier Paris designers transformed a humdrum 1960s office building into one of the city's liveliest fashion-centric boutique hotels. **Pros:** great location; charming garden; in-room tea and coffee. **Cons:** air-conditioned only after May 1; small bathrooms; some rooms tiny. [$] *Rooms from: €200* ✉ *52 rue Galilée, Champs-Élysées* ☎ *01–53–76–09–05* 🌐 *www.hotelekta.com* 🛏 *25 rooms* 🍴 *No Meals* [M] *George V.*

Hôtel Elysia

$$$$ | **HOTEL** | Discreet and contemporary sums up this seven-story town house steps from the hustle and bustle of the Champs-Élysées. **Pros:** extremely elegant rooms; central location; friendly, attentive service. **Cons:** pricey breakfast; rooms impeccably clean but some need sprucing up; small spa and gym. [$] *Rooms from: €449* ✉ *35 rue de Berri, Champs-Élysées* ☎ *01–53–53–20–20* 🌐 *www.hotelelysia.fr* 🛏 *35 rooms* 🍴 *No Meals* [M] *St-Philippe-du-Roule, George V.*

Hôtel Barrière Fouquet's

$$$$ | **HOTEL** | Adjacent to the legendary Fouquet's Brasserie at the corner of the Champs-Élysées and Avenue George V, this luxury hotel is recognizable by its uniformed valets, parked sports cars, and elegant Haussmannian entryway. **Pros:** many rooms overlook the Champs-Élysées; beautiful spa and pool; very close to the métro. **Cons:** corporate events give the place a business-hotel feel; bars can get overcrowded; expensive. [$] *Rooms from: €1000* ✉ *46 av. George V, Champs-Élysées* ☎ *01–40–69–60–00* 🌐 *www.hotelsbarriere.com/en/paris/le-fouquets.html* 🛏 *114 rooms* 🍴 *No Meals* [M] *George V.*

★ Hôtel Grand Powers

$$$$ | **HOTEL** | No detail was left to chance at this ravishing hotel in a restored 1920s building located on a posh corner of the Golden Triangle. **Pros:** small spa and 24-hour fitness room; quality in-hotel dining; excellent location close to public transportation. **Cons:** limited fitness room; not all rooms have views; rooms are pricey. [$] *Rooms from: €450* ✉ *52 rue François 1er, Champs-Élysées* ☎ *01–47–23–91–05* 🌐 *www.hotelgrandpowersparis.com* 🛏 *50 rooms* 🍴 *No Meals* [M] *George V.*

★ Hôtel Keppler

$$$ | **HOTEL** | **FAMILY** | Like your own classy pied-à-terre, the Keppler—set on a quiet street not far from the Champs-Éysées—combines traditional French and contemporary style for a comfy, lived-in elegance that invites total relaxation. **Pros:** luxurious common spaces; elegant neighborhood; great in-hotel bar. **Cons:** no spa; a walk to the nearest métro; some rooms quite small. [$] *Rooms from: €297* ✉ *10 rue Kepler, Champs-Élysées* ☎ *01–47–20–65–05* 🌐 *www.keppler.fr* 🛏 *44 rooms* 🍴 *No Meals* [M] *George V.*

Hôtel Lancaster

$$$$ | **HOTEL** | Once a Spanish nobleman's town house, this luxurious retreat dating from 1889 dazzles with its elegant decor, lush courtyard, and acclaimed restaurant. **Pros:** steps from the Champs-Élysées and five minutes from the métro; peaceful street; excellent seasonal menus at Monsieur Restaurant. **Cons:** no spa; decor looks tired; size of rooms varies greatly. [$] *Rooms from: €480* ✉ *7 rue de Berri, Champs-Élysées* ☎ *01–40–76–40–76* 🌐 *www.hotel-lancaster.com* 🛏 *56 rooms* 🍴 *No Meals* [M] *George V.*

★ Hôtel Le Bristol

$$$$ | **HOTEL** | **FAMILY** | The historic Bristol ranks among Paris's most exclusive hotels and has numerous accolades to prove it, as does its Michelin-starred restaurant. **Pros:** rooftop pool with views of Sacré-Coeur; one of the best restaurants

in Paris; location on luxury shopping street. **Cons:** very expensive rates; old-fashioned atmosphere may not be for everyone; a few blocks from the nearest métro. $ *Rooms from: €1100* ✉ *112 rue du Faubourg St-Honoré, Champs-Élysées* ☎ *01–53–43–43–00* ⊕ *www.oetkercollection.com/hotels/le-bristol-paris* ⊷ *188 rooms* ❖ *No Meals* Ⓜ *Miromesnil.*

★ Hôtel Le 123 Elysées

$$ | HOTEL | Italian marble, exposed brick, rough concrete, and sleek wood mix with leather, feathers, Swarovski crystals, and fiber-optic fairy lights to give this boutique hotel a genuinely eclectic atmosphere. **Pros:** chic decor; hotel bar open daily; near luxury shopping. **Cons:** some rooms quite small for the price; no on-site restaurant; service can be impolite. $ *Rooms from: €200* ✉ *123 rue du Faubourg St-Honoré, Champs-Élysées* ☎ *01–53–89–01–23* ⊕ *www.astotel.com/hotel/hotel-le-123-elysees/overview* ⊷ *41 rooms* ❖ *No Meals* Ⓜ *St-Philippe du Roule, Franklin D. Roosevelt.*

★ Hôtel Plaza Athénée

$$$$ | HOTEL | FAMILY | Distinguished by the scarlet flowers cascading over its elegant facade, this glamorous landmark hotel sits on one of the most expensive avenues in Paris. **Pros:** Eiffel Tower views; Dior Institute spa; great restaurant and bar. **Cons:** small fitness room; exorbitant prices; attracts oligarchs. $ *Rooms from: €1200* ✉ *25 av. Montaigne, Champs-Élysées* ☎ *01–53–67–66–65* ⊕ *www.dorchestercollection.com/en/paris/hotel-plaza-athenee* ⊷ *208 rooms* ❖ *No Meals* Ⓜ *Alma-Marceau.*

Hôtel Prince des Galles

$$$$ | HOTEL | This lustrous Art Deco gem—originally intended as a Paris dwelling for Prince Edward VIII until he married Wallis Simpson—is a sleek and refined alternative to the area's stuffier palaces. **Pros:** great neighborhood; fabulous bar and lounge; some rooms have spacious balconies with views. **Cons:** breakfast is expensive; no pool; some rooms on the small side. $ *Rooms from: €800* ✉ *33 av. George V, Champs-Élysées* ☎ *01–53–23–77–77* ⊕ *www.marriott.com/hotels/travel/parlc-prince-de-galles-a-luxury-collection-hotel-paris* ⊷ *159 rooms* ❖ *No Meals* Ⓜ *George V.*

Hôtel Raphael

$$$$ | HOTEL | FAMILY | This discreet palacelike hotel was built in 1925 to cater to travelers spending a season in Paris, so every space is generously sized for long, lavish stays. **Pros:** a block from the Champs-Élysées and Arc de Triomphe; intimate hotel bar frequented by locals; rooftop garden terrace. **Cons:** neighborhood far from the action; some soundproofing issues; decor can feel worn and dowdy. $ *Rooms from: €460* ✉ *17 av. Kléber, Champs-Élysées* ☎ *01–53–64–32–00* ⊕ *www.raphael-hotel.com* ⊷ *83 rooms* ❖ *No Meals* Ⓜ *Kléber.*

★ Hôtel du Rond Point des Champs-Élysées

$$$ | HOTEL | FAMILY | A stylish Art Deco upgrade gave this 19th-century mansion two blocks from the Champs-Élysées a sleek period look enhanced by refined contemporary touches. **Pros:** staff couldn't be friendlier or more helpful; excellent location, near the Grand Palais, Concorde, and walking distance to Louvre; reasonable prices for this neighborhood. **Cons:** spa has only two treatment rooms; small pool; some rooms quite small. $ *Rooms from: €236* ✉ *10 rue de Ponthieu, Champs-Élysées* ☎ *01–53–89–14–14* ⊕ *www.paris-hotel-rondpoint-champselysees.com* ⊷ *36 rooms* ❖ *No Meals* Ⓜ *Champs-Élysées–Clémenceau.*

Hotel Vernet

$$$ | HOTEL | A glamorous centenary update added 21st-century luxuries while remaining true to the beautiful bones of this boutique hotel, which first opened in the waning years of the Belle Époque. **Pros:** larger than average rooms; quiet street close to sights and shopping; beautiful stained-glass ceilings designed by G. Eiffel. **Cons:** in-hotel dining quite expensive; extras can be pricey; coffee machines only in deluxe rooms. $ Rooms from: €349 ✉ 25 rue Vernet, Champs-Élysées ☎ 01–44–31–98–00 ⊕ www.hotelvernet-paris.com ⇆ 50 rooms |O| No Meals Ⓜ George V, Étoile.

La Maison Champs Élysées

$$$ | HOTEL | This chic boutique hotel, in the heart of the Golden Triangle and a 10-minute walk from the city's most famous avenue, lures an art-minded fashion crowd with an eclectic twist on a historical Haussmannian *belle demeure*. **Pros:** quiet street close to métro; unique decor; excellent location near both the Grand and Petit Palais. **Cons:** expensive bar; no fitness center; some rooms seem tired. $ Rooms from: €350 ✉ 8 rue Jean Goujon, Champs-Élysées ☎ 01–40–74–64–65 ⊕ www.lamaisonchampselysees. com ⇆ 57 rooms |O| No Meals Ⓜ Franklin D. Roosevelt.

★ La Réserve

$$$$ | HOTEL | Set in a splendid 19th-century mansion just steps from the presidential palace and the American embassy, this aristocratic lodging is one of the city's most elegant small hotels. **Pros:** top-notch spa with pool; excellent dining; splendid views over the Champs-Élysées and Eiffel Tower. **Cons:** out-of-the-way neighborhood; can be snobby; very expensive. $ Rooms from: €1100 ✉ 42 av. Gabriel, Champs-Élysées ☎ 01–58–36–60–60 ⊕ www.lareserve-paris.com ⇆ 40 rooms |O| No Meals Ⓜ Franklin D. Roosevelt.

Le Royal Monceau Raffles Paris

$$$$ | HOTEL | FAMILY | The glamorous Royal Monceau Raffles offers tons of luxury, great dining, and an artsy atmosphere along with a hefty dose of cool. **Pros:** ethereal spa and fitness center; nice terrace garden; chic private apartments. **Cons:** fitness room is small; away from the heart of Paris; hefty prices. $ Rooms from: €950 ✉ 37 av. Hoche, Champs-Élysées ☎ 01–42–99–88–00 ⊕ www.

leroyalmonceau.com ⇆ 149 rooms |O| No Meals Ⓜ Charles-de-Gaulle–Étoile.

Marignan

$$$$ | HOTEL | Set smack-dab in the middle of Paris's Golden Triangle, just off the Champs-Élysées, this sleek five-star hotel is a paragon of contemporary style that includes fine in-hotel dining and some breathtaking terrace views. **Pros:** stellar views from upper terraces; great location; prices good for this standard of luxury. **Cons:** lack of outlets in bathrooms; not all rooms have great views; a few rooms on the smaller side. $ Rooms from: €488 ✉ 12 rue de Marignan, Champs-Élysées ☎ 01–40–76–34–56 ⊕ www.hotelmarignanelyseesparis.com ⇆ 50 rooms |O| No Meals Ⓜ Franklin D. Roosevelt.

★ Monsieur George

$$$ | HOTEL | This cosmopolitan, five-star boutique hotel, two minutes from the Champs-Élysées, brings a welcome frisson of romance to the neighborhood, with opulent, jewellike decor featuring glittering mirrors, luxe fabrics, and design-conscious furnishings. **Pros:** designed by superstar Anouska Hempel; lovely bar and dining room; spacious rooms and bathrooms. **Cons:** not ideal for families; spa quite small; set on a slightly drab but quiet side street. $ Rooms from: €350 ✉ 17 rue Washington, Champs-Élysées ☎ 01–87–89–48–48 ⊕ www.monsieurgeorge.com ⇆ 46 rooms |O| No Meals Ⓜ George V.

★ The Peninsula Paris

$$$$ | HOTEL | FAMILY | A €900 million renovation restored the luster of this lavishly appointed 1908 gem and raised the bar for luxury hotels in Paris. **Pros:** world-class dining; amazing views from higher floors; fabulous spa and pool. **Cons:** stuffy neighborhood; not centrally located; price out of reach for most. $ Rooms from: €950 ✉ 19 av. Kléber, Champs-Élysées ☎ 01–58–12–28–88 ⊕ www.peninsula.com/en/

paris/5-star-luxury-hotel-16th-arron-dissement 200 rooms ❄ No Meals Ⓜ Kléber, Charles de Gaulle–Étoile.

Renaissance Paris Arc de Triomphe
$$$$ | HOTEL | This American-style hotel catering to corporate executives is in a predominantly business district between the Arc de Triomphe and Place des Ternes. **Pros:** walking distance to métro; good discounts with Marriott points; spacious rooms. **Cons:** rather unfriendly service; filled with business conferences; neighborhood lacks character. Ⓢ *Rooms from: €435* ✉ *39 av. de Wagram, Champs-Élysées* ☎ *01–55–37–55–37* ⊕ *www.marriott.fr/hotels/travel/parwg-re-naissance-paris-arc-de-triomphe-hotel* *138 rooms* ❄ *No Meals* Ⓜ *Ternes.*

Room Mate Alain Champs-Élysées
$$ | HOTEL | The contemporary design, modern comforts, and close proximity to the Arc de Triomphe and Champs-Élysées—a 10-minute walk away—are big draws at this stylish boutique hotel. **Pros:** good prices for the area; quiet residential street; friendly, welcoming service. **Cons:** breakfast costs extra; no extra beds for children and limited closet space; some rooms quite small. Ⓢ *Rooms from: €190* ✉ *1–5 rue d'Argentine, Champs-Élysées* ☎ *01–45–02–76–76* ⊕ *room-matehotels.com/en/alain* *36 rooms* ❄ *No Meals* Ⓜ *Argentine.*

▼ Nightlife

As the sun sets, Paris's most elegant neighborhood comes to life. Join the fashionistas for a *coupe de Champagne* in an opulent hotel bar, spend a night clubbing with the jet set, or indulge in a bit of over-the-top French "culture" at a cabaret.

BARS
Apicius
BARS | Mere steps from the Champs-Élysées, Apicius offers sublime elegance. Wander through the luxe front garden and château restaurant to the sleekly modern black bar where couture cocktails are concocted to suit any cultured taste. ✉ *20 rue d'Artois, 8e, Champs-Élysées* ☎ *01–43–80–19–66* ⊕ *www.restaurant-apicius.com* Ⓜ *George V.*

Blind Bar, Maison Champs Élysées
BARS | This romantic spot in the ultra-chic Maison Champs Élysées offers a wood fire in winter and a quiet terrace in warmer months. Its impressive range of Champagnes and impeccable cocktails is well worth the stellar prices. The separate all-black cigar bar is one of the few remaining in Paris. ✉ *8 rue Jean Goujon, 8e, Champs-Élysées* ☎ *01–40–74–64–65* ⊕ *www.lamaisonchampselysees.com* Ⓜ *Franklin D. Roosevelt, Champs-Élysées–Clémenceau.*

Le Bar Anglais
BARS | You might find diplomats and other dignitaries discussing state affairs at this rich red den of masculinity in L'Hôtel Raphael, a stone's throw from the Arc de Triomphe. The hotel's Rooftop Bar, a well-guarded Parisian secret, was voted the best bar in Europe in recent years. ✉ *17 av. Kléber, 16e, Champs-Élysées* ☎ *01–53–64–32–00* ⊕ *www.raphael-hotel.com* Ⓜ *Kléber, Charles de Gaulle–Etoile.*

Le Bar at George V
BARS | An ultraluxe, clubby hideaway in the Four Seasons Hotel, Le Bar at George V is perfect for stargazing from the plush wine-red armchairs, cognac in hand. Its charm still lures the glitterati, especially during Fashion Weeks. Be sure to notice the hotel's signature—and stunning—flower arrangements. ✉ *31 av. George V, 8e, Champs-Élysées* ☎ *01–49–52–70–00* ⊕ *www.fourseasons.com/paris/dining/lounges/le_bar* Ⓜ *George V.*

Le Bar at the Hôtel Plaza Athénée
BARS | This hotel bar par excellence has a clubby feel that lures a younger fashion crowd. Lounge in leather chairs under an Yves Klein–blue ceiling installation while sipping stylish cocktails, like the

signature Rose Royal (Champagne, raspberry, and a splash of cognac). Mood lighting and music spun by a live DJ Thursday through Saturday set the tone for a glam late-night rendezvous. ⊠ *25 av. Montaigne, 8e, Champs-Élysées* ☎ *01–53–67–66–00* ⊕ *www.dorchestercollection.com* Ⓜ *Alma–Marceau.*

★ Le Bar du Bristol

BARS | Apparently not satisfied with its usual rich and powerful clientele, this tony spot is now vying for the impossibly hip, too. Along with enticing cocktails and rarified spirits, Le Bar promises exceptional wines and tapas. Weekdays from 7 pm to 9:30 pm, it also showcases curated art videos on its behind-the-bar mirror screen. Chic Paris DJs heat up the scene between 9:30 pm and 2 am on Friday and Saturday. ⊠ *112 rue du Faubourg St-Honoré, 8e, Champs-Élysées* ☎ *01–53–43–43–00* ⊕ *www.oetkercollection.com/hotels/le-bristol-paris/restaurants-bar/le-bar-du-bristol* Ⓜ *Miromesnil.*

Le Marta Paris

BARS | Swanky decor and luscious drinks are drawing the cocktail cognoscenti to this intimate lounge hidden away in the legendary Le Fouquet's Hotel. If you prefer daylight, the hotel offers two other superchic bars: Le Joy and L'Escadrille. ⊠ *Le Fouquet's Paris, 46 av. George V, 8e, Champs-Élysées* ☎ *01–40–69–60–00* ⊕ *www.hotelsbarriere.com* Ⓜ *Georges V.*

Publicis Drugstore

BARS | A stone's throw from the Arc de Triomphe, this trendy spot—equal parts concept store, pharmacy, cinema, and brasserie-café—is stocked with an ever-changing array of upscale wares from designer handbags and diamond bracelets to fine wine and cigars. When you're done browsing, enjoy a bite at the on-site eatery (a prix-fixe menu is available) or stop by the bakery for food to take away. ⊠ *133 av. des Champs-Élysées, 8e, Champs-Élysées* ☎ *01–44–43–79–00* ⊕ *www.publicisdrugstore.com* Ⓜ *Charles de Gaulle–Étoile.*

Ran

COCKTAIL LOUNGES | Splashes of neon add a dash of glitz to this Japanese-chic bar attached to a sophisticated Nipponese restaurant set in an elegant Paris town house. A choice menu of exotic Asian-themed cocktails (e.g., the Akira, with rum, apricot liqueur, jasmine syrup, wasabi, mango, and green tea) is accompanied by Japanese finger food. ⊠ *8 rue d'Anjou, 8e, Champs-Élysées* ☎ *01–40–17–04–77* ⊕ *ran-paris.com* Ⓜ *Concorde, Madeleine.*

CABARET

★ Crazy Horse

CABARET | This world-renowned cabaret has elevated the striptease to an art form. Founded in 1951, it's famous for gorgeous dancers and naughty routines characterized by lots of humor and very little clothing. What garments there are have been dazzlingly designed by the likes of Louboutin and Alaïa and shed by top divas (including Dita Von Teese). Reserved seats for the show start at €87. ⊠ *12 av. George V, 8e, Champs-Élysées* ☎ *01–47–23–32–32* ⊕ *www.lecrazyhorseparis.com* Ⓜ *Alma-Marceau.*

Lido

CABARET | The legendary Lido now adds a modern-day dose of awe-inspiring stage design to the cabaret's trademark style. The 100-minute productions—still featuring those beloved Bluebell Girls and 12 "Lido boys"—run at 9 pm and 11 pm, 365 days a year. Dinner-for-two packages (including a vegetarian option) range from €145 for dinner and the show to €330 for dinner, drinks (half bottle of bubbly, wine, and coffee), and the show. Yes, those prices are per person, but this is Paris nightlife as it's meant to be experienced. It's best to book your tickets in advance online. ⊠ *116 bis, av. des Champs-Élysées, 8e, Champs-Élysées* ☎ *01–40–76–56–10* ⊕ *www.lido.fr* Ⓜ *George V.*

Paris Cinemas

Paris is a city for cinephiles, and it's a shame that language barriers often keep French cinema off-limits to Anglophone visitors. Luckily, the company Lost in Frenchlation has set out to change all that. The organization offers a weekly program of the latest French releases and beloved classics, all with English subtitles. The main screening venue is Club de L'Étoile, near the Arc de Triomphe, which offers four screenings a month, as well as a venue in the Marais (Luminor Hôtel de Ville) and one in Montmartre (Studio 28). Most screenings offer convivial drinks and snacks beforehand, where you can mingle with English-speaking expats and visitors. For more information check out the website (www.lostinfrenchlation.com).

CLUBS

★ Manko

PIANO BARS | This is a lavish spot for fashionistas and upscale revelers seeking chic thrills. Outrageous weekend cabarets, themed party nights, and a *branché* vibe—plus some very spiffy cocktails—put this happening club high on Paris's nightclub A-list. ✉ *15 av. Montaigne, 8e, Champs-Élysées* ☎ *01–82–28–00–15* ⊕ *www.manko-paris.com* ⊙ *Closed Sun.* Ⓜ *Alma-Marceau, Champs-Élysées–Clemenceau.*

JAZZ CLUBS

Jazz Club Étoile

LIVE MUSIC | This moody club at Le Méridien Hotel hosts a roster of top-billed international musicians in a classy set of rooms. Check out the Sunday afternoon jazz brunch buffet and the interior garden. ✉ *Le Méridien Hotel, 81 bd. Gouvion-St-Cyr, 17e, Champs-Élysées* ☎ *01–40–68–30–42* ⊕ *www.jazzclub-paris.com* Ⓜ *Porte Maillot.*

🎭 Performing Arts

Comédie des Champs-Élysées

THEATER | Next door to the Théâtre des Champs-Élysées, the Comédie des Champs-Élysées offers intriguing productions in its small theater. ✉ *15 av. Montaigne, 8e, Champs-Élysées* ☎ *01–53–23–99–19* ⊕ *www.comediedeschampselysees.com* Ⓜ *Alma-Marceau.*

Salle Gaveau

MUSIC | The 1,020-seat Salle Gaveau is a perfectly appointed gold-and-white hall with remarkable acoustics and a distinctly Parisian allure. It hosts chamber music, orchestral, piano, and vocal recitals. ✉ *45–47 rue la Boétie, 8e, Champs-Élysées* ☎ *01–49–53–05–07* ⊕ *www.sallegaveau.com* Ⓜ *Miromesnil.*

Salle Pleyel

CONCERTS | Once one of Paris's major classical music venues, these days Salle Pleyel's packed concert calendar focuses mostly on contemporary music, entertainment, and events, as well as hosting the annual César Awards, France's answer to the Oscars. Tickets range from €10–€80. ✉ *252 rue du Faubourg St-Honoré, 8e, Concorde* ☎ *01–42–56–13–13* ⊕ *www.sallepleyel.com* Ⓜ *Ternes.*

Théâtre des Champs-Élysées

ARTS CENTERS | This was the scene of 1913's infamous Battle of the Rite of Spring, when police had to be called in after the audience ripped up seats in outrage at Stravinsky's *Le Sacre du Printemps* score and Nijinsky's choreography. Today Théâtre des Champs-Élysées is elegantly restored and worthy of a visit if only for the architecture. (It's one of Paris's most striking examples of Art Deco.) The theater also hosts first-rate opera and dance performances, along with orchestral, chamber, and Sunday morning concerts. ⊠ *15 av. Montaigne, 8e, Champs-Élysées* ☎ *01–49–52–50–50* ⊕ *www.theatrechampselysees.fr* Ⓜ *Alma-Marceau.*

Shopping

Step into your Chanel suit, gird your loins, and plunge into Paris's most desirable (and most daunting) hunting grounds, where royals, jet-setters, starlets, and other glitterati converge in pursuit of the high life. The Golden Triangle—bordered by Avenues Montaigne, George V, and Champs-Élysées, with Rue François 1er in between—is home to almost all the luxury Goliaths, and what you don't find there you're bound to find on the Champs-Élysées or the Rue du Faubourg St-Honoré.

BEAUTY

Guerlain

PERFUME | This opulent address is a fitting home for Paris's first—and most famous—perfumer. Still the only Paris outlet for legendary perfumes like Shalimar and L'Heure Bleue, it has added several new signature scents (including Myrrhe et Délires and Cuir Beluga). Personalized bottles in several sizes can be filled on demand, or, for a mere €30,000, a customized scent can be blended just for you. Sybarites will also appreciate Guerlain's makeup, scented candles, and spa featuring its much-adored skin-care line. There's an elegant gourmet restaurant for lunch or tea too. ⊠ *68 av. des Champs-Élysées, 8e, Champs-Élysées* ☎ *01–45–62–52–57* ⊕ *www.guerlain.com* Ⓜ *Franklin D. Roosevelt.*

Parfums de Nicolaï

PERFUME | This perfumerie is run by Guerlain family member Patricia de Nicolaï. Children's, women's, and men's scents are on offer (including some unisex), as are sprays for the home and fragrant candles. ⊠ *69 av. Raymond Poincaré, 16e, Louvre* ☎ *01–44–55–02–00* ⊕ *www. pnicolai.com* Ⓜ *Victor Hugo.*

CHILDREN'S CLOTHING
★ Bonpoint

CHILDREN'S CLOTHING | Outfit the prince or princess in your life at Bonpoint (yes, royalty *does* shop here). The prices are high, but the quality is exceptional, and the adorable miniduds couldn't be more stylish: picture a perfect hand-smocked Liberty-print dress, a velvety lambskin vest, or a double-breasted cashmere sweater for Little Lord Fauntleroy. The Avenue Raymond Poincaré boutique is one of more than a dozen citywide. ⊠ *64 av. Raymond Poincaré, 16e, Champs-Élysées* ☎ *01–47–27–60–81* ⊕ *www. bonpoint.com* Ⓜ *Trocadéro.*

CLOTHING
Balmain

MIXED CLOTHING | Slinky silhouettes, bare midriffs, sequins, crystals, frills, and furbelows, not to mention plenty of silver, patent leather, and cutouts. In other words, Balmain is not for shrinking violets. This may sound like a break from the couture house's ultrafeminine backstory (a favorite of '50s Hollywood idols), but in the hands of Olivier Rousteing being feminine translates to being at home in your skin first, then dressing it up—his glamorous, highly Instagrammable flights of fancy are catnip for models, singers, and reality stars. The elegantly minimal boutique in the heart of the Golden Triangle carries the full collection and is a lovely backdrop for these opulent street wear–meets–boudoir fashions. ⊠ *44 rue François 1er, 8e, Champs-Élysées* ☎ *01–47–20–57–58* ⊕ *www.balmain.com* Ⓜ *Franklin D. Roosevelt, George V.*

★ Céline

MIXED CLOTHING | Phoebe Philo, who defined this bohemian-chic label for a decade, single-handedly redefined the codes of fashion for professional women, garnering a huge and fiercely loyal following for her streamlined, minimal designs, featuring flowing pants, long, unstructured jackets, and the Cabas bag. All heads turned when bad boy Hedi Slimane, who left Saint Laurent in 2016 after rocking (or rock 'n' rolling) the label to its core, was tapped to fill Philo's comfy shoes. After his first season's glittery minis tanked, Slimane did an about-face, channeling a bourgeois art-house look that felt distinctly Parisian. Now, he's relegated the sultry looks to evening and sells tailored blouses and contoured jackets that are singularly sexy. ⊠ *53 av. Montaigne, 8e, Champs-Élysées* ☎ *01–40–70–07–03* ⊕ *www.celine.com* Ⓜ *Franklin D. Roosevelt.*

★ Chanel

WOMEN'S CLOTHING | Elegant, modern looks with sex appeal and lasting value are Chanel's stock-in-trade. Although the spectacularly beautiful Avenue Montaigne flagship takes shoppers' breath away, the heart of this revered fashion house is still the boutique at 31 rue Cambon, where Chanel once perched high up on the mirrored staircase watching audience reactions to her collection debuts. Great investments include all of Coco's favorites: the perfectly tailored suit, a lean soigné dress, or a quilted bag with a gold chain. Handbags, jewelry, shoes, and accessories are all found at the fabulous 42 avenue Montaigne boutique, opposite the flagship store. ⊠ *51 av. Montaigne, 8e, Champs-Élysées* ☎ *01–44–50–73–00* ⊕ *www.chanel.com* Ⓜ *Franklin D. Roosevelt.*

★ Dior

MIXED CLOTHING | Maria Grazia Chiuri, Dior's first female designer for a label that's traditionally defined the feminine, has quickly made the House of Dior thoroughly her own. Her feminist perspective—which brings together the glamour, high style, and comfort women of all ages really want, instead of a fantastical notion best-suited for models—has transformed the house of Dior, raising it to one of the most exciting Parisian designer brands in the city, not to mention the most profitable. Furthermore, the reopening of Dior's refurbished Avenue Montaigne flagship store ushered in a new benchmark for Paris boutiques. Covering more than 105,000 square feet, this pearl of a flagship brings together haute couture and ready-to-wear items, beauty, and menswear, along with a restaurant (Monsieur Dior) and pastry shop (by chef Jean Imbert of the Plaza Athénée), three gardens, guest suites, and a superb gallery space bound to rival the Musée Yves Saint Laurent. ⊠ *30 av. Montaigne, 8e, Champs-Élysées* ☎ *01–40–73–73–73,* ⊕ *www.dior.com* Ⓜ *Franklin D. Roosevelt.*

Dolce & Gabbana

MIXED CLOTHING | Dolce & Gabbana offers a sexy, young-Italian-widow vibe with a side of moody boyfriend. Svelte silk dresses, sharply tailored suits, and plunging necklines are made for drama. Women's clothes are at the Avenue Montaigne location; men's are at 3 rue Faubourg St-Honoré. ⊠ *54 av. Montaigne, 8e, Champs-Élysées* ☎ *01–42–25–68–78* ⊕ *www.dolcegabbana.com* Ⓜ *Alma-Marceau.*

Maison Ullens

WOMEN'S CLOTHING | A glam Golden Triangle location, a Rem Koolhaas–designed boutique, sumptuous clothes—the Belgian label's first Paris outpost hits all the marks and then some. Founded in 2013, Maison Ullens puts the focus on luxe fabrics and skins in classic-chic designs with plenty of staying power. It has everything you need for après-ski or weekends on Capri. ⊠ *4 rue de Marignan, 8e, Champs-Élysées* ☎ *01–47–20–23–56* ⊕ *www.maisonullens.com* Ⓜ *Franklin D. Roosevelt.*

Marni

MIXED CLOTHING | Marni started out as a little Italian label that put a quirky spin on classic styles, employing retro-ish prints and colors (think citron yellow or seaweed green) and funky fabrics (such as rubberized cotton and filmy silks).

Now it has evolved into a major player on the edgy fashion scene. Each season has something new to say—whether it's an inventive take on bold ethnic prints, ingenious knits, or eloquent color schemes. Sought-after shoes and jewelry never make it to sale time. ⊠ 57 av. Montaigne, 8e, Champs-Élysées ☎ 01–56–88–08–08 ⊕ www.marni.com Ⓜ Franklin D. Roosevelt.

★ Petit Bateau

MIXED CLOTHING | FAMILY | This iconic clothing store, originally for kids, provides a fundamental part of the classic French wardrobe from cradle to teen and beyond. The signature T-shirt—cut close to the body, with smallish shoulders—works equally well with school uniforms or vintage Chanel. Thanks to timeless designs, the high-grade cotton clothes remain wardrobe staples year after year; however, lines in cotton-silk or cotton-cashmere and popular collaborations with chic designers like Christian Lacroix or Inès de la Fressange mean there's now even more in store. There are boutiques in all the major shopping neighborhoods. Stock up: if you can find this brand back home, the prices are sure to be higher. ⊠ 116 av. des Champs-Élysées, 8e, Champs-Élysées ☎ 01–40–74–02–03 ⊕ www.petit-bateau. fr Ⓜ George V.

Prada

MIXED CLOTHING | Prada spins gold out of fashion straw. Knee-length skirts, peacock colors, cardigan sweaters, geometric prints: the waiting lists cross continents. Shoes, bags, and other accessories for men and women perennially become cult items. ⊠ 10 av. Montaigne, 8e, Champs-Élysées ☎ 01–53–23–99–40 ⊕ www.prada.com Ⓜ Alma-Marceau.

Saint Laurent Paris

WOMEN'S CLOTHING | Anthony Vaccarello has calmed the waters at Saint Laurent with an assuredness and sleight of hand that fashion editors appreciate more

every year. His recent collections have inspired the kind of praise that marks a sea change in fashion, dispensing with the rock 'n' roll glitz and overt sexiness for something less rebel-with-a-cause and more timelessly elegant. Silver evening gowns shimmer like water, and oversized suits are cut to revive movie-star glamour worthy of Katharine Hepburn. At this austere flagship store, done all in chrome and marble, you'll find ready-to-wear items (think leggings, cropped leather jackets, exquisite trenches in satin, cashmere, or leather, and bias-cut evening dresses and gowns) and all the brand's coveted accessories and jewelry too. ⊠ 53 av. Montaigne, 8e, Champs-Élysées ☎ 01-53-83-84-68 ⊕ www.ysl.com/en-fr Ⓜ Franklin D. Roosevelt.

SHOES, HANDBAGS, AND LEATHER GOODS

Berluti

SHOES | Berluti has been making exquisite and expensive men's shoes for more than a century. "Nothing is too beautiful for feet" is Olga Berluti's motto; she even exposes her creations to the moonlight to give them an extra-special patina. One model is named after Andy Warhol; other famous clients of the past include the Duke of Windsor, Fred Astaire, and James Joyce. ⊠ 26 rue Marbeuf, 8e, Champs-Élysées ☎ 01–53–93–97–97 ⊕ www.berluti.com Ⓜ Franklin D. Roosevelt.

★ Christian Louboutin

SHOES | It seems the world's romance with heels so high they're potentially lethal will never end, thanks in no small part to the king of the iconic red-soled stiletto. Louboutin artfully weaves fantasy, glamour, and good cheeky fun into his towering heels, which have graced red carpets and the gangways of private jets. But you can also find more prudent models, including kitten-heeled mules and spiky sneakers, as well as chic and functional bags and a selection of lipsticks and nail polish that blend right in with your soles. His new, 3,000-square-foot boutique—done up in Louboutin red, of course—offers three floors of pure fetishistic pleasure. ⊠ *400 rue St-Honoré, 8e, Champs-Élysées* ⊕ *eu.christian-louboutin.com* Ⓜ *Concorde.*

Giuseppe Zanotti Design

SHOES | Every pair of shoes here is fetish-worthy, if not downright dangerous. Sky-scraping spike heels, buckle stilettos, slinky python booties, and jewel-encrusted black-satin pumps beg to be noticed. More toned-down models, like over-the-knee leather flats, and even sneakers, can be had too. ⊠ *12 av. Montaigne, 8e, Champs-Élysées* ☎ *01–47–20–07–85* ⊕ *www.giuseppezanotti.com* Ⓜ *Franklin D. Roosevelt.*

Jimmy Choo

SHOES | This is the place for vampy stilettoes, strappy flats, and biker boots. Recent *Belle de Jour*–inspired kitten heels are a nice respite from the famous mile-high styles that put Choo on the map. Beautiful bags, clutches, and small leather items in animal print, reptile, and metallics are deservedly popular. ⊠ *34 av. Montaigne, 8e, Champs-Élysées* ☎ *01–47–23–03–39* ⊕ *www.jimmychoo.com* Ⓜ *Franklin D. Roosevelt.*

★ Louis Vuitton

HANDBAGS | Louis Vuitton has spawned a voracious fan base from Texas to Tokyo with its mix of classic leather goods and saucy revamped versions orchestrated by Marc Jacobs. His 2013 exit left tall boots to fill, but Nicholas Ghesquière—a daring designer who single-handedly resurrected the Balenciaga label—has done an admirable job. Melding his signature edgy modernism with vintage touches and colors, Ghesquière is taking the legendary luxe label to a glorious new level. ⊠ *101 av. des Champs-Élysées, 8e, Champs-Élysées* ☎ *01–53–57–52–00* ⊕ *www.louisvuitton.com* Ⓜ *George V.*

★ Renaud Pellegrino

HANDBAGS | Just steps from the Arc de Triomphe, Renaud Pellegrino is a black-book address for style icons like Catherine Deneuve and Paloma Picasso, who eschew status labels in favor of individuality and staying power. A black lace-over-leather bag or an azure tote with tiny silver grommets brings glamour to daytime looks, and a Mondrian-esque patchwork of silk-satin adds magnificence to evening wear. ⊠ *8 av. Victor Hugo, 16e, Louvre* ☎ *01–42–61–75–32* ⊕ *www.renaudpellegrino.com* Ⓜ *Charles de Gaulle–Étoile.*

Chapter 6

AROUND THE LOUVRE

Updated by
Emily Monaco

◉ Sights	🍴 Restaurants	🛏 Hotels	🛍 Shopping	🍸 Nightlife
★★★★☆	★★☆☆☆	★★★★☆	★★★★★	★★☆☆☆

NEIGHBORHOOD SNAPSHOT

GETTING HERE

The neighborhoods here include the 1er and 2e arrondissements, from the Faubourg St-Honoré to Les Halles. If you're heading to the Louvre, take the métro Line 1 to the Palais-Royal–Musée du Louvre stop. For the Tuileries, use the Tuileries stop on the same line. For Place de la Concorde, use the Concorde stop on Line 1, 8, or 12. This is a good starting point for a walk on Rue St-Honoré. If you're going to Les Halles, take Line 4 to Les Halles or Line 1 to Châtelet.

MAKING THE MOST OF YOUR TIME

Try to devote two days or more—one for the Louvre alone—to these vastly different neighborhoods. Along the narrow sidewalks of the Faubourg St-Honoré, you'll find some of the finest Parisian boutiques. Place de la Concorde is the gateway to the Tuileries gardens, which lead to the looming Louvre itself. At the eastern end of the area, Les Halles (the old market district) is booming with shops and eateries around cobbled Rue Montorgueil, where traffic is mercifully restricted.

If you're headed to the Musée du Louvre, it's best to have a game plan. First step: buy your ticket online at ⊕ www.louvre.fr. If there is a crowd waiting to enter I. M. Pei's imposing glass pyramid, use the entrance in the underground mall, the Carrousel du Louvre, 99 rue de Rivoli.

VIEWFINDER

Standing under the ornate Arc de Triomphe du Carrousel (on the Place du Carrousel), you can witness Paris's history unfolding: to one side, your eye lands on the Louvre itself, a former palace with roots in the 12th century but ultimately bearing the characteristics of its Renaissance renovation. Look to the other side, and your eye will land on the pristine, manicured Tuileries gardens, designed by André Le Nôtre, the 17th-century royal landscape architect who would later design Versailles. Past the gardens looms the Luxor obelisk, one of a pair taken from Egypt by Napoléon.

TOP REASONS TO GO

■ **Musée du Louvre.** The world's first great art museum—which displays such renowned works as the serenely smirking *Mona Lisa* (La Joconde, in French) and the statuesque *Venus de Milo*—deserves a long visit. Plan on three hours or more.

■ **Tuileries to Place de la Concorde.** For centuries, Parisians and visitors alike have strolled the length of this magnificent garden from the Louvre's Arc du Carrousel to the gold-tipped obelisk at Place de la Concorde.

■ **Galerie Vivienne.** The prettiest of the glass-roofed 19th-century shopping arcades that remain in Paris, this *passage* is worth a stop to shop and photo op.

■ **Palais-Royal.** Visit these arcades and the romantic garden to understand why French writer Colette called the view from her window "a little corner of the country."

■ **Rue Montorgueil.** This historic market street is lined with food shops and cafés and is a stone's throw from some of the city's trendiest restaurants and bars.

The neighborhoods from the très chic Faubourg St-Honoré to trendy Les Halles are a study in contrasts, with the Louvre in the midst of the bustle.

The posh **Rue du Faubourg St-Honoré,** once the stomping ground of kings and queens, is now home to the French president and assorted foreign ambassadors. Beloved by fashionistas for three centuries, it's as popular today as when royal mistresses shopped here—which explains the plethora of high-end stores (almost every luxury brand is represented). Not surprisingly, ritzy restaurants and haute hotels are here as well.

To the east, **Les Halles** (pronounced leh- *ahl*) has risen from its roots as a down-and-out market district, once described by Emile Zola as the "belly of Paris," to become a culinary destination of a wholly different kind. Vermin-infested cobbled streets have given way to trendy shops, cafés, and bars centered around Rue Montorgueil. A sweeping multiyear renovation of the former wholesale food market (which closed in 1969) gave a much-needed face-lift to the plaza aboveground and the vast shopping mall below.

Between Faubourg St-Honoré and Les Halles, you can find some of Paris's main draws—namely the mighty **Musée du Louvre** and, just next door, the majestic **Jardin des Tuileries.** The garden is home to the **Musée de l'Orangerie,** with its curved galleries built for the express purpose of showcasing Monet's *Water Lilies.* Nearby, **Les Arts Décoratifs** is a must for design buffs.

In Place Colette, the stately **Comédie Française** theater is still going strong after 400 years. At the edge of the square is the psychedelic sculpture—doubling as a *métro* entrance—of the *kiosque des noctambules* (kiosk of the nightcrawlers), designed by artist Jean-Michel Othoniel.

Hidden just off Place Colette is the **Palais-Royal,** a romantic garden ringed by arcades with boutiques selling everything from old-fashioned music boxes to fashion-forward frocks and bedecked with the oh-so-Instagrammable *colonnes de Buren* (Buren's columns). A stone's throw away is **Galerie Vivienne,** an exquisitely restored 19th-century shopping arcade with a beautiful glass ceiling.

◉ Sights

★ Bourse de Commerce–Collection Pinault Paris

ART MUSEUM | Capping one of the art world's great rivalries, the Collection Pinault Paris opened in spring 2021, adding another gem to the city's cultural roster. After years of false starts, tycoon François Pinault is now showcasing his billion-dollar trove of contemporary works by bold-faced names such as Mark Rothko and Damien Hirst under the historic iron-and-glass dome of the 19th-century Commerce Exchange, one of the city's most stunning, if underused, buildings. After losing a previous bid to open a museum outside Paris—taking his works to Venice instead—Gucci owner Pinault could only watch as archrival Bernard Arnault opened his Frank Gehry–designed Fondation Louis Vuitton in 2014. Not one to be outdone, Pinault tapped star Japanese architect Tadao Ando to carry out a nearly $140 million redesign of the edifice—Paris' former

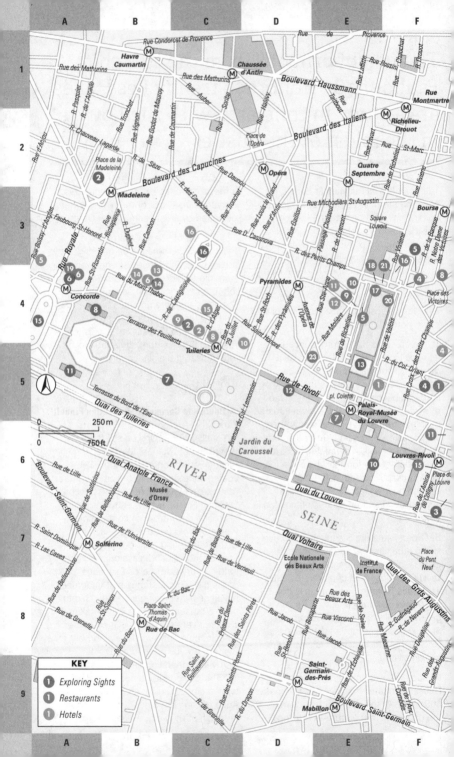

Around the Louvre

Sights ▼

1 Bourse de Commerce-Collection Pinault Paris............. G5
2 Église de la Madeleine B2
3 Église St-Germain l'Auxerrois F6
4 Galerie Véro-Dodat...... F5
5 Galerie Vivienne F4
6 Hôtel de la Marine...... A4
7 Jardin des Tuileries..... B5
8 Jeu de Paume........... A4
9 Les Halles............... G5
10 The Louvre................ E6
11 Musée de l'Orangerie.............. A5
12 Musée des Arts Décoratifs (MAD)....... D5
13 Palais-Royal.............. E5
14 Passage du Grand-Cerf.............. H4
15 Place de la Concorde A4
16 Place Vendôme C3
17 Rue Montorgueil........ H4
18 Saint-Eustache........... H5
19 Tour Jean Sans Peur... H4
20 Tour Saint-Jacques.......I7

Restaurants ▼

1 A l'Epi d'Or.............. F5
2 Angelina C4
3 Au Rocher de Cancale H4
4 Bistrot Vivienne F4
5 Café Kitsuné.............. E4
6 Café Lapérouse A4
7 Café Marly............... E6
8 Chez Georges F4
9 Ellsworth................ E4
10 Juvéniles E4
11 La Dame de Pic F6
12 La Poule au Pot G6
13 La Régalade Saint-Honoré............ G6
14 L'Ardoise................ B4
15 Le Fumoir F6
16 Le Grand Colbert........ F4
17 Le Grand Véfour........ E4
18 Macéo E4
19 Mimosa A4
20 Restaurant du Palais-Royal.............. F4
21 Willi's Wine Bar.......... E4
22 Yam'Tcha G6
23 Zen D5

Hotels ▼

1 Grand Hotel du Palais Royal E5
2 Hôtel Brighton............ C4
3 Hôtel Britannique H7
4 Hôtel Crayon F5
5 Hôtel de Crillon.......... A3
6 Hôtel du Continent...... B4
7 Hotel Konfidentiel....... G6
8 Hotel La Tamise.......... C4
9 Hôtel Le Meurice C4
10 Hôtel Le Pradey......... D5
11 Hôtel Louvre Sainte-Anne.............. E4
12 Hôtel Thérèse E4
13 Mandarin Oriental Paris..................... B4
14 Meliá Vendôme B4
15 Renaissance Paris Vendôme................. C4
16 The Ritz C3

grain exchange—in 2017. Inside, four levels of exhibition space spiral skyward along a giant concrete cylinder ringed at the top by a walkway offering a bird's-eye view of the galleries below. The sparsity of the collections only contributes to the spaceshiplike appeal of the contemporary renovation, with a handful of 19th-century details remaining: double-helix stone staircases, wooden display cases dating to 1889, the engine room on the lower level, and the realist mural adorning the underside of the dome, displaying seasonal panoramas of French traders engaged in commerce with the rest of the world. Paris Mayor Anne Hidalgo, who supplied a 50-year lease, called Pinault's creation an "immense gift" to the city. Free 20-minute tours depart daily from the ground-floor level; on the hour, tours explore the collection, while on the half-hour, they delve into the history and architecture of the building. A children's area allows kids to engage with a tour guide, discovering the collection by way of games and books, while the Halle aux Graines restaurant from Michelin-starred father-and-son team Michel and Sébastien Bras allows you to discover a tasting menu in three, five, or seven courses or an à la carte selection of upscale, contemporary French specialties. Don't miss the 100-foot-tall Medici Column on the back side of the building. It was once the stargazing perch of Marie de Medici's powerful astrologer, Cosimo Ruggieri. Legend has it that on stormy nights, a silhouetted figure can be seen in the metal cage at the top. ✉ 2 rue de Viarmes, Louvre ☎ 01/55–04–60–60 ⊕ www.collectionpinaultparis.com ✎ €14 ⊘ Closed Tues. Ⓜ Les Halles; RER: Châtelet–Les Halles.

Église de la Madeleine

CHURCH | With its rows of uncompromising columns, this enormous neoclassical edifice in the center of Place de la Madeleine was consecrated as a church in 1842, nearly 78 years after construction began. Initially planned as a Baroque building, it was later razed and begun anew by an architect who had the Roman Pantheon in mind. Interrupted by the Revolution, the site was razed yet again when Napoléon decided to transform it into a Greek-inspired temple dedicated to the glory of his army. Those plans changed when the army was defeated and the emperor deposed. Other ideas for the building included making it into a train station, a market, and a library. Finally, Louis XVIII decided it should be a church, which it still is today. Classical concerts are held here regularly, some of them free. ✉ Pl. de la Madeleine, Louvre ☎ 01–44–51–69–00 ⊕ www.eglise-lamadeleine.com Ⓜ Madeleine.

Église Saint-Germain l'Auxerrois

CHURCH | Founded in 500 AD, this grand church across from the Louvre's eastern end is one of the city's oldest. It was destroyed during the Norman siege in 885–886, rebuilt in the 11th century, and subsequently expanded until the current edifice was finished in 1580. The bell, named Marie, dates to 1527. During the renovation of Notre-Dame Cathedral, Saint-Germain l'Auxerrois is hosting the cathedral's liturgy services and is the temporary home of the crown of thorns relic, saved from the conflagration. ✉ 2 pl. du Louvre, Louvre ☎ 01–42–60–13–96 ⊕ www.saintgermainauxerrois.fr Ⓜ Louvre–Rivoli.

Galerie Véro-Dodat

PEDESTRIAN MALL | A lovely 19th-century passage that's been gorgeously restored, the Véro-Dodat has a dozen artsy boutiques selling objets d'art, textiles, furniture, and accessories. The headliner tenant is Christian Louboutin at Rue Jean-Jacques Rousseau, whose red-soled stilettos are favored by Angelina Jolie, Madonna, and other members of the red-carpet set. On the opposite end, at the Rue du Bouloi entrance, star cosmetics maker Terry De Gunzburg has a boutique, By Terry. ✉ Main entrance at

19 rue Jean-Jacques Rousseau, Louvre ⊗ *Closed Sun.* Ⓜ *Palais-Royal–Louvre.*

★ Galerie Vivienne

PEDESTRIAN MALL | Considered the grande dame of Paris's 19th-century *passages couverts*—the world's first shopping malls—this graceful arcade evokes an age of gaslights and horse-drawn carriages. Once, Parisians came to passages like this one to tread tiled floors instead of muddy streets; to see and be seen browsing boutiques under the glass-and-iron roofs. Today, the Galerie Vivienne still attracts unique retailers selling clothing, accessories, and housewares. La Marelle (No. 25) stocks secondhand designer labels, and wine merchant Legrand Filles & Fils (1 rue de la Banque) is the place for an upscale tasting. The Place des Victoires, a few steps away, is one of Paris's most picturesque squares. In the center is a statue of an outsized Louis XIV (1643–1715), the Sun King, who appears almost as large as his horse. ⊠ *Main entrance at 4 rue des Petits-Champs, Louvre* ⊗ *Closed Sun.* Ⓜ *Palais-Royal–Louvre, Bourse.*

★ Hôtel de la Marine

OTHER MUSEUM | FAMILY | This splendid museum is the closest you'll get to Versailles in Paris. It took more than 200 skilled artisans and nearly $160 million to achieve what is hands down Paris's most ravishing museum to date, allowing the public a glimpse behind the elegant facade of a masterpiece of French 18th-century interior design for the first time in 250 years. No detail was overlooked in the restoration: wallpaper and curtains were painted or sewed by hand in the original 18th-century techniques; the woodwork was painstakingly stripped, restored, and gilded by master craftspeople; and decorative features were created in Paris's most rarified workshops.

The mansion is one of two twin structures built in 1758 for Louis XV to mark a new square created in his honor (now Place de la Concorde). Both buildings sat unused before the eastern facade—now the Hôtel de Crillon—was auctioned off to the Duc d'Aumont. The western edifice became the Garde-Meuble de la Couronne, the institution in charge of selecting, maintaining, and storing the king's furniture. In 1789 it became the headquarters for the navy ministry, which remained in the building for 226 years. The decrees ending slavery and the slave trade in France were signed here in 1794. Visitors can learn about the building's history through state-of-the-art interactive displays in the grand ballroom and loggia, a sprawling balcony facing Place de la Concorde with impressive views of the Assemblée Nationale and the Eiffel Tower. You can take a guided visit (in English) or grab a state-of-the-art headset; well worth it to discover the museum's fascinating history.

The museum also houses the exquisite Al Thani collection, featuring objects and artwork spanning 6,000 years and myriad civilizations. Another great pleasure of your visit is lunch, teatime, or a cocktail at the romantic Café Lapérouse (the first offshoot of the historic Paris restaurant) or Mimosa, across the courtyard, helmed by chef Jean-François Piège, one of Paris's star chefs. Both restaurants offer sumptuous interiors and outdoor dining in the interior courtyard or under the pillars overlooking Place de la Concorde. ⊠ *2 Place de la Concorde, 8e, Champs-Élysées* ☎ ⊕ *www.hotel-de-la-marine. paris/en* ⊠ *Free, guided tours from €13* Ⓜ *Concord, Madeleine.*

★ Jardin des Tuileries

CITY PARK | FAMILY | This quintessential French garden, with its verdant lawns, rows of manicured trees, and gravel paths, was designed by André Le Nôtre for Louis XIV. After the king moved his court to Versailles in 1682, the Tuileries became *the* place for stylish Parisians to stroll. (Ironically, the name derives from the decidedly unstylish factories that once occupied this area: they produced *tuiles,* or roof tiles, fired in kilns called *tuileries.*) Monet and Renoir captured the garden with paint and brush. It's no wonder the Impressionists loved it—the gray, austere light of Paris's famously overcast days make the green trees appear even greener.

The garden still serves as a setting for one of the city's loveliest walks. Laid out before you is a vista of must-see monuments, with the Louvre at one end and the Place de la Concorde at the other. The Eiffel Tower is on the Seine side, along with the Musée d'Orsay, reachable across a footbridge in the center of the garden. A good place to begin is at the Louvre end, at the Arc du Carrousel, a stone-and-marble arch commissioned by Napoléon to showcase the bronze horses he stole from St. Mark's Cathedral in Venice. The horses were eventually returned and replaced here with a statue of a quadriga, a four-horse chariot. On the Place de la Concorde end, twin buildings bookend the garden. On the Seine side, the former royal greenhouse is now the exceptional Musée de l'Orangerie, home to the largest display of Monet's lovely *Water Lilies* series, as well as a sizable collection of early-20th-century paintings. On the opposite end is the Jeu de Paume, which hosts some of the city's best photography exhibitions.

Note that the Tuileries is one of the best places in Paris to take kids if they're itching to run around. There's a carousel, trampolines, and, in summer, a funfair. If you're hungry, look for carts serving gelato from Amorino or sandwiches from the chain bakery Paul at the eastern end near the Louvre. Within the gated part of the gardens are four cafés with terraces. Pavillon des Tuileries near Place de la Concorde is a good place to stop for late-afternoon tea or an apéritif. ⊠ *Bordered by Quai des Tuileries, Pl. de la Concorde, Rue de Rivoli, and the Louvre,* *Louvre* ☎ *01–40–20–90–43* 🖪 *Free* Ⓜ *Tuileries, Concorde.*

Jeu de Paume

ART MUSEUM | This Napoléon III–era building at the north entrance of the Jardin des Tuileries began life in 1861 as a place to play *jeu de paume* (or "palm game"), a forerunner of tennis. It later served as a transfer point for art looted by the Germans during World War II. Today, it displays some of the city's best photography, serving as an ultramodern, white-walled showcase for up-and-comers as well as icons such as Diane Arbus, Richard Avedon, Cindy Sherman, and Robert Frank. In 2022, the museum launched the first annual Jeu de Paume festival, a celebration of multiple media that marries exhibits, screenings, concerts, and more. As of this writing, entry times must be booked in advance online. ⊠ *1 pl. de la Concorde, Louvre* ☎ *01–47–03–12–50* ⊕ *www.jeudepaume. org* 🖪 *€12* ⊘ *Closed Mon.* Ⓜ *Concorde.*

Les Halles

BUSINESS DISTRICT | For 800 years, Paris was fed by the acres of food halls overflowing with meats, fish, and vegetables that made up this district. Sensuously described in Émile Zola's novel *The Belly of Paris,* Les Halles was teeming with life—though not all of it good. Hucksters and the homeless shared these streets with prostitutes, and the plague of cat-size rats didn't cease until the market moved to the suburbs in 1969. Today, you can still see stuffed pests hanging by their tails in the windows of the circa-1872 shop Julien Aurouze (8 rue des Halles) whose sign, *Destruction des Animaux Nuisibles* (Vermin Extermination), says it all. All that remains of the 19th-century iron-and-glass market buildings designed by architect Victor Baltard is a portion of the superstructure on the southern edge of the Jardins des Halles. The Fontaine des Innocents, from 1550, at Rues Berger and Pierre Lescot, marks the site of what was once a vast

cemetery before the bones were moved to the Catacombs.

After years of delays, Les Halles finally underwent one of the city's most ambitious public works projects: a sweeping €500 million renovation, completed in 2018, that has transformed the plaza, and the much-maligned underground concrete mall called the Forum des Halles, into a must-go destination. While the project was not without opponents, even famously grumpy Parisians were satisfied by the prospect of a prettier Les Halles—and a spruced-up train station underground. (The métro and RER station at Les Halles is one of the city's busiest transport hubs.) In an echo of the past, a 48-foot iron-and-glass canopy floats over the entrance, flooding light into the caverns below. Aboveground, a 10-acre park called the Jardin Nelson Mandela is dotted with trees, decorative pools, and play areas for kids. On the northern end, a redesigned Place René Cassin has tiered steps centered around L'Ecoute, Henri de Miller's giant head and hand sculpture. Looming behind is the magnificent church of Saint-Eustache, a Gothic gem. Movie buffs should check out the Forum des Images, which stages screenings of quirky or older films, often with notables on hand such as director Oliver Stone. Or sample some of the 7,000 films available for viewing on individual screens. To find it, enter the mall on the side of the church at the Porte Saint-Eustache.

The streets surrounding Les Halles have boomed in recent years with boutiques, bars, and restaurants that have sent rents skyrocketing. Historic Rue Montorgueil is home to food shops and cafés. Running parallel, Rue Montmartre, near the church, still has a few specialty shops selling foie gras and other delicacies, though these merchants, like the butchers and bakers before them, are slowly being pushed out by trendy clothing boutiques. Steps away, Rue du Nil has recently become a foodie haven thanks to the Frenchie family of restaurants as well as shops from locavore trendsetters Terroirs d'Avenir. The area is also well-known for kitchen supply stores frequented by cooking amateurs and professionals alike; E. Dehillerin (18 rue Coquillière) is rife with old-fashioned charm, while Mora (13 rue Montmartre) is a bit more sterile but easier to navigate. ⊠ *Garden entrances on Rues Coquillière, Berger, and Rambuteau. Mall entrances on Rues Pierre Lescot, Berger, and Rambuteau, Louvre* Ⓜ *Les Halles; RER: Châtelet–Les Halles.*

★ **The Louvre**

ART MUSEUM | Simply put, the Louvre is the world's greatest art museum—and the largest, with 675,000 square feet of works from almost every civilization on Earth. The *Mona Lisa* is, of course, a top draw, along with the *Venus de Milo* and *Winged Victory.* These and many more of the globe's most coveted treasures are displayed in three wings—Richelieu, Sully, and Denon—which are arranged like a horseshoe around I. M. Pei's Pyramide. The giant glass pyramid surrounded by a trio of smaller ones opened in 1989 over the new entrance in the Cour Napoléon. Book your obligatory timed entry online in advance, and for an excellent overview, join a 90-minute English-language tour (€12, or €26 in combination with museum admission, daily at 11 and 2). Slick Nintendo 3DS multimedia guides (€5), available at the entrance to each wing, offer a self-guided alternative.

Having been first a fortress and later a royal residence, the Louvre represents a saga that spans nine centuries. Its medieval roots are on display underground in the Sully wing, where vestiges of the foundation and moat remain. Elsewhere in this wing you can ogle the largest display of Egyptian antiques outside of Cairo, most notably the magnificent statue of Ramses II (Salle 12). Upstairs is the armless Venus de Milo, a 2nd-century representation of Aphrodite (Salle 7). Highlights of the wing's collection of French paintings from the 17th century onward include *The Turkish Bath* by Jean-August-Dominique Ingres (Salle 60). American Cy Twombly's contemporary ceiling in Salle 32 adds a 21st-century twist. In the Denon wing, climb the sweeping marble staircase (Escalier Daru) to see the sublime *Winged Victory of Samothrace,* carved in 305 BC. This wing is also home to the iconic, enigmatic *Mona Lisa* (Salle 711); two other Leonardo da Vinci masterpieces hang in the nearby Grand Galerie. The museum's most recent architectural wonder is here as well—the 30,000-square-foot Arts of Islam exhibition space, which debuted in 2012. Topped with an undulating golden roof evoking a flowing veil, its two-level galleries contain one of the largest collections of art from the Islamic world. After admiring it, be sure to visit the Richelieu wing and the Cour Marly, with its quartet of horses carved for Louis XIV and Louis XV. On the ground floor, the centerpiece of the Near East Antiquities Collection is the Lamassu, carved 8th-century winged beasts (Salle 4). The elaborately decorated Royal Apartments of Napoléon III are on the first floor. On the second floor, French and Northern School paintings include Vermeer's *The Lacemaker* (Salle 38). ⊠ *Palais du Louvre, Louvre* ☏ *01–40–20–53–17* ⊕ *www. louvre.fr* ⊠ *€17, includes entrance to the charming Musée National Eugène-Delacroix within 2 days of use* ⊗ *Closed Tues.* ⚲ *Timed entrance obligatory; book online* Ⓜ *Palais-Royal–Louvre, Louvre–Rivoli.*

★ **Musée de l'Orangerie**
ART MUSEUM | In high season, the lines to see Claude Monet's massive, meditative *Water Lilies* (*Les Nymphéas*) can stretch into the pretty Tuileries Gardens, but the paintings are well worth the wait. These works, displayed in two curved galleries designed in 1914 by the master himself, are the highlight of the Orangerie's small but excellent collection, which also features early-20th-century paintings by other Impressionist masters like Renoir, Cézanne, and Matisse. Many hail from the private holdings of high-powered art dealer Paul Guillaume (1891–1934), among them the dealer's portrait by Modigliani entitled *Novo Pilota* (*New Pilot*). Temporary exhibitions are typically quirky and well curated. Originally built in 1852 to shelter orange trees, the long rectangular building, a twin of the Jeu de Paume across the garden, includes a portion of the city's 16th-century wall (you can see remnants on the lower floor). A small café and gift shop are here too. Entrance is by timed entry and must be booked online. ⊠ *Jardin des Tuileries at Pl. de la Concorde, Louvre* ☏ *01–44–77–80–07* ⊕ *www.musee-orangerie.fr* ⊠ *€12.50* ⊗ *Closed Tues.* Ⓜ *Concorde.*

Musée des Arts Décoratifs (MAD)
ART MUSEUM | The city's leading showcase of French design, Les Arts Décoratifs was rechristened the Musée des Arts Décoratifs—or MAD—in 2018 in an effort to better carve out a niche for itself. Sharing a wing of the Musée du Louvre, but with a separate entrance and admission charge, MAD is actually three museums in one spread over nine floors. The stellar collection of decorative arts, fashion, and graphics includes altarpieces from the Middle Ages and furnishings from the Italian Renaissance to the present day. There are period rooms reflecting different eras, such as the early 1820s salon of the Duchesse de Berry (who actually lived in the building), plus several rooms reproduced from designer Jeanne Lanvin's 1920s apartment. Don't miss the gilt-and-green-velvet bed of the Parisian courtesan who inspired the boudoir in Émile Zola's novel *Nana*; you can hear Zola's description of it on the free English audioguide, which is highly recommended. The second-floor jewelry gallery is another must-see.

Continued on page 150

MUSÉE DU LOUVRE

Try to wrap your mind around this: The Louvre has more than 37,000 pieces of art in its collection, representing nearly every civilization on earth, and more than 675,000 square feet of exhibition space. It's gone through countless cycles of construction and demolition, expansion and renovation, starting as a medieval fortress, then becoming a royal residence before opening its doors as the Museum Central des Arts at the end of the 18th century.

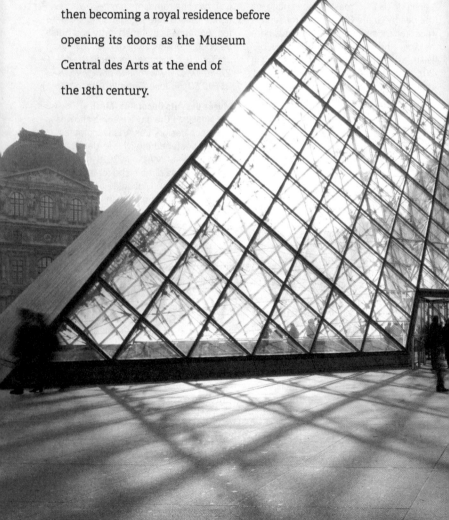

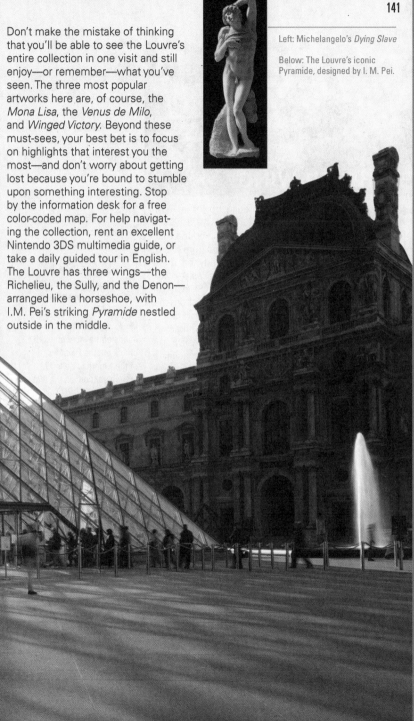

Don't make the mistake of thinking that you'll be able to see the Louvre's entire collection in one visit and still enjoy—or remember—what you've seen. The three most popular artworks here are, of course, the *Mona Lisa*, the *Venus de Milo*, and *Winged Victory*. Beyond these must-sees, your best bet is to focus on highlights that interest you the most—and don't worry about getting lost because you're bound to stumble upon something interesting. Stop by the information desk for a free color-coded map. For help navigating the collection, rent an excellent Nintendo 3DS multimedia guide, or take a daily guided tour in English. The Louvre has three wings—the Richelieu, the Sully, and the Denon—arranged like a horseshoe, with I.M. Pei's striking *Pyramide* nestled outside in the middle.

Left: Michelangelo's *Dying Slave*

Below: The Louvre's iconic Pyramide, designed by I. M. Pei.

RICHELIEU WING

COLLECTIONS
Near East Antiquities
French Painting
French Sculpture
Northern Schools
Decorative Arts

Below Ground & Ground Floor. Entering from the *Pyramide*, head upstairs to the sculpture courtyards, Cour Marly and Cour Puget. In Cour Marly you'll find the Marley Horses (see right). Salle 2 has fragments from Cluny, the powerful Romanesque abbey in Burgundy that dominated 11th-century French Catholicism. Salles 4–6 follow the evolution of French sculpture, and in Salles 7–10 you'll find funerary art. In Cour Puget, products from the Académie Royale, the art school of 18th-century France, fill Salles 25–33. Behind this is the Near East Antiquities Collection. Salle 3's centerpiece is the Codex of Hammurabi, an 18th-century BC black-diorite stela containing the world's oldest written code of laws. In Salle 4, you'll find Lamassu (see right).

First Floor. Head straight through Decorative Arts to see the magnificently restored Royal Apartments of Napoléon III *(see right).*

Second Floor. Much of this floor is dedicated to French and Northern School paintings. At the entrance is a 14th-century painting of John the Good—the oldest-known individual portrait from the north of Italy. In Salle 4 hangs *The Madonna of Chancellor Rolin,* by the 15th-century Early Netherlandish master Jan van Eyck (late 14th century–1441). Peter Paul Rubens's (1577–1640) the *Disembarkation of Marie de' Medici at the Port of Marseille* is in Salle 18. In Salle 31 are several paintings by Rembrandt van Rijn (1606–69), including *Bathsheba*, his largest nude. The masterpiece of the Dutch collection is Vermeer's *The Lacemaker (see right).*

TIPS

■ The 25 paintings by Rubens commisioned by Marie de Medici for the Luxembourg Palace in Salle 18 on the second floor each mark an event in the queen's life.

■ To see what's on the minds of the museum staff, check out the Painting of the Month in Salle 17, French section, on the 2nd floor.

■ Take a hot chocolate break in the Café Richelieu on the first floor, run by the upscale confiseur (confectioner) Angelina. There is an outdoor terrace in summer and a tempting lunch menu.

■ Save your ticket and duck out for lunch at one of the nearby cafés.

DON'T MISS

LAMASSU, 8TH CENTURY   SALLE 4

With their fierce beards and gentle eyes, these massive winged beasts are benevolent guardians straight from the dreamworld. Magical for children and adults, the strangely lifelike sculptures are located in the Near Eastern antiquities collection. The winged bull demigods are part of the Cour Khorsabad, a re-creation of the temple erected by Assyrian king Sargon II. ✛ *Richelieu, ground floor*

Lamassu

THE LACEMAKER, 1669–1671   SALLE 38

This is a small but justifiably famous gem of Dutch optical accuracy (and a must-see for fans of the movie and book, *Girl With a Pearl Earring*, to see how his style evolved over a 5-year period.) Here, Jan Vermeer (1632–75) painted the red thread in the foreground as a slightly blurred jumble, just as one would actually see it if focusing on the girl. The lacemaker's industriousness represents domestic virtue, but the personal focus of the painting is far more engaging than a simple morality tale. ✛ *Richelieu, second floor*

The Lacemaker

MARLY HORSES, 1699–1740   COUR MARLY

During the dramatic 1989 reorganization of the Louvre, two courtyards were elegantly glassed over to match the entrance pyramid. The dramatic glass-roofed Marly sculpture court houses several works from Louis XIV's garden at Marly, including two magnificent winged horses by Antoine Coysevox. Later, the artist's nephew, Guillaume Coustou, created two accompanying earth-bound horse sculptures for Louis XV; their fame was such that, during the Revolution, these sculptures were moved to the Tuileries gardens for public viewing. Now the four original horses greet visitors to the Richelieu Wing, ready to gallop off into the museum; replicas stand guard in the Tuileries. ✛ *Richelieu, lower ground floor*

The Marly Horses

ROYAL APARTMENTS OF NAPOLÉON III, 1860s   SALLE 87

These dozen reception rooms, hung with crystal chandeliers, elaborate mirrors, and imperial velour, are a gilt-covered reminder that the Louvre was a palace for centuries, regally designed to impress. En route, you'll pass decorative items like the solid-crystal Restoration dressing table (Salle 77) that prepare you for the eye-popping luxury of the Second Empire. ✛ *Richelieu, first floor*

Royal Apartments of Napoléon

SULLY WING

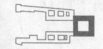

COLLECTIONS
History of the Louvre
Ancient Egypt
Near East Antiquities
Greek, Roman, & Etruscan
Antiquities
French Painting
Graphic Arts
Northern Schools
Decorative Arts

Below Ground & Ground Floor. Start your visit with a journey to the roots of the Louvre—literally. From the *Pyramide* entrance, tour the 13th-century foundations of the original fortress and the **Medieval Moat** (see right). In Salle 12, you'll find towering **Ramses II** (see right). Check out the mummies and rare examples of Egyptian funerary art in Salles 14 and 15.

Upstairs, the north galleries of the Sully continue the ancient Iranian collection begun in the Richelieu Wing. Salle 16 has the 2nd-century BC **Venus de Milo** *(see right)*, anchoring the Greek collection of Salles 7–17.

First Floor. The northern galleries of the first floor continue with the Decorative Arts collection, including works from all over Europe, and connect with the Napoléon III apartments.

Second Floor. Sully picks up French painting in the 17th century where the Richelieu leaves off. The Académiciens are best exemplified by Nicolas Poussin (1594–1665, Salle 19), the first international painting star from France. The antithesis of this style was the candlelit modest work by outsider Georges de La Tour (Salle 28), as in his *Magdalene of Night Light*.

The Académie Royale defined the standards of painting through revolution, republic, and empire. Exoticism wafted in during the Napoleonic empire, as in **The Turkish Bath** (see right) painting of Jean-Auguste-Dominique Ingres (1780–1867). Fresh energy crackled into French painting in the 18th century. Antoine Watteau (1684–1721), was known for his theatrical scenes and *fêtes galantes*, portrayals of well-dressed figures in bucolic settings. In *Pilgrimage to the Island of Cythera* (Salle 36), he used delicate brushstrokes and soft tones to convey the court set, here depicted arriving on (or departing from) Cythera, the mythical isle of love.

TIPS

■ There is a little-known collection of pieces by Monet, Renoir, and Cezanne in Salle C on the second floor, the only Impressionist works in the Louvre.

■ There's a surprise in Salle 17 on the ground floor—the *Sleeping Hermaphrodite* by the entrance.

■ Be sure to look up as you make your way up Escalier Henri II. It took four years to complete this 16th-century vaulted ceiling.

■ Need a bathroom? There are some tucked between Salles 22 and 23 on the first floor. (And admire the colorful, 4,000-year-old Seated Scribe in Salle 22.)

■ For a breather, head to the bench in Salle 33 on the first floor and enjoy the sedate three-part ceiling by Georges Braque (1955) called *Les Oiseux (The Birds)*.

DON'T MISS

RAMSES II, APPROX. 1200 BC   **SALLE 12**

The sphinx-guarded Egyptian Wing contains the biggest display of Egyptian antiquities in the world after the Cairo museum—not surprising, considering that Egyptology as a Western concept was invented by a Frenchman, Champollion, founder of the Louvre's Egypt collection and translator of the hieroglyphics on the Rosetta Stone. This statue from the site of Tanis, presumed to be Ramses II, never fails to stop visitors' breath with its gleaming stone, beatific expression, and perfect proportions. ✛ *Sully, ground floor*

Ramses II

VENUS DE MILO, **APPROX. 120 BC**   **SALLE 16**

After countless photographs and bad reproductions, the original Aphrodite continues to dazzle. The armless statue, one of the most recognizable works of art in the world, is actually as beautiful as they say. She was unearthed on the Greek island of Milos in the 19th century and sold for 6,000 francs to the French ambassador in Constantinople, who presented her to King Louis XVIII. ✛ *Sully, ground floor*

Venus de Milo

MEDIEVAL MOAT, 13TH CENTURY   **MEDIEVAL LOUVRE**

Wander around the perimeter of the solidly built original moat to reach the remarkable Salle Saint-Louis with its elegant columns and medieval artifacts. Keep an eye out for the parade helmet of Charles VI, which was dug up in 169 fragments and astonishingly reassembled. ✛ *Sully, lower ground floor*

Medieval Moat

THE *TURKISH BATH,* **1862**   **SALLE 60**

Though Jean-August-Dominique Ingres' (1780–1867) long-limbed women hardly look Turkish, they are singularly elegant, and his polished immaculate style was imitated by an entire generation of French painters. This painting is a prime example of Orientalism, where Western artists played out fantasies of the Orient in their work. Popular as a society portrait painter, Ingres returned repeatedly to langorous nudes—compare the women of *The Turkish Bath* with the slinky figure in his *La Grande Odalisque,* in the Denon Wing. ✛ *Sully, second floor*

The Turkish Bath

THE DENON WING

COLLECTIONS
Ancient Egypt
Greek, Roman, & Etruscan Antiquities
French Painting
Italian & Spanish Painting
Graphic Arts
Italian, Spanish, & Northern Sculpture
African, Asian, Oceanic, & American Arts
Arts of Islam

TIPS

■ Don't skip the coat check on the ground floor. Much of the museum is hot and stuffy.

■ Don't miss the glass case near *Winged Victory of Samothrace* on the first floor. It contains her two-fingered hand.

■ Need a bathroom? There are some tucked away at the end of the wing on the first floor near Salle 13.

Below Ground & Ground Floor. The stunning Arts of Islam wing with 30,000 square feet of gallery space is built into the Cour Visconti and topped with an undulating glass roof meant to evoke a floating head scarf. Here you'll find Europe's largest collection of treasures from across the Islamic world, including the Ottoman Empire. On the lower level, don't miss the Baptistery of Saint Louis, a 14th-century sculpted golden basin. The galleries to the south and east of the *Pyramide* entrance display early Renaissance Italian sculpture, including a 15th-century *Madonna and Child* by Florentine Dontallo (1386–1466). Drift upstairs to the Italian sculptures on the ground level, where you'll find Michelangelo's exquisite *Slaves* (1513–15) in Salle 4.

First Floor. Walk up the marble Escalier Daru to discover the sublime **Winged Victory of Samothrace** *(see right)*, cleaned in 2014. Then head to the stunning Galerie d'Apollon (Apollo Gallery). Built in 1661 but not finished until 1851, the hall was a model for Versailles's Hall of Mirrors.

Back out and into Paintings, you'll find four by Leonardo da Vinci (1452–1519). His enigmatic, androgynous *St-John the Baptist* hangs here, along with more overtly religious works such as the 1483 *Virgin of the Rocks*. Take a close look at the pretty portrait of *La Belle Ferronnière*, which Leonardo painted a decade before the **Mona Lisa** *(see right)*; it will give you something to compare with Mona when you finally get to meet her in the Salle des Etats, near Salles 5 and 6. Head across to Salle 75 for an artistic 180°: the gleaming pomp and circumstance of a new empire with the **Coronation of Napoléon** *(see right)* by French classicist Jacques-Louis David (1748–1825).

In Salle 77 is the graphic 1819 **The Raft of the Medusa,** *(see right)* by Théodore Géricault (1791–1824).

DON'T MISS

MONA LISA, 1503   SALLE 7

The most famous painting in the world, *La Gioconda* (*La Joconde* in French) is tougher than she looks: the canvas was stolen from the Louvre by an Italian nationalist in 1911, recovered from a Florentine hotel, and survived an acid attack in 1956. She is believed to be the wife of Francesco del Giocondo, a Florentine millionaire, and was probably 24 when she sat for this painting; some historians believe the portrait was actually painted after her death. Either way, she has become immortal through da Vinci's ingenious "sfumato" technique, which combines glowing detail with soft, depth-filled brushwork. ⚜ *Denon, first floor*

Mona Lisa

THE RAFT OF THE MEDUSA, 1819   SALLE 77

Théodore Géricault was inspired by the grim news report that survivors of a wrecked French merchant ship were left adrift on a raft without supplies. Géricault interviewed survivors, visited the morgue to draw corpses, and turned his painting of the disaster into a strong indictment of authority, the first time an epic historical painting had taken on current events in this way. Note the desperate energy from the pyramid construction of bodies on the raft and the manipulation of greenish light. ⚜ *Denon, first floor*

The Raft of the Medusa

WINGED VICTORY OF SAMOTHRACE, 305 BC   STAIRS

Poised for flight at the top of the Escalier Daru, this exhilarating statue was found on a tiny Greek island in the northern Aegean. Depicted in the act of descending from Olympus, *Winged Victory*, or Nike to the Ancient Greeks, was carved to commemorate the naval victory of Demetrius Poliorcetes over the Persians. ⚜ *Denon, first floor*

Winged Victory of Samothrace

CORONATION OF NAPOLÉON, 1805   SALLE 75

Classicist Jacques-Louis David (1748–1825) was the ultimate painter-survivor: he began his career under the protection of the king, became official designer of the Revolutionary government, endured two rounds of exile, and became one of the greatest of Napoléon's painters. Here, David avoided the politically fraught moment of December 2, 1804—when Napoléon snatched the crown from the hands of Pope Pius VII to place it upon his own head—choosing instead the romantic moment when the new emperor turned to crown Joséphine. ⚜ *Denon, first floor*

Detail from the *Coronation of Napoléon*

PLANNING YOUR VISIT

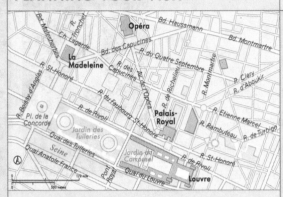

TOURS

There are 90-minute guided tours in English daily. The meeting point is at "Accueil des Groups" under the pyramid. There are also free leaflets that map out various themed, self-guided tours—some designed especially for kids. The Louvre has a phenomenal program of courses and workshops (mostly in French); see website for details.

ACCESSIBILITY

Those using wheelchairs or strollers can skip the long entry line and use the marvelous cylindrical elevator inside the entrance pyramid.

WITH KIDS

Begin your tour in the Sully Wing at the Medieval Moat, which leads enticingly to the sphinx-guarded entrance of the Egyptian Wing, a must for mummy enthusiasts. For a more in-depth visit, you can reserve private kid-centric family tours such as the Paris Muse Clues. Don't forget the Tuileries is right next door (with carnival rides in summer).

ENTRY TIPS

You can order your ticket online (€15 plus €2 fee) at ⊕ www. ticketlouvre.fr. Or save the fee and buy your ticket at the official Paris tourist office a short walk from the museum at 29 rue de Rivoli. See ⊕ www.en.parisinfo.com for more information.

Shorten your wait by avoiding the main entrance at the Pyramide and head for the entrance in the underground mall, Carrousel du Louvre. Automatic ticket machines are available. Note that crowds are thinner on Wednesday and Friday nights, when the museum is open late. Be sure to check the website for room closings; renovations are always taking place. Remember the Louvre is closed on Tuesday.

A WHIRLWIND TOUR

If you've come to Paris and feel you must go to the Louvre to see the Big Three—*Venus de Milo, Winged Victory,* and *Mona Lisa*—even though you'd rather be strolling along the Champs-Elysees, it can be done in an hour or less if you plan well. Start in Denon and head upstairs through Estruscan and Greek antiquities, walking down the long hall of sculptures until you see the *Winged Victory* in front of you. Take a right and head up the staircase through French painting to the *Mona Lisa*. Then go back down under the *Pyramide* to Sully to see the *Venus de Milo*.

✉ Palais du Louvre, Louvre/Tuileries

☎ 01–40–20–53–17 (information)

⊕ www.louvre.fr

🕐 Mon., Thurs., and weekends 9–6; Wed., Fri., and first Sat. of the month, 9 am–9:30 pm; closed Tues.

Ⓜ Palais-Royal-Louvre, Louvre-Rivoli

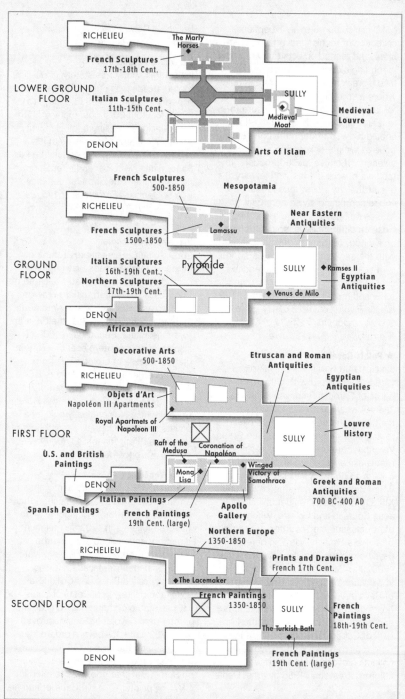

LOWER GROUND FLOOR

RICHELIEU

The Marly Horses

French Sculptures
17th-18th Cent.

Italian Sculptures
11th-15th Cent.

SULLY

Medieval Moat

Medieval Louvre

DENON

Arts of Islam

GROUND FLOOR

French Sculptures
500-1850

Mesopotamia

RICHELIEU

French Sculptures
1500-1850

Lamassu

Near Eastern Antiquities

Italian Sculptures
16th-19th Cent.;
Northern Sculptures
17th-19th Cent.

Pyramide

SULLY

Ramses II

Egyptian Antiquities

Venus de Milo

DENON

African Arts

FIRST FLOOR

Decorative Arts
500-1850

Etruscan and Roman Antiquities

Egyptian Antiquities

RICHELIEU

Objets d'Art
Napoléon III Apartments

Royal Apartmets of
Napoleon III

Louvre History

U.S. and British Paintings

Raft of the Medusa

Coronation of Napoléon

DENON

Mona Lisa

Winged Victory of Samothrace

Italian Paintings

Spanish Paintings

French Paintings
19th Cent. (large)

Apollo Gallery

SULLY

Greek and Roman Antiquities
700 BC-400 AD

SECOND FLOOR

Northern Europe
1350-1850

RICHELIEU

Prints and Drawings
French 17th Cent.

The Lacemaker

French Paintings
1350-1850

SULLY

French Paintings
18th-19th Cent.

The Turkish Bath

DENON

French Paintings
19th Cent. (large)

MAD is also home to an exceptional collection of textiles, advertising posters, films, and related objects that are shown in rotating exhibitions. Before leaving, take a break at the restaurant Le Loulou, where an outdoor terrace is an ideal spot for lunch or afternoon tea (be sure to reserve—spots fill up quickly!) Shoppers should browse through the on-site boutique as well. Stocked with an interesting selection of books, paper products, toys, tableware, accessories, and jewelry, it's one of the city's best museum shops. If you're combining a visit here with the Musée du Louvre, note that the two close on different days, so don't come on Monday or Tuesday. If you're pairing it with the exquisite Nissim de Camondo, joint tickets are available at a reduced cost. Admission is currently by timed entry and must be booked online. ⊠ *107 rue de Rivoli, Louvre* ☎ *01–44–55–57–50* ⊕ *www.madparis.fr* 🗺 *€14* ⊘ *Closed Mon.* Ⓜ *Palais-Royal–Louvre.*

★ **Palais-Royal**
OTHER ATTRACTION | This truly Parisian garden is enclosed within the former home of Cardinal Richelieu (1585–1642). The 400-year-old arcades now house boutiques and one of the city's oldest restaurants, the haute-cuisine Le Grand Véfour, where brass plaques recall former regulars like Napoléon and Victor Hugo. Built in 1629, the *palais* became royal when Richelieu bequeathed it to Louis XIII. Other famous residents include Jean Cocteau and Colette, who wrote of her pleasurable "country" view of the *province à Paris*. It was also here, two days before the Bastille was stormed in 1789, that Camille Desmoulins gave an impassioned speech sowing the seeds of Revolution. Today, the garden often hosts giant temporary art installations sponsored by another tenant, the Ministry of Culture. The courtyard off Place Colette is outfitted with an eye-catching collection of squat black-and-white columns created in 1986 by artist Daniel

Buren. ⊠ *Pl. du Palais-Royal, Louvre* Ⓜ *Palais-Royal–Louvre.*

Passage du Grand-Cerf
PEDESTRIAN MALL | This stately, glass-roofed arcade was built in 1825 and expertly renovated in 1988. Today, it's home to about 20 shops, many of them small designers selling original jewelry, accessories, and housewares. If it's apéritif time, stop by the popular Le Pas Sage, with a wine bar and a restaurant flanking either side of the entrance at Rue St-Denis. ⊠ *Entrances at 145 rue St-Denis and 8 rue Dussoubs, Louvre* ⊘ *Closed Sun.* Ⓜ *Étienne Marcel.*

Place de la Concorde
PLAZA/SQUARE | This square at the foot of the Champs-Élysées was originally named after Louis XV. It later became the Place de la Révolution, where crowds cheered as Louis XVI, Marie-Antoinette, and some 2,500 others lost their heads to the guillotine. Renamed in 1836, it also got a new centerpiece: the 75-foot granite Obelisk of Luxor, a gift from Egypt quarried in the 8th century BC. Among the handsome 18th-century buildings facing the square is the Hôtel Crillon, which was originally built as a private home by Gabriel, the architect of Versailles's Petit Trianon. ⊠ *Rue Royale, Louvre* Ⓜ *Concorde.*

Place Vendôme
PLAZA/SQUARE | Jules-Hardouin Mansart, an architect of Versailles, designed this perfectly proportioned octagonal plaza near the Tuileries in 1702. To maintain a uniform appearance, he gave the surrounding *hôtels particuliers* (private mansions) identical facades. It was originally called Place des Conquêtes to extoll the military conquests of Louis XIV, whose statue on horseback graced the center until Revolutionaries destroyed it in 1792. Later, Napoléon ordered his likeness erected atop a 144-foot column modestly modeled after Trajan's Column in Rome. But that, too, was toppled in 1871 by painter Gustave Courbet and his

band of radicals. The Third Republic raised a new column and sent Courbet the bill, though he died in exile before paying it. Chopin lived and died at No. 12, which is also where Napoléon III enjoyed trysts with his mistress; since 1902 it has been home to the high-end jeweler Chaumet. ✉ *Pl. Vendôme, Louvre* Ⓜ *Tuileries.*

★ Rue Montorgueil

STREET | Rue Montorgueil was once the gritty oyster hub of Les Halles. Now lined with food shops and cafés, the cobbled street—whose name translates to Mount Pride—is the heart of one of the city's trendiest neighborhoods. History runs deep here. Monet captured the scene in 1878 when Montorgueil was ablaze with tricolor flags during the World's Fair (see the painting in the Musée d'Orsay). Honoré de Balzac and his 19th-century band of scribes frequented Au Rocher de Cancale at No. 78, whose famously crumbling facade has been painstakingly restored with gilt panache. Other addresses have been around for centuries: Stohrer at No. 51 has been baking elaborate pastries since 1730, and L'Escargot Montorgueil at No. 38, a favorite of Charlie Chaplin, is still graced by a giant golden snail evoking its most popular menu item. Relative newcomers include the luxury Nuxe spa at Nos. 32–34 and the Fou de Pâtisseries pastry shop at No. 45. The street extends onto Rue des Petits-Carreaux just before Sentier métro, home to an outpost of excellent Breton crêperie Breizh Café and specialty grocer Maison Plisson—both at No. 14. Browse the boutiques on Rue Montmartre, which runs parallel, or shop for cookware at Julia Child's old haunt, E. Dehillerin, still in business at 18–20 rue Coquillière. Rue Tiquetonne is rife with bistros, and once sleepy Rue St-Sauveur became a destination when the Experimental Cocktail Club (No. 37) moved in, joined by other trendy eating and drinking spots. The diminutive Rue du Nil is a foodie haven, home to Frenchie restaurant (No. 5) and wine bar (No.

6) as well as Terroirs d'Avenir's locavore shops and Plaq (No. 4), known for bean-to-bar chocolate. Even the area around Rue d'Aboukir, once far scruffier, is now a hipster fave thanks to the arrival of American-style baked goods like Boneshaker's doughnuts (No. 86) and Cookie Love's cookies (No. 84), as well as brunch spots Echo (No. 95) and Maafim (5 rue des Forges). ✉ *Rue Montorgueil, off Rue de Turbigo, Louvre* ☉ *Many shops closed Mon.* Ⓜ *Sentier, Les Halles.*

Saint-Eustache

CHURCH | Built as the market neighborhood's answer to Notre-Dame, this massive church is decidedly squeezed into its surroundings. Constructed between 1532 and 1640 with foundations dating from 1200, the church mixes a Gothic exterior, complete with impressive flying buttresses, and a Renaissance interior. On the east end (Rue Montmartre), Dutch master Rubens's *Pilgrims of Emmaus* (1611) hangs in a small chapel. Two chapels to the left is Keith Haring's *The Life of Christ,* a triptych in bronze and white-gold patina. It was given to the church after the artist's death in 1990, in recognition of the parish's efforts to help people with AIDS. On the Rue Montmartre side of the church, look for the small door to Saint Agnes's crypt, topped with a stone plaque noting the date, 1213, below a curled fish, an indication the patron made his fortune in fish. There's free entry to the weekly organ concerts. ✉ *2 impasse St-Eustache, Louvre* ⊕ *www.saint-eustache.org* Ⓜ *Les Halles; RER: Châtelet–Les Halles.*

Tour Jean Sans Peur

NOTABLE BUILDING | FAMILY | This fascinating little tower is the only remnant of a sprawling complex built on the edge of the original city walls in 1369. It is named for Jean Sans Peur (John the Fearless), the Duke of Burgundy, who gained power in 1407 after ordering the assassination of his rival, the king's brother. In 1409, as civil war raged, he had the tower erected and put his bedroom on a high floor with a bird's-eye view of approaching enemies. Carved into the vaulted second-floor ceiling—a masterwork of medieval architecture—is an ornate sculpture of an oak tree entwined with plants representing the duke's family. Children (and curious adults) will enjoy the climb up to see the restored red-velvet-lined latrine, a state-of-the-art comfort in its time. Kitschy costumed mannequins and medieval-themed exhibits covering subjects from food to furniture to hygiene lend the tower added kid appeal. Be sure to ask for English information at the entry. Note that it's open in the afternoon only. ✉ *20 rue Étienne Marcel, Louvre* ☎ *01–40–26–20–28* 🌐 *www.tourjeansanspeur.com* 🎟 *€6* 🕒 *Closed mornings and Mon. and Tues.* [M] *Étienne Marcel.*

★ **Tour Saint-Jacques** (*Saint-Jacques Tower*)
VIEWPOINT | For centuries, this 170-foot bell tower guided pilgrims to a starting point of the Chemin de St-Jacques (Way of Saint James). Built in 1508 in the Flamboyant Gothic style, it's all that remains of the Église St-Jacques-de-la-Boucherie, which was destroyed in the French Revolution. Purchased by the city in 1836, the tower languished until a three-year renovation, completed in 2009, restored 660 tons of stone and statues, including the gargoyles hanging from the upper reaches and the figure of Saint James gracing the top. Blaise Pascal was among the medieval scientists who conducted experiments here (his involved gravity), which is why his statue sits at the base. If you wish to enter the tower, guided tours are occasionally offered in summer and fall by reservation only; schedule one online at *www.desmotsetdesarts.com.* ✉ *39 rue de Rivoli, Louvre* 🎟 *Tours €12* [M] *Châtelet.*

🍴 Restaurants

Home to the city's wholesale food market until the 1960s, Les Halles is still the place to go for late-night onion soup or steak *frites,* washed back with gulps of cheap and tasty red wine. The foodie hub around Rue Montorgueil is a can't-miss for pastry, fresh produce, trendy restaurants, and more. The streets grow more subdued around the Louvre and Palais Royal, where you can slurp oysters at a classic brasserie, indulge in more experimental haute cuisine, or hang out at one of a handful of trendy wine bars.

A l'Epi d'Or
$$ | **FRENCH** | Jean-François Piège has breathed new life into A l'Epi d'Or, harking back to the 20s, when Paris was filled with delightful classic bistros. The allure of the old-fashioned zinc bar, tiled floor, and dark wood tables invites you in; the mastery of authentic French cuisine—such as duck confit with potatoes or *moules-frites*—begs you to stay. **Known for:** homey, traditional dining room; daily comfort-food specials; simple and straightforward prix-fixe menu with a handful of à la carte options. [$] *Average main: €22* ✉ *25 rue Jean-Jacques Rousseau, Louvre* ☎ *01–42–36–38–12* 🌐 *www.alepidorparis.com* 🕒 *Closed weekends* [M] *Louvre–Rivoli.*

★ **Angelina**
$ | **CAFÉ** | Founded in 1903 and patronized by literary luminaries like Marcel Proust and Gertrude Stein, Angelina is famous for its *chocolat "l'Africain,"* ultrarich hot chocolate topped with whipped cream, as well as for its beautiful chestnut "Mont Blanc" pastry. Book well in advance online to avoid being disappointed. **Known for:** table 45—Coco Chanel's favorite; opulent, Belle Époque setting; the most famous hot chocolate in Paris. [$] *Average main: €15* ✉ *226 rue de Rivoli, Louvre* ☎ *01–42–60–82–00* 🌐 *www.angelina-paris.fr* [M] *Tuileries.*

Au Rocher de Cancale

$ | FRENCH | As its impressive facade attests, this café has a special history. It opened in 1846, when Balzac was a regular, and Rue Montorgueil was *the* place to buy oysters, though these days, the menu is more modern with salads, burgers, and brunch options, as well as a handful of classics like escargots and French onion soup. **Known for:** beautiful terrace with views over the bustling rue Montorgueil; lovely dining room with panels showing scenes of 18th-century life; all-day service from 8 am to 2 am. $ *Average main: €17* ✉ *78 rue Montorgueil, Louvre* ☎ *01–42–33–50–29* Ⓜ *Les Halles.*

Bistrot Vivienne

$$ | FRENCH | Set in the Galerie Vivienne, Paris's loveliest covered passage, this charmingly authentic 19th-century bistro feels both cozy and welcoming, and the food and drink are well above average. With all-day hours as well as a double terrace either inside Galerie Vivienne or on a picturesque street a few steps from the Palais Royal gardens, this is a satisfying spot for a quick coffee or glass of wine, a snack, or a full meal. **Known for:** good vegetarian options; great location in the Galerie Vivienne; all-day service until 11 pm. $ *Average main: €23* ✉ *4 rue des Petits Champs, 2e, Louvre* ☎ *01–49–27–00–50* ⊕ *www.bistrotvivienne.com* Ⓜ *Bourse, Palais-Royal–Musée du Louvre.*

Café Kitsuné

$ | CAFÉ | This Japanese-inspired mini-chain of coffeehouses is the place to be seen during Paris Fashion Week. There are three locations: one at 208 rue de Rivoli, one at 2 place André Malraux, and this one—the original and persistent favorite, thanks in large part to views over the Palais Royal gardens. **Known for:** lovely pastries from Chef Kévin Lacote; iced matcha lattes perfect for cooling down in summer; branded apparel and coffee mugs. $ *Average main: €5* ✉ *51 Galerie Montpensier, Louvre* ☎ *01–40–15–62–31* ⊕ *www.maisonkitsune.com* Ⓜ *Palais-Royal–Louvre.*

Café Lapérouse

$$ | FRENCH | A charming and much less infamous version of its sumptuous mothership—the legendary 250-year-old Parisian restaurant Lapérouse—this light-drenched café, housed within the beautiful Hôtel de la Marine, has all the romance of a 19th-century luxury cruiseliner bound for exotic shores: plush banquettes in sorbet colors, glittering chandeliers, and touches from faraway places. Here you can nibble on a crisp salad topped with a flurry of shaved truffles or indulge in a rich langoustine *parmentier*, a Lapérouse classic. **Known for:** beautiful decor; charming outdoor dining; great location on Place de la Concorde. $ *Average main: €20* ✉ *Hôtel de la Marine, 2 Pl. de la Concorde, Champs-Élysées* ☎ *01–53–93–65–53* ⊕ *www. hotel-de-la-marine.paris/Autour-de-la-visite/Gastronomie/Le-Cafe-Laperouse* Ⓜ *Concorde.*

Café Marly

$$$ | CAFÉ | Run by the Costes brothers, this café overlooking the main courtyard of the Louvre and its famous glass pyramid is a stylish place to meet for a drink or a coffee, whether in the chic, jewel-toned dining rooms or on the Louvre's long, sheltered terrace. Regular café service shuts down during meal times, when fashion-conscious folks dig into Asian-inspired salads and pseudo-Italian pasta dishes. **Known for:** all-day hours; great views of the Louvre; a see-and-be-seen atmosphere. $ *Average main: €30* ✉ *Cour Napoléon du Louvre, enter from Louvre courtyard, 93 rue de Rivoli, 1er, Louvre* ☎ *01–49–26–06–60* ⊕ *www.cafe-marly.com* Ⓜ *Palais-Royal.*

Chez Georges

$$$ | BISTRO | If you were to ask Parisian bankers, aristocrats, or antiques dealers to name their favorite bistro for a three-hour weekday lunch, many would choose Chez Georges. The traditional fare is very

good, and the atmosphere is better, compensating for the steep prices. **Known for:** lively historic atmosphere evoking 1940s Paris; buttery sole meunière; excellent wine list including options by the glass. [$] *Average main: €32* ✉ *1 rue du Mail, 2e, Louvre* ☎ *01–42–60–07–11* ⏲ *Closed weekends, Aug., and 1 wk at Christmas* [M] *Sentier.*

Ellsworth

$$$ | **FRENCH FUSION** | This spot is on Ina Garten's must-visit list in Paris, and it's not hard to see why. The succinct menu of seasonal cuisine is fresh and light, served in a simple dining room with lovely decor including wooden windowpanes and white marble tables. **Known for:** Paris's best fried chicken; panoply of plant-based options; slight American accents on a contemporary French menu. [$] *Average main: €28* ✉ *34 rue de Richelieu, Louvre* ☎ *01–42–60–59–66* 🌐 *www.ellsworthparis.com* ⏲ *Closed Sun.–Tues. No lunch.* [M] *Pyramides.*

★ Juvéniles

$$$ | **WINE BAR** | A favorite with the French and expats alike, this neighborhood bistro blends great dining with an inspired wine list and a handy location a stone's throw from the Louvre. Exquisite French ingredients are given an inspired, often slightly lighter makeover by Chef Romain Roudeau, although hearty house-made terrines and foie gras as well as slow-cooked meat and game are frequently featured on the eclectic menu. **Known for:** small space, so best to reserve in advance; phenomenal wine selection on-site and takeaway; great cheese selection from Neal's Yard and neighboring Madame Hisada. [$] *Average main: €28* ✉ *47 rue de Richelieu, 1er, Louvre* ☎ *01–42–97–46–49* 🌐 *www.juvenileswinebar.com* ⏲ *Closed Sun. and Mon.* [M] *Bourse, Pyramides.*

La Dame de Pic

$$$$ | **FRENCH** | This Michelin-starred establishment from Anne-Sophie Pic features a Provençal-accented menu of specialties from the chef's native Valence, with produce-driven dishes and Southern cheeses. The dining room leans into the chef's feminine side, with pale pink accenting the cozy space otherwise decked out in leather and wood. **Known for:** open Sundays and Mondays, when many other top establishments are closed; steps from the Louvre; four-, five-, and seven-course prix fixe menus with wine pairings. [$] *Average main: €90* ✉ *20 rue du Louvre, Louvre* ☎ *01–42–60–40–40* 🌐 *www.anne-sophie-pic.com.*

La Poule au Pot

$$$$ | **FRENCH** | When Jean-François Piège took over this restaurant overlooking the former Les Halles market, he gave it a much-needed makeover while also retaining its vintage appeal. Slide into one of the red leather banquettes and peruse the menu of exquisite upscale bistro classics with prices to match. **Known for:** house-made tarts for dessert; superb French bistro fare, like frogs' legs and French onion soup; gorgeous vintage setting and atmosphere. [$] *Average main: €40* ✉ *9 rue Vauvilliers, Louvre* ☎ *01–42–36–32–96* 🌐 *www.lapouleaupot.fr* ⏲ *Closed Sun. and Mon.* [M] *Louvre–Rivoli.*

L'Ardoise

$$$ | **BISTRO** | Despite the chic, updated decor, this tiny, reliable bistro hasn't sacrificed substance for style. The servers are friendly, the wine list is small but well curated, and the dining is first-rate, with a three-course dinner menu (you can order à la carte, but it's less of a bargain) of original dishes marrying terroir-driven ingredients—like Charolais beef, fois gras from the Landes, and organic eggs—with contemporary touches and pretty plating. **Known for:** can be noisy and crowded due to its popularity; ever-changing traditional fare with contemporary twists; good-value prix-fixe menus. [$] *Average main: €27* ✉ *28 rue du Mont Thabor, 1er, Louvre* ☎ *01–42–96–28–18* 🌐 *www.lardoise-paris.com* ⏲ *No lunch Sun.* [M] *Concorde.*

★ La Régalade Saint-Honoré

$$$ | MODERN FRENCH | After taking over the original La Régalade, chef Bruno Doucet kept some of what made the old restaurant so popular (country terrines, reasonably priced wines, convivial atmosphere), but he also had a few tricks under his toque, notably creating a successful haute-cuisine-meets-comfort-food destination. With a good quality-to-price ratio, this chic bistro has evolved into a good stalwart, and thanks to takeaway options, hearty braises like the house beef bourguignon reheat well at home. **Known for:** good-value prix-fixe menu for lunch and dinner; comfort-food desserts like rice pudding or soufflé; contemporary iterations of French bistro classics like escargots or beef bourguignon. $ *Average main: €25* ⊠ *123 rue St-Honoré, 1er, Louvre* ☎ *01–42–21–92–40* ⊕ *www.laregalade.paris* ⊗ *Closed Sun. and Mon.* Ⓜ *Louvre–Rivoli.*

Le Fumoir

$$$$ | FRENCH | Equal parts café, bar, and restaurant, Le Fumoir is a timelessly popular place to sip coffee and read the paper or enjoy an after-dinner drink. Reservations are recommended for dinner as well as for the copious Sunday brunch from Chef Henrik Andersson. **Known for:** reasonable prix fixe menu; good vegetarian options; French fare with slightly Scandinavian influences. $ *Average main: €36* ⊠ *Pl. du Louvre, 6 rue de l'Amiral-Coligny, Louvre* ☎ *01–42–92–00–24* ⊕ *www.lefumoir.com* Ⓜ *Louvre–Rivoli.*

Le Grand Colbert

$$$ | BRASSERIE | FAMILY | With its globe lamps and molded ceilings, this neighborhood institution feels elegant yet not overpolished, attracting a wonderfully Parisian mix of elderly lone diners, business lunchers, tourists, couples, and the post-theater crowd, all of whom come for the enormous seafood platters, duck foie gras with Sauternes jelly, steak tartare, and roasted chicken rendered famous by Diane Keaton in *Something's Gotta Give*. Open every day, Le Grand Colbert is also a pleasant destination for a quick bite between 3 pm and 6 pm, when most everything else is closed. **Known for:** delightful roast chicken; standout historic decor and ambience; towering seafood platters. $ *Average main: €30* ⊠ *2 rue Vivienne, 2e, Louvre* ☎ *01–42–86–87–88* ⊕ *www.legrandcolbert.fr* Ⓜ *Bourse.*

★ Le Grand Véfour

$$$ | MODERN FRENCH | One of the area's most historic spots has welcomed everyone from Napoléon to Colette to Jean Cocteau beneath its mirrored ceiling and is still a contender for the most beautiful restaurant in Paris. This once-Michelin-starred spot has made a few changes of late, transitioning to an all-day menu of far more reasonable (but still delicious) fare. **Known for:** a prix fixe including an ever-changing plat du jour; sumptuous historic decor dating from the 18th century; one of the city's most romantic restaurants. $ *Average main: €30* ⊠ *17 rue de Beaujolais, 1er, Louvre* ☎ *01–42–96–56–27* ⊕ *www.grand-vefour.com* ⊗ *Closed Sun. and Mon.* Ⓜ *Palais-Royal.*

Macéo

$$$ | MODERN FRENCH | With a reasonably priced set menu, this restaurant from the owners of Willi's Wine Bar is an ideal spot for a relaxed meal after visiting the Louvre. Natural light streams through the interior, and a broad, curved staircase leads to a spacious upstairs salon: the perfect place to enjoy the seasonally motivated menu. **Known for:** convenient to the Louvre and Palais Royal gardens; phenomenal wine list; seasonal French fare with an Italian accent. $ *Average main: €32* ⊠ *15 rue des Petits-Champs, 1er, Louvre* ☎ *01–85–15–22–56* ⊕ *maceorestaurant.com* ⊗ *Closed Sun. and 3 wks in Aug. No lunch Sat.* Ⓜ *Palais-Royal.*

★ Mimosa

$$$$ | FRENCH | Two-Michelin-star chef Jean-Michel Piège takes the Mediterranean Sea as his inspiration in this

beautiful dining room housed in the Hôtel de la Marine. Delicacies from land and sea are perfectly grilled over a wood fire, such as octopus with tiny chickpeas and coriander, a luscious whole grilled lobster, or the catch of the day with fennel fondant and a Menton lemon emulsion. **Known for:** delightful grilled seafood; well-known Parisian chef; romantic setting and terrace. 🟊 *Average main: €45* ✉ *2 rue Royale, 8e, Champs-Élysées* 🕾 *01–53–93–65–52* ⊕ *www.mimosa-rueroyale.com* Ⓜ *Concord, Madeleine.*

★ Restaurant du Palais-Royal

$$$$ | **FRENCH** | This stylish modern bistro serves stunning gourmet cuisine to match its gorgeous location under the arcades of the Palais-Royal. Philip Chronopoulos' menu more than delivers on the promise, with a revered suckling pig centerpiece supported by dishes mainly taking full advantage of exquisite fish and shellfish. **Known for:** baba au rhum that evolves with the seasons; phenomenal tasting menu with wine pairings; Mediterranean-accented choices from a young Greek chef. 🟊 *Average main: €75* ✉ *Jardins du Palais-Royal, 110 Galerie Valois, 1er, Louvre* 🕾 *01–40–20–00–27* ⊕ *www.restaurantdupalaisroyal.com* 🕓 *Closed Sun. and Mon.* Ⓜ *Palais-Royal.*

Willi's Wine Bar

$$ | **MODERN FRENCH** | More restaurant than wine bar, this British-owned spot is a stylish haunt for Parisians and visiting gourmands who might stop in for a glass of wine at the oak bar or settle into the wood-beamed dining room. The selection of reinvented classic dishes from Chef François Yon changes daily and in accordance with the seasons. **Known for:** good-value, three-course, prix-fixe menu; fine choice of wines by the glass; upscale expat hangout. 🟊 *Average main: €20* ✉ *13 rue des Petits-Champs, 1er, Louvre* 🕾 *01–42–61–05–09* ⊕ *www.williswinebar.com* 🕓 *Closed Mon. in Aug. and Sun.* Ⓜ *Bourse.*

★ Yam'Tcha

$$$$ | **FRENCH FUSION** | Dishes here rely on Chinese flavors and very precise technique, and they're paired with teas by the tea sommelier, who introduces diners to earthy or grassy flavors that complement the prix-fixe menus (€70 lunch, €150 dinner). The team also owns nearby Lai'Tcha (7 rue du Jour), which offers exquisite dim sum and takeaway dishes. **Known for:** close to the Louvre and Centre Pompidou; one of Paris's star chefs, Adeline Grattard; rare and unique tea pairings. 🟊 *Average main: €150* ✉ *121 rue St. Honoré, 1er, Louvre* 🕾 *01–40–26–08–07* ⊕ *www.yamtcha.com* 🕓 *Closed weekends. No lunch Mon. and Tues.* Ⓜ *Louvre–Rivoli, Les Halles.*

Zen

$ | **JAPANESE** | There's no shortage of Japanese restaurants around the Louvre, but this one is a cut above much of the competition. The menu has something for every palate, from warming *donburi* to sushi and sashimi. **Known for:** bright, modern space; plentiful seating; good value, especially at lunchtime. 🟊 *Average main: €17* ✉ *8 rue de l'Echelle, 1er, Louvre* 🕾 *01–42–61–93–99* ⊕ *www.restaurantzenparis.fr* 🕓 *Closed 10 days in mid-Aug.* Ⓜ *Pyramides, Palais-Royal.*

🛏 Hotels

With a central location and many attractions—from the stately Palais Royal gardens to a plethora of fine museums—the area around the Louvre is a great place to hang your hat. Hotels here run the gamut from stylishly refurbished 18th-century mansions to colorful and reasonably priced boutique properties.

★ Grand Hotel du Palais Royal

$$$$ | **HOTEL** | Despite its splashy name, this gracious five-star hotel, housed in an 18th-century mansion just steps from the Palais Royal gardens, keeps a surprisingly relaxed profile, its focus less on flagrant luxury and more on the essentials that make a hotel truly grand—service, quality, comfort, refinement, and quiet. **Pros:** wonderful seasonal cuisine indoors and out at Café 52; great location steps from the Louvre and Palais Royal; an island of quiet and calm in a bustling neighborhood. **Cons:** small fitness room; no pool; not all rooms come with balconies. $ *Rooms from: €500* ✉ *4 rue de Valois, Louvre* ☎ *01–42–96–15–35* 🌐 *www.grandhoteldupalaisroyal.com* 🛏 *68 rooms* 🍴 *No Meals* [M] *Palais Royal–Musée du Louvre.*

Hôtel Brighton

$$$ | **HOTEL** | **FAMILY** | A few of the city's most prestigious hotels face the Tuileries or Place de la Concorde, but the 19th-century Brighton occupies the same prime real estate and offers a privileged stay for a less daunting price. **Pros:** convenient central location; great room service in collaboration with local restaurants; friendly service. **Cons:** no restaurant on-site; only half of rooms have a view; some areas in need of repair. $ *Rooms from: €295* ✉ *218 rue de Rivoli, Louvre* ☎ *01–47–03–61–61* 🌐 *www.paris-hotel-brighton.com* 🛏 *62 rooms* 🍴 *No Meals* [M] *Tuileries.*

Hôtel Britannique

$$$ | **HOTEL** | Open since 1861, just a stone's throw from the Louvre and near the banks of the Seine, the romantic Britannique blends courteous English service with old-fashioned French elegance. **Pros:** on calm side street; copious breakfast buffet for a reasonable fee; less than a block from the métro/RER station. **Cons:** decor a bit stodgy; soundproofing could be better; small rooms. $ *Rooms from: €230* ✉ *20 av. Victoria, Louvre* ☎ *01–42–33–74–59* 🌐 *www.hotel-britannique.fr* 🛏 *39 rooms* 🍴 *No Meals* [M] *Châtelet.*

Hôtel Crayon

$$ | **HOTEL** | Managed by artists, this hotel near the Louvre distinguishes itself with an eclectic pop-art decor—expect an unusual canvas of local and international guests that's just as colorful. **Pros:** hand-painted graffiti walls; curated and curious mix of modern objets d'art; very friendly staff. **Cons:** lobby lounge lacks coziness and warmth; basement breakfast area; small bathrooms. $ *Rooms from: €150* ✉ *25 rue du Bouloi, Louvre* ☎ *01–42–36–54–19* 🌐 *www.hotelcrayon.com* 🛏 *26 rooms* 🍴 *No Meals* [M] *Louvre.*

★ **Hôtel de Crillon**

$$$$ | **HOTEL** | One of the city's most historic properties reopened in 2017 after a four-year renovation and is now more sumptuous and majestic than ever. **Pros:** two suites designed by Karl Lagerfeld; beautiful bar with a mile-long Champagne list; well-equipped gym with personal trainers available on request. **Cons:** very expensive; extra beds not available in smaller rooms; small pool with tough-to-find changing rooms. $ *Rooms from: €1300* ✉ *10 pl. de la Concorde, Louvre* ☎ *01–44–71–15–00* 🌐 *www.rosewood-hotels.com* 🛏 *124 rooms* 🍴 *No Meals* [M] *Concorde.*

★ **Hôtel du Continent**

$$ | **HOTEL** | You'd be hard-pressed to find a budget hotel this stylish anywhere in Paris, let alone in an upscale neighborhood close to many of the city's top attractions. **Pros:** very friendly staff; prime Parisian location just steps from Rue St-Honoré, arguably the city's best shopping street; all modern amenities. **Cons:** bold decor not for everyone; tiny bathrooms; no lobby. $ *Rooms from: €167* ✉ *30 rue du Mont-Thabor, Louvre* ☎ *01–42–60–75–32* 🌐 *www.hotelcontinent.com* 🛏 *25 rooms* 🍴 *No Meals* [M] *Concorde, Tuileries.*

Hôtel Konfidentiel

$$$$ | **HOTEL** | **FAMILY** | Sleep beneath the pre-guillotined head of Marie-Antoinette or amid the turmoil of the French Revolution in one of six individually themed rooms, including the Eiffel duplex suite with a stately spiral staircase. **Pros:** terrific location near the Louvre; friendly staff; comfortable, unique rooms. **Cons:**

kitschy decor doesn't suit every taste; no bathtubs in bathrooms; can feel a bit enclosed. $ *Rooms from: €370* ⊠ *64 rue de l'Arbre Sec, Louvre* ☎ *01–55–34–40–40* ⊕ *www.konfidentiel-paris.com* ⇨ *6 rooms* ⊗ *No Meals* Ⓜ *Louvre–Rivoli.*

★ Hôtel La Tamise

$$ | **HOTEL** | In 1878, what was a stately home owned by a noble French family was converted to an intimate hotel favored by aristocrats and, later, fashion icons. **Pros:** location on a quiet street in the heart of Paris; free Mariage Frères teas on arrival; just steps from super-lative shopping. **Cons:** limited views of the Tuileries; no balconies; small lobby. $ *Rooms from: €219* ⊠ *4 rue d'Alger, Louvre* ☎ *01–40–41–14–14* ⊕ *www.paris-hotel-la-tamise.com* ⇨ *19 rooms* ⊗ *No Meals* Ⓜ *Tuileries, Concorde.*

★ Hôtel Le Meurice

$$$$ | **HOTEL** | **FAMILY** | Since 1835, Paris's first palace hotel has welcomed royalty and celebrities from the Duchess of Windsor to Salvador Dalí and continues to enchant with service, style, and views. **Pros:** stunning art and architecture; Michelin-starred dining; views over the Tuileries gardens. **Cons:** very expensive; front-desk service at times inattentive; some amenities lacking like in-room coffee machine. $ *Rooms from: €900* ⊠ *228 rue de Rivoli, Louvre* ☎ *01–44–58–10–09* ⊕ *www.dorchestercollection.com* ⇨ *208 rooms* ⊗ *No Meals* Ⓜ *Tuileries, Concorde.*

Hôtel Le Pradey

$$ | **HOTEL** | This compact boutique hotel near the Tuileries has a luxe feel, paying homage to Parisian style with rooms split between traditional *chambres* and Paris-themed suites like the Louvre and Grand Palais. **Pros:** choice of copious breakfast buffet or quick coffee and crois-sant; Pierre Marcolini chocolates and Hermès and Nuxe toiletries; designer touches throughout. **Cons:** few servic-es; rooms vary greatly in style; smaller rooms lack closet space. $ *Rooms from:*

€200 ⊠ *5 rue St-Roch, Louvre* ☎ *01–42–60–31–70* ⊕ *www.lepradey.com* ⇨ *28 rooms* ⊗ *No Meals* Ⓜ *Tuileries.*

Hôtel Louvre Sainte-Anne

$$ | **HOTEL** | Walk to many major sites from this small, low-key, budget property exceptionally located between the Opéra and the Louvre, and offering rooms decorated in pastel colors with a country theme and little extras like heated towel racks and feather duvets. **Pros:** conven-ient location; reduced-mobility room available; hot-and-cold breakfast buffet (for a fee) served in a stone-vaulted cellar. **Cons:** breakfast area slightly claustro-phobic; district can feel un-Parisian; very small rooms. $ *Rooms from: €155* ⊠ *32 rue Ste-Anne, Louvre* ☎ *01–40–20–02–35* ⊕ *www.paris-hotel-louvre.com* ⇨ *20 rooms* ⊗ *No Meals* Ⓜ *Pyramides.*

Hôtel Thérèse

$$ | **HOTEL** | Tucked away from the traffic and crowds of Avenue de l'Opéra, this five-floor hotel named after the wife of Louis XIV is a stone's throw from regal sites like the Louvre, Palais Royal, and the historic Comédie Française theater. **Pros:** on a quiet street; breakfast (for a fee) can be served in room; cozy, nicely decorated rooms. **Cons:** no restaurant or gym; breakfast area located in basement; rooms are relatively small for price. $ *Rooms from: €180* ⊠ *5/7 rue Thérèse, Louvre* ☎ *01–42–96–10–01* ⊕ *www. hoteltherese.com* ⇨ *40 rooms* ⊗ *No Meals* Ⓜ *Pyramides.*

★ Mandarin Oriental Paris

$$$$ | **HOTEL** | Of Paris's palace hotels, the Mandarin Oriental is among the most contemporary, with a soaring marble entryway and a sleek, luxe style that is a welcome contrast to the historic grande dames. **Pros:** superlative hotel spa (con-tender for Paris's very best); two gourmet restaurants helmed by Michelin-starred chef Thierry Marx and in-house pastry shop; many rooms with terraces. **Cons:** very pricey; noise from courtyard during special events; not much variation in

Apartment Rentals

If you favor extra space plus that special feeling of living like a local, try renting a Paris apartment. Rentals can also offer savings, especially for groups.

Check out the **Paris Tourism Office** website (⊕ en.parisinfo.com) for reputable agency listings. Policies differ, but you can expect a minimum required stay ranging from three to seven days, a refundable deposit payable on arrival, a possible agency fee, and maid and linen service. The following is a list of property hunters, good-value and luxury apartments, and apartment services.

Paris Perfect (⊕ parisperfect.com) manages more than 100 apartments in varying sizes around Paris, mostly on the Left Bank in the upscale 7e arrondissement. Many apartments, which are designed to feel like your very own chic *pied-à-terre*, have Eiffel Tower views. Luxury services, like concierge and gourmet food tours, are often available. **Cattalan Johnson** (⊕ cattalanjohnson.com) is an established, fee-based agency specializing in rental properties. The multilingual staff has a citywide inventory of thousands of furnished apartments available for durations ranging from one week to a few years. **Citadines Apart Hotel** (☎ 01–41–05–79–05; ⊕ citadines.com) is a chain of apartment-style hotel accommodations. They're somewhat generic but offer many services and are a good value for short stays. Well-established **Home Rental** (☎ 01–42–25–65–40; ⊕ home-rental.com) doesn't charge agency fees and rents everything from studios to six-bedroom units on a short- (one-week minimum) or long-term basis, all furnished. Maid service, cable, and Wi-Fi are included. **Lodgis Paris** (☎ 01–70–39–11–11; ⊕ lodgis.com/en) has one of the largest inventories in Paris; note, however, that the agency fee makes it cheaper *per diem* to rent for more than one week. **Paris Attitude** (☎ 01–42–96–31–46; ⊕ pari-sattitude.com) offers a large selection of furnished rentals, from studios to five-bedroom units, for stays from a week to a year. **Paris Vacation Apartments** (☎ 06–63–60–67–14; ⊕ parisvacationapartments.com) specializes in luxury rentals, with all-inclusive prices by the week. **Paris-Hospitality** (☎ 01–47–83–75–91; ⊕ paris-hospitality.com) lists more than 350 units in prime locations throughout Paris for short- or long-term visits. Concierge services are available.

standard rooms. [$] *Rooms from: €1250* ✉ *251 rue St-Honore, Louvre* ☎ *01–70–98–78–88* ⊕ *www.mandarinoriental.com/paris* 🛏 *135 rooms* 🍽 *No Meals* Ⓜ *Tuileries, Concorde.*

Meliá Vendôme
$$ | HOTEL | In a prestigious neighborhood a few minutes from the Jardin des Tuileries, Place de la Concorde, Opéra Garnier, and the Louvre, the Meliá Vendôme has handsome and spacious rooms that exude understated elegance. **Pros:** outstanding location in the city center; elegant, immaculate rooms; near world-class shopping. **Cons:** in-room cooling system unreliable; no spa or pool; expensive breakfast. [$] *Rooms from: €222* ✉ *8 rue Cambon, Louvre* ☎ *01–44–77–54–00* ⊕ *www.melia.com* 🛏 *83 rooms* 🍽 *No Meals* Ⓜ *Concorde, Madeleine.*

★ Renaissance Paris Vendôme
$$$$ | HOTEL | FAMILY | Hiding behind a classic, 19th-century facade is this fresh, 1930s-influenced hotel, which

was fully remodeled in 2018 by designer Didier Gomez. **Pros:** light-drenched suite and patio rooms with private terraces; full-service spa and fitness room; trendy restaurant with Mediterranean-accented cuisine and 24-hour room service. **Cons:** packed with business groups; public lounges noisy at times; lacks authentic French character. $ *Rooms from: €450* ⊠ *4 rue du Mont Thabor, Louvre* ☎ *01–40–20–20–00* ⊕ *www.marriott.com* 📢 *97 rooms* ⊙ *No Meals* Ⓜ *Tuileries.*

★ The Ritz

$$$$ | **HOTEL** | In novels, songs, and common parlance, there's not a word that evokes the romance and luxury of Paris better than the Ritz. **Pros:** spacious swimming pool; top-notch service; superlative selection of bars and restaurants including a fantastic pastry counter. **Cons:** astronomical prices; paparazzi magnet; easy to get lost in the vast hotel. $ *Rooms from: €1000* ⊠ *15 pl. Vendôme, Louvre* ☎ *01–43–16–30–30* ⊕ *www.ritzparis.com* 📢 *143 rooms* ⊙ *No Meals* Ⓜ *Opéra.*

🌙 Nightlife

The cocktail craze has taken off in this atmospheric neighborhood, where dusky speakeasies and cozy hotel bars provide the perfect prelude to an evening of jazz or dancing until dawn at hip all-night clubs. The area is also known for a plethora of both classic and trendy wine bars, offering everything from essential old-world vintages to contemporary natural bottles.

BARS

Bar 8

BARS | Ever since the monolithic marble bar at the Mandarin Oriental Hotel opened its doors, it has been the "in" game in town. There's an extensive Champagne list and an internationally inspired menu of bar snacks. The outdoor terrace is especially busy during Fashion Weeks. ⊠ *251 rue St-Honoré, 1er, Louvre* ☎ *01–70–98–78–88* ⊕ *www.*

mandarinoriental.com Ⓜ *Concorde, Tuileries.*

Bar 228

BARS | Hôtel Le Meurice converted its ground-floor Fontainebleau library into the intimate Bar 228, with wood paneling and huge murals depicting the royal hunting forests of Fontainebleau. Its loyal fashion crowd is continually wooed by Philippe Starck's decor updates and lubricated with the bar's famous Bellinis. Try the Meurice Millennium cocktail, made with Champagne, rose liqueur, and Cointreau. ⊠ *228 rue de Rivoli, 1er, Louvre* ☎ *01–44–58–10–66* ⊕ *www.dorchester-collection.com* Ⓜ *Tuileries.*

★ Bar Hemingway & the Ritz Bar

BARS | Literature lovers, cocktail connoisseurs, and other drink-swilling devotees flock to these two iconic bars within the Ritz Hotel. A $400 million renovation happily didn't alter the chill vibe or the wood-paneled, club-chair decor of tiny Bar Hemingway, where mixologist mainstay and twice-named "Best Head Barman in the World" Colin Field will fix you a bespoke cocktail. Try the Serendipity, the bar's most popular drink, combining Champagne with Calvados and mint. Across the elegant corridor, the more spacious Ritz Bar's 2021 renovation paved the way for an astrologically themed experience. In a style evoking Belle Époque Paris, the space's circular bar is topped by a monumental lantern whose projection of stars and constellations begins each evening at 5:30 exactly. Signature cocktails continue the zodiac theme, with creations for each astrological sign, as well as a menu of spirits, wines, and shared small plates. Electro music from French DJs Polo and Pan was specifically created for the space. ⊠ *15 pl. Vendôme, 1er, Louvre* ☎ *01–43–16–33–74* ⊕ *www.ritzparis.com* Ⓜ *Opéra.*

★ Experimental Cocktail Club

BARS | Fashioned as a speakeasy on a tiny brick-paved street, this was one of the first bars to bring the cocktail revolution to Paris. Colorful, innovative, and ever-changing drinks are mixed with aplomb by friendly (and attractive) bartenders. By 11 pm, the bar is always packed with a mix of locals, professionals, and fashionistas. ⊠ *37 rue St-Sauveur, 2e, Louvre* ☎ *01–45–08–88–09,* ⊕ *www.experimentalgroup.com* Ⓜ *Réamur–Sébastopol.*

Jefrey's

BARS | A custom-DJ'd soundtrack, enticing love seats, and truly inventive cocktails make this an easy choice for an intimate evening in sophisticated surroundings. Need further incentive to return? Jefrey's lets you keep your bottle stored on the shelf, with your name on it, for next time. ⊠ *14 rue St-Sauveur, 2e, Louvre* ☎ *01–42–33–60–77* Ⓜ *Étienne Marcel.*

L'Assaggio Bar

BARS | At this gracious bar and tea salon in the Hôtel Castille (Coco Chanel's old stomping grounds), enjoy a selection of French and Italian wines, a glass of Champagne, or one of a few signature cocktails alongside a short-and-sweet bar menu of Italian-accented nibbles. ⊠ *37 rue Cambon, 1er, Louvre* ☎ *01–44–58–44–58* ⊕ *www.castille.com* Ⓜ *Concorde, Madeleine.*

Le Café Noir

BARS | Parisians from *bobos* (bourgeois-bohemians) to *pompiers* (firefighters) are lured to Le Café Noir's elegantly worn digs for organic coffee during the day or a glass of natural wine come evening. In addition to cool drinks and friendly staff, the place features a pipe-smoking papier-mâché fish and a vintage leopard-print-covered motorbike. On weekends, a DJ spins electro or funk. (The restaurant with the same name is unrelated.) ⊠ *65 rue Montmartre, 2e, Louvre* ☎ *01–40–39–07–36* Ⓜ *Étienne Marcel.*

Le Garde-Robe

WINE BARS | One of the first bars to bring natural wine to the capital, Le Garde-Robe unites a casual atmosphere and truly knowledgeable staff. Order a platter of cheese or charcuterie to accompany your sulfite-free bottles. ⊠ *41 rue de l'Arbre-Sec, Louvre* ☎ *01–49–26–90–60* ⊕ *www.legarderobe.fr* Ⓜ *Louvre–Rivoli.*

★ Les Ambassadeurs

PIANO BARS | The ultimate in elegance, Les Ambassadeurs, located within the magnificent Hôtel de Crillon, is perhaps the closest you'll come to experiencing the royal treatment in a real palace—it was built by order of Louis XV in 1758. Sink into one of the cozy armchairs and enjoy a *coupe* of Champagne from a list as long as the marble walls are high, or select one of a curated list of signature cocktails. All the right touches are preserved, including a frescoed ceiling adorned with twinkling chandeliers and gilt—lots of it. Live music accompanies your evening Thursday through Saturday starting at 8. ⊠ *10 pl. de la Concorde, Louvre* ☎ *01–44–71–15–00* ⊕ *www. rosewoodhotels.com* Ⓜ *Concorde.*

CLUBS

Kong

DANCE CLUBS | This bar is glorious not only for its panoramic skyline views but also for its manga-inspired decor and kooky, disco-ball-and-kid-sumo-adorned bathrooms. A menu of Japanese-inspired fare is offered at the rooftop restaurant, and top-shelf DJs keep patrons dancing on weekends. Valet parking is available starting at 7:30 pm. ⊠ *1 rue du Pont Neuf, 1er, Louvre* ☎ *01–40–39–09–00* ⊕ *www.kong.fr* Ⓜ *Pont Neuf.*

JAZZ CLUBS

Duc des Lombards

LIVE MUSIC | The Duc's cozy interior and top-class jazz acts make this iconic club one of the city's most popular small venues. It's best to purchase advance tickets online or arrive early to guarantee a spot at the twice-nightly concerts at 7:30 and

10. Jam sessions Friday and Saturday begin at midnight and last until 4 am. ⊠ *42 rue des Lombards, 1er, Louvre* ☏ *01–42–33–22–88* ⊕ *www.ducdeslombards.com* Ⓜ *Châtelet–Les Halles.*

Sunset-Sunside

LIVE MUSIC | This two-part club hosts French and American jazz musicians: the Sunside upstairs is devoted mostly to acoustic jazz, while the Sunset downstairs features everything from electronic jazz, fusion, and groove to classic and swing. Jam sessions have been known to last well into the wee hours. ⊠ *60 rue des Lombards, 1er, Louvre* ☏ *01–40–26–46–60* ⊕ *www.sunset-sunside.com* Ⓜ *Châtelet–Les Halles.*

WINE BARS

Ô Château

WINE BARS | This wine bar–cum–tasting space is the go-to for Anglophones wanting to deepen their wine knowledge and refine their palates. With more than 1,000 options, it's ideal for sampling the best French vintages. Classes in wine tasting are offered, starting at €69 for an hour-long "Tour de France" in English, with more in-depth options available. Although the restaurant is closed Sunday and Monday, tastings are available daily. ⊠ *68 rue Jean-Jacques Rousseau, Les Halles* ☏ *1–44–73–97–80* ⊕ *www.o-chateau.com* Ⓜ *Etienne-Marcel.*

Les Caves du Louvre

WINE BARS | This 18th-century wine cellar was built by Trudon, the sommelier to King Louis XV, and tastings here are truly an experience fit for royalty. Book your experience, which can include a tour or wine-and-cheese workshop, online in advance. ⊠ *52 rue de l'Arbre Sec, Louvre* ☏ *01–40–28–13–11* ⊕ *www.cavesdulouvre.com* Ⓜ *Louvre-Rivoli.*

🎭 Performing Arts

★ Comédie Française

THEATER | Founded in 1680, the Comédie Française is the most hallowed institution in French theater. It specializes in splendid classical French plays by the likes of Racine, Molière, and Marivaux. Buy tickets at the box office, by telephone, or online. If the theater is sold out, the Salle Richelieu offers steeply discounted last-minute tickets an hour before each performance. ⊠ *Salle Richelieu, Pl. Colette, 1er, Louvre* ☏ *01–44–58–15–15* ⊕ *www.comedie-francaise.fr* Ⓜ *Palais-Royal–Musée du Louvre.*

Le Forum des Images

FILM | The Forum organizes thematic viewings in five state-of-the-art screening rooms, often presenting discussions with directors or film experts beforehand. Archival films and videos, workshops, and lectures are also on the schedule here. Movie tickets cost €7 (€9 for virtual reality Saturdays), but roundtables, discussions, and access to the film library are free; you can also download the Forum app for smartphones. ⊠ *Forum des Halles, 2 rue du Cinéma, Louvre* ☏ *01–44–76–63–00* ⊕ *www.forumdesimages.fr* Ⓜ *Châtelet–Les Halles (St-Eustache exit).*

Théâtre du Palais-Royal

THEATER | **FAMILY** | Located in the former residence of Cardinal Richelieu, this plush, 716-seat, Italian-style theater is bedecked in gold and purple. It specializes in lighter fare, like comedies and theatrical productions aimed at the under-12 set. ⊠ *38 rue de Montpensier, 1er, Louvre* ☏ *01–42–97–59–76* ⊕ *theatrepalaisroyal.com* Ⓜ *Palais-Royal.*

🛍 Shopping

The flagship stores of big luxury brands rub elbows here with independent boutiques and concept stores notable for their fashion cachet. The fabulous Rue St-Honoré—a bastion of Parisian chic—is the area's retail spine, but the Marché St-Honoré and the Faubourg provide tempting detours. Whatever you do, don't miss the gorgeous Palais-Royal gardens, where flashy fashion stars mix with the discreet purveyors of handmade gloves.

BEAUTY
Anne Sémonin
SKINCARE | This boutique with its own spa sells tailor-made skin-care products popular with top models. Products feature seaweed and trace elements, as well as essential oils. ⊠ 2 rue des Petits-Champs, 2e, Louvre ☎ 01–42–60–94–66 ⊕ www.annesemonin.com Ⓜ Palais-Royal–Louvre.

Annick Goutal
PERFUME | Annick Goutal sells its own line of signature scents, which come packaged in gilded gauze purses. Gardenia, Passion, Petite Chérie, and l'Eau d'Hadrien are perennial favorites. ⊠ 14 rue de Castiglione, 1er, Louvre ☎ 01–42–60–52–82 ⊕ www.annickgoutal.com Ⓜ Concorde.

By Terry
COSMETICS | This small, refined store is the brainchild of Terry de Gunzburg, Yves Saint Laurent's former director of makeup, whose brand of ready-to-wear cosmetics is a favorite among French actresses and socialites. Upstairs, specialists create what de Gunzburg calls haute couleur, exclusive makeup tailored to each client (it's very expensive, and takes three weeks to create). ⊠ 36 Galerie Véro-Dodat, 1er, Louvre ☎ 01–44–76–00–76 ⊕ www.byterry.com Ⓜ Palais-Royal–Louvre.

★ Guerlain
PERFUME | The world's oldest perfumer has a gorgeous Parisian flagship store, just blocks from its very first shop founded by Pierre-François Guerlain in 1828. The outpost is a sumptuous affair and offers more personalized services and customization than ever before. A tablet helps you define your olfactory profile, and experts are on hand to guide you through a private consultation in a special room decked out in blushing velvets; or you can have a private consultation with a house "nose" to design your own fragrance. If those options are out of your price range (as they are for most mortals), you can still personalize any of the perfumer's 110 fragrances from the "perfume bar," choosing from several crystal bottles and selecting the color of your label and ribbons. ⊠ 356 rue St-Honoré, 1er, Louvre ☎ 01–42–60–68–61 ⊕ www.guerlain.com Ⓜ Tuileries, Pyramides.

Jovoy
PERFUME | Representing 100 artisanal perfumers, Jovoy is the largest independent purveyor of fragrances in the world—indeed, the brand calls itself the "embassy of rare perfumes." Owner François Hénin is often on hand expounding on the unique qualities and fascinating histories of different fragrances, some of which date back hundreds of years, and many that are exclusive to the boutique. The shop also carries fragrances for the home and a range of beautifully packaged scented candles. ⊠ 4 rue de Castiglione, 1er, Louvre ☎ 01–40–20–06–19 ⊕ www.jovoyparis.com Ⓜ Tuileries, Concorde.

★ Les Salons du Palais-Royal Serge Lutens
PERFUME | Every year, Serge Lutens dreams up two new fragrances, which are then sold exclusively in this boutique. Each is compellingly original, from the strong somptueux scents (often with musk and amber notes) to intense florals (Rose de Nuit). Bottles can be etched and personalized for gifts. The shop itself boasts a beautiful spiral staircase. ⊠ Jardins du Palais-Royal, 142 Galerie de Valois, 1er, Louvre ☎ 01–49–27–09–09 ⊕ www.sergelutens.com Ⓜ Palais-Royal–Louvre.

BOOKS AND STATIONERY
Librairie Galignani
BOOKS | Dating to 1520s Venice, this venerable bookstore opened in Paris in 1801 and was the first to specialize in English-language books. Its present location, across from the Tuileries Garden on Rue de Rivoli, opened in 1856, and the

wooden bookshelves, creaking floors, and hushed interior provide the perfect atmosphere for perusing Paris's best collection of contemporary and classic greats in English and French, plus a huge selection of gorgeous art books. ✉ *224 rue de Rivoli, 1er, Louvre* ☎ *01–42–60–76–07* ⊕ *www.galignani.com* ☽ *Closed Sun.* Ⓜ *Tuileries.*

Smith&Son

BOOKS | This bookseller formerly associated with chain WHSmith has stepped out on its own with this newer, independent shop that remains a must-visit for Anglophone bibliophiles, with a multitude of travel and language guides, cookbooks, and fiction for adults and children. It also has the best selection of foreign magazines and newspapers in Paris. Upstairs, enjoy a delightful afternoon tea in George Washington's former Paris apartment. ✉ *248 rue de Rivoli, 1er, Louvre* ☎ *01–53–45–84–40* ⊕ *www.smithandson.com* Ⓜ *Concorde.*

CLOTHING

★ Acne Studios

MIXED CLOTHING | Justly famous for its sexy, derriere-shaping jeans, this Swedish label daringly mixes genders and genres in body-hugging or oversized, asymmetrical styles that rival some of the best catwalk looks. Standout shoes, boots, and accessories—all exhibiting the brand's underplayed cool—are sold here too. ✉ *124 Galerie de Valois, 1er, Louvre* ☎ *01–42–60–16–62* ⊕ *www.acnestudios. com* Ⓜ *Palais-Royal–Louvre.*

agnès b.

MIXED CLOTHING | This shop embodies the quintessential French approach to easy but stylish dressing. There are many branches, and the clothes are also sold in department stores, but for the fullest range go to Rue du Jour, where agnès takes up much of the street (women's and children's wear are at No. 6, menswear at No. 3). For women, classics include sleek black leather jackets, flattering black jersey separates, and

trademark wide-stripe T-shirts. Children love the two-tone T-shirts proclaiming their age. And the stormy-gray velour or corduroy suits you see on those slouchy, scarf-clad men? agnès b. ✉ *3 and 6 rue du Jour, 1er, Louvre* ☎ *01–45–08–56–56* ⊕ *www.agnesb.eu* Ⓜ *Châtelet–Les Halles.*

★ Alexander McQueen

MIXED CLOTHING | The Paris flagship of this lauded label, whose global fame only skyrocketed with the design of the Duchess of Cambridge's wedding gown, is glorious to behold. The late McQueen's hallmarks—tons of lace, gossamer fabrics, tartans, death's heads, and voluminous silhouettes—are all lavishly on display. But, while staying true to McQueen's vision, creative director Sarah Burton isn't as intent on pushing the boundaries as she is on creating her own magic in lavish gowns and dramatic ready-to-wear attire. Shoes, accessories, and surprisingly affordable jewelry to go with the garments are available as well. ✉ *372 rue St-Honoré, 1er, Louvre* ☎ *01–70–80–78–00* ⊕ *www.alexander-mcqueen.com* Ⓜ *Tuileries.*

& Other Stories

MIXED CLOTHING | H&M's upscale "style lab" covers all the major fashion bases, appealing to women of different tastes and ages. Unlike the minimalist COS—another H&M spawn—& Other Stories offers the kind of au courant looks and well-made basics that are beloved by urban sophisticates who wouldn't be caught dead buying the parent brand but still want style on a budget. The shoe collection downstairs is a serious draw all on its own. Accessories, lingerie, and makeup are also available. ✉ *277 rue St-Honoré, 8e, Louvre* ☎ *01–76–77–56–20* ⊕ *www.stories.com* Ⓜ *Concorde.*

★ Chloé

WOMEN'S CLOTHING | Much like the clothes it sells, Chloé's flagship boutique is softly feminine and modern without being stark. Housed in an 18th-century mansion, its creamy marble floors, gold sconces, and walls in the brand's signature rosy beige are the perfect backdrop for designer Clare Waight Keller's beautifully tailored yet fluid designs. Shoppers are met with the kind of sincere attention that is all but extinct in most high-end Paris shops. Whether it's for a handbag or a whole new wardrobe, VIP rooms and professional stylists are available to assist anyone who calls for an appointment. ⊠ *253 rue St-Honoré, 1er, Louvre* ☎ *01–55–04–03–30* ⊕ *www.chloe.com* Ⓜ *Franklin D. Roosevelt.*

★ Didier Ludot

WOMEN'S CLOTHING | The incredibly charming Didier Ludot inspired a fervent craze for vintage couture, and rifling through his racks of well-preserved, French-made pieces from the '20s to the '80s can yield wonderful Chanel suits, Balenciaga dresses, and Hermès scarves. You may even see one of these Oscar-worthy hand-me-downs swishing along a red carpet. Ludot has two adjacent boutiques in Galerie Montpensier: No. 20 houses his amazing vintage couture collection, while No. 24 has vintage ready-to-wear and accessories. ⊠ *Jardins du Palais-Royal, 20–24 Galerie Montpensier, 1er, Louvre* ☎ *01–42–96–06–56* ⊕ *www.didierludot.fr* Ⓜ *Palais-Royal–Musée du Louvre.*

Gabrielle Geppert

WOMEN'S CLOTHING | Gabrielle Geppert's unique boutique shop takes its inspiration from 20th-century fashion's greatest hits. One part luxury vintage and one part Geppert's eponymous brand, her Palais Royal shop has it all. ⊠ *32–33 Galerie Montpensier, 1er, Louvre* ☎ *01–42–61–53–52* Ⓜ *Palais-Royal–Musée du Louvre.*

Loris Azzaro

WOMEN'S CLOTHING | When Azzaro saw his 1970s designs, now collector's items, worn by stars like Nicole Kidman and Kate Winslet, he decided to update his bestsellers. He's a master of the dramatic dress: picture floor-length columns with jeweled collars and sheer gowns with strategically placed sequins. ⊠ *65 rue de Faubourg St-Honoré, 8e, Louvre* ☎ *08–93–02–53–54* ⊕ *www.azzaro-couture.com* Ⓜ *Concorde.*

★ Louis Vuitton

MIXED CLOTHING | The Paris-based luxury leather goods and fashion house par excellence is resplendent in an 18th-century mansion on the elegant Place Vendôme. Part fashion boutique and part art gallery, this impeccably restored locale retains the original woodwork, gilding, and stone, adding contemporary chrome, glass, and colorful works from more than 30 contemporary artists and sculptors. Covering three floors, the grand Place Vendôme store offers the entire Vuitton collection, including high-end jewelry and watches, bags and accessories, fashion, luggage, and some fabulous home furnishings on the top floor. ⊠ *2 pl. Vendôme, 1er, Louvre* ☎ *09–77–40–40–77* ⊕ *www.louisvuitton. com* Ⓜ *Concorde.*

Maison Martin Margiela

MIXED CLOTHING | This famously elusive Belgian designer has earned a devoted following for his avant-garde styling and his innovative technique, from spiraling seams to deconstructed shirts. Women's fashion is sold at 28 rue de Richelieu, menswear at No. 26. ⊠ *26 and 28 rue de Richelieu, 1er, Louvre* ☎ *01–40–15–07–55* ⊕ *www.maisonmartinmargiela.fr* Ⓜ *Palais-Royal–Musée du Louvre.*

Miu Miu

MIXED CLOTHING | This Faubourg St-Honoré boutique dispenses with Miu Miu's Modernist ethos in favor of a Neo-Baroque sensibility—and it influences everything from the velvet wallpaper to, perhaps, a lavish pair of ruby slippers. Although the shoes and accessories scream glitz, the clothes still have a sleek refinement, with the designer's notorious tension between minimalism and opulence. ⊠ *1 rue du Faubourg St-Honoré, 8e, Louvre* ☎ *01–58–62–53–20* ⊕ *www.miumiu.com* Ⓜ *Concorde.*

Rick Owens

MIXED CLOTHING | Rick Owens expertly finessed the jump from L.A. rock-star chic to Paris offbeat elegance. Lately defined more by glamour than grunge, his lush fabrics and asymmetrical designs have evolved to a new level of artistry—and wearability. Owens still loves a paradox (shrouding while revealing) and mixes high luxury with a bit of the tooth and the claw. You'll also find shoes, furs, jewelry, and accessories. ✉ *130–133 Galerie de Valois, 1er, Louvre* ☎ *01–40–20–42–52* ⊕ *www.rickowens.eu* Ⓜ *Palais-Royal–Musée du Louvre.*

Saint Laurent

MIXED CLOTHING | Yves Saint Laurent revolutionized women's wear in the 1970s, putting pants in couture shows for the first time. His safari jackets, "le smoking" suits, Russian-boho collections, and tailored *Belle de Jour* suits are considered fashion landmarks. Taking the helm in 2012, Hedi Slimane caused a major stir, renaming the brand, moving its headquarters, and bringing his own street-smart L.A. chic while nose-tweaking fashion journalists. In the ever-evolving game of musical chairs shaking up the major fashion houses, Anthony Vaccarello took the reins in 2017, keeping the sexy, street-smart look and adding his signature razor-sharp styling with plenty of metallics, feathers, and beading. ✉ *38 rue du Faubourg St-Honoré, 8e, Louvre* ☎ *01–42–65–74–59* ⊕ *www.ysl.com* Ⓜ *Concorde.*

DEPARTMENT STORES

★ Samaritaine

DEPARTMENT STORE | After standing empty for 16 years, the Samaritaine department store finally reopened in 2021 following an ambitious renovation by new owners LVMH. The space dating to 1870 retains many of its Art Deco details, including its beautiful facade overlooking the Seine, and is also now home to the city's Cheval Blanc hotel. You can enter the store via Rue de la Monnaie, encountering labels from more than 600 fashion brands, including Alexander McQueen, Balenciaga, Stella McCartney, and Moschino. The new Samaritaine is also home to a spa and several eateries, including a gorgeous fifth-floor restaurant, Voyage, where you can dine on seasonal, international dishes beneath the department store's beautiful glass roof. ✉ *19 Rue de la Monnaie, Louvre* ☎ *01–88–88–60–00* ⊕ *www.dfs.com* Ⓜ *Pont-Neuf.*

FOOD AND TREATS

Jean-Paul Hévin

CHOCOLATE | Forty masterful varieties of chocolate and some of the best pastries in Paris earned Jean-Paul Hévin his world-class chocolatier status. Devotees will be pleased to know that there are several other outposts in the capital, including one nearby at 108 rue St-Honoré. ✉ *231 rue St-Honoré, 1er, Louvre* ☎ *01–55–35–35–96* ⊕ *www.jeanpaulhevin.com* Ⓜ *Tuileries.*

Ladurée

FOOD | Founded in 1862, Ladurée oozes period atmosphere—even at the big Champs-Élysées branch (No. 75)—but nothing beats the original tearoom on Rue Royale, with its pint-size tables and frescoed ceiling. Ladurée claims a familial link to the invention of the *macaron*, so it's no surprise that there's a huge selection on offer. Unfortunately, service has lagged at all three of the tearooms in recent years, and the crowded space feels more like an ersatz tourist destination than the historic tearoom that it is. Still, Ladurée's stylish boxes make memorable, delicious gifts. ✉ *16 rue Royale, 8e, Louvre* ☎ *01–42–60–21–79* ⊕ *www.laduree.com* Ⓜ *Madeleine.*

★ Terroirs d'Avenir

FOOD | This shop has been at the heart of the Parisian locavore movement since 2008, when it began uniting innovative chefs with small local producers. Today, Terroirs d'Avenir also caters to individuals, with no fewer than five shops on the tiny Rue du Nil: a bakery (No. 3), butcher shop (No. 6), cheesemonger (No. 8), greengrocer (No. 7), and fishmonger (No. 8). Even if you're not planning a purchase, the picturesque cobbled street is worth a stop for a photo op. ⊠ *7 rue du Nil, 2e, Louvre* ☏ *01–84–79–88–07* ⊕ *www.terroirs-avenir.fr* Ⓜ *Sentier.*

HOME DECOR
A. Simon
HOUSEWARES | Parisian chefs have been coming here for their kitchen needs for more than a century—from plates and glasses to pans and wooden spoons. The shop also offers a great selection of white porcelain. ⊠ *48-52 rue Montmartre, 2e, Louvre* ☏ *01–42–33–71–65* Ⓜ *Étienne Marcel.*

Astier de Villatte
HOUSEWARES | Come here for tongue-in-chic interpretations of 18th-century table settings and furniture; live out your Baroque or Empire fancies with milk-white china sets and lots of mahogany. Moody candles and incense complete the atmosphere. ⊠ *173 rue St-Honoré, 1er, Louvre* ☏ *01–42–60–74–13* ⊕ *www. astierdevillatte.com* Ⓜ *Tuileries.*

★ E. Dehillerin
HOUSEWARES | Never mind the creaky stairs: E. Dehillerin has been around for almost 200 years and clearly knows its business. The huge range of professional cookware in enamel, stainless steel, and fiery copper is gorgeous; rely on the knowledgeable staff to locate specific items in the vast expanse of this store. During her years in Paris, Julia Child was a regular. ⊠ *18–20 rue Coquillière, 1er, Louvre* ☏ *01–42–36–53–13* ⊕ *www. edehillerin.fr* Ⓜ *Les Halles.*

JEWELRY AND ACCESSORIES
Dary's
JEWELRY & WATCHES | This family-run cavern teeming with artists, actors, models, and jewelry lovers offers an Ali Baba–ish shopping experience. You'll need to take your time, as the walls are filled with row upon row of antique jewels from every era, as well as more modern secondhand

jewelry and vintage one-of-a-kinds. ⊠ *362 rue St-Honoré, 1er, Louvre* ☏ *01–42–60–95–23* ⊕ *www.darys-bijouterie-paris.fr* Ⓜ *Tuileries.*

LINGERIE
★ Alice Cadolle
LINGERIE | Selling lingerie to Parisians since 1889, Alice Cadolle offers some of the city's most sumptuous couture undergarments. Ready-to-wear bras, corsets, and sleepwear fill this eponymous boutique. ⊠ *4 rue Cambon, 1er, Louvre* ☏ *01–42–60–94–22* ⊕ *www.cadolle.com* Ⓜ *Concorde.*

MARKETS
★ Rue du Nil
MARKET | Just steps from the popular market street Rue Montorgueil, this diminutive passage has become a foodie mecca ever since Frenchie chef Grégory Marchand set up shop here in 2009. Not only is the street home to Marchand's Michelin-starred restaurant (No. 5), wine bar (No. 6), to-go shop (No. 9), and wine cellar (No. 9), but it also features five shops from locavore trendsetters Terroirs d'Avenir peddling everything from cheese (No. 8) to produce (No. 7) to baked goods (No. 3). Chocoholics won't want to miss Plaq at No. 4 selling exquisite single-origin chocolates, cakes, and hot cocoa. ⊠ *Rue du Nil, 2e, Louvre* Ⓜ *Sentier.*

SHOES, HANDBAGS, AND LEATHER GOODS
Christian Louboutin
SHOES | These shoes carry their own red carpet with them thanks to their trademark crimson soles. Whether tasseled, embroidered, or strappy, in Charvet silk or shiny patent leather, the heels are always perfectly balanced. No wonder they set off such legendary legs as Tina Turner's and Gwyneth Paltrow's. The men's shop is next door at No. 17, while No. 21 is home to a leather goods outpost. ⊠ *19 rue Jean-Jacques Rousseau, 1er, Louvre* ☏ *08–00–94–58–04* ⊕ *www. christianlouboutin.com* Ⓜ *Palais-Royal–Musée du Louvre.*

Goyard

HANDBAGS | These colorful totes are the choice of royals, blue bloods, and the like (clients have included Sir Arthur Conan Doyle, Gregory Peck, and the Duke and Duchess of Windsor). Parisians swear by their durability and longevity; they're large enough to transport a baguette and durable enough for a magnum of Champagne. Dog owners won't want to miss the "Le Chic du Chien" boutique farther down at No. 352. ⊠ *233 rue St-Honoré, 1er, Louvre* ☎ *09–73–87–45–60* ⊕ *www. goyard.com* Ⓜ *Tuileries.*

★ Hermès

OTHER ACCESSORIES | The go-to for those who prefer their logo discreet yet still crave instant recognition, Hermès was established as a saddlery in 1837, then went on to create the eternally chic Kelly (named for Grace Kelly) and Birkin (named for Jane Birkin) handbags. The silk scarves are legendary, known for their rich colors and intricate designs, which change yearly. Other accessories are also extremely covetable: enamel bracelets, dashing silk-twill ties, and small leather goods. During semiannual sales, in January and July, prices are slashed by up to 50%, and the crowds line up for blocks. ⊠ *24 rue du Faubourg St-Honoré, 8e, Louvre* ☎ *01–40–17–46– 00* ⊕ *www.hermes.com* ☉ *Closed Sun.* Ⓜ *Concorde.*

Lancaster

HANDBAGS | A household name in France for 100 years, Lancaster has a reputation for style and craftsmanship. Its bags are chic and sporty, with an emphasis on practicality, and all the classic models are available in this spaceship-modern boutique. Look for the popular cross-body Besace bag (it's made of patent leather or soft cowhide and comes in a rainbow of colors). ⊠ *422 rue St-Honoré, 8e, Louvre* ☎ *01–42–28–88–88* ⊕ *www. lancaster.com* Ⓜ *Concorde.*

Maison Fabre

HATS & GLOVES | Until you've eased on an exquisite pair of gloves handcrafted by Fabre, you probably haven't experienced the sensation of having a second skin far superior to your own. Founded in 1924, this historic *gantier* is known for styles ranging from classic to haute: picture elbow-length croc leather, coyote-fur mittens, and peccary driving gloves. ⊠ *128–129 Galerie de Valois, Louvre* ☎ *01–42–60–75–88* ⊕ *www.maisonfabre. com* Ⓜ *Palais-Royal–Musée du Louvre.*

Pierre Hardy

SHOES | With Vivier and Louboutin, Pierre Hardy completes the triumvirate of anointed Paris shoe designers. Armed with a pedigree—Dior, Hermès, Balenciaga—Hardy opened his own boutique in 2003 and made serious waves. The luxe bags are ever popular, and the shoes are unmistakable: sky-scraping platforms and wedges or demure kitten heels double as sculpture with breathtaking details and luscious colors. ⊠ *Palais-Royal Gardens, 156 Galerie de Valois, 1er, Louvre* ☎ *01–42–60–59–75* ⊕ *www.pierrehardy. com* Ⓜ *Palais-Royal–Musée du Louvre.*

Roger Vivier

SHOES | Long known for his Pilgrim-buckle shoes and inventive heels, Roger Vivier's name is being resurrected through the creativity of über-Parisienne Inès de la Fressange and the expertise of shoe designer Gherardo Felloni. The results are easily some of the best shoes in town: leather boots that mold to the calf perfectly, towering rhinestone-encrusted or feathered platforms for evening, and vertiginous crocodile pumps. ⊠ *29 rue du Faubourg St-Honoré, 8e, Louvre* ☎ *01–53–43–00–85* ⊕ *www.rogervivier. com* Ⓜ *Concorde.*

Chapter 7

LES GRANDS BOULEVARDS

Updated by
Jennifer Ladonne

● Sights	🍴 Restaurants	🛏 Hotels	👜 Shopping	🍸 Nightlife
★★★☆☆	★★★☆☆	★★★★★	★★★★★	★★★★★

NEIGHBORHOOD SNAPSHOT

GETTING HERE

This neighborhood covers parts of the 2e, 3e, 8e, and 9e arrondissements. There are myriad ways of getting to the major sights in these areas; however, for the major landmarks we mention, take the *métro* to the Opéra station, named for the opulent opera house. Just behind it, you can find the department stores Galeries Lafayette and Au Printemps, each with three buildings (women's, men's, home) along Baron Haussmann's wide avenues known as the Grands Boulevards. If you're planning to visit the numerous small and wonderful museums, take the métro to Parc Monceau for the Musée Nissim Camondo, Musée Cernuschi, and Musée Jacquemart-André (if you don't mind a little walk). For the Musée Gustave Moreau, the métro stop St-George is the closest, but you can also head to Pigalle, stop in at the Musée de la Vie Romantique, and walk through the still-elegant historic Nouvelle Athènes neighborhood, where such artistic luminaries as Georges Sand, Frédéric Chopin, Eugène Delacroix, and Jean Auguste Dominique Ingres lived, worked, and played.

MAKING THE MOST OF YOUR TIME

If you're a serious shopper, plan to spend a full day in this neighborhood, beginning with the department stores near the Opéra *métro* stop (best to go on weekday mornings when the crowds are thinner). Then check out the shopping and food scene on the Rue d'Aboukir and around the elegant shops surrounding the Place des Victoires. From here, head east on the Rue Étienne Marcel, lined with boutiques, as well as the Rues Montmartre, du Louvre, and du Jour. Don't miss the historic covered galleries (Paris's first shopping malls): the soaring glass Passages Jouffroy and Verdeau, and Paris's oldest, the Passage des Panoramas, just across the street.

If shopping isn't your bag, plan on a long afternoon's visit: tour the Opéra Garnier and one or two museums, or bring a picnic lunch to lovely Parc Monceau on the western edge.

TOP REASONS TO GO

■ **Les Grands Magasins.** Sample a new perfume under the magnificent dome at Galeries Lafayette; update your look, wander the sumptuous food halls, or gaze at Parisian rooftops from the eighth-floor outdoor restaurant terraces at Au Printemps.

■ **Opéra Garnier.** It may not be haunted by the Phantom, but this 19th-century opera house still dazzles. Enjoy a ballet or an opera, take the guided tour, or simply ogle the halls bedecked in marble and gold leaf.

■ **Parc Monceau.** Join the well-dressed children of well-heeled Parisians and frolic on some of the prettiest lawns in the city.

■ **Musée Jacquemart-André.** Once home of husband-and-wife art collectors, the superb permanent collection in their home, still dressed as it was when they lived here, is well worth a view, and the temporary exhibitions are some of the best in Paris (as is their adorable tearoom).

■ **Les Passages Couverts.** Stroll the passages Jouffroy, Verdeau, and Panoramas to experience what the original shopping malls were like 200 years ago.

In Belle Époque Paris, the Grands Boulevards were the place to see and be seen: in the cafés, at the opera, or in the ornate *passages couverts* (glass-roofed arcades that served as the world's first malls).

If you close your eyes, you can almost imagine the Grands Boulevards immortalized on canvas by the Impressionists, with well-attired Parisians strolling wide avenues dotted with shops, cafés, grand hotels, and horse-drawn carriages—all set against a backdrop of stately Haussmannian buildings. Today, despite the chain stores, sidewalk vendors, and fast-food joints, the Grands Boulevards remain one of the city's shopping epicenters, home to the most popular *grands magasins* (department stores), Galeries Lafayette and Au Printemps, near Place de l'Opéra.

Shopping aside, the Grands Boulevards are a cultural destination anchored by the magnificent **Opéra Garnier,** commissioned by Napoléon III. The neighborhood is also home to some of the city's best small museums, all former private collections housed in 19th-century *hôtels particuliers* (mansions) that alone are worth the trip. The exquisite **Musée Jacquemart-André** displays an impressive collection of Italian Renaissance art, while the jewel-box **Musée Nissim de Camondo** remembers one family's tragic end. The **Musée Cernuschi** has a dazzling array of Asian art, the **Musée National Gustave-Moreau** is an offbeat tribute to the Symbolist master, and the **Musée de la Vie Romantique,** with a hidden garden café, is the perfect place to spend an afternoon.

◉ Sights

★ Au Printemps
STORE/MALL | Encompassing a trio of upscale department stores (Printemps Mode, Printemps Beauté-Maison-Enfant, and Printemps Homme), this vast, venerable retailer has been luring shoppers since 1865 and has lately upped its glamour quotient with a series of elegant storewide restorations. Besides the clothes, shoes, housewares, and everything else, there are appealing dining options here. Two floors of the main building (Printemps Homme) have been completely renovated and are now home to Printemps du Goût, a celebration of French cuisine. If you are a do-it-yourselfer, you can find the best of French foodstuffs on the seventh floor. But if you want to eat in style while taking in spectacular views, either from inside via floor-to-ceiling windows or outside on the wraparound terrace, continue on to the eighth floor, where noted chefs and food artisans—including master cheese-maker Laurent Dubois, chef *pâtissier* Nina Métayer, and artisanal baker Gontran Cherrier—oversee a gourmet cornucopia. You can also opt for a leisurely shopping break at La Brasserie Printemps, under the famous stained-glass cupola, or the magnificent terrace of restaurant Perruche, with 360-degree views over Paris. Shoppers will be pleased to know that Paris's grand department stores are now open Sunday. ⊠ *64 bd. Haussmann, 9e,*

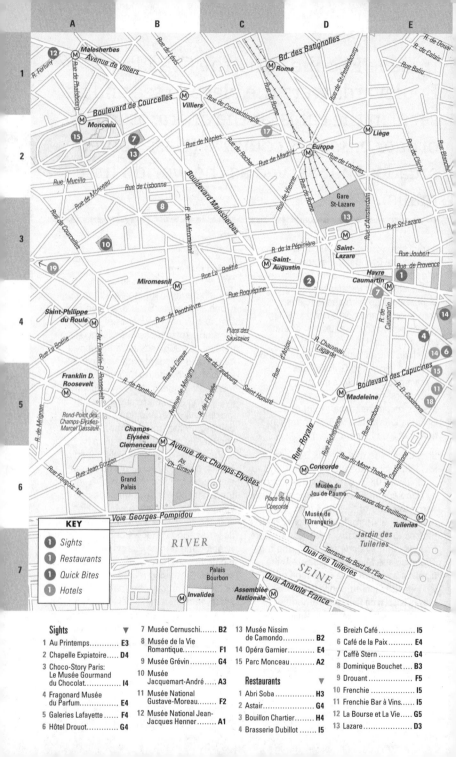

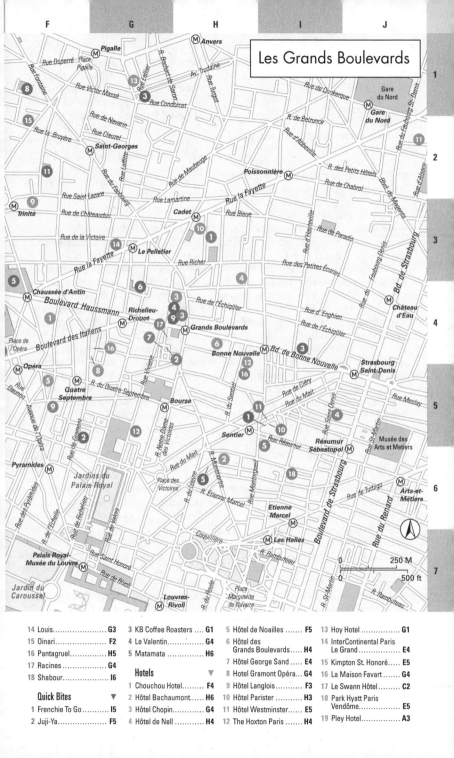

Les Grands Boulevards

Grands Boulevards ☎ *01–42–82–50–00* ⊕ *www.printemps.com* Ⓜ *Havre-Caumartin, St-Lazare.*

Chapelle Expiatoire

CHURCH | Commissioned in 1815, this neoclassical temple marks the original burial site of Louis XVI and Marie-Antoinette. After the deposed monarchs took their turns at the guillotine on Place de la Concorde, their bodies were taken to a nearby mass grave. A loyalist marked their place, and their remains were eventually retrieved by the dead king's brother, Louis XVIII, who moved them to the Basilica of St-Denis. He then ordered the monument (which translates to Expiatory, or Atonement, Chapel) built on this spot, in what is now the leafy Square Louis XVI off Boulevard Haussmann. Two massive white-marble sculptures by François Joseph Bosio show the king and queen being succored by angels, while stone tablets below are inscribed with the last missives of the doomed royals, including pleas to God to forgive their Revolutionary enemies. ⊠ *Square Louis-XVI, 29 rue Pasquier, 8e, Grands Boulevards* ☎ *01–42–65–35–80* ⊕ *www. chapelle-expiatoire-paris.fr* 🎟 *€6* ⊘ *Oct.– Mar.: closed Sun.–Tues.; Apr.–Sept.: closed Sun. and Mon.* Ⓜ *St-Augustin.*

Choco-Story Paris: Le Musée Gourmand du Chocolat

OTHER MUSEUM | **FAMILY** | Considering that a daily dose of chocolate is practically obligatory in Paris, it's hard to believe that this spot (opened in 2010) is the city's first museum dedicated to the sweet stuff. Exhibits on three floors tell the story of chocolate from the earliest traces of the "divine nectar" in Mayan and Aztec cultures, through to its introduction in Europe by the Spanish, who added milk and sugar to the spicy dark brew and launched a Continental craze. There are detailed explanations in English, with many for the kids. While the production of chocolate is a major topic, there is also a respectable collection of some 1,000 chocolate-related artifacts, such as terracotta Mayan sipping vessels (they blew into straws to create foam) and delicate chocolate pots in fine porcelain that were favored by the French royal court. Frequent chocolate-making demonstrations finish with a free tasting. ⊠ *28 bd. de Bonne Nouvelle, 10e, Grands Boulevards* ☎ *01–42–29–68–60* ⊕ *www. museeduchocolat.fr* 🎟 *€12; €15 with a cup of hot chocolate* Ⓜ *Bonne-Nouvelle, Strasbourg, St-Denis.*

Fragonard Musée du Parfum

OTHER MUSEUM | More of a showroom than a museum, the small exhibit run by *parfumier* Fragonard above its boutique on Rue Scribe is heavy on decorative objects associated with perfume, including crystal bottles, gloves, and assorted bibelots. The shop is a good place to find gifts, like body lotion made with royal jelly, myriad soaps, and, of course, perfume. True fragrance aficionados can double their pleasure by visiting the Théâtre Musée des Capucines-Fragonard, another mini-museum nearby at 39 bd. des Capucines. ⊠ *3–5 sq. de l'Opéra Louis Jouvet, 9e, Grands Boulevards* ☎ *01–40–06–10–09* ⊕ *musee-parfum-paris.fragonard.com* 🎟 *Free* ⊘ *Closed Sun.* Ⓜ *Opéra.*

★ Galeries Lafayette

STORE/MALL | The stunning Byzantine glass *coupole* (dome) of the city's most famous department store is not to be missed. Amble to the center of the main store, amid the perfumes and cosmetics, and look up. If you're not in the mood for shopping, visit the (free) first-floor Galerie des Galeries, an art gallery devoted to fashion, applied arts, and design; or have lunch at one of the restaurants, including a rooftop bar and restaurant in the main store—it has some of the best panoramic views of the city. On your way down, the top floor of the main store is a good place to pick up interesting Parisian souvenirs. Across the street in Galeries Maison, the gourmet food hall has one

The interior of the Galeries Lafayette department store—especially the ceiling—almost outshines the fabulous merchandise.

of the city's best selections of delicacies and several restaurants, including the elegant Maison de la Truffe lunch bar. Try a classic *madeleine* filled with pistachio or lemon at YC Café Yann Couvreur's popular teatime. The luxurious Bar Kaspia, under the main building's famous coupole, serves caviar and all things from the sea. Don't miss Duclot La Cave on Galeries Maison/Gourmet's first floor, where 2,500 bottles of wine from France and around the world are on display. ⊠ *35–40 bd. Haussmann, 9e, Grands Boulevards* ☎ *01–42–82–34–56* ⊕ *www.galerieslafayette.com* Ⓜ *Chaussée d'Antin–La Fayette, Havre–Caumartin.*

Hôtel Drouot

MARKET | Hidden away in a small antiques district, not far from the Opéra Garnier, is Paris's central auction house, said to be the oldest in the world. Drouot sells it all: vintage clothes, haute-couture gowns, tchotchkes, ornate Chinese lacquered boxes, rare books, art, and wine. Anyone can attend the sales and viewings, which draw a mix of art dealers, ladies who

lunch, and art amateurs hoping to discover an unknown masterpiece. Check the website to see what's on the block. Don't miss the small galleries and antiques dealers in the Quartier Drouot, a warren of small streets around the auction house, notably on Rues Rossini and de la Grange-Batelière. ⊠ *9 rue Drouot, 9e, Grands Boulevards* ☎ *01–48–00–20–20* ⊕ *www.drouot.com* 🎟 *Free* 🕐 *Closed Sun.* Ⓜ *Richelieu-Drouot.*

★ Musée Cernuschi

ART MUSEUM | Wealthy Milanese banker and patriot Enrico (Henri) Cernuschi fled to Paris in 1850 after the new Italian government collapsed, only to be arrested during the 1871 Paris Commune. He subsequently decided to wait out the unrest by traveling and collecting Asian art. Upon his return 18 months later, he had a special mansion built on the edge of Parc Monceau to house his treasures, notably a two-story bronze Buddha from Japan. Reopened in spring 2020 after a yearlong restoration, France's second-most-important collection of Asian art, after the

Musée Guimet, expanded its galleries to include objects never before displayed, widening the collection to include more works from Japan, Korea, and Vietnam. Cernuschi had an eye not only for the bronze pieces he adored but also for Neolithic pottery (8000 BC), *mingqi* tomb figures (AD 300–900), and an impressive array of terra-cotta figures from various dynasties. A collection highlight is La Tigresse, a bronze wine vessel in the shape of a roaring feline (11th century BC) purchased after Cernuschi's death. Although the museum is free, there is a charge for temporary exhibitions: previous shows have featured Japanese drawings, Iranian sculpture, and Imperial Chinese bronzes. ✉ *7 av. Velasquez, 8e, Grands Boulevards* ☎ *01–53–96–21–50* ⊕ *www.cernuschi.paris.fr* ✉ *Free; €8 for temporary exhibitions* ☉ *Closed Mon.* Ⓜ *Monceau.*

Musée de la Vie Romantique
OTHER MUSEUM | A visit to the charming Museum of Romantic Life (recently reopened after a yearlong renovation), dedicated to novelist George Sand (1804–76), will transport you to the countryside. Occupying a pretty 1830s mansion in a tree-lined courtyard, the small permanent collection features drawings by Delacroix and Ingres, among others, though Sand is the undisputed star. Displays include glass cases stuffed with her jewelry and even a mold of the hand of composer Frédéric Chopin—one of her many lovers. The museum, about a five-minute walk from the Musée National Gustave-Moreau, is in a picturesque neighborhood once called New Athens, a reflection of the architectural tastes of the writers and artists who lived and worked in the area. There is usually an interesting temporary exhibit here too. The garden café (open mid-March to mid-October) is a lovely spot for lunch or afternoon tea. ✉ *16 rue Chaptal, 9e, Grands Boulevards* ☎ *01–55–31–95–67* ⊕ *www.museevieromantique.paris.fr*

✉ *Free; €9 temporary exhibits* ☉ *Closed Mon.* Ⓜ *Blanche, Pigalle, St-Georges.*

Musée Grévin
OTHER MUSEUM | FAMILY | If you like wax museums, this one founded in 1882 ranks among the best. Pay the steep entry price and ascend a grand Phantom of the Opera–like staircase into the Palais des Mirages, a mirrored salon from the 1900 Paris Exposition that transforms into a hokey light-and-sound show the kids will love. (It was a childhood favorite of designer Jean-Paul Gaultier, who is in the collection, of course.) From there, get set for a cavalcade of nearly 300 statues, from Elvis to Ernest Hemingway, Picasso to Queen Elizabeth. Every king of France is here, along with Mick Jagger and George Clooney, plus scores of French singers and celebrities. ✉ *Passage Jouffroy, 10 bd. Montmartre, 9e, Grands Boulevards* ☎ *01–47–70–85–05* ⊕ *www.grevin-paris.com* ✉ *From €25* Ⓜ *Grands Boulevards.*

Paris's Covered Arcades

Before there were the *grands magasins*, there were the *passages couverts*, covered arcades that offered the early-19th-century Parisian shopper a hodgepodge of shops under one roof and a respite from the mud and grit of streets that did not have sidewalks. Until the rise of department stores in the latter part of the century, they would rule as the top places not just to shop but also to wander, socialize, and take tea. Technical and architectural wonders of the time, the vaulting structures of iron and frosted glass inspired artists and writers such as Émile Zola.

Of the 150 arcades built around Paris in the early 1800s, only about a dozen are still in business today, mostly in the 2e and 9e arrondissements. Two arcades still going strong are the fabulously restored **Galerie Vivienne** (⌑ *4 rue Petits Champs, 2e*) and the **Galerie Véro-Dodat** (⌑ *19 rue Jean-Jacques Rousseau, 1er*), both lined with unique and glamorous boutiques. Three other modest passages enjoying a renaissance can be found end to end off the Grands Boulevards, east of Place de l'Opéra. Begin with the most refined, the **Passage Jouffroy** (⌑ *10–12 bd. Montmartre, 9e*), which is home to the Musée Grévin and the

well-regarded, budget-friendly Hôtel Chopin. There's an eclectic array of shops, including Galerie Fayet at No. 34, founded in 1909, which sells a wildly eccentric collection of umbrellas and walking sticks capped with animal heads and whatnot. You can outfit your dollhouse at Pain d'Épices (⌑ *No. 29*), which stocks thousands of miniatures. Pop out at the northern end of Passage Jouffroy and cross Rue de la Grange-Batelière into the **Passage Verdeau** (⌑ *9e*), where the charming Le Bonheur des Dames sells everything for embroideries like your grandma used to make (⌑ *No. 8*) or Thierry Ruby's art- and exotica-filled cabinet of curiosities at No. 12. On the southern end of the Passage Jouffroy, across Boulevard Montmartre, is the **Passage des Panoramas** (⌑ *2e*), the granddaddy of the arcades. Opened in 1799, Passage des Panoramas became the first public space in Paris equipped with gaslights in 1817. A few philatelist shops remain, though the arcade is now dominated by restaurants, including two popular wine bar–bistros, Racines (⌑ *No. 8*) and Coinstot Vino (⌑ *No. 26, bis*), the chic Astair bistro (⌑ *No. 19*), and the perfect spot for an Italian coffee or teatime at Caffè Stern (⌑ *No. 47*).

★ Musée Jacquemart-André

ART MUSEUM | Among the city's best small museums, the opulent Musée Jacquemart-André is home to a huge collection of art and furnishings lovingly assembled in the late 19th century by banking heir Edouard André and his artist wife, Nélie Jacquemart, when this was their home. Their midlife marriage in 1881 raised eyebrows—he was a dashing bachelor and a Protestant,

and she, no great beauty, hailed from a modest Catholic family. Still, theirs was a happy union fused by a common passion for art. For six months every year, the couple traveled, most often to Italy, where they hunted down works from the Renaissance, their preferred period. Their collection also includes French painters Fragonard, Jacques-Louis David, and François Boucher, plus Dutch masters Van Dyke and Rembrandt. The Belle Époque mansion itself is a major attraction. The elegant ballroom, equipped with collapsible walls operated by then-state-of-the-art hydraulics, could hold 1,000 guests. The winter garden was a wonder of its day, spilling into the *fumoir,* where André would share cigars with the *grands hommes* (important men) of the time. You can tour the separate bedrooms—his in dusty pink, hers in pale yellow. The former dining room, now an elegant café, features a ceiling by Tiepolo. Don't forget to pick up the free audioguide in English, and do inquire about the current temporary exhibition, which is usually top-notch. Plan on a Sunday visit, and enjoy the popular brunch (€29.50) in the café from 11 am to 2:30 pm. Reservations are not accepted, so come early or late to avoid waiting in line. ⊠ *158 bd. Haussmann, 8e, Grands Boulevards* ☎ *01–45–62–11–59* ⊕ *www. musee-jacquemart-andre.com* ⊠ *From €12* Ⓜ *St-Philippe du Roule, Miromesnil.*

Musée National Gustave-Moreau

ART MUSEUM | Visiting the quirky town house and studio of painter Gustave Moreau (1826–98) is well worth your time. With an eye on his legacy, Moreau—a high priest of the Symbolist movement—created an enchanting gallery to showcase his dark paintings, drawings, and sculpture. The recently refurbished first-floor rooms, closed to the public for more than a decade, now trace Moreau's "sentimental journey"; their walls are festooned with family portraits and works offered by close friends and allies like Chassériau, Fromentin, and Degas. The two light-flooded top floors house Moreau's vast workshops, where hundreds of paintings, watercolors, and more than 4,000 drawings give a broad overview of his techniques and subjects. Some of the pieces appear unfinished, such as *Unicorns* (No. 213) inspired by the medieval tapestries in the Musée de Cluny: Moreau refused to work on it further, spurning the wishes of a wealthy would-be patron. His interpretation of Biblical scenes and Greek mythology

combine flights of fantasy with a keen use of color, shadow, and tracings influenced by Persian and Indian miniatures. There are wax sculptures and cupboards with sliding vertical doors containing small-format paintings. The Symbolists loved objects, and Moreau was no different. His cramped private apartment on the second floor is jam-packed with bric-a-brac, and artworks cover every inch of the walls. ⊠ *14 rue de la Rochefoucauld, 9e, Grands Boulevards* ☎ *01–48–74– 38–50* ⊕ *www.musee-moreau.fr* ⊠ *€7* ☉ *Closed Tues.* Ⓜ *Trinité, St-Georges.*

Musée National Jean-Jacques Henner

ART MUSEUM | French artist Jean-Jacques Henner (1829–1905) was a star in his day, and although his luminous nudes and clear-eyed portraits are largely forgotten now, the handsomely renovated 19th-century mansion-cum-museum stocked with his works is an interesting stop for art enthusiasts. Henner painted more than 400 portraits, including a substantial number sold in America, with a Realist's eye, yet there is much beauty here as well: witness *Lady with Umbrella,* a portrait of a fur-clad aristocrat with glistening blue eyes. Many of his soft-featured nudes betray other influences. Don't miss them in the light-filled atelier on the museum's third floor, where they share space with a series of religious paintings, notably the haunting *Saint Sebastian* and a stark portrayal of a lifeless Christ, whose luminescent white skin is offset by a shock of flaming red hair. There is some information in English. ⊠ *43 av. de Villiers, 17e, Parc Monceau* ☎ *01–47–63–42–73* ⊕ *www. musee-henner.fr* ⊠ *€6* ☉ *Closed Tues.* Ⓜ *Malesherbes.*

★ **Musée Nissim de Camondo**

HISTORIC HOME | The story of the Camondo family is steeped in tragedy, and it's all recorded within the walls of this superb museum. Patriarch Moïse de Camondo, born in Istanbul to a successful banking family, built his showpiece mansion in

1911 in the style of the Petit Trianon at Versailles and stocked it with some of the most exquisite furniture, wainscoting, artworks, and bibelots of the mid-to-late 18th century. Despite his vast wealth and purported charm, his wife left him five years into their marriage. Then his son, Nissim, was killed in World War I. Upon Moïse's death in 1935, the house and its contents were left to the state as a museum named for his lost son. A few years after Moïse's death, daughter Béatrice, her husband, and two children were deported from France and murdered at Auschwitz. No heirs remained, and the Camondo name died out. Today, the house is an impeccable tribute to Moïse's life. Recent renovations have opened several rooms to the public, including some of the family's private apartments, the kitchen, scullery, and the servant's dining room. There's also a chic contemporary café with a lovely terrace set in the adjoining former garage. ⊠ *63 rue de Monceau, 8e, Grands Boulevards* ☎ *01–53–89–06–50* ⊕ *madparis.fr/francais/musees/musee-nissim-de-camondo* ⊡ *€12; €20 joint ticket with Musée des Arts Décoratifs* ☉ *Closed Mon. and Tues.* Ⓜ *Villiers, Monceau.*

★ Opéra Garnier

PERFORMANCE VENUE | Haunt of the Phantom of the Opera and the real-life inspiration for Edgar Degas's dancer paintings, the gorgeous Opéra Garnier is one of two homes of the National Opera of Paris. The building, the Palais Garnier, was begun in 1860 by then-unknown architect Charles Garnier, who finished his masterwork 15 long years later, way over budget. Festooned with (real) gold leaf, colored marble, paintings, and sculpture from the top artists of the day, the opera house was about as subtle as Versailles and sparked controversy in post-Revolutionary France. The sweeping marble staircase, in particular, drew criticism from a public skeptical of its extravagance. But Garnier, determined to make a landmark that would last forever,

spared no expense. The magnificent grand foyer is one of the most exquisite salons in France. In its heyday, the cream of Paris society strolled all 59 yards of the vast hall at intermission, admiring themselves in the towering mirrors. To see the opera house, buy a ticket for an unguided visit, which allows access to most parts of the building, including a peek into the auditorium. There is also a small ballet museum with a few works by Degas and the tutu worn by prima ballerina Anna Pavlova when she danced her epic *Dying Swan* in 1905. To get to it, pass through the unfinished entrance built for Napoléon III and his carriage (construction was abruptly halted when the emperor abdicated in 1870). On the upper level, you can see a sample of the auditorium's original classical ceiling, which was later replaced with a modern version painted by a septuagenarian Marc Chagall. His trademark willowy figures encircling the dazzling crystal chandelier—today the world's third largest—shocked an unappreciative public upon its debut in 1964. Critics who fret that Chagall's masterpiece clashes with the fussy crimson-and-gilt decor can take some comfort in knowing that the original ceiling is preserved underneath, encased in a plastic dome.

The Opéra Garnier hosts the Paris Ballet as well as a few operas each season (most are performed at the Opéra Bastille). Tickets cost €10–€230 and should be reserved as soon as they go on sale—typically a month ahead at the box office, earlier by phone or online; otherwise, try your luck last-minute. To learn about the building's history, and get a taste of aristocratic life during the Second Empire, take an entertaining English-language tour (daily at 11 am and 2:30 pm, €14) or rent an audioguide (€5) and proceed at your own pace. To complete the experience, dine at Coco—an over-the-top Belle Époque *folie* recalling the glamorous 1920s and helmed by chef Julien Chicoisne—or browse through the Palais Garnier gift shop for ballet-inspired wares, fine Bernardaud porcelain depicting the famous Chagall ceiling, a jar of honey from the Opéra's own rooftop hives, and an exceptional selection of themed DVDs and books. ✉ *Pl. de l'Opéra, 9e, Grands Boulevards* ☎ *08–92–89–90–90 (€0.35 per min), 01–71–25–24–23 from outside France* 🌐 *www.operadeparis.fr* 🎟 *€11; €12 with temporary exhibition; €16 for tours* [M] *Opéra.*

Parc Monceau

CITY PARK | FAMILY | This exquisitely landscaped park began in 1778 as the Duc de Chartres's private garden. Though some of the land was sold off under the Second Empire (creating the exclusive real estate that now borders the park), the refined atmosphere and some of the fanciful faux ruins have survived. Immaculately dressed children play under the watchful eye of their nannies, while lovers cuddle on the benches. In 1797, André Garnerin, the world's first-recorded parachutist, staged a landing in the park. The rotunda—known as the Chartres Pavilion—is surely the city's grandest public restroom: it started life as a tollhouse. ✉ *Entrances on Bd. de Courcelles, Av. Velasquez, Av. Ruysdaël, and Av. van Dyck, 8e, Grands Boulevards* [M] *Monceau.*

🍴 Restaurants

One of Paris's most atmospheric and up-and-coming neighborhoods, this area is also a culinary melting pot. You'll find everything from minuscule Japanese noodle shops lining Rue Ste-Anne to authentic 19th-century brasseries that evoke the old working-class *bouillons*. In Art Nouveau–style Belle Époque dining rooms, a new generation of young, talented chefs cooks up some of the city's most exciting cuisine.

★ Abri Soba

$$ | JAPANESE | Those unable to score a sought-after table at chef Katsuaki Okiyama's restaurant Abri should have better luck at this small soba bar tucked away on a back street off the Faubourg-Montmartre. The chef's savory homemade buckwheat noodles are the big draw—enjoy them hot or cold, paired with duck and leeks, fried tofu and mushrooms, or more imaginative concoctions like eel, cod intestine, and the freshest sashimi. **Known for:** no reservations—try to arrive early; crème brûlée with matcha–sesame seed ice cream; good selection of natural wines and Japanese whiskies. [$] *Average main: €20* ✉ *10 rue Saulnier, 9e, Grands Boulevards* ☎ *01–45–23–51–68* 🕒 *Closed Sun. and Mon.* [M] *Cadet.*

★ Astair

$$ | BRASSERIE | This classy brasserie in the heart of the Passage des Panoramas, Paris's oldest and most picturesque covered gallery, has much more going for it than just good looks. Every item on its tempting menu of French classics—from *oeufs mayonnaise* and *soupe à l'oignon* to frogs' legs and octopus *à la Provençal*, a house specialty—is made with the freshest market ingredients and perfectly cooked, beautifully presented, and served with a smile. **Known for:** exceptional dining without breaking the bank; friendly and welcoming atmosphere; beautiful historic setting. [$] *Average main: €22* ✉ *19 Passage des Panoramas, 2e, Sentier* ☎ *09–81–29–50–95* 🌐 *www.astair.paris* 🕒 *Closed Sun. and Mon.* [M] *Grands Boulevards, Bourse.*

Bouillon Chartier

$ | BISTRO | FAMILY | So-named to call one of the Parisian soup restaurants popular among workers in the early 20th century, Bouillon Chartier is a part of the Gérard Joulie group of bistros and brasseries, which discreetly updated the menu without changing the fundamentals. People come here more for the *bonhomie* and the stunning 1896 interior than the cooking, which could be politely described as unambitious—then again, where else can you find a plate of foie gras for €7.50? **Known for:** extensive menu with gentle prices; 19th-century ambience; Paris's last truly authentic bouillon. [$] *Average main: €12* ✉ *7 rue du Faubourg-Montmartre, 9e, Grands Boulevards* ☎ *01–47–70–86–29* 🌐 *www.bouillon-chartier.com* [M] *Montmartre.*

Brasserie Dubillot

$ | **BRASSERIE** | **FAMILY** | There's nothing quite like a good old-fashioned Paris brasserie...except, perhaps, for a good old-fashioned Paris neobrasserie, a lively new genre that takes the best of the classic eatery—lively atmosphere, copious menu options, all-day hours, classic decor—and adds a 21st-century vibe, all at reasonable prices. At Dubillot, you'll find the French classics—*oeufs mayonnaise*, house-made country pâté, steak tartare, smoked trout, leg of lamb, crispy frites—along with well-priced wines by the bottle or glass. **Known for:** brasserie classics with locally sourced ingredients; fun and lively ambience; affordable wines. [$] *Average main: €15* ✉ *222 rue St-Denis, 2e, Grands Boulevards* ☎ *01–88–61–51–24* 🌐 *www.nouvelle-gardegroupe.com* [M] *Réaumur-Sébastopol, Strasbourg Saint-Denis.*

Breizh Café

$ | **FRENCH** | **FAMILY** | This most stalwart of Breton addresses in the French capital is known for its savory buckwheat galettes and sweet wheat-flour crêpes, best enjoyed with a glass of local Breton cider. The city boasts several outposts of this restaurant; this one quite near the Les Halles market area is known for its cozy vaulted cider cellar, with more than 40 ciders to sample. **Known for:** organic buckwheat galettes with fillings like truffled ham, Basque chorizo, and raw-milk raclette cheese; outdoor tables overlooking a lively pedestrian shopping street; nonstop service throughout the day. [$] *Average main: €15* ✉ *14 rue des Petits Carreaux, 2e, Les Halles* ☎ *01–42–33–97–78* 🌐 *www.breizhcafe.com* [M] *Sentier.*

Café de la Paix

$$$ | **FRENCH** | A pinnacle of Second Empire opulence, this Paris landmark was once an obligatory stop on the sophisticated gastronome's tour of Paris and a favorite watering hole among the likes of Victor Hugo, Gustave Flaubert, Arthur Conan Doyle, Josephine Baker, and Marlene Dietrich. While super-fresh heaping seafood platters are your best bet here, you'll do just as well with a classic French dish or an *apéro* on the terrace as the sun sets over the Opéra Garnier across the street—a magical Parisian scene indeed. **Known for:** spectacular buffet brunch; Paris institution with a history; breathtaking decor. [$] *Average main: €25* ✉ *5 pl. de l'Opéra, 9e, Grands Boulevards* ☎ *01–40–07–36–36* 🌐 *www.cafedelapaix.fr* [M] *Opéra, Havre-Caumartin.*

★ **Caffè Stern**

$$$ | **ITALIAN** | Lodged in one of Paris's most picturesque historic passages, the Italian Caffè Stern—a listed monument updated by designer Philippe Starck—is loaded with the sort of antique charm that makes a cup of coffee and dessert feel like a romantic moment in time. Full meals are a more elegant—and expensive—affair, though teatime (3 pm–6 pm, €26) and the prix-fixe lunch make for a more manageable splurge. **Known for:** top-notch food; gorgeous decor; superb historic setting in the Passage des Panoramas. [$] *Average main: €26* ✉ *47 Passage des Panoramas, 2e, Grands Boulevards* ☎ *01–75–43–63–10* 🌐 *www.alajmo.it* ⏲ *Closed Sun. and Mon.* [M] *Grands Boulevards, Bourse.*

Dominique Bouchet

$$$$ | **BISTRO** | To taste the cooking of one of the city's revered chefs, head to Dominique Bouchet's elegant modern bistro, where contemporary art brightens cream-color walls. On the menu, refined

French technique meets country-style cooking, as in leg of lamb braised in wine with roasted cocoa bean and potato puree or a chocolate éclair with black cherries and ice cream. **Known for:** well-deserved Michelin star; attentive service in a small dining room; master chef of French technique. [$] *Average main: €38* ✉ *11 rue Treilhard, 8e, Champs-Élysées* ☎ *01–45–61–09–46* 🌐 *www.dominique-bouchet.com* 🕒 *Closed weekends and 3 wks in Aug.* [M] *Miromesnil.*

Drouant

$$$ | MODERN FRENCH | FAMILY | Best known for the literary prizes awarded here since 1914, Drouant has shed its dusty image to become a forward-thinking restaurant. The playful menu revisits the French hors d'oeuvres tradition with starters that come as a series of four plates; diners can pick from themes such as French classics (like a deconstructed leek salad) or convincing minitakes on Thai and Moroccan dishes. **Known for:** elegant atmosphere; good for same-day reservations; France's most prestigious literary prize, the Prix Goncourt, awarded here. [$] *Average main: €27* ✉ *16–18 pl. Gaillon, 2e, Grands Boulevards* ☎ *01–42–65–15–16* 🌐 *www.drouant.com* [M] *Pyramides.*

★ Frenchie

$$$$ | BISTRO | Set in a brick-and-stone-walled building on a pedestrian street near Rue Montorgueil, Frenchie has quickly become one of the most hard-to-book bistros in town, with tables booked months in advance, despite two seatings each evening. This success is due to the good-value, five-course dinner menu (prix fixe only); boldly flavored dishes such as calamari gazpacho with squash blossoms or melt-in-the-mouth braised lamb with roasted eggplant and spinach are excellent options. **Known for:** graciously accommodating to vegetarians; extensive and original wine list; casual laid-back atmosphere that belies the ultrasophisticated dishes. [$] *Average main: €34* ✉ *5 rue du Nil, 2e, Grands Boulevards* ☎ *01–40–39–96–19* 🌐 *www.frenchie-restaurant.com* 🕒 *Closed weekends, 2 wks in Aug., and 10 days at Christmas. No lunch Mon.–Wed.* [M] *Sentier.*

★ Frenchie Bar à Vins

$$ | WINE BAR | If this weren't one of Paris's most outstanding wine bars, the wait and metal tractor seats might be a deterrent. Yet wine lovers would be hard-pressed to find a better venue for sampling a great list of French wines and inspired selections from Italy and Spain—every one of them sold by the bottle or glass—with superb tapas to match. **Known for:** long waits unless you get there right when it opens (7 pm); rare expertise in natural, organic, and biodynamic wines; choice selection of natural wines from France and Europe. [$] *Average main: €18* ✉ *6 rue du Nil, 2e, Grands Boulevards* ☎ *No phone* 🌐 *www.frenchie-bav.com* 🕒 *Closed weekends. No lunch* [M] *Sentier.*

★ La Bourse et La Vie

$$$$ | BISTRO | After a takeover by the French-trained American star chef Daniel Rose, this bistro stalwart transformed from a duckling to a swan, with elegant revamps of its bistro decor and an upgrade on its deeply satisfying French comfort-food classics. All meals begin with superb *gougères* (warm cheesy puffs), and, if you're wise, will end with dessert. **Known for:** one of the best tartes tatin in Paris; rich veal pot-au-feu stew; buttery, melt-in-your-mouth steak frites. [$] *Average main: €35* ✉ *12 rue Vivienne, 2e, Louvre* ☎ *01–42–60–08–83* 🌐 *www.labourselavie.com* 🕒 *Closed weekends* [M] *Bourse.*

Lazare

$$ | BRASSERIE | With so many of Paris's fabled brasseries co-opted by upscale chains, the 2013 opening by three-Michelin-star chef Eric Frechonof of this modern take on the traditional brasserie in the St-Lazare train station was met with curiosity and joy. Though prices are commensurate with his status, Frechon doesn't skimp on the classics: steak tartare, escargot, and charcuterie all make memorable appearances. **Known for:** classic brasserie atmosphere and cooking; can usually snag a seat sans reservation; quick dining before catching a train. $ *Average main: €24* ⊠ *108 rue Saint-Lazare, 8e, Grands Boulevards* ☎ *01–45–23–42–06* ⊕ *www.lazare-paris. fr* Ⓜ *St-Lazare.*

★ Louis

$$$$ | **FRENCH** | It may not be the most glamorous or the most well known of the city's Michelin-starred restaurants, but this intimate, prix-fixe dining room in an authentic part of town is one of the best. Be prepared to be both wowed and surprised, with choices from chef Stéphane Pitré, who is known for his precise, original dishes that offer Asian touches without a hint of pretension. **Known for:** excellent options at lunchtime, outstanding options at dinner; happily accommodating to those with food preferences and allergies; intimate dining room with individual attention. $ *Average main: €81* ⊠ *23 rue de la Victoire, 9e, Grands Boulevards* ☎ *01–55–07–86–52* ⊕ *www.louis. paris* ☉ *Closed weekends* Ⓜ *Le Peletier, Notre-Dame-de-Lorette.*

Oinari

$ | **JAPANESE** | Small but mighty when it comes to fresh and delicious Japanese comfort food in the form of *inari age*: sushi rice wrapped in fried tofu (that used here is imported from Kyoto) and topped with vegetables, fish, or meat. The menu also features delicious udon, donburi, gyoza, and mochi for dessert. **Known for:** good-value bento boxes; expert sake pairings; near Sacré-Coeur. $ *Average main: €13* ⊠ *34 rue la Bruyère, 9e, Grands Boulevards* ☎ *06–60–06– 08–10* ⊕ *www.oinariparis.com* ☉ *Closed weekends* Ⓜ *St-Georges, Blanche.*

Pantagruel

$$$$ | **FRENCH** | Chef Jason Gouzy won a Michelin star less than a year after the 2020 opening of this sought-after

restaurant, where each dish resembles a gemlike work of art. The sleekly romantic dining room perfectly mirrors what's on the menu: dishes of exceptional imagination and refinement with an emphasis on seasonal market-fresh vegetables, seafood, and meticulously sourced meats. **Known for:** lovely atmosphere; excellent wines by the glass; good prices for this quality of cuisine. $ *Average main: €45* ⊠ *24 rue du Sentier, 2e, Grands Boulevards* ☎ *01–73–74–77–28* ⊕ *www.restaurant-pantagruel.com* ☉ *Closed Weekends* Ⓜ *Grands Boulevards, Sentier.*

Racines

$$$ | **WINE BAR** | Originally a *cave à manger* (a wine bar/bistro) serving natural wines and top-quality French fare, the foodie world rejoiced when adulated chef Simone Tondo took the helm and introduced a small but stellar menu of Italian comfort dishes mixed with French stalwarts. The old tile floors, wooden tables, and location in the atmospheric Passage des Panoramas, Paris's oldest covered arcade, only add to the ambience. **Known for:** homemade tagliatelli with slow-cooked beef; hard-to-find Italian wines; wonderful atmosphere in a historic passage. $ *Average main: €26* ⊠ *8 Passage des Panoramas, 2e, Grands Boulevards* ☎ *01–40–13–06–41* ⊕ *www. racinesparis.com* ☉ *Closed weekends and 3 wks in Aug.* Ⓜ *Grands Boulevards, La Bourse.*

Shabour

$$ | **MEDITERRANEAN** | You could hear the buzz for miles when this beautiful dining room opened in 2019, and it's only gotten louder thanks to a shiny new Michelin star. Jerusalem-born chef Assaf Granit brings his formidable talent and imagination to Israeli and Asian-inspired dishes. Candlelit at night, the small but beautiful dining room is the perfect backdrop to an unforgettable meal. **Known for:** unusual wines; perfect for a romantic dinner; to-die-for desserts. $ *Average main: €22* ⊠ *19 rue St-Sauveur, 2e, Sentier*

☎ 06–95–16–32–87 ⊕ www.restaur-antshabour.com ⊗ Closed weekends Ⓜ Réamur-Sébastopol, Sentier, Bonne Nouvelle.

☕ Coffee and Quick Bites

Frenchie To Go

$ | MODERN FRENCH | FAMILY | An outpost of Frenchie's Rue du Nil empire, Frenchie To Go capitalizes on three of the latest Paris food trends: breakfast, fast-food, and takeaway. The hot dogs and tasty pastrami (almost unheard of in Paris) are meticulously sourced, as is pretty much everything else—Brittany lobster for the lobster rolls and line-caught hake for the scrumptious fish-and-chips. **Known for:** homemade ginger beer; quick breakfasts or take-out lunches; good value for top-quality ingredients. Ⓢ Average main: €10 ⊠ 9 rue du Nil, 2e, Louvre ☎ 01–40–39–96–19 ⊕ www.frenchie-ftg.com Ⓜ Sentier.

Juji-Ya

$ | JAPANESE | One of Paris's first bento-box cafés (it's also a Japanese grocer), this cozy spot on storied Rue Ste-Anne offers an array of delicious eats, from smoked eel and grilled salmon to crispy chicken, fried tofu, and yummy veggie sides like marinated seaweed—a house specialty—and sesame spinach. For a meal on the go, this is the place. **Known for:** bento boxes to go; Japanese gourmet groceries; long lines. Ⓢ Average main: €14 ⊠ 46 rue Ste-Anne, 9e, Grands Boulevards ☎ 01–42–86–02–22 ⊕ www.jujiya-bento.com ⊗ Closed Sun.–Wed. No dinner Ⓜ Pyramides, Bourse, Quatre-Septembre.

KB Coffee Roasters

$ | CAFÉ | Set at a leafy crossroads on the lively Rue des Martyrs, this is a top pick in this vibrant neighborhood for a quick stop or to linger with a device. The coffee (roasted at their atelier-café Back in Black) is always good, as are the many other beverage options, both hot and cold, and the food—from healthy salads and sandwiches to yummy pastries—exactly what's needed to get you revved up for your next Paris adventure. **Known for:** open daily; healthy snacks; spacious outdoor setting. Ⓢ Average main: €6 ⊠ 53 av. Trudaine, 9e, Grands Boulevards ☎ 01–56–92–12–41 ⊕ www.kbcafeshop.com ⊗ No dinner Ⓜ Anvers, Notre-Dame-de-Lorette.

★ Le Valentin

$ | BAKERY | A head-turning variety of luscious pastries, classic French breakfast sweets and breads, ice cream, chocolates, and homemade jams will tempt every sweet tooth at this charming bakery and tearoom. Tucked into the historic covered Passage Jouffroy, Le Valentin is a picturesque spot for breakfast, lunch, or teatime—or buy a box of irresistible French-Alsatian sweets to enjoy on the go. **Known for:** French-Alsatian specialties; charming place to sit for breakfast, lunch, or dessert; set in an 1845 covered passage. Ⓢ Average main: €6 ⊠ 30–32 Passage Jouffroy, 9e, Grands Boulevards ☎ 01–47–70–88–50 ⊕ www.facebook.com/salondethelevalentin Ⓜ Grands Boulevards.

★ Matamata

$ | CAFÉ | This tiny gem of a coffee shop may not have the ambience of Paris's historic brasserie cafés, but it does have something you won't find in any brasserie in Paris—reliably excellent coffee served with care and enthusiasm. What's more, a small menu of delicious homemade sweets and sandwiches and salads at lunchtime pretty much covers all your restorative needs in a warm and friendly atmosphere. **Known for:** friendly atmosphere; quality beans sourced from around the world; consistently great coffee drinks of all kinds. Ⓢ Average main: €6 ⊠ 58 rue d'Argout, 2e, Grands Boulevards ☎ 01–71–39–44–58 ⊕ www.matamatacoffee.com ⊗ Closed Sun. No dinner Ⓜ Sentier.

Hotels

This bustling historic district is tops for both travelers on a budget and those willing to shell out a bit more to indulge at a grande dame. Some savvy newcomers have enlivened this central area's eclectic lodging scene, especially around the magnificent Opéra Garnier. Among the many reasons to make this area your base is how easy it is to get almost anywhere you want on foot. But the Opéra métro stop is also a hub for several lines.

Chouchou Hotel

$$$ | HOTEL | A distinctly bohemian vibe reigns in this oh-so-Parisian hotel, which opened in 2020 in a 19th-century Haussmannian building that's just a stone's throw from the Opéra Garnier. **Pros:** central location; top-quality bath products; excellent restaurant, oyster bar, and lounge. **Cons:** no fitness room (but there are yoga classes); suites are expensive; rooms are rather cozy. $ *Rooms from: €230* ✉ *11 rue du Helder, Grands Boulevards* ☎ *01–87–44–54–79* ⊕ *www. chouchouhotel.com* ⇱ *63 rooms* ❑ *No Meals* Ⓜ *Chaussée d'Antin-Lafayette, Opéra.*

★ Hôtel Bachaumont

$$ | HOTEL | This sleek 2015 revival of a 100-year-old neighborhood hotel that closed in the 1970s is a newfound favorite with the international set, whether staying the night or just stopping in for a stylish bite or drink at the wildly popular cocktail bar. **Pros:** central location in a vibrant up-and-coming neighborhood; retro interiors; chic nightlife on the premises. **Cons:** gym small and basic; room service can be slow; nearby metro can disturb sensitive sleepers in lower rooms. $ *Rooms from: €229* ✉ *18 rue Bachaumont, Grands Boulevards* ☎ *01–81–66–47–00* ⊕ *www.hotelbachaumont.com* ⇱ *49 rooms* ❑ *No Meals* Ⓜ *Sentier.*

Hôtel Chopin

$$ | HOTEL | A unique mainstay of the district, the Chopin—set within the atmospheric Passage Jouffroy—recalls its 1846 birth date with a creaky-floored lobby, aged woodwork, and its own homey charm. **Pros:** charmed location; great nightlife district; close to major métro station. **Cons:** few amenities; single rooms are very small; thin walls. $ *Rooms from: €140* ✉ *10 bd. Montmartre, Grands Boulevards* ☎ *01–47–70–58–10* ⊕ *www.hotelchopin-paris-opera. com* ⇱ *36 rooms* ❑ *No Meals* Ⓜ *Grands Boulevards.*

★ Hôtel de Nell

$$$$ | HOTEL | Tucked in a picturesque corner of a chic, up-and-coming neighborhood ripe for exploration, this serenely beautiful hotel offers contemporary luxury with clean lines and uncluttered spaces designed by French starchitect Jean-Michelle Wilmotte. **Pros:** good dining and bar on premises; beautiful rooms; interesting neighborhood to explore. **Cons:** lacks a spa; far from the major Paris attractions; area deserted at night. $ *Rooms from: €385* ✉ *9 rue du Conservatoire, Grands Boulevards* ☎ *01–44–83–83–60* ⊕ *www.hoteldenell. com* ⇱ *33 rooms* ❑ *No Meals* Ⓜ *Bonne Nouvelle.*

Hôtel de Noailles

$$$ | HOTEL | With a nod to the work of postmodern designers like Putman and Starck, this stylish boutique hotel is both contemporary and cozy. **Pros:** 15- to 20-minute walk to the Louvre and Opéra; free Wi-Fi; a block from the airport bus. **Cons:** small elevator; some bathrooms in need of renovation; no interesting views. $ *Rooms from: €290* ✉ *9 rue de la Michodière, Grands Boulevards* ☎ *01–47–42–92–90* ⊕ *www.hotelnoailles.com* ⇱ *56 rooms* ❑ *No Meals* Ⓜ *Opéra.*

★ Hôtel des Grands Boulevards

$$$ | HOTEL | At this chic hotel, tucked away in plain sight on the Boulevard Poissonière, even the smallest of the

minimalist jewel-toned rooms (some with balconies or garden terraces) feels elegant, with tall windows, marble touches, and Marie-Antoinette–worthy draped headboards. **Pros:** beautifully designed rooms; lots of outdoor spaces and some fabulous private terraces; chic on-site cocktail bar, restaurant, and rooftop bar. **Cons:** some rooms quite tiny; not every room has a balcony; rooms facing the courtyard bar can be noisy at night if windows are open. $ *Rooms from: €280* ✉ *17 bd. Poissonnière, Grands Boulevards* ☎ *01–85–73–33–33* ⊕ *www. grandsboulevardshotel.com* ↻ *50 rooms* ⚍ *No Meals* Ⓜ *Bonne Nouvelle, Grands Boulevards.*

Hôtel George Sand
$$$ | **HOTEL** | This family-run hotel, where the 19th-century writer George Sand once lived, feels up-to-date while preserving some of its original architectural details. **Pros:** near two famous department stores; simple but comfortable rooms; historic atmosphere. **Cons:** some rooms are quite small; can hear métro rumble on lower floors; noisy street. $ *Rooms from: €250* ✉ *26 rue des Mathurins, Grands Boulevards* ☎ *01– 47–42–63–47* ⊕ *www.hotelgeorgesand. com* ↻ *20 rooms* ⚍ *No Meals* Ⓜ *Havre Caumartin.*

Hôtel Gramont Opéra
$$ | **HOTEL** | Near the Opéra Garnier and some of the city's best department stores, this family-owned boutique hotel has lots of little extras that make it a great value. **Pros:** breakfast buffet (for a fee) with eggs made to order; connecting rooms for families; personal and professional service. **Cons:** elevator doesn't go to top floor; small bathrooms; singles have no desk. $ *Rooms from: €210* ✉ *22 rue Gramont, Grands Boulevards* ☎ *01–42–96–85–90* ⊕ *www.hotelgramontparis.com* ↻ *25 rooms* ⚍ *No Meals* Ⓜ *Quatre-Septembre.*

Hôtel Langlois
$$ | **HOTEL** | This darling hotel gained a reputation as one of the more atmospheric budget sleeps in the city, although rates have since crept up. **Pros:** excellent views from the top floor; historic decor; close to department stores and Opéra Garnier. **Cons:** some sagging furniture and worn fabrics; a bit out of the way; noisy street. $ *Rooms from: €185* ✉ *63 rue St-Lazare, Grands Boulevards* ☎ *01–48–74–78–24* ⊕ *www.hotel-langlois.com* ↻ *27 rooms* ⚍ *No Meals* Ⓜ *Trinité.*

★ Hôtel Parister
$$$ | **HOTEL** | A glamorous addition to the fabulous (if off-the-beaten-path) 9e arrondissement, the Parister flaunts its design creds in even the tiniest of details, from its gorgeous common spaces to its sparse but elegant rooms. **Pros:** great neighborhood; elegant on-site restaurant; pool, steam room, and fitness center. **Cons:** some rooms on the small side; a little pricey for the location; neighborhood off the beaten path. $ *Rooms from: €280* ✉ *19 rue Saulnier, Grands Boulevards* ☎ *01–80–50–91–91* ⊕ *www.paristerhotel. com* ↻ *45 rooms* ⚍ *No Meals* Ⓜ *Cadet.*

Hôtel Westminster
$$$ | **HOTEL** | On one of the most prestigious streets in Paris, between the Opéra and Place Vendôme, this mid-19th-century inn happily retains its old-world feel. **Pros:** prestigious location near major sights; popular jazz bar; soothing steam room. **Cons:** poor bathroom plumbing; some rooms overlook an air shaft; a bit old-fashioned. $ *Rooms from: €315* ✉ *13 rue de la Paix, Grands Boulevards* ☎ *01–42–61–57–46* ⊕ *www.warwick-hotels.com* ↻ *102 rooms* ⚍ *No Meals* Ⓜ *Opéra.*

The Hoxton Paris
$$$ | **HOTEL** | In 2017, the urban-chic trendsetting Hoxton brand transformed an 18th-century mansion in Paris's up-and-coming Sentier district into this hip hostelry with a chic restaurant, three cocktail bars—including the charming

Jacques Bar tucked away on the second floor—and a welcoming community vibe. **Pros:** cool neighborhood with lots to explore; memorable bar scene; historic mansion setting. **Cons:** the most affordable rooms have very few frills; restaurant is just average; off-the-radar neighborhood not for everyone. $ *Rooms from: €310 ⊠ 30–32 rue du Sentier, Grands Boulevards* ☎ *01–85–65–75–00* ⊕ *www.thehoxton.com* ⤴ *172 rooms* ⏹ *Free Breakfast* Ⓜ *Grands Boulevards, Bonne Nouvelle.*

Hoy Hotel
$$$ | **HOTEL** | Ethical, sustainable, "zero waste," and entirely focused on your well-being, this distinctive property with feng shui–correct rooms and "indulge and enjoy" as its motto has made quite a splash since its 2020 debut. **Pros:** numerous healthy details; superb bar and plant-based restaurant; yoga and wellness classes offered on-site. **Cons:** not ideal for hedonists; no TVs; wellness classes cost extra. $ *Rooms from: €235 ⊠ 68 rue des Martyrs, Grands Boulevards* ☎ *01–77–37–87–20* ⊕ *www.hoyparis.com* ⤴ *19 rooms* ⏹ *No Meals* Ⓜ *Pigalle, St-Georges.*

★ InterContinental Paris Le Grand
$$$$ | **HOTEL** | Sarah Bernhardt and Sir Arthur Conan Doyle adored this elegant Belle Époque hotel, an epitome of Haussmannian grandeur inaugurated in 1862 by the Empress Eugenie herself, and in 2021 it was given a dazzling renovation—the 458 rooms, many with eye-popping views of the Opéra Garnier, blend old-world luxury with 21st-century glamour. **Pros:** terraces with breathtaking Parisian views; the best breakfast buffet in Paris; stupendous duplex apartments. **Cons:** the 4 miles of hallways can get confusing; some rumbling from the métro below on lower floors; not all terraces overlook the opera house. $ *Rooms from: €500 ⊠ 2 rue Scribe, 9e, Grands Boulevards* ☎ *01–40–07–32–32* ⊕ *www.parislegrand.*

intercontinental.com ⤴ *458 rooms* ⏹ *No Meals* Ⓜ *Opéra.*

★ Kimpton St Honoré
$$$$ | **HOTEL** | The chic Kimpton line's first Parisian outpost opened in 2021 inside a stunning Art Nouveau landmark building—once part of the luxury Samaritaine department store—and each of the 149 Deco-inspired rooms is different: some offer balconies, others stellar views to the Eiffel Tower or the Opéra a stone's throw away. **Pros:** walking distance to major sights; stellar rooftop cocktail bar with astounding panoramas; some rooms have balconies with great views. **Cons:** only two rooms in the spa; bar can get crowded; pricey restaurant. $ *Rooms from: €480 ⊠ 27–29 bd. des Capucines, 2e, Grands Boulevards* ☎ *01–80–40–76–10* ⊕ *www.kimptonsthonoreparis.com* ⤴ *149 rooms* ⏹ *No Meals* Ⓜ *Opéra.*

La Maison Favart
$$$ | **HOTEL** | An atmospheric indoor pool, relaxing sauna, and around-the-clock concierge are some of the reasons this jewel-box hotel is such a popular choice—add 18th-century charm, reasonable rates, good service, and beautifully decorated rooms, and it's no wonder why this hotel, named after the founders of the Comic Opera, pleases those who demand discreet elegance and creature comforts. **Pros:** lovely rooms and interior design; easy walking distance to the sights; spacious bathrooms. **Cons:** no spa; impractical use of space in some rooms; high demand for best rooms. $ *Rooms from: €340 ⊠ 5 rue de Marivaux, Grands Boulevards* ☎ *01–42–97–59–83* ⊕ *www.lamaisonfavart.com* ⤴ *39 rooms* ⏹ *No Meals* Ⓜ *Quatre-Septembre.*

Le Swann Hôtel
$$$ | **HOTEL** | This original, modern *hôtel littéraire* pays homage to France's greatest literary lion, Marcel Proust. **Pros:** not far from the big department stores; views from some rooms; good breakfasts. **Cons:** bathrooms are minuscule; most rooms on the small side; some street

noise. $ *Rooms from: €240* ✉ *15 rue de Constantinople, Grands Boulevards* ☎ *01–45–22–80–80* ⊕ *www.hotel-leswann.com* ⤴ *81 rooms* ⦿ *No Meals* Ⓜ *Europe, Villiers, Rome.*

★ Park Hyatt Paris Vendôme
$$$$ | **HOTEL** | Understated luxury with a contemporary Zen vibe differentiates this Hyatt from its more classic neighbors between Place Vendôme and Opéra Garnier. **Pros:** stylish urban-chic design; only in-suite spa tubs in Paris; the latest technology. **Cons:** very expensive; many corporate events held here; as part of a chain, it can feel anonymous. $ *Rooms from: €950* ✉ *3–5 rue de la Paix, Grands Boulevards* ☎ *01–58–71–12–34* ⊕ *www. hyatt.com* ⤴ *148 rooms* ⦿ *No Meals* Ⓜ *Concorde, Opéra.*

Pley Hotel
$$ | **HOTEL** | Life's one big playground at this chic hotel that adds lightness and fun—not to mention serious style—to a neighborhood that can be a bit uppity. **Pros:** fun decor that nods to Paris's radio history; good location between Arc de Triomphe and Parc Monceau; excellent rooftop bar with Eiffel Tower views. **Cons:** cozy rooms can feel small; no proper spa; traffic noise from street-side rooms. $ *Rooms from: €190* ✉ *214 rue du Faubourg St-Honoré, Champs-Élysées* ☎ *01-42-25-26-27* ⊕ *www.pley-hotel.com* ⤴ *100 rooms* ⦿ *No Meals* Ⓜ *George V, Ternes.*

Nightlife

The up-and-coming Sentier district continues to brings a welcome infusion of chic to area nightlife. Besides the Hoxton Hotel's cozy Jacques bar, the Sequoia rooftop space at the Kimpton Saint Honoré, and The Shell at Hôtel Grands Boulevards—all excellent choices—a handful of smart newcomers have amped up the scene. For homesick Anglos, an assortment of venerable hotel bars and well-established British-Irish pubs offers an authentic facsimile of home in this many-faceted neighborhood that bustles by day and empties out at night.

BARS
★ Bonhomie
BARS | This cocktail bar does a highly successful three in three—drinks, food, and ambience—a feat not to be taken lightly. What's more, the high-quality drinks include sourced coffees, tasty craft cocktails, and small-producer wines; basically anything your finicky heart desires. A menu of Mediterranean-inspired dishes is great for lunch, dinner, or sharing over cocktails or a glass of wine, and the café's late-morning and late-evening hours are a big plus in this neighborhood. ✉ *22 rue d'Enghien, 10e, Grands Boulevards* ☎ *07–64–30–39–68* ⊕ *www.bonhomie.paris* Ⓜ *Bonne Nouvelle, Château d'Eau.*

Corcoran's Irish Pub
PUBS | This roomy pub, with several locations in central Paris, has an ample menu, a sleek bar, a pool table, and old-timey photos and quotations on the walls—such as "He who opens his mouth most is the one who opens his purse least." It's basically a classic Irish pub. Copious plates of pub food and frosty glasses of beer fuel conversation. Dancing at night has a regulated guy-to-girl ratio, so men shouldn't try coming alone. ✉ *23 bd. Poissonière, 2e, Grands Boulevards* ☎ *01–40–39–00–16* ⊕ *www. corcoransirishpubs.com* Ⓜ *Grands Boulevards.*

Duke's Bar
BARS | A favorite not only for its prestigious location between Opéra and Place Vendôme, but also for its worn-leather chairs and English-private-club feel, the Westminster Hotel's bar offers drinks like the "James Bond" and "Duke's Martini." At times, you get the feeling that Monsieur Hercule Poirot is lurking just behind that wing chair. ✉ *13 rue de la Paix, 2e, Grands Boulevards* ☎ *01–42–61–57–46*

⊕ www.warwickhotels.com/hotel-west-
minster ⓂOpéra.

Harry's Bar

BARS | Also known as Harry's New York
Bar, this cozy, wood-paneled hangout
decorated with dusty college pennants
is popular with expats and American-lov-
ing French people who welcome the
ghosts of Ernest Hemingway and F.
Scott Fitzgerald, both of whom drank
themselves unconscious here. Gershwin
composed *An American in Paris* in the
piano bar downstairs, and the Bloody
Mary is said to have originated on-site.
✉ 5 rue Daunou, 2e, Grands Boulevards
☎ 01–42–61–71–14 ⊕ www.harrysbar.fr
Ⓜ Opéra.

★ Jacques' Bar

BARS | Tucked away beyond a cob-
bled courtyard and up a winding back
stairway, this cozy (only 24 seats) bar
achieves an intimate, parloresque ambience thanks to floral chintz wallpaper,
plush armchairs and poufs, and Asian
rugs. For a hotel bar it has well-priced
Moroccan-inspired cocktails and small
plates, making settling in for the evening
a tempting option. Considering the Hoxton Hotel's other bustling spaces, this is
a nice little getaway. It gets crowded, so
arrive early. ✉ 30–32 rue du Sentier, 2e,
Grands Boulevards ☎ 01–85–65–75–01
⊕ thehoxton.com/paris/jacques-bar
Ⓜ Bonne Nouvelle.

★ Kouto

BARS | At this cozy lounge, decorated
with the owners' grandfathers' old knives
(get it, *couteau*?), partners Marie and
Chirine Cabaret-Besenval share their passion for the overlooked and underappreci-
ated in eight superlative cocktail choices
designed to be delicious with or without
alcohol. Grapes, corn, chestnut foam,
and homemade liqueurs are a few of the
unexpected ingredients you'll find on the
constantly evolving menu. There's also
craft beer on tap, wine, French cider, and
homemade sodas, plus some wonderful
artisanal cheese and charcuterie plates
for snacking. ✉ 40 rue d'Enghien, Grands
Boulevards ☎ 06–49–28–28–45 ⊕ kouto.
business.site Ⓜ Grands Boulevards,
Bonne Nouvelle.

Magniv

BARS | One of the newer outposts in a
neighborhood with plenty to choose
from, this scene-y hangout strikes a cool
balance between a cocktail lounge, a
Mediterranean restaurant, and a club—
it's all of these. Set on three floors,
Magniv has streamlined, vaguely futuristic decor, arched mirrors, and dusky
lighting—perfect for dining, drinking, or
dancing. Expect inventive tapas and truly
delicious cocktails. ✉ 37 rue du Sentier,
2e, Grands Boulevards ☎ 01–40–26–14–
94 ⊕ www.magnivrestaurant.fr Ⓜ Bonne
Nouvelle.

★ The Shell

BARS | Parisian cocktail lovers squeeze
into this beautiful intimate space—the
beating heart of the Hôtel des.Grands
Boulevards—to imbibe some of the city's
most ingenious and delicious cocktails
concocted by a trailblazing mixologist.
But the innovation doesn't end there. The
Shell specializes in "mocktails" and lets
drinkers watching their intake choose
their dosage of alcohol, with commen-
surate prices, starting at €8. Anyone can
get behind The Shell's motto: "No more
hangovers."✉ 17 bd. Poissonnière, 2e,
Grands Boulevards ☎ 01–85–73–33–32
⊕ www.grandsboulevardshotel.com.

CLUBS

Le Rex

DANCE CLUBS | Open Wednesday through
Sunday, this temple of techno and house
is popular with students. One of France's
most famous DJs, Laurent Garnier, is
sometimes at the turntables. ✉ 5 bd.
Poissonnière, 2e, Grands Boulevards
☎ 01–42–36–10–96 ⊕ rexclub.com ☞ €15
cover charge Ⓜ Grands Boulevards.

Silencio

DANCE CLUBS | David Lynch named his nightclub after a reference in his Oscar-nominated hit, *Mulholland Drive.* Silencio, which hosts concerts, films, and other performances, is open only to members and their guests until 11 pm; after that everyone is allowed. Guest DJs spin until 4 am Tuesday through Thursday, and until 6 am on Friday and Saturday. ✉ *142 rue Montmartre, 2e, Grands Boulevards* ☎ *01–40–13–12–33* ⊕ *www.facebook.com/silencioclubparis* Ⓜ *Bourse.*

JAZZ CLUBS
★ New Morning

LIVE MUSIC | At New Morning—the premier spot for serious fans of avant-garde jazz, folk, and world music—the look is spartan, and the mood reverential. ✉ *7 rue des Petites-Ecuries, 10e, Grands Boulevards* ☎ *01–45–23–51–41* ⊕ *www.newmorning.com* Ⓜ *Château d'Eau.*

🎭 Performing Arts

This central neighborhood's lively performing arts scene represents a real slice of authentic Parisian life. It's home to the city's grandest movie and opera houses, and you'll also find the kind of small theaters—often architectural gems—that Parisians love, as well as one of the city's top venues for live music, featuring everything from jazz and gospel to French chanson.

Ateliers Berthier

ARTS CENTERS | The outlying atelier for the more illustrious Théâtre de l'Odéon is in the 17e, a bit off the beaten path; the upside is that on Sunday it often has a 3 pm matinee in addition to the evening show (usually at 8 pm). ✉ *1 rue André Suarès, 17e, Batignolles ✛ Corner of Bd. Berthier* ☎ *01–44–85–40–00* ⊕ *www.theatre-odeon.eu* Ⓜ *Porte de Clichy.*

Casino de Paris

THEATER | Once a favorite of the immortal Serge Gainsbourg, Casino de Paris has a horseshoe balcony and a cramped

but cozy music-hall feel, and it presents everything from performances by touring musicals to Lorde and Belle & Sebastian concerts. This is where Josephine Baker performed in the early '30s with her leopard, Chiquita. ✉ *16 rue de Clichy, 9e, Grands Boulevards* ☎ *08–92–69–89–26 €0.40 per min* ⊕ *www.casinodeparis.fr* Ⓜ *Trinité.*

★ Folies Bergère

MUSIC | Many an arts career was launched at this institution, where Josephine Baker charmed the city clad in nothing but a banana skirt and pearls, and icons such as Charlie Chaplin, Maurice Chevalier, and Mistinguett made their big Paris debuts. The 1926 Art Deco facade is a listed historic monument, but the opulent interiors hark back to its Belle Époque heyday as Paris's most daring cabaret. Nowadays, Dita Von Teese and other cabaret acts perform here regularly, but you'll also find more family-style shows, including dance, solo acts, and musicals. ✉ *32 rue Richer, 9e, Grands Boulevards* ☎ *01–44–79–98–60* ⊕ *www.foliesbergere.com/uk.*

★ Le Grand Rex

FILM | Since it opened in 1932, the Grand Rex—a designated historic landmark—has been Europe's largest cinema, with 2,800 seats in its main auditorium and Paris's largest screen. The cinema's history is almost as colorful as its superb Art Deco architecture, considered some of the finest in the city. Although some films are in French or are dubbed in French, many of the international films are in their original language (including many in English) with French subtitles. ✉ *1 bd. Poissonnière, 2e, Grands Boulevards* ☎ *01–45–08–93–89* ⊕ *www.legrandrex.com* Ⓜ *Bonne Nouvelle, Grands Boulevards.*

★ L'Olympia

CONCERTS | Paris's legendary music hall hosts an eclectic roster of performances encompassing genres that range from gospel and jazz to French chanson to rock. Edith Piaf rose to fame after a series of Olympia concerts, and Jeff Buckley's famous *Live at the Olympia* was recorded here. Nowadays, you can see top acts ranging from Beach House to Lady Gaga to George Benson. ✉ *28 bd. des Capucines, 9e, Grands Boulevards* ☎ *08–92–68–33–68* ⊕ *www.olympiahall.com* Ⓜ *Madeleine, Opéra.*

★ Opéra Comique

OPERA | France's third-oldest theatrical institution is a gem of an opera house whose reputation was forged by its former director, *enfant terrible* Jérôme Savary. In addition to staging operettas, the hall hosts modern dance, classical concerts, and vocal recitals. Tickets range from €6 to €120 and can be purchased at the theater, online, or by phone. ✉ *1 pl. Boieldieu, 2e, Grands Boulevards* ☎ *01–70–23–01–00* ⊕ *www.opera-comique.com* Ⓜ *Richelieu-Drouot.*

★ Salle Cortot

MUSIC | This acoustic jewel was built in 1929 by Auguste Perret, who promised to construct "a concert hall that sounds like a Stradivarius." You can buy tickets for jazz and classical concerts only at the box office 30 minutes before each show; check the website for information on advance purchases. Free student recitals are offered at 12:30 pm on Tuesday and Thursday from October to April, and on some Wednesday afternoons from January to May. ✉ *78 rue Cardinet, 17e, Batignolles* ☎ *01–47–63–47–48* ⊕ *www.sallecortot.com* Ⓜ *Malesherbes.*

★ Théâtre Mogador

THEATER | One of Paris's most sumptuous theaters features musicals and other productions with a pronounced popular appeal (think *The Lion King* or *Holiday on Ice*). Many of the shows here are subtitled in English, thanks to Theatre in Paris. ✉ *25 rue de Mogador, 9e, Grands Boulevards* ☎ *01–53–32–32–32* ⊕ *www.theatremogador.com* Ⓜ *Trinité.*

Shopping

From Paris's great *grands magasins* on Boulevard Haussmann (namely Galeries Lafayette and Printemps) to the scores of chic boutiques lining the Rue Étienne Marcel, Rue du Louvre, and Rue Montmartre, there's no shortage of shopping opportunities here. Once you add in the area's elegant covered passages, there's enough to keep you busy for a weekend, if not an entire week.

BARGAIN SHOPPING

Monoprix

DEPARTMENT STORE | **FAMILY** | With branches throughout the city, this is *the* French dime store par excellence, stocking everyday items like cosmetics, groceries, toys, kitchenwares, and more. Monoprix also has a line of stylish, inexpensive, basic wearables for the whole family—particularly adorable kids' clothes—and isn't a bad place to stock up on French chocolate, jams, or *confit de canard* at reasonable prices. ✉ *21 av. de l'Opéra, 1er, Grands Boulevards* ☎ *01–42–61–78–08* ⊕ *www.monoprix.fr* Ⓜ *Opéra.*

BEAUTY

Make Up For Ever

COSMETICS | Poised at the back of a courtyard, this store is a must-stop for makeup artists, models, actresses, and divas of all stripes. The riotous color selection includes hundreds of hues for foundation, eye shadow, powder, and lipstick. ✉ *5 rue de la Boétie, 8e, Grands Boulevards* ☏ *01–53–05–93–30* ⊕ *www. makeupforever.com* Ⓜ *St-Augustin.*

★ Nose

PERFUME | Off the bustling Rue Montmartre, this unique concept store is Paris's perfume and skin-care central—a must for seekers of that elusive perfect fragrance. After installing you at the bar (with refreshment) you'll be given a detailed questionnaire on the in-house iPad to pinpoint five or 10 scents from 500 niche perfumes that correspond to your deepest self. There's also a super range of European skin-care products, scented candles, and other delicious surprises. ✉ *20 rue Bachaumont, 2e, Grands Boulevards* ☏ *01–40–26–46–03* ⊕ *noseparis.com* Ⓜ *Sentier, Étienne Marcel.*

CLOTHING

Anouschka

WOMEN'S CLOTHING | Anouschka has set up shop in her apartment (open by appointment only, Monday through Saturday), and has rack upon rack of vintage clothing dating from the 1930s to the '80s. It's the perfect place to find a '50s cocktail dress in mint condition or a mod jacket for him. A former model herself, she calls this a "designer laboratory," and teams from top fashion houses often pop by looking for inspiration. ✉ *6 av. du Coq, 9e, Grands Boulevards* ☏ *01–48–74–37–00* Ⓜ *St-Lazare, Trinité.*

★ By Marie

OTHER SPECIALTY STORE | At her multibrand concept store, jewelry designer and general fashionista-about-town Marie Gas does the work for you, mixing designers you already know and love (Golden Goose, Ulla Johnson) with French and European *créateurs* that you definitely want to know (and will love). Her own line of jewelry is also wildly popular. Browse a seasonal collection of everything from ready-to-wear to jewelry, leather goods, perfume, and design objects for the home. ✉ *44 rue Étienne Marcel, 2e, Grands Boulevards* ☏ *01–42–33–36–04* ⊕ *www.bymarie.com* Ⓜ *Sentier, Étienne Marcel.*

Charvet

MIXED CLOTHING | The Parisian equivalent of a Savile Row tailor, Charvet is a conservative, aristocratic institution. It's famed for made-to-measure shirts, exquisite ties, and accessories; for garbing John F. Kennedy, Charles de Gaulle, and the Duke of Windsor; and for its regal address. Although the exquisite silk ties, in hundreds of colors and patterns, and custom-made shirts for men are the biggest draws, refined pieces for women and girls, as well as adorable miniatures for boys, round out the collection. ✉ *28 pl. Vendôme, 1er, Grands Boulevards* ☏ *01–42–60–30–70* Ⓜ *Opéra.*

Éric Bompard

MIXED CLOTHING | This cashmere shop provides stylish Parisians with luxury cashmere in every color, style, and weight; yarns range from light as a feather to a hefty 50-ply for the jaunty caps. The store caters to men and women (there are some kids' models too). Styles are updated seasonally yet tend toward the classic. ✉ *75 bd. Haussmann, 8e, Grands Boulevards* ☏ *01–42–68–00–73* ⊕ *www. eric-bompard.com* Ⓜ *Miromesnil.*

★ Y's Yohji Yamamoto

MIXED CLOTHING | Yamamoto's voluminous, draped, and highly coveted Y's label fully expresses itself in this sleek backdrop of white and chrome. Don't expect a varied palette; the clothing comes mostly in his signature black, with splashes of red, beige, and white. But do expect sophisticated, classic clothes that never go out of style. ✉ *25 rue du Louvre, 2e, Grands*

Boulevards ☎ 01–42–21–42–93 ⊕ www.
yohjiyamamoto.co.jp Ⓜ Étienne Marcel,
Bourse, Louvre-Rivoli.

FOOD AND TREATS
À la Mère de Famille
CANDY | FAMILY | This enchanting shop
dates from 1761 and is the oldest
continuously open confectionary in Paris.
Though it has gone the way of the chain,
with multiple boutiques in Paris, À la
Mère de Famille retains its authenticity
and is well versed in French regional specialties as well as old-fashioned bonbons,
chocolates, marzipan, ice creams, and
more. ⊠ 35 rue du Faubourg-Montmar-
tre, 9e, Grands Boulevards ☎ 01–47–
70–83–69 ⊕ www.lameredefamille.com
Ⓜ Cadet.

Fauchon
FOOD | The most iconic of Parisian food
stores is expanding globally, but its flagship is still behind the Madeleine church.
Established in 1886, Fauchon sells
renowned pâté, honey, jelly, tea, and
private-label Champagne. Expats come
for hard-to-find foreign foods (think U.S.
pancake mix or British lemon curd), while
those with a sweet tooth make a beeline
to the pâtisserie for airy, ganache-filled
macarons. There's also a café for a quick
bite. Be prepared, though: prices can be
eye-popping—marzipan fruit for €100
a pound? ⊠ 26 pl. de la Madeleine, 8e,
Grands Boulevards ☎ 01–70–39–38–00
⊕ www.fauchon.com Ⓜ Madeleine.

★ G. Detou
FOOD | Join Paris's chefs and head for
G. Detou (get it, j'ai de tout—I have
everything), just off the wonderful
Marché Montorgeuil, for an absolutely
astounding range of baking staples, nuts,
chocolate, canned rarities, and other
French and European delicacies. Basi-
cally, a bit of, well … everything. ⊠ 58
rue Tiquetonne, 2e, Grands Boulevards
☎ 01–42–36–54–67 Ⓜ Étienne Marcel,
Réaumur Sébastopol.

★ Rrraw
CHOCOLATE | Just when Paris thought its
already phenomenal chocolate scene
couldn't get any better, chocolatier
Frédéric Marr opened this chic chocolate
factory and boutique in 2007. Now the
words "healthy" and "chocolate" appear
together in the organic, nondairy, vegan
(and yes, tasty) confections made here
from unheated raw beans to preserve all
the nutrients, subtle flavors, and (minimal) natural sugars. There's no resisting
the chic metal boxes filled with bite-size
truffles perfumed with flavors like sesa-
me-rose, hazelnut-vanilla, or honey-pol-
len, as well as tablettes (bars) and baking
chocolate, a boon for vegan cooks. It's
known for its vegan, gluten-free, organic,
and low-sugar products, but it also has
delicious hot chocolate. Plus, you can
watch chocolate being made on the
premises. ⊠ 8 rue de Mulhouse, 2e,
Grands Boulevards ☎ 01–45–08–84–04
⊕ www.rrraw.fr Ⓜ Bonnes Nouvelle.

★ Stohrer
FOOD | This institution opened in 1730,
thanks to Louis XV's Polish bride, who
couldn't bear to part with her pastry chef
and thus brought Nicholas Stohrer along
with her to Paris. Today, it has all the
to-die-for pastries that made the bakery's
name, including the famous baba au
rhum that originated here, as well as a
tantalizing range of other sweets, breads,
and savory prepared foods to go. ⊠ 51
rue Montorgueil, 2e, Grands Boulevards
☎ 01–42–33–38–20 ⊕ stohrer.fr Ⓜ Étienne Marcel, Réaumur–Sébastopol.

HOME DECOR
★ Design et Nature
ANTIQUES & COLLECTIBLES | Harking back
to the Victorian era, when every chic
household had a stuffed bird or small
mammal, this outstanding cabinet of curiosities mixes jewel-like butterflies and
insects with astonishing specimens of
wild animals, including giraffes, lions and
tigers, polar bears, antelopes, zebras, and
exquisite birds (all of the animals died of

natural causes in zoos). More comical or whimsical pieces include pastel-colored chickens, winged monkeys or mice, and the Poe chandelier, complete with a raven. All items come with certification for easy export and can be shipped anywhere. ✉ *4 rue d'Aboukir, 2e, Grands Boulevards* ☎ *01–43–06–86–98* ⊕ *www.designetnature.fr* Ⓜ *Étienne Marcel, Pyramides, Palais Royal–Musée du Louvre.*

JEWELRY AND ACCESSORIES
Alexandre Reza
JEWELRY & WATCHES | One of Paris's most exclusive jewelers, Alexandre Reza is first and foremost a gemologist. He travels the world looking for the finest stones and then works them into stunning pieces, many of which are replicas of jewels of historical importance. ✉ *21 pl. Vendôme, 1er, Grands Boulevards* ☎ *01–42–61–51–21* ⊕ *www.alexandrereza.com* Ⓜ *Opéra.*

Chanel Jewelry
JEWELRY & WATCHES | Chanel Jewelry feeds off the iconic design elements of the pearl-draped designer: witness the quilting (reimagined for gold rings), camellias (now brooches), and shooting stars (used for her first jewelry collection in 1932, now appearing as diamond rings). ✉ *18 pl. Vendôme, 1er, Grands Boulevards* ☎ *01–40–98–55–55* ⊕ *www.chanel.com* Ⓜ *Tuileries, Opéra.*

Dinh Van
JEWELRY & WATCHES | Just around the corner from Place Vendôme's titan jewelers, Dinh Van thumbs its nose at in-your-face opulence. The look here is refreshingly spare. Best sellers include a hammered-gold-orb necklace and leather-cord bracelets joined with geometric shapes in white or yellow gold, some with pavé diamonds. ✉ *16 rue de la Paix, 2e, Grands Boulevards* ☎ *01–42–61–74–49* ⊕ *www.dinhvan.com* Ⓜ *Opéra.*

LINGERIE
Erès
LINGERIE | This brand revolutionized the bathing suit in the free-spirited '60s. Engineered to move freely with the body, these ingenious cuts liberated women from bones and padding. Lingerie followed in 1998, offering the same flawless craftsmanship and supreme comfort. Sexy without a hint of trashiness, Erès puts out some of the finest and most sophisticated lingerie and bathing suits in Paris season after season. ✉ *2 rue Tronchet, 8e, Grands Boulevards* ☎ *01–47–42–28–82* ⊕ *www.eresparis.com* Ⓜ *Madeleine.*

MARKETS
★ Marché Montorgueil
MARKET | One of Paris's oldest and most colorful market streets, with its roots in the 12th century, still harbors addresses that hark back to the 18th century. To get the full effect, start at Rue Réaumur, and walk this cobbled pedestrian street all the way to the Forum des Halles, past shops displaying every French delicacy, from cheese and chocolate to oysters and pastry, interspersed with bustling cafés. Stop in at Société des Huîtres d'Étretat (1777), at Nos. 61–63, purveyors of oysters to Marie-Antoinette, or grab a divine pastry at Stohrer (1730) at No. 51. ✉ *Rue Montorgueil, 2e, Grands Boulevards* Ⓜ *Étienne Marcel, Réaumur–Sébastopol.*

★ Rue du Nil
NEIGHBORHOODS | Once a sordid spot where grifters convened to count the daily take, this minuscule street, tucked away in the up-and-coming Sentier neighborhood in arrondissement 2e, is now foodie central. It all began with the Frenchie empire—takeout, wine bar, and gastronomic restaurant—then their suppliers decided to follow. Now, the cobbled street is lined with chic eateries and purveyors of everything from fresh fish and fruits to tempting breads and pastries, and boasts one of Paris's best

gourmet coffee shops (L'Arbre à Café). ✉ *Rue du Nil, Grands Boulevards.*

Rue Lévis

MARKET | This market, near Parc Monceau, is one of Paris's more vibrant and oldest market streets, dating back to the 1600s. Though some cut-rate boutiques lately encroached, you'll find plenty of the authentic good stuff, from cured Iberian ham to every French specialty under the sun. ✉ *Rue Lévis, 17e, Grands Boulevards* Ⓜ *Villiers.*

SHOPPING GALLERIES

Passage des Panoramas

MARKET | Built in 1799, the city's oldest extant arcade has become a foodie paradise, with no fewer than a dozen gourmet destinations, including Racines, Alstair, Caffè Sterne, and Coinstot Vino wine bar. ✉ *11 bd. Montmartre, 2e, Grands Boulevards* Ⓜ *Opéra, Grands Boulevards.*

Passage Jouffroy

MARKET | This passage is full of eclectic shops selling toys, Asian furnishings, cinema posters, and more. Pain d'Épices, at No. 29, specializes in dollhouse decor. ✉ *10–12 bd. Montmartre, 9e, Grands Boulevards* Ⓜ *Grands Boulevards.*

Passage Verdeau

MARKET | Across from Passage Jouffroy, Passage Verdeau has shops carrying antique cameras, comic books, and engravings. Au Bonheur des Dames, at No. 8, has all things embroidery. ✉ *4–6 rue de la Grange Batelière, 9e, Grands Boulevards* Ⓜ *Grands Boulevards.*

TOYS
★ Pain d'Épices

TOYS | FAMILY | This shop has anything you can imagine for the French home (and garden) in miniature, including Lilliputian croissants, wine decanters, and minuscule instruments in their cases. Build-it-yourself dollhouses include a 17th-century town house and a *boulangerie* storefront. Upstairs are do-it-yourself teddy-bear kits and classic toys. ✉ *29 Passage Jouffroy, 9e, Grands Boulevards* ☎ *01–47–70–08–68* ⊕ *www.paindepices. fr* Ⓜ *Grands Boulevards.*

WINE

Les Caves Augé

WINE/SPIRITS | One of the best wine shops in Paris, Les Caves Augé has been in operation since 1850. It's just the ticket, whether you're looking for a rare vintage, a select Bordeaux, or a seductive bubbly for a tête-à-tête. English-speaking experts are on hand to guide you through an excellent selection of small-producer, organic, and natural wines and select grower-producer Champagnes. ✉ *116 bd. Haussmann, 8e, Grands Boulevards* ☎ *01–45–22–16–97* Ⓜ *St-Augustin.*

Chapter 8

MONTMARTRE

Updated by
Jack Vermee

⊚ Sights	🍴 Restaurants	🛏 Hotels	⊖ Shopping	🍸 Nightlife
★★★★☆	★★★☆☆	★★☆☆☆	★★★☆☆	★☆☆☆☆

NEIGHBORHOOD SNAPSHOT

MAKING THE MOST OF YOUR TIME

Devote a day to this neighborhood if you want to see more than the obligatory Sacré-Coeur Basilica. If possible, avoid weekends, when the narrow—and extremely hilly—streets are jam-packed.

GETTING HERE

Montmartre is in the 18e arrondissement. Take Line 2 to Anvers *métro* station, and then take the funicular (one métro ticket) up to Sacré-Coeur. Or take Line 12 to Abbesses station and take your time wandering the cobbled streets and staircases that lead up to the basilica. For a scenic tour, hop the public bus, Montmartrobus (one métro ticket). An easy starting point is the métro station Jules-Joffrin (Line 12): the bus winds up the hilly streets, with a convenient stop at Sacré-Coeur. Alternatively, pile the kids onto Le Petit Train de Montmartre (€4.50–€7), a bus disguised as a minitrain that runs a circuit every 30 minutes (every hour in winter) from Place Blanche.

PAUSE HERE

Directly behind the Sacré-Coeur Basilica sits the lovely park and green space formally known as the Square Marcel Bleustein Blanchet. With great views of Paris's northeast quadrant, it is the perfect spot to recharge your batteries before tackling Sacré-Coeur itself.

TOP REASONS TO GO

■ **Basilique du Sacré-Coeur.** The best view of Paris is worth the climb—or the funicular ride—especially at twilight when the city lights create a magnificent panorama below the hill of Montmartre.

■ **Place du Tertre.** This bustling square beside Sacré-Coeur teems with crowds of tourists and hordes of street artists clamoring to paint them.

■ **Place des Abbesses.** Capture the village ambience that makes Montmartre special by exploring the tiny streets branching out from this picturesque square.

■ **Carré Roland Dorgelès.** Bring your camera to this little square overlooking a pair of classic Montmartre sights: the city's only vineyard and the famous Au Lapin Agile cabaret.

Montmartre has become almost too charming for its own good. Yes, it feels like a village (if you wander off the beaten path); yes, there are working artists here (though far fewer than there used to be); and yes, the best view of Paris is yours for free from the top of the hill (if there's no haze).

That's why on any weekend day, year-round, you can find scores of visitors crowding these cobbled alleys, scaling the staircases that pass for streets, and queuing to see Sacré-Coeur, the "sculpted cloud," at the summit.

If you're lucky enough to have a little corner of Montmartre to yourself, you'll understand why locals love it so. Come at nonpeak times, on a weekday, or in the morning or later in the evening. Stroll around **Place des Abbesses,** where the rustic houses and narrow streets escaped the heavy hand of urban planner Baron Haussmann. Until 1860 the area was, in fact, a separate village, dotted with windmills. Always a draw for bohemians and artists, many of whom had studios at what is now the **Musée de Montmartre** and the **Bateau-Lavoir,** Montmartre has been home to such painters as Suzanne Valadon and her son Maurice Utrillo, Picasso, Van Gogh, Géricault, Renoir, and, of course, Henri de Toulouse-Lautrec, whose iconic paintings of the cancan dancers at the **Moulin Rouge** are now souvenir-shop fixtures. While you can still see shows at the Moulin Rouge in Place Blanche and the pocket-size cabaret **Au Lapin Agile,** much of the entertainment here is on the seedier side—the area around Pigalle is the city's largest

red-light district, though it's far tamer than it used to be. Boulevard de Clichy was virtually an artists' highway at the turn of the 20th century: Degas lived and died at No. 6, and Picasso lived at No. 11. The *quartier* is a favorite of filmmakers (the blockbuster *Moulin Rouge* was inspired by it), and visitors still seek out Café des Deux Moulins at 15 rue Lepic, the real-life café (unfortunately with a remodeled look) where Audrey Tautou waited tables in 2001's *Amélie.* In 1928, **Studio 28** opened as the world's first cinema for experimental films.

Sights

★ Basilique de St-Denis
CHURCH | Built between 1136 and 1286, St-Denis Basilica is one of the most important Gothic churches in France. It was here, under dynamic prelate Abbé Suger, that Gothic architecture (typified by pointed arches and rib vaults) was said to have made its first appearance. The kings of France soon chose St-Denis as their final resting place, and their richly sculpted tombs—along with what remains of Suger's church—can be seen in the choir area at the east end. The basilica was battered during the Revolution; afterward, however, Louis

XVIII reestablished it as the royal burial site by moving the remains of Louis XVI and Marie-Antoinette here to join centuries' worth of monarchial bones. The vast 13th-century nave is a brilliant example of structural logic; its columns, capitals, and vault are a model of architectural harmony. The facade, retaining the rounded arches of the Romanesque that preceded the Gothic period, is set off by a small rose window, reputedly the oldest in France. Check out the extensive archaeological finds, such as a Merovingian queen's grave goods. Guided tours in English are available (see website for times); if you'd rather explore on your own, audioguides are available for €3, as is a free English-language information leaflet. ⊠ *1 rue de la Légion d'Honneur, St-Denis* ☎ *01–48–09–83–54* ⊕ *www. saint-denis-basilique.fr* ⊠ *€9.50* Ⓜ *Basilique de St-Denis.*

★ **Basilique du Sacré-Coeur**
CHURCH | It's hard not to feel as though you're ascending to heaven when you visit Sacred Heart Basilica, the white castle in the sky, perched atop Montmartre. The French government commissioned it in 1873 to symbolize the return of self-confidence after the devastating years of the Commune and Franco-Prussian War, and architect Paul Abadie employed elements from Romanesque and Byzantine styles when designing it—a mélange many critics dismissed as gaudy. Construction lasted until World War I, and the church was finally consecrated in 1919. Many people now come to Sacré-Coeur to admire the superlative view from the top of its 271-foot-high dome. But if you opt to skip the climb up the spiral staircase, the view from the front steps is still ample compensation for the trip.

Inside, expect another visual treat—namely the massive golden mosaic set high above the choir. Created in 1922 by Luc-Olivier Merson, *Christ in*

Majesty depicts Christ with a golden heart and outstretched arms, surrounded by various figures, including the Virgin Mary and Joan of Arc. It remains one of the largest mosaics of its kind. In the basilica's 262-foot-high campanile hangs La Savoyarde, one of the world's heaviest bells, weighing about 19 tons.

The best time to visit Sacré-Coeur is early morning or early evening, and preferably not on a Sunday, when the crowds are thick. If you're coming to worship, there are daily Masses.

■ **TIP→ To avoid the steps, take the funicular, which costs one métro ticket each way.** ⊠ *Pl. du Parvis-du-Sacré-Coeur, 18e, Montmartre* ☎ *01–53–41–89–00* ⊕ *www. sacre-coeur-montmartre.com* ⊠ *Basilica free, dome €7* Ⓜ *Anvers, plus funicular; Jules Joffrin plus Montmartrobus.*

Bateau-Lavoir
HISTORIC HOME | The birthplace of Cubism isn't open to the public, but a display in the front window details this unimposing spot's rich history. Montmartre poet Max Jacob coined the name because the original structure here reminded him of the laundry boats that used to float in the Seine, and he joked that the warren of paint-splattered artists' studios needed a good hosing down (wishful thinking, because the building had only one water tap). It was in the Bateau-Lavoir that, early in the 20th century, Pablo Picasso, Georges Braque, and Juan Gris made their first bold stabs at Cubism, and Picasso painted the groundbreaking *Les Demoiselles d'Avignon* in 1906–07. The experimental works of the artists weren't met with open arms, even in liberal Montmartre. All but the facade was rebuilt after a fire in 1970. Like the original building, though, the current incarnation houses artists and their studios. ⊠ *13 pl. Émile-Goudeau, 18e, Montmartre* Ⓜ *Abbesses.*

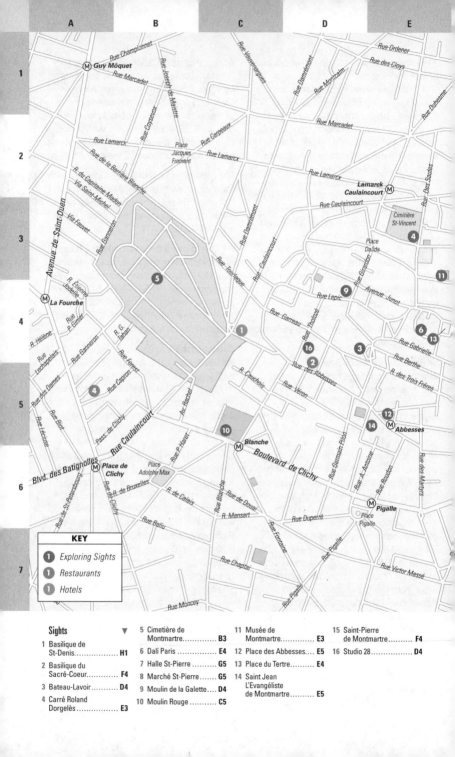

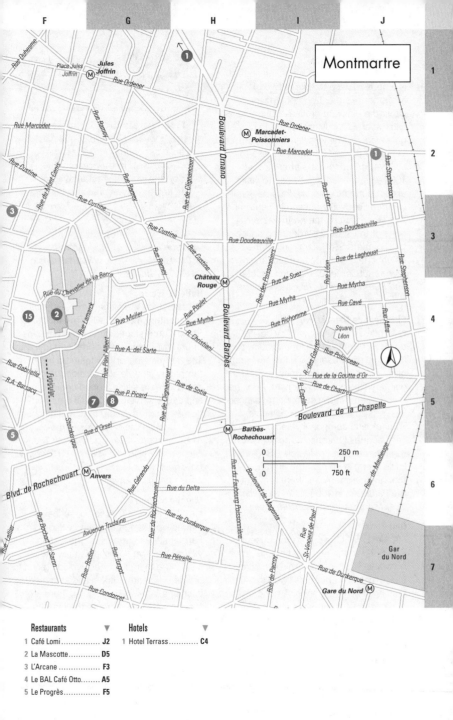

Montmartre

Carré Roland Dorgelès

PLAZA/SQUARE | This unassuming square is a perfect place to take in two of Montmartre's most photographed sites: the pink-and-green Au Lapin Agile cabaret and Clos Montmartre, Paris's only working vineyard. While the former, famously painted by Camille Pissarro, still welcomes revelers after almost 160 years, the latter is closed to visits except during the annual Fête de Jardins (Garden Festival) weekend in September. The stone wall on the northwestern edge of the square borders the peaceful Cimetière St-Vincent, one of the neighborhood's three atmospheric cemeteries. ✉ *Corner of Rue des Saulnes and Rue St-Vincent, 18e, Montmartre* Ⓜ *Lamarck-Caulaincourt.*

Cimetière de Montmartre

CEMETERY | Overshadowed by better-known Père-Lachaise, this cemetery is just as picturesque. It's the final resting place of a host of luminaries, including painters Degas and Fragonard; Adolphe Sax, inventor of the saxophone; dancer Vaslav Nijinsky; filmmaker François Truffaut; and composers Hector Berlioz and Jacques Offenbach. The Art Nouveau tomb of novelist Émile Zola (1840–1902) lords over a lawn near the entrance—though Zola's remains were moved to the Panthéon in 1908. ✉ *20 av. Rachel, 18e, Montmartre* Ⓜ *Blanche.*

Dalí Paris

ART MUSEUM | One of several museums dedicated to the Surrealist master, the permanent collection in this exhibition space includes about 300 works, mostly etchings and lithographs. Among the two dozen sculptures are versions of Dalí's melting bronze clock and variations on the *Venus de Milo.* Since he was a multimedia pioneer ahead of his time, there are videos with Dalí's voice, and temporary exhibits have included the mustachioed man's foray into holograms. There's plenty of information in English, and audioguides can be rented for €3.

Picasso Lived Here

Montmartre is virtually littered with "Picasso Lived Here" plaques. The artist resided at three different addresses in the area: on Rue Gabrielle when he first arrived; at the Bateau-Lavoir; and at 11 bd. de Clichy.

✉ *11 rue Poulbot, 18e, Montmartre* ☎ *01–42–64–40–10* ⊕ *www.daliparis.com* 🎫 *€13* Ⓜ *Abbesses.*

Halle St-Pierre

ART MUSEUM | The elegant iron-and-glass, 19th-century market hall at the foot of Sacré-Coeur stages dynamic exhibitions of *art brut,* "raw" or outsider and folk art. The international artists featured are contemporary in style and outside the mainstream. There's also a good bookstore and a café serving light, well-prepared dishes, such as savory tarts and quiches with salad on the side, plus homemade desserts. ✉ *2 rue Ronsard, 18e, Montmartre* ☎ *01–42–58–72–89* ⊕ *www. hallesaintpierre.org* 🎫 *€9* ⊗ *Closed weekends in Aug.* Ⓜ *Anvers.*

Marché St-Pierre

MARKET | FAMILY | This self-described "fabric kingdom" has been selling Parisians their curtains for more than 60 years. With five floors, it actually stocks a lot more than draperies, including bolts of fine silk, feather boas, and spangled cushions. Among the regulars here are the designers who create the famous windows at Hermès. The Marché anchors a fabric district that extends to the neighboring streets; each shop is a bit different from the next. ✉ *2 rue Charles Nodier, 18e, Montmartre* ☎ *01–42–06–92–25* ⊕ *www.marchesaint-pierre.com* ⊗ *Closed Sun.* Ⓜ *Anvers.*

Moulin de la Galette

WINDMILL | Of the 14 windmills (*moulins*) that used to sit atop this hill, only two remain. They're known collectively as Moulin de la Galette, a name taken from the bread the owners once produced. The more storied of the two is Le Blute-Fin: in the late 1800s there was a dance hall on the site, famously captured by Renoir (you can see the painting in the Musée d'Orsay). A face-lift restored the windmill to its 19th-century glory; however, it is on private land and can't be visited. Down the street is the other moulin, Le Radet. ⊠ *Le Blute-Fin, at corner of Rue Lepic and Rue Girardon, 18e, Montmartre* Ⓜ *Abbesses.*

Moulin Rouge

PERFORMANCE VENUE | When this world-famous cabaret opened in 1889, aristocrats, professionals, and the working classes alike all flocked to ogle the scandalous performers (the cancan was considerably kinkier in Toulouse-Lautrec's day, when girls kicked off their knickers). There's not much to see from the outside except for tourist buses and sex shops; if you want to catch a show inside, ticket prices start at €88. Souvenir seekers should check out the Moulin Rouge gift shop (around the corner at 11 rue Lepic), which sells official merchandise, from jewelry to sculptures, by reputable French makers. ⊠ *82 bd. de Clichy, 18e, Montmartre* ☎ *01–53–09–82–82* ⊕ *www. moulinrouge.fr* Ⓜ *Blanche.*

Musée de Montmartre

ART MUSEUM | During its turn-of-the-20th-century heyday, this building—now home to Montmartre's historical museum—was occupied by painters, writers, and cabaret artists. Foremost among them was Pierre-Auguste Renoir, who painted *Le Moulin de la Galette* (an archetypal scene of sun-drenched revelers) while living here. Recapping the area's colorful past, the museum has a charming permanent collection, which includes many Toulouse-Lautrec posters and original Eric Satie scores. An ambitious renovation, completed in 2014, doubled its space by incorporating both the studio apartment once shared by mother-and-son duo Suzanne Valadon and Maurice Utrillo (now fully restored) and the adjoining Demarne Hotel (which has been redesigned to house temporary exhibitions). The lovely surrounding gardens—named in honor of Renoir—have also been revitalized. An audioguide is included in the ticket price. ⊠ *12 rue Cortot, 18e, Montmartre* ☎ *01–49–25–89–39* ⊕ *www.museedemontmartre.fr* ✉ *€14 (€5 gardens only)* ⊗ *Closed Tues.* Ⓜ *Lamarck–Caulaincourt.*

Place des Abbesses

PLAZA/SQUARE | This triangular square is typical of the countrified style that has made Montmartre famous. Now a hub for shopping and people-watching, the *place* is surrounded by hip boutiques, sidewalk cafés, and shabby-chic restaurants—a prime habitat for the young, neo-bohemian crowd and a sprinkling of expats. Trendy streets like Rue Houdon and Rue des Martyrs have attracted small designer shops, trendy secondhand clothing stores, and even a *pâtisserie* specializing in meringues. Many retailers remain open on Sunday afternoon. ⊠ *Rue des Abbesses at Rue la Vieuville, 18e, Montmartre* Ⓜ *Abbesses.*

Place du Tertre

PLAZA/SQUARE | Artists have peddled their wares in this square for centuries. Busloads of tourists have changed the atmosphere, but if you come off-season—when the air is chilly and the streets are bare—you can almost feel what it was like when up-and-coming Picassos lived in the houses that today are given over to souvenir shops and cafés. ⊠ *East end of Rue Norvin, Pl. du Tertre, 18e, Montmartre* Ⓜ *Abbesses.*

Saint Jean L'Evangéliste de Montmartre

CHURCH | This eye-catching church with a compact Art Nouveau interior was the first modern house of worship built in

Paris (1897–1904) and the first to be constructed of reinforced cement. Architect Anatole de Baudot's revolutionary technique defied the accepted rules at the time with its use of unsupported masonry; critics, who failed to stop construction, feared the building would crumble under its own weight. Today the church attracts a steady flow of visitors curious about its unusual Moorish-inspired facade of redbrick and curved arches. Note the tiny clock at the top left of the bell tower and the handsome stained-glass windows. Free concerts and art exhibitions are staged in the church from time to time. ✉ *19 rue des Abbesses, 18e, Montmartre* ☎ *01–46–06–43–96* ⊕ *www.saintjeandemontmartre.com* Ⓜ *Abbesses.*

Saint-Pierre de Montmartre

CHURCH | Tucked in the shadow of mighty Sacré-Coeur is one of the oldest churches in Paris. Built in 1147 on the site of a 5th-century temple to the god Mars, this small sanctuary with its impressive sculpted metal doors was once part of a substantial Benedictine abbey. Besides the church, all that remains is a small cemetery, now closed (you can see it through the ornate metal door on the left as you enter the courtyard). Renovated multiple times through the ages, Saint-Pierre combines various styles. Interior elements, such as the columns in the nave, are medieval; the facade dates to the 18th century, with renovations in the 19th century; and the stained-glass windows are 20th century. Maurice Utrillo's 1914 painting of the titular saint hangs in the Musée de l'Orangerie. Admission is free; English audioguides are €3. ✉ *2 rue du Mont Cenis, off Pl. du Tertre, 18e, Montmartre* ☎ *01–46–06–57–63* ⊕ *www.saintpierredemontmartre.net* Ⓜ *Anvers.*

Studio 28

OTHER ATTRACTION | This little movie house has a distinguished history. When it opened in 1928, it was the first theater in the world purposely built for *art et essai,* or experimental film, and Luis Buñuel and Salvador Dalí's *L'Age d'Or* caused a riot when it premiered here. Through the years artists and writers came to see "seventh art" creations by directors such as Jean Cocteau, François Truffaut, and Orson Welles. Today it's a repertory cinema, showing first-runs, just-runs, and previews—usually in their original language. Movies are screened beginning at 3 pm daily, and tickets cost €9.50. In the back of the movie house is a cozy bar and café that has a quiet outdoor terrace decorated with murals of film stars. Oh, and those charmingly bizarre chandeliers in the *salle*? Cocteau designed them. ✉ *10 rue Tholozé, 18e, Montmartre* ☎ *01–46–06–47–45* ⊕ *www.cinema-studio28.fr* 🎟 *Movie tickets €9.50* Ⓜ *Abbesses.*

🍴 Restaurants

Perched above central Paris, Montmartre is buzzing with a hip vibe. Idyllic as the portrayal of Montmartre might seem in Jean-Pierre Jeunet's film *Amélie,* it's surprisingly close to reality. Though decidedly out of the way, Montmartre is still one of the most desirable areas in Paris, seamlessly blending the trendy and the traditional. The less picturesque neighborhood around Gare du Nord and Gare de l'Est is making its mark on the culinary milieu: besides classic brasseries, tucked-away bistros, and the city's most authentic Indian restaurants, there is a new generation of cafés and gastro-bistros exploding onto the scene.

Café Lomi

$ | CAFÉ | A trailblazer on the Paris gastro-coffee scene, out-of-the-way Café Lomi first supplied expertly roasted single-origin coffees to the first wave of barista cafés and top restaurants. Now Lomi's industrial-chic loft is equal parts roaster, café, workshop, and pilgrimage stop for hard-core coffee lovers, serving a range of splendid brews along with a menu of warm and cold dishes and a hearty brunch on weekends. **Known**

Perhaps the most famous cabaret in the world, the Moulin Rogue is where the cancan dance is said to have originated.

for: consistently excellent brews; coffee roasted on the premises; industrial-chic space. $ *Average main: €10* ✉ *3 ter rue Marcadet, 18e, Montmartre* ☎ *09–51–27–46–31* ⊕ *www.lomi.coffee* ⊘ *Closed Sun., Mon., and 3 wks in Aug.* Ⓜ *Marcadet-Poissonière.*

La Mascotte
$$$ | BRASSERIE | Though everyone talks about the "new Montmartre," exemplified by a wave of chic residents and throbbingly cool cafés and bars, the old Montmartre is alive and well at the untrendy-and-proud-of-it Mascotte. This old-fashioned café-brasserie—which dates from 1889, the same year that saw the opening of the Tour Eiffel and the Moulin Rouge—is a local favorite. **Known for:** typical Belle Époque Montmartre atmosphere; sidewalk dining in summer; copious oyster and seafood platters. $ *Average main: €32* ✉ *52 rue des Abbesses, 18e, Montmartre* ☎ *01–46–06–28–15* ⊕ *www.la-mascotte-montmartre.com* Ⓜ *Abbesses.*

★ L'Arcane
$$$$ | FRENCH | Once a well-guarded foodie secret, a Michelin star brought this singular restaurant, tucked behind the Sacré-Coeur, richly deserved acclaim. Now the dining room is packed with diners enjoying impeccable contemporary French cuisine that's gorgeously presented and full of flavor. **Known for:** very friendly service; location near the Sacré-Coeur; vividly imagined cuisine on multicourse tasting menus. $ *Average main: €135* ✉ *52 rue Lamarck, 18e, Montmartre* ☎ *01–46–06–86–00* ⊕ *www. restaurantlarcane.com* ⊘ *Closed Sun., Mon., Aug., 1 wk in mid-Apr., and last wk of Dec.* Ⓜ *Lamarck-Cauliancourt.*

★ Le BAL Café Otto
$ | CAFÉ | FAMILY | Set in a bright, modern space on a tiny street in the lower reaches of Montmartre, the popular Le BAL Café Otto caters to a diverse clientele who come for the great coffee, delicious homey food, lively crowd, and the art gallery/bookstore. Italian-and French-inspired cuisine (like spelt

A Scenic Walk in Montmartre

One of Paris's most charming walks begins at the Abbesses métro station (Line 12). Explore the streets ringing **Place des Abbesses**, or begin the walk immediately by heading west along Rue des Abbesses. Turn right on Rue Tholozé and note the historic movie house, **Studio 28**, at No. 10. At the top of the street is Le Blute-Fin, a windmill portrayed in a well-known work by Renoir; a right on Rue Lepic takes you past the only other windmill still standing, Le Radet. Take a left here onto Rue Girardon, to **Place Dalida**, marked with a voluptuous bust of the beloved French singer who popularized disco. (Yolanda Gigliotti, aka Dalida, lived until her death in 1987 at 11 bis, rue d'Orchampt, one of the city's narrowest streets, opposite Le Radet.)

The stone house behind Dalida's bust is the 18th-century **Château des Brouillards**, whose name, Castle of the Mists, is taken from the light fog that used to cloak this former farmland. Detour down the romantic alley of the same name. Renoir is said to have lived in the château before moving to the small house across the way at No. 8. From Place Dalida, head down winding Rue de l'Abreuvoir, one of the most photographed streets in Paris. Pissarro kept a pied-à-terre at No. 12. The stone-and-wood-beam house at No. 4 was once home to a historian of the Napoleonic wars whose family symbol was an eagle. Notice the wooden sundial with a rooster and the inscription: "When you chime, I'll sing." At the pink-and-green **Maison Rose** restaurant, committed to canvas by resident artist Maurice Utrillo, turn left on Rue des Saules, where you'll find Paris's only working vineyard, **Clos de Montmartre.**

Across the street is the famous cabaret **Au Lapin Agile**, still going strong. On the opposite corner, a stone wall rings the **Cimetière Saint-Vincent**, one of the city's smallest cemeteries, where Utrillo is buried. Backtrack up Rue des Saules and take the first left onto Rue Cortot to the **Musée de Montmartre**, once home to a bevy of artists. Renoir rented a studio here to store his painting of Le Blute-Fin. A few doors down, at No. 6, the composer Erik Satie, piano player at Le Chat Noir nightclub, lived during a penniless period in a 6-by-4-foot flat with a 9-foot ceiling (and two pianos, stacked on top of each other). At the corner of Rue Mont-Cenis, the white water tower Château d'Eau still services the neighborhood. Turn right to reach **Place du Tertre**, a lively square packed with tourists and street artists. Easily overlooked is **Saint-Pierre de Montmartre**, one of the city's oldest churches, founded in 1147. End your walk at the basilica **Sacré-Coeur**, and enjoy one of the best views of Paris from the city's highest point.

risotto with mushrooms, hazelnuts, and creamed spinach) during the week rests alongside a traditional weekend brunch menu featuring items like tender pancakes, fried eggs with ham and roasted tomatoes, and buttery scones with jam. **Known for:** outdoor terrace on a quiet passageway; art gallery on the premises; great brunches and reliably good coffee. [$] *Average main: €16* ✉ *6 impasse de la Défense, 18e, Montmartre* ☎ *01–44–70–75–51* 🌐 *www.le-bal.fr/le-bal-cafe-x-otto* 🕒 *Closed Mon. and Tues.* [M] *Place de Clichy.*

Le Progrès

$ | **BRASSERIE** | This photo op–ready corner café draws a quirky mix of hipsters, artists, and discriminating tourists. The food is good and includes classics like steak tartare. **Known for:** excellent cheeseburger and fries; good value for your money; lively atmosphere. [$] *Average main: €17* ✉ *7 rue des Trois Frères, 18e, Montmartre* ☎ *01–42–64–07–37* 🌐 *www.facebook.com/leprogresmontmartre* [M] *Abbesses.*

Hotels

Like a village unto itself, off-the-beaten-path Montmartre and its equally picturesque hotels provide a homey retreat after a day of sightseeing. There's much to explore here, and the old cobbled streets and hidden historic corners harbor lodgings as varied as old, gated mansions and quaint mom-and-pop hotels.

★ Hotel Terrass

$$ | **HOTEL** | **FAMILY** | If you feel like being away from it all, but in a reasonably priced, fairly self-sufficient setting with a good on-site restaurant and a chic bar with stupendous views, this is the place. **Pros:** panoramic views of all of Paris; welcoming common areas with complimentary coffee; awesome terrace bar. **Cons:** some street noise; restaurant could be better; basic rooms are small. [$] *Rooms from: €220* ✉ *12–14 rue Joseph de Maistre, Montmartre* ☎ *01–46–06–72–85* 🌐 *www.terrass-hotel.com* 🛏 *92 rooms* 🍴 *No Meals* [M] *Blanche, Abbesses.*

Nightlife

Vestiges of this *quartier's* absinthe-tinged heyday, immortalized by Toulouse-Lautrec and Renoir, still endure in the cabarets and clubs that extend from the heights of Montmartre down to louche Pigalle's newly vibrant cocktail bar and dance scene.

BARS

Café la Fourmi

BARS | One of Pigalle's trendiest addresses, Café la Fourmi has a funky, spacious bar-café where cool locals party. It's open until 2 am every night but Friday and Saturday, when it's open until 4 am. ✉ *74 rue des Martyrs, 18e, Montmartre* ☎ *01–42–64–70–35* [M] *Pigalle.*

Cave des Abbesses

WINE BARS | Locals head to this charming retro-looking *caviste* (wineshop) and wine bar for a glass of something special with a side of oysters, or perhaps La Grande Mixte, a platter of charcuterie, terrine, and cheese (€17). ✉ *43 rue des Abbesses, 18e, Montmartre* ☎ *01–42–52–81–54* 🌐 *www.cavesbourdin.fr/cave-des-abbesses-montmartre* 🕒 *Closed Mon.* [M] *Abbesses.*

★ Dirty Dick

COCKTAIL LOUNGES | An updated version of the classic tiki lounge, this stylish option in the hip South Pigalle (SoPi) neighborhood comes complete with lurid lighting, life-size totems, and retro rattan furniture. All the exotic drinks you'd expect at a Polynesian beach hut (or '60s motel lounge) are here—including fruity cocktails, a range of rums, and punch bowls with names like Amazombie. ✉ *10 rue Frochot, 9e, Montmartre* ☎ *01–48–78–74–58* [M] *Pigalle.*

Le Rendez-Vous des Amis

BARS | This makes an intriguing midway breather if you climb the hill of Montmartre by foot. Le Rendez-Vous des Amis has a jovial staff, eclectic music, and a century's worth of previous patrons immortalized in painted murals. ✉ *23 rue Gabrielle, 18e, Montmartre* ☎ *01–46–06–01–60* [M] *Abbesses.*

Le Sancerre

BARS | Café/restaurant by day, Le Sancerre turns into an essential watering hole for Montmartrois and artists at night (until 2 am), with Belgian beers on tap and an impressive list of cocktails. Locals

Did You Know?

Like many of the "streets" in Montmartre, Rue du Calvaire, off Place du Tertre, is actually a staircase, and a scenic way down from the top of the hill.

love its traditional old-school vibe. ✉ *35 rue des Abbesses, 18e, Montmartre* ☎ *01–42–58–08–20* ⊕ *www.lesancerre-paris.com* Ⓜ *Abbesses.*

★ Paname Brewing Company

BREWPUBS | One of Paris's first and best microbreweries on the city's exploding brewery scene, Paname offers a dozen masterful craft beers, plus limited-time specials, and a fabulous terrace on a plum spot facing the Canal de la Villette. ✉ *41 bis, quai de la Loire, Montmartre* ☎ *01–40–36–43–55* ⊕ *www.paname-brewingcompany.com* Ⓜ *Crimée, Laumière, Ourcq.*

CABARET

★ Au Lapin Agile

CABARET | An authentic survivor from the 19th century, Au Lapin Agile considers itself the doyen of cabarets. Founded in 1860, it inhabits the same modest house that was a favorite subject of painter Maurice Utrillo. It became the home-away-from-home for Braque, Modigliani, Apollinaire, and Picasso—who once paid for a meal with one of his paintings, then promptly exited and painted another that he named after this place. There are no topless dancers; this is a genuine French cabaret with songs, poetry, and humor (in French) in a publike setting. Entry (one drink included) is €35, and it's cash only. ✉ *22 rue des Saules, 18e, Montmartre* ☎ *01–46–06–85–87* ⊕ *aulapinagile.fr* Ⓜ *Lamarck–Caulaincourt.*

Chez Michou

CABARET | Although the always-decked-out-in-blue owner, Michou, passed away in early 2020, the over-the-top show dances on. It features performers on stage in extravagant drag, with high camp for a radically different cabaret experience. Dinner shows are €120 and €160, or you can watch from the bar for €60. ✉ *80 rue des Martyrs, 18e, Montmartre* ☎ *01–46–06–16–04* ⊕ *michou.com* Ⓜ *Pigalle.*

🎭 Performing Arts

Cinéma des Cinéastes

FILM | FAMILY | Catch previews of feature films, as well as documentaries, shorts, children's movies, and rarely shown flicks at Cinéma des Cinéastes. Near the Montmartre neighborhood, it's an old cabaret transformed into a movie house and wine bar. ✉ *7 av. de Clichy, 17e, Montmartre* ☎ *01–53–42–40–20* ⊕ *www.cinema-des-cineastes.fr* 🎟 *€10* Ⓜ *Place de Clichy.*

★ La Cigale

CONCERTS | Artists like Maurice Chevalier and Arletty were once a staple of this small concert hall in the storied Pigalle neighborhood before cabaret and vaudeville moved in. Today it's one of Paris's top pop and contemporary music venues; artists like Adele and Coldplay played here in their early days. ✉ *120 bd. de Rochechouart, 18e, Montmartre* ☎ *01–49–25–89–99* ⊕ *www.lacigale.fr* Ⓜ *Pigalle, Anvers.*

★ Le Louxor

FILM | First opened in 1921, Le Louxor has since been returned to its original Egyptian-themed splendor. Now the city's grandest cinema, this Art Deco beauty is gorgeously appointed—all in rich ocher with jewel-toned velvet seating—and shows a roster of contemporary international art films in three cinemas. Have a drink at the top-floor bar or balcony for spectacular views of the neighborhood and Sacré-Coeur. ✉ *170 bd. Magenta, 10e, Montmartre* ☎ *01–44–63–96–96* ⊕ *www.cinemalouxor.fr* 🎟 *€10* Ⓜ *Barbès–Rochechouart.*

Théâtre des Abbesses

THEATER | Part of the Théâtre de la Ville, Théâtre des Abbesses is a 400-seat venue in Montmartre. It features lesser-known theater acts, musicians, and up-and-coming choreographers, who often make it onto the program in the

Théâtre de la Ville the following year. ✉ *31 rue des Abbesses, 18e, Montmartre* ☎ *01–42–74–22–77* ⊕ *www.theatre-delaville-paris.com* Ⓜ *Abbesses.*

Shopping

To avoid an uphill climb, the Abbesses métro stop on Rue de la Vieuville is a good starting point for serious shoppers. From here, descend picturesque Rue des Martyrs all the way down to Notre-Dame-de-Lorette. The route promises a cornucopia of captivating boutiques that sell everything from chic antiques and offbeat fashion to gourmet food.

CLOTHING

A.P.C. Surplus

MIXED CLOTHING | A.P.C. opened its surplus store steps away from Sacré-Coeur. No need to wait for sales; funky classics can always be found here for a whopping 50% off. ✉ *20 rue André del Sarte, 18e, Montmartre* ☎ *01–42–62–10–88* ⊕ *www.apc.fr* Ⓜ *Château Rouge.*

Spree

MIXED CLOTHING | When Spree first opened, its mission was to give young designers a venue; it has since branched out to include fashion elites like Comme des Garçons, Isabel Marant, Golden Goose, and Christian Wijnants. The expertly chosen inventory seems almost curated. A great selection of accessories and jewelry, along with cool furniture and a revolving exhibition of artwork by international artists, complete the gallery feel. ✉ *16 rue la Vieuville, 18e, Montmartre* ☎ *01–42–23–41–40* ⊕ *www.spree.fr* Ⓜ *Abbesses.*

MARKETS

★ Marché aux Puces St-Ouen

(*Clignancourt*)

MARKET | This picturesque market on the city's northern boundary still lures crowds on Friday from 8 am to 12 pm and Saturday through Monday from 10 am to 6 pm, but its once-unbeatable prices are now a relic. Packed with antiques booths and *brocante* stalls, the century-old, miles-long labyrinth has been undergoing a mild renaissance lately: its 15 covered "marchés" now house all manner of artisans and creators as well as buzzworthy shops and galleries (some of which keep weekend-only hours). Destination eateries—including the popular Philippe Starck–designed Ma Cocotte and the chic MOB Hotel—also attract a hip Paris contingent. Arrive early to pick up the best loot, then linger over a meal or *apéro*. Be warned, though: if there's one place in Paris where you need to know how to bargain, this is it. If you're arriving by métro, walk under the overpass and take the first left at the Rue de Rosiers to reach the center of the market. Note that stands selling dodgy odds and ends (think designer knockoffs and questionable gadgets) set up around the overpass. These blocks are crowded and gritty; be careful with your valuables here and throughout the marché. ✉ *18e, Montmartre* ⊕ *www.marcheauxpuces-saintouen.com* Ⓜ *Porte de Clignancourt, Garibaldi, Mairie de Saint-Ouen.*

Chapter 9

THE MARAIS

Updated by
Jennifer Ladonne

👁 **Sights**
★★★★★

🍴 **Restaurants**
★★★★☆

🛏 **Hotels**
★★★★☆

🛍 **Shopping**
★★★★★

🍸 **Nightlife**
★★★★☆

NEIGHBORHOOD SNAPSHOT

MAKING THE MOST OF YOUR TIME

One day in the Marais might seem painfully short, but it would allow you to take a do-it-yourself walking tour, peek into private courtyards, and picnic in the Place des Vosges as you proceed. Leave at least two days if your itinerary includes the Centre Pompidou and the Musée Picasso. In three days you could cover some of the smaller museums, which are well worth visiting as many are housed in exquisite mansions. If time permits, wander the edges of the 3e arrondissement to see the charming streets, away from the crowds, or drop into the quirky-artsy Musée de la Chasse et de la Nature or science-centric Musée des Arts et Métiers. Sunday afternoon is a lively time to come because many shops are open. As Paris's most concentrated—and chicest—shopping neighborhood, you'll want to reserve at least an afternoon for discovering its many-splendored boutiques. This neighborhood thrives after dark as well: business is brisk at cafés and bars—particularly those favored by the LGBTQ+ community.

GETTING HERE

The Marais includes the 3e and 4e arrondissements. It's a pleasant walk from Beaubourg—the area around Centre Pompidou—into the heart of the Marais. Rue Rambuteau turns into Rue des Francs-Bourgeois, which runs into Place des Vosges. If you're going by *métro*, the most central stops are St-Paul or Hôtel de Ville on Line 1. If you're going to the Pompidou, take Line 1 to Hôtel de Ville or Line 11 to Rambuteau. For the Musée Picasso, the closest stop is St-Sébastien–Froissart on Line 8. For the 3e arrondissement, you can get off at any of the stops on métro Line 8: République, Filles du Calvaire, St-Sébastien–Froissart, or Chemin Vert.

TOP REASONS TO GO

■ **Centre Pompidou.** Paris's leading modern art museum is also a vast (and architecturally ambitious) arts center that presents films, theater, performance art, and dance performances.

■ **Place des Vosges.** The prettiest square in the French capital surrounds a manicured park, where benches and inviting patches of grass are ideal if you're in need of a siesta.

■ **Musée National Picasso-Paris.** Spectacularly renovated, this museum is a must-see for fans of the Spanish master, who painted some of his best work while living in the city.

■ **Shopping.** This is Paris's largest, most diverse, and most fashionable neighborhood, with more boutiques than you could visit in a week, let alone a day.

■ **Jewish history.** The old Jewish quarter has two world-class sites: Mémorial de la Shoah (the Holocaust Memorial) and the Musée d'Art et d'Histoire du Judaïsme.

■ **Hidden cultural gems.** The Marais is home to a wealth of not-to-miss smaller museums and cultural centers that often fall under the tourist radar.

From swampy to swanky, the Marais has a fascinating history, having remade itself many times and today retaining several identities. It's the city's epicenter of cool, with hip boutiques, designer hotels, and art galleries galore. It's also the hub of Paris's LGBTQ+ community, and, though fading, it's the nucleus of Jewish life. You could easily spend your entire visit to Paris in this neighborhood—there is that much to do.

"Marais" means swamp, and that is exactly what this area was until the 12th century, when it was converted to farmland. In 1605, Henri IV began building the Place Royale (today's Place des Vosges, the oldest square in Paris), which touched off a building boom, and the wealthy and fabulous moved in. Despite the odors—the area was one of the city's smelliest—it remained the chic quarter until Louis XIV transferred his court to Versailles, trailed by dispirited aristocrats unhappy to decamp to the country. Merchants took over their exquisite *hôtels particuliers* (private mansions), which are some of the city's best surviving examples of French Baroque and Renaissance architecture. Here you can see the hodgepodge of narrow streets that so vexed Louis Napoléon and his sidekick, Baron Haussmann, who feared a redux of the famous *barricades* that Revolutionaries threw up to thwart the monarchy. Haussmann leveled scores of blocks like these, creating the wide, arrow-straight

avenues that are a hallmark of modern Paris. Miraculously, the Marais escaped destruction, though much of it fell victim to neglect and ruin. Thanks to restoration efforts over the past half-century, the district is enjoying its latest era of greatness, and the apartments here—among the city's oldest—are also some of the most in demand, with *beaucoup* charm, exposed beams, and steep crooked staircases barely wide enough for a supermodel. (Should you be lucky enough to find an elevator, don't expect it to fit your suitcase.) Notice the impressive *portes cochères,* the huge doors built to accommodate aristocratic carriages that today open into many sublime courtyards and hidden gardens.

The 4e arrondissement, the Marais's glitzier half, is sandwiched between two opposite poles—the regal **Place des Vosges** in the east and the eye-teasing modern masterpiece **Centre Pompidou** in the west. Between these points you'll find most of the main sites, including the

Musée Picasso, the **Maison Européenne de la Photographie,** and the **Musée Carnavalet,** set in a splendid Renaissance mansion and the best place to see how the city evolved through the ages. To tour an exquisitely restored 17th-century hôtel particulier, visit the **Musée Cognacq-Jay** or wander into the manicured back garden of the magnificent **Hôtel de Sully.** The quieter 3e arrondissement of the Marais, around Rue de Bretagne, has become one of Paris's most in-demand residential areas—and one of the most interesting to explore. Here you'll find intriguing, off-the-tourist-track boutiques, bars, and galleries, plus notable attractions such as the **Musée des Arts and Métiers,** Europe's oldest science museum, and the **Musée de la Chasse et de la Nature,** one of Paris's most delightful museums.

Paris's **Jewish quarter** (the Pletzl, Yiddish for "little place") has existed in the Marais in some form since the 13th century and still thrives around Rue des Rosiers, even as hipster hangouts encroach on the traditional bakeries and delis. Not far away is the beating heart of the gay Marais, radiating out from Rue Vieille du Temple and the Rue des Archives, along Rue St-Croix de la Bretonnerie to Rue du Temple. It's filled with trendy shops, cool cafés, and lively nightspots popular with LGBTQ folks but welcoming to all.

Sights

Agoudas Hakehilos Synagogue
SYNAGOGUE | Art Nouveau genius Hector Guimard built this unique synagogue (also called Synagogue de la Rue Pavée) in 1913 for a Polish-Russian Orthodox association. The facade resembles an open book: Guimard used the motif of the Ten Commandments to inspire the building's shape and its interior, which can only rarely be visited. Knock on the door, and see if the caretaker will let you upstairs to the balcony, where you can admire Guimard's well-preserved decor.

Like other Parisian synagogues, its front door was dynamited by Nazis on Yom Kippur, 1941. The Star of David over the door was added after the building was restored. ✉ *10 rue Pavé, 4e, Marais Quarter* ☎ *01–48–87–21–54* Ⓜ *St-Paul.*

Archives Nationales
ARCHIVE | Thousands of important historical documents are preserved inside the Hôtel de Soubise and Hôtel de Rohan—a pair of spectacular buildings constructed in 1705 as private homes. Fans of the decorative arts will appreciate a visit to the former, where the well-preserved private apartments of the Prince and Princess de Soubise are among the first examples of the rococo style, which preceded the more somber Baroque opulence of Louis XIV. The Hôtel de Soubise also has a museum that displays documents dating from 625 to the 20th century. Highlights include the Edict of Nantes (1598), the Treaty of Westphalia (1648), the wills of Louis XIV and Napoléon, and the Declaration of Human Rights (1789). Louis XVI's diary is also here, containing his sadly clueless entry for July 14, 1789—the day the Bastille was stormed and the French Revolution was launched. The Hôtel de Rohan, open to the public only during Patrimony Weekend in September, was built for Soubise's son, Cardinal Rohan. Before you leave, notice the medieval turrets in the courtyard: this is the Porte de Clisson, all that remains of a stately 14th-century mansion. ✉ *60 rue des Francs-Bourgeois, 3e, Marais Quarter* ☎ *01–40–27–60–96* ⊕ *www.archives-nationales.culture.gouv. fr* ✉ *Hôtel de Soubise €5 (free 1st Sun. of month); €8 for temporary exhibitions* ⊘ *Closed Tues.* Ⓜ *Rambuteau.*

★ Centre Pompidou
ART MUSEUM | FAMILY | Love it or hate it, the Pompidou is certainly a unique-looking building, and it holds some of the city's best contemporary art, from the 20th century to the present day. Most

Parisians have warmed to the industrial, Lego-like exterior that caused a scandal when it opened in 1977. Named after French president Georges Pompidou (1911–74), it was designed by then-unknown architects Renzo Piano and Richard Rogers, who put the building's guts on the outside and color-coded them: water pipes are green, air ducts are blue, electrics are yellow, and things like elevators and escalators are red.

The Musée National d'Art Moderne (Modern Art Museum, entrance on Level 4) occupies the top two levels. Level 5 is devoted to modern art from 1905 to 1960, including major works by Matisse, Modigliani, Marcel Duchamp, and Picasso. Level 4 is dedicated to contemporary art from the '60s on, including video installations. The Galerie d'Enfants (Children's Gallery) on the mezzanine level has interactive exhibits designed to keep the kids busy. Outside, next to the museum's sloping plaza—where throngs of teenagers hang out (and where there's free Wi-Fi)—is the Atelier Brancusi. This small, airy museum contains four rooms reconstituting Brancusi's Montparnasse studios with works from all periods of his career. On the opposite side, in Place Igor-Stravinsky, is the Stravinsky fountain, which has 16 gyrating mechanical figures in primary colors, including a giant pair of ruby red lips. On the opposite side of Rue Rambuteau, on the wall at the corner of Rue Clairvaux and Passage Brantôme, is the appealingly bizarre, mechanical, brass-and-steel clock, *Le Défenseur du Temps*.

The Pompidou's permanent collection takes up very little of the massive building, which also contains temporary exhibition galleries, including a special wing for design and architecture; the free, highly regarded reference library (university students often line up on Rue Renard to get in); and the basement, with its two cinemas, theater, dance

venue, and a small, free exhibition space. On your way up the escalator, you'll have spectacular views of Paris, ranging from Tour Montparnasse to the left, around to the hilltop Sacré-Coeur on the right. ⊠ *Pl. Georges-Pompidou, 4e, Marais Quarter* ☎ *01–44–78–12–33* ⊕ *www.centrepompidou.fr* ✉ *Center access free, Atelier Brancusi free, museum and exhibits €14 (free 1st Sun. of month)* ☉ *Closed Tues.* Ⓜ *Rambuteau.*

Église Saint-Merry

CHURCH | This impressive Gothic church in the shadow of the Centre Pompidou was completed in 1550. Notable features include the turret (it contains the oldest bell in Paris, cast in 1331) and an 18th-century pulpit supported on carved palm trees. There are free concerts here Saturday at 8 pm and Sunday at 4 pm. ⊠ *76 rue de la Verrerie, 4e, Marais Quarter* ☎ *01–42–71–93–93* ⊕ *www. saintmerry.org* Ⓜ *Hôtel de Ville.*

★ Fondation Henri Cartier-Bresson

ART MUSEUM | Henri Cartier-Bresson, the legendary artist-photojournalist and co-creator of the Magnum photo agency, launched this foundation with his wife Martine Franck, a British-Belgian portrait and documentary photographer, and their daughter Melanie. The soaring, light-filled gallery showcases a collection of 50,000 original prints along with an exceptional series of solo exhibitions from notable photographers. The foundation's bookstore itself is a draw for photography buffs. ⊠ *79 rue des Archives, 3e, Marais Quarter* ☎ *01–40–61–50–50* ⊕ *www. henricartierbresson.org* ✉ *€9* ☉ *Closed Sun.* Ⓜ *République, Filles du Calvaire, Rambuteau.*

Hôtel de Sens

CASTLE/PALACE | One of the few remaining structures in Paris from the Middle Ages, this little castle was most famously the home of Queen Margot, who took up residence here in 1605 after her

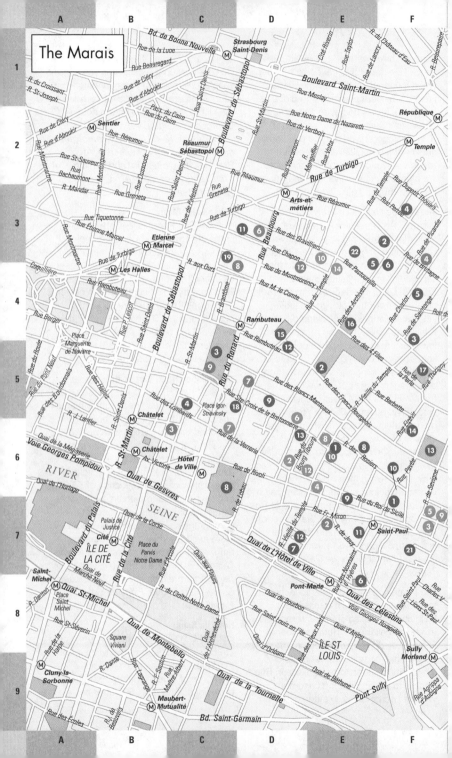

The Marais

Sights ▼

1 Agoudas Hakehilos
   Synagogue **F7**
2 Archives Nationales..... **E5**
3 Centre Pompidou **C5**
4 Église Saint-Merry....... **C5**
5 Fondation Henri
   Cartier-Bresson.......... **E4**
6 Hôtel de Sens **E8**
7 Hôtel de Sully **G7**
8 Hôtel de Ville **C6**
9 Lafayette
   Anticipations **D5**
10 Maison de
   Victor Hugo.............. **G7**
11 Maison Européenne
   de la Photographie **E7**
12 Mémorial de
   la Shoah **D7**
13 Musée Carnavalet....... **F6**
14 Musée Cognacq-Jay.... **F6**
15 Musée d'Art et d'Histoire
   du Judaïsme (mahJ).... **D4**
16 Musée de la Chasse
   et de la Nature **E4**
17 Musée National
   Picasso-Paris **F5**
18 Musée Pierre Cardin,
   Passé-Présent-Futur... **D5**
19 Nicolas Flamel's
   Home..................... **C3**
20 Place des Vosges....... **G7**
21 St-Paul–St-Louis....... **F7**
22 3e Arrondissement **E3**

Restaurants ▼

1 Assemblages............ **G7**
2 Au Bourguignon
   du Marais................ **E7**
3 Benoît **C6**
4 Café Charlot.............. **F4**
5 Café des Musées **G6**
6 Datsha Underground... **D3**
7 Grand Coeur............ **D5**
8 L'Ambassade
   d'Auvergne **C4**
9 Le Georges **C5**
10 Les Philosophes **E6**
11 Ogata..................... **F4**
12 Parcelles................ **D4**

Quick Bites ▼

1 Au Petit Fer à Cheval.... **E6**
2 Bontemps................. **F3**
3 Breizh Café **F5**
4 The Broken Arm Café ... **F3**
5 Chez Alain
   Miam Miam **F4**
6 Gramme................... **F4**
7 La Caféothèque **D7**
8 L'As du Fallafel **E6**
9 La Tartine **E7**
10 Le Loir dans
   La Théière **F6**
11 Loustic **D3**
12 Pain de Sucre **D5**
13 Une Glace à Paris **D6**

Hotels ▼

1 Cour des Vosges........ **G7**
2 Hôtel Bourg Tibourg.... **D6**
3 Hôtel Caron.............. **F7**
4 Hôtel Caron de
   Beaumarchais **E6**
5 Hôtel de JoBo........... **F7**
6 Hôtel de la
   Bretonnerie............. **D6**
7 Hôtel Duo **C6**
8 Hôtel Dupont-Smith..... **E6**
9 Hôtel Jeanne-d'Arc **G7**
10 Hôtel Jules & Jim....... **E3**
11 Hôtel Sookie............. **G4**
12 9Confidential **E6**
13 Pavillon de la Reine..... **G6**
14 Sinner **E4**

KEY

1 *Exploring Sights*
1 *Restaurants*
1 *Quick Bites*
1 *Hotels*

marriage to Henry IV was annulled. Margot was known for her many lovers (she supposedly wore wigs made from locks of their hair) and reputedly ordered a servant beheaded in the courtyard after he ridiculed one of her companions. The street is said to be named after a fig tree she ordered cut down because it was inconveniencing her carriage. Perhaps for that reason there's a fig tree planted in the elegant rear garden, which is open to the public. Notice the cannonball lodged in the front facade commemorating a battle here during the three-day revolution in July 1830. Built for the archbishop of Sens in 1475, the castle was extensively renovated in the 20th century and is today home to the Bibliothèque Forney, a library that also stages temporary exhibitions drawn from its extensive collection of fine and graphic arts. ✉ *1 rue du Figuier, 4e, Marais Quarter* ☎ *01–42–78–14–60* 🖰 *Library free; free to €6 for exhibitions* ⊘ *Closed Sun. and Mon.* Ⓜ *Pont Marie.*

Hôtel de Sully (*Hôtel de Béthune-Sully*)
NOTABLE BUILDING | This early Baroque gem, built in 1624, is one of the city's loveliest hôtels particuliers. Like much of the area, it fell into ruin until the 1950s, when it was rescued by the institute for French historic monuments (the Centre des Monuments Nationaux), which is based here. The renovated headquarters aren't open to the public, but you're welcome to enjoy the equally lovely garden. Stroll through it, past the Orangerie, to find a small passage into nearby Place des Vosges. Sully's best buddy, King Henri IV, would have lived there had he not been assassinated in 1610. An on-site bookstore (with a 17th-century ceiling of exposed wooden beams) sells specialized English-language guides to Paris. ✉ *62 rue St-Antoine, 4e, Marais Quarter* ☎ *01–44–61–20–00* ⊕ *www.hotel-de-sully.fr* ⊘ *Bookstore closed Mon.* Ⓜ *St-Paul.*

Hôtel de Ville
GOVERNMENT BUILDING | Overlooking the Seine, City Hall contains the residence and offices of the mayor. The original Renaissance structure was built by François I in 1535–51 and added to by both Henry IV and Louis XIII in the early 17th century. In 1871 it was sacked and burned during the final days of the Paris Commune. Rebuilt in an almost exact replica of the original in 1874, it is one of Paris's most stunning buildings, made all the more dramatic by elaborate nighttime lighting. The adjoining public library stages frequent free exhibits celebrating famous photographers like Doisneau or Atget and their notable subjects, often the city itself. (The entrance is on the side across from the department store BHV.) Alas, the impressive interior of the main administrative building, with its lavish reception halls and staircases, is open only for independent visits during Patrimony Weekend in September. If your French is good, however, free guided tours are given biweekly in summer, weekly in other seasons (call two months ahead for information and reservations). The grand public square out front is always lively, playing host to events and temporary exhibitions. There's a carousel and a beach volleyball court (or similar) in summer, and an ice-skating rink (with skate rental available) in winter. ✉ *Pl. de l'Hôtel-de-Ville, 4e, Marais Quarter* ☎ *01–42–76–43–43 tours* ⊕ *www.paris.fr* 🖰 *Free* ⊘ *Closed weekends* ☞ *Access for visits at 29 rue de Rivoli* Ⓜ *Hôtel de Ville.*

Lafayette Anticipations
ART GALLERY | In 2018, at the behest of the Fondation Entreprise Galeries Lafayette, Rem Koolhaas and his OMA studio transformed this 19th-century industrial space into a streamlined, six-floor "laboratory of innovation" that supports and exhibits the work of up-and-coming contemporary artists and designers. Each year, the foundation choses three or four artists

and presents their work over a span of three months, enhanced by live performances and discussions. The space also features a branch of the popular café Wild & the Moon, with healthy, ethically sourced snacks, juices, and artisanal coffee, plus Atelier E.B., a chic boutique full of limited-edition clothing, objects, and gifts by artists and designers. ⊠ *9 rue du Plâtre, 4e, Marais Quarter* ☎ *01–57–40– 64–17* ⊕ *www.lafayetteanticipations.com* ⊠ *Free; events €5 to €15* ⊘ *Closed Tues.* Ⓜ *Hôtel de Ville.*

Maison de Victor Hugo

HISTORIC HOME | France's most famous scribe lived in this house on the southeast corner of Place des Vosges between 1832 and 1848. It's now a museum dedicated to the multitalented author. In Hugo's apartment on the second floor, you can see the tall desk, next to the short bed, where he began writing his masterwork *Les Misérables* (as always, standing up). There are manuscripts and early editions of the novel on display, as well as others such as *Notre-Dame de Paris*, known to English readers as *The Hunchback of Notre-Dame.* You can see illustrations of Hugo's writings, including Bayard's rendering of the impish Cosette holding her giant broom (which has graced countless *Les Miz* T-shirts). The collection includes many of Hugo's own, sometimes macabre, ink drawings (he was a fine artist), and furniture from several of his homes. Particularly impressive is the room of carved and painted Chinese-style wooden panels that Hugo designed for the house of his mistress, Juliet Drouet, on the island of Guernsey, when he was exiled there for agitating against Napoléon III. Try to spot the intertwined Vs and Js (hint: look for the angel's trumpet in the left corner). A recent restoration not only spiffed up the house but made the museum fully accessible to people with physical or mental disabilities and impaired sight or hearing, with improved touch screens

and audioguides. It also added a lovely garden and a café by Paris's famous pastry shop Maison Mulot. ⊠ *6 pl. des Vosges, 4e, Marais Quarter* ☎ *01–42–72– 10–16* ⊕ *www.maisonsvictorhugo.paris.fr* ⊠ *Free; from €6–€9 for temporary exhibitions* ⊘ *Closed Mon.* Ⓜ *St-Paul, Bastille.*

★ Maison Européenne de la Photographie
(*Center for European Photography*)

ART MUSEUM | Much of the credit for the city's ascendancy as a hub of international photography goes to Maison Européenne de la Photographie (MEP). Set in a landmark 17th-century mansion with a contemporary addition, MEP hosts up to four simultaneous exhibitions, which change about every three months, along with themed visits, workshops, and programs for kids. Shows feature an international crop of photographers and video artists. Works by superstar Annie Leibovitz or the late designer-photographer Karl Lagerfeld may overlap with a collection of self-portraits by an up-and-coming artist, and there are also regular retrospectives of photos by Doisneau, Cartier-Bresson, Man Ray, and other classics from MEP's vast private collection. The center has an excellent library, bookstore, and a café that spills out into the courtyard in warm months. Programs are available in English, and English-language tours are sometimes offered. ⊠ *5/7 rue de Fourcy, 4e, Marais Quarter* ☎ *01–44–78–75–00* ⊕ *www. mep-fr.org* ⊠ *€7–€13* ⊘ *Closed Mon. and Tues., between exhibitions* Ⓜ *St-Paul.*

Mémorial de la Shoah (*Memorial to the Holocaust*)

HISTORY MUSEUM | The first installation in this compelling memorial and museum is the deeply moving Wall of Names, tall plinths honoring the 76,000 French Jews deported from France to Nazi concentration camps, of whom only 2,500 survived. Opened in 2005, the center has an archive on the victims, a library, and a gallery hosting temporary exhibitions.

The permanent collection includes riveting artifacts and photographs from the camps, along with video testimony from survivors. The children's memorial is particularly poignant and not for the faint of heart—scores of backlit photographs show the faces of many of the 11,000 murdered French children. The crypt, a giant black marble Star of David, contains ashes recovered from the camps and the Warsaw ghetto. You can see the orderly drawers containing small files on Jews kept by the French police. (France officially acknowledged the Vichy government's role only in 1995.) The history of anti-Semitic persecution in the world is revisited, as well as the rebounding state of Jewry today. There is a free guided tour in English the second Sunday of every month at 3. ✉ *17 rue Geoffroy l'Asnier, 4e, Marais Quarter* ☎ *01–42–77–44–72* ⊕ *www.memorialdelashoah.org* ✆ *Free* ⊙ *Closed Sat.* Ⓜ *Pont Marie, St-Paul.*

★ **Musée Carnavalet**
HISTORY MUSEUM | If it has to do with Parisian history, it's here. Spruced up after a four-year renovation, this fascinating hodgepodge of artifacts and art ranges from prehistoric canoes used by the Parisii tribes to the cork-lined bedroom where Marcel Proust labored over his evocative novels. Thanks to scores of paintings, drawings, photographs, furniture, and scale models, nowhere else in Paris can you get such a precise picture of the city's evolution through the ages. The museum fills more than 100 rooms in two adjacent mansions, the Hôtel Le Peletier de St-Fargeau and the Hôtel Carnavalet. The latter is a Renaissance jewel that was the home of writer Madame de Sévigné from 1677 to 1696. Throughout her long life, she wrote hundreds of frank and funny letters to her daughter in Provence, giving an incomparable view of both public and private life during the time of Louis XIV. The museum offers a glimpse into her world, but its collection covers far more than just the 17th century. The exhibits on the Revolution are especially interesting, with scale models of guillotines and a replica of the Bastille prison carved from one of its stones. Louis XVI's prison cell is reconstructed along with mementos of his life, even medallions containing locks of his family's hair. Other impressive interiors are reconstructed from the Middle Ages through the rococo period and into Art Nouveau—showstoppers include the Fouquet jewelry shop and the Café de Paris's original furnishings. The sculpted garden at 16 rue des Francs-Bourgeois is open from April to the end of October. ✉ *16 rue des Francs-Bourgeois, 4e, Marais Quarter* ☎ *01–44–59–58–58* ⊕ *www.carnavalet. paris.fr* ✆ *Free; around €7 for temporary exhibitions* Ⓜ *St-Paul.*

Musée Cognacq-Jay
ART MUSEUM | One of the loveliest museums in Paris, this 16th-century, rococo-style mansion contains an outstanding collection of mostly 18th-century artwork in its rooms of *boiserie* (intricately carved wood paneling). A tour through them allows a rare glimpse into the lifestyle of wealthy 19th-century Parisians. Ernest Cognacq, founder of the department store La Samaritaine, and his wife, Louise Jay, amassed furniture, porcelain, and paintings—notably by Fragonard, Watteau, François Boucher, and Tiepolo—to create one of the world's finest private collections of this period. Some of the best displays are also the smallest, like the tiny enamel medallion portraits showcased on the second floor, and on the third floor, the glass cases filled with exquisite inlaid snuff boxes, sewing cases, pocket watches, perfume bottles, and cigar cutters. Exhibits are labeled in French only, but free pamphlets and €5 audioguides are available in English. ✉ *8 rue Elzévir, 3e, Marais Quarter* ☎ *01–40–27–07–21* ⊕ *www.museecognacqjay.paris.fr* ✆ *Free; €8 for temporary exhibitions* ⊙ *Closed Mon.* Ⓜ *St-Paul.*

The Musée Picasso Paris highlights various works from Pablo Picasso, including his longtime devotion to sculpture.

★ Musée d'Art et d'Histoire du Judaïsme (mahJ)

HISTORY MUSEUM | This excellent museum traces the tempestuous backstory of French and European Jews through art and history. Housed in the refined 17th-century Hôtel St-Aignan, exhibits have good explanatory texts in English, but the free English audioguide adds another layer of insight; guided tours in English are also available on request (€4 extra). Highlights include 13th-century tombstones excavated in Paris; a wooden model of a destroyed Eastern European synagogue; a roomful of early paintings by Marc Chagall; and Christian Boltanski's stark two-part tribute to Shoah (Holocaust) victims in the form of plaques on an outer wall naming the (mainly Jewish) inhabitants of the Hôtel St-Aignan in 1939, and canvas hangings with the personal data of the 13 residents who were deported and died in concentration camps. The museum also mounts excellent temporary exhibitions, like the recent "Chagall, Modigliani, Soutine: Paris as a School, 1940." The rear-facing windows offer a view of the Jardin Anne Frank. To visit the garden, use the entrance on Impasse Berthaud, off Rue Beaubourg, just north of Rue Rambuteau. ✉ *71 rue du Temple, 3e, Marais Quarter* ☎ *01–53–01–86–60* ⊕ *www.mahj.org* ✉ *€10.50 with temporary exhibitions* ⊙ *Closed Mon.* Ⓜ *Rambuteau, Hôtel de Ville.*

★ Musée de la Chasse et de la Nature

HISTORY MUSEUM | FAMILY | Mark this down as one of Paris's most distinctive—and fascinating—collections around the theme of "humans and nature." The museum, housed in the gorgeous 17th-century Hôtel de Guénégaud, features lavishly appointed rooms stocked with animal- and hunt-themed art and sculpture by the likes of Rubens and Gentileschi, as well as antique weaponry and taxidermy interspersed with contemporary works by artists such as Jeff Koons, Sophie Calle, and Walton Ford. In a tribute to Art Nouveau, the decor incorporates chandeliers and railings curled like antlers. Older kids will appreciate the jaw-dropping Trophy Room's impressive menagerie of beasts, not to mention the huge polar bear stationed outside. There is a lovely multimedia exhibit on the myth of the unicorn, as well as charming interactive displays on antique weaponry and bird calls. Temporary exhibits take place on the first floor, with works scattered throughout the permanent collection. There's also a spacious café. ⊠ *62 rue des Archives, 3e, Marais Quarter* ☎ *01–53–01–92–40* ⊕ *www.chassenature.org* ☑ *€12.50* ⊘ *Closed Mon.* Ⓜ *Rambuteau.*

★ Musée National Picasso-Paris

ART MUSEUM | Home to the world's largest public collection of Picasso's inimitable oeuvre, this spectacular museum covers almost 54,000 square feet in two buildings: the splendid 17th-century Hôtel Salé and a sprawling structure in the back garden dedicated to temporary exhibitions. Diego Giacometti's exclusively designed furnishings in the former are a bonus. The 200,000-plus paintings, sculptures, drawings, documents, and other archival materials (most of them donated to the City of Paris by Picasso or his family members) span the artist's entire career. Although it doesn't include his most recognizable works, it does contain many of the pieces Picasso himself treasured most. The first two floors cover his work from 1895 to 1972. The top floor illustrates his relationship to his favorite artists: landscapes, nudes, portraits, and still life works taken from his private collection detail his "artistic dialogue" with Cézanne, Gauguin, Degas, Rousseau, Matisse, Braque, Renoir, Modigliani, Miró, and others. The basement centers around Picasso's workshops, with photographs, engravings, paintings, and sculptures that document or evoke key pieces created at the Bateau Lavoir, Château de Boisgeloup, Grands-Augustins, Villa La Californie, and his farmhouse,

Notre-Dame-de-Vie, in Mougins. With excellent temporary exhibitions and plenty of multimedia components and activities that cater to kids, this is ideal for children and adult art lovers alike. ∎ **TIP→ Buy tickets online well in advance of your planned visit. Also, try to avoid visiting on weekends, when the crowds are largest.** ⊠ *5 rue de Thorigny, 3e, Marais Quarter* ☎ *01–85–56–00–36* ⊕ *www. museepicassoparis.fr* ☑ *€14* ⊘ *Closed Mon.* Ⓜ *St-Sébastien–Froissart.*

Nicolas Flamel's Home

HISTORIC HOME | Built in 1407 and reputed to be the oldest house in Paris (though other buildings also claim that title), this abode has a mystical history. Harry Potter fans should take note: this was the real-life residence of Nicolas Flamel, the alchemist whose sorcerer's stone is the source of immortality in the popular book series. A wealthy scribe, merchant, and dabbler in the mystical arts, Flamel willed his home to the city as a dormitory for the poor—on the condition that boarders pray daily for his soul. Today, the building contains apartments and a restaurant. ⊠ *51 rue Montmorency, 3e, Marais Quarter* Ⓜ *Rambuteau.*

★ Place des Vosges

PLAZA/SQUARE | **FAMILY** | The oldest square in Paris and—dare we say it—the most beautiful, Place des Vosges represents an early stab at urban planning. The precise proportions offer a placid symmetry, but things weren't always so calm here. Four centuries ago, this was the site of the Palais des Tournelles, home to King Henry II and Queen Catherine de Medici. The couple staged regular jousting tournaments, and Henry was fatally lanced in the eye during one of them in 1559. Catherine fled to the Louvre, abandoning her palace and ordering it destroyed. In 1612, the square became Place Royale on the occasion of Louis XIII's engagement to Anne of Austria. Napoléon renamed it Place des Vosges to honor the northeast

On a beautiful day, one of the best places to soak up the sun in the city is Place des Vosges.

region of Vosges, the first in the country to pony up taxes to the Revolutionary government. At the base of the 36 redbrick-and-stone houses—nine on each side of the square—is an arcaded, covered walkway lined with art galleries, shops, and cafés. There's also an elementary school, a synagogue (whose barrel roof was designed by Gustav Eiffel), and several chic hotels. The formal, gated garden's perimeter is lined with chestnut trees; inside are a children's play area and a fountain. Aside from hanging out in the park, people come here to visit the house, now a museum, of the man who once lived at No. 6—Victor Hugo, the author of *Les Misérables* and *Notre-Dame de Paris* (aka *The Hunchback of Notre-Dame*).

■ TIP→ One of the best things about this park is that you're actually allowed to sit—or snooze or snack—on the grass during spring and summer.

There is no better spot in the Marais for a picnic: you can pick up fixings at the nearby street market on Thursday and Sunday mornings. (It's on Boulevard Richard Lenoir between Rues Amelot and St-Sabin.) The most likely approach to Place des Vosges is from Rue de Francs-Bourgeois, the main shopping street. However, for a grander entrance, walk along Rue St-Antoine until you get to Rue de Birague, which leads directly into the square. ⊠ *Off Rue des Francs-Bourgeois, near Rue de Turenne, 4e, Marais Quarter* Ⓜ *Bastille, St-Paul.*

St-Paul–St-Louis

CHURCH | The leading Baroque church in the Marais, its dome rising 180 feet above the crossing, was begun in 1627 by the Jesuits, who modeled it after their Gesù church in Rome. Recently cleaned on the outside but dark and brooding inside, it contains Delacroix's *Christ on the Mount of Olives* in the transept and a shell-shape holy-water font at the entrance. The font was donated by

Victor Hugo, who lived in nearby Place des Vosges. Hugo's beloved daughter, Léopoldine, was married here in 1843, though she met a tragic end less than seven months later, when she fell into the Seine and drowned, along with her husband Charles, who tried to save her. ⊠ *99 rue St-Antoine, 4e, Marais Quarter* ☎ *01–42–72–30–32* ⊕ *www.spsl.fr* Ⓜ *St-Paul.*

★ 3e Arrondissement

NEIGHBORHOOD | In recent years, the 3e arrondissement, known at the "haut Marais," or upper Marais, has morphed into one of the city's hottest neighborhoods. Its charming old notions and hardware shops have been replaced by cool cafés, art galleries, and trendy boutiques. To enjoy this alluring *quartier* like a local, first head to Rue de Bretagne, the main drag. Stop for lunch at one of the food stalls in the Marché des Enfants Rouges (No. 39, open Tuesday through Sunday); it's the oldest covered market in Paris. Next, explore narrow side streets, like Rues Charlot, Debelleyme, and Poitou, lined with art galleries and small boutiques. Stop for a famous *chausson aux pommes* at Poilâne bakery (38 rue Debelleyme), or treat yourself to a homemade gelato at Pastelli Mary Gelateria (60 rue du Temple) before a visit to one of Paris's most original small museums, the Musée de la Chasse et de la Nature (62 rue des Archives).

The park attached to the City Hall (Mairie) of the 3e arrondissement is a fine place to picnic or relax and watch the world go by, complete with a children's playground, a charming duck pond, and lovely greenery. Across the street is the 19th-century cast-iron-and-glass Carreau du Temple, which is now a locally driven arts and sports community center. This is the site of the former Templar Tower, where Louis XIV and Marie-Antoinette were imprisoned before the king's date with the guillotine. (Napoléon later razed

it.) For your evening apéritif, make a bee-line for the buzzy Café Charlot at 38 rue de Bretagne. If you're in the mood for a cocktail, try the Little Red Door speakeasy at No. 60 rue Charlot. ⊠ *Marais Quarter* Ⓜ *Arts et Métiers, Filles du Calvaire.*

🍴 Restaurants

Historic Marais is the epitome of chic, but you can still find reminders of its down-to-earth past along Rue des Rosiers, where falafel shops and Eastern European delis jostle with designer boutiques. Truly ambitious restaurants are few and far between in the Marais, but picturesque old bistros—like Benoît and neighborhood stalwart Café des Musées—remain, and smaller veggie-centric eateries are popping up all over. A new generation of barista cafés serving gourmet snacks for breakfast and lunch has created its own niche, answering a need for better coffee and faster sit-down dining. The popular Breizh Café attracts young and old alike with its inexpensive and authentic *galettes* (buckwheat crêpes) made with quality ingredients and best enjoyed with a crisp, delicious *cidre* from Normandy or Brittany.

★ Assemblages

$ | WINE BAR | At this restaurant set on a pretty street leading right into the Place des Vosges, it's hard to know if you've landed in someone's chic private *salon* or their woodworking studio. Carpenter and wine lover Eric Wilmot shares his passion for wood and wine (and Harley-Davidsons) in this stylishly intimate space, featuring Persian rugs and velvet chaises, where you can indulge in some stupendous wines handpicked by the owner and served alongside a tempting array of nibbles—homemade foie gras, smoked salmon, artisanal cheeses, and some seriously decadent desserts. **Known for:** gorgeous interiors; intimate atmosphere with a carpentry shop behind glass; hard-to-find wines. Ⓢ *Average main: €15* ✉ *7 rue de Birague, 4e, Marais Quarter* ☎ *09–52–58–61–12* ⊕ *www.facebook. com/assemblagesparis* ⊗ *Closed Mon.* Ⓜ *St-Paul, Bastille, Chemin Vert.*

Au Bourguignon du Marais
$$ | BISTRO | This handsome, contemporary Marais bistro and wine bar is the perfect place to enjoy traditional fare and excellent Burgundies served by the glass and bottle. Unusual for Paris, food is served nonstop from noon to 11 pm, and you can drop by just for a glass of wine in the afternoon. **Known for:** sidewalk dining with nice views of the Marais; hearty Burgundian cuisine; traditional bistro atmosphere. Ⓢ *Average main: €23* ✉ *52 rue François-Miron, 3e, Marais Quarter* ☎ *01–48–87–15–40* ⊕ *aubourguignondu-marais.fr* Ⓜ *St-Paul.*

Benoît
$$$$ | BISTRO | Without changing the vintage 1912 setting, superchef Alain Ducasse and Thierry de la Brosse of L'Ami Louis have subtly improved the menu, with dishes such as marinated salmon, frogs' legs in a morel-mushroom cream sauce, and an outstanding *cassoulet* served in a cast-iron pot. It's a splurge to dine here, so go all the way, and top off your meal with the caramelized tarte tatin or a rum-doused baba. **Known for:** charming outdoor terrace in warm weather; affordable prix-fixe lunch menu; glorious Marais setting overlooking the Seine with equally romantic interior. Ⓢ *Average main: €39* ✉ *20 rue St-Martin, 4e, Marais Quarter* ☎ *01–42–72–25–76* ⊕ *www. benoit-paris.com* ⊗ *Closed Aug. and 1 wk in Feb.* Ⓜ *Châtelet.*

Café Charlot
$$ | CAFÉ | It may not have the healthiest food in the Marais, and the coffee may not be third wave, but that doesn't keep chic locals from packing into it on a sunny (or even not-so-sunny) day. The people-watching from this choice spot—at

the intersection of the à la mode shopping street Rue Charlot and the bustling Rue de Bretagne—is top-notch, and the café's 1950s film noir charm is irresistible. **Known for:** open daily from 7 am to 2 am; chic, lively atmosphere; hearty, delicious French staples and well-priced wines by the glass. Ⓢ *Average main: €20* ✉ *38 rue de Bretagne, 3e, Marais Quarter* ☎ *01–44–54–03–30* ⊕ *www. lecharlot-paris.com* Ⓜ *Filles du Calvaire.*

Café des Musées
$ | BISTRO | A true neighborhood haunt, this bustling little bistro near the Musée Picasso offers a convivial slice of Parisian life at a good value. Traditional French bistro fare is adapted to a modern audience. **Known for:** proximity to Marais museums; warm and friendly service; reliable bistro fare. Ⓢ *Average main: €17* ✉ *49 rue de Turenne, 3e, Marais Quarter* ☎ *01–42–72–96–17* ⊕ *www.lecafedesmu-sees.fr* Ⓜ *St-Paul.*

Datsha Underground
$$$ | FRENCH FUSION | If you're seeking good food among a chicest-of-chic crowd, this beautifully designed restaurant—whose sole aim is to provide you a "sensorial experience"—is just the place. Chef Baptiste Trudel, a *Top Chef* contender, concocts gastronomic dishes that you might find at a fantasy of a Russian country getaway—beef tartare with red wine–shallot "caviar" or a rich black pudding of squid and mushrooms—paired with wines from a truly impressive list. **Known for:** great people-watching; knowledgeable sommelier; innovative French-Russian fare. Ⓢ *Average main: €25* ✉ *57 rue des Gravilliers, 3e, Marais Quarter* ☎ *01–43–56–95–09* ⊕ *www.datshaunderground. com* ⊗ *Closed Sun. and Mon. No lunch.* Ⓜ *Arts et Métiers.*

Grand Coeur
$$$ | MODERN FRENCH | Soaring ceilings with exposed beams, globe lighting, velvet chairs, and marble-top tables give this superchic eatery the look of

a classic brasserie gone upscale. The menu, designed by three-star chef Mauro Colagreco of the world-renowned Mirazur restaurant on the Riviera, features market-fresh French classics complemented by a wine list with plenty of by-the-glass offerings. **Known for:** menu designed by a "World's Best Chef"; chic decor; spacious courtyard terrace. $ *Average main: €27* ⊠ *41 rue du Temple, 4e, Marais Quarter* ☎ *01–58–28–18–90* ⊕ *www.grandcoeur.paris* Ⓜ *Hôtel de Ville, Rambuteau.*

L'Ambassade d'Auvergne

$$ | **BISTRO** | The rare authentic Parisian bistro that refuses to change, Les Ambassade claims one of the city's great restaurant characters: maître d' Francis Panek, with his handlebar mustache and gravelly voice. Settle into the dining room in an ancient Marais house to try rich, rib-sticking dishes from the Auvergne, a sparsely populated region in central France. **Known for:** chocolate mousse for dessert; excellent price-to-quality ratio; copious quantities of classic French cuisine. $ *Average main: €22* ⊠ *22 rue du Grenier St-Lazare, 3e, Marais Quarter* ☎ *01–42–72–31–22* ⊕ *ambassade-auvergne.fr* Ⓜ *Rambuteau.*

Le Georges

$$$ | **MODERN FRENCH** | One of those showstopping rooftop venues so popular in Paris, Le Georges preens atop the Centre Pompidou. Part of the Costes brothers' empire, the establishment trots out fashionable dishes such as sesame-crusted tuna and coriander-spiced beef fillet flambéed with cognac. **Known for:** hit-or-miss pricey food; indifferent service; stunning views of central Paris and beyond from the terrace. $ *Average main: €31* ⊠ *Centre Pompidou, 6th fl., 19 rue Beaubourg, 4e, Louvre* ☎ *01–44–78–47–99* ⊕ *www.restaurantgeorgesparis.com* ⊘ *Closed Tues.* Ⓜ *Rambuteau.*

Les Philosophes

$$ | **FRENCH** | All of Paris seems to collide at this lively corner café in the heart of the Marais, where you'll find pretty much whatever is your pleasure any time of the day or night. Slide into a red banquette, or take a seat on the wide wraparound terrace to watch the world go by while indulging in generous servings of all the French classics, a glass of wine, or coffee and dessert. **Known for:** decent prices; lively atmosphere; extensive menu. $ *Average main: €19* ⊠ *28 rue Vieille du Temple, 4e, Marais Quarter* ☎ *01–48–87–49–64* ⊕ *www.cafeine.com* Ⓜ *Hôtel de Ville.*

Ogata

$$$$ | **JAPANESE** | Housed in an 18th-century Marais mansion on a picturesque backstreet, this Japanese restaurant, bar, tearoom, pastry shop, and boutique redefines preciousness. It took four years for the architect and owner to construct, and every detail is a triumph of Japanese craftsmanship—from the rough *wabi-sabi* walls to the graceful sculptural touches to the ethereal porcelain tea and dinnerware used in the restaurant and for sale in the boutique. **Known for:** more than the usual Parisian attitude; top-quality products in the restaurant, tearoom … and everywhere else!; jaw-droppingly beautiful. $ *Average main: €41* ⊠ *16 rue Debelleyme, 3e, Marais Quarter* ☎ *01–42–60–30–21* ⊕ *ogata.com/paris* ⊘ *Closed Mon. and Tues.* Ⓜ *Filles-du-Calvaire, St-Paul.*

★ Parcelles

$$ | **FRENCH** | One of the city's best-kept secrets, this gem of bistro has been a fixture since 1936, and the new owners have retained the old-world vibe that's ever harder to come by in Paris, especially in the Marais. Cozy and full of charm—with beamed ceilings, stone walls, and a timeless decor—the atmosphere perfectly highlights chef Julien Chevallier's deliciously down-to-earth

and seasonally inspired meats, fish, and charcuterie. **Known for:** excellent selection of natural wines; charming old-world feel; lovely terrace seating. [$] *Average main: €22* ✉ *13 rue Chapon, 3e, Marais Quarter* ☎ *01–43–37–91–64* 🌐 *www.parcelles-paris.fr* 🕒 *Closed Sun.* [M] *Arts et Métiers, Rambuteau.*

Coffee and Quick Bites

Au Petit Fer à Cheval

$ | **BISTRO** | This cozy bar is always packed, and tables often spill out onto the sidewalk. Come for a hearty meal, a cup of coffee, or a glass of wine. **Known for:** sidewalk seating; open till 2 am; well-prepared classics like beef tartare and duck confit. [$] *Average main: €15* ✉ *30 rue Vieille du Temple, 4e, Marais Quarter* ☎ *01–2–72–47–47* 🌐 *www.cafeine.com* 🕒 *Closed Mon. and Tues.* [M] *Hôtel-de-Ville, St-Paul.*

★ Bontemps

$ | **FRENCH** | This charming courtyard café-tearoom grew out of an adorable pastry shop (next door) specializing in the French *sablé*, those classic melt-in-your-mouth butter cookies, with an assortment of ethereal cream fillings. Marble-topped tables, velvet chairs, and other vintagelike touches make this one of the neighborhood's most charming spots for lunch, brunch, or dessert. **Known for:** high prices; top-notch homemade food and pastries; vintage atmosphere. [$] *Average main: €17* ✉ *57 rue de Bretagne, 3e, Marais Quarter* ☎ *01–42–74–10–68* 🌐 *www.facebook.com/bontempspatisserie* 🕒 *Closed Mon. and Tues.*

★ Breizh Café

$ | **FRENCH** | **FAMILY** | Eating a crêpe in Paris might seem clichéd, until you venture into this modern offshoot of a Breton crêperie. The plain, pale-wood decor is refreshing, but what really makes the difference are the ingredients—farmers' eggs, unpasteurized Gruyère, shiitake mushrooms, Valrhona chocolate, homemade caramel, and extraordinary butter from a Breton dairy farmer. **Known for:** Cancale oysters on the half shell; adventurous ingredients; some of the best crêpes in Paris. [$] *Average main: €12* ✉ *109 rue Vieille du Temple, 3e, Marais Quarter* ☎ *01–42–72–13–77* 🌐 *www.breizhcafe.com* 🕒 *Closed Aug.* [M] *St-Sébastien–Froissart.*

★ The Broken Arm Café

$ | **CAFÉ** | This stylish café, attached to an oh-so-chic concept store, is a tad roomier than the profusion of postage-stamp-size cafés that have sprung up all over the Marais. It's especially nice on warm days, when you can sit on the spacious sidewalk terrace across from a pretty park. **Known for:** chic atmosphere—it's attached to one of the Marais's chicest concept stores; excellent coffee; healthy dishes for lunch or snacking. [$] *Average main: €15* ✉ *12 rue Perrée, 3e, Marais Quarter* ☎ *01–44–61–53–60* 🌐 *www.the-broken-arm.com/en/189-cafeteria* 🕒 *Closed Sun. and Mon. No dinner* [M] *République.*

Chez Alain Miam Miam

$ | **SANDWICHES** | You may be tempted to call it a sandwich stand, but for Parisians it's more of a pilgrimage point at the beloved Marché des Enfants-Rouges. Alain's inspired creations burst with organic vegetables (raw or roasted), artisanal cheeses, locally cured ham, roast chicken, or pastrami, among other gourmet fillings, lodged between slices of bread, a buckwheat galette, or a *socca* (a Provençale flatbread made with chickpea flour). **Known for:** a favorite Parisian address; top ingredients; good price for the quantity and quality. [$] *Average main: €10* ✉ *26 rue Charlot, 3e, Marais Quarter* ☎ *09–86–17–28–00* 🕒 *Closed Mon. No dinner* [M] *Filles-du-Calvaire.*

Gramme

$ | CAFÉ | "Gastro-café" may be the best description of this pint-size coffee shop with an inventive menu of seasonal fare. You can enjoy your artisanal coffee, homemade lemonade, kombucha, or glass of organic wine with dishes inspired by Paris's cultural mix: pulled pork banh mi, a "dwitch" sandwich on brioche with caramelized bacon, fried egg, and miso topped with fresh herbs. **Known for:** great coffee; delicious pastries and inventive snacks; all-day hours. ⓢ *Average main: €11* ⊠ *86 rue des Archives, 3e, Marais Quarter* ☎ *09–50–92–20–23* ⊕ *www.grammeparis.fr* ⊘ *Closed Mon. No dinner* Ⓜ *Arts-et-Métiers, Filles-du-Calvaire.*

★ La Caféothèque

$ | CAFÉ | This was Paris's first coffee bar, founded by former Guatemalan ambassador to France turned coffee ambassador, Gloria Montenegro. With three spacious rooms, all coffee preparations under the sun, and a daily special brew chosen from among dozens of varieties of meticulously sourced beans from plantations around the globe, this is a Paris institution. **Known for:** all roasting done in-house; excellent coffee of the day; rigorously sourced, hard-to-find beans. ⓢ *Average main: €4* ⊠ *52 rue de l'Hotel de Ville, 4e, Marais Quarter* ☎ *01–53–01–83–84* ⊕ *www.lacafeotheque.com* ⊘ *No dinner.* Ⓜ *Pont Marie, St-Paul.*

L'As du Fallafel

$ | MIDDLE EASTERN | FAMILY | For one of the cheapest, tastiest meals in Paris, look no further than the fantastic falafel stands on the pedestrian Rue de Rosiers, where L'As (the Ace) is widely considered the best of the bunch, with lunchtime lines that extend down the street. A falafel sandwich costs €6 to go or €8 in the dining room, and it's heaping with grilled eggplant, cabbage, hummus, tahini, and hot sauce. **Known for:** shawarma sandwiches; fast takeout or seated

service at lunch; the best, freshest, and biggest falafel sandwich in town. ⓢ *Average main: €10* ⊠ *34 rue des Rosiers, 4e, Marais Quarter* ☎ *01–48–87–63–60* ⊘ *Closed Sat. No dinner Fri.* Ⓜ *St-Paul.*

La Tartine

$ | FRENCH | This calm café-brasserie on busy Rue de Rivoli is a local favorite with an extensive wine list. Though the food is nothing to write home about, its authentic brasserie atmosphere and inexpensive wines by the glass from every region of France make it a great place for a quick pick-me-up or an apéro on the go. **Known for:** reasonably priced Champagne; total lack of snobbery; authentic Art Deco interior. ⓢ *Average main: €16* ⊠ *24 rue de Rivoli, Marais Quarter* ☎ *01–42–72–76–85* ⊕ *www.latartineparis.fr* Ⓜ *St-Paul.*

Le Loir dans la Théière

$ | FRENCH | Sink into a comfy armchair at this popular tearoom, whose name translates to "the Dormouse in the Teapot" (from *Alice in Wonderland*). The savory tarts are good, but the real stars are desserts like the decadent chocolate crumble tart or mile-high lemon meringue pie. **Known for:** shabby-chic setting; scrumptious desserts; Sunday brunch. ⓢ *Average main: €15* ⊠ *3 rue des Rosiers, 4e, Marais Quarter* ☎ *01–42–72–90–61* ⊕ *www.leloirdanslatheiere.com* ⊘ *No dinner.* Ⓜ *St-Paul.*

★ Loustic

$ | CAFÉ | One of the Marais's first specialty coffee bars, it's also one of its most stylish—and one of the best. The coffee here is excellent, the staff friendly, and the food—for breakfast, lunch, or just a coffee break—is reliably good *and* healthy. **Known for:** popular weekend brunch; cool crowd; chic but friendly ambience. ⓢ *Average main: €6* ⊠ *40 rue Chapon, 3e, Marais Quarter* ☎ *09–80–31–07–06* Ⓜ *Arts et Métiers.*

★ Pain de Sucre

$ | **BAKERY** | A dazzling array of gourmet pastries here includes all the classics in imaginative and delicious flavor combinations. There are also impossibly moist individual cakes, Paris's best *baba au rhum*, sublime cookies, and the specialty *guimauve*, a flavored, melt-in-your-mouth marshmallow. **Known for:** takeout options for picnics; gourmet sandwiches; some of Paris's best pastries. Ⓢ *Average main: €8 ✉ 14 rue Rambuteau, 3e, Marais Quarter ☎ 01–45–74–68–92 ⊕ www.patisseriepaindesucre.com ☾ Closed Tues. and Wed. No dinner.* Ⓜ *Rambuteau.*

★ Une Glace à Paris

$ | **ICE CREAM** | Smoked chocolate … orange-carrot-ginger … coffee–black cardamom … these are just a few of the intriguing ice cream and gelato flavors featured at Paris's Instagram-famous *glacier*. Expect only the best seasonal ingredients plus cream and sugar in the ice creams and loads of fresh fruit in the nondairy sorbets. **Known for:** free samples; lots of nondairy and gluten-free choices; imaginative and creative flavor pairings. Ⓢ *Average main: €6 ✉ 15 rue saint Croix de la Bretonnerie, 4e, Marais Quarter ☎ 01–49–96–98–33 ⊕ uneglaceaparis.fr ☾ Closed Mon.–Tues. No dinner.*

Hotels

A major shopping mecca and a center of LGBTQ and Jewish life in the city, the trendy Marais is a vibrant and stylish mosaic in motion. Like the neighborhood, the lodgings are all about history and style: historic Grand Dames abut hidden gardens and small boutique hotels harbor chic cocktail bars where guests can blend in with trendsetting locals.

★ Cour des Vosges

$$$$ | **HOTEL** | This luxurious hotel that opened in 2019 and is set in a 16th-century building right on the city's most beautiful square is quite splendid, with its opulent guest rooms and suites decked out with beamed ceilings, bespoke furnishings, and a vast collection of contemporary artworks. **Pros:** gorgeous, art-centric decor; butler service; an enchanting pâtisserie-tearoom with a terrace. **Cons:** very expensive; restaurant serves only light dinner fare; discreetly exclusive vibe may not suit everyone. Ⓢ *Rooms from: €770 ✉ 19 pl. des Vosges, Marais Quarter ☎ 01–42–50–30–30 ⊕ www.courdesvosges.com ☞ 12 rooms* ⦿ *No Meals* Ⓜ *St-Paul, Chemin Vert, Bastille.*

Hôtel Bourg Tibourg

$$$ | **HOTEL** | Subdued lighting and rich jewel tones announce the blend of romance and chic cultivated by the Hôtel Bourg Tibourg, designed by Paris superstar Jacques Garcia. **Pros:** in the heart of the trendy Marais; great nightlife district; moderate prices. **Cons:** lounge area gets crowded; no restaurant; small and poorly lit rooms. Ⓢ *Rooms from: €290 ✉ 19 rue du Bourg Tibourg, Marais Quarter ☎ 01–42–78–47–39 ⊕ www.bourgtibourg.com ☞ 30 rooms* ⦿ *No Meals* Ⓜ *Hôtel de Ville.*

Hôtel Caron

$$$ | **HOTEL** | On a relatively quiet side street, this contemporary boutique bed-and-breakfast may be petite, but many thoughtful extras—free Wi-Fi and non-alcoholic minibar beverages, L'Occitane toiletries—make it as accommodating as bigger hotels. **Pros:** excellent location in center of Paris; great amenities; friendly staff. **Cons:** tight space in bathrooms; no hotel restaurant or bar; only enough storage for small suitcases. Ⓢ *Rooms from: €249 ✉ 3 rue Caron, Marais Quarter ☎ 01–40–29–02–94 ⊕ www.hotelcaron.com ☞ 18 rooms* ⦿ *No Meals* Ⓜ *St-Paul.*

★ Hôtel Caron de Beaumarchais

$$ | **HOTEL** | For that traditional French feeling, book into this intimate, affordable,

romantic hotel—the theme is the work of former next-door-neighbor Pierre-Augustin Caron de Beaumarchais, a supplier of military aid to American revolutionaries and the playwright who penned *The Marriage of Figaro* and *The Barber of Seville*. **Pros:** cozy Parisian decor of yesteryear; excellent location within easy walking distance of major monuments; breakfast in bed served until noon. **Cons:** may feel old-fashioned for younger crowd; busy street of bars and cafés can be noisy; small rooms with few amenities. $ *Rooms from: €185* ✉ *12 rue Vieille du Temple, Marais Quarter* ☎ *01–42–72–34–12* ⊕ *www.carondebeaumarchais.com* ⇥ *19 rooms* ⦿| *No Meals* Ⓜ *Hôtel de Ville.*

★ Hôtel de JoBo

$$$ | **HOTEL** | On a small street, just steps from the Place des Vosges and the Musée Picasso, this hotel takes its name and stylish spirit from Joséphine Bonaparte herself. **Pros:** excellent location close to the Seine; steps from the métro; small, intimate atmosphere. **Cons:** fire station across the street can mean lots of sirens; breakfast not included in standard rates; common area can feel claustrophobic. $ *Rooms from: €280* ✉ *10 rue d'Ormesson, Marais Quarter* ☎ *01–48–04–70–48* ⊕ *www.hoteldejobo.paris* ⇥ *24 rooms* ⦿| *No Meals* Ⓜ *St-Paul, Bastille.*

Hôtel de la Bretonnerie

$$ | **HOTEL** | This small hotel with exposed wooden beams and traditional styling sits on a side street in a 17th-century *hôtel particulier* (a grand town house) that's just a few minutes from the Centre Pompidou and the numerous bars and cafés of Rue Vieille du Temple. **Pros:** typical Parisian character; free Wi-Fi access; moderate prices for the area. **Cons:** rooms facing street can be noisy; no air-conditioning; quality and size of the rooms vary greatly. $ *Rooms from: €154* ✉ *22 rue Ste-Croix-de-la-Bretonnerie, Marais Quarter* ☎ *01–48–87–77–63*

⊕ *www.hotelparismaraisbretonnerie.com* ⇥ *29 rooms* ⦿| *No Meals* Ⓜ *Hôtel de Ville.*

Hôtel Duo

$$$ | **HOTEL** | Architect Jean-Philippe Nuel used bold colors and dramatic lighting in his update of this hotel, and although some rooms still have the original 16th-century beams, the overall feel is functional urban-chic. **Pros:** central location near shops and cafés; decent prices for this neighborhood; walking distance to major monuments. **Cons:** small standard rooms and bathrooms; service not always delivered with a smile; neighborhood noise, especially in ground-floor rooms. $ *Rooms from: €250* ✉ *11 rue du Temple, Marais Quarter* ☎ *01–42–72–72–22* ⊕ *www.duo-paris.com* ⇥ *58 rooms* ⦿| *No Meals* Ⓜ *Hôtel de Ville.*

★ Hôtel Dupond-Smith

$$$ | **HOTEL** | If it weren't your chic destination for the night, you could easily walk right by this boutique hotel set on a tiny street. **Pros:** quality buffet breakfast; ideally located; in-room massage service. **Cons:** small staff; limited honor bar; small common area. $ *Rooms from: €331* ✉ *2 rue des Guillemites, Marais Quarter* ☎ *01–42–76–88–99* ⊕ *www.hoteldupondsmith.com* ⇥ *8 rooms* ⦿| *No Meals* Ⓜ *Hôtel de Ville.*

Hôtel Jeanne-d'Arc

$$ | **HOTEL** | This hotel is prized for its unbeatable location off tranquil Place du Marché Ste-Catherine, one of the city's lesser-known pedestrian squares, and for its gentler prices in an ever more costly neighborhood. **Pros:** charming street close to major attractions; lots of drinking and dining options nearby; good value for the Marais. **Cons:** no air-conditioning; rooms quite small; noisy garbage trucks and late-night revelers on the square after midnight. $ *Rooms from: €199* ✉ *3 rue de Jarente, Marais Quarter* ☎ *01–48–87–62–11* ⊕ *www.hoteljeannedarc.com* ⇥ *35 rooms* ⦿| *No Meals* Ⓜ *St-Paul.*

★ Hôtel Jules & Jim

$$$ | **HOTEL** | In the less-traveled corner of the trendy Marais district, this contemporary boutique hotel with an easy-to-miss industrial facade and three buildings set around a historic courtyard feels almost like an art gallery. **Pros:** bright and modern; close to public transportation; stylish bar. **Cons:** no in-room coffeemakers; no restaurant; the small "Jules" rooms are best for those traveling light or staying just one night. [$] *Rooms from: €240* ✉ *11 rue des Gravilliers, Marais Quarter* ☎ *01–44–54–13–13* 🌐 *www.hoteljulesetjim.com* 🛏 *23 rooms* 🍴 *No Meals* [M] *Arts et Métiers.*

Hôtel Sookie

$$ | **HOTEL** | Set at one of the Haut Marais's trendiest crossroads, this vintage-themed and jazz-inspired newcomer (its name comes from a tune by guitarist Grant Green) fits perfectly into the beating heart of the neighborhood. **Pros:** top-notch café; excellent location in the heart of the Marais; super-friendly staff. **Cons:** rooms are a bit small (but cozy); tiny bathrooms; breakfast not included in rates. [$] *Rooms from: €225* ✉ *2 bis rue Commines, 3e, Marais Quarter* ☎ *01–40–29–01–33* 🌐 *www.hotelsookie.com* 🛏 *50 rooms* 🍴 *No Meals* [M] *Filles du Calvaire, St-Sébastien-Froissart.*

9Confidentiel

$$$$ | **HOTEL** | This glamorous Philippe Starck–designed property takes the art and poetry of Cocteau-era Paris as its theme and couldn't be more stylish or better located. **Pros:** luxury touches, like the Codage amenities and sophisticated tearoom; small but very helpful and friendly staff; nice views from some rooms (be sure to ask). **Cons:** no fitness center; many rooms quite small; on the pricey side. [$] *Rooms from: €360* ✉ *58 rue du Roi de Sicile, Marais Quarter* ☎ *01–86–90–23–33* 🌐 *www.hotel-9confidentiel-paris.fr* 🛏 *29 rooms* 🍴 *No Meals* [M] *St-Paul, Hôtel de Ville.*

Pavillon de la Reine

$$$$ | **HOTEL** | Hidden off regal Place des Vosges behind a stunning garden courtyard, this enchanting château has gigantic beams, chunky stone pillars, and a weathered fireplace that speaks to its 1612 origins. **Pros:** historic character; free loaner bikes; quiet setting. **Cons:** the interior design lacks a uniform theme; nearest métro is a few blocks away; expensive for the area and the room size. [$] *Rooms from: €500* ✉ *28 pl. des Vosges, 3e, Marais Quarter* ☎ *01–40–29–19–19* 🌐 *www.pavillon-de-la-reine.com* 🛏 *54 rooms* 🍴 *No Meals* [M] *Bastille, St-Paul.*

Sinner

$$$$ | **HOTEL** | The crowd of chic locals and bank of fog rolling out over the bar are the first clues that you've stepped into one of the Marais's trendiest addresses. **Pros:** super comfy beds; cozy spa; great location. **Cons:** expensive across the board; teensy pool; extremely dark hallways. [$] *Rooms from: €520* ✉ *116 rue du Temple, Marais Quarter* ☎ *01–42–72–20–00* 🌐 *www.sinnerparis.com* 🛏 *43 rooms* 🍴 *No Meals* [M] *Arts et Métiers, Filles du Calvaire, République.*

Nightlife

A first-class shopping destination by day, by night this superchic neighborhood draws a diverse and trendy crowd for its *branché* cocktail bars and the city's most vibrant gay and lesbian scene.

BARS

Bar at the Hotel Jules & Jim

BARS | The look here is something between a chic contemporary Paris apartment and a low-key lounge. Enjoy a cocktail over a good book from the bar library, or relax with a smooth drink in front of the outdoor fireplace. ✉ *11 rue des Gravilliers, 3e, Marais Quarter* ☎ *01–44–54–13–13* 🌐 *www.hoteljulesetjim.com* [M] *Arts et Métiers, Rambuteau.*

★ Candelaria

BARS | Steamy Candelaria is a taquería by day and a cocktail lounge by night. The tang of tequila hangs in the air at this hip hideaway, where deftly crafted drinks are poured for a contented crowd. ✉ *52 rue de Saintonge, 3e, Marais Quarter* ☎ *01–42–74–41–28* ⊕ *www.facebook. com/candelariaparis* Ⓜ *Filles du Calvaire.*

Grazie

BARS | Equal parts cocktail bar and gourmet pizzeria, this stylish offspring of the übercool concept store Merci promises top-quality libations and stone-oven-baked pizza. The decor is industrial-rustic, with pressed-tin ceilings and a corrugated-iron bar, all enhanced by mood lighting. It's jam-packed with neighborhood hipsters, so reservations are a must. ✉ *91 bd. Beaumarchais, 3e, Marais Quarter* ☎ *01–42–78–11–96* ⊕ *www.graziegrazie.fr* Ⓜ *St-Sébastien–Froissart.*

La Belle Hortense

BARS | This spot is heaven for anyone who ever wished they had a book in a bar (or a drink in a bookstore). The *bar littéraire* is the infamous spot where gal-about-town Catherine M. launched her *vie sexuelle* that became a bawdy best seller. ✉ *31 rue Vielle-du-Temple, 4e, Marais Quarter* ☎ *01–48–04–74–60* Ⓜ *St-Paul.*

★ Le Mary Celeste

BARS | Half-price oysters at happy hour (6 pm–7 pm) aren't the only reason this refreshingly unpretentious cocktail bar is wildly popular. One of a trilogy of super-hip watering holes (including Candelaria and Glass) opened by a trio of expat restaurateurs, its craft cocktails, microbrews, natural wines, and standout tapas menu deliver the goods and then some. If you're planning to dine, reserve ahead online. ✉ *1 rue Commines, 3e, Marais Quarter* ☎ *No phone* ⊕ *www.lemaryceleste.com* Ⓜ *St-Sébastian–Froissart.*

Le Trésor

BARS | On a tiny street that's a tad separated from the sometimes-madding crowd of the Marais, this large, lively Auvernian café has mismatched Baroque furnishings and a chill vibe, but its biggest appeals are the sprawling outdoor terrace (heated in winter) and late weekend hours. ✉ *9 rue du Trésor, 4e, Marais Quarter* ☎ *01–42–71–35–17* ⊕ *www.restaurantletresor.com* Ⓜ *St-Paul.*

Little Red Door

BARS | Behind the red door, you'll discover a dark, cozy lounge that has style, sophistication, and atmosphere without the attitude. Creative cocktails—supplemented by artisanal beers and well-chosen wines by the glass (the last of which aren't always easy to come by in a cocktail bar)—can be enjoyed from a cushy velour bar stool or cubbyhole alcove. ✉ *60 rue Charlot, 3e, Marais Quarter* ☎ *01–42–71–19–32* ⊕ *www.lrdparis.com* Ⓜ *Filles du Calvert.*

★ Sherry Butt

BARS | On a quiet street close to the Bastille, Sherry Butt's relaxed loftlike atmosphere, imaginative drinks, whiskey flights, and tasty bar menu draw a lively crowd that appreciates meticulously crafted cocktails. A DJ spins on weekends. ✉ *20 rue Beautreillis, 4e, Marais Quarter* ☎ *09–83–38–47–80* ⊕ *www.sherrybuttparis.com* Ⓜ *Bastille, Sully-Morland.*

LGBTQ+ BARS

Café Cox

BARS | "Le Cox" is a prime gay pickup joint that's known for its live DJ sets. Its extended Sunday happy hour—from 6 pm to 2 am—is a rollicking good time. ✉ *15 rue des Archives, 4e, Marais Quarter* ☎ *01–42–72–08–00* ⊕ *www.cox.fr* Ⓜ *Hôtel de Ville.*

Duplex Bar

BARS | Young tortured-artist types flock to this low-key club—one of the oldest gay bars in the city—to enjoy the frequent art exhibitions, alternative music, and mood-inspiring ambient lighting. It's open from 8 pm to 2 am, except on Friday and Saturday when it's open till 4 am. ⊠ *25 rue Michel-Le-Comte, 3e, Louvre* ☎ *01–42–72–80–86* Ⓜ *Rambuteau.*

Open Café

BARS | Drawing everyone from suits to punks, this spot is less of a hookup spot than neighboring Café Cox. Relaxed and always packed, it has a disco-café vibe. ⊠ *17 rue des Archives, 4e, Marais Quarter* ☎ *01–42–72–26–18* ⊕ *www.opencafe. fr* Ⓜ *Hôtel de Ville.*

Raidd Bar

BARS | The ever-popular Raidd has a dark downstairs bar and potent drinks. The men are hot, and so is the steamy shower show presented after 11 pm—not for timid voyeurs. ⊠ *23 rue du Temple, 3e, Marais Quarter* ☎ *01–42–77–04–88* ⊕ *www.facebook.com/leraiddparis* Ⓜ *Hôtel de Ville, St-Paul.*

🎭 Performing Arts

Café de la Gare

THEATER | This spot offers an opportunity to experience a particularly Parisian form of entertainment, the *café-théâtre*—part satire, part variety revue—jazzed up with slapstick humor and performed in a café salon. You'll need a good grasp of French slang and current events to keep up with the jokes. There's no reserved seating; doors open 15 minutes before showtime. ⊠ *41 rue du Temple, 4e, Marais Quarter* ☎ *01–42–78–52–51* ⊕ *www.cdlg.org* Ⓜ *Hôtel de Ville.*

👜 Shopping

The Marais has stolen the show as the city's hippest shopping destination—and, for sheer volume, it can't be beat. Rue des Francs-Bourgeois and Rue Vieille de Temple form the central retail axis from which the upper and lower Marais branch out. The newest frontier is its northeastern edge (the Haut Marais), which is known for ultrastylish boutiques, vintage stores, made-in-Paris, and design ateliers.

ANTIQUES AND COLLECTIBLES

Village St-Paul

ANTIQUES & COLLECTIBLES | This clutch of streets, in the beautiful historic nether-world, tucked between the fringes of the Marais and the banks of the Seine, has many antiques shops. ⊠ *Enter from Rue St-Paul, 4e, Marais Quarter* ⊕ *www. levillagesaintpaul.com* Ⓜ *St-Paul.*

BARGAIN SHOPPING

L'Habilleur

MIXED CLOTHING | L'Habilleur is a favorite with the fashion press and anyone looking for a deal. For women, there's a great selection from Harley of Scotland, Roberto Collina, and Henrik Vibskov. Men can find elegant suits from Scandinavian designers. ⊠ *44 rue de Poitou, 3e, Marais Quarter* ☎ *01–48–87–77–12* ⊕ *habilleur.fr* Ⓜ *St-Sébastien–Froissart.*

Zadig & Voltaire Stock

MIXED CLOTHING | Here you'll find new unsold stock from last season. There's a great selection of beautiful cashmere sweaters, silk slip dresses, rocker jeans, and leather jackets, all in their signature luscious colors, for 33%–60% off. ⊠ *22 rue Bourg Tibourg, 4e, Marais Quarter* ☎ *01–44–59–39–64* ⊕ *www.zadig-et-vol-taire.com* Ⓜ *Hôtel de Ville.*

BEAUTY

★ Officine Universelle Buly 1803

PERFUME | This elegant little "pharmacy" could have been here for a hundred years, thanks to the genteel ambience of the shop featuring a line of irresistible all-natural fragrances and luscious beauty concoctions for the face and body. Choose from a range of lotions in delicate scents like tuberose, orange blossom, and damask rose or create your own according to skin type. The charming tea and coffee bar, where you can sit for a snack or drink, was imported straight from Italy. ⊠ *45 rue de Saintonge, 3e, Marais Quarter* ☎ *01–42–72–28–92* ⊕ *www.buly1803.com* Ⓜ *Filles du Calvaire.*

BOOKS AND STATIONERY

Comptoir de l'Image

BOOKS | This is where designers John Galliano and Marc Jacobs stock up on old copies of *Vogue, Harper's Bazaar,* and *The Face.* You'll also find trendy magazines like *Dutch, Purple,* and *Spoon,* plus designer catalogs from the past and rare photo books. Don't arrive early: whimsical opening hours tend to start after lunch. ⊠ *44 rue de Sévigné, 3e, Marais Quarter* ☎ *01–42–72–03–92* Ⓜ *St-Paul.*

Ofr

NEWSSTAND | Ofr gets magazines from the most fashionable spots in the world before anyone else. The store is messy, but you can rub shoulders with photo and press agents while checking out the latest in underground, art, and alternative monthlies. ⊠ *20 rue Dupetit-Thouars, 3e, Marais Quarter* ☎ *01–42–45–72–88* Ⓜ *St-Paul.*

CHILDREN'S CLOTHING

Bonton

CHILDREN'S CLOTHING | FAMILY | Bonton takes the prize for most-coveted duds among those who like to think of children as fashion accessories. (Moms may find some useful wardrobe pointers too.) Sassy separates in saturated colors layer beautifully, look amazing, and manage to be perfectly kid-friendly. Bonton sells toys and furniture too. ⊠ *5 bd. des Filles du Calvaire, 3e, Marais Quarter* ☎ *01–42–72–34–69* ⊕ *www.bonton.fr* Ⓜ *Filles du Calvaire.*

CLOTHING

AB33

WOMEN'S CLOTHING | AB33 is like a sleek boudoir—complete with comfy chairs and scented candles—and the clothes here are unabashedly feminine. Separates in luxury fabrics from top designers, irresistible silk lingerie, dainty jewelry, and a selection of accessories celebrate that certain French *je ne sais quoi.* ⊠ *33 rue Charlot, 3e, Marais Quarter* ☎ *01–42–71–02–82* ⊕ *www.ab33.fr* Ⓜ *Filles du Calvaire.*

The Broken Arm

MIXED CLOTHING | Like the ready-made Duchamp "artwork" for which it is named, the Broken Arm projects a minimalist cool that puts the concept back in concept store. A hypercurated selection of A-list brands for men and women includes vivid separates from the likes of Martin Margiela, Raf Simons, and the sublime Christophe Lemaire. A choice selection of objects and accessories (books, hats, shoes, jewelry, and leather goods) elevates the everyday to art. ⊠ *12 rue Perrée, 3e, Marais Quarter* ☎ *01–44–61–53–60* ⊕ *www.the-broken-arm.com* Ⓜ *Temple.*

Comptoir des Cotonniers

WOMEN'S CLOTHING | Comfortable, affordable, *au courant* clothes make this chain popular. Its reputation is built on smart, wearable styles that stress ease over fussiness. Separates in natural fibers—cotton, silk, and cashmere blends—can be light and breezy or cozy and warm, but they are always soft, flattering, and in a range of beautiful colors. ⊠ *33 rue des Francs-Bourgeois, 4e, Marais Quarter* ☎ *01–42–76–95–33* ⊕ *www.comptoirdescotonniers.com* Ⓜ *St-Paul.*

COS

MIXED CLOTHING | COS—which stands for Collection of Style—is the H&M group's answer to fashion sophisticates, who flock here in droves for high-concept, minimalist designs with serious attention to quality tailoring and fabrics at a reasonable price. Classic accessories and shoes look more expensive than they are. ⊠ *4 rue des Rosiers, 4e, Marais Quarter* ☎ *01–44–54–37–70* ⊕ *www.cosstores. com* Ⓜ *St-Paul.*

★ The Frankie Shop

MIXED CLOTHING | This small-but-mighty boutique has quickly become chic Parisians' go-to place for affordable, eminently wearable, and ever-stylish urban classics. From stunning leather trenches to flowing suits and elegant evening wear, you'll find all the best in urban basics for home, office, and evening. These beautiful basics will never go out of style. ⊠ *14 rue St-Claude, 3e, Marais Quarter* ☎ *01–49–96–52–39* ⊕ *eu.thefrankieshop. com* Ⓜ *St-Sébastien Froissart.*

Free 'P' Star

MIXED CLOTHING | Don't let the chaos at Free 'P' Star discourage you—there's gold in them there bins. Determined seekers on a budget can reap heady rewards, at least according to the young hipsters who flock here for anything from a floor-sweeping peasant skirt to a cropped chinchilla cape. A second Marais branch—at 61 rue de la Verrerie—is equally stuffed to the gills. ⊠ *52 rue de la Verrerie, 4e, Marais Quarter* ☎ *01–42–76–03–72* ⊕ *www.freepstar.com* Ⓜ *Hôtel de Ville.*

FrenchTrotters

MIXED CLOTHING | The flagship store features an understated collection of contemporary French-made clothes and accessories for men and women that emphasize quality fabrics, classic style, and cut over trendiness. You'll also find a handpicked collection of exclusive collaborations with cutting-edge French brands (like sleek leather-and-suede booties by Avril Gau for FrenchTrotters), as well as FrenchTrotters' namesake label and a limited selection of housewares for chic Parisian apartments. ⊠ *128 rue Vieille du Temple, 3e, Marais Quarter* ☎ *01–44–61–00–14* ⊕ *www.frenchtrotters.fr* Ⓜ *St-Sébastien–Froissart.*

L'Eclaireur

MIXED CLOTHING | This Rue de Sevigné boutique is Paris's touchstone for edgy, up-to-the-second styles. L'Eclaireur's knack for uncovering new talent and championing established visionaries is legendary—no surprise after 30 years in the business. Hard-to-find geniuses, like leather wizard Isaac Sellam and British prodigy Paul Harnden, coexist with luxe labels such as Ann Demeulemeester, Jil Sander, and Maison Margiela. ⊠ *40 rue de Sevigné, 3e, Marais Quarter* ☎ *01–48–87–10–22* ⊕ *leclaireur.com* Ⓜ *St-Paul.*

★ Lemaire

MIXED CLOTHING | Even during his time as creative director at Hermès, Christophe Lemaire kept his own eponymous label, designed with his wife, Sarah-Linh Tran. Their refined little boutique in the fashionable Haut Marais is Lemaire's sole dedicated outpost in Paris and remains an absolute fashion mecca season after season. The chicest Parisians flock here for choice, beautifully tailored, minimalist designs in classic neutrals and dreamy hues. The boutique also carries the designers' choice selection of shoes and leather goods. ⊠ *28 rue de Poitou, 3e, Marais Quarter* ☎ *01–44–78–00–09* ⊕ *eu. lemaire.fr* Ⓜ *Filles du Calvaire.*

Majestic Filatures

MIXED CLOTHING | Wearing a Majestic cashmere-cotton blend T-shirt, dress, cardigan, or blazer is like spending the day cocooned in your favorite jammies. Fans have been known to buy five pairs of the silky-soft leggings in one go, just to be sure they never run out. The fact that you'll look totally stylish is the icing on the cake. ⊠ *7 rue des Francs-Bourgeois, 4e, Marais Quarter* ☎ *01–57–40–62–34* ⊕ *www.majesticfilatures.com* Ⓜ *St-Paul.*

★ Merci

MIXED CLOTHING | Paris's favorite concept store assembles top fashions for men and women, home furnishings (including those irresistible French bed and bath linens), vintage, jewelry, and housewares all plucked straight from top-tier French, European, and American designers. Every two months the store features a new design concept in the main entrance, with themes that range from Merci en Rose (featuring all things pink) to American Surf & Skate. The store's three cafés make lingering among Paris's fashion elite a pleasure. ⊠ *111 bd. Beaumarchais, 3e, Marais Quarter* ☎ *01–42–77–00–33* ⊕ *www.merci-merci. com* Ⓜ *St-Sebastien–Froissart.*

Pretty Box

SECOND-HAND | The owners of Pretty Box have scoured Europe for unique pieces from the '20s through the '80s. Women love the superstylish belts, shoes, and bags—many in reptile—sold here for a fraction of what they'd cost new, along with an eccentric selection of cool separates and Bettie Page–era lingerie. The men's collection includes vintage French military coats, sharkskin suits, and a gaggle of riotously patterned shirts. ⊠ *46 rue de Saintonge, 3e, Marais Quarter* ☎ *01– 48–04–81–71* Ⓜ *St-Sébastien–Froissart.*

★ Roseanna

WOMEN'S CLOTHING | An absolute favorite address for the kind of beautifully designed, offbeat yet sexy wardrobe staples we've come to expect from Paris designers. First carried only in top boutiques and concept stores, this sought-after label opened its own boutique only recently. You'll find tons here to love that you won't see on anyone else, including shoes and accessories. ⊠ *5 rue Froissart, 3e, Marais Quarter* ☎ *09–86–62–58–32* ⊕ *roseanna.fr* Ⓜ *St-Sébastien–Froissart, Filles du Calvaire.*

Studio W

WOMEN'S CLOTHING | If you're nostalgic for the days of Studio 54, sashay over to Studio W, where a rare Loris Azzaro gold-chain top or a plunging Guy Laroche beaded couture dress in crimson mousseline has Liza and Bianca written all over it. With plenty of jewelry, shoes, bags, and even gloves to match, this elegant boutique is a must-see for fashion divas who don't mind spending a little more for sublimity. ⊠ *21 rue du Pont aux Choux, 3e, Marais Quarter* ☎ *01–44–78–05–02* Ⓜ *St-Sébastien–Froissart.*

Tom Greyhound

MIXED CLOTHING | This sleek, streamlined concept store gets you down to business. Not only will you find a handpicked selection of clothes and accessories for men and women by top-name designers, but there are also plenty of smaller, cooler labels to discover. ⊠ *19 rue de Saintonge, 3e, Marais Quarter* ☎ *01–44– 61–36–59* ⊕ *www.tomgreyhound.com* Ⓜ *Filles du Calvaire.*

★ Valentine Gauthier

WOMEN'S CLOTHING | Glamour, nonchalance, and serious chic are what make these highly sophisticated separates standouts for the contemporary woman-on-the-go. Even Gauthier's more tailored, masculine styles manage to feel feminine and romantic, and she doesn't shy away from gauzy silks or colorful prints. A Paris insider favorite, her sleek boutique—on an up-and-coming Haut Marais shopping street not far from the concept store Merci—carries clothes, accessories, and her sought-after shoes. ⊠ *88 bd. Beaumarchais, 3e, Marais Quarter* ☎ *01–75–57–14–33* ⊕ *valentinegauthier. com* Ⓜ *St-Sébastien–Froissart, Chemin Vert, Richard Lenoir.*

Vintage Clothing Paris

SECOND-HAND | It's worth a detour to the Marais's outer limits to visit Vintage Clothing Paris, where the racks read like an A-list of designer greats—Margiela, Valentino, Comme des Garçons, and

Mugler, just to name a few. Brigitte Petit's minimalist shop is the fashion insider's go-to spot for rare pieces that stand out in a crowd, like a circa-1985 Alaïa suede skirt with peekaboo grommets and a jaunty Yves Saint Laurent Epoch Russe hooded cape. ⊠ *10 rue de Crussol, 11e, Marais Quarter* ☎ *01–48–07–16–40* ⊕ *www.vintageclothingparis.com* Ⓜ *Filles du Calvaire, Oberkampf.*

Zadig & Voltaire

MIXED CLOTHING | Zadig & Voltaire rocks the young fashionistas by offering street wear at its best: racy camisoles, cashmere sweaters in gorgeous colors, cropped leather jackets, and form-fitting pants to cosset those tiny French derrieres. Branches abound in every chic corner of Paris. ⊠ *42 rue des Francs-Bourgeois, 3e, Marais Quarter* ☎ *01–44–54–00–60* ⊕ *www.zadig-et-voltaire.com* Ⓜ *St-Paul.*

DEPARTMENT STORES
★ BHV

DEPARTMENT STORE | Short for Bazar de l'Hôtel de Ville, Le BHV Marais houses an enormous basement hardware store that sells everything from doorknobs to cement mixers and has to be seen to be believed. The fashion offerings for men, women, and kids feature many of the top labels, and there's a fabulous, not-too-crowded lingerie department on the fifth floor. But BHV is most noted for its high quality home-decor items, electronics, stationery, and office supplies. If you're looking for typically French housewares (like those heavy, gold-rimmed café sets, gorgeous linens, or Savon de Marseille), this is the place. The extensive men's store is across the street at 36 rue de la Verrerie. Perched on the top level is Le Perchoir, a cozy rooftop cocktail bar overlooking the city skyline. ⊠ *52 rue de Rivoli, 4e, Marais Quarter* ☎ *09–77–40–14–00* ⊕ *www.bhv.fr* Ⓜ *Hôtel de Ville.*

FOOD AND TREATS
★ Artefact

OTHER SPECIALTY STORE | Tea lovers will adore this art-centric tea boutique and *salon* set in a 17th-century stone building in the upper Marais, near the Centre Pompidou. In contrast to the behemoth sellers—Mariage Frères, Palais des Thés, and Dammann Frères—who focus on quantity over quality, this shop's hand-selected varieties come from surprising places around the world (oolong from Georgia, anyone?) and small artisanal producers. The friendly owners, a husband-and-wife team, love to share their extensive knowledge, and a tasting flight of four pots in the adorable tearoom is a delight. Upstairs is reserved for artists' books and limited-edition artworks. There's also a tempting array of handmade porcelain teaware. ⊠ *23 rue des Blancs Manteaux, 3e, Marais Quarter* ☎ *01–40–09–96–58* ⊕ *www. artefact-marais.com* Ⓜ *Rambuteau, Hôtel de Ville.*

Izraël

FOOD | This place isn't called the "*épicerie du monde*" for nothing. Izraël is a one-stop shop for any spice under the sun, plus those hard-to-find items you'd otherwise spend days tracking down. Bins overflowing with every variety of candied fruit, nuts, beans, olives, pickles, and preserved fish give this tiny shop the air of an exotic bazaar. You'll also find all manner of canned goods, candies, rare spirits, and baking necessities. ⊠ *30 rue François Miron, 4e, Marais Quarter* ☎ *01–42–72–66–23* Ⓜ *St-Paul.*

Jacques Genin

CHOCOLATE | Genin offers great chocolate: not too sweet, with handpicked seasonal ingredients for the velvety ganaches. The tea salon is a great spot to sample one of Genin's masterful takes on classic French pastries and a voluptuous *chocolat chaud*. ⊠ *133 rue de Turenne, 3e, Marais Quarter* ☎ *01–45–77–29–01* ⊕ *www.jacquesgenin.fr* Ⓜ *Filles du Calvaire, Oberkampf.*

Le Palais des Thés

OTHER SPECIALTY STORE | White tea, green tea, black tea, tea from China, Japan, Indonesia, South America, and more: you can expect a comprehensive tea experience here. Try one of the flavored varieties, such as Hammam, a traditional Turkish recipe with date pulp, orange flower, rose, and red berries. ⊠ *64 rue Vieille du Temple, 3e, Marais Quarter* ☎ *01–48–87–80–60* ⊕ *www.palaisdesthes.com* Ⓜ *St-Paul.*

Mariage Frères

OTHER SPECIALTY STORE | Mariage Frères, with its colonial *charme* and wooden counters, has 100-plus years of tea purveying behind it. Choose from more than 450 blends from 32 countries, not to mention teapots, teacups, books, and tea-flavor biscuits and candies. High tea and light lunches are served here and at several other Paris locations. ⊠ *30 rue du Bourg-Tibourg, 4e, Marais Quarter* ☎ *01–42–72–28–11* ⊕ *www.mariagefreres.com* Ⓜ *Hôtel de Ville.*

Méert

FOOD | The first Paris offshoot of the famous patisserie and tea salon in Lille (one of France's oldest) specializes in the *gauffre*, a delicate waffle handmade in the original 19th-century molds and wrapped in gilt-paper packages. Native to Belgium and northern France, Méert's version is treasured for its light cream center perfumed with Madagascar vanilla. There are also chocolates, pastries, and flavored *guimauves*, the airy French marshmallows. ⊠ *16 rue Elzévir, 3e, Marais Quarter* ☎ *01–49–96–56–90* ⊕ *www.meert.fr* Ⓜ *St-Paul.*

HOME DECOR

★ Empreintes

HOUSEWARES | The *raison d'être* of the organization Métiers d'Art is to reward and promote French *savoir faire*—the traditional expertise of France's many fine craftspeople and artists passed down from generation to generation. To this end—and to the delight of local bobos (short for *bourgeois-bohème* or bourgeois-bohemians) decorating their Marais lofts—Métiers d'Art opened the capital's first crafts "concept store," which assembles the work of dozens of craftspeople and artists on four floors, including impeccably crafted glassware, porcelain, jewelry, leather goods, furnishings, housewares, fine art, and much more. It's an excellent place for a souvenir of French *art de vivre.* ⊠ *5 rue de Picardie, 3e, Marais Quarter* ☎ *01–40–09–53–80* ⊕ *www.empreintes-paris.com* Ⓜ *Temple, République, Filles du Calvaire.*

Le Monde Sauvage

HOUSEWARES | Le Monde Sauvage is a must-visit for home accessories. Expect reversible silk bedspreads in rich colors, velvet throws, hand-quilted bed linens, silk floor cushions, colorful rugs, and the best selection of hand-embroidered curtains in silk, cotton, linen, or velvet. ⊠ *21 rue Sévigné, 4e, Marais Quarter* ☎ *01–44–61–02–61* ⊕ *www.lemondesauvage.com* Ⓜ *St-Paul.*

Muji

HOUSEWARES | *Kanketsu* (simplicity) is the guiding philosophy at Muji, and the resulting streamlined designs are all the rage in Europe. Must-haves include a collection of mini-necessities—travel essentials, wee office gizmos, purse-size accoutrements, plus the best notebooks and pens around. They're so useful and adorable you'll want them all. ⊠ *47 rue des Francs–Bourgeois, 4e, Marais Quarter* ☎ *01–49–96–41–41* ⊕ *www.muji.eu* Ⓜ *St-Paul.*

Van der Straeten

HOUSEWARES | Paris designer Hervé van der Straeten started out creating jewelry for Saint Laurent and Lacroix, designed a perfume bottle for Christian Dior, and then moved on to making rather baroque and often wacky furniture. In his loft gallery-cum-showroom, furniture, lighting, and startling mirrors are on display. ⊠ *11* rue Ferdinand Duval, 4e, Marais Quarter ☎ 01–42–78–99–99 ⊕ www.vanderstraet-en.fr Ⓜ St-Paul.

JEWELRY AND ACCESSORIES

Audrey Langlois

JEWELRY & WATCHES | Beautiful, affordable, wearable—these are just a few of the words that spring to mind to describe this Parisian designer's line of sumptuous creations that mix rich gold-plate with semiprecious stones—lapis, turquoise, azurite, and agate—with designs that can be both fragile and bold. These pieces for all occasions put just the right touch on any outfit. The beautiful, cozy boutique is a must-visit for lovers of unique, one-off pieces you won't find anywhere else. ✉ 66 rue du Temple, 3e, Marais Quarter ☎ no phone ⊕ www.audreylanglois-paris. fr Ⓜ Rambuteau.

Les Néréides

JEWELRY & WATCHES | You'd be hard pressed to find a more charming line of vibrant, adorable, colorful, and feminine costume jewelry, and everything is completely distinct and a lot of fun. This Nice-based brand's necklaces, bracelets, earrings, and rings mix leaves, flowers, fruit, and a colorful array of faux gemstones in fanciful bouquets. You'll also find colorful creatures, such as ladybugs, unicorns, ballerinas, bird's nests, and a couple of koala bears swinging from a golden vine among green gems. You'll get a lift just trying them on. ✉ 30 Rue de Sévigné, 4e, Marais Quarter ☎ 09–82–41–56–53 ⊕ www.lesnereides.com Ⓜ St-Paul, Chemin Vert.

★ Titlee

JEWELRY & WATCHES | This whimsical jewelry line finally open a dedicated boutique, home to its entire cast of lovable creatures—from ghosts and jack-o-lanterns to owls and dolphins to rocket ships and PAC-MAN—all so colorful and captivating you can't stop at just one. There's also a superchic line of bracelets,

necklaces, and rings, but the real show-stoppers are the pins, perfect accents on anything from an evening gown to a jean jacket. This stylish boutique also stocks original artwork, ceramics, books, toys, and an irresistible line of stationery. ✉ 29 rue des Gravilliers, 3e, Marais Quarter ☎ 01–45–25–26–23 ⊕ www.titlee.fr Ⓜ Arts-et-Métiers.

★ WHITE bIRD

JEWELRY & WATCHES | Irresistible is the word for this shop's scintillating collection of jewels—from an assemblage of top-echelon international designers—that ranges from the daintiest of diamond rings, bracelets, and necklaces to brilliantly colored stones in edgy settings. This spare boutique, a stone's throw from concept store Merci, may be tiny, but it's had a big impact on fashion jewelry in Paris. If you're looking for a piece to be worn every day or a statement piece that goes from day to night, this is your place. Trunk shows and openings are held at WHITE bIRD's first and larger boutique at 38 rue du Mont Thabor, just off the Rue Saint-Honoré. ✉ 7 bd. des Filles du Calvaire, 3e, Marais Quarter ☎ 01–40–24–27–17 ⊕ www.whitebirdjewellery. com Ⓜ Filles du Calvaire.

SHOES, HANDBAGS, AND LEATHER GOODS

★ Isaac Reina

HANDBAGS | It takes up to several days of painstaking work to create one of Isaac Reina's refined handbags, satchels, totes, backpacks, or small leather goods. Meticulous detailing and gorgeous finishes are just some of the trademarks of this Barcelona native's elegant designs, all handcrafted in Paris in his sleek boutique near the Musée Picasso. These luxury bags are for people who appreciate superlative quality but don't care to flash a logo. ✉ 12 rue de Thorigny, 3e, Marais Quarter ☎ 01–42–78–81–95 ⊕ www. isaacreina.com Ⓜ St-Paul, Chemin Vert.

K. Jacques

SHOES | K. Jacques has shod everyone from Brigitte Bardot to Drew Barrymore. The famous St-Tropez–based maker of strappy leather-soled flats has migrated to the big time while still keeping designs classic and comfortable. From gladiator style to lightweight cork platforms, metallics to neutrals, these are perennial favorites. ⊠ *16 rue Pavée, 4e, Marais Quarter* ☎ *01–40–27–03–57* ⊕ *www.kjacques.fr* Ⓜ *St-Paul.*

Mademoiselle Chapeau

HATS & GLOVES | This is the only hatmaker in Paris where you can see jaunty cloches, fedoras, and flat-topped straw boaters being made with centuries-old techniques in an on-site atelier. Classic models in straw, wool, rabbit felt, or silk in a huge range of colors come in a dozen styles, from a charming pillbox to an elegant wide-brim model so light and graceful it could easily pair with an evening suit or wedding gown. ⊠ *15 rue des Tournelles, 4e, Marais Quarter* ☎ *01–72–60–77–68* ⊕ *www.mademoisellechapeaux.com* Ⓜ *Bastille, St-Paul.*

Chapter 10

EASTERN PARIS

Updated by
Jennifer Ladonne

⊙ Sights	🍴 Restaurants	🛏 Hotels	🛍 Shopping	🍸 Nightlife
★★☆☆☆	★★★★☆	★★☆☆☆	★★★★☆	★★★★★

NEIGHBORHOOD SNAPSHOT

GETTING HERE

Eastern Paris includes the 10e, 11e, 12e, 19e, and 20e arrondissements. The Bastille métro stop, on Lines 1, 5, and 8, is a good place to start. For the Canal St-Martin, use the Place de la République stop (Lines 3, 5, 8, 9, 11) and walk along Rue Faubourg du Temple; use the Gare de l'Est stop (Lines 4, 5, 7) and walk along Rue des Récollets; or choose the Jaurès stop (Lines 2, 5, and 7 bis), take the Boulevard de Villette exit, and walk a mere 80 feet south. For the Cimetière du Père-Lachaise, take Line 2 or 3 to the eponymous stop.

MAKING THE MOST OF YOUR TIME

The Canal St-Martin is one of the most popular destinations in the city, particularly on Sunday afternoon, when the streets are closed to cars. Walk along the leafy canal, have lunch in a sidewalk café, then grab a Vélib' rental bike, and follow the canal all the way to Parc de la Villette. A Sunday morning trip to the picturesque Marché d'Aligre, which includes the covered Marché Beauvau, is also recommended, even if you're not buying (it's open every morning but Monday). The heaps of fresh produce and colorful flowers sold by spirited vendors are worth seeing. On any day Place de la Bastille is a lively spot to stop for drinks or lunch. If time is limited, save this neighborhood for after dark, when the streets around Place de la Bastille and Oberkampf really come to life.

PAUSE HERE

One of the oldest and prettiest parks in Paris, the towering Parc de Belleville is also its highest, affording spectacular panoramas of the city. Its winding *allées*, sprawling lawns, and shady lanes lead to fountains, woods, and gardens, with lovely spots for picnicking along the way. Famous for its taverns since the 14th century, it is now home to one of Paris's five wine-producing vineyards.

TOP REASONS TO GO

■ **Canal St-Martin.** This scenic canal, built by Napoleon Bonaparte, is now one of the city's hottest, hippest hangouts—it's great for strolling, with plenty of galleries, shops, and cafés.

■ **Place de la Bastille.** The flashpoint of the French Revolution still draws unruly crowds, but not so much agitators as partiers. It's also home to the Opéra Bastille.

■ **Cimetière du Père-Lachaise.** Fans of celebrities, from Frédéric Chopin and Oscar Wilde to Gertrude Stein and Jim Morrison, come to pay tribute at their final resting place.

■ **Parc de la Villette.** As the site of the city's esteemed science museum and planetarium, this is a great destination for curious kids and grown-up science buffs. For music lovers, it's also the site of the Cité de la Musique and the stunning Philharmonie de Paris.

■ **Coulée Verte René-Dumont/Promenade Plantée (Viaduc des Arts).** This abandoned railway extending 5 km (3 miles) from Bastille all the way to the Bois de Vincennes, was transformed into a beautiful tree-lined walkway perched atop a brick viaduct.

The Bastille is so much more than just history. The lively bars and cafés around the Place de la Bastille give way to a hive of smaller streets lined with one-off boutiques, A-list restaurants, and buzzy cocktail bars and clubs. Add world-class performances at the Opéra Bastille and this a must-see area, day and night.

There are also noteworthy attractions, like the nearby **Coulée verte René-Dumont (Viaduc des Arts),** an urban-renewal project that transformed an old elevated rail line into arcaded, design-focused studios and shops. Along the top, the Promenade Plantée makes for a lovely stroll through the 12e arrondissement, which includes stately apartment buildings and pretty Square Trousseau, gateway to the **Marché d'Aligre.**

The **Canal St-Martin,** once the down-and-out cousin on the northern border, is now trend-spotting central, brimming with funky bars, cafés, bistros, and boutiques. The scene is similar on Rues Oberkampf, St-Maur, Folie Méricourt, and Jean-Pierre-Timbaud, where artists, small designers, and gastronomic bistros have set up shop, and where a substantial slice of the city's *bobo* (bourgeois-bohemian) contingent is buying up the no-longer-so-affordable apartments.

Continuing east, you'll find the city's largest and most scenic cemetery, **Père-Lachaise,** with a roster of famous tenants lining its winding cobbled streets. Heading north, the impressively wild **Parc Buttes-Chaumont,** with grassy fields, a small Greek-style temple, and sweeping hilltop views of Paris, is a perennial favorite. It's the perfect place to take a picnic lunch and let museum-weary kids blow off some steam. The eastern section is also home to three other popular parks: the **Parc de la Villette,** which contains a pair of engaging museums and the monumental Philharmonie de Paris to the northeast; the sky-high **Parc de Belleville**; and the **Bois de Vincennes,** home to the Château de Vincennes, the Parc Floral, and the city's largest zoo to the southeast.

South of the Bastille, the old wine warehouses at **Bercy** have become a veritable village of shops and restaurants bordering Parc de Bercy. Directly across the Seine is the **Bibliothéque Nationale François Mitterrand,** the National Library of France, and the Piscine Joséphine Baker, the only swimming pool in the Seine.

Bastille, Bercy, Nation, and Around

The cafés and clubs of bustling Bastille give way to a less-touristed area around the Gare de Lyon and Bercy. You'll find fascinating Art Deco remnants of the 1931 Paris Colonial Exposition in the stunning Palais de la Port Dorée, which houses the Musée Nationale de l'Histoire de l'Immigration and Paris's most charming aquarium—and the many riches of the Bois de Vincennes.

Sights

Bercy

NEIGHBORHOOD | FAMILY | Tucked away south of the Gare de Lyon in the 12e arrondissement, blocks of stone warehouses that once stored wine are now home to **Bercy Village** (✉ *28 rue François Truffaut 08–25–16–60–75*) a collection of boutiques and eateries that stay open unusually late for Paris—many shops until 9 pm, Monday to Saturday; some restaurants until 2 am daily. You can still see the old train tracks used to transport the wine barrels from the provinces. Adjacent to the shops is the tranquil **Parc de Bercy**, with lawns, ponds, and flower beds crisscrossed by gravel paths, and the Jardin Yitzhak Rabin, a garden named for the late Nobel peace prize winner. Nearby, at 51 rue de Bercy, a Cubist building by Frank Gehry houses the **Cinémathèque Française**, a film buff's paradise, showing classic films, many in English; there are frequent homages to directors and actors, plus a cinema bookshop and museum. ✉ *Bercy* Ⓜ *Cour St-Emilion, Bercy.*

Bibliothèque Nationale François Mitterrand

LIBRARY | The National Library of France, across the sleek Simone de Beauvoir footbridge from Bercy Park, is a stark complex comprising four 22-story L-shape buildings representing open books. Commissioned by President Mitterrand, the €1 billion library was said to be the world's most modern when it opened in 1998—a reputation quickly sullied when it was discovered that miles of books and rare documents were baking in the glass towers, unprotected from the sun (movable shutters were eventually installed). Some of the most important printed treasures of France are stored here, though the majority of them are available only to researchers. Visitors can see the impressive 17th-century Globes of Coronelli, a pair of 2-ton orbs made for Louis XIV. There's a sunken center garden with tall trees (open to the public the first weekend in June) ringed by low-ceilinged reading rooms, which are nothing special. A first-floor gallery hosts popular temporary exhibitions on subjects such as the life of Casanova. Enter through the easternmost tower. ✉ *Quai François Mauriac, 13e, Bibliothèque* ☎ *01–53–79–59–59* ⊕ *www.bnf.fr* ✉ *Globes gallery free; all other entries from €4* ⊘ *Closed Mon.* Ⓜ *Bibliothèque, Quai de la Gare.*

★ Bois de Vincennes

CITY PARK | FAMILY | Like the Bois de Boulogne to the west, this much-loved retreat on the city's eastern border was landscaped by Napoléon III. Its roots, however, reach back to the 13th century, when Philippe Auguste created a hunting preserve in the shadow of the royal Château de Vincennes, which once ranked as the largest château in Europe. In 1731 Louis XV created a public park here, and the *bois* (or woods) now features a Japanese garden, La Grande Pagode (a Buddhist temple containing the largest golden statue of the Buddha in Europe), and the exquisite Parc Floral, with acres of flower gardens, a huge kids' park, and summertime jazz and classical concerts. Horse races at the restored Vincennes Hippodrome de Paris are an event for the whole family, but perhaps not the Espace Naturiste, Paris's first area for nudists, opened in 2017. Rowboats are for hire at a pair of lakes: Lac Daumesnil, which has two islands, and Lac des Minimes, which has three. For the kids, there are pony rides, a miniature train, and numerous play areas. Here, too, you'll find the stunning Palais de la Porte Dorée, home to an immigration museum and tropical aquarium. Through late summer, the Parc Floral hosts two beloved music festivals, the Paris Jazz Festival and the Festival Classique au Vert. Grab a picnic and a blanket and enjoy classical music or jazz in the amphitheater or on the lawn in Paris's prettiest park. ⊠ *Bois de Vincennes, 12e, Bois de Vincennes* Ⓜ *Château de Vincennes, Porte Dorée.*

★ Château de Vincennes

CASTLE/PALACE | This imposing high-walled château, on the northern edge of the Bois de Vincennes, was France's medieval version of Versailles. Built and expanded by various kings between the 12th and 14th centuries, it is now surrounded by a dry moat and dominated by a 170-foot keep, the last of nine original towers. The royal residence eventually became a prison holding, notably, convicts of both sexes—and "the doors did not always remain closed between them," as one tour guide coyly put it. Inmates included the philosopher Diderot and the Marquis de Sade, and the alleged spy Mata Hari was executed in its dry moat bed. Both the château and its cathedral, Ste-Chapelle—designed in the style of the Paris church of the same name—have undergone a spectacular restoration, returning them to their previous glory. If you speak French, the free 90-minute tour is worthwhile; otherwise, consider spending €3 for the English audioguide. The entrance to the lovely Parc Floral de Paris is just behind the chateau. ⊠ *Av. de Paris, 12e, Bois de Vincennes* ☎ *01–43–28–15–48* ⊕ *www.chateau-vincennes.fr* ⊠ *€9.50* Ⓜ *Château de Vincennes.*

★ Coulée Verte René-Dumont/Promenade Plantée (*La Coulée Verte*)

CITY PARK | Once a train line from the Paris suburbs to Bastille, this redbrick viaduct (often referred to as Le Viaduc des Arts) is now one of the park highlights of the unpretentious 12e arrondissement. The rails have been transformed into a 4½-km (3-mile) walkway lined with trees, bamboo, and flower gardens, offering a bird's-eye view of the stately Haussmannian buildings along Avenue Daumesnil. Below, the *voûtes* (arcades) have been transformed by the city into artisan boutiques, many focused on decor and design. There are also temporary galleries showcasing art and photography. The Promenade, which gained fame as a setting in the 2004 film *Before Sunset,* was the inspiration for New York's High Line. It ends at the Bastille. From there, you can continue your walk to the Bois de Vincennes. If you're hungry, grab a bite at L'Arrosoir, a cozy café under the viaduct at 75 avenue Daumesnil. ⊠ *1–129 av. Daumesnil, 12e, Bastille* ☎ *01–86–95–95–07* ⊕ *www.leviaducdesarts.com* Ⓜ *Bastille, Gare de Lyon.*

★ Marché d'Aligre

MARKET | Place d'Aligre has two of Paris's best markets: the lively outdoor Marché d'Aligre and the covered Marché Beauvau. Open every day but Monday, both are great places to pick up picnic essentials, which you can enjoy nearby in the small park at Square Trousseau or on the Promenade Plantée. The picturesque outdoor market has dozens of boisterous vendors, their stands laden with fresh fruits and vegetables, flower bouquets, and regional products such as jam, honey, and dried sausage. Many vendors are happy to give you a taste of whatever they're selling. The covered market, Marché Beauvau, stocks everything from cheeses and olive oil to brewed-in-Paris craft beer. Sunday morning, when the accompanying flea market is in full swing, is the liveliest time to visit. Stop for a plate of fresh oysters, *charcuterie* and a glass of *rouge* (even on Sunday morning) at one of the city's quirkiest wine bars, Le Baron Rouge (1 rue Théophile Roussel) or one of the many chic cafés in the neighborhood. ⊠ *Pl. d'Aligre, 12e, Bastille* ☉ *Closed Mon.* Ⓜ *Ledru-Rollin, Bastille.*

★ Opéra Bastille

PERFORMANCE VENUE | This mammoth ultramodern facility, designed by architect Carlos Ott and inaugurated in 1989, long ago took over the role of Paris's main opera house from the Opéra Garnier (although both operate under

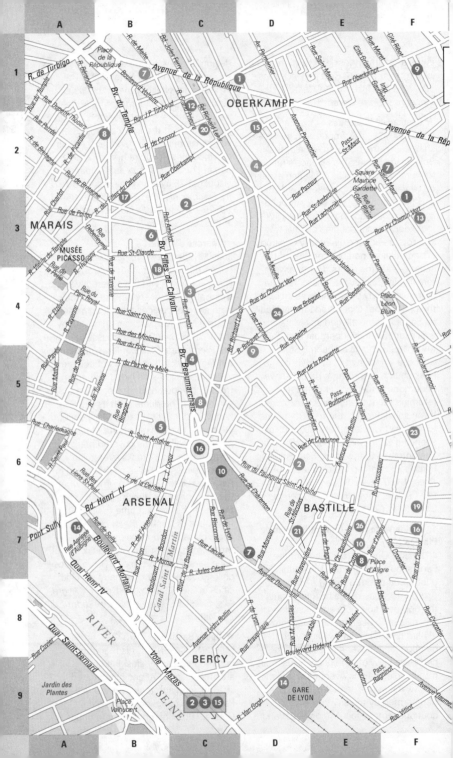

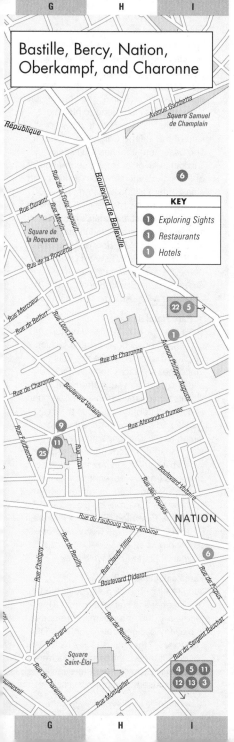

Bastille, Bercy, Nation, Oberkampf, and Charonne

KEY

1 Exploring Sights

1 Restaurants

1 Hotels

Sights ▼

1 Atelier des Lumières **F3**
2 Bercy..................... **C9**
3 Bibliothèque Nationale
   François Mitterrand **C9**
4 Bois de Vincennes... **I9**
5 Château de Vincennes... **I9**
6 Cimetière du
   Père-Lachaise **I3**
7 Coulée Verte
   René-Dumont/
   Promenade Plantée ... **D7**
8 Marché d'Aligre **E7**
9 Musée Edith Piaf......... **F1**
10 Opéra Bastille............. **C6**
11 Palais de la
   Porte Dorée **I9**
12 Parc Floral de Paris....... **I9**
13 Parc Zoologique de
   Paris.......................... **I9**
14 Pavillon de l'Arsenal.... **A7**
15 Piscine
   Josephine Baker......... **C9**
16 Place de la Bastille **C6**

Restaurants ▼

1 Astier..................... **D1**
2 Au Passage............... **C3**
3 Au Trou Gascon.......... **I9**
4 Back in Black Coffee.... **C5**
5 Bubar..................... **B6**
6 Cantine Merci............ **B3**
7 Double Dragon........... **F2**
8 Jacques Genin
   Salon de Thé **B2**
9 La Chocolaterie
   Cyril Lignac.............. **G6**
10 Le Baron Rouge.......... **E7**
11 Le Bistrot Paul Bert..... **G6**
12 Le Rigmarole **C1**
13 Le Servan................. **F3**
14 Le Train Bleu **D9**
15 Le Villaret **D2**
16 L'Ébauchoir **F7**
17 Lily of the Valley......... **B3**
18 Maison Plisson.......... **B4**
19 Mokonuts................. **F7**
20 Ober Mamma **C2**
21 Passerini................. **D7**
22 Sadarnac **I4**
23 Septime **F6**
24 Ten Belles Bread **D4**
25 Unico..................... **G6**
26 Virtus **E7**

Hotels ▼

1 Eden Lodge................ **I5**
2 Hôtel Antoine............ **D6**
3 Hôtel Bastille de
   Launay **C4**
4 Hôtel Fabric **D2**
5 Hôtel Mama Shelter..... **I4**
6 Hotel Paradiso **I7**
7 Le Général Hôtel........ **B1**
8 Le Petit
   Beaumarchais **C5**
9 Maison Bréguet......... **D5**

the same Opéra de Paris umbrella). The fabulous acoustics of the steeply sloping, stylish auditorium have earned more plaudits than the modern facade. Like the building, performances tend to be on the avant-garde side—you're as likely to see a contemporary adaptation of *La Bohème* as you are to hear Kafka set to music. Tickets for Opéra de Paris productions run €15–€230 and generally go on sale at the box office a month before shows, earlier by phone and online. Once the doors open, "standing places" can be purchased for €10 from vending machines in the lobby, but you'll need coins or a credit card (no bills) and patience to snag one, as the lines are long. The opera season usually runs September through July; the box office is open Monday through Saturday 11:30–6:30 and one hour before curtain call. If you just want to look around inside, you can also buy tickets for a 90-minute guided tour (in French only) for €17. ⊠ *Pl. de la Bastille, 12e, Bastille* ☎ *08–92–89–90–90 tickets and tour information, 01–71–25–24–23 from outside of France* ⊕ *www.operadeparis.fr* ⊙ *Closed mid-July–Aug. Box office closed Sun. and after 6:30 pm, except 1 hr before curtain call* Ⓜ *Bastille.*

Palais de la Porte Dorée

HISTORIC SIGHT | FAMILY | If you're bound for the Bois de Vincennes, pay a visit to the Palais de la Porte Dorée. Built for the 1931 Colonial Exhibition, it's one of the best examples of Art Deco architecture in Paris. The ornate facade features bas-relief sculptures representing France's erstwhile empire. Inside, the elaborate marble, ornate metalwork, frescoes, and original lighting are all beautifully maintained. Entry to the ground floor is free. On either end are furnished salons, one representing Asia, the other Africa (a Gucci commercial was filmed in the latter); peek into the central room, called the Forum, where restored Africa-inspired mosaics line the walls. The

upper floors are occupied by the **Musée Nationale de l'Historie de l'Immigration**, a fascinating modern museum tracing the history of immigration in France through photographs, artworks, and first-person accounts. It's also home to blockbuster exhibits, like the recent show on king-of-the-stiletto Christian Louboutin. The basement contains **L'Aquarium Tropical**, a favorite among generations of Parisians, who all visited as kids, with a pair of rare albino alligators, plus 300 species of exotic marine life. ■TIP➜ **Be sure to check out the Palais's excellent program of temporary exhibitions.** ⊠ *293 av. Daumesnil, 12e, Bois de Vincennes* ☎ *01–53–59–58–60* ⊕ *www.palais-porte-doree.fr* ⊠ *Ground floor free; museum €8; aquarium €8; combined ticket €12* ⊙ *Closed Mon.* Ⓜ *Porte Dorée.*

★ Parc Floral de Paris

CITY PARK | FAMILY | A lake, a butterfly garden, a bonsai pavillion, and seasonal displays of blooms make the Bois de Vincennes's 70-acre floral park a lovely place to spend a warm afternoon. Kids will also enjoy the extensive playgrounds and the marionette (*guignol*) theater. A café and a sit-down tea salon make dining easy, but picnicking under the trees is highly recommended, especially when the park hosts jazz and classical concerts (most weekends from June through September). In winter months, some attractions may be closed. ⊠ *12e, Rte. de la Pyramide, Bois de Vincennes* ☎ *01–49–57–24–81* ⊕ *www.parcfloraldeparis.com* ⊠ *€2.50 May–Oct.; free rest of year* Ⓜ *Château de Vincennes.*

Parc Zoologique de Paris

ZOO | FAMILY | The 35-acre zoo in the Bois de Vincennes is France's largest. This facility's 1,000 or so animals are housed in cleverly designed environments (aka "biozones") that mix species as Mother Nature intended; these include a free-range aviary you can walk through and a greenhouse that recreates a slice of the rain forest. ✉ *53 av. de St-Maurice, 12e, Bois de Vincennes* ✈ *Entrance at intersection of Av. Daumesnil and Rte. de Ceinture du Lac Daumesnil* ☎ *08–11–22–41–22* ⊕ *www.parczoologiquedeparis.fr* 🎟 *€20* ⊘ *Closed Tues. in Nov. and Dec.* Ⓜ *Porte Dorée.*

Pavillon de l'Arsenal

HISTORY MUSEUM | FAMILY | If your knowledge of Paris history is *nul* (nil), stop here for an entertaining free tutorial. Built in 1879 as a private museum, the Pavillon today is a restored structure of glass and iron that showcases the city's urban development through the ages. A giant model of Paris traces its evolution (with information in English). There are photos, maps, and videos, plus a giant digital interactive model detailing what Paris is predicted to look like in the future. Reconstruction plans—called Grand Paris—are vast and will extend to the 2024 Olympics and beyond. The Pavillon also has a café-bookstore and hosts frequent architecture-themed temporary exhibits. ✉ *21 bd. Morland, 4e, Bastille* ☎ *01–42–76–33–97* ⊕ *www.pavillon-arsenal.com* 🎟 *Free* ⊘ *Closed Mon.* Ⓜ *Sully-Morland, Bastille.*

Piscine Josephine Baker

POOL | FAMILY | This modern aquatic center, which floats on the Seine and is named after the much-beloved American entertainer, features a pool with a retractable glass roof, two solariums, a steam room, Jacuzzis, and a gym. Check the opening hours and schedule of classes online. ✉ *Porte de la Gare, 21 quai François Mauriac, 13e, Bibliothèque* ☎ *01–56–61–96–50* ⊕ *www.piscine-baker.fr* 🎟 *Pool €4 (€6.50 in summer); fees may apply for other activities* Ⓜ *Quai de la Gare, Bibilothèque.*

Place de la Bastille

HISTORIC SIGHT | Almost nothing remains of the infamous Bastille prison, destroyed more than 225 years ago, though tourists still ask bemused Parisians where to find it. Until the late 1980s, there was little more to see here than a busy traffic circle ringing the Colonne de Juillet (July Column), a memorial to the victims of later uprisings in 1830 and 1848. The opening of the Opéra Bastille in 1989 rejuvenated the area, however, drawing art galleries, bars, and restaurants to the narrow streets, notably along Rue de Lappe—once a haunt of Edith Piaf—and Rue de la Roquette.

Before it became a prison, the Bastille St-Antoine was a defensive fortress with eight immense towers and a wide moat. It was built by Charles V in the late 14th century and transformed into a prison during the reign of Louis XIII (1610–43). Famous occupants included Voltaire, the Marquis de Sade, and the Man in the Iron Mask. On July 14, 1789, it was stormed by an angry mob that dramatically freed all of the remaining prisoners (there were only seven), thereby launching the French Revolution. The roots of the revolt ran deep. Resentment toward Louis XVI and Marie-Antoinette had been building amid a severe financial crisis. There was a crippling bread shortage, and the free-spending monarch was blamed. When the king dismissed the popular finance minister, Jacques Necker, enraged Parisians took to the streets. They marched to Les Invalides, helping themselves to stocks of arms, then continued on to the Bastille. A few months later, what was left of the prison was razed—and 83 of its stones were carved into miniature Bastilles and sent to the provinces as a memento (you can see one of them in the Musée Carnavalet). The key to the prison was given to George Washington by Lafayette and has remained at Mount Vernon ever since. Today, nearly every major street demonstration in Paris—and there are many—passes through this square. ✉ *Bastille* Ⓜ *Bastille.*

🍽 Restaurants

Au Trou Gascon

$$$$ | BISTRO | This elegant establishment off Place Daumesnil offers a refined take on the cuisine of Gascony, a region renowned for its pork, foie gras, lamb, and duck. Most popular with the regulars are the surprisingly light cassoulets (all the meats are grilled before going into the pot) with big white Tarbais beans and a superb duck or goose confit. **Known for:** splurge-worthy wine list; time-honored specialty of roasted milk-fed lamb; gourmet take on the rich gastronomy of southwest France. $ *Average main: €38* ✉ *40 rue Taine, 12e, Bastille* ☎ *01–43–44–34–26* ⊕ *www.autrougascon.fr* ⊘ *Closed weekends, Aug., and 1 wk in Jan.* Ⓜ *Daumesnil.*

★ Back in Black Coffee

$ | FRENCH | This sleek 2,000-square-foot café—an easy walk from Place de la Bastille and the Marais—is a favorite spot for breakfast, veggie-centric nibbles, and exceptional scones, breads, and sweet rolls served all day, seven days a week. Mornings are a good time to enjoy the fragrance of fresh roasting coffee, performed in full view. **Known for:** famous scones; some of the best café food around; excellent brunch (reserve ahead of time). $ *Average main: €6* ✉ *25 rue Amelot, 11e, Bastille* ☎ ⊕ *backinblackcoffee.com* Ⓜ *Bastille, Chemin Vert.*

Bubar

$ | WINE BAR | In summer, look for the crowd spilling out the front of this signless wine bar named for Jean-Louis, the bartender (*bubar* or *barbu* is French slang for "bearded"). The wine menu—with many selections available by the glass—features French wines and small-batch vintages from South Africa, Chile, and Argentina. **Known for:** bring-your-own snacks option; wines to discover, guided by a knowledgeable and generous owner; low-lit, almost clandestine atmosphere. $ *Average main: €12* ✉ *3 rue des*

Tournelles, 4e, Marais Quarter ☎ *01–40–29–97–72* ⊘ *No lunch* Ⓜ *Bastille.*

★ Le Baron Rouge

$ | WINE BAR | This laid-back wine bar near the Place d'Aligre market is a throwback to another era, with just a few tables plus giant wine barrels along the walls for filling and refilling your take-home bottles. A fun time to come is Sunday morning (yes, morning) when it's packed with locals who have just been to the market and want to linger over good food and that first *petit blanc* of the day. **Known for:** oysters on a winter evening; authentic neighborhood atmosphere; wine by the barrel with refills to take home. $ *Average main: €11* ✉ *1 rue Théophile Roussel, 12e, Bastille* ☎ *01–43–43–14–32* ⊕ *www.lebaronrouge.net* Ⓜ *Ledru-Rollin.*

L'Ébauchoir

$$ | BISTRO | From its traditional bentwood bistro chairs to its well-priced menu of contemporary French classics, this is the kind of neighborhood bistro we dream about when we think of Paris. Friendly service, a convivial atmosphere, a top-notch wine list, and delicious market-fresh fare all add up to the kind of place you want to keep all to yourself. **Known for:** reliably excellent food; a local favorite; warm and welcoming service (in English). $ *Average main: €22* ✉ *43–45 Rue de Cîteaux, 12e, Bastille* ☎ *01–43–42–49–31* ⊕ *lebauchoir.com* ⊘ *Closed Sun. No lunch Mon.* Ⓜ *Faidherbe-Chaligny, Reuilly-Diderot.*

★ Le Train Bleu

$$$$ | FRENCH | Paris's grandest Belle Époque beauty, hidden within the Gare de Lyon train station, has been fully restored to a culinary status almost befitting its eye-popping decor. The menu of French classics is not cheap, though the €49 "travelers menu" for lunch assures you'll be wined, dined, and on your train in 45 minutes. **Known for:** tasty and creative cocktails; gorgeous setting; unique historic atmosphere. $ *Average main: €38* ✉ *Pl. Louis-Armand, 12e, Bastille*

☎ 01–43–43–09–06 ⊕ www.le-train-bleu. com/en Ⓜ Gare de Lyon.

★ Maison Plisson

$ | **MODERN FRENCH** | The deep sidewalk terrace at this three-in-one gourmet grocer, restaurant, and café is a great place to linger over lunch and a glass of wine. The daily menu of hot dishes, soups, and salads complements a wide selection of tasty pastries and classic sandwiches made with top-notch ingredients. **Known for:** snob appeal; good sandwiches to stay or take away; French specialties from every corner of the country. Ⓢ Average main: €10 ✉ 93 bd. Beaumarchais, 3e, Marais Quarter ☎ 01–71–18–19–09 ⊕ www.lamaisonplisson.com ◷ No dinner weekends. Ⓜ St-Sébastien–Froissart, Chemin Vert.

★ Passerini

$ | **ITALIAN** | Chef Giovanni Passerini, a favorite Parisian chef, has done it again with this wine-focused spot, the companion to his wildly popular Italian restaurant just a few steps away. Wine bar, gastro-bistro, and pasta factory all in one, the oh-so-good plates of high-brow Italian comfort food are served with his typically masterful selection of well-priced French and Italian wines. **Known for:** fun, laid-back atmosphere; always excellent Italian classics; tons of finds on the wine list. Ⓢ Average main: €15 ✉ 44 rue Traversière, 12e, Bastille ☎ 01–56–61–23—61 ⊕ www.passerini.paris ◷ Closed Sun. and Mon. No lunch Tues.–Sat. Ⓜ Lédru-Rollin.

Ten Belles Bread

$ | **CAFÉ** | The two British chefs behind this bustling café set in an industrial-style loft on an up-and-coming corner of the 11e are known around town for their gourmet take on healthy foods. Here the emphasis is on breakfast, lunch, and brunch, with a range of salads, savory pies, and pastries all made in the on-site bakery. **Known for:** top-notch coffee; gourmet take-out lunches; rustic whole-grain breads made fresh throughout the

day. Ⓢ Average main: €7 ✉ 17–19 rue Breguet, 11e, Bastille ☎ 01–47–00–08–19 ⊕ tenbelles.com Ⓜ Bréguet-Sabin, Richard Lenoir, Chemin Vert.

★ Virtus

$$$$ | **FRENCH** | Two young chefs bring their heritage (Argentine and Japanese) and impressive cooking credentials to bear in their beautiful restaurant, steps from the Marché d'Aligre, that's almost worth a visit for the decor alone. But it's the food that has earned them a passionate following among Parisians, for its range, imagination, quality, and sheer deliciousness. **Known for:** gem of a wine list; vegetarian and non-gluten friendly; exquisite pairings of seafood and vegetables. Ⓢ Average main: €39 ✉ 29 rue de Cotte, 12e, Bastille ☎ 09–80–68–08–08 ⊕ www.virtus-paris.com ◷ Closed Sun. and Mon. Ⓜ Ledru-Rollin.

Hotels

★ Hôtel Antoine

$$ | **HOTEL** | If you want designer digs in a well-located boutique hotel that won't break the budget, this is a great spot for you. **Pros:** location on the area's best fashion shopping street; spacious suites; quiet, cozy lobby with complimentary coffee. **Cons:** breakfast not always complimentary; gym is minuscule; double rooms on the smaller side. Ⓢ Rooms from: €176 ✉ 12 rue de Charonne, Bastille ☎ 01–55–28–30–11 ⊕ www.hotelantoineparis.com ⇌ 38 rooms ◉| No Meals Ⓜ Bastille, Ledru-Rollin.

Hôtel Bastille de Launay

$$ | **HOTEL** | The no-frills decor might seem spartan at first, but this tidy boutique hotel also offers modern amenities like free Wi-Fi, a perfect location a few blocks from the regal Place des Vosges, and outstanding prices for the area. **Pros:** homey touches; reasonably spacious for the neighborhood; attentive service. **Cons:** basic bathrooms; some small rooms; tiny elevator. Ⓢ Rooms from: €155 ✉ 42

rue Amelot, Bastille ☎ *01–47–00–88–11* 🌐 *bastilledelaunay.com* 🛏 *35 rooms* 🍴 *No Meals* [M] *Chemin Vert.*

Hotel Paradiso

$$$ | **HOTEL** | Film buffs might opt to forego the light of day at MK2 Cinema's hotel, where each of the 36 cozy rooms sports an overhead projector and giant screen. **Pros:** superb design and lighting; 2,500 DVDs to choose from; plush private cinema. **Cons:** technology can be complicated; limited bar menu; smallish rooms. [$] *Rooms from: €350* ✉ *135 bd. Diderot, Bastille* ☎ *01–56–61–23–61* 🌐 *www.mk2hotelparadiso.com* 🛏 *34 rooms* 🍴 *No Meals* [M] *Ledru-Rollin.*

Le Petit Beaumarchais

$$ | **HOTEL** | Parisian fashion designer Stella Cadente let her formidable imagination run wild in this whimsical 38-room boutique hotel where no two rooms are alike. **Pros:** excellent location between the Bastille and the Marais; whimsical, unique decor; well priced for a boutique hotel in this location. **Cons:** be aware that some tubs are in the room; no spa, only a sauna; some rooms on the smaller side. [$] *Rooms from: €228* ✉ *8 bd. Beaumarchais, Bastille* ☎ *01–47–00–91–50* 🌐 *www.hotelpetitbeaumarchaisparis.com* 🛏 *38 rooms* 🍴 *No Meals* [M] *Bastille, Bréguet-Sabin.*

★ Maison Bréguet

$$$ | **HOTEL** | Tucked away on a quiet street so close and yet far enough from the bustling Bastille, this is one of Paris's more elegant boutique lodgings. **Pros:** beautiful rooms with plenty of light; five-minute walk to Bastille; lovely hammam and pool on-site. **Cons:** some rooms on the small side; pool could be bigger; not as good a deal as it used to be. [$] *Rooms from: €261* ✉ *8 rue Breguet, Bastille* ☎ *01–58–30–32–31* 🌐 *www.maisonbreguet.com* 🛏 *53 rooms* 🍴 *No Meals* [M] *Bréguet-Sabin, Bastille.*

Nightlife

BARS

★ Calbar

BARS | This off-the-beaten-path watering hole, where the drinks are so good, the music so cool, and the atmosphere so right, is a big draw for a laid-back but knowing crowd. Relax on the big leather sofa while sipping a well-priced craft cocktail that pairs perfectly with your plate of Iberian ham or cheese and charcuterie. ✉ *82 rue de Charenton, 12e, Bastille* ☎ *01–84–06–18–90* 🌐 *lecalbar-cocktail.com.*

Moonshiner

BARS | In true Prohibition-era fashion, this 1920s-style speakeasy is reached through a freezer door in the depths of a pizzeria, so don't be alarmed at first glance (it's quite obvious when you're there). House cocktails are imaginative and delicious, but the friendly bartenders are equally adept at the classics—and the pizza's good, too. ✉ *5 rue Sedaine, 11e, Bastille* ☎ *09–50–73–12–99* 🌐 *www.moonshinerbar.fr* [M] *Bastille, Bréguet-Sabin.*

Performing Arts

★ Cinémathèque Française

FILM | This mecca for cinephiles brought up on Federico Fellini, Igmar Bergman, and Alain Resnais is known for its superb, and exhaustive, retrospectives of world cinema past and present. Its spectacular home—in the former American Center, designed by Frank Gehry—includes elaborate museum exhibitions plus three cinemas and a video library. British and American films are always screened in the original language with French subtitles. ✉ *51 rue de Bercy, 12e, Bastille* ☎ *01–71–19–33–33* 🌐 *www.cinematheque.fr* [M] *Bercy.*

Théâtre de la Bastille

MODERN DANCE | An example of the innovative activity in the Bastille area, Théâtre de la Bastille has an enviable record as a launchpad for tomorrow's modern-dance stars. ✉ *76 rue de la Roquette, 11e, Bastille* ☎ *01–43–57–42–14* ⊕ *www. theatre-bastille.com* Ⓜ *Bastille.*

UGC Ciné-Cité Bercy

FILM | This mammoth 18-screen complex is in the Bercy Village shopping area. For sound and seating, it's one of the best. ✉ *2 cour St- Emilion, 12e, Bercy* ☎ *01–76–64–79–64* ⊕ *www.ugc.fr* Ⓜ *Cour St-Emilion.*

 Shopping

★ Amélie Pichard

SHOES | You'll feel positively cinematic sporting the shoes of this wildly creative young designer, whose career was jump-started in 2014 by a collaboration with her idol Pamela Anderson. Whether in zebra stripe, scarlet suede, or pink patent leather, the shoes, boots, bags, and small leather goods are always thrilling, showing loads of glamour and more than a hint of daring. You'll also find tartan, faux fur, crocodile, and basket weave. Pichard's adorable boutique is on a cobbled street just off the lucrative shopping fields of the Rue de Charonne. ✉ *34 rue de Lappe, 11e, Bastille* ☎ *01–71–20–94–08* ⊕ *www.ameliepichard.com* Ⓜ *Bastille, Charonne, Ledru-Rollin.*

Marché Bastille

MARKET | Paris's largest market is as much an event as a place to shop. Blocks of specialized stalls—including ones devoted to rare wines, regional cheeses, game, seafood, and flowers—cater to scores of Parisian chefs and epicures. It's open Thursday and Sunday 8:30 am to 1:30 pm. ✉ *Bd. Richard Lenoir, between Rues Amelot and St-Sabin, 11e, Bastille* Ⓜ *Ledru-Rollin.*

Oberkampf and Charonne

Paris's hip Oberkampf and Charonne neighborhoods form a rectangle between Nation and République, extending from the eastern border of the Marais all the way to Père Lachaise cemetery. In this central area—popular with Parisians but sometimes overlooked by visitors—you'll find some of the city's most exciting dining and shopping opportunities, not to mention chic boutique hotels and irresistible cocktail bars.

 Sights

★ Atelier des Lumières

ARTS CENTER | An abandoned iron foundry in the hip 11e arrondissement is the soaring backdrop for Culturespace's newest feast for the eyes and the senses, where visitors are invited to actually step into the midst of some of the great masterpieces of 19th- and 20th-century painting (many found in famous Parisian museums). More than 100 video projectors cast vivid scenes of gorgeously colored artwork on the walls, ceilings, and floors, accompanied by a dynamic soundtrack for total immersion into a 30-minute explosion of color and sound. ✉ *38–40 rue St-Maur, 11e, Père Lachaise* ☎ *01–80–98–46–00* ⊕ *www. atelier-lumieres.com* 🎟 *€16* Ⓜ *Voltaire, Rue St-Maur, Père Lachaise.*

★ Cimetière du Père-Lachaise

CEMETERY | Bring a red rose for "the Little Sparrow" Edith Piaf when you visit the cobblestone avenues and towering trees that make this 118-acre oasis of green perhaps the world's most famous cemetery. Named for Père François de la Chaise, Louis XIV's confessor, Père-Lachaise is more than just a who's who of celebrities. The Paris Commune's final battle took place here on May 28, 1871, when 147 rebels were lined up and shot against the Mur des Fédérés (Federalists'

Famed cemetery Père-Lachaise is the final resting place for artists like Edith Piaf, Jim Morrison, Marcel Proust, Oscar Wilde, and many more.

Wall) in the southeast corner. Aside from the sheer aesthetic beauty of the cemetery, the main attraction is what (or who, more accurately) is belowground.

Two of the biggest draws are Jim Morrison's grave (with its own guard to keep Doors fans under control) and the life-size bronze figure of French journalist Victor Noir, whose alleged fertility-enhancing power accounts for the patches of bronze rubbed smooth by hopeful hands. Other significant grave sites include those of 12th-century French philosopher Pierre Abélard and his lover Héloïse; French writers Colette, Honoré de Balzac, and Marcel Proust; American writers Richard Wright, Gertrude Stein, and Alice B. Toklas; Irish writer Oscar Wilde; French actress Sarah Bernhardt; French composer Georges Bizet; Greek-American opera singer Maria Callas; Franco-Polish composer Frédéric Chopin; painters of various nationalities including Georges-Pierre Seurat, Camille Pissaro, Jean-Auguste-Dominique Ingres, Jacques-Louis David, Eugène Delacroix, Théodore Géricault, Amedeo Clemente Modigliani, and Max Ernst; French jazz violinist Stephane Grappelli; French civic planner Baron Haussmann; French playwright and actor Molière; and French singer Edith Piaf. (To visit the grave sites of a few other famous French men and women, head south to Cimetière du Montparnasse, north to Cimetière de Montmartre, or west to Passy Cemetery.) ■TIP→ **Pinpoint grave sites on the website before you come, but buy a map anyway outside the entrances—you'll still get lost, but that's part of the fun.**

One of the best days to visit is on All Saints' Day (November 1), when Parisians bring flowers to adorn the graves of loved ones or favorite celebrities. ✉ *Entrances on Rue des Rondeaux, Bd. de Ménilmontant, and Rue de la Réunion, Père Lachaise* ☎ *01–55–25–82–10* ⊕ *www.pere-lachaise.com* 🎟 *Free* Ⓜ *Gambetta, Philippe-Auguste, Père-Lachaise.*

Musée Edith Piaf

HISTORIC HOME | Devotees will appreciate the tiny two-room apartment where the "little sparrow" lived for a year when she was 28 years old and sang in the working-class cafés on Rue Oberkampf. The flat was obtained by Les Amis d'Edith Piaf in 1978 and is now a shrine to the petite crooner, whose life-size photo (she was just 4 feet, 9 inches tall) greets visitors at the door. The red walls are covered with portraits of Piaf done by her many artist friends, and her personal letters are framed. On display, you'll see her books and handbags, as well as a few dresses, her size 4 shoes, and a touching pair of old boxing gloves belonging to one of her great loves—champion pugilist Marcel Cerdan. (A reservation is required; no English spoken.) ✉ *5 rue Crespin du Gast, 11e, Oberkampf* ☎ *01–43–55–52–72* ⊕ *en.parisinfo.com/paris-museum-monument/71402/Musee-Edith-Piaf* 🎫 *Free, donations strongly encouraged* ⊘ *Closed Fri.–Sun.* Ⓜ *Ménilmontant.*

🍴 Restaurants

Astier

$$ | BISTRO | FAMILY | There are three good reasons to go to Astier: the generous cheese platter plunked on your table atop a help-yourself wicker tray, the exceptional wine cellar with bottles dating back to the 1970s, and the French bistro fare (even if portions seem to have diminished over the years). Dishes like marinated herring with warm potato salad, sausage with lentils, and baba au rhum are classics on the frequently changing set menu, which includes a selection of no less than 20 cheeses. **Known for:** excellent choice for authentic French cooking; traditional atmosphere; same-day reservations possible. 💲 *Average main: €24* ✉ *44 rue Jean-Pierre Timbaud, 11e, République* ☎ *01–43–57–16–35* ⊕ *www.restaurant-astier.com* Ⓜ *Parmentier.*

Au Passage

$$ | WINE BAR | This *bistrot à vins* has the lived-in look of a longtime neighborhood hangout—which it was until two veterans of the raging Paris wine-bar scene reinvented the place, keeping the vintage, laid-back atmosphere and adding a serious foodie menu that's one of the best deals in town. A blackboard lists a selection of tapas, including several house-made pâtés, fresh tomato or beet salads, a superb seafood carpaccio, and artisanal charcuterie and cheeses. **Known for:** roasted lamb haunch to share; friendly, low-key vibe; gastronomy on a budget. 💲 *Average main: €19* ✉ *1 bis, passage St-Sébastien, 11e, République* ☎ *01–43–55–07–52* ⊕ *www.restaurant-aupassage.fr* ⊘ *Closed Sun. No lunch* Ⓜ *St-Ambroise, Saint-Sébastien–Froissart, Richard Lenoir.*

Cantine Merci

$ | MODERN FRENCH | On the lower garden level of a chic concept store you'll find the perfect spot for a quick and healthy lunch between bouts of shopping. Highlights include a small soup menu, a risotto of the day, and hearty vegetarian salads. **Known for:** rosé by the glass; fresh juices and mint iced tea; quick lunchtime spot. 💲 *Average main: €17* ✉ *111 bd. Beaumarchais, 3e, Marais Quarter* ☎ *01–42–77–79–28* ⊕ *www.merci-merci.com* ⊘ *Closed Sun. No dinner* Ⓜ *St-Sébastien–Froissart.*

★ Double Dragon

$ | CHINESE | Anyone with a hankering for enticing, well-priced, gourmet-inflected Chinese fare in a chic setting need look no further. Friendly to both carnivores and herbivores alike, the fried tofu filled with Comté cheese, the cold noodles, and the cucumber salad are just as good as the perfectly crisp caramelized pork or fried chicken. **Known for:** Chinese classics with a French flair; local beers and natural wines; affordable lunch menu. 💲 *Average main: €14* ✉ *52 rue St-Maur, 11e,*

Oberkampf ☎ *0-71-32-41-95* 🌐 *www.doubledragonparis.com* 🕒 *Closed Mon. and Tues.* [M] *St-Ambroise, Rue St-Maur.*

★ **Jacques Genin Salon de Thé**

$ | **BAKERY** | Master chocolatier Jacques Genin's sophisticated *carrés* are like small jewels, perfumed with ganaches of exquisite subtlety in seasonal flavors like rosemary, Szechuan pepper, or bergamot. The glorious pastries served in this tea-room and chocolate boutique (one of the loveliest in Paris) are no longer available for takeaway but rather are assembled to order, to be eaten fresh on the premises. **Known for:** melt-in-your-mouth caramels; some of the city's best chocolates and pastries; sinful chocolat chaud. [$] *Average main: €10* ✉ *133 rue de Turenne, 3e, Marais Quarter* ☎ *01-45-77-29-01* 🌐 *www.jacquesgenin.fr* 🕒 *Closed Mon.* [M] *Filles du Calvaire.*

★ **La Chocolaterie Cyril Lignac**

$ | **MODERN FRENCH** | You don't have to be a chocoholic to appreciate this cozy little nook of a café focused on all things derived from the cocoa bean: decadent cakes and pastries, chocolates and *tablettes* (bars of chocolate), and a most sinful *chocolat chaud.* There are also coffee and other beverages to linger over inside or at a sidewalk table. **Known for:** classic Parisian hot chocolate; good spot for coffee; top-notch chocolate in every form. [$] *Average main: €8* ✉ *25 rue Chanzy, 11e, Charonne* ☎ *01-55-87-21-40* 🌐 *www.lachocolateriecyrillignac.com* [M] *Rue des Boulets.*

★ **Le Bistrot Paul Bert**

$$$ | **BISTRO** | The Paul Bert delivers everything you could want from a traditional Paris bistro (faded 1930s decor, thick steak with real frites, and good value), so it's no wonder its two dining rooms fill every night with a cosmopolitan crowd. The impressively stocked wine cellar helps, as does the heaping cheese cart, the laid-back yet efficient staff, and hearty dishes such as monkfish with white beans and duck with pears. **Known for:** sidewalk seating in summer; delicious dessert soufflés; excellent, and abundant, cheese trolley. [$] *Average main: €25* ✉ *18 rue Paul Bert, 11e, Charonne* ☎ *01-43-72-24-01* 🌐 *www.bistrotpaulbert.fr* 🕒 *Closed Sun. and Mon.* [M] *Rue des Boulets.*

★ **Le Rigmarole**

$$$$ | **MODERN FRENCH** | This small, most earnest of gastronomic restaurants quickly became one of the hottest tickets in town and won its first Michelin star in 2020. French-American chef Robert Compagnon and his partner, pastry chef Jessica Yang, preside over a totally unique dining experience focused around Japanese yakitori: small plates of meat, fish, and vegetables delicately grilled over a white odorless charcoal. **Known for:** inventive wine pairings; vegetarian friendly; unique dining experience. [$] *Average main: €38* ✉ *10 rue du Grand Prieuré, 11e, Oberkampf* ☎ *01-71-24-58-44* 🌐 *www.lerigmarole.com* 🕒 *Closed Mon. No lunch Tues.* [M] *Oberkampf.*

★ **Le Servan**

$$ | **MODERN FRENCH** | The impressive but unfussy gastronomic menu here features Asian-inflected dishes that express the food's far-flung influences. A starter of "zakouskis," several small dishes that may include deep-fried giblets, fresh radishes with anchovy butter, or herb-infused cockles, warms you up for a sublime entrée of whole lacquered quail, cod with spicy black-bean reduction, or crispy melt-in-your mouth pork on a bed of braised leeks. **Known for:** lovely, intimate setting; accommodating to vegetarians; great-value lunch menu. [$] *Average main: €22* ✉ *32 rue St-Maur, 11e, Père Lachaise* ☎ *01-55-28-51-82* 🌐 *www.leservan.fr* 🕒 *Closed weekends. No lunch Mon.* [M] *Voltaire, Rue St-Maur, Parmentier.*

★ **Le Villaret**

$$$ | **BISTRO** | Classic bistros are making a comeback in Paris, and this

neighborhood favorite embodies everything people love about this French institution. Here, traditional fare is lovingly prepared with top-quality ingredients and served in generous portions paired with a wine list that's so good it's a draw unto itself. **Known for:** a local favorite; exceptional wines to go with a menu of French classics; wonderful service. $ *Average main: €30* ⊠ *13 rue Ternaux, 11e, Oberkampf* ☎ *01–43–57–89–76* ⊕ *www. levillaret-restaurant.fr/en/* ⊗ *Closed Sun. and Mon.* Ⓜ *St-Ambroise.*

Lily of the Valley

$ | CAFÉ | If you're hankering for a good cup of tea, head to this adorable *salon de thé.* Teatime (which is anytime) is served on vintage china and includes a great choice of handpicked teas and a tempting array of treats made fresh every day from organic ingredients with a minimal sugar. **Known for:** a wide range of teas for sale; teas from around the world; delicious homemade pastries. $ *Average main: €6* ⊠ *7 rue Commines, République* ☎ *01–57–40–82–80* ⊕ *www. lilyofthevalleyparis.com* ⊗ *Closed Sun. and Mon.* Ⓜ *St-Sébastien Froissart, Filles du Calvaire.*

★ Mokonuts

$ | CONTEMPORARY | One of the city's best examples of the casual gourmet cafés popping up around Paris, Mokonuts is run by a talented husband-and-wife team who create delicious dishes and pastries that are as pleasing to the eye as they are to the palate. Prepare for crowds at breakfast and teatime, when you can choose from chunky multigrain cookies, sweet or savory muffins, tarts, and other sweet goodies. **Known for:** small space so it gets crowded fast; late hours for a café (open until 6 pm); excellent coffee. $ *Average main: €13* ⊠ *5 rue Saint-Bernard, 11e, Oberkampf* ☎ *09–80–81–82–85* ⊕ *www.mokonuts.com* ⊗ *No dinner* Ⓜ *Faidherbe-Chaligny, Ledru-Rollin.*

Ober Mamma

$ | ITALIAN | FAMILY | This chic trattoria draws an enthusiastic local crowd for its fabulous wood-oven-fired pizzas, copious pasta dishes, and refreshing craft cocktails. You can sit in the soaring dining room or relax with a plate of Italian charcuterie and a drink at the very popular, and often crowded, cocktail bar. **Known for:** lively atmosphere; large pizzas; good price-to-quality ratio. $ *Average main: €15* ⊠ *107 bd. Richard Lenoir, 11e, Oberkampf* ☎ *01–58–30–62–78* ⊕ *www. bigmammagroup.com* Ⓜ *Oberkampf, République.*

Sadarnac

$ | FRENCH | If you love to discover Paris's authentic corners and hidden culinary gems this is a place for you. In a pretty dining room set on a charming cobbled street five minutes from Père-Lachaise, chef Lise Deveix crafts memorable dishes that mix her passion for healthy local ingredients with an outsized talent that has won her a following from the four corners of the city. **Known for:** gourmet cooking with an emphasis on healthy and local; excellent prices; award-winning young chef. $ *Average main: €15* ⊠ *17 rue Saint-Blaise, 20e, Belleville* ☎ *01–72–60–72–06* ⊕ *restaurantsadarnac.fr* ⊗ *Closed Sun. and Mon.* Ⓜ *75020.*

★ Septime

$$$ | BISTRO | With amazing food and a convivial, unpretentious atmosphere, Septime has become one of the hottest tables in town. Seasonal ingredients, inventive pairings, and excellent natural wines bring in diners ready for exciting and sophisticated dishes like creamy gnochetti in an orange-rind-flecked Gouda sauce sprinkled with coriander flowers. **Known for:** reservations needed far in advance; one Michelin star; exceptional Parisian bistro. $ *Average main: €32* ⊠ *80 rue de Charonne, 11e, Charonne* ☎ *01–43–67–38–29* ⊕ *www.septime-charonne.fr* ⊗ *Closed weekends. No lunch Mon.* Ⓜ *Ledru Rollin, Charonne.*

Unico

$$$ | MODERN ARGENTINE | An architect and a photographer, both Parisians born in Argentina, teamed up to open one of Bastille's hottest restaurants—literally hot, too, because the Argentinean meat served here is grilled over charcoal. Whichever cut of beef you choose (the ultimate being *lomo*, or fillet), it's so melt-in-your-mouth that the sauces served on the side seem almost superfluous. **Known for:** excellent value prix-fixe menus; chic retro atmosphere; tender Argentinean beef, aged and grilled. $ *Average main: €30* ✉ *15 rue Paul-Bert, 11e, Charonne* ☎ *01–43–67–68–08* ⊕ *www.resto-unico.com* ⊗ *Closed Sun. No lunch Mon.* Ⓜ *Faidherbe–Chaligny.*

 Hotels

★ Eden Lodge

$$ | B&B/INN | FAMILY | Set in a hidden tree-shaded courtyard off a nondescript street minutes from Père-Lachaise cemetery, no lodging in the capital is quite as unobtrusively fabulous as this trailblazing, 100% sustainable, five-room eco-lodge. **Pros:** chic contemporary decor; spacious terraces in all rooms; tons of great restaurants in the neighborhood. **Cons:** not on the prettiest street; no in-house bar; low-key neighborhood. $ *Rooms from: €225* ✉ *175 rue de Charonne, Père Lachaise* ☎ *01–43–56–73–24* ⊕ *www.edenlodgeparis.net* ⟿ *5 rooms* ⦿ *Free Breakfast* Ⓜ *Père Lachaise, Charonne.*

★ Hôtel Fabric

$$ | HOTEL | This urban-chic hotel tucked away on an old artisan street is fully in tune with the pulse of the lively Oberkampf neighborhood and close to fabulous nightlife, cocktail bars, restaurants, bakeries, and shopping (and the Marais and Canal St-Martin). **Pros:** all-you-can-eat breakfast for €18; warm and helpful staff; lots of great sightseeing within walking distance. **Cons:** might be too party-focused for some; very popular so book well in advance; rooms can be noisy.

$ *Rooms from: €220* ✉ *31 rue de la Folie Méricourt, Oberkampf* ☎ *01–43–57–27–00* ⊕ *www.hotelfabric.com* ⟿ *33 rooms* ⦿ *No Meals* Ⓜ *St-Ambroise, Oberkampf.*

★ Hôtel Mama Shelter

$$ | HOTEL | Close to Père-Lachaise in the up-and-coming 20e arrondissement, this large hotel is an experiment in quirky postmodern countercultural cool, with a fun and funky interior designed by Philippe Starck. **Pros:** trendy design without designer prices; entertainment center in each room; fun vibe with hip bar on-site. **Cons:** small rooms; nearby club can be noisy; 10-minute walk to métro. $ *Rooms from: €159* ✉ *109 rue de Bagnolet, Belleville* ☎ *01–43–48–48–48* ⊕ *www.mamashelter.com* ⟿ *172 rooms* ⦿ *No Meals* Ⓜ *Gambetta.*

Le Général Hôtel

$$$ | HOTEL | Designer Jean-Philippe Nuel applied his sleek styling to Le Général, one of Paris's first affordable, high-design hotels. **Pros:** friendly service; in popular nightlife district; smart design. **Cons:** basic breakfast (not included); not within easy walking distance of major tourist attractions; noisy neighborhood. $ *Rooms from: €280* ✉ *5–7 rue Rampon, République* ☎ *01–47–00–41–57* ⊕ *www.legeneralhotel.com* ⟿ *46 rooms* ⦿ *No Meals* Ⓜ *République; Oberkampf.*

 Nightlife

BARS

Bluebird

BARS | Its swank Mad Men–meets–tiki bar atmosphere and dynamic gin-centric cocktails have earned this dusky cocktail den an avid following. ✉ *12 rue Saint-Bernard, 11e, Charonne* Ⓜ *Faidherbe-Chaligny, Rue des Boulets.*

★ Dirty Lemon

BARS | When Palestinian chef Ruba Khoury (a veteran of several Michelin-starred kitchens) struck out on her own, she surprised everyone by opening a cocktail bar, "made by women for women." But no one's complaining: along with some of the city's most splendid cocktails and mocktails, highlighting fresh fruit and veggie juices, her accompanying menu of scintillating finger food makes settling in for the evening a pleasure. ☒ 24 rue de la Folie Méricourt, 11e, Charonne ☎ 01–43–38–77–02 ⊕ www.dirtylemonbar.com Ⓜ St-Ambroise.

★ Le Lone Palm

BARS | Knock back a few classic cocktails in a vintage 1950s atmosphere, where the booths and records are vinyl, the vibe is laid-back, and the prices are as enjoyable as the drinks. ☒ 21 rue Keller, 11e, Bastille ☎ 01–48–06–03–95 ⊕ www.lonepalm.fr Ⓜ Voltaire, Bastille.

CLUBS

Le Nouveau Casino

DANCE CLUBS | You'll find this concert hall and club tucked behind the Café Charbon. Pop and rock concerts prevail during the week, and the revelry continues on Friday and Saturday from midnight until dawn. Hip-hop, house, disco, and techno DJs are the standard. ☒ 109 rue Oberkampf, 11e, Oberkampf ☎ 01–43–57–57–40 ⊕ www.nouveaucasino.fr Ⓜ Parmentier.

Pop-In

DANCE CLUBS | On a backstreet just off the Boulevard Beaumarchais (which links the Bastille to République), this dark, hard-partying boho playhouse has a pronounced English-rocker feel. ☒ 105 rue Amelot, 4e, Oberkampf ☎ 01–48–05–56–11 Ⓜ St-Sebastien–Froissart.

🎭 Performing Arts

Cirque d'Hiver Bouglione

CIRCUSES | Cirque d'Hiver Bouglione brings together two famous circus institutions: the beautiful Cirque d'Hiver hall, constructed in 1852, and the Bouglione troupe, known for its rousing assembly of acrobats, jugglers, clowns, trapeze artists, tigers, and house cats that leap through rings of fire. Shows run mid-October to March, with a new production each season. ☒ 110 rue Amelot, 11e, République ☎ 01–47–00–28–81 ⊕ www.cirquedhiver.com Ⓜ Filles du Calvaire.

Shopping

CLOTHING

★ FrenchTrotters

MIXED CLOTHING | A handpicked selection of the best in French and European fashion for men and women (hard to find outside Europe) is gathered in this sleek duplex boutique. There's also a small selection of accessories, including scarves, bags and leather goods, outerwear, jewelry, perfume, and scented candles. ☒ 30 rue de Charonne, 11e, Charonne ☎ 01–47–00–84–35 ⊕ frenchtrotters.fr.

Isabel Marant

WOMEN'S CLOTHING | The clothes from this full-fledged design star rock out bohemian French stylishness. The separates skim the body without constricting: look for layered miniskirts, loose peekaboo sweaters ready to slip from a shoulder, and super full-length shearling vests to pair with slouchy boots. The secondary line, Étoile, offers a less expensive take. ☒ 16 rue de Charonne, 11e, Charonne ☎ 01–49–29–71–55 ⊕ www.isabelmarant.com Ⓜ Ledru-Rollin.

Sessùn

MIXED CLOTHING | Designer Emma François's main inspiration is traveling to faraway places, where she picks up ideas for the textures, prints, and colors of her versatile collection of fashion staples. Separates range from neutral basics—a lace inset top or camisole, a wraparound jumpsuit, a knitted cape—to brilliantly colored or natty print sweaters, trousers, blouses, and blazers. The collection is completed with a gently priced line of shoes, boots, scarves, and accessories. The Rue de Charonne concept store, the largest of her three Paris shops, also has a gallery featuring the work of French artists and artisans and a selection of handmade textiles, housewares, and jewelry. ⊠ *34 rue de Charonne, 11e, Charonne* ☎ *01–48–06–55–66* ⊕ *boutique. sessun.com* Ⓜ *Bastille.*

HOME DECOR
★ Borgo delle Tovaglie

HOUSEWARES | This Naples-based label's soaring concept store eschews sterile minimalism for an opulence well suited to its lavish Italian linen sheets and pillows. Crafted by hand in yummy colors that change with the seasons, they can be paired with a chic array of dishes, candles, and other treasures for the home. Linger at the stylish bistro—a neighborhood hipster hangout—for an espresso, a glass of wine, or a plate of Italian charcuterie. ⊠ *4 rue du Grand Prieuré, 11e, Oberkampf* ☎ *09–82–33–64–81* ⊕ *www. borgodelletovaglie.com* Ⓜ *Oberkampf.*

JEWELRY AND ACCESSORIES
★ Yves Gratas

JEWELRY & WATCHES | With a knack for pairing gems of varying sizes, brilliance, and texture, Yves Gratas allows each stone to influence the design. Whether it's a spectacular necklace of sapphire beads to be worn long or doubled, or a simple agate sphere tipped in gold and dangling like a tiny planet, these stellar jewels feel like one organic whole. ⊠ *9 rue Oberkampf, 11e, Oberkampf* ☎ *01–49–29–00–53* ⊕ *www.yvesgratas.com* Ⓜ *Filles du Calvaire, Oberkampf.*

SHOES
★ La Botte Gardiane

SHOES | Craftsmanship and style that won't wreck your budget—that's the trademark of this artisan bootmaker that hails from the Camargue, a wild area of Provence where gypsies and cowboys require durable boots to rustle the wild horses. That doesn't mean the boutique is short on chic. La Botte Gardiane has impeccably designed and beautifully classic full-length boots, slouchy booties, chukkas, espadrilles, and strappy sandals in suede, python, shearling, and the supplest calf leather from the tanner that supplies Hermès. Look for styles for men, women, and kids. ⊠ *25 rue de Charonne, 11e, Charonne* ☎ *09–51–11–05–15* ⊕ *www.labottegardiane.com* Ⓜ *Bastille, Charonne.*

Canal St-Martin and République

The Place de la République stands as a crossroads between the upper Marais and Oberkampf neighborhoods and as a gateway to the 10e arrondissement and the Canal St-Martin. This lively, fashionable area was once overlooked but is now a big draw for its chic, offbeat boutiques and many top-notch cafés, restaurants, and cocktail bars along with its scenic walks by the leafy canal.

⊙ Sights
★ Canal St-Martin

HISTORIC SIGHT | This once-forgotten canal has morphed into one of the city's trendiest places to wander. A good time to come is Sunday afternoon, when the Quai de Valmy is closed to cars and some of the shops are open. Rent a bike at any of the many Vélib' stations, stroll along the banks, or go native and cuddle quai-side in the sunshine with someone special.

In 1802 Napoléon ordered the 4.3-km (2.7-mile) canal dug as a source of clean drinking water after cholera and other epidemics swept the city. When it finally opened 23 years later, it extended north from the Seine at Place de la Bastille to the Canal de l'Ourcq, near La Villette. Baron Haussmann later covered a 1.6-km (1-mile) stretch of it, along today's Boulevard Richard Lenoir. It nearly became a highway in the 1970s, before

Did You Know?

Many people take boat rides on the Seine, but there are also several companies that offer trips along the Canal St-Martin.

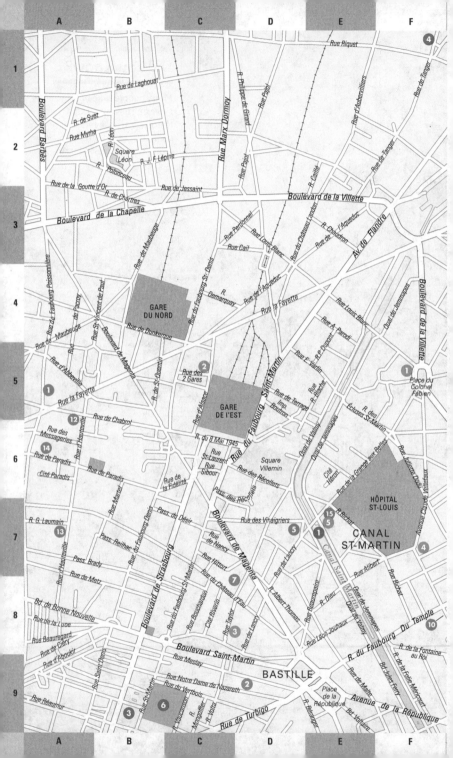

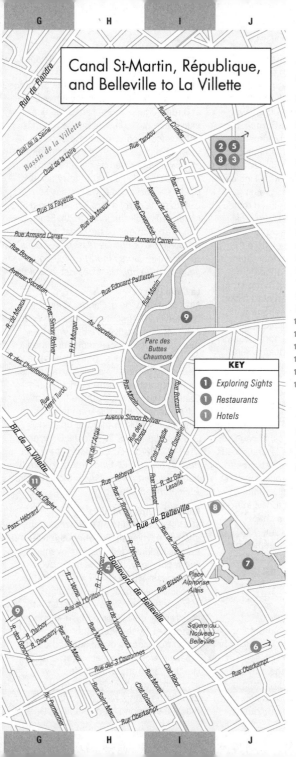

Canal St-Martin, République, and Belleville to La Villette

KEY

① *Exploring Sights*
① *Restaurants*
① *Hotels*

the city's urban planners regained their senses. These days you can take a boat tour from end to end through the canal's nine locks: along the way, the bridges swing or lift open. The drawbridge with four giant pulleys at Rue de Crimée, near La Villette, was a technological marvel when it debuted in 1885. In recent years gentrification has transformed the once-dodgy canal, with artists taking over former industrial spaces and creating studios and galleries. The bar and restaurant scene is hipster central, and small designers have arrived, fleeing expensive rents in the Marais. To explore this evolving quartier, set out on foot. Start on the Quai de Valmy at Rue Faubourg du Temple (use the République métro stop). Here, at Square Frédéric Lemaître facing north, there is a good view of one of the locks (behind you the canal disappears underground). As you head north, detour onto side streets like Rue Beaurepaire, a fashionista destination with several "stock" (or surplus) shops for popular brands, some open on Sunday. Rues Lancry and Vinaigriers are lined with bars, restaurants, and small shops.

A swing bridge across the canal connects Lancry to the Rue de la Grange aux Belles, where you'll find the entrance to the massive Hôpital Saint-Louis, built in 1607 to accommodate plague victims and still a working hospital today. In front of you is the entrance to the chapel, which held its first Mass in July 1610, two months after the assassination of the hospital's patron, Henry IV. Stroll the grounds, flanked by the original brick-and-stone buildings with steeply sloping roofs. The peaceful courtyard garden is a neighborhood secret.

Back on Quai Valmy, browse more shops near the Rue des Récollets. Nearby is the Jardin Villemin, the 10e arrondissement's largest park (4½ acres) on the former site of another hospital. The nighttime scene, especially in summer, is hopping with twentysomethings spilling out of cafés and bars and onto the canal banks. If you've made it this far, reward yourself with a fresh taco or burrito at the tiny and authentically Mexican El Nopal taqueria at 3 rue Eugène Varlin. Farther up, just past Place Stalingrad, is the La Rotonde Ledoux (commonly called Rotonde de la Villette), a lively square with restaurants and twin MK2 cinemas on either side of the canal, plus a boat to ferry ticket holders across. Canauxrama (www.canauxrama.com) offers 2½-hour boat cruises through the locks (€20). Embarkation is at each end of the canal: at Bassin de la Villette or Port de l'Arsenal. ⊠ *Canal St-Martin* Ⓜ *Jaurès (north end), République (south end), Gare de l'Est (middle).*

La Gaîté Lyrique

ARTS CENTER | One of Paris's younger (it opened in 2011) contemporary-art venues combines innovative exhibits with live musical performances and a multimedia space that features a library, movies, and free video games. Think of it as a smaller, more interactive Centre Pompidou. La Gaîté Lyrique occupies three floors of a 19th-century theater—remnants of which are visible in the café upstairs. ⊠ *3 bis, rue Papin, 3e, Marais Quarter* ☎ *01–53–01–52–00* ⊕ *www.gaite-lyrique. net* 🖾 *Free; €7–€14 for temporary exhibitions; concert prices vary* ⊗ *Closed Mon.* Ⓜ *Réaumur-Sébastopol.*

Musée des Arts et Métiers

SCIENCE MUSEUM | **FAMILY** | Science buffs should not miss this cavernous museum, Europe's oldest dedicated to invention and technology. It's a treasure trove of wonkiness with 80,000 instruments, machines, and gadgets—including 16th-century astrolabes, Pascal's first mechanical calculator, and film-camera prototypes by the Frères Lumière. You can watch video simulations of ground-breaking architectural achievements, like the cast-iron dome, or see how Jacquard's mechanical loom revolutionized clothmaking. Kids will love the flying machines (among them the first plane to cross the English Channel) and the impressive display of old automobiles in the high-ceilinged chapel of St-Martin-des-Champs. Also in the chapel is a copy of Foucault's Pendulum, which proved to the world in 1851 that the Earth rotated (demonstrations are staged daily at noon and 5). The building, erected between the 11th and 13th centuries, was a church and priory that was confiscated during the Revolution, and, after incarnations as a school and a weapons factory, became a museum in 1799. Most displays have information in English, but renting an English audioguide (€5) helps. If you're arriving via the métro, check out the platform of Line 11 in the Arts and Métiers station—one of the city's most elaborate—which is made to look like the inside of a Jules Verne–style machine, complete with copper-color metal walls, giant bolts, and faux gears. ✉ *60 rue Réaumur, 3e, Marais Quarter* ☎ *01–53–01–82–75* 🌐 *www.arts-et-metiers.net* 🎫 *€8* 🕒 *Closed Mon.* [M] *Arts et Métiers.*

🍴 Restaurants

★ Abri

$$$ | MODERN FRENCH | This tiny storefront restaurant's immense popularity has much to do with the fresh and imaginative food, the friendly servers, and great prices. The lauded Japanese chef works from a small open kitchen behind the zinc bar, putting forth skillfully prepared dishes like lemon-marinated mackerel topped with micro-thin slices of beet and honey vinaigrette, or succulent duck breast with vegetables au jus. **Known for:** need to make reservations weeks in advance; casual atmosphere and great prices; daily changing menu of inventive French-Japanese cuisine. [$] *Average main: €25* ✉ *92 rue du Faubourg-Poissonnière, 10e, Pigalle* ☎ *01–83–97–00–00* 🌐 *www.abrirestaurant.fr* 🕒 *Closed Sun., Mon., 1 wk at Christmas, and Aug.* [M] *Poissonnière, Cadet.*

★ Addommè

$$ | PIZZA | One of Paris's newer pizza places, in the Haut Marais, is also one of the best, serving irresistible handmade Neapolitan pies with top-quality Italian toppings: *bresaola, fior di latte,* burrata, hot Calabria salami, figs, fresh herbs, nuts, and creamy *stracciatella.* Try the sweet version for dessert, topped with a gourmet version of Nutella, among other dreamy confections. **Known for:** good wines by the glass; well-curated toppings; delicious crispy crust. [$] *Average main: €22* ✉ *26 rue Notre-Dame de Nazareth, 3e, Paris* ☎ *09–83–27–63–80* 🌐 *www.addomme.com* 🕒 *Closed Sun. No lunch Sat., no dinner Mon.* [M] *Temple, République.*

Early June

$ | FRENCH | To taste the sheer love of cooking get thee to this unassuming canal-side café—named for that most delicious time of year. The outrageously talented young couple at the helm, veterans of notable Parisian kitchens, are truly delighted when diners exalt over the luscious dishes placed before them: scallops Saint-Jacques with pistachio and trout eggs; white asparagus with *gochujang* hot sauce, Gorgonzola, and sesame, all paired with some stunning wines or craft beer made in Paris (that you can purchase at the little shop). **Known for:** vegetarian and food-allergy friendly; exceptional price-to-value quotient; welcoming service and atmosphere. [$] *Average main: €14* ✉ *19 rue Jean Poulmarch, 10e, Canal St-Martin* ☎ *01–42–85–40–74* 🌐 *early-june.fr* [M] *Jacques Bonsergent, Gare de l'Est.*

★ Holybelly

$ | CAFÉ | FAMILY | A welcome addition to the Canal St-Martin area, this spacious, modern coffee bar caters to Paris's blossoming breakfast and brunch scene with a menu of American-style classics. Homemade granola, pancakes topped with fruit, and bacon and eggs are served all day long, accompanied by hearty sandwiches, healthy salads (with kale!), and homemade desserts. **Known for:** spacious enough to accommodate groups; lively, friendly atmosphere; wonderful coffee. $ *Average main: €12* ✉ *19 rue Lucien Sampaix, 10e, Canal St-Martin* ☎ *01–82–28–00–80* ⊕ *holybellycafe. com* ⊗ *Closed Tues. and Wed. No dinner* Ⓜ *Jacques Bonsergent.*

Le Chateaubriand

$$$$ | MODERN FRENCH | A chef who once presented a single, peeled apple pip (really) on a plate has no ordinary approach to food. Self-taught Basque cook Inaki Aizpitarte is undeniably provocative, but he gets away with it because (a) he's young and extremely cool and (b) he has an uncanny sense of which unexpected ingredients go together, as in a combination of oysters and lime zest in chicken stock. **Known for:** service can be haughty; lively and hip crowd; inventive but approachable cuisine. $ *Average main: €45* ✉ *129 av. Parmentier, 11e, Canal St-Martin* ☎ *01–43–57–45–95* ⊕ *www.lechateaubriand.net* ⊗ *Closed Sun., Mon., and 1 wk at Christmas. No lunch* Ⓜ *Goncourt.*

Le Dauphin

$$ | WINE BAR | The avant-garde chef Inaki Aizpitarte transformed what was a dowdy café into a sleek, if chilly, all-marble watering hole (designed by Rem Koolhaus) for late-night cuisinistas. Honing his ever-iconoclastic take on tapas, the dishes served here are a great way to get an idea of what all the fuss is about. **Known for:** tapas by a star chef; good wines by the glass; late-night revelry. $ *Average main: €20* ✉ *131 av. Parmentier, 11e, Canal St-Martin* ☎ *01–55–28–78–88* ⊕ *www.restaurantledauphin. net* ⊗ *Closed Sun., Mon., and 1 wk at Christmas. No lunch Tues.* Ⓜ *Parmentier.*

★ Le Galopin

$$$ | BISTRO | Across from a pretty square on the border of two up-and-coming neighborhoods, this light-drenched spot

is one of Paris's standout gastro-bistros. By adhering to a tried-and-true formula—meticulously sourced produce, natural wines, and an open kitchen—the dishes here are small wonders of texture and flavor. **Known for:** veggie-centric dishes; hip, laid-back atmosphere; daily changing, market-fresh gastronomic menu. $ *Average main: €25* ✉ *34 rue Sainte-Marthe, 10e, Canal St-Martin* ☎ *01–42–06–05–03* ⊕ *le-galopin.paris/fr* ⊗ *Closed weekends. No lunch Mon.–Wed.* Ⓜ *Goncourt, Belleville, Colonel Fabien.*

★ Mâche

$$ | FRENCH | Don't let the casual decor and laid-back atmosphere here fool you, this is a seriously ambitious restaurant full of Parisian foodies who would be happy to keep this gem all to themselves. Starters like smoked eel and cabbage topped with a delicate *tuille* of black rice, smoked zucchini ravioli with lemon butter, or roasted pigeon are gorgeously presented and so deliciously complex they defy description. **Known for:** the best of Paris bistronomique cuisine; very reasonable prices for this level of dining; top-notch produce. $ *Average main: €21* ✉ *61 rue de Chabrol, 10e, Canal St-Martin* ☎ *09–83–40–60–04* ⊕ *www.mache.restaurant* ⊗ *Closed Sun. and Mon.* Ⓜ *Poissonière, Gare de l'Est, Gare du Nord.*

★ Restaurant Eels

$$$ | FRENCH | Don't be put off by the name—and the must-try signature dish—at this terrific eatery, where young chef Adrien Ferrand's complex dishes are as magnificent to taste as they are to behold. From a crisp-tender grilled suckling pig to the delicious smoked eel with apple, and a roster of exquisite desserts—Granny Smith broth with hazelnut sabayon or "craquant" of chocolate with caramel cream and banana marmalade—a meal here is a delight from start to finish. **Known for:** very laid-back for this quality of cuisine; superlovely staff;

gorgeous food presentation. $ *Average main: €29* ✉ *27 rue d'Hauteville, Canal St-Martin* ☎ *01–42–28–80–20* 🌐 *restaurant-eels.com* 🕒 *Closed Sun. and Mon.* [M] *Château d'Eau.*

Sapid

$ | **FRENCH** | Organic, plant-based, no-waste, accessible: this isn't exactly what we think of when we think of the haute-cuisine world of Alain Ducasse, chef extraordinaire of 20 Michelin stars. But in partnership with the skilled Peruvian chef Marvic Medina, this spot works. thanks to dishes like roasted white asparagus with fresh herbs, poached burrata with Paris mushrooms, and smoked fish and roasted celery root sandwich on gluten-free bread—all served semi-cafeteria style (at lunch) at large marble tables in a pleasing and adventurous (and well-priced) mix of high-meets-low. **Known for:** exceptional prices; top-notch products; inventive, sustainable dining. $ *Average main: €13* ✉ *54 rue de Paradis, 10e, Canal St-Martin* ☎ *06–31–90–87–73* 🌐 *www.sapid.fr* 🕒 *Sat., Sun.* [M] *Poissonière.*

Ten Belles

$ | **CAFÉ** | Ten Belles is where pedigreed baristas cater to a hip crowd of good-brew connoisseurs, with an accompanying menu of delicious sandwiches, soups, snacks, and pastries. For Sunday brunch, head over to sister café Ten Belles Bread, at 17–19 bis, rue Bréguet Paris, in the 11e arrondissement, where the crusty organic breads and pastries are baked on the premises. **Known for:** small space; homemade everything; reliably good coffee. $ *Average main: €6* ✉ *10 rue de la Grange aux Belles, 10e, Canal St-Martin* ☎ *01–42–40–90–78* 🌐 *www.tenbelles.com* 🕒 *No dinner* [M] *Jacques Bonsergent, République.*

Hotels

Hotel Les Deux Gares

$ | **HOTEL** | There's no way to be glum at this chic, colorful hotel set in a bustling neighborhood between two of Paris's main railway stations, Gare de l'Est and the Gare du Nord. **Pros:** near Paris's Little India (for great Indian food); wonderful chic decor; reasonably priced. **Cons:** bustling neighborhood at all hours can be overwhelming; breakfast not included; café isn't located right in the hotel. $ *Rooms from: €100* ✉ *2 rue des Deux Gares, 10e, Canal St-Martin* ☎ *01–85–73–11–83* 🌐 *www.hoteldeuxgares.com* 🛏 *40 rooms* 🍴 *No Meals* [M] *Gare de l'Est, Gare du Nord.*

Hôtel Taylor

$$ | **HOTEL** | Tucked away on a tiny one-way street between République and Canal St-Martin, Hôtel Taylor offers large rooms (by Parisian standards) at affordable prices in the edgy 10e arrondissement. **Pros:** close to the métro; larger than average rooms; Wi-Fi available in rooms. **Cons:** open-plan bathrooms; street can seem intimidating at night; bathrooms and some rooms need refurbishment. $ *Rooms from: €159* ✉ *6 rue Taylor, Canal St-Martin* ☎ *01–42–40–11–01* 🌐 *www.paris-hotel-taylor.com* 🛏 *54 rooms* 🍴 *No Meals* [M] *République.*

La Planque Hotel

$$ | **HOTEL** | Just two blocks from the Canal St-Martin, and within walking distance of shopping, restaurants, and both the Gare du Nord and the Gare du l'Est, lies this pretty, little hotel full of vintage charm that's also easy on the wallet. **Pros:** impeccably clean; well-priced buffet breakfast (€13) and free coffee and tea in breakfast room; stylish, functional rooms and bathrooms. **Cons:** small but charming bathrooms; not a central location; rooms are quite small. $ *Rooms from: €135* ✉ *3 rue Arthur Groussier, Canal St-Martin*

☎ *01–88–32–73–15* 🌐 *laplanquehotel.com* 🛏 *36 rooms* 🍴 *No Meals* [M] *Goncourt, Belleville.*

★ Le Citizen Hôtel

$$ | HOTEL | With direct views over the historic Canal St-Martin and also close to the Marais, Le Citizen's minimalist-chic decor and high-tech touches like loaner iPads melds a modern ethos with the cool eastern Paris vibe. **Pros:** trendy neighborhood; friendly, attentive staff; cool perks. **Cons:** about 20 minutes by métro from top attractions; noisy street; the smallest rooms are best for one person. [$] *Rooms from: €199* ✉ *96 quai de Jemmapes, Canal St-Martin* ☎ *01–83–62–55–50* 🌐 *www.lecitizenhotel.com* 🛏 *12 rooms* 🍴 *No Meals* [M] *Jacques Bonsergent.*

Nightlife

BARS

Chez Prune

BARS | Epitomizing the effortless cool of this arty neighborhood, Chez Prune is a well-loved spot. It offers the designers, architects, and journalists who gather here a prime terrace for gazing out at the arched footbridges and funkier locales of Canal St-Martin. ✉ *36 rue Beaurepaire, 10e, Canal St-Martin* ☎ *01–42–41–30–47* [M] *République, Jacques Bonsergent.*

★ CopperBay

BARS | This sleek and chic cocktail bar's nautical theme extends to its lustrous wood bar and bright, generous spaces where no one has to fight for elbow room. Imaginative drinks change with the season (with hot choices in cold weather), the atmosphere is friendly, and the service is top-notch. ✉ *5 rue Bouchardon, 10e, Canal St-Martin* 🌐 *www.copperbay.fr* [M] *Strasbourg–Saint-Denis, Jacques Bonsergent.*

★ Gravity Bar

BARS | On a street crammed with hip restaurants and bars, you'll find the area's best craft cocktails here, concocted with unusual house-made ingredients. An excellent dining menu is served around a circular bar or at one of the few tables under an undulating wood ceiling. It's small and popular so it's best to come early or late. ✉ *44 rue des Vinaigriers, 10e, Canal St-Martin* ☎ *06–98–54–92–49* [M] *Château d'Eau, Jacques Bonsergent.*

Performing Arts

Théâtre de la Renaissance

THEATER | Belle Époque superstar Sarah Bernhardt, who directed and performed at this beautiful theater from 1893 to 1899, put the Théâtre de la Renaissance on the map. Big French stars often perform here. Note that the theater is on the second floor, and there's no elevator. ✉ *20 bd. St-Martin, 10e, Canal St-Martin* ☎ *01–42–02–47–35* 🌐 *www.theatredelarenaissance.com* [M] *Strasbourg–St-Denis.*

Théâtre des Bouffes du Nord

THEATER | Welcome to the wonderfully atmospheric, slightly decrepit home of Peter Brook. The renowned British director regularly delights with his quirky experimental productions in French and, sometimes, English. ✉ *37 bis, bd. de la Chapelle, 10e, Stalingrad* ☎ *01–46–07–34–50* 🌐 *www.bouffesdunord.com* [M] *La Chapelle.*

Shopping

BOOKS AND STATIONERY

★ Artazart

BOOKS | The best design bookstore in France carries tomes on everything from architecture to tattoo art: there are sections dedicated to photography, fashion, graphic art, typography, illustration, package design, color, and more. ✉ *83 quai de Valmy, 10e, Canal St-Martin* ☎ *01–40–40–24–00* 🌐 *www.artazart.com* [M] *République.*

CLOTHING
agnès b.
MIXED CLOTHING | A household name in Paris, agnès b. has earned rock-star status among two generations of fashionistas. Her artsy-yet-classic aesthetic translates to a slew of well-made staples in quality fabrics that you'll mix and match for years to come. Look for the signature striped cotton T-shirts, travel clothes that never wrinkle, and irresistible accessories. ⊠ *13 rue de Marseille, 10e, Canal St-Martin* ☎ *01–42–06–66–58* ⊕ *www.agnesb.eu* Ⓜ *République.*

Antoine & Lili
WOMEN'S CLOTHING | This bright, fuchsia-colored store is packed with an international assortment of eclectic objects and items from Antoine & Lili's own clothing line. There's an ethnic-rummage-sale feel, with old Asian posters, small lanterns, and basket upon basket of inexpensive doodads, baubles, and trinkets for sale. The clothing itself has simple lines, and there are always plenty of raw-silk pieces to pick from. ⊠ *95 quai de Valmy, 10e, Canal St-Martin* ☎ *01–40–37–41–55* ⊕ *www.antoineetlili.com* Ⓜ *Jacques Bonsergent.*

★ Centre Commercial
MIXED CLOTHING | **FAMILY** | This store's A-list fashion credentials come with a big bonus—everything here is ethically and ecologically sourced. Peruse racks of men's and women's wear from hand-picked European and U.S. labels, then head to the stellar shoe department to complete your look. Beneath glass skylights as clear as your conscience, you'll also find a fine selection of natural candles, leather goods, and jewelry. The kids' store just around the corner (*22 rue Yves Toudic*) is one of the city's best, with toys, decor, and color-coordinated togs that express canal-side cool. ⊠ *2 rue de Marseille, 10e, Canal St-Martin* ☎ *01–42–02–26–08* ⊕ *www.centrecommercial.cc* Ⓜ *Jacques Bonsergent.*

Des Petits Hauts
WOMEN'S CLOTHING | This poetic brand charmed its way into the local fashion idiom with chic yet beguilingly feminine styles. Fabrics are soft, and styles are casual with a tiny golden star sewn into each garment for good luck. ⊠ *21 rue Beaurepaire, 10e, Canal St-Martin* ☎ *01–75–44–05–83* ⊕ *www.despetitshauts.com* Ⓜ *République.*

★ Thanx God I'm A V.I.P.
MIXED CLOTHING | If you don't find something you absolutely love among the color-coordinated racks jam-packed with vintage designer and simply fabulous clothing here, we'll eat our cashmere beret. Look for Hermès, Corrèges, Vivian Westwood, Yves Saint Laurent, and so much more for both men and women. Check out the new arrivals of the week on the website, but don't get there too early, as the boutique is open from 2 pm to 8 pm, Monday through Saturday. ⊠ *12 rue de Lancry, 10e, Canal St-Martin* ☎ *01–42–03–02–09* ⊕ *www.thanxgod.com* Ⓜ *Jacques Bonsergent, République.*

HOME DECOR
Idéco
HOUSEWARES | Little items for the home in a riot of colors are sold at Idé Co. But you'll also find fabulous rubber jewelry and funky stuff for kids big and small. ⊠ *19 rue Beaurepaire, 10e, Canal St-Martin* ☎ *01–42–01–19–69* ⊕ *www.idecoparis.com* Ⓜ *République.*

La Trésorerie
HOUSEWARES | No place outfits chic Canal St-Martin lofts better than this soaring eco-friendly boutique. Housed in a historic treasury, it assembles the crème de la crème of French and European kitchen and dining ware, linens, bath products, small furnishings, hardware, lighting, paint, and more. Local hipsters come to La Trésorerie's bright, Scandinavian-style café for all things fresh, organic, and delicious. ⊠ *11 rue du Château d'Eau, 10e, Canal St-Martin* ☎ *01–40–40–20–46*

⊕ www.latresorerie.fr Ⓜ Jacques Bonsergent.

JEWELRY AND ACCESSORIES
Médecine Douce
JEWELRY & WATCHES | Sculptural pieces that combine leather, suede, rhinestones, agate, or resin with whimsical themes can be found at Médecine Douce. The wildly popular lariat necklace can be looped and dangled according to your mood du jour. ⊠ 10 rue de Marseille, 10e, Canal St-Martin ☎ 01–82–83–11–53 ⊕ www.bijouxmedecinedouce.com Ⓜ République.

Viveka Bergström
JEWELRY & WATCHES | Whether it's a bracelet of gigantic rhinestones, a ring of fluorescent pink resin, or a pair of floating angel wings on a necklace, each Viveka Bergström piece has an acute sense of style while not taking itself too seriously. ⊠ 23 rue de la Grange aux Belles, 10e, Canal St-Martin ☎ 01–40–03–04–92 ⊕ viveka-bergstrom.com Ⓜ République.

SHOES, HANDBAGS, AND LEATHER GOODS
Jamin Puech Inventaire
HANDBAGS | These are last season's models, but no one will guess; savings are 30% to 60%. ⊠ 61 rue d'Hauteville, 10e, Canal St-Martin ☎ 01–40–22–08–32 ⊕ www.jamin-puech.com Ⓜ Poissonnière.

Patricia Blanchet
SHOES | Do not hesitate to run for that taxi in a pair of superchic pumps, flats, or booties from Patricia Blanchet, which are neither too high nor too low but just the right height. Though the designer doesn't swerve from her five or six basic styles, her beautifully hued leathers, including metallics and exotic skins like pony and stingray, change with the season. Booties may come with metallic piping or colorful insets and cutouts, and are cut low for a sexy peek at the ankle. ⊠ 20 rue Beaurepaire, 10e, Canal St-Martin ☎ 01–42–02–35–85 ⊕ www.patriciablanchet.com Ⓜ République.

Belleville to La Villette

This sprawling area of eastern Paris between up-and-coming Belleville and La Villette contains three of Paris proper's largest and most appealing parks: the vertiginous Parc de Belleville, with tremendous views of the city and one of Paris's last two wine-producing vineyards; Parc des Buttes Chaumonts, a lovely, bucolic place to stroll; and La Villette, packed with cultural activities and known for its many musical events in the summer. A great area to explore, you'll find plenty in the way of culture here as well as nightlife, too.

◉ Sights

Cité des Sciences et de l'Industrie (Museum of Science and Industry)
SCIENCE MUSEUM | FAMILY | Occupying a colorful three-story industrial space that recalls the Pompidou Center, this ambitious science museum in Parc de la Villette is packed with things to do—all of them accessible to English speakers. Scores of exhibits focus on subjects like space, transportation, and technology. Hands-on workshops keep the kids entertained, and the planetarium is invariably a hit. Temporary exhibitions, like a recent exploration of cinematic special effects, are always multilingual and usually interactive. ⊠ Parc de la Villette, 30 av. Corentin-Cariou, La Villette ☎ 01–40–05–70–00, 01–85–53–99–74 interactive voice response ⊕ www.cite-sciences.fr ⊠ Permanent and temporary exhibitions and planetarium €12 ◷ Closed Mon. Ⓜ Porte de la Villette.

★ Le 104
ARTS CENTER | Le Cent Quatre takes its name from its address in a rough-around-the-edges corner of the 19e arrondissement, near Parc de la Villette. The former site of the city morgue, this cavernous art hub is home to an offbeat collection of performance venues, shops,

and studios (artists of all genres compete for free studio space, and sometimes you can get a peek of them at work). Contemporary art exhibits, some of which charge admission, are staged here, as are concerts. On-site you'll also find a restaurant, a café, a bookstore, a secondhand shop, and a play area for children. Check the website before going to see what's on. ⊠ *5 rue Curial, 19e, La Villette* ☎ *01–53–35–50–00* ⊕ *www.104.fr* ✉ *Free, prices for exhibits and concerts vary* ⊘ *Closed Mon.* Ⓜ *Stalingrad, Riquet.*

Musée de la Musique

OTHER MUSEUM | FAMILY | Parc de la Villette's music museum contains four centuries' worth of instruments from around the world—about 1,000 in total, many of them exquisite works of art. Their sounds and stories are evoked on numerous video screens and via commentary you can follow on headphones (ask for a free audioguide in English). Leave time for the excellent temporary exhibitions, like a recent one on the life and music of French chanteuse Barbara. On the plaza adjacent to the museum, the outdoor terrace at Café des Concerts (☎ *01–42–49–74–74*) is an inviting place to have a drink on a sunny day. ⊠ *Parc de la Villette, 221 av. Jean Jaurès, 19e, Eastern Paris* ☎ *01–44–84–44–84* ⊕ *www.philharmoniedeparis.fr/fr/musee-de-la-musique* ✉ *From €9* ⊘ *Closed Mon.* Ⓜ *Porte de Pantin.*

Parc de Belleville

CITY PARK | Lofty Parc de Belleville is Paris's highest-altitude park and one of its prettiest. Traversed by shaded winding lanes interspersed with woods, gardens, and sloping grassy fields, it's a lovely spot to have a picnic while taking in spectacular panoramic views of Paris. The park is also home to one of the city's five cultivated vineyards, with vines of Chardonnay and Pinot Meunier, that produce a slightly sparkling wine called Piquette. You are welcome to join in the grape harvest during the last week of September.

⊠ *47 rue des Couronnes, Eastern Paris* ☎ *01–43–15–20–20* ⊕ *www.paris.fr/equipements/parc-de-belleville-1777* ✉ *Free* Ⓜ *Couronnes, Pyrénées.*

Parc de la Villette

CITY PARK | FAMILY | This former *abattoir* (slaughterhouse) is now an ultramodern, 130-acre park. With lawns and play areas, an excellent science museum, a music complex, and a cinema, it's the perfect place to entertain kids. You could easily spend a whole day here. The park itself was designed in the 1980s by postmodern architecture star Bernard Tschumi, who melded industrial elements, children's games (don't miss the dragon slide), ample green spaces, and funky sculptures along the canal into one vast yet unified playground. Loved by picnickers, the lawns also attract rehearsing samba bands and pickup soccer players. In summer there are outdoor festivals and a free open-air cinema, where people gather at dusk to watch movies on a huge inflatable screen.

In cold weather you can visit an authentic submarine and the Espace Chapiteaux (a circus tent featuring contemporary acrobatic theater performances) before hitting the museums. The hands-on one at the Cité des Sciences et de l'Industrie is a favorite stop for families and a must for science fans; its 3-D Omnimax cinema (La Géode) is housed in a giant mirrored ball. Arts-oriented visitors of all ages will marvel at the excellent, instrument-filled Musée de la Musique. The park has even more in store for music lovers in the form of the Philharmonie de Paris, a striking 2,400-seat concert hall designed by Jean Nouvel. All that's left of the slaughterhouse that once stood here is La Grande Halle, a magnificent iron-and-glass building currently used for exhibitions, performances, and trade shows. ⊠ *211 av. Jean Jaurès, 19e, La Villette* ☎ *01–40–03–75–75* ⊕ *lavillette.com* Ⓜ *Porte de Pantin, Porte de la Villette.*

Parc des Buttes-Chaumont

CITY PARK | FAMILY | If you're tired of perfectly manicured Parisian parks with lawns that are off-limits to your weary feet, this place is for you. Built in 1863 on abandoned gypsum quarries and a former gallows, it was northern Paris's first park, part of Napoléon III's planned greening of the city (the emperor had spent years in exile in London, where he fell in love with the public parks). Today the lovely 61-acre hilltop expanse in the untouristy 19e arrondissement has grassy fields, shady walkways, waterfalls, and a picturesque lake dotted with swans. Rising from the lake is a rocky cliff you can climb to find a mini Greek-style temple and a commanding view of Sacré-Coeur Basilica. A favorite of families, the park also has pony rides and an open-air puppet theater—Guignol de Paris (€5; shows at 3:30 pm and 4:45 pm Wednesday and Saturday, and at 11:15 am, 3:30 pm, and 4:45 pm on Sunday, year-round)—not far from the entrance at the Buttes-Chaumont métro stop. When you've worked up an appetite, grab a snack at the Rosa Bonheur café (www.rosabonheur.fr), or reserve a table for weekend lunch at Le Pavillon du Lac restaurant. ⊠ *Entrances on Rue Botzaris or Rue Manin, 19e, Belleville* Ⓜ *Buttes-Chaumont, Botzaris, Laumière.*

 Restaurants

Au Boeuf Couronné

$$$ | BRASSERIE | Parc de La Villette once housed the city's meat market, and this brasserie devoted to fine beef (whether French or Irish) soldiers on as if nothing has changed. It's worth the trek here to sample one of the 16 takes on the beef theme (plus a gargantuan marrow bone) or good fish and seafood dishes, such as sole or scallops (in season). **Known for:** convenient to the Philharmonie de Paris; spacious outdoor terrace with plants and a vegetal wall; authentic atmosphere. Ⓢ *Average main: €28* ⊠ *188 av. Jean-Jaurès, 19e, La Villette* ☎ *01–42–39–44–44* ⊕ *www.boeuf-couronne.com* Ⓜ *Porte de Pantin.*

Dong Huong

$ | VIETNAMESE | While not quite a secret, these two undecorated dining rooms on a Belleville side street can be hard to find, but this is where Chinese and Vietnamese locals come for a reassuring bowl of pho (noodle soup) or plate of grilled lemongrass-scented meat with rice. Spicy, peanuty *saté* soup is a favorite, and at this price, you can also spring for a plate of crunchy imperial rolls, to be wrapped in accompanying lettuce and mint. **Known for:** exceptionally fresh bo bun; good prices; authentic Asian cuisine. Ⓢ *Average main: €11* ⊠ *14 rue Louis-Bonnet, 11e, Belleville* ☎ *01–43–32–25–74* ⊕ *pho-donghuong. fr* ⊘ *Closed Tues. and 3 wks in Aug.* Ⓜ *Belleville.*

★ Fripon

$$ | FRENCH | *Top Chef* contestant Pauline Séné's beautiful marble-clad dining room has created a major buzz across Paris for the kind of subtle and imaginative cuisine you'd expect to find in one of Paris's more tony addresses. The meal gets off to a revelatory start with fresh oysters on the half shell delicately seasoned with cilantro, nuoc-mâm, pickled onions, and kumquat, then just keeps going: melt-in-your-mouth lamb, bacon-wrapped Saint-Jacques scallops and pale Jerusalem artichokes, and a sublime crunchy peanut chocolate mousse for dessert, all accompanied by a fine menu of natural wines. **Known for:** Michelin-star quality cuisine (get here before they do); natural wine discoveries; up-and-coming chef. Ⓢ *Average main: €18* ⊠ *108 rue de Ménilmontant, 20e, Belleville* ☎ *09–81–89–27–40* ⊘ *Closed weekends* Ⓜ *Gambetta.*

Le Baratin

$$ | BISTRO | It's been around for more than 20 years, but Le Baratin is still one of the more sought-after out-of-the-way bistros in Paris. The key to its success is the combination of fresh, comforting cooking and a lovingly selected list of organic and natural wines from small producers. **Known for:** affordable lunch menu; late hours; artisanal charcuterie. [$] *Average main: €23* ✉ *3 rue Jouye Rouve, 20e, Belleville* ☎ *01–43–49–39–70* ⏲ *No lunch Sat. Closed Sun., Mon., and Aug.* [M] *Pyrénées, Belleville.*

Hotels

Generator Paris

$ | **HOTEL** | **FAMILY** | It's impossible to find better lodging for €80 a night in Paris, especially one this close to edgy Belleville and Canal St-Martin, with panoramic views of the city and Sacré-Coeur Basilica to boot. **Pros:** in-house nightclub and lots of lounging areas; close to great nightlife, restaurants, and the Parc du Buttes-Chaumont; private rooms available. **Cons:** beware if you're the antisocial type—it's very bustling and friendly; breakfast food can run out; shared rooms have only bunk beds. [$] *Rooms from: €80* ✉ *9–11 pl. du Colonel Fabien, Belleville* ☎ *01–70–98–84–00* 🌐 *staygenerator.com/hostels/paris* 🛏 *199 rooms* 🍴 *Free Breakfast* [M] *Colonel Fabien, Jaurès.*

Nightlife

BARS

★ Combat

BARS | The three skilled mixologists at this streamlined cocktail bar have earned serious accolades in Paris's cocktail scene for their fresh, original, and artful creations. ✉ *63 rue de Belleville, 19e, Belleville* ☎ *09–80–84–78–60* [M] *Pyrénées, Belleville.*

★ La Commune

BARS | This lively cocktail bar is a favorite watering hole among the cocktail cognoscenti and local hipsters. The design is a mix of high-low (think concrete, marble, and velvet), with a lovely plant-filled terrace. Visitors come for a taste of the mightily delicious cocktails and silver punch bowls filled with ambrosial concoctions. The menu of shared plates will help keep you on your stool. ✉ *80 bd. de Belleville, 20e, Belleville* ☎ *07–54–29–71–40* [M] *Couronnes, Belleville.*

Mama Shelter

BARS | It's not just hotel guests who flock to this hotel's Island Bar, one of the coolest spots around Belleville. Local hipsters also appreciate the live music and DJ nights, foosball, and even the adjacent pizza bar. In summer, the fun extends to the bar's rooftop cocktail lounge, especially popular on weekend evenings. ✉ *109 rue de Bagnolet, 20e, Belleville* ☎ *01–43–48–48–48* 🌐 *www.mamashelter.com* [M] *Alexandre Dumas.*

Performing Arts

Centre National de la Danse

MODERN DANCE | Occupying a former administrative center in the Paris suburb of Pantin, this space is dedicated to supporting professional dancers by offering classes, rehearsal studios, and a multimedia dance library. A regular program of free and reasonably priced performances, expositions, screenings, and conferences is open to the public from October to July. ✉ *1 rue Victor Hugo, Paris* ☎ *01–41–83–27–27* 🌐 *www.cnd.fr* [M] *Hoche; RER: Pantin.*

Espace Chapiteaux

CIRCUSES | Parc de la Villette is home to Espace Chapiteaux: a circus-tent complex that hosts guest circus troupes several times a year, as well as students from the National Circus Arts Center. ✉ *211 av. Jean-Jaurès, 19e, La Villette* ☎ *01–40–03–75–75* 🌐 *www.villette.com* [M] *Porte de Pantin.*

La Géode

FILM | It's hard to miss La Géode—a giant steel globe in Parc de La Villette. The theater screens wide-angle Omnimax films—including kid-friendly documentaries—on a gigantic spherical surface. ✉ *At Cité des Sciences et de l'Industrie, Parc de La Villette, 26 av. Corentin Cariou, 19e, La Villette* ☎ *01–40–05–79–99* ⊕ *www.lageode.fr* Ⓜ *Porte de La Villette.*

Philharmonie de Paris

ARTS CENTERS | Designed by French architect Jean Nouvel, this is one of the world's finest and most expensive auditoriums. It can accommodate 2,400 music lovers, and the adjustable modular seating means you'll be able to see the stage no matter where you sit. Because the hall is home to the Orchestre de Paris, concerts are mostly classical; however, programming includes guest artists and, on weekends, pop, jazz, and world music performances appeal to patrons with more diverse tastes—and smaller budgets. Part of the same complex (formerly known as the Cité de la Musique), **Philharmonie 2** features a 1,000-seat concert hall and a 250-seat amphitheater and presents an eclectic range of concerts (some of which are free) in a postmodern setting. The Philharmonie de Paris is a 45-minute métro ride from downtown. If you're driving, there are 600 parking spaces available. ✉ *221 av. Jean Jaurès, 19e, La Villette* ☎ *01–44–84–44–84* ⊕ *www.philharmoniedeparis.fr* Ⓜ *Porte de Pantin.*

Théâtre Darius Milhaud

THEATER | This theater stages classics by Camus and Baudelaire, as well as occasional shows for children. Performances are in French, but if your language skills are up to it, this is the perfect place to appreciate a classic production. ✉ *80 allée Darius Milhaud, 19e, Buttes-Chaumont* ☎ *01–42–01–92–26* ⊕ *www.theatredariusmilhaud.fr* Ⓜ *Porte de Pantin.*

★ Théâtre Équestre Zingaro

CIRCUSES | FAMILY | Ready for a variation on the circus theme? If you're lucky enough to be visiting during the two months Zingaro performs at home (usually in late fall), you'll have the chance to witness a truly unique spectacle. Since 1985, France's foremost horse whisperer, who goes by the name of Bartabas, has created captivating equestrian shows that mix theater, dance, music, and poetry. The 500-seat theater-in-the-round on the outskirts of Paris is part of a caravan, where trainers and their families, 45 horses, and Bartabas himself live and work. The horses perform in close proximity to the audience in astonishing displays of choreography and acrobatic skill. If you can't make it for Zingaro, there is a consolation prize: in 2003, Bartabas created the Académie du Spectacle Équestre at the royal stables of Versailles (Grandes Écuries). Audiences can catch a decidedly more elegant show there on weekends (Saturday at 6 pm, Sunday at 3 pm) and on certain weekdays during school holidays. Expect to pay €21 to €42 for tickets. ✉ *176 av. Jean Jaurès, Aubervilliers* ☎ *01–48–39–18–03* ⊕ *www.bartabas.fr* Ⓜ *Fort d'Aubervilliers.*

Chapter 11

THE LATIN QUARTER

Updated by
Jack Vermee

⦿ Sights	🍴 Restaurants	🛏 Hotels	🛍 Shopping	🍸 Nightlife
★★★★☆	★★★☆☆	★★★★☆	★★★☆☆	★★★☆☆

NEIGHBORHOOD SNAPSHOT

GETTING HERE

The Latin Quarter is in the 5e arrondissement. Take métro Line 4 to St-Michel to start exploring at the Lucifer-slaying fountain near Shakespeare & Company, across the Seine from Notre-Dame. Go to the Cluny stop on Line 10 if you're heading to the Musée de Cluny. The Place Monge stop on Line 7 puts you near the Panthéon and Rue Mouffetard, the Mosquée de Paris, and the Jardin des Plantes. Les Gobelins neighborhood straddles the 5e, 13e, and 14e arrondissements but is considered part of the 5e because of the Manufacture des Gobelins.

MAKING THE MOST OF YOUR TIME

The Latin Quarter is the perfect place to wander sans itinerary, though there is no shortage of sites worth seeing. Shopping here is generally more affordable (but less original) than in other neighborhoods, and there are lots of new- and used-book stores, many of which stock English-language titles. Pick up picnic supplies in the food shops along Rue Mouffetard or the open-air market at Place Monge (Wednesday, Friday, and Sunday until midafternoon), then enjoy your finds on a bench at the Jardin des Plantes. Linger over mint tea at the lovely Grande Mosquée de Paris or take in a terrific view from the roof of the Institut du Monde Arabe. Stroll the hilly streets around the Panthéon on your way to see the treasures at the Musée de Cluny. Finish with a sunset apéritif on one of the barge cafés (open spring to fall) along the Seine, across from Notre-Dame.

PAUSE HERE

Boasting a number of cafés to choose from, the Place de la Contrescarpe is a favorite place to pause among Latin Quarter locals. Located at the north end of Rue Mouffetard, it's a lovely place for a coffee or a glass of wine after visiting the nearby market at Place Monge or cruising Mouffetard's many shops.

TOP REASONS TO GO

■ **Musée de Cluny.** On the site of an ancient Roman bath, this former abbey is home to the famous *The Lady and the Unicorn* tapestries; the building, tranquil garden, and extensive collection have the hush of a medieval monastery.

■ **Shakespeare & Company.** This legendary English-language bookstore is more than a shopping destination; it's a meeting place for young expats and literature-loving travelers alike.

■ **Rue Mouffetard.** Whether you're a gastronome or just plain hungry, you'll be enthralled by the array of characteristically French edibles sold on this winding market street.

■ **Jardin des Plantes.** This garden is a great spot to enjoy a picnic or to rest your tired feet on one of the many shaded benches.

■ **La Grande Mosquée de Paris.** Relax with a little glass of mint tea in the leafy courtyard café at Paris's most beautiful mosque.

The Latin Quarter is the heart of student Paris—and has been for more than 800 years. France's oldest university, La Sorbonne, was founded here in 1257, and the neighborhood takes its name from the fact that Latin was the common language of the students, who came from all over Europe. Today the area is full of cheap and cheerful cafés, bars, and shops.

The main drag, **Boulevard St-Michel,** is a busy street where bookshops have given way to chain clothing stores and fast-food joints—but don't let that stop you. There are (almost) as many French people wandering the streets here as there are tourists. At **Place St-Michel,** the symbolic gateway to the *quartier,* notice the 19th-century fountain depicting Saint Michael slaying the "great dragon," Satan—a symbolic warning to rebellious locals from Napoléon III. Today the fountain serves as a meeting spot and makes a rather fine metaphor for the boulevard it anchors: a bit grimy but extremely popular.

When you've had enough of the crowds, turn off the boulevard and explore the side streets, where you can find quirky boutiques and intimate bistros. Or stop for a *demi* (a half pint of draft beer) at one of the cafés on **Place de la Sorbonne,** ground zero for students (and their many noisy demonstrations). Around the winding streets behind the **Panthéon,** where French luminaries are laid to rest, you can still encounter plenty of academics arguing philosophy while sipping espresso,

but today the 5e arrondissement is also one of Paris's most charming and sought-after (read: expensive) places to live.

Shop along **Rue Mouffetard** as Parisians do—all the while complaining about the high prices—for one of the best selections of runny cheeses, fresh breads, and charcuterie. Grab a seat in a bustling café, or follow the locals' lead and stand at the bar, where drinks are always cheaper. Film buffs won't have to look far to find one of the small cinema revival houses showing old American films in English (look for v.o., for *version originale*). Not far from le Mouffe is the gorgeous white **Grande Mosquée de Paris** with its impressive minaret. Just beyond the mosque is the **Jardin des Plantes**—a large, if somewhat bland, botanical garden that is home to three natural history museums, most notably the **Grande Galerie de l'Évolution.** Inside, kids can marvel at enormous whale skeletons, along with all sorts of taxidermy. Some of Paris's most intriguing sites are in this neighborhood, including the **Musée de Cluny** and the innovative **Institut du Monde**

Arabe. See ancient history mingle with modern life at the **Arènes de Lutèce,** a Roman amphitheater and favorite soccer pitch for neighborhood kids.

The villagelike neighborhood of La Butte aux Cailles (in the 13e arrondissement, south of Place d'Italie) is a fun destination with a hip crowd, not far from the Latin Quarter if you want a break from the tourists.

Sights

Arènes de Lutèce
RUINS | FAMILY | This Roman amphitheater, designed as a theater and circus, was almost completely destroyed by barbarians in AD 280. The site was rediscovered in 1869, and you can still see part of the stage and tiered seating. Along with the remains of the baths at Cluny, the arena constitutes rare evidence of the powerful Roman city of Lutetia that flourished on the Rive Gauche in the 3rd century. Today it's a favorite spot for picnicking, pickup soccer, or *boules.* ⊠ *Entrances on Rues Monge, de Navarre, and des Arènes, Latin Quarter* ☎ *01–45–35–02–56* ☒ *Free* Ⓜ *Place Monge, Cardinal Lemoine, Jussieu.*

Grande Galerie de l'Évolution
SCIENCE MUSEUM | FAMILY | With a parade of taxidermied animals ranging from the tiniest dung beetle to the tallest giraffe, this four-story natural history museum in the Jardin des Plantes will perk up otherwise museum-weary kids. The flagship of three natural history museums in the garden, this restored 1889 building has a ceiling that changes color to suggest storms, twilight, or the hot savanna sun. Other must-sees are the gigantic skeleton of a blue whale and the stuffed royal rhino (he came from the menagerie at Versailles, where he was a pet of Louis XV). Kids ages 6 to 12 enjoy La Galerie d'Enfants (The Children's Gallery): it has bilingual interactive exhibits about the natural world. A lab

stocked with microscopes often offers free workshops, and most of the staff speaks some English. Hang on to your ticket—it will get you a discount at the other museums within the Jardin des Plantes. ⊠ *36 rue Geoffroy-St-Hilaire, Latin Quarter* ☎ *01–40–79–56–01* ⊕ *www. grandegaleriedelevolution.fr* ☒ *From €10* ☉ *Closed Tues.* Ⓜ *Place Monge, Censier–Daubenton.*

Institut du Monde Arabe
ARTS CENTER | FAMILY | This eye-catching metal-and-glass tower by architect Jean Nouvel cleverly uses metal diaphragms in the shape of square Arabic-style screens to work like a camera lens, opening and closing to control the flow of sunlight. The vast cultural center's layout is a reinterpretation of the traditional enclosed Arab courtyard. Inside, there are various spaces, among them a museum that explores the culture and religion of the 22 Arab League member nations. With the addition of elements from the Louvre's holdings and private donors, the museum's impressive collection includes four floors of Islamic art, artifacts, ceramics, and textiles. There is also a performance space, a sound-and-image center, a library, and a bookstore. Temporary exhibitions usually have information and an audioguide in English. Glass elevators whisk you to the ninth floor, where you can sip mint tea in the rooftop restaurant, Le Zyriab, while feasting on one of the best views in Paris. ⊠ *1 rue des Fossés-St-Bernard, Latin Quarter* ☎ *01–40–51–38–38* ⊕ *www.imarabe.org* ☒ *€8* ☉ *Closed Mon.* Ⓜ *Jussieu.*

★ Jardin des Plantes
GARDEN | FAMILY | Opened in 1640 and once known as the Jardin du Roi (King's Garden), this sprawling patch of greenery is a neighborhood gem. It's home to several gardens and various museums, all housed in 19th-century buildings that blend glass with ornate ironwork. The botanical and rose gardens are impressive, and plant lovers won't want to

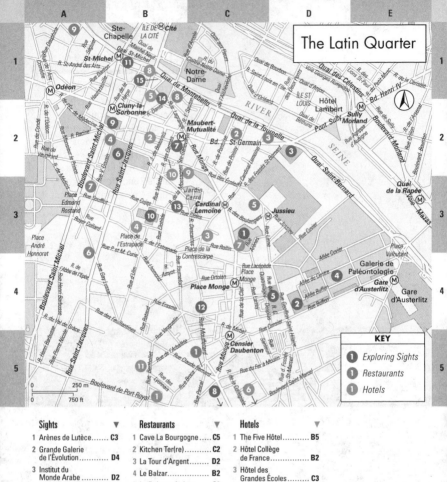

The Latin Quarter

KEY

- **1** Exploring Sights
- **1** Restaurants
- **1** Hotels

miss the towering greenhouses (*serre* in French)—they are filled with one of the world's most extensive collections of tropical and desert flora. If you have kids, take them to the excellent Grande Galerie de l'Évolution or one of the other natural history museums here: the Galerie de Paléontologie, replete with dinosaur and other skeletons, and the recently renovated Galerie de Minéralogie. If the kids prefer fauna, visit the Ménagerie, a small zoo founded in 1794 whose animals once fed Parisians during the 1870 Prussian siege. The star attractions are Nénette, the grande-dame orangutan from Borneo, and her swinging friends in the monkey and ape house. ■**TIP→ If you need a break, there are three kiosk cafés in the Jardin.** ✉ *Entrances on Rue Geoffroy-St-Hilaire, Rue Cuvier, Rue de Buffon, and Quai St-Bernard, Latin Quarter* ☏ *01–40–79–56–01* ⊕ *www.jardindesplantesdeparis.fr/en* ✉ *Museums from €7, zoo €13, greenhouses €7, gardens free* ⊘ *Museums and greenhouses closed Tues.* Ⓜ *Gare d'Austerlitz, Jussieu; Place Monge, Censier–Daubenton for Grande Galerie de l'Évolution.*

La Grande Mosquée de Paris
MOSQUE | This awe-inspiring white mosque, built between 1922 and 1926, has tranquil arcades and a minaret decorated in the style of Moorish Spain. Enjoy sweet mint tea and an exotic pastry in the charming courtyard tea salon or tuck into some couscous in the restaurant. Prayer rooms are not open to sightseers, but there are inexpensive—and quite rustic—hammams, or Turkish steam baths, with scrubs and massages offered to women and men on separate days (check website for times and prices). ✉ *2 bis, pl. du Puits de l'Ermite, entrance to tea salon and restaurant at 39 rue Geoffroy St-Hillaire, Latin Quarter* ☏ *01–45–35–97–33* ⊕ *www.mosqueedeparis.net* ✉ *€3* ⊘ *Closed Fri. (open for worshippers only)* Ⓜ *Place Monge.*

La Sorbonne
COLLEGE | Unless your French is good enough to justify joining a 90-minute group tour (€15, by online reservation only), you can't get into the city's most famous university without a student ID—but it's still fun to hang out with the young scholars. Although La Sorbonne remains the soul of the Quartier Latin, it is only one of several campuses that make up the public Université de Paris. ✉ *1 rue Victor Cousin, Latin Quarter* ☏ *01–40–46–22–11* ⊕ *www.sorbonne.fr* ⊘ *Closed Sun.* Ⓜ *Cluny–La Sorbonne.*

Le Musée de la Préfecture de Police
OTHER MUSEUM | Crime buffs will enjoy this museum hidden on the second floor of the 5e arrondissement's police station. Although the exhibits are in French only, the photographs, letters, drawings, and memorabilia pertaining to some of the city's most sensational crimes are easy enough to follow. Among the 2,000-odd relics you'll find a guillotine, old uniforms, and remnants of the World War II occupation—including what's left of a firing post, German machine guns, and the star insignias worn by Jews. ✉ *4 rue de la Montagne Ste-Geneviève, Latin Quarter* ☏ *01–44–41–52–50* ✉ *Free* ⊘ *Closed Sun. and Mon.* Ⓜ *Maubert-Mutualité.*

Manufacture des Gobelins
ARTS CENTER | Tapestries have been woven at this spot in southeastern Paris, on the banks of the long-covered Bièvre River, since 1662. The Galerie des Gobelins stages exhibitions on two light-flooded floors, highlighting tapestries, furnishings, timepieces, and other treasures mostly drawn from the state collection. Guided visits to the Manufacture (in French, by reservation only) allow a fascinating look at weavers—from students to accomplished veterans—as they work on tapestries and rugs that take years to complete. Also on-site is a highly selective school that teaches weaving, plus a workshop charged with repairing and restoring furnishings belonging to

the French government, which are also stored here in a vast concrete warehouse. ✉ *42 av. des Gobelins, Latin Quarter* ☎ *08–25–05–44–05 reservations* ⊕ *www.mobiliernational.culture.gouv.fr* 🎫 *€8 temporary exhibits (free 1st Sun. of month); €15.50 guided tour of workshops* 🕐 *Gallery closed Mon.* Ⓜ *Gobelins.*

★ Musée de Cluny

HISTORY MUSEUM | Built on the ruins of Roman baths, the Hôtel de Cluny has been a museum since medievalist Alexandre Du Sommerard established his collection here in 1844. The ornate 15th-century mansion was created for the abbot of Cluny, leader of the mightiest monastery in France. Symbols of the abbot's power surround the building, from the crenellated walls that proclaimed his independence from the king to the carved Burgundian grapes twining up the entrance that symbolize his valuable vineyards. The scallop shells (*coquilles St-Jacques*) covering the facade are a symbol of religious pilgrimage, another important source of income for the abbot; the well-traveled pilgrimage route to Spain once ran around the corner along Rue St-Jacques. The highlight of the museum's collection is the world-famous *La Dame à la Licorne* (*The Lady and the Unicorn*) tapestry series, woven in the 16th century, probably in Belgium, and now presented in refurbished surroundings. The vermillion tapestries are an allegorical representation of the five senses. In each, a unicorn and a lion surround an elegant young woman against an elaborate *millefleur* (literally, "1,000 flowers") background. The enigmatic sixth tapestry is thought to be either a tribute to a sixth sense, perhaps intelligence, or a renouncement of the other senses; "To my only desire" is inscribed at the top. The collection also includes the original sculpted heads of the *Kings of Israel and Judah* from Notre-Dame, decapitated during the Revolution and discovered in 1977 in the basement of a French bank. The *frigidarium* is a stunning reminder of the city's cold-water Roman baths; the soaring space, painstakingly renovated, houses temporary exhibits. Also notable is the pocket-size chapel with its elaborate Gothic ceiling. Outside, in Place Paul Painlevé, is a charming medieval-style garden where you can see flora depicted in the unicorn tapestries. The English audioguide (€3) is highly recommended. For a different kind of auditory experience, check the event listings; concerts of medieval music are often staged Sunday afternoon and Monday at lunchtime (€7). Following extensive renovations, intended to vastly improve accessibility and transform the museum experience, the museum was expected to reopen in May 2022. ✉ *6 pl. Paul-Painlevé, Latin Quarter* ☎ *01–53–73–78–16 (reservations)* ⊕ *www.musee-moyenage.fr* 🎫 *€12 (free 1st Sun. of month)* 🕐 *Closed Tues.* Ⓜ *Cluny–La Sorbonne.*

★ Panthéon

NOTABLE BUILDING | Rome has St. Peter's, London has St. Paul's, and Paris has the Panthéon, whose enormous dome dominates the Left Bank. Built as the church of Ste-Geneviève, the patron saint of Paris, it was later converted to an all-star mausoleum for some of France's biggest names, including Voltaire, Zola, Dumas, Rousseau, and Hugo. Pierre and Marie Curie were reinterred here together in 1995, and feminist-politician Simone Veil became only the fifth woman in this illustrious group when she was entombed in 2018. Begun in 1764, the building was almost complete when the French Revolution erupted. By then, architect Jacques-German Soufflot had died—supposedly from worrying that the 220-foot-high dome would collapse. He needn't have fretted: the dome was so perfect that Foucault used it in his famous pendulum test to prove the Earth rotates on its axis. Today the crypt, nave, and dome still sparkle (the latter offering great views), and Foucault's pendulum still holds pride of place on the main

Hemingway's Paris

There is a saying: "Everyone has two countries, his or her own—and France." For the Lost Generation after World War I, these words rang particularly true. Lured by favorable exchange rates, free-flowing alcohol, and a booming arts scene, many American writers, composers, and painters moved to Paris in the 1920s and 1930s, Ernest Hemingway among them. He arrived in Paris with his first wife, Hadley, in December 1921 and headed for the Rive Gauche—the Hôtel de l'Angleterre, to be exact (still operating at 44 rue Jacob).

Hemingway worked as a journalist and quickly made friends with expat writers such as Gertrude Stein and Ezra Pound. In 1922 the Hemingways moved to 74 rue du Cardinal Lemoine, a bare-bones apartment with no running water (his writing studio was around the corner, on the top floor of 39 rue Descartes). Then, in 1924, they and their baby son settled at 113 rue Notre-Dame des Champs. Much of *The Sun Also Rises*, Hemingway's first serious novel, was written at nearby café La Closerie des Lilas. These were the years in which he forged his writing style, paring his sentences down to the pith—as he noted in *A Moveable Feast*, "hunger was good discipline." There were some especially hungry months when Hemingway gave up journalism for short-story writing, and the family was "very poor and very happy."

They weren't happy for long: in 1926, as *The Sun Also Rises* made him famous, Hemingway left Hadley. The next year, he wed his mistress, Pauline Pfeiffer, and moved to 6 rue Férou, near the Musée du Luxembourg.

For gossip and books, and to pick up his mail, Hemingway would visit Shakespeare & Company (then at 12 rue de l'Odéon). For cash and cocktails, he usually headed to the upscale Rive Droite. He collected the former at the Guaranty Trust Company, at 1 rue des Italiens. He found the latter, when he was flush, at the bar of the landmark Hôtel de Crillon, on Place de la Concorde next to the American Embassy, or, when poor, at the Caves Mura, at 19 rue d'Antin, or Harry's Bar, still in brisk business at 5 rue Daunou. Hemingway's loyal and legendary association with the Hôtel Ritz was sealed during the Liberation in 1944, when he strode in at the head of his platoon and "liberated" the joint by ordering martinis all around. Here Hemingway asked Mary Welsh to become his fourth wife, and here also, the story goes, a trunk full of notes regarding his first years in Paris turned up in the 1950s, giving him the raw material for writing *A Moveable Feast*.

floor, slowly swinging in its clockwise direction and reminding of us of earth's eternal spin. ✉ *Pl. du Panthéon, Latin Quarter* ☎ *01–44–32–18–00* ⊕ *www. paris-pantheon.fr* 🎫 *€11.50; €15 with dome access* ☉ *Dome closed Nov.–Mar.* Ⓜ *Cardinal Lemoine; RER: Luxembourg.*

Place St-Michel

PLAZA/SQUARE | This square was named for Gabriel Davioud's grandiose 1860 fountain sculpture of St. Michael vanquishing Satan—a loaded political gesture from Napoléon III's go-to guy, Baron Haussmann, who hoped St-Michel would quell the Revolutionary fervor of the neighborhood. The fountain is often used as a meeting point for both local students and young tourists. ✉ *Latin Quarter* Ⓜ *Métro or RER: St-Michel.*

★ Rue Mouffetard

NEIGHBORHOOD | This winding cobblestone street is one of the city's oldest and was once a Roman road leading south from Lutetia (the Roman name for Paris) to Italy. The upper half is dotted with restaurants and bars that cater to tourists and students; the lower half is the setting of a lively morning market, Tuesday through Sunday. The highlight of le Mouffe, though, is the stretch in between where the shops spill into the street with luscious offerings such as roasting chickens and potatoes, rustic *saucisson,* pâtés, and pungent cheeses, especially at Androuët (No. 134). If you're here in the morning, Le Mouffetard Café (No. 116) is a good place to stop for a continental breakfast (about €10). If it's apéritif time, head to Place de la Contrescarpe for a cocktail, or enjoy a glass of wine at Cave La Bourgogne (No. 144). Prefer to just do a little noshing? Sample the chocolates at Mococha (No. 89) or the gelato at Gelati d'Alberto (No. 45). Note that most shops are closed on Monday. ✉ *Latin Quarter* Ⓜ *Place Monge, Censier-Daubenton.*

★ Shakespeare & Company

STORE/MALL | The English-language bookstore Shakespeare & Company is one of Paris's most eccentric and lovable literary institutions. Founded by George Whitman, the maze of new and used books has offered a sense of community (and often a bed) to wandering writers since the 1950s. The store takes its name from Sylvia Beach's original Shakespeare & Co., which opened in 1919 at 12 rue d'Odéon, welcoming the likes of Ernest Hemingway, James Baldwin, and James Joyce. Beach famously bucked the system when she published Joyce's *Ulysses* in 1922, but her original store closed in 1941. After the war, Whitman picked up the gauntlet, naming his own bookstore after its famous predecessor.

When Whitman passed away in 2011, heavy-hearted locals left candles and flowers in front of his iconic storefront. He is buried in the literati-laden Père-Lachaise cemetery; however, his legacy lives on through his daughter Sylvia, who runs the shop and welcomes a new generation of Paris dreamers. Walk up the almost impossibly narrow stairs to the second floor and you'll still see laptops and sleeping bags tucked between the aging volumes and under dusty daybeds; it's sort of like a hippie commune. A revolving cast of characters helps out in the shop or cooks meals for fellow residents. They're in good company; Henry Miller, Samuel Beckett, and William Burroughs are among the famous writers to benefit from the Whitman family hospitality.

Today, you can still count on a couple of characters lurking in the stacks, a sometimes spacey staff, the latest titles from British presses, and hidden second-hand treasures in the odd corners and crannies. Check the website for readings and workshops throughout the week. ✉ *37 rue de la Bûcherie, Latin Quarter* ☎ *01–43–25–40–93* ⊕ *www.shakespeare-andcompany.com* Ⓜ *St-Michel.*

St-Étienne-du-Mont

CHURCH | This jewel box of a church has been visited by several popes paying tribute to Ste-Geneviève (the patron saint of Paris), who was buried here before Revolutionaries burned her remains. Built on the ruins of a 6th-century abbey founded by Clovis, the first king of the Franks, it has a unique combination of Gothic, Renaissance, and early Baroque elements, which adds a certain warmth that is lacking in other Parisian churches of pure Gothic style. Here you'll find the only rood screen left in the city—an ornate 16th-century masterwork of carved stone spanning the nave like a bridge, with a spiral staircase on either side. Observe the organ (dating from 1631, it is the city's oldest), the ornate wood-carved pulpit, and the marker in the floor near the entrance that commemorates an archbishop of Paris who was stabbed to death here by a defrocked priest in 1857. Guided tours are free, but a small offering is appreciated; call for times. ✉ *Pl. Ste-Geneviève, 30 rue Descartes, Latin Quarter* ☎ *01–43–54–11–79* 🌐 *www.saintetiennedumont.fr* [M] *Cardinal Lemoine.*

St-Julien-le-Pauvre

CHURCH | This tiny shrine in the shadow of Notre-Dame is one of the three oldest churches in Paris. Founded in 1045, it became a meeting place for university students in the 12th century and was Dante's church of choice when he was in town writing his *Divine Comedy*. Today's structure dates mostly from the 1600s, but keep an eye out for older pillars, which crawl with carvings of demons. You can maximize your time inside by attending one of the classical or gospel concerts frequently held here. Alternately, go outside and simply perch on a bench in the lovely garden and gaze across the Seine. ✉ *1 rue St-Julien-le-Pauvre, Latin Quarter* ☎ *01–43–54–52–16* [M] *St-Michel.*

🍴 Restaurants

Thanks to its student population, the Latin Quarter caters to those on a budget with kebab shops, crêpe stands, fast-food joints, and no-nonsense bistros. Look beyond the pedestrian streets such as Rue de la Huchette and Rue Mouffetard for less touristy eateries preferred by locals. As you might expect in an area known for its *gauche caviar* (wealthy intellectuals who vote Socialist), the Latin Quarter brims with atmospheric places to linger over a tiny cup of black coffee.

Cave La Bourgogne

$ | **BRASSERIE** | Settle in on the terrace for lunch (try the beef carpaccio or salmon tartare) or join the locals along the zinc bar at this Latin Quarter favorite. Nestled at the foot of the gently sloping rue Monge, it offers friendly service amidst an old-school bistro ambience. **Known for:** late night hours until 2 am; authentic bistro atmosphere; excellent value. [$] *Average main: €16* ✉ *144 rue Mouffetard, Latin Quarter* ☎ *01–47–07–82–80* [M] *Censier-Daubenton.*

★ Kitchen Ter(re)

$$ | **FRENCH FUSION** | Michelin-starred chef William Ledeuil flexes his genius for France-meets-Asia flavors at this chic address—his third—a few blocks from the Île St-Louis and Notre-Dame. Ledeuil is known and loved for his fearless pairings of bold and subtle flavors, like veal tartare pasta with crunchy peanuts and pungent bonito flakes or Thai beef soup with luscious Iberian ham, mushrooms, and sweet pear. **Known for:** easy walk from many tourist sites; excellent-value lunch menus; Asian-inflected contemporary French cuisine. [$] *Average main: €21* ✉ *26 bd. St-Germain, 5e, Latin Quarter* ☎ *01–42–39–47–48* 🌐 *www.zekitchen-galerie.fr* 🕒 *Closed Sun., Mon., and 2nd wk of Jan.* [M] *Cardinal Lemoine, Maubert Mutualité.*

Paris Café Culture 🍴

The café capital of the world is making room for the new barista cafés sweeping cities across the globe. For discerning coffee lovers this is good news indeed. Scattered throughout Paris's most compelling neighborhoods, most of these contemporary third-wave cafés—many with multiple branches—have a character all their own and, alongside superb gastronomic coffee, offer a selection of top-notch snacks or even meals. Some of the very best include Bal Café, Café Coutume, and Ten Belles.

★ La Tour d'Argent

$$$$ | **MODERN FRENCH** | You can't deny the splendor of this legendary Michelin-starred restaurant's setting overlooking the Seine; if you don't want to break the bank on dinner, treat yourself to the three-course lunch menu for €120. This entitles you to succulent slices of one of the restaurant's numbered ducks (the great duck slaughter began in 1919 and is now well past the millionth mallard, as your certificate will attest). **Known for:** fabulous Seine-side setting with glorious views; one of the city's best wine lists; duck in all its glorious forms. [$] *Average main: €110* ✉ *15–17 quai de la Tournelle, 5e, Latin Quarter* ☎ *01–43–54–23–31* 🌐 *www.tourdargent.com* 🕓 *Closed Sun., Mon., and Aug.* 👔 *Jacket and tie* [M] *Cardinal Lemoine.*

Le Balzar

$$$ | **BRASSERIE** | Regulars grumble about the uneven cooking at Le Balzar, but they continue to come back because they can't resist the waiters' wry humor and the dining room's amazing people-watching possibilities. The restaurant attracts politicians, writers, tourists, and local eccentrics—and remains one of the city's classic brasseries: the perfect stop before or after a film in a local art-house cinema. **Known for:** drinks on the terrace; famous patrons; standard French bistro menu. [$] *Average main: €25* ✉ *49 rue des Écoles, 5e, Latin Quarter* ☎ *01–43–54–13–67* 🌐 *www.brasseriebalzar.com* [M] *Cluny–La Sorbonne.*

★ Le Buisson Ardent

$$$ | **BISTRO** | **FAMILY** | This charming Quartier Latin bistro with woodwork and murals dating from 1925 is always packed and boisterous. A glance at the affordable menu makes it easy to understand why: dishes such as chestnut soup with spice bread, sea bass marinated in lime and coconut, and apple and quince tatin (upside-down tart) with gingerbread ice cream put a fresh twist on French classics. **Known for:** you can take home your wine if you don't finish it; excellent value daily prix-fixe lunch menu; authentic Parisian bistro atmosphere. [$] *Average main: €25* ✉ *25 rue Jussieu, 5e, Latin Quarter* ☎ *01–43–54–93–02* 🌐 *www.facebook.com/lebuissonardent.paris* 🕓 *Closed Sun.* [M] *Jussieu.*

★ Les Papilles

$$$$ | **WINE BAR** | Part wineshop and épicerie, part restaurant, Les Papilles has a winning formula—pick any bottle off the well-stocked shelf, and pay €7 corkage to sip it with your meal. You can also savor one of several superb wines by the glass at your table while enjoying the excellent set menu of dishes made with top-notch, seasonal ingredients. **Known for:** excellent wines by the glass or bottle; market menu that changes daily; lively, authentic atmosphere. [$] *Average main: €38* ✉ *30 rue Gay-Lussac, 5e, Latin Quarter* ☎ *01–43–25–20–79* 🌐 *www.lespapillesparis.fr* 🕓 *Closed Sun., Mon., last wk of July, and 2 wks in Aug.* [M] *Cluny–La Sorbonne.*

Les Patios

$ | **BRASSERIE** | If you're young—or young at heart—come here to hang with the Sorbonne crowd at this bustling brasserie on a shaded pedestrian lane. It's steps from campus and also near Le Jardin du Luxembourg. **Known for:** pizza and burgers; colorful people-watching; extensive outdoor seating. [$] *Average main: €16* ✉ *5 pl. de la Sorbonne, Latin Quarter* ☎ *01–43–54–34–43* [M] *Cluny–La Sorbonne.*

★ Sola

$$$$ | **ECLECTIC** | This foodie sanctuary is where dishes like miso-lacquered foie gras or sake-glazed suckling pig—perfectly crisp on the outside and melting inside—pair traditional Japanese and French ingredients to wondrous effect. The seven-course set dinner menu (€130, with an option to add a pairing of five glasses of wine or sake), while not

cheap, offers a choice of fish or meat and finishes with some stunning confections. **Known for:** traditional Japanese dining downstairs; contemporary French-Japanese cooking at its finest; beautiful atmosphere in a 17th-century building. $ *Average main: €130* ✉ *12 rue de l'Hôtel Colbert, 5e, Latin Quarter* ☎ *01–42–02–39–24* ⊕ *www.restaurant-sola.com* ⊘ *Closed Sun. and Mon. No lunch Tues.–Thurs.* Ⓜ *Maubert–Mutualité.*

★ Ze Kitchen Galerie

$$$$ | **FRENCH FUSION** | The name of this contemporary bistro might not be inspired, but the cooking shows creativity and a sense of fun. From a deliberately deconstructed menu featuring raw fish, soups, pastas, and grills, you can choose a five-course (€95) or a seven-course (€115) menu. **Known for:** locally sourced vegetables and spices; exquisitely presented French-Asian fusion dishes; perfect location near the Seine. $ *Average main: €95* ✉ *4 rue des Grands-Augustins, 6e, Latin Quarter* ☎ *01–44–32–00–32* ⊕ *www.zekitchengalerie.fr* ⊘ *Closed weekends* Ⓜ *St-Michel.*

Hotels

Leafy and bookish, this quiet quartier at the heart of the city retains all the charm of Old Paris, as do its hotels, which tend to be smaller, family-owned establishments or budget chains with character.

The Five Hôtel

$ | **HOTEL** | Small is beautiful at this design hotel on a quiet street near the Rue Mouffetard market and the Latin Quarter. **Pros:** unique design; quiet side street; personalized welcome. **Cons:** most rooms only have showers, not tubs; the nearest métro is a 10-minute walk; most rooms are too small for excessive baggage. $ *Rooms from: €116* ✉ *3 rue Flatters, Latin Quarter* ☎ *01–43–31–74–21* ⊕ *www.thefivehotel.com* ⇱ *25 rooms* ⦿ *No Meals* Ⓜ *Gobelins.*

Hôtel Collège de France

$$ | **HOTEL** | Exposed stone walls, wooden beams, and medieval artwork echo the style of the Musée Cluny, two blocks from this charming, family-run hotel. **Pros:** walk to Rive Gauche sights; ceiling fans; free Wi-Fi. **Cons:** old-fashioned bathrooms; no air-conditioning; thin walls between rooms. $ *Rooms from: €135* ✉ *7 rue Thénard, Latin Quarter* ☎ *01–43–26–78–36* ⊕ *www.hotel-collegedefrance.com* ⇱ *29 rooms* ⦿ *No Meals* Ⓜ *Maubert–Mutualité, St-Michel, Cluny–La Sorbonne.*

Hôtel des Grandes Écoles

$$ | **HOTEL** | Distributed among a trio of three-story buildings set back in a quiet cobbled courtyard, Madame Le Floch's rooms have a distinct grandmotherly vibe because of their flowery wallpaper and lace bedspreads, but they're spacious for this part of Paris. **Pros:** close to Latin Quarter nightlife spots; good value; lovely courtyard. **Cons:** no room TVs; walls are thin, meaning some internal noise; uphill walk from the métro. $ *Rooms from: €160* ✉ *75 rue du Cardinal Lemoine, Latin Quarter* ☎ *01–43–26–79–23* ⊕ *www.hoteldesgrandesecoles.com* ⇱ *51 rooms* ⦿ *No Meals* Ⓜ *Cardinal Lemoine.*

Hôtel des Grands Hommes

$$$ | **HOTEL** | The "great men" this hotel honors with its name rest in peace within the towering Panthéon monument across the street. **Pros:** major Latin Quarter sights within walking distance; lovely views from many rooms; comfortable and attractive rooms. **Cons:** high price for this area; neighborhood can be loud after dark; closest métro is a 10-minute walk. $ *Rooms from: €350* ✉ *17 pl. du Panthéon, Latin Quarter* ☎ *01–46–34–19–60* ⊕ *www.hoteldesgrandshommes.com* ⇱ *30 rooms* ⦿ *No Meals* Ⓜ *RER: Luxembourg.*

11

The Latin Quarter

Hôtel Henri IV Rive Gauche

$$ | **HOTEL** | About 50 paces from Notre-Dame and the Seine, this elegant hotel has identical, impeccable rooms with beige and rose linens and framed prints of architectural drawings. **Pros:** comfortable decor; friendly reception staff; close to major sights and RER station. **Cons:** furnishings showing their age; single rooms are small; on a busy street full of late-night bars. [$] *Rooms from: €209* ✉ *9–11 rue St-Jacques, Latin Quarter* ☎ *01–46–33–20–20* 🌐 *www.henri-paris-hotel.com* 🛏 *23 rooms* 🍴 *No Meals* [M] *St-Michel.*

Hôtel La Manufacture

$ | **HOTEL** | **FAMILY** | Just behind Place d'Italie and a short stroll from both the Jardin des Plantes and Rue Mouffetard, La Manufacture's lesser-known location makes you feel like a *vrai* (real) Parisian. **Pros:** easy access to major métro and bus lines; bright breakfast room; safe, nontouristy district. **Cons:** small rooms; a long stroll to the center of Paris; street noise. [$] *Rooms from: €120* ✉ *8 rue Philippe de Champagne, Latin Quarter* ☎ *01–45–35–45–25* 🌐 *www.hotel-la-manufacture.com* 🛏 *57 rooms* 🍴 *No Meals* [M] *Place d'Italie.*

★ Hotel Monge

$$ | **HOTEL** | Chic, cozy, and welcoming, you couldn't land in a more charming—and reasonably priced—Parisian boutique hotel. **Pros:** excellent neighborhood close to sights and legendary markets; lovely spa; great views from balconies. **Cons:** quiet neighborhood with few restaurants; open-design showers; not all rooms have balconies. [$] *Rooms from: €198* ✉ *55 rue Monge, Latin Quarter* ☎ *01–43–54–55–55* 🌐 *www.hotelmonge.com* 🛏 *30 rooms* 🍴 *No Meals* [M] *Jussieu, Cardinal Lemoine, Place Monge.*

Hôtel Notre-Dame Saint-Michel

$$ | **HOTEL** | If you love the quirky and eclectic fashions of Christian Lacroix and don't mind hauling your bags up some steps, this unique boutique hotel overlooking Notre-Dame may be for you. **Pros:** beautiful design by Christian Lacroix; comfortable beds; stunning views of the cathedral and river. **Cons:** some low ceilings; no minibar in rooms; stairs can be tricky with large bags. [$] *Rooms from: €214* ✉ *1 quai Saint-Michel, Latin Quarter* ☎ *01–43–54–20–43* 🌐 *www.hotelnotredameparis.com* 🛏 *26 rooms* 🍴 *No Meals* [M] *St-Michel.*

Hôtel Résidence Henri IV

$$ | **HOTEL** | **FAMILY** | This small hotel on a quiet cul-de-sac is perfect for travelers—especially those with children—who need a home base where they can kick back, make their own meals, and feel at home. **Pros:** handy kitchenettes; charming rooms; close to Latin Quarter attractions. **Cons:** decor a bit dated; some rooms on the small side; closest métro is a few blocks away. [$] *Rooms from: €180* ✉ *50 rue des Bernadins, Latin Quarter* ☎ *01–44–41–31–81* 🌐 *www.residence-henri4.com* 🛏 *13 units* 🍴 *No Meals* [M] *Maubert–Mutualité.*

Hôtel Saint-Jacques

$$ | **HOTEL** | *Quaint* is the word that springs to mind at this well-located hotel, bedecked with faux-marble trompe-l'oeil, Renoiresque murals on walls and ceilings, and all those cozy details that remind you of a classic Parisian living room. **Pros:** unique Parisian decor; free Wi-Fi; close to Latin Quarter sights. **Cons:** decor needs some refurbishment; thin walls between rooms; busy street can be noisy in summer. [$] *Rooms from: €175* ✉ *35 rue des Écoles, Latin Quarter* ☎ *01–44–07–45–45* 🌐 *www.paris-hotel-stjacques.com* 🛏 *36 rooms* 🍴 *No Meals* [M] *Maubert–Mutualité.*

Hotel Seven

$$ | **HOTEL** | The "seven" may refer to the level of heaven you'll find at this wacky boutique hotel, but most likely

it means the seven suites, where a team of designers and artists were let loose to riff on imaginative themes like Secret Agent, Sublime, and Nuit Chic. **Pros:** fun design elements; quiet location near Mouffetard market street; copious breakfast buffet for a fee. **Cons:** design detail can be a bit much; several blocks to closest métro; small closets. [$] *Rooms from: €159* ✉ *20 rue Berthollet, Latin Quarter* ☎ *01–43–31–47–52* 🌐 *www.sevenhotelparis.com* 🛏 *35 rooms* 🍴 *No Meals* [M] *Censier–Daubentin.*

Nightlife

The smoke may have cleared from the jazz clubs in the city's historically bohemian quarter, but the atmosphere's still hopping.

CABARET

Paradis Latin

CABARET | Occupying a building that's attributed to Gustav Eiffel, Paradis Latin peppers its quirky show with acrobatics and eye-popping lighting effects, making this the liveliest and trendiest cabaret on the Left Bank. Prices range from €70 (for the show only) to €200 (with the top-of-the-line dinner option and wine added in). ✉ *28 rue du Cardinal Lemoine, 5e, Latin Quarter* ☎ *01–43–25–28–28* 🌐 *www.paradislatin.com* [M] *Cardinal Lemoine.*

JAZZ CLUBS

Caveau de la Huchette

LIVE MUSIC | One of the few surviving cellar clubs from the 1940s has the "best boppers" in the city and packs 'em in for swing dancing and Dixieland tunes. It's a killer jazz spot for everyone but claustrophobics. The music continues until 4 am on Friday and Saturday. ✉ *5 rue de la Huchette, 5e, Latin Quarter* ☎ *01–43–26–65–05* 🌐 *www.caveaudelahuchette.fr* [M] *St-Michel.*

Performing Arts

For fans of the seventh art, the Latin Quarter is heaven on earth: the numerous small and not-so-small cinemas that dot the neighborhood are still going strong, many showing Hollywood classics in *version originale* (original English versions).

Les Écoles Cinéma Club

FILM | Formerly Le Desperado, then Les Écoles 21, the refurbished Les Écoles Cinéma Club continues the tradition of presenting version originale American classics and cult films for €9 on four screens. ✉ *23 rue des Écoles, 5e, Latin Quarter* ☎ *01–43–25–72–07* 🌐 *www.pariscinemaclub.com/ecoles* [M] *Maubert-Mutualité.*

Saint-André des Arts

FILM | One of a number of popular cinemas near the Sorbonne, Saint-André des Arts is also one of the best cinemas in Paris. It hosts an annual festival devoted to a single director (like Bergman or Tarkovsky) and shows indie films every day at 1 pm. Some of the latter are part of "Les Découvertes de Saint-André" series, which focuses on the work of young filmmakers; these screenings are followed by a discussion (check the website for details). ✉ *30 rue St-André des Arts, 6e, Latin Quarter* ☎ *01–43–26–48–18* 🌐 *www.cinesaintandre.fr* [M] *St-Michel.*

Théâtre de la Huchette

THEATER | This tiny Rive Gauche venue has been staging the titanic Romanian-French writer Ionesco's *The Bald Soprano* and *The Lesson* since 1957: before the COVID-19 pandemic, it held the world record for a nonstop theater run with 19,000 performances viewed by more than 2.5 million people. You can see both shows on the same day for €40; Wednesday shows have English subtitles. Other productions are also mounted, and single tickets cost €28. ✉ *23 rue de la*

Huchette, 5e, Latin Quarter ☎ *01–43–26–38–99* ⊕ *www.theatre-huchette.com* Ⓜ *St-Michel.*

Shopping

Considering this fabled quartier is home to the Sorbonne and historically one of Paris's intellectual-bohemian centers, it's not surprising that it has a rich selection of bookstores—not just for students but for collectors and bargain hunters, too. Gastronomes, meanwhile, flock in to shop at the outstanding charcuteries and fromageries along Rue Mouffetard.

BOOKS AND STATIONERY
Abbey Bookshop
BOOKS | Paris's Canadian bookstore has books on Canadian history as well as new and secondhand Québécois and English-language novels. The Canadian Club of Paris also organizes regular poetry readings and literary conferences here. ⊠ *29 rue de la Parcheminerie, 5e, Latin Quarter* ☎ *01–46–33–16–24* ⊕ *www.abbeybookshop.org* Ⓜ *Cluny–La Sorbonne.*

HOME DECOR
Avant-Scène
FURNITURE | Head to Avant-Scène for original, poetic furniture. Owner Elisabeth Delacarte commissions limited-edition pieces from artists like Mark Brazier-Jones, Franck Evennou, Elizabeth Garouste, and Hubert Le Gall. ⊠ *4 pl. de l'Odéon, 6e, Latin Quarter* ☎ *01–46–33–12–40* ⊕ *www.avantscene.fr* Ⓜ *Odéon.*

MARKETS
Rue Mouffetard
MARKET | This colorful market street near the Jardin des Plantes reflects its multicultural neighborhood: vibrant, with a laid-back feel that still smacks of old Paris. It's best on weekends (although it closes Sunday afternoon and Monday as well). ⊠ *5e, Latin Quarter* ⊕ *www.rue-mouffetard.com/market.html* Ⓜ *Monge.*

Chapter 12

ST-GERMAIN-DES-PRÉS

Updated by
Virginia Power Jestin

 Sights
★★★★★

 Restaurants
★★★☆☆

 Hotels
★★★★★

 Shopping
★★★★★

 Nightlife
★★☆☆☆

NEIGHBORHOOD SNAPSHOT

GETTING HERE

The St-Germain neighborhood is in the 6e arrondissement and a bit of the 7e. To get to the heart of this area, take the Line 4 *métro* to St-Germain-des-Prés. For shopping, use this station or St-Sulpice. From either of those stops, it's a short walk to the Jardin du Luxembourg, or take the RER B line to the Luxembourg station. For the Musée d'Orsay, take the Line 12 métro to Solferino or the RER C line to the Musée d'Orsay.

MAKING THE MOST OF YOUR TIME

Aim for an early start—savor a *café crème* at a café along the river and get to the Musée d'Orsay early, when crowds are thinner. Leave some time for window-shopping around Boulevard St-Germain and Rue de Rennes on your way to the Jardin du Luxembourg. You might want to plan your visit on a day other than Monday, when the d'Orsay, many of the art galleries, and even some shops are closed.

PAUSE HERE

Don't miss the Taras Chevtchenko Square, a small, public garden on the corner of Boulevard St-Germain and Rue des Saint-Pères, where you'll find a statue of the 19th-century Ukrainian poet who fought for his country's independence. The garden backs up to the Ukrainian cathedral Saint Volodymyr Le Grand de Paris. Formerly connected to a long-disaffected hospital, the garden is also home to a much older statue of famous French physician René Laennec, inventor of the stethoscope.

TOP REASONS TO GO

■ **Musée d'Orsay.** The magnificent vaulted ceiling and abundant natural light inside this train station-turned-art museum are reminders of why the Impressionist painters thought *les gares* ("the train stations") were the cathedrals of the 19th century.

■ **Jardin du Luxembourg.** Wander the tree-lined gravel paths, take in a puppet show, or simply laze by the fountain in a chair in one of the city's most elegant gardens.

■ **Boulevard St-Germain.** The main artery of this chic neighborhood is edged with shops and galleries. Most of top galleries are on the small streets between the Musée d'Orsay and Rue Dauphine.

■ **Café Life.** This is prime people-watching territory, so find a seat at a comfy café, order a coffee, beer, or *kir*, and watch the world go by.

If you had to choose the most classically Parisian neighborhood, this would be it. St-Germain-des-Prés has it all: genteel blocks lined with upscale art galleries, storied cafés, designer boutiques, atmospheric restaurants, and a fine selection of museums. Cast your eyes upward after dark and you may spy a frescoed ceiling in a tony apartment. These historic streets can get quite crowded, especially in summer, so mind your elbows and plunge in.

This *quartier* is named for the oldest church in Paris, **St-Germain-des-Prés,** and it's become a prized address for Parisians and expats alike. Despite its pristine facade, though, this wasn't always silver-spoon territory. Claude Monet and Auguste Renoir shared a cramped studio at 20 rue Visconti, and the young Picasso barely eked out an existence in a room on Rue de Seine. By the 1950s St-Germain bars bopped with jazz, and the likes of Albert Camus, Jean-Paul Sartre, and Simone de Beauvoir puffed away on Gauloises while discussing the meaninglessness of life at Café de Flore. Nearby, in the 7e arrondissement, the star attraction is the **Musée d'Orsay,** home to a world-class collection of Impressionist paintings in a converted Belle Époque railway station along the Seine. It's famous for having some of Paris's longest lines, so a visit to the Orsay should be planned with care. There are also several smaller museums worth a stop here, including the impressive **Musée Maillol,** a private collection dedicated to the work of sculptor Aristide Maillol, in an elegant mansion. The **Musée Delacroix,** in lovely Place Furstenberg, is home to a small collection of the Romantic master's works. Not far away is the stately **Église St-Sulpice,** where you can see two impressive Delacroix frescoes.

Paris is a city for walking, and St-Germain is one of the most enjoyable places to practice the art of *le flâneur,* or one who strolls. Make your way to the busy crossroads of **Carrefour de Buci,** dotted with cafés, bakeries, and greengrocers. Rue de l'Ancienne Comédie is so named because it was the first home of the legendary Comédie Française; it cuts through to busy Place de l'Odéon and Rue St-André des Arts. Along the latter you can find the historic **Cour du**

The Jardin du Luxembourg is one of the most charming parks in Paris.

Commerce St-André (opposite No. 66), a charming cobbled passageway filled with cafés—including, halfway down on the left, Paris's oldest, Le Procope.

Make sure you save some energy for the exquisite **Jardin du Luxembourg,** a 57-acre French garden whose tree-lined paths have attracted fashionable fresh-air fans through the ages.

Sights

Carrefour de Buci

STREET | FAMILY | Just behind the neighborhood's namesake St-Germain church, this colorful crossroads (*carrefour* means "intersection") was once a notorious Rive Gauche landmark. During the French Revolution, the army enrolled its first volunteers here. It was also here that thousands of royalists and priests lost their heads during the 10-month wave of public executions known as the Reign of Terror. There's certainly nothing sinister about the area today, though; brightly colored flowers are for sale alongside take-out ice cream and other gourmet treats. Devotees of the superb, traditional bakery Carton (6 rue de Buci) line up for fresh breads and pastries (try the *pain aux raisins, tuiles* cookies, and *tarte au citron*). ⊠ *Intersection of Rues Mazarine, Dauphine, and de Buci, St-Germain-des-Prés* Ⓜ *Mabillon.*

Cour du Commerce St-André

HISTORIC SIGHT | Like an 18th-century engraving come to life, this charming street arcade is a remnant of *ancien* Paris, with its uneven cobblestones, antique roofs, and old-world facades. Famed for its rabble-rousing inhabitants—journalist Jean-Paul Marat ran the Revolutionary newspaper *L'Ami du Peuple* at No. 8, and the agitator Georges Danton lived at No. 20—it is also home to Le Procope, Paris's oldest café. The passageway contains a turret from the 12th-century wall of Philippe-Auguste. ⊠ *Linking Bd. St-Germain and Rue St-André-des-Arts, St-Germain-des-Prés* Ⓜ *Odéon.*

École Nationale des Beaux-Arts

SCHOOL | Occupying three large mansions near the Seine, the national fine arts school—today the breeding ground for painters, sculptors, and architects—was once the site of a convent founded in 1608 by Marguerite de Valois, the first wife of Henri IV. After the Revolution the convent was turned into a museum for works of art salvaged from buildings attacked by the rampaging French mobs. In 1816 the museum was turned into a school. Today its peaceful courtyards host contemporary installations and exhibits. Note that public access to the school is limited, except during temporary exhibitions. ⊠ *14 rue Bonaparte, St-Germain-des-Prés* ☎ *01–47–03–50–00* ⊕ *www. beauxartsparis.fr* ⊠ *Free* ⊙ *Closed Aug. and weekends except during temporary exhibits* Ⓜ *St-Germain-des-Prés.*

Église St-Germain-des-Prés

CHURCH | Paris's oldest church was built to shelter a simple shard of wood, said to be a relic of Jesus's cross brought back from Spain in AD 542. Vikings came down the Seine and sacked the sanctuary, and Revolutionaries used it to store gunpowder. Yet the elegant building has defied history's abuses: its 11th-century Romanesque tower continues to be the central symbol of the neighborhood. The colorful 19th-century frescoes in the nave are by Hippolyte Flandrin, a pupil of the classical master Ingres, while the Saint Benoit chapel contains the tomb of philosopher René Descartes. Step inside for spiritual nourishment, or pause in the square to people-watch—there's usually a street musician tucked against the church wall, out of the wind. The church also stages superb organ concerts and recitals; see the website for details. ⊠ *Pl. St-Germain-des-Prés, St-Germain-des-Prés* ☎ *01–55–42–81–10* ⊕ *www.eglise-sgp.org* ⊠ *Free* Ⓜ *St-Germain-des-Prés.*

★ Église St-Sulpice

CHURCH | Dubbed the Cathedral of the Rive Gauche, this enormous 17th-century Baroque church has entertained some unlikely christenings—among them those of the Marquis de Sade and Charles Baudelaire—as well as the nuptials of novelist Victor Hugo. More recently, the church played a supporting role in the best-selling novel *The Da Vinci Code,* and it now draws scores of tourists to its obelisk (part of a gnomon, a device used to determine exact time and the equinoxes, built in the 1730s). Other notable features include the exterior's asymmetrical towers and two magnificent Delacroix frescoes, which can be seen in a chapel to the right of the entrance. In the square just in front, view Visconti's magnificent 19th-century fountain—it's especially beautiful at night. ⊠ *Pl. St-Sulpice, 2 rue Palatine, St-Germain-des-Prés* ☎ *01–42–34–59–60* ⊕ *www.paris.catholique. fr/-saint-sulpice* Ⓜ *St-Sulpice, St-Germain-des-Pres, Mabillon.*

Institut de France

GOVERNMENT BUILDING | The Institut de France is one of the country's most revered cultural institutions, and its golden dome is one of the Rive Gauche's most impressive landmarks. The site was once punctuated by the Tour de Nesle (a "tour" is a tower): forming part of Philippe-Auguste's medieval fortification wall, the tower had many royal occupants, including Henry V of England. Then, in 1661, wealthy Cardinal Mazarin willed 2 million French *livres* (pounds) for the construction of a college here. It's also home to the Académie Française, the protectors of the French language. The edicts issued by this esoteric group of 40 *perpétuel* (lifelong) members are happily ignored by the French public. The interior is off-limits to visitors. ⊠ *Pl. de l'Institut, St-Germain-des-Prés* ⊕ *www. institut-de-france.fr* Ⓜ *Pont Neuf.*

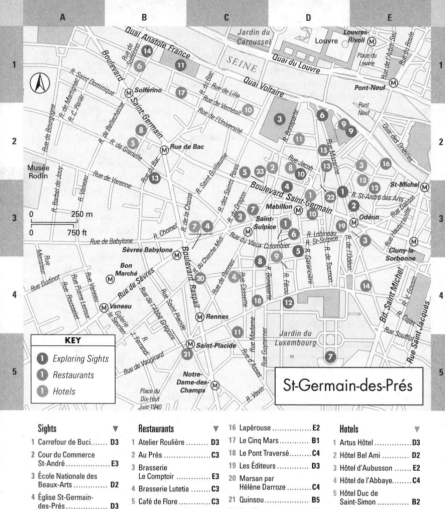

St-Germain-des-Prés

★ **Jardin du Luxembourg**

GARDEN | FAMILY | Everything that is charming, unique, and befuddling about Parisian parks can be found in the Luxembourg Gardens: groomed trees, ironed-and-pressed walkways, sculpted flower beds, and immaculate emerald lawns meant for admiring, not necessarily for lounging. The tree- and bench-lined paths are a marvelous reprieve from the bustle of the neighborhoods it borders: the Quartier Latin, St-Germain-des-Prés, and Montparnasse. Beautifully austere during the winter months, the garden grows intoxicating as spring brings blooming beds of daffodils, tulips, and hyacinths, and the circular pool teems with wooden sailboats nudged along by children. The park's northern boundary is dominated by the Palais du Luxembourg, which houses the Sénat (Senate), one of two chambers that make up the Parliament. The original inspiration for the gardens came from Marie de Medici, who was nostalgic for the Boboli Gardens of her native Florence; she is commemorated by the recently restored Fontaine de Medicis, a favorite spot in summer for contemplative readers.

Les Marionettes du Théâtre du Luxembourg is a timeless attraction, where, on weekend mornings and afternoons, along with Wednesday afternoons, you can catch classic *guignols* (marionette shows) for €7. The wide-eyed kids might be the real attraction—their expressions of utter surprise, despair, and glee have fascinated the likes of Henri Cartier-Bresson and François Truffaut. The park also has a merry-go-round, swings, and pony rides. The bandstand on the eastern side of the park hosts free concerts on summer afternoons.

As you stroll the paths, you might be surprised by a familiar sight: one of the original (miniature) casts of the Statue of Liberty was installed in the gardens in 1906. There are over 100 other statues in the gardens too. Check out the rotating photography exhibits hanging on the perimeter fence near the entrance on Boulevard St-Michel. And if you want to burn off that breakfast *pain au chocolat*, there's a well-maintained trail around the perimeter that is frequented by gentrified joggers. Gendarmes regularly walk the grounds to ensure park rules are enforced; follow guidelines posted on entry gates. ⊠ *Bordered by Bd. St-Michel and Rues de Vaugirard, de Medicis, Guynemer, Auguste-Comte, and d'Assas, St-Germain-des-Prés ⊕ www.senat.fr/ visite/jardin ⊠ Free ⊙ Closed dusk–dawn* Ⓜ *Odéon; RER: B Luxembourg.*

Mairie du 6e

GOVERNMENT BUILDING | The *mairie* (town hall) of the 6e arrondissement often stages impressive free art exhibitions and concerts. Stop by the *accueil* (reception desk) on the ground floor to see what's on or to pick up information on other timely happenings around this artsy district. ⊠ *78 rue Bonaparte, St-Germain-des-Prés* ☎ *01–40–46–75–06 ⊕ www. mairie06.paris.fr ⊠ Free ⊙ Closed Sun.* Ⓜ *St-Sulpice.*

Monnaie de Paris

HISTORY MUSEUM | FAMILY | Louis XVI transferred the royal Mint to this imposing mansion in the late 18th century. It was moved again (to Pessac, near Bordeaux) in 1973; however, weights and measures, medals, and limited-edition coins are still made here, and the site houses a museum devoted to currency. There is an extensive collection of coins and related artifacts, plus workshops where you can watch artisans in action as they mint, mold, sculpt, polish, and engrave using century-old techniques. Public spaces host cultural programs and temporary contemporary art exhibitions. Check the website for Wednesday and Saturday afternoon craft workshops for children. The museum is also home to the three-star Guy Savoy restaurant (reservations required: *reserv@guysavoy.com*) and the simpler café Frappé par Bloom. ✉ *11 quai de Conti, St-Germain-des-Prés* ☎ *01–40–46–56–66* ⊕ *www.monnaiedeparis. fr* ⛟ *€12* 🕑 *Closed Mon.* Ⓜ *Pont Neuf, Odéon.*

Musée Delacroix

ART MUSEUM | The final home of artist Eugène Delacroix (1798–1863) contains only a small collection of his sketches and drawings, but you can see the lovely studio he had built in the large garden out back to work on frescoes he created for St-Sulpice Church, where they remain on display today. The museum also plays host to temporary exhibitions, such as Delacroix's experiments with photography. France's foremost Romantic painter had the good luck to live on Place Furstenberg, one of the smallest, most romantic squares in Paris; seeing it is reason enough to come. ✉ *6 rue Furstenberg, St-Germain-des-Prés* ☎ *01–44–41–86–50* ⊕ *www.musee-dela-croix.fr* ⛟ *€7; €17 with admission to the Louvre within 48 hours* 🕑 *Closed Tues.* Ⓜ *St-Germain-des-Prés.*

★ Musée d'Orsay

ART MUSEUM | **FAMILY** | Opened in 1986, this gorgeously renovated Belle Époque train station displays a world-famous collection of Impressionist and Postimpressionist paintings on three floors. To visit the exhibits in a roughly chronological manner, start on the ground floor, take the escalators to the top, and end on the middle floor. If you came to see the biggest names here, head straight for the top floor and work your way down. English audioguides and free color-coded museum maps (both available just past the ticket booths) will help you plot your route.

Galleries off the main alley feature early works by Manet and Cézanne in addition to pieces by masters such as Delacroix and Ingres. The Pavillon Amont has Courbet's masterpieces *L'Enterrement à Ornans* and *Un Atelier du Peintre.*

Hanging in Salle 14 is Édouard Manet's *Olympia,* a painting that pokes fun at the fashion for all things Greek and Roman (his nubile subject is a 19th-century courtesan, not a classical goddess). Impressionism gets going on the top floor, with iconic works by Degas, Pissarro, Sisley, and Renoir. Don't miss Monet's series on the cathedral at Rouen and, of course, samples of his water lilies. Other selections by these artists are housed in galleries on the ground floor. On the middle floor, you'll find an exquisite collection of sculpture as well as Art Nouveau furniture and decorative objects. There are rare surviving works by Hector Guimard (designer of the swooping green Paris métro entrances), plus Lalique and Tiffany glassware. Postimpressionist galleries include work by Van Gogh and Gauguin, while Neo-Impressionist galleries highlight Seurat and Signac.

■**TIP→ To avoid the lines here, which are among the worst in Paris, book ahead online or buy a Museum Pass, then go directly to Entrance C. Otherwise, go early.**

Thursday evening the museum is open until 9:45 pm and less crowded. Don't miss the views of Sacré-Coeur from the balcony—this is the Paris that inspired the Impressionists. The Musée d'Orsay is closed Monday, unlike the Pompidou and the Louvre, which are closed Tuesday. ✉ *1 rue de la Légion d'Honneur, St-Germain-des-Prés* ☎ *01–40–49–48–14* ⊕ *www.musee-orsay.fr* ⛟ *€16* 🕑 *Closed Mon.* Ⓜ *Solférino; RER: Musée d'Orsay.*

Musée du Luxembourg

ART GALLERY | Located in the northwestern corner of the Luxembourg Gardens, this former orangerie (a greenhouse for orange and other trees) for the Palais du Luxembourg became the city's first public painting gallery in 1884. It now features excellent temporary exhibitions that are well worth a visit. ✉ *19 rue de Vaugirard, St-Germain-des-Prés* ☎ *01–40–13–62–00* ⊕ *www.museeduluxembourg. fr* ⛟ *€13* Ⓜ *Rennes, St-Sulpice.*

Dueling Cafés

Les Deux Magots (⊠ 6 pl. St-Germain-des-Prés) and the neighboring **Café de Flore** (⊠ 172 bd. St-Germain) have been duking it out on this busy corner in St-Germain for more than a century. Les Deux Magots, the snootier of the two, is named for the two Chinese figurines, or magots, inside, and has hosted the likes of Oscar Wilde, Ernest Hemingway, James Joyce, and Richard Wright. Jean-Paul Sartre and Simone du Beauvoir frequented both establishments, though they are claimed by the Flore. The two cafés remain packed, but these days you're more likely to rub shoulders with tourists than with philosophers. Still, if you're in search of that certain *je ne sais quoi* of the Rive Gauche, you can do no better than to station yourself at one of the sidewalk tables—or at a window table on a wintry day—to watch the passing parade. Stick to a croissant and an overpriced coffee, or enjoy an early-evening aperitif; the food is expensive and nothing special.

Musée Maillol

ART MUSEUM | Bronzes by Art Deco sculptor Aristide Maillol (1861–1944), whose voluptuous, stylized nudes adorn the Tuileries Gardens, can be admired at this handsome mansion lovingly restored by his former model and muse, Dina Vierny. The museum is particularly moving because it's Vierny's personal collection. The stunning life-size drawings upstairs are both erotic and tender—age gazing on youth with fondness and longing. Access to the museum is possible only when temporary exhibits are staged. ⊠ 61 rue de Grenelle, St-Germain-des-Prés ☎ 01–42–22–59–58 ⊕ www.musee-maillol.com ☎ €15 Ⓜ Rue du Bac.

Musée National de la Légion d'Honneur (Hôtel de Salm)

HISTORY MUSEUM | A must for military-history buffs, the National Museum of the Legion of Honor is dedicated to French and foreign military leaders. Housed in an elegant mansion just across from the Musée d'Orsay, it features a broad collection of military decorations, themed paintings, and video tributes to various luminaries—including U.S. general Dwight Eisenhower, a Légion member who led the Allied liberation of France in 1944. The palatial complex was completed in 1788 and acquired by the Legion of Honor in 1804. Admission includes an English audioguide. ⊠ 2 rue de la Légion d'Honneur, St-Germain-des-Prés ☎ 01–40–62–84–25 ⊕ www.legiondhonneur.fr ☎ Free ⊙ Closed Mon. and Tues. Ⓜ Solférino; RER: Musée d'Orsay.

🍴 Restaurants

St-Germain is enjoying a revival as a foodie haunt, with Yves Camdeborde's Brasserie Le Comptoir the perfect example of the kind of market-inspired bistro that Parisians (and foreigners) adore. The neighborhood's old leftist roots and new *bobo* (short for bourgeois-bohemian) sensibility blend together nicely in eateries that are down-to-earth yet reflect a discerning touch. You'll find everything from top Paris chefs (Hélène Darroze, Pierre Gagnaire) to neighborhood favorites so good (Semilla, La Boissonnerie) that they draw Parisians from bordering arrondissements—and that's saying a lot.

Atelier Roulière

$$$ | **BISTRO** | If it's steak you're craving, put your faith in Jean-Luc Roulière, a fifth-generation butcher who opened this long, narrow bistro near St-Sulpice church. Partner Franck Pinturier is from the Auvergne region, which is also known for its melt-in-the-mouth meat, so start with a marinated octopus salad or a rich marrow bone before indulging in a generous slab of Limousin or Salers beef, excellent veal kidney, or, for the meat-shy, roast monkfish with fresh green beans. **Known for:** all things meat; superb price-to-quality ratio; friendly service. [$] *Average main: €26* ✉ *24 rue des Canettes, 6e, St-Germain-des-Prés* ☎ *01–43–26–25–70* 🌐 *www.facebook.com/AtelierRouliere* ⏲ *Closed Aug.* [M] *Mabillon.*

Au Prés

$$$$ | **FUSION** | Young, talented, and now famous chef Cyril Lignac has nabbed three small sites all within a few feet of each other to create a trio of intimate signature spaces. The main address is Au Prés, which serves Angus rib-eye steaks and Japanese-inspired delights such as teriyaki lamb chops or miso-carmelized black cod. **Known for:** terrific steaks; excellent cocktails; intimate speakeasy vibe. [$] *Average main: €35* ✉ *27 rue du Dragon, St-Germain-des-Prés* ☎ *01–45–48–29–68* 🌐 *www.restaurantauxpres.com* [M] *St-Germain-des-Pres, Sevres-Babylone.* Restaurant

Brasserie Le Comptoir

$$$ | **BISTRO** | Run by legendary bistro chef Yves Camdeborde, this small, Art Deco restaurant gets booked up early for its satisfying menu of traditional French cuisine. Favorites include classics like rib steak with potato purée and grilled salmon. **Known for:** sidewalk dining; no reservations so expect a long wait; lively atmosphere. [$] *Average main: €30* ✉ *5 carrefour de l'Odéon, 6e, St-Germain-des-Prés* ☎ 🌐 *www.camdeborde.com/en/restaurants/brasserie-le-comptoir* [M] *Odéon.*

Brasserie Lutetia

$$$$ | **BRASSERIE** | This casual-chic eatery within the Hotel Lutetia is the most relaxed of the hotel's restaurants. The extensive menu has a respectable oyster and shellfish selection, plus classics like escargot, steak tartare, and roast chicken as well as fish and vegetarian options. **Known for:** gathering spot for upscale locals; lively atmosphere; excellent shellfish. [$] *Average main: €40* ✉ *45 bd. Raspail, 6e, St-Germain-des-Prés* ☎ *01–49–54–46–00* 🌐 *www.hotellutetia.com/brasserie* [M] *Sevres-Babylone.*

Café de Flore

$$ | **CAFÉ** | Picasso, Chagall, Sartre, and de Beauvoir, attracted by the luxury of a heated café, worked and wrote here in the early 20th century. Today you'll find more tourists than intellectuals, and prices are hardly aimed at struggling artists, but the outdoor terrace is popular with Parisians and great for people-watching. **Known for:** touristy reputation; scenic, central location; simple menu. [$] *Average main: €22* ✉ *172 bd. St-Germain, 6e, St-Germain-des-Prés* ☎ *01–45–48–55–26* 🌐 *www.cafedeflore.fr* [M] *St-Germain-des-Pres.*

Café de la Mairie

$$ | **FRENCH** | Overlooking the St-Sulpice church, this retro café recalls the Paris of yesteryear, before the proliferation of luxury boutiques and trendy eateries. It is a favorite spot for locals for a coffee, drink, or simple meal. **Known for:** excellent location; good food; classic Parisian feel. [$] *Average main: €20* ✉ *8 pl. St-Sulpice, 6e, St-Germain-des-Prés* ☎ *01–43–26–67–82* [M] *St-Sulpice.*

Eggs & Co.

$ | **BISTRO** | **FAMILY** | With a cheerfully bright and tiny, wood-beamed dining room—there's more space in the loftlike upstairs—this spot is devoted to the egg in all its forms. Whether you like yours baked with smoked salmon, whisked into an omelet with truffle shavings, or beaten into fluffy pancakes, there will be something for you on the blackboard menu. **Known for:** cheerful, child-friendly atmosphere; special-order coffee; great breakfast and brunch spot. $ *Average main: €15* ⊠ *11 rue Bernard Palissy, 6e, St-Germain-des-Prés* ☎ *01–45–44–02–52* ⊕ *www.eggsandco.fr* ⊗ *Closed Wed.* Ⓜ *St-Germain-des-Prés.*

★ Gaya

$$$$ | **MODERN FRENCH** | If you can't fathom paying hundreds of euros per person to taste the cooking of Pierre Gagnaire, one of France's foremost chefs, at his eponymous restaurant, but would still like to encounter one of his outstanding culinary experiences, book a table at his Left Bank fish restaurant. At Gaya, Gagnaire uses seafood as a palette for his creative impulses. **Known for:** truly exceptional dining experience; fresh, artfully presented seafood; intimate, cozy atmosphere. $ *Average main: €50* ⊠ *6 rue Saint Simon, 7e, St-Germain-des-Prés* ☎ *01–45–44–73–73* ⊕ *www.pierregagnaire.com/restaurants/gaya* ⊗ *Closed Sun. and Mon.* Ⓜ *Rue du Bac.*

★ Guy Savoy

$$$$ | **MODERN FRENCH** | Within the beautifully restored Monnaie de Paris, you'll find star chef Guy Savoy's hallowed dining room. The market-fresh menu features à la carte classics such as artichoke truffle soup or red mullet fish, but if you want the ultimate gourmet dining experience, splurge on the 13-course, €500 tasting menu (the price does not include wine). **Known for:** one of Paris's most highly rated dining experiences; intimate, art-filled dining rooms; gorgeous setting overlooking the Seine. $ *Average main: €250* ⊠ *11 quai de Conti, 6e, St-Germain-des-Prés* ☎ *01–43–80–40–61* ⊕ *www.guysavoy.com* ⊗ *Closed Sun. and Mon., and 1 wk at Christmas. No lunch Sat.* ⌂ *Jacket required* Ⓜ *St-Germain-des-Pres.*

Huîtrerie Régis

$$$$ | **SEAFOOD** | It's all about oysters at this bright 14-seat restaurant with crisp white tablecloths and pleasant service, popular with the area's chic set. If you find yourself puzzled over the relative merits of *fines de claires* and *spéciales,* you can always go with the €39 prix fixe that includes a glass of Sancerre and a dozen No. 3 (medium) oysters—or ask the knowledgeable waiters for advice. **Known for:** fruit pie for dessert; freshness and variety of oysters; location right in the heart of St-Germain shopping. $ *Average main: €39* ⊠ *3 rue de Montfaucon, 6e, St-Germain-des-Prés* ☎ *01–44–41–10–07* ⊕ *huitrerie-regis.com* ⊗ *Closed early July–early Sept.* Ⓜ *Mabillon.*

Judy

$$ | **VEGETARIAN** | **FAMILY** | Proving that an organic, vegetarian, lactose- and sugar-free menu can, indeed, be delicious, Judy was founded with the conviction that our well-being is directly connected to what we eat and how we live. The cheerful, inviting space comes with a sunny sidewalk terrace where seats are coveted by locals. **Known for:** vegan and gluten-free options; delicous fresh-pressed organic juices; fresh veggie bowls. $ *Average main: €20* ⊠ *18 rue d'Assas, 6e, Paris* ☎ *01–43–25–54–14* ⊕ *www.judy-paris.com* ⊗ *No dinner.*

KGB

$$$ | **MODERN FRENCH** | After extravagant success with his Asian-infused cuisine at Ze Kitchen Galerie, master-chef William Ledeuil extended his artistry to annex KGB (Kitchen Galerie Bis) just down

the street, this time with a more casual focus and gentler prices. Order the "zors-d'oeuvres" plate of two, three, or four minidish appetizers, followed by a main course, which allows diners to really explore the flavors that make Ledeuil's cooking so alluring. **Known for:** casual-chic setting; small plates perfect for sharing; a taste of master-chef William Ledeuil's cooking at less-steep prices. $ *Average main: €32* ⊠ *25 rue des Grands Augustins, 6e, St-Germain-des-Prés* ☎ *01–46–33–00–85* ⊕ *www.zekitchen-galerie.fr* ۞ *Closed Sun., Mon., early Jan., and Aug.* Ⓜ *Odéon, St-Michel.*

★ La Boissonnerie

$$$ | BISTRO | A perennial favorite, this lively, unpretentious bistro is prized by expats and locals for its friendly atmosphere, consistently good food, solid wine list, and English-speaking staff—a quartet sorely lacking in the neighborhood. Dishes like velvety black squid-ink risotto, roasted cod with tender braised fennel, or duck breast with creamy polenta always hit the spot, especially when followed by decadent molten chocolate cake or poached pear with white wine and sorbet. **Known for:** good-value menu that changes daily; excellent selection of natural wines; convivial atmosphere. $ *Average main: €26* ⊠ *69 rue de Seine, 6e, St-Germain-des-Prés* ☎ *01–43–54–34–69* ⊕ *www.fishlaboissonnerie.com* Ⓜ *St-Germain-des-Prés, Odéon.*

La Ferrandaise

$$ | BISTRO | Portraits of cows adorn the stone walls of this no-nonsense bistro near the Luxembourg Gardens, hinting at the kitchen's penchant for meaty cooking (Ferrandaise is a breed of cattle). Still, there's something for every taste on the market-inspired menu, which changes monthly and lists at least one fish, one poultry, and one vegetarian main. **Known for:** à la carte options; daily blackboard menu; excellent prices for

this area. $ *Average main: €24* ⊠ *8 rue de Vaugirard, 6e, St-Germain-des-Prés* ☎ *01–43–26–36–36* ⊕ *www.laferrandaise. com* ۞ *Closed Sun., and 3 wks in Aug. No lunch Mon. and Sat.* Ⓜ *Odéon; RER: Luxembourg.*

La Palette

$$ | FRENCH | The terrace of this corner café, opened in 1902, is a favorite haunt of local gallery owners and Beaux-Arts students. Light fare is available throughout the day. **Known for:** old-world feel; proximity to art galleries; lively outdoor terrace. $ *Average main: €20* ⊠ *43 rue de Seine, 6e, St-Germain-des-Prés* ☎ *01–43–26–68–15* ⊕ *www.lapalette-paris.com* Ⓜ *Mabillon, Odéon.*

Lapérouse

$$$$ | FRENCH | Self-described as a *Maison de Plaisir* (House of Pleasure) since 1766, this 17th-century wood-paneled townhouse flaunts its naughty history with a dark, boudoir-style decor; Émile Zola, George Sand, and Victor Hugo were regulars here, and the restaurant's mirrors still bear diamond scratches from the days when mistresses would use them to double-check the value of their jewels. The classic menu includes caviar and truffle-flavored specials. **Known for:** high romance factor; location right on the Seine; charming historic setting. $ *Average main: €60* ⊠ *51 quai des Grands Augustins, 6e, St-Germain-des-Prés* ☎ *01–43–26–68–04* ⊕ *www. laperouse.com* ۞ *Closed Sun. No lunch* Ⓜ *St-Michel.*

Le Cinq Mars

$$ | BISTRO | This quaint, casual bistro a few blocks from the Musée d'Orsay is open seven days a week and serves its own scrumptious versions of the deeply satisfying French classics like a country terrine, *brandade de morue* (a garlicky, salty cod and mashed potato dish) and *blanquette de veau* (a delicious, creamy

veal dish). Desserts are also traditionally French, and the giant dollop of chocolate mousse is to die for. **Known for:** friendly atmosphere; reasonable prices, especially for wines by the glass; top-notch, market-fresh dishes. [$] *Average main: €24* ✉ *51 rue de Verneuil, 7e, Eiffel Tower* ☎ *01–45–44–69–13.*

Le Pont Traversé

$ | **FRENCH FUSION** | **FAMILY** | What used to be a rare bookshop has been carefully reinvented into a coffee shop and gourmet deli serving casual fare like an egg and salmon breakfast, creative pasta dishes, and mixed veggie salads. The vintage hand-painted storefront and tile floors have been preserved and make the space utterly charming; these are the details that make people fall in love with Paris. **Known for:** tasty lentil salad; fresh-pressed juices; good to-go spot for picnics in the Luxembourg Gardens. [$] *Average main: €16* ✉ *62 rue de Vaugirard, 6e, St-Germain-des-Prés* ☎ *01–45–44–60–15* 🌐 *www.leponttraverse.com* [M] *St-Sulpice.*

Les Editeurs

$$ | **BRASSERIE** | This lively and popular brasserie is open from 8 am to 2 am seven days a week, serving a copious morning breakfast, brunch on weekends, and a full menu of everything from warm goat cheese salad to *magret de canard* from noon until 1 am. In keeping with the area's literary past and its name (Les Editeurs means "the publishers"), the book-lined space hosts monthly discussions with best-selling contemporary authors. **Known for:** delicious food; lively atmosphere; cool literary vibe. [$] *Average main: €24* ✉ *4 carrefour de l'Odeon, St-Germain-des-Prés* ☎ *01–43–26–67–76* 🌐 *www.lesediteurs.fr* [M] *Odeon.* Brasserie

Marsan par Hélène Darroze

$$$$ | **FRENCH** | Michelin-starred chef Hélène Darroze made a name for herself decades ago, and her long-established restaurant in Paris has been revamped and renamed Marsan, a nod to her birthplace in the country's southwest. It's prix-fixe only, at lunch and dinner, whether you opt for the elegant upstairs dining room, the semiprivate table for six with a view of the open kitchen, or the more casual large table on the street-level surrounded by the wine cellar. **Known for:** modern, elegant atmosphere; legendary chef; excellent variety of prix-fixe menus. [$] *Average main: €175* ✉ *4 rue d'Assas, St-Germain-des-Prés* ☎ *01–42–22–00–11* 🌐 *www.marsanhelenedarroze.com* 🕓 *Closed Sun. and Mon.* [M] *Sevres Babylone.* Luxury

★ Quinsou

$$$$ | **FRENCH** | The serious, unpretentious, and mightily creative cuisine here quickly catapulted Quinsou to culinary fame. An emphasis on first-rate growers and suppliers puts vegetables in the limelight, though fish, shellfish, and game also make welcome appearances in the small number of market-fresh dishes that grace the daily menu. **Known for:** good value prix-fixe menus (especially for lunch); warm and welcoming service; highly original seasonal cuisine. [$] *Average main: €86* ✉ *33 rue de l'Abbé Grégoire, St-Germain-des-Prés* ☎ *01–42–22–66–09* 🌐 *www.quinsourestaurant.fr* 🕓 *Closed Sun. and Mon. No lunch Tues.* 👔 *casual* [M] *Rennes, St-Placide.*

Semilla

$$$ | **BISTRO** | The duo behind the popular neighborhood bistro La Boissonerie and the excellent wine shop La Dernière Goutte have poured their significant expertise into this laid-back bistro in the heart of tony St-Germain-des-Prés. Its sophisticated cuisine, superb wines by the bottle or glass, and total lack of

pretension have quickly made Semilla the toast of the town. **Known for:** open kitchen serving plenty of bistro classics; great options for vegetarians; convivial dining room with a lively, appreciative crowd. [$] *Average main: €28* ✉ *54 rue de Seine, 6e, St-Germain-des-Prés* ☎ *01–43–54–34–50* 🌐 *www.semillaparis.com* [M] *Odéon, St-Germain-des-Prés.*

Yen

$$$ | **JAPANESE** | If you're having what is known in French as a *crise de foie* (liver crisis), the result of overindulging in rich food, this chic Japanese noodle house with a summer terrace and a second dining room upstairs is the perfect antidote. The blond-wood walls soothe the senses, and the freshly made soba (buckwheat noodles), served in soup or with a restorative dipping broth, will give you the courage to face another round of caramelized foie gras. **Known for:** light, delicious tempura; artisanal sake and other Japanese spirits; authentic Japanese noodles. [$] *Average main: €29* ✉ *22 rue St-Benoît, 6e, St-Germain-des-Prés* ☎ *01–45–44–11–18* 🌐 *www.yen-paris.fr* 🕒 *Closed Sun. and 2 wks in Aug.* [M] *St-Germain-des-Prés.*

Hotels

True to its Rive Gauche bourgeois-bohemian vibe, lodgings here are an eclectic bunch. You'll find everything from posh L'Hôtel (Oscar Wilde's final dwelling) to other small hotels with loads of character as well as some good budget options.

Artus Hôtel

$$$ | **HOTEL** | **FAMILY** | One of the best things about this comfortable six-story hotel is that it's smack in the middle of Rue de Buci, in the lively St-Germain-des-Prés district. **Pros:** helpful concierge; sauna in basement; excellent location on a market street. **Cons:** Mad Men–esque decor not for everyone; no on-site restaurant; rooms are small. [$] *Rooms from: €230* ✉ *34 rue de Buci, St-Germain-des-Prés* ☎ *01–43–29–07–20* 🌐 *www.artushotel.com* 🛏 *27 rooms* 🍴 *No Meals* [M] *Mabillon.*

Hôtel Bel Ami

$$$$ | **HOTEL** | A short stroll from the famous Café de Flore, the Bel Ami hides its past as an 18th-century textile factory behind its contemporary lobby, low-slung furnishings, computer stations, and flat-screen TVs. **Pros:** central St-Germain-des-Prés location; spacious fitness center and spa; very modern. **Cons:** books up quickly; pretty pricey; some guests report loud noise between rooms. [$] *Rooms from: €450* ✉ *7–11 rue St-Benoît, St-Germain-des-Prés* ☎ *01–42–61–53–53* 🌐 *www.hotelbelami-paris.com* 🛏 *108 rooms* 🍴 *No Meals* [M] *St-Germain-des-Prés.*

★ **Hôtel d'Aubusson**

$$$$ | **HOTEL** | **FAMILY** | The showpiece at this 17th-century town house in the heart of St-Germain-des-Prés is the stunning front lobby, spanned by massive beams and a gigantic stone fireplace reminiscent of French aristocratic homes of yore. **Pros:** central location near shops and major sights; on-site spa and popular jazz club; spacious rooms. **Cons:** can seem touristy; street and bar can be noisy; some rooms lack character. [$] *Rooms from: €504* ✉ *33 rue Dauphine, St-Germain-des-Prés* ☎ *01–43–29–43–43* 🌐 *www.hoteldaubusson.com* 🛏 *51 rooms* 🍴 *No Meals* [M] *Odéon.*

★ **Hôtel de l'Abbaye**

$$$$ | **HOTEL** | In an 18th-century convent, this atmospheric hotel on a tranquil side street near St-Sulpice welcomes guests with a cobblestone ante-courtyard, lovely rooms, and a spacious garden terrace. **Pros:** tranquil setting; historic Paris charm; upscale neighborhood. **Cons:** old-fashioned decor not for everyone; some bathrooms are quite small; rooms differ greatly in size and style. $ *Rooms from: €352* ✉ *10 rue Cassette, St-Germain-des-Prés* ☎ *01–45–44–38–11* ⊕ *www.hotelabbayeparis.com* ➧ *44 rooms* |○| *Free Breakfast* Ⓜ *St-Sulpice.*

Hôtel Duc de Saint-Simon

$$$ | HOTEL | For pure French flavor, including rooms decorated in floral chintz, check out this intimate hotel in a hidden-away location between Boulevard St-Germain and Rue du Bac. Four of the antiques-filled rooms have spacious terraces overlooking the courtyard. **Pros:** upscale neighborhood close to St-Germain-des-Prés; friendly service; historic character. **Cons:** no room service; cramped bathrooms; rooms in the annex are smaller and have no elevator. $ *Rooms from: €295* ✉ *14 rue St-Simon, St-Germain-des-Prés* ☎ *01–44–39–20–20* ⊕ *www.hotelducdesaintsimon.com* ➧ *34 rooms* |○| *No Meals* Ⓜ *Rue du Bac.*

Hôtel Le Bellechasse Saint Germain

$$$ | HOTEL | If you like eclectic modern interior design, this tiny boutique hotel, where the decor was overseen by Christian Lacroix, is a good choice, and it's also around the corner from the Musée d'Orsay. **Pros:** central location near top museums; helpful staff; one-of-a-kind style. **Cons:** open bathrooms lack privacy; street-facing rooms can be noisy; busy, colorful decor not for everyone. $ *Rooms from: €279* ✉ *8 rue de Bellechasse, St-Germain-des-Prés* ☎ *01–45–50–22–31* ⊕ *www.lebellechasse.com* ➧ *33 rooms* |○| *No Meals* Ⓜ *Solferino.*

★ Hôtel Lutetia

$$$$ | HOTEL | The crown jewel of Left Bank hotels, this magnificent Art Nouveau behemoth has a long history of hosting illustrious painters and writers such as Matisse, Picasso, James Joyce, and many others. **Pros:** ultramodern amenities including spa and pool; fascinating history; home to one of the best bars in town. **Cons:** too sleek for some;

very expensive; lacks some of its former old-world charm. $ *Rooms from: €1182* ✉ *45 bd. Raspail, St-Germain-des-Prés* ☎ *01–49–54–46–00* ⊕ *www.hotellutetia.com* ➧ *138 rooms* |○| *No Meals* Ⓜ *Sevres-Babylone.*

Hôtel Millésime

$$$$ | HOTEL | The graceful stone archway of this 17th-century city mansion in St-Germain-des-Prés was the original entrance to the Saint-Germain Abbey, but now leads to a captivating boutique hotel that's the height of Left Bank style. **Pros:** upscale shopping nearby; beautiful chic decor; quiet patio for relaxing. **Cons:** some rooms quite small; elevator stops at the fourth floor; ground-floor rooms can be noisy. $ *Rooms from: €379* ✉ *15 rue Jacob, St-Germain-des-Prés* ☎ *01–44–07–97–97* ⊕ *www.millesimehotel.com* ➧ *20 rooms* |○| *No Meals* Ⓜ *St-Germain-des-Prés.*

★ Hôtel Recamier

$$$ | HOTEL | This discreet boutique hotel in a quiet corner overlooking Eglise St-Sulpice is perfect if you're seeking a romantic and cozy hideaway in the sought-after St-Germain-des-Prés district. **Pros:** peaceful garden courtyard; beautiful views from some rooms; complimentary afternoon tea and aperitifs. **Cons:** no fitness area, spa, or restaurant on-site; room service only until 11 pm; small bathrooms. $ *Rooms from: €330* ✉ *3 bis, pl. St-Sulpice, St-Germain-des-Prés* ☎ *01–43–26–04–89* ⊕ *www.hotelrecamier.com* ➧ *24 rooms* |○| *No Meals* Ⓜ *Mabillon.*

Hôtel Verneuil

$$$ | HOTEL | A short walk from the Museé d'Orsay and the Louvre, this intimate boutique hotel is on a quiet street in the heart of St-Germain. **Pros:** historic charm; tasty breakfast (costs extra); near-it-all location on Left Bank. **Cons:** no gym or spa; no restaurant; stairs to reach all rooms but one. $ *Rooms from: €300*

✉ *8 rue de Verneuil, St-Germain-des-Prés* ☎ *01–42–60–82–14* 🌐 *www.hotel-verneuil-saint-germain.com* 🛏 *26 rooms* 🍴 *No Meals* [M] *Rue de Bac.*

★ L'Hôtel

$$$$ | **HOTEL** | There's something just a bit playful in the air at this sumptuously beautiful boutique hotel, thanks to its history as an 18th-century *pavillon d'amour* (inn for trysts) and as the place where Oscar Wilde died in 1900 (Room 16 to be exact). **Pros:** interesting history; romantic swimming pool in the basement; elegant bar. **Cons:** only a few rooms have a terrace; opulent decor not for everyone; some rooms are on the small side. [$] *Rooms from: €352* ✉ *13 rue des Beaux-Arts, St-Germain-des-Prés* ☎ *01–44–41–99–00* 🌐 *www.l-hotel.com* 🛏 *20 rooms* 🍴 *No Meals* [M] *St-Germain-des-Prés.*

★ Relais Christine

$$$$ | **HOTEL** | You'll find discrete old-world service and tranquility at this venerable hotel set back off a quiet street among its own flagstone courtyard and gardens. **Pros:** beautiful decor and historic character; 24-hour room service; lovely spa. **Cons:** small bathtubs; only four rooms have garden access; some duplex rooms have stairs. [$] *Rooms from: €540* ✉ *3 rue Christine, St-Germain-des-Prés* ☎ *01–40–51–60–80* 🌐 *www.relais-christine.com* 🛏 *46 rooms* 🍴 *No Meals* [M] *Odéon.*

Nightlife

Exclusivity is the theme in the bobo Left Bank, where clubs draw celebs and fashionistas, and stylish cocktail bars cater to an urbane mix of students, gallerists, expats, and urban sophisticates.

BARS

Alcazar

BARS | Sir Terence Conran's makeover of a 17th-century Parisian *jeu de paume* court features a stylish mezzanine-level bar under a greenhouse-glass roof. DJs and "sound designers" spin mixes into the wee hours Wednesday through Saturday. Themes for the night often change weekly. ✉ *62 rue Mazarine, 6e, St-Germain-des-Prés* ☎ *01–53–10–19–99* 🌐 *www.alcazar.fr/en* [M] *Odéon.*

Bar du Marché

BARS | Waiters wearing red overalls and revolutionary *gavroche* hats serve drinks every day of the week at this local institution (they demonstrate particular zeal around happy hour). With bottles of wine at about €25, it draws a quintessential Rive Gauche mix of expats, fashion-house interns, and even some professional rugby players. Sit outside on the terrace and enjoy the prime corner location. ✉ *75 rue de Seine, 6e, St-Germain-des-Prés* ☎ *01–43–26–55–15* [M] *Mabillon, Odéon.*

★ Bar Josephine

PIANO BARS | Inside the magnificent, historic Hôtel Lutetia, Bar Josephine has been restored beyond its former glory. The vast Art Nouveau frescoed ceiling, wrought-iron balcony, and colorful, carefully selected spirits—all lit by abundant natural light coming through the vast window facing Boulevard Raspail—make this beautiful space the place to see and be seen. There is live piano music from 7:30 pm to 9:30 pm most evenings. ✉ *45 bd. Raspail, St-Germain-des-Prés* ☎ *01–49–54–46–00* 🌐 *www.hotellutetia.com* [M] *Sevres-Babylone.*

Chez Georges

BARS | Chez Georges has been serving red wine, pastis, and beer for the past 60-odd years in pretty much the same *caveau* that still packs in devotees today. Older students and locals fill sofas and crowd around tiny, candle-topped tables in the cellar bar before grinding to pulsing world music every night until 2 am. ✉ *11 rue de Canettes, 6e, St-Germain-des-Prés* ☎ *01–43–26–79–15* [M] *Mabillon.*

Compagnie des Vins Surnaturels

THEMED ENTERTAINMENT | After jump-starting the Paris cocktail bar scene, the partners behind the Experimental Cocktail Club and the Ballroom du Beef Club applied the same winning formula to this hybrid wine bar–nightclub. Plush surroundings, an extensive wine list, and a tasty tapas menu draw a crowd of hip young Parisians who can hone their wine-tasting skills on classics in every price range. ⊠ *7 rue Lobineau, 6e, St-Germain-des-Prés* ☎ *09–54–90–20–20* ⊕ *compagniedesvinssurnaturels.com* Ⓜ *Odéon, Mabillon.*

L'Hôtel

BARS | The hushed Baroque bar at L'Hôtel is ideal for a discreet rendezvous. Designed in typically opulent Jacques Garcia style, the hideaway evokes the decadent spirit of onetime resident Oscar Wilde. ⊠ *13 rue des Beaux-Arts, 6e, St-Germain-des-Prés* ☎ *01–44–41–99–00* ⊕ *www.l-hotel.com* Ⓜ *St-Germain-des-Prés.*

JAZZ CLUBS
★ Café Laurent

LIVE MUSIC | Bookcases on the wall and the glossy central piano recall this jazz bar's earlier incarnation as the Café Tabou, when Paris's postwar artists and intellectuals argued and partied the night away to the strains of New York jazz. Nowadays, the plush seating and low lights still draw a crowd of die-hard jazz lovers. ⊠ *33 rue Dauphine, 6e, St-Germain-des-Prés* ☎ *01–43–29–03–33* ⊕ *www.parisjazzclub.net/en/12/club/ cafe-laurent* Ⓜ *St-Germain-des-Prés, Mabillon, Pont Neuf.*

🛍 Shopping

Ever since Yves Saint Laurent arrived in the 1960s, the Rive Gauche has been synonymous with iconoclastic style. Trendsetting stores line a jumble of streets in the 6e arrondissement, and

exciting boutiques await between Place de l'Odéon and Église St-Sulpice. In the 7e arrondissement, don't miss Rue du Four, Rue Bonaparte, Rue du Bac, and that jewel of a department store, Le Bon Marché. St-Germain-des-Prés is also known for its multitude of signature chocolate shops.

ANTIQUES AND COLLECTIBLES
★ Carré Rive Gauche

ANTIQUES & COLLECTIBLES | Head to the streets between Rue du Bac, Rue de l'Université, Rue de Lille, and Rue des Saints-Pères to unearth museum-quality pieces. The more than 100 shops in this association of galleries and antiques dealers are marked with a small, blue square banner on their storefronts. ⊠ *Between St-Germain-des-Prés and Musée d'Orsay, 7e, St-Germain-des-Prés* ⊕ *www.carrerivegauche.com* Ⓜ *St-Germain-des-Prés, Rue du Bac.*

★ Deyrolle

ANTIQUES & COLLECTIBLES | FAMILY | This wonderful 19th-century taxidermist has long been a stop for curiosity seekers. A 2008 fire destroyed what was left of the original shop, but it has been lavishly restored and remains a cabinet of curiosities par excellence. Create your own box of butterflies or metallic beetles from scores of bug-filled drawers or just enjoy the menagerie that includes stuffed zebras, monkeys, lions, bears, and more. Also in stock: collectible shells, corals, and crustaceans, plus a generous library of books and posters that once graced every French schoolroom. There is a line of decorative wallpaper murals, too. ⊠ *46 rue du Bac, 7e, St-Germain-des-Prés* ☎ *01–42–22–30–07* ⊕ *www.deyrolle.com* Ⓜ *Rue du Bac.*

BEAUTY
★ Buly 1803

COSMETICS | Although it only opened in 2014, you can be forgiven for thinking Buly 1803 is an antique apothecary—those jars overflowing with exotic herbs, powders, and elixirs are used to recreate 200-year-old recipes for the all-natural skin-care line. Delicious-smelling hand, body, and face products come in scents like rose and Scottish moss. All the products are organic, beautifully packaged, and impossibly chic. ⊠ 6 rue Bonaparte and in Le Bon Marché, 6e, St-Germain-des-Prés ☎ 01–43–29–02–50 ⊕ www.buly1803.com Ⓜ St-Germain-des-Prés.

Editions de Parfums Frédéric Malle

PERFUME | This perfumery is based on a simple concept: take the most famous noses in France and have them edit singular perfumes. The result? Exceptional, highly concentrated fragrances. Le Parfum de Thérèse, for example, was created by famous Dior nose Edmond Roudnitska exclusively for his wife who entrusted the formula to Frédéric Malle after her husband's death. Other iconic scents include rose-infused Portrait of a Lady and ultrachic rose, saffron, and frankincense-infused The Night by Dominique Ropion. Monsieur Malle has devised high-tech ways to keep each smelling session here unadulterated: at the Rue de Grenelle store, individual scents are released in glass columns— just stick your head in and sniff. ⊠ 37 rue de Grenelle, 7e, St-Germain-des-Prés ☎ 01–42–22–76–40 ⊕ www.frederic-malle.com Ⓜ Rue du Bac.

CHILDREN'S CLOTHING

★ Bonpoint

CHILDREN'S CLOTHING | Stroll through the ground floor of this high-end children's clothing store, inside a 17th-century mansion, and you'll feel like royalty on a private visit to a friend's estate, which happens to have beautiful clothing for babies and children on display. The rooms wrap around a large, private garden and helpful salespeople will assist in finding the perfect gift. ⊠ 6 rue de Tournon, 6e,

St-Germain-des-Prés ☎ 01–40–51–98–02 ⊕ www.bonpoint.com Ⓜ Mabillon.

Marie Puce

CHILDREN'S CLOTHING | FAMILY | The simplicity and style of these handmade children's clothes has helped Marie Puce acquire a loyal clientele since it was created in 2003. Made to withstand everyday wear and tear, the cotton pants and Liberty of London dresses can be passed down from one sibling to another. ⊠ 60 rue du Cherche Midi, St-Germain-des-Prés ☎ 01–45–48–30–90 ⊕ www.mariepuce.com Ⓜ St-Placide or Sevres-Babylone.

Pom d'Api

CHILDREN'S CLOTHING | FAMILY | Pom d'Api lines up footwear for babies and young children in quality leathers and vivid colors. Expect well-made, eye-catching fashion—bright fuchsia sneakers and leopard suede boots, as well as classic Mary Janes in shades of silver, pink, and gold. There are also utility boots, sandals, and sturdy rain gear. ⊠ 28 rue du Four, 6e, St-Germain-des-Prés ☎ 01–45–48–39–31 ⊕ www.pomdapi.fr Ⓜ St-Germain-des-Prés.

CLOTHING

agnès b.

WOMEN'S CLOTHING | A loyal clientele has been devoted to agnès b. since the clothing brand was created in 1975. The simple-yet-innovative modern designs are paired with lasting quality in pieces like the signature "snap" cardigan available in a variety of colors, fitted T-shirts, and leather bags and jackets that last for decades. Her men's clothing collection is next door at number 10. ⊠ 6 rue du Vieux Colombier, 6e, St-Germain-des-Prés ⊕ www.agnesb.fr Ⓜ St-Sulpice.

A.P.C.

MIXED CLOTHING | The A.P.C. brand may be antiflash and minimal, but a knowing eye can always pick out its jeans in a crowd. The clothes here are rigorously well made and worth the investment in lasting style. Prime wardrobe pieces include dark indigo and black denim, zip-up cardigans, peacoats, and streamlined ankle boots. Their surplus store at 40 rue Jacob has a sampling of last year's accessories, shoes, and clothing at reduced prices. ⊠ *38 rue Madame, 6e, St-Germain-des-Prés* ☎ *01–42–22–12–77* ⊕ *www.apc.fr* Ⓜ *St-Sulpice.*

Carven

WOMEN'S CLOTHING | Daringly original designs that are sexy yet wearable account for Carven's steady rise into the fashion stratosphere. Artistic director Guillame Henry was tapped in 2014 to revive the label; however, in 2017, Serge Ruffieux from Dior began bringing his own ingenue-meets-grandma take to the brand's meticulous tailoring and sleek silhouettes. ⊠ *13 rue de Grenelle, St-Germain-des-Prés* ☎ *01–42–22–24–93* ⊕ *www.carven.com* Ⓜ *St-Sulpice, Sevres-Babylone.*

Karl Lagerfeld

MIXED CLOTHING | The titular late designer's own chiseled profile is still a key design element in this St-Germain flagship store. Inside, look for very chic ready-to-wear collections for men and women, playing to the fashion-conscious twenty- and thirtysomethings who want to strut their stuff (think body-slimming jackets, jeans, and geometric-print T-shirts, mostly in black and white with a splash of color). The store also stocks signature caps, keychains, eyewear, accessories, bags, shoes, fragrances, and—you guessed it—Lagerfeld's signature fingerless leather gloves. ⊠ *194 bd. St-Germain, 7e, St-Germain-des-Prés* ☎ *01–42–22–74–99* ⊕ *www.karl.com* Ⓜ *Rue du Bac.*

L'Habit Français

MIXED CLOTHING | This small, ambitious clothing boutique specializes in all things made in France. The owner can tell you the story of each creator or manufacturer of every item in her shop. If your size or preferred color are not on hand, she can most likely have the local artisan who made it whip one up for you on short notice. Check out the beautifully made cotton blouses, hand-knit sweaters, and leather bags. ⊠ *99 rue de Seine* ☎ *01–77–32–68–98* ⊕ *lhabitfrancais.com* Ⓜ *Odeon.* Gift shop

Saint James

MIXED CLOTHING | Created near the chilly coast of Normandy, this company of "master spinners" has been making quality fishermen's clothes since 1889. Once family owned, it was bought out by a devoted team of skilled employees, and the majority of their items are still made in France. The wool nautical sweaters and sailor caps are built for warmth and wear, and the striped, long-sleeve Breton T-shirts are classic French. ⊠ *66 rue de Rennes, 6e, St-Germain-des-Prés* ⊕ *fr. saint-james.com* Ⓜ *St-Sulpice.*

Tara Jarmon

WOMEN'S CLOTHING | The bases are all covered here, when it comes to that coveted French élan: sleek designs, excellent quality, luxe fabrics, and prices well within the stratosphere. With styles that vie with the high-profile designers, and accessories to match, this label is fast becoming the chic Parisian's wardrobe essential. Jarmon has two boutiques in the 6th arrondissement; the other is at 75 rue des Saints-Pères. ⊠ *18 rue du Four, 6e, St-Germain-des-Prés* ☎ *01–46–33–26–60* ⊕ *www.tarajarmon. com* Ⓜ *Mabillon, St-Germain-des-Prés.*

DEPARTMENT STORES

★ Le Bon Marché

DEPARTMENT STORE | Founded in 1852, Le Bon Marché has emerged as the city's chicest department store. The fact that it isn't nearly as crowded as the department stores on the Right Bank is an added bonus. On the ground floor of the main building, look for makeup, perfume, and accessories; this is where celebs duck in for essentials while everyone pretends not to notice. On the floor above, you can do laps through chic labels (Givenchy, Stella McCartney) and überhip (Margiela, Dries Van Noten) ones. The next floor up is home to streetwise designers and edgy secondary lines. Under the restored glass ceiling, the gleaming Le Soulier shoe department assembles the crème de la crème of European shoes. Meanwhile, the menswear department has consumed the entire basement level and has even added a barbershop. Across the street, the home-goods store in the sister building is a great place to stock up on French linens, porcelain, cookware, and luggage, or just relax over tea or a gourmet lunch in the soaring atrium restaurant. Before leaving, be sure to visit the spectacular La Grande Épicerie and *cave* (wine shop) on the ground floor of the main building; it's the haute couture of grocery stores. Artisanal jams, olive oils, and much more make great gifts, and the luscious pastries, fruit, and huge selection of prepared foods beg to be chosen for a meal or snack. ⊠ *24 rue de Sèvres, 7e, St-Germain-des-Prés* ☏ *01–44– 39–80–00* ⊕ *www.lebonmarche.com* Ⓜ *Sèvres-Babylone.*

FOOD AND TREATS

Debauve & Gallais

CHOCOLATE | The two former chemists who founded Debauve & Gallais in 1800 became the royal chocolate purveyors and were famed for their "health chocolates," made with almond milk. Test the benefits yourself with ganache, truffles, or *pistoles* (flavored dark-chocolate disks). ⊠ *30 rue des Sts-Pères, 7e, St-Germain-des-Prés* ☏ *01–45–48– 54–67* ⊕ *www.debauve-et-gallais.fr* Ⓜ *St-Germain-des-Prés.*

Henri Le Roux

CHOCOLATE | The originator of the renowned *caramel au beurre salé*, Henri Le Roux pairs a Breton pedigree with Japanese flair. Brilliant confections result. ⊠ *1 rue de Bourbon le Château, 6e, St-Germain-des-Prés* ☏ *01–82– 28–49–80* ⊕ *www.chocolatleroux.com* Ⓜ *St-Germain-des-Prés.*

Jean-Charles Rochoux

CHOCOLATE | Rochoux makes three superb collections of artisanal chocolates: the Ephemeral, with fresh fruit; Made-to-Measure, in the form of animals and figurines; and the Permanent Collection of everyday favorites. ⊠ *16 rue d'Assas, 6e, St-Germain-des-Prés* ☏ *01–42–84–29–45* ⊕ *jcrochoux.com* Ⓜ *Rennes.*

La Maison du Chocolat

CHOCOLATE | A bit less artisanal than most of the others, the silky ganaches still have subtlety and flavor. See the website for a full list of Paris locations. ⊠ *19 rue de Sèvres, 6e, St-Germain-des-Prés* ☏ *01–45–44–20–40* ⊕ *www.lamaisonduchocolat.fr* Ⓜ *Sèvres-Babylone.*

Michalak

FOOD | After years of working with the best and brightest in the Paris pastry world, superstar Christophe Michalakis is now opening boutiques, writing books, and promoting his skills. His signature pastries are smooth, eye-popping ovals of glazed perfection, whether the bright orange mango mousse with crunchy textures or the green pistachio coconut version. If you're less adventurous, the small vanilla cake is rich and flavorful. ⊠ *8 rue du Vieux Colombier, St-Germain-des-Prés* ☏ *01–45–49–44–90* ⊕ *www.christophe-michalak.com/magasins* Ⓜ *St-Sulpice.*

Patrick Roger

CHOCOLATE | Paris's bad-boy chocolatier likes to shock with provocative shapes and wicked humor, but it all tastes sinfully good. He designs every detail in his shops, including the presentation tables and futuristic decor. The Boulevard St-Germain shop, his very first, is one of four in the neighborhood and 10 citywide. The other three nearby are at 19 rue de

12

St-Germain-des-Prés

Sevres, 91 rue de Rennes, and 2–4 pl. St. Sulpice. ✉ *108 bd. St-Germain, 6e, St-Germain-des-Prés* ☎ *01–43–29–38–42* ⊕ *www.patrickroger.com* Ⓜ *Odéon.*

★ Pierre Hermé

CHOCOLATE | Pierre Hermé might just be Paris's most renowned pâtissier, and this shop has the peerless cakes and macarons, and many chocolate delights (classic varieties, like the dark-chocolate and orange-rind batons, are perennial favorites). It sells a wonderful, zesty lemon pound cake preboxed and dense enough to survive the trip home—if you can resist eating it. There are several small cafés in St-Germain-des-Prés (and around the city) that feature his creations, one just across from this original boutique, at 61 rue Bonaparte. Other locations include 126 boulevard St-Germain, 43 rue St-Placide, and 53–57 rue de Grenelle, in the quiet, contemporary Beaupassage. ✉ *72 rue Bonaparte, 6e, St-Germain-des-Prés* ☎ *01–43–54–47–77* ⊕ *www.pierreherme.com* Ⓜ *Odéon.*

Pierre Marcolini

CHOCOLATE | Sourcing his star ingredient from independent farmers, Pierre Marcolini proves it's all in the bean. His specialty *saveurs du monde* ("flavors of the world") collection of Belgian chocolates are each made with a single cacao from a single location, such as Madagascar or Ecuador—thus, each has a distinct flavor. ✉ *89 rue de Seine, 6e, St-Germain-des-Prés* ☎ *01–44–07–39–07* ⊕ *www.marcolini.com* Ⓜ *Mabillon.*

Richart

CHOCOLATE | How do I love thee? The ways are too numerous to count. As the name implies, each tiny square of Richart chocolate is a colorful work of art that dazzles the eye and elevates the palate. ✉ *27 rue Bonaparte, 6e, St-Germain-des-Prés* ☎ *01–46–33–24–94* ⊕ *www.chocolats-richart.com* Ⓜ *St-Germain-des-Prés.*

Sadaharu Aoki

OTHER FOOD & DRINK | The gorgeous, delicate pastry creations made by Japanese-born Sadaharu Aoki are a delightful mix of traditional French with his signature Asian flavor and design touches. Look for green tea, black sesame, and yuzu versions of updated classics like éclairs, mille-feuille, and other elegant baked goods, as well as artfully presented colorful batons of chocolate. ✉ *35 rue de Vaugirard, 6e, St-Germain-des-Prés* ☎ *01-45-44-48–90* ⊕ *www.sadaharuaoki. com/boutique/paris-en.html* Ⓜ *St-Sulpice.*

HOME DECOR

Alexandre Biaggi

FURNITURE | Alexandre Biaggi specializes in lamps, tables, and chairs from the 1920s and 1930s and also commissions pieces from such talented designers as Patrick Naggar and Hervé van der Straeten. ✉ *14 rue de Seine, 6e, St-Germain-des-Prés* ☎ *01–44–07–34–73* ⊕ *www.alexandrebiaggi.com* Ⓜ *St-Germain-des-Prés.*

★ Cire Trudon

HOUSEWARES | The candles made by Cire Trudon have illuminated the great palaces and churches of Paris since the 1600s. Nowadays their products provide the atmosphere for tony restaurants and exclusive soirées. The all-vegetal, atmospherically scented wares come in elegant black glass, pillars of all sizes, or busts of clients past—like Napoléon and Marie-Antoinette. ✉ *78 rue de Seine, 6e, St-Germain-des-Prés* ☎ *01-43-26-46-50* ⊕ *www.ciretrudon.com* Ⓜ *Odéon.*

Conran Shop

FURNITURE | The brainchild of British entrepreneur Terence Conran, this shop carries expensive contemporary furniture, beautiful bed linens, and items for every other room in the house—all marked by a balance of utility and not-too-sober style. Conran makes the most ordinary household items fun. ✉ *117* rue du Bac, 7e, St-Germain-des-Prés 🕿 01–42–84–10–01 ⊕ www.conranshop. fr Ⓜ Sèvres-Babylone.

De Gournay

HOUSEWARES | Although de Gournay has been decorating homes with hand-painted wallpaper for a mere 30 years (compare that to Zuber's 200 years), the results are timeless and enviable. If you've always dreamed of transforming your living room into a colorful jungle, your sunroom into a lemon orchard, or your bathroom into a gold-leaf boudoir, de Gournay will help you create your desired universe. ⊠ 15 rue des Saint-Pères, 6e, St-Germain-des-Prés 🕿 01–40–20–08–97 ⊕ www.degournay.com Ⓜ St-Germain-des-Pres.

★ Diptyque

HOUSEWARES | A Paris mainstay since 1961, Diptyque's flagship shop is famous for its candles, eaux de toilette, and home fragrances in a huge range of sophisticated scents like myrrh, fig tree, wisteria, and quince. They're delightful but not cheap; the candles, for instance, cost nearly $1 per hour of burn time. ⊠ 34 bd. St-Germain, 6e, St-Germain-des-Prés 🕿 01–43–26–77–44 ⊕ www. diptyqueparis.fr Ⓜ Maubert–Mutualité.

★ Librarie Elbé

ANTIQUES & COLLECTIBLES | Elbé has been selling rare, original serigraphs, lithographs, and vintage posters since 1976, specializing in artists such as Roger Broders and Keith Haring. Air France's graphic posters featuring exotic destinations, a Brigitte Bardot movie classic, or Sean Connery in the French version of one of his roles as 007 are just a few examples of the large, frameable *affiches* (posters) sold here. ⊠ 213 bis, bd. St Germain, 7e, St-Germain-des-Prés 🕿 01–45–48–77–97 ⊕ www.elbe.paris/en Ⓜ Rue du Bac.

Marin Montagut

OTHER SPECIALTY STORE | Artist and illustrator Marin Montagut's whimsical boutique near the Luxembourg Gardens is filled with hand-painted porcelain, glasses, paper boxes, globes, notebooks, and just about anything that is decorative and useful. His tea towels and silk scarves, which feature original illustrations in cheerful pastel colors of the gardens' famous green chairs, or a map of the gardens themselves are perfect souvenirs for lovers of the Left Bank. ⊠ 48 rue Madame, St-Germain-des-Prés 🕿 09–81–22–53–44 ⊕ en.marinmontagut. com Ⓜ Rennes. Gift shop

R&Y Augousti

FURNITURE | Paris-based couple Ria and Yiouri Augousti have been a designing duo for over three decades. Their signature revival of the artisanal technique of shagreen also includes other exotic materials such as parchment, snakeskin, nacre, and metal. Each piece, whether a desk, table, or chair, is a one-of-a-kind work of art. Though they travel the world for international commissions their flagship store in Paris is still home. ⊠ 103 rue du Bac, St-Germain-des-Prés 🕿 01–42–22–22–21 ⊕ www.augousti. com Ⓜ Rue du Bac. Home decor

Zuber

ANTIQUES & COLLECTIBLES | Have you always wanted to imitate the grand homes of Paris? Here's your chance. Zuber has operated nonstop for more than two centuries as the world's oldest producer of prestige hand-printed wallpapers, renowned for their magnificent panoramic scenes. Warning: with only one scene produced per year, the wait can be nearly a decade long. Opulent Restoration-era wallpapers (including metallics, silks, velvets, and pressed leather) make modern statements and can be purchased in 32-foot rolls for slightly less than a king's ransom. ⊠ 36 *rue Bonaparte, 6e, St-Germain-des-Prés* ☎ *01–42–77–95–91* ⊕ *www.zuber.fr* Ⓜ *St-Germain-des-Prés.*

JEWELRY AND ACCESSORIES

Adelline

JEWELRY & WATCHES | Entering this jewelry shop is like landing in Ali Baba's cave: each piece is more gorgeous than the last, and the bounty of beautiful shapes and styles satisfies a large range of tastes (and budgets). Cabochon rings can be pebble-size or rocklike, jeweled cuffs sport diamonds in a web of gold, and simple cord-and-gem bracelets cannot fail to make a statement. ✉ *54 rue Jacob, 6e, St-Germain-des-Prés* ☎ *01–47–03–07–18* ⊕ *www.adelline.com* Ⓜ *St-Germain-des-Prés.*

Alexandra Sojfer

JEWELRY & WATCHES | The proprietress of this legendary little store is the queen of walking sticks (the late president François Mitterrand bought his here). Alexandra Sojfer also carries an amazing range of umbrellas, parasols, small leather goods, and other accessories for men and women. ✉ *218 bd. St-Germain, 7e, St-Germain-des-Prés* ☎ *01–42–22–17–02* ⊕ *www.alexandrasojfer.com* Ⓜ *Rue du Bac.*

Arthus-Bertrand

JEWELRY & WATCHES | Dating back to 1803, Arthus-Bertrand has glass showcases full of designer jewelry and many wonderful objects to celebrate all kinds of occasions. ✉ *54 rue Bonaparte, 6e, St-Germain-des-Prés* ☎ *01–49–54–72–10* ⊕ *www.arthus-bertrand.com* Ⓜ *St-Germain-des-Prés.*

★ Hermès

OTHER ACCESSORIES | Ever the statement maker, luxury brand Hermès has reopened its Left Bank store in an Art Deco former swimming pool. Their signature silk scarves, jewelry, home furnishings, and fragrances are arrayed around the tastefully decorated cavernous space

with hand-painted walls by Matthieu Cossé. There is also a small café. ✉ *17 rue de Sevres, 6e, St-Germain-des-Prés* ⊕ *www.hermes.com* Ⓜ *Sevres Babylone.*

LINGERIE

★ Sabbia Rosa

LINGERIE | One could easily walk straight past this discreet, boudoir-like boutique. It is, however, one of the world's finest lingerie stores and the place where actresses Catherine Deneuve and Isabelle Adjani (among many others) buy superb French underthings. ✉ *73 rue des Sts-Pères, 6e, St-Germain-des-Prés* ☎ *01–45–48–88–37* Ⓜ *St-Germain-des-Prés.*

MARKETS

Boulevard Raspail

MARKET | The city's major *marché biologique,* or organic market, is on Boulevard Raspail between Rue du Cherche-Midi and Rue de Rennes. Bursting with produce, fish, and eco-friendly products, it's open every Sunday from 9 to 3. (A nonorganic market operates at this location on Tuesday and Friday, from 7 to 2:30.) ✉ *Allée Sonia Rykiel, 6e, St-Germain-des-Prés* Ⓜ *Rennes.*

Le Marché Saint-Germain

MARKET | With a history that dates back to the 16th century, the Marché Saint-Germain has undergone many transformations in its lifetime. The current structure of stone arcades, which wrap around an entire city block, was built in 1817. The ground floor of this elegant complex is now home to an Apple store, a Uniqlo, a Nespresso shop, and a gourmet food court, including the *marché couvert* Saint-Germain, an indoor space for epicureans. This market is home to greengrocers, fishmongers, cheesemongers, butchers, bakers, florists, and a number of international food stalls and is open every day except Monday. ✉ *4–6 rue Lobineau, 6e, St-Germain-des-Prés* ⊕ *www.marchesaintgermain.com* Ⓜ *Mabillon.*

Rue de Buci

MARKET | Vendors at this market, which is really on the Rue de Seine, just at the corner of Rue de Buci, often tempt you with tastes of their wares, from slices of sausage and cheese to slivers of peaches and mandarins. Paul bakery on the corner is a great place to grab a snack. ✉ *Rue de Seine at Rue de Buci, 6e, St-Germain-des-Prés* Ⓜ *Odéon.*

SHOES, HANDBAGS, AND LEATHER GOODS

★ Avril Gau

SHOES | After designing a dozen collections for Chanel, Gau struck out on her own, opening this neo-Baroque boutique on the charming Rue des Quatre Vents. She takes her inspiration from glamorous French movie icons, dreaming up styles that are elegant and sexy without being trashy. Sleek pumps, wedge booties, ballerina flats, and riding boots (all in the finest quality calf, reptile, and lambskin) are as classy as they come. Bags share the spotlight, with updated riffs on the classics. ✉ *17 rue des Quatre Vents, 6e, St-Germain-des-Prés* ☎ *01–43–29–49–04* ⊕ *www.avrilgau.com* Ⓜ *Odéon.*

Bensimon Concept Store

SHOES | The Bensimon brothers started their brand over 40 years ago with their now iconic "tennis Bensimon," flat canvas sneakers with rubber soles and tips, which they bought from an army surplus store and dyed in a variety of colors. The shoes were an instant hit, whose popularity has continued to endure, and the brand has since expanded into prêt-à-porter, accessories, and home decor. The simple, classic designs favor cheerful, solid colors, which are wearable day after day and year after year. ✉ *54 rue de Seine, St-Germain-des-Prés* ☎ *01–43–54–64–47* ⊕ *www.bensimon. com* Ⓜ *St-Germain-des-Prés.*

Carel

SHOES | This company made a name for itself in the 1950s with its youthful designs that were made to match with the modern fashions of iconic designer Christian Dior. The playful, low-heeled, and comfortable shoes and boots have remained popular thanks to their classic designs. ✉ *12 rue du Four, 6e, St-Germain-des-Prés* ☎ *01–43–54–11–69* ⊕ *www.carel.fr* Ⓜ *Mabillon.*

Jamin Puech

HANDBAGS | Nothing's plain Jane at Jamin Puech, which thinks of its bags not just as a necessity, but as jewelry. Beaded purses swing from thin link chains; fringes flutter from dark embossed-leather totes; and small evening clutches are covered with shells, oversize sequins, or hand-dyed crochet. The collections fluctuate with the seasons but never fail to be whimsical and imaginative. ✉ *43 rue Madame, 6e, St-Germain-des-Prés* ☎ *01–45–48–14–85* ⊕ *www.jamin-puech. com* Ⓜ *St-Sulpice.*

Jérôme Dreyfuss

HANDBAGS | The newest star in the city's handbag universe has captivated *le tout Paris* with his artsy take on hobo, Birkin, and messenger bags. Unique styles (like the twee-mini) are impossibly cute, though you may need to take out a second mortgage to tote around a luxe matte-python model. A line of gorgeous, high-heeled footwear is equally chic. ✉ *4 rue Jacob, 6e, St-Germain-des-Prés* ☎ *01–43–54–70–93* ⊕ *www.jerome-drey-fuss.com* Ⓜ *St-Germain-des-Prés.*

Repetto

SHOES | Rose Repetto, mother of Roland Petit, started making ballet slippers for her dancer-choreographer son in the 1940s. She soon became the dance-slipper maker of choice for the choreographers and dancers of le tout Paris. Along the way, she created Brigitte Bardot's signature ballerina shoes and Zizi

Jeanmarie's jazz shoes, which are still popular today and sold in a rainbow of colors. For €275 and up, you can design your own ballerina shoes. Repetto has branched out to making boots, leather handbags, and clothes, but still specializes in ready-to-dance and custom-made ballet and pointe footware. ✉ *51 rue du Four, St-Germain-des-Prés* ☎ *01–45–44–98–65* ⊕ *www.repetto.fr* Ⓜ *St-Sulpice.*

WINE

★ La Dernière Goutte

WINE/SPIRITS | This inviting *cave* (literally wine store or wine cellar) focuses on wines by small French producers. Each is handpicked by the owner, along with a choice selection of estate Champagnes, Armagnac, and the classic Vieille Prune (plum brandy). The friendly and knowledgable English-speaking staff makes browsing a pleasure. Check the schedule for classes and tastings. ✉ *6 rue de Bourbon le Château, 6e, St-Germain-des-Prés* ☎ *01–43–29–11–62* ⊕ *ldgparis.com* Ⓜ *Odéon.*

La Maison du Whisky and Fine Spirits

WINE/SPIRITS | LMDW has more than 1,000 items to entice collectors of whiskey, as well as all kinds of fine spirits from around the world, including 400 types of rum. ✉ *6 carrefour de l'Odeon, St-Germain-des-Prés* ☎ *01–46–34–70–20* ⊕ *www.whisky.fr* Ⓜ *Odeon.*

Ryst-Dupeyron

WINE/SPIRITS | This shop specializes in fine wines and liquors, with port, Calvados, and Armagnacs that date from 1878. Looking for a great gift idea? Find a bottle from the year of a friend's birth and have it labeled with their name. Personalized bottles can be ordered and delivered on the same day. ✉ *79 rue du Bac, 7e, St-Germain-des-Prés* ☎ *01–45–48–80–93* ⊕ *www.maisonrystdupeyron.com* Ⓜ *Rue du Bac.*

MONTPARNASSE

Updated by
Virginia Power Jestin

⦿ Sights	🍴 Restaurants	🛏 Hotels	💼 Shopping	🍸 Nightlife
★★★☆☆	★★★☆☆	★★★☆☆	★★★☆☆	★★☆☆☆

NEIGHBORHOOD SNAPSHOT

GETTING HERE

Montparnasse includes parts of the 6e, 14e, and 15e arrondissements. Take Line 4, 6, 12, or 13 to Montparnasse–Bienvenue for the Tour Montparnasse or take Line 4 to Vavin and you'll be right at the neighborhood's famous cafés. Take Line 4 or 6 to the Raspail métro stop for the Cimetière du Montparnasse. To visit the Catacombs, take the 4 or 6 line to Denfert–Rochereau. Other nearby métro stops include the Edgar Quinet stop on the 6 line and the Gaîté stop on the 13 line.

MAKING THE MOST OF YOUR TIME

Boulevard du Montparnasse is famous for its spacious and historic bars and restaurants, but for cultural sights, don't miss the charming Musée Zadkine, the Fondation Cartier pour l'Art Contemporaine, or the spooky Catacombs (all closed Monday). The Cimetière du Montparnasse is open daily. Currently closed for renovations, the observation deck on top of the Tour Montparnasse has the best views of Paris on a clear day. When it reopens in 2024, you'll be rewarded with a vista unmatched in all of Paris.

PAUSE HERE

Approach the Luxembourg Gardens from the rue Vavin, which intersects boulevard Montparnasse, or from the rue Michelet, which is just steps from the Musée Zadkine. On the corner of rue Michelet and avenue de l'Observatoire is a surprising brick edifice built in the 1920s for the Université de Paris art history department. Just past this, pause on the grass or one of the many benches in the Jardin des Grands Explorateurs on avenue de l'Observatoire. The southern end of the garden features a 19th-century bronze statue of four women, each representing a different continent, holding up a globe. The big white dome further south in the distance is the Paris Observatory (rarely open to the public). To the north is Luxembourg Gardens, which one can enter on the rue Auguste Comte.

TOP REASONS TO GO

■ **Catacombs.** History buffs, lovers of the macabre, and the just plain curious can make an unforgettable descent into Paris's underground bastion of bones. Claustrophobic folks, however, should be wary.

■ **Fondation Cartier Pour L'art Contemporain.** Connoisseurs of cutting-edge art will appreciate what's on view here. The building itself was designed by Jean Nouvel, the avant-garde darling of Paris architecture.

■ **Musee Zadkine.** Once sculptor Ossip Zadkine's home and studio, this little-known gem of a museum is just steps from the Luxembourg Gardens.

■ **Cimetière de Montparnasse.** Take a break from the bustle of the city in this peaceful, green enclave, where you can admire the historic tombstones of some of France's most notable artists, writers, politicians, and scholars. Some of the small monuments are works of art themselves.

Once a warren of artists' studios and swinging cafés, part of Montparnasse was leveled in the 1960s to make way for a train station and the Tour Montparnasse, Paris's only—and much maligned—skyscraper. Nevertheless, the neighborhood has maintained its reputation as a hub for lively cafés and the kind of real-life vibe lost in some of the trendier sections of the city.

The **Tour Montparnasse** is currently undergoing a much needed refresh, which is schedule to be completed in 2024. Once finished, the rooftop terrace, restaurant, and hotel rooms on floors 42–45 will provide some of the best views of Paris.

The other star attraction of Montparnasse is underground. The labyrinthine tunnels of the Paris **Catacombs** contain the bones of centuries' worth of Parisians, moved here when disease, spread by rotting corpses, threatened the city center.

The bohemian café society that flourished in Montparnasse in the early 20th century—artists and intellectuals including Picasso, Modigliani, Hemingway, Man Ray, and even Trotsky raised a glass here—is still evident along Boulevard du Montparnasse. The Art Deco interior of **La Coupole** attracts diners seeking piles of golden choucroute.

Along Boulevard Raspail you can see today's art stars at the **Fondation Cartier pour l'Art Contemporain** or pay your respects to Baudelaire, Alfred Dreyfus, or Simone de Beauvoir in the **Cimetière du Montparnasse**.

Sights

★ Cimetière du Montparnasse

CEMETERY | Many of the neighborhood's most illustrious residents rest here, a stone's throw from where they lived and loved: Charles Baudelaire, Frédéric Bartholdi (who designed the Statue of Liberty), Alfred Dreyfus, and Guy de Maupassant, as well as photographer Man Ray, playwright Samuel Beckett, writers Marguerite Duras, Jean-Paul Sartre, and Simone de Beauvoir, actress Jean Seberg, and singer-songwriter Serge Gainsbourg. Opened in 1824, the ancient farmland is the second-largest burial ground in Paris and is spread over 47 acres—so if you go late in the day, give yourself plenty of time to get back to the gate before the exits are locked. Note that this is not the largest cemetery in Paris—that honor goes to the Cimetière du Père-Lachaise, in eastern Paris. ✉ *Entrances on Rue Froidevaux, Bd. Edgar Quinet, Montparnasse* 🖾 *Free* ☉ *Closed dusk–dawn* Ⓜ *Raspail, Edgar Quinet, Gaîté.*

Spooky yet fascinating, the underground passages known as Les Catacombes hold some 6 million bones of former Parisians.

Closerie des Lilas

RESTAURANT | It's now a popular and pricey bar-restaurant, but the Closerie is also a staple of Parisian literary tours for its storied history. Commemorative plaques are bolted to the bar as if they were still saving seats for their former clientele: an impressive list of literati including Zola, Baudelaire, Rimbaud, Apollinaire, Beckett, and, of course, Hemingway. ("Papa" wrote pages of *The Sun Also Rises* here and lived around the corner at 115 rue Notre-Dame-des-Champs.) Although the lilacs that once graced the garden—and shaded such habitués as Ingres, Whistler, and Cézanne—are gone, the terrace still opens onto a garden wall of luxuriant foliage. There is live music in the piano bar. ⊠ *171 bd. du Montparnasse, Montparnasse* ☎ *01–40–51–34–50* ⊕ *www.closeriedeslilas.fr* Ⓜ *Vavin; RER: Port Royal.*

Fondation Cartier Pour L'art Contemporain

ART MUSEUM | **FAMILY** | There's no shortage of museums in Paris, but this eye-catching gallery may be the city's premier place to view cutting-edge art. Funded by luxury giant Cartier, the foundation is at once an architectural landmark, a traveling corporate collection, and an exhibition space. Architect Jean Nouvel's 1993 building looks rather like a glass house of cards, layered seamlessly between the boulevard and the garden. The foundation regularly hosts *Soirées Nomades* (Nomadic Nights) featuring lectures, dance, music, film, or fashion on various evenings. Some are in English. Family tours and creative workshops for children ages 9 to 13 are available. There are free guided tours of exhibits at 6 pm Tuesday through Friday, depending on space. ⊠ *261 bd. Raspail, Montparnasse* ☎ *01–42–18–56–50* ⊕ *www.fondationcartier.com* ⌨ *€11* ⊙ *Closed Mon.* Ⓜ *Raspail.*

Jardin Atlantique

GARDEN | Built above the tracks of Gare Montparnasse, this park nestled among tall modern buildings is named for its assortment of trees and plants typically found in coastal regions near the Atlantic Ocean. In the center of the park, what looks like a quirky piece of metallic sculpture is actually a meteorological center, with a battery of flickering lights reflecting temperature, wind speed, and monthly rainfall. ⊠ *1 pl. des Cinq-Martyrs-du-Lycee-Buffon, Montparnasse* 🖃 *Free* Ⓜ *Montparnasse–Bienvenüe.*

★ Les Catacombes

CEMETERY | The catacombs are a fascinating haunt for anyone with morbid interests. A visit starts with a descent through dark, clammy passages that bring you to Paris's principal ossuary, which also once served as a hideout maze for the French Resistance. Bones from the defunct Cimetière des Innocents were the first to arrive in 1786, when decomposing bodies started seeping into the cellars of the market at Les Halles, drawing swarms of ravenous rats. The legions of bones were dumped here over the course of several decades by parish and by type—rows of skulls, packs of tibias, and piles of spinal disks, often rather artfully arranged. Among the nameless 6 million or so are the bones of Madame de Pompadour (1721–64), laid to rest with the riffraff after a lifetime spent as the mistress of Louis XV. One of the most interesting aspects of the catacombs is one you probably won't see: so-called *cataphiles,* or urban explorers, mostly art students, have found alternate entrances into the 300 km (186 miles) of tunnels and come to make art, party, and purportedly raise hell. For regular visits, arrive early as the line is always long and only 200 people can enter at a time. It's not recommended for people who are claustrophobic or young children. ⊠ *1 av. du Colonel Henri Roi-Tanguy,* *Montparnasse* 🕾 *01–43–22–47–63* ⊕ *www.catacombes.paris.fr* 🖃 *€15* 🕓 *Closed Mon.* ⚹ *You can buy tickets in advance for double the door price to avoid the long line* Ⓜ *Métro or RER: Denfert-Rochereau.*

Marché Edgar Quinet

MARKET | To experience local living in one of the best ways, visit this excellent street market that takes place every Wednesday and Saturday. On Wednesday there are produce stands, but also inexpensive clothing, jewelry, and fun knickknacks. Saturday is a food lover's paradise with multiple stands selling fresh produce, spices, olives, fish, cheese, meat, and other gastronomic pleasures. It's a good place to pick up lunch on the go before paying your respects at Cimetière du Montparnasse across the street. ⊠ *Bd. du Edgar Quinet at métro Edgar Quinet, Montparnasse* 🕓 *Closed Sun.–Tues., Thurs., and Fri.* Ⓜ *Edgar Quinet.*

Musée Bourdelle

ART MUSEUM | FAMILY | Antoine Bourdelle was a life-long artist and prolific sculptor who worked with Auguste Rodin before breaking away to pursue his own style. He received commissions for prestigious projects, both small and monumental, many of which are documented in his cavernous, former workplace. This lesser-known museum has undergone a few renovations and extensions but still has preserved some of the artist's original spaces and the small garden with towering sculptures. ⊠ *18 rue Antoine Bourdelle, Montparnasse* 🕾 *01–49–54–73–73* ⊕ *www.bourdelle.paris.fr/en* 🖃 *Free* 🕓 *Closed Mon.* Ⓜ *Montparnasse or Falguière.* Museum

Musee de la Liberation de Paris

HISTORY MUSEUM | Designed by Claude-Nicolas Ledoux in the late 18th century, this landmark structure was originally built as a custom station for

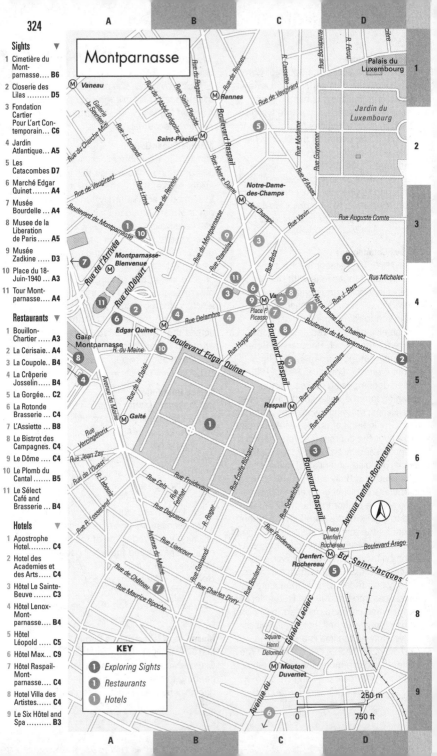

Montparnasse

KEY

1 *Exploring Sights*

1 *Restaurants*

1 *Hotels*

merchandise entering Paris. Today, it's home to the two museums formerly located above the Gare Montparnasse, dedicated to World War II and the French heroes of resistance and liberation of Paris. The museum features a fascinating collection of historic memorabilia, photographs, documents, and video archives. ⊠ *4 av. du Colonel Henri Rol-Tanguy, Montparnasse* ⊕ *www.museeliberation-leclerc-moulin.paris.fr* ☞ *Free except for temporary exhibits* ⊗ *Closed Mon.* Ⓜ *Denfert-Rochereau.*

★ Musée Zadkine

ART MUSEUM | The sculptor Ossip Zadkine spent nearly four decades living in this bucolic retreat near the Jardin du Luxembourg, creating graceful, elongated figures known for their clean lines and simplified features. Zadkine, a Russian-Jewish émigré, moved to Paris in 1910 and fell into a circle of avant-garde artists. His early works, influenced by African, Greek, and Roman art, later took a Cubist turn, no doubt under the influence of his friend, the founder of the Cubist movement: Pablo Picasso. This tiny museum displays a substantial portion of the 400 sculptures and 300 drawings bequeathed to the city by his wife, artist Valentine Prax. There are busts in bronze and stone reflecting the range of Zadkine's style, and an airy back room filled with lithe female nudes in polished wood. The charming, leafy garden contains a dozen statues nestled in the trees, including *The Destroyed City,* a memorial to the Dutch city of Rotterdam, destroyed by the Germans in 1940. ⊠ *100 bis, rue d'Assas, Montparnasse* ☎ *01–55–42–77–20* ⊕ *www.zadkine.paris.fr* ☞ *Free; €9 during temporary exhibitions* ⊗ *Closed Mon.* Ⓜ *Vavin, Notre-Dame-des-Champs; RER: Port Royal.*

Place du 18-Juin-1940

HISTORIC SIGHT | At the busy intersection of Rue de Rennes and Boulevard du Montparnasse, this small square commemorates an impassioned radio broadcast Charles de Gaulle made from London on June 18, 1940. In it he urged the French to resist Nazi occupiers (who had invaded the month prior), thereby launching the French Resistance Movement. It was also here that German military governor Dietrich von Choltitz surrendered to the Allies in August 1944, ignoring Hitler's orders to destroy the city as he withdrew. The square (in fact, a triangle) has been restored and now has a bench and one of the city's sculpted, cast-iron Wallace drinking fountains, which run with clean clear water and where you can fill up your water bottle. There are about 100 of these fountains around the city, most of them painted green (though there is at least one red one in Chinatown) and named after Sir Richard Wallace, an English art collector who funded the project in the 19th century. ⊠ *Montparnasse* ✛ *Off Blvd. du Montparnasse* Ⓜ *Montparnasse–Bienvenüe.*

Tour Montparnasse

VIEWPOINT | Paris's least regarded architectural eyesore is currently undergoing a major overhaul and will have a sparkling new facade, with planted terraces for the planned reopening and a renovated, ground-level shopping center by 2024. When it reopens a quick elevator ride will whisk visitors to the top of one of continental Europe's tallest skyscrapers, where you can take in panoramic vistas of Paris from the glass-enclosed observation deck on the 56th floor. On a clear day, you can see for 40 km (25 miles). Built in 1973, the 680-foot building will also sport a rooftop restaurant as well as hotel rooms on the 42nd to 45th floors, from which one can enjoy some of the the best views of Paris and beyond. ⊠ *Rue de L'Arrivee, Montparnasse* ☎ *01–45–38–52–56* ⊕ *www.tourmontparnasse56.com* Ⓜ *Montparnasse–Bienvenüe.*

🍴 Restaurants

Bouillon-Chartier

$ | **FRENCH** | **FAMILY** | The exceptional Art Nouveau decor and inexpensive menu are strong magnets for diners who are willing to stand in line for a seat at this historic brasserie, all to enjoy a three-course meal for as little as €20. The food is average and service brisk, but it's worth a visit between traditional meal times when there is no line. **Known for:** affordable prices; long lines; great decor. [$] *Average main: €10* ✉ *59 blvd du Montparnasse, Montparnasse* ☎ *01–45–49–19–00* 🌐 *www.bouillon-chartier.com/montparnasse* [M] *Montparnasse.* Brasserie

La Cerisaie

$$ | **BISTRO** | If you can nab a seat in this small, unremarkable dining room (be sure to call ahead), you'll be rewarded with food prepared with such attention to detail that it will restore your faith in humanity. Since the chef is from southwest France, foie gras makes several appearances on the chalkboard menu, as does a delicious cassoulet, but you can also find freshly caught fish and perhaps farmer's pork straight from Gascony, a rarity in Paris. **Known for:** daily blackboard menu; intimate dining room; skillfully prepared southwest France specialties. [$] *Average main: €18* ✉ *70 bd. Edgar Quinet, 14e, Montparnasse* ☎ *01–43–20–98–98* 🌐 *www.restaurantlacerisaie.com* ⏲ *Closed weekends, mid-July–mid-Aug., and 1 wk at Christmas* [M] *Edgar Quinet.*

★ La Coupole

$$$ | **BRASSERIE** | This world-renowned, cavernous spot with Art Deco murals practically defines the term *brasserie*. It's been popular since Jean-Paul Sartre and Simone de Beauvoir were regulars, and it's still great fun. Today it attracts a mix of bourgeois families, tourists, and lone diners treating themselves to a dozen oysters. **Known for:** historic setting; lively atmosphere; classic brasserie menu. [$] *Average main: €30* ✉ *102 bd. du Montparnasse, 14e, Montparnasse* ☎ *01–43–20–14–20* 🌐 *www.lacoupole-paris.com* [M] *Vavin.*

Montparnasse Oysters 🍴

Ever since the first trains from Brittany brought oyster-loving settlers to Montparnasse, the neighborhood has had a proud seafood tradition. The knobbly shelled *creuses* tend to be larger, elongated, fresh-flavored, and more common than the rounder *plates*, which are cultivated in deeper waters, are more intensely flavored, and are more expensive. Oysters can be dressed with vinegar and shallots, but a squeeze of lemon—or nothing at all—might be the best accompaniment.

La Crêperie Josselin

$ | **MODERN FRENCH** | **FAMILY** | With lacy curtains, beamed ceilings, and carved wood walls, this might be the closest you'll get to an authentic Breton crêperie without heading to the coast. Tuck into a hearty buckwheat galette, perfectly crisped on the edges and filled with, perhaps, a classic combo of country ham, egg, cheese, and mushrooms, accompanied by a pitcher of refreshing dry Breton cider. **Known for:** perfect for families; quick and efficient service; authentic Breton crêpes. [$] *Average main: €12* ✉ *67 rue du Montparnasse, 14e, Montparnasse* ☎ *01–43–20–93–50* ⏲ *Closed Mon., Aug., and 2 wks in Jan.* [M] *Vavin, Edgar Quinet.*

La Gorgée

$$ | **FRENCH** | This neighborhood bistro is a local favorite for its fresh, seasonal menu, friendly service, and excellent

qualité prix. The creamy roast endive soup with foie gras starter, followed by the wild fish and celery root risotto, will make you glad you came to Paris. **Known for:** good wines; creative seasonal dishes; casual atmosphere. $ *Average main: €20* ⊠ *22 rue de Fleurus, Montparnasse* ☎ *01–43–22–41–14* ⊕ *www.la-gorgee-paris.fr/en* ☉ *Closed Sun.* Ⓜ *Notre-Dame-des-Champs, Rennes.* Brasserie

La Rotonde Brasserie
$$$$ | FRENCH | A second home to foreign artists and political exiles in the 1920s and 1930s, La Rotonde has a less exotic but faithful clientele today. It's still a very pleasant place to have coffee or a meal on the sunny terrace. **Known for:** people-watching on the outdoor terrace; former home base of writers and artists; traditional French dining. $ *Average main: €35* ⊠ *105 bd. Montparnasse, Montparnasse* ☎ *01–43–26–48–26* Ⓜ *Vavin.*

★ L'Assiette
$$$ | BISTRO | David Rathgeber spent 12 years working for celebrity-chef Alain Ducasse before taking over this landmark restaurant, where he has created his own menu and welcomes a devoted clientele. Expect classics with a subtle modern touch, such as the signature cassoulet with six different meats, and crème caramel with salted butter—all executed with the precision you would expect of a Ducasse veteran. **Known for:** famous cassoulet; generous portions and good price-to-quality ratio; reliably excellent food. $ *Average main: €32* ⊠ *181 rue du Château, 14e, Montparnasse* ☎ *01–43–22–64–86* ⊕ *www.restaurant-lassiette.com* ☉ *Closed Mon., Tues., Aug., and 1 wk at Christmas* Ⓜ *Pernety, Mouton-Duvernet.*

Le Bistrot des Campagnes
$$ | FRENCH | This small, casual French restaurant is nestled on a tiny street that runs between two major boulevards.

The welcome is warm, and relaxed and the extensive, traditional menu of market-fresh produce makes it difficult to choose. **Known for:** tasty, unfussy dishes; friendly service; good wines at reasonable prices. $ *Average main: €20* ⊠ *6 rue Leopold Robert, Montparnasse* ☎ *01–40–47–91–27* ⊕ *www.lebistrotdes-campagnes.fr* ☉ *Closed Sun.* Ⓜ *Vavin, Raspail.*

Le Dôme
$$$$ | BRASSERIE | Now a fancy fish brasserie serving seafood delivered fresh from Normandy every day, this restaurant began as a dingy meeting place for exiled artists and intellectuals like Lenin and Picasso. The family-owned institution has hired star Japanese chef Yoshikiko Miura to modernize its menu while keeping some enduring classics. **Known for:** great oysters; authentic ambience; heaping seafood platters. $ *Average main: €38* ⊠ *108 bd. Montparnasse, 14e, Montparnasse* ☎ *01–43–35–25–81* ☉ *Closed Sun. and Mon. in July and Aug.* Ⓜ *Vavin.*

Le Plomb du Cantal
$$ | FRENCH | This lively café in the heart of the Left Bank theater district specializes in meats, wines, and cheeses from the Auvergne region of France, famous for its prize beef cattle. If you don't want meat but love cheese and mashed potatoes, try the aligot, a hearty recipe of potato purée, melted cheese, cream, and garlic. **Known for:** very lively atmosphere; casual and friendly service; good house wines. $ *Average main: €23* ⊠ *3 rue de la Gaîté, Montparnasse* ☎ *01–43–35–16–92* ⊕ *www.leplombducantal.com* ☉ *Closed Tues.*

Le Sélect Café and Brasserie
$$$ | FRENCH | Legendary performers and artists, including the likes of Isadora Duncan and Hart Crane, used to hang out here, and now it's a popular place for a coffee, glass of wine, or well-made cocktail. Not as "hip" as the equally

historic cafés in St-Germain-des-Prés, Le Select is a low-key way of soaking in the Left Bank historic café scene without the hubbub. **Known for:** old-world Paris café atmosphere; quiet, intellectual crowd; large, classic brasserie menu. $ *Average main: €25* ✉ *99 bd. Montparnasse, Montparnasse* ☎ *01–45–48–38–24* Ⓜ *Vavin.*

 ## Hotels

Apostrophe Hotel
$$ | HOTEL | Those enamored of the artistic and literary history of Paris's Left Bank will appreciate this whimsical family-run hotel between Montparnasse and the Luxembourg Garden. **Pros:** friendly, multilingual staff; close to métro; quiet street in charming area. **Cons:** no restaurant or bar; little privacy with bathrooms opening up directly to rooms; limited closet space. $ *Rooms from: €190* ✉ *3 rue de Chevreuse, Montparnasse* ☎ *01–56–54–31–31* ⊕ *www.apostrophe-hotel.com* ➟ *16 rooms* ⦾ *No Meals* Ⓜ *Vavin.*

★ Hôtel Léopold
$$ | HOTEL | The colors of this hotel are a cheerful mix of smoky blues, pinks, and yellows, paired with William Morris prints, making it feel fresh, whimsical, and soothing all at once. **Pros:** central location; friendly service; good breakfast. **Cons:** no on-site restaurant; standard rooms are small; no courtyard. $ *Rooms from: €200* ✉ *225 blvd Raspail, Montparnasse* ☎ *01–43–20–35–82* ⊕ *www.leopoldhotelparis.com* ➟ *40 rooms* ⦾ *No Meals* Ⓜ *Raspail.*

Hôtel des Académies et des Arts
$$$ | HOTEL | Directly across the street from the historic art studio, Académie de la Grande Chaumière, where drawing and painting lessons are still given, this hotel embraces the creative history and significance of the neighborhood, once home to many painters and artists. **Pros:** location on a charming street; close to Montparnasse and Luxembourg Gardens; unique artistic feel. **Cons:** small rooms; no courtyard; might be too austere for some. $ *Rooms from: €250* ✉ *15 rue de la Grande Chaumière, Montparnasse* ☎ *01–43–26–66–44* ⊕ *www.hoteldesacademies.fr* ➟ *20 rooms* ⦾ *No Meals* Ⓜ *Vavin.* Hotel

Hôtel Lenox-Montparnasse
$$ | HOTEL | Set in a typical 19th-century Haussmannian building on a small street lined with food shops, restaurants, and bars, this six-story hotel gets points for its proximity to Montparnasse and the Jardin du Luxembourg, as well as for its sleek decor. **Pros:** lively district close to Montparnasse and Rue de la Gaîté; friendly, multilingual staff; well-stocked honesty bar. **Cons:** attracts business clientele; noisy street; standard rooms are small. $ *Rooms from: €215* ✉ *15 rue Delambre, Montparnasse* ☎ *01–43–35–34–50* ⊕ *www.paris-hotel-lenox.com* ➟ *52 rooms* ⦾ *No Meals* Ⓜ *Vavin.*

Hôtel Le Sainte-Beuve
$$$ | HOTEL | On a tranquil street between the Jardin du Luxembourg and Montparnasse's cafés and brasseries sits this pleasant six-story hotel. **Pros:** cozy, colorful decor; close to major métro lines; good location without the tourist crowds. **Cons:** unremarkable service; small rooms and elevator; 20-minute walk to the Latin Quarter or St-Germain-des-Prés. $ *Rooms from: €290* ✉ *9 rue Ste-Beuve, Montparnasse* ☎ *01–45–48–20–07* ⊕ *www.hotelsaintebeuve.com* ➟ *22 rooms* ⦾ *No Meals* Ⓜ *Vavin.*

Hôtel Max
$$ | HOTEL | FAMILY | A sleek Scandinavian design with lively splashes of color, bright comfortable rooms, and a warm and welcoming atmosphere make this 19-room hotel one of Paris's best-kept secrets. **Pros:** good prices; quiet, residential neighborhood; intimate feel. **Cons:** no bathtubs; rooms on the small side; a métro ride to most sights. $ *Rooms from: €150* ✉ *34 rue d'Alésia, Montparnasse* ☎ *01–43–27–60–80* ⊕ *www.hotel-max.fr* ➟ *19 rooms* ⦾ *No Meals* Ⓜ *Alésia.*

Hôtel Raspail-Montparnasse

$$ | HOTEL | FAMILY | Montparnasse was the art capital of the world in the 1920s and '30s, and this hotel captures some of that spirit by naming its rooms after artists who lived in the neighborhood while also providing excellent service at hard-to-beat prices. **Pros:** some rooms have balconies and/or views of the Eiffel Tower; friendly staff; many markets and cafés nearby. **Cons:** not all rooms have Eiffel Tower views; some rooms small; traffic noise on first floor. $ *Rooms from: €135* ⊠ *203 bd. Raspail, Montparnasse* ☎ *01–43–20–62–86* ⊕ *www.hotelraspail-montparnasse.com* ⇌ *38 rooms* ⦿| *No Meals* Ⓜ *Vavin.*

Hôtel Villa des Artistes

$$ | HOTEL | On a small street famous for its nearby historic art studio, this 54-room hotel gives a distinct bow to modern art and its different movements. **Pros:** modern and sleek design; great location; pretty garden courtyard. **Cons:** breakfast not included; no air-conditioning; lacking character a bit. $ *Rooms from: €215* ⊠ *9 rue de la Grande Chaumière, Montparnasse* ☎ *01–43–26–60–86* ⊕ *www.villa-artistes.com* ⇌ *54 rooms* ⦿| *No Meals* Ⓜ *Vavin.*

★ Le Six Hôtel and Spa

$$$ | HOTEL | FAMILY | Modern, cheerful, and very zen, Le Six Hôtel and Spa has a fireplace-equipped common room, a small library, and elegant, quiet rooms with individual Nespresso machines. **Pros:** free use of a hammam; great breakfast; elegant atmosphere. **Cons:** no views; expensive; some rooms are small. $ *Rooms from: €300* ⊠ *14 rue Stanislas, Montparnasse* ☎ *01–42–22–00–75* ⊕ *www.hotel-le-six.com* ⇌ *41 rooms* ⦿| *No Meals* Ⓜ *Notre-Dame-des-Champs, Vavin.*

Nightlife

BARS

Le Rosebud

BARS | Step through the Art Nouveau front door of Jean-Paul Sartre's onetime haunt and you're instantly immersed in the dark, moody, fourth dimension of Old Montparnasse, where white-jacketed servers and red-lacquered tables transport you into the past. ⊠ *11 rue Delambre, 14e, Montparnasse* ☎ *01–43–35–38–54* Ⓜ *Vavin.*

 Performing Arts

★ La Comédie Italienne

THEATER | The Rue de la Gaîté has been a Left Bank entertainment hub since the late 18th century. Once dotted with dance halls and cabarets, this street is still home to a multitude of lively bars and several historic theaters that feature well-known actors and offer a selection of dramas, musicals, and concerts. Check out the decorative La Comédie Italienne at No. 19, specializing in original plays and Carlos Goldoni Italian classics. All performances are in French. The theater, with whimsical trompe l'oeil paintings, can also be rented for private events. ⊠ *19 rue de la Gaite, 14e, Montparnasse* ⊕ *www.comedie-italienne.fr* Ⓜ *Edgar Quinet, Gaîté.*

Le Lucernaire

ARTS CENTERS | Occupying an abandoned factory, Le Lucernaire wins a standing ovation as far as cultural centers are concerned. With three theaters staging a total of six performances per day, plus three movie screens, a bookstore, photography exhibitions, a lively restaurant-bar, and the equally animated surrounding neighborhood of Vavin, it caters to a local audience of young intellectuals. ⊠ *53 rue Notre-Dame-des-Champs, 6e, Montparnasse* ☎ *01–45–44–57–34* ⊕ *www.lucernaire.fr* Ⓜ *Notre-Dame-des-Champs.*

Théâtre de la Cité Internationale

ARTS CENTERS | In the heart of the Cité Internationale Universitaire de Paris, this complex includes three theaters, an international student residence community, a casual daytime restaurant, and a park. Conceived in the 1930s with a visionary concept of pacifism and international peace, the Cité U campus is home to thousands of students and researchers from around the world. The theaters host young, avant-garde dance, music, theater, and circus performances, as well as debates, meetings, and workshops. Forty percent of the productions are by foreign artists. ⊠ *17 bd. Jourdan, 14e, Montparnasse* ☎ *01–43–13–50–50* ⊕ *www.theatredelacite.com* Ⓜ *RER: Cité Universitaire.*

Shopping

CHILDREN'S CLOTHING

Rue Vavin

CHILDREN'S CLOTHING | FAMILY | Rue Vavin, which runs between boulevard de Montparnasse and the Luxembourg Gardens, is lined with charming children's boutiques. Stop in Jacadi and Petit Bateau (No. 26) for timeless cotton classics or Catimini (No. 10) for more modern togs. Along the way, you'll pass Oxybul (No. 19), an educational toy store for babies and children, and Le Petit Souk (No. 17), which has a creative collection of games, toys, baby clothes, and decorative and practical items. For exceptional handmade smock dresses, l'Ile aux Fées at 66 rue Notre-Dames-des-Champs is worth the very short detour. When you're tired from all the shopping, grab some gelato at Amorino (No. 4) and head to the Luxembourg Gardens, which is literally steps away. ⊠ *Rue Vavin, Montparnasse* Ⓜ *Vavin.*

MARKETS

Les Puces des Vanves

MARKET | This small flea market is a hit with the fashion and design set. It specializes in easily portable items (like textiles or clothing) and collectible objects that include books, posters, postcards, and glassware. With tables sprawling along both sides of the sidewalk, there's an extravagant selection—just be sure to bargain with vendors. It's open on weekends from 8 am to 2pm, but come early for the real deals as good stuff goes fast. ⊠ *Av. de le Porte de Vanves at Av. Marc Sangnier, 14e, Montparnasse* ⊕ *www. pucesdevanves.fr* Ⓜ *Porte de Vanves.*

TOYS AND GAMES

★ Rouge et Noir

TOYS | FAMILY | Opened in 1977, this family-owned boutique specializes in high-end traditional board games such as chess and backgammon, but also many you've never heard of like Nain Jaune ("Yellow Dwarf," a very old French game), and other ancient card games. With over 2,000 items in stock, many made by French artisans, the game-passionate staff has an endless number of suggestions and advice to help you find the perfect original gift that no one else will have back home. ⊠ *24 rue Vavin, Montparnasse* ☎ *06–52–66–35–50* ⊕ *www.rouge-et-noir.fr* Ⓜ *Vavin.*

Chapter 14

WESTERN PARIS

Updated by
Jack Vermee

◉ Sights	🍴 Restaurants	🛏 Hotels	🛍 Shopping	🍸 Nightlife
★★★☆☆	★★★☆☆	★★☆☆☆	★☆☆☆☆	★★☆☆☆

NEIGHBORHOOD SNAPSHOT

GETTING HERE

Western Paris includes the 16e and 17e arrondisse-ments. Take Line 9 to La Muette métro stop for the Musée Marmottan Monet or to the Jasmin stop (also Line 9) to explore Rue Jean de la Fontaine. Take Line 6 to the Passy stop for the Musée du Vin or to reach the main drag, Rue de Passy. Alternatively, take Bus 72 from the Hôtel de Ville or 63 from St. Sulpice. For the main entrance of the Bois de Boulogne, take Line 2 to Porte Dauphine or RER C to Avenue Foch. For the Jardin d'Acclimatation, enter the park from Les Sablons or Porte Maillot métro stops on Line 1. If you're heading out to La Défense, it's the terminus of Line 1.

MAKING THE MOST OF YOUR TIME

If this isn't your first time in Paris, or even if it is and you've had enough of the touristy central part of the city, this neighborhood is a great choice and can be treated like a day trip. Spend the morning admiring the Monets at the uncrowded Musée Marmottan Monet, then take in the Art Nouveau architecture on Rue Jean de la Fontaine. Or while away the day in the leafy Bois de Boulogne.

VIEWFINDER

At 360 feet high, the promenade atop the Grande Arche de la Défense offers stunning vistas in all directions. Constructed along the same axis as the Arc de Triomphe and the Louvre pyramid, this is Western Paris's best vantage point for shutterbugs. The glassed-in elevator ride to the top also dazzles. Take métro Line 1 to La Défense.

TOP REASONS TO GO

■ **Fondation Louis Vuitton.** Contemporary art meets iconoclastic architecture at this wood, steel, and glass museum designed by Frank Gehry.

■ **Musée Marmottan Monet.** Full of Claude Monet paintings, this gem tucked away deep in the 16e, near the Jardin du Ranelagh, is a must for fans of the Impressionist master.

■ **Bois de Boulogne.** Whether you spend your afternoon in a rowboat or wandering gardens filled with foliage, the Bois is a perfect escape from the city.

■ **Jardin d'Acclimatation.** With rides, animals, a train, and more, what child under the age of five wouldn't love this amusement park on the northern edge of the Bois de Boulogne?

Meet Paris at its most prim and proper. This genteel area is a study in smart urban planning, with classical architecture and newer construction cohabiting as easily as the haute bourgeoisie inhabitants mix with their expat neighbors.

There's no shortage of celebrities seeking seclusion here, but you're just as likely to find well-heeled families who decamped from the center of the city in search of a spacious apartment. Passy, once a separate village and home to American ambassadors Benjamin Franklin and Thomas Jefferson, was incorporated into the city in 1860 under Napoléon III.

A walk along the main avenues gives you a sense of Paris's finest Art Nouveau and Modernist buildings, including **Castel-Béranger,** by Hector Guimard, and the **Fondation Le Corbusier** museum, a prime example of the titular architect's pioneering style (it was one of Le Corbusier's first Paris commissions).

This neighborhood is also home to one of the city's best and most overlooked museums—the **Musée Marmottan Monet**—which has an astonishing collection of Impressionist art. Enjoy a *dégustation* (tasting) at the **Musée du Vin,** or simply find a café on Rue de Passy and savor a moment in one of the city's most exclusive enclaves.

For outdoor adventures, the **Bois de Boulogne** is the place to be, especially if you have kids in tow. At *le Bois,* you can explore the Pré Catelan and peacock-filled Bagatelle gardens, both meticulously landscaped and surrounded by woods. You can also admire contemporary art in the **Fondation Louis Vuitton,** head to the old-fashioned amusement park at the Jardin d'Acclimatation, take a rowboat out on one of the park's two bucolic lakes, or rent a bike and hit 14 km (9 miles) of marked trails.

◉ Sights

★ Bois de Boulogne
CITY PARK | FAMILY | When Parisians want to experience the great outdoors without going too far from home, they head to the Bois de Boulogne. Once a royal hunting ground, the Bois is like a vast tamed forest where romantic lakes and wooded paths are complemented by formal gardens and family-friendly amusements. On nice days, it's filled with cyclists, rowers, rollerbladers, and joggers. Art lovers also flock here thanks to the Fondation Louis Vuitton, a stunning exhibition space dedicated to contemporary art.

The Parc de Bagatelle is a floral garden with irises, roses, tulips, water lilies, and roaming peacocks, while the Pré Catelan contains one of Paris's largest trees: a copper beech more than 200 years old. Romantic Le Pré Catelan restaurant (three Michelin stars), a Belle Époque classic with an elegant terrace, still draws diners and wedding parties. The Jardin Shakespeare inside the Pré Catelan has

The Bois de Boulogne is the ultimate Parisian way to experience the outdoors without venturing too far from the city.

a sampling of the flowers, herbs, and trees mentioned in Shakespeare's plays, and it becomes an open-air theater for the Bard's works in spring. The Jardin d'Acclimatation is an amusement park that attracts hordes of preschoolers on summer Sundays. Boats or bikes can be rented for a few euros at Lac Inférieur. You can row or take a quick "ferry" to the island restaurant, Le Chalet des Îles. Two popular horse-racing tracks are also in the park: the Hippodrome de Longchamp and the Hippodrome d'Auteuil. Fans of the French Open can visit its home base, Stade Roland-Garros.

The main entrance to the Bois is off Avenue Foch near the Porte Dauphine métro stop on Line 2; it is best for accessing the Pré Catelan and Jardin Shakespeare, both off the Route de la Grande-Cascade by the lake. For the Jardin d'Acclimatation and the Fondation Louis Vuitton, off Boulevard des Sablons, take Line 1 to Les Sablons or Porte Maillot, where you can walk or ride the Petit Train to the amusement park, which is next door to

the foundation. The foundation also offers a €2 return-trip shuttle from Place de l'Étoile. The Parc de Bagatelle, off Route de Sèvres-à-Neuilly, can be accessed from either Porte Dauphine or Porte Maillot, though it's a bit of a hike. You'll want to leave the park by dusk, as the Bois—potentially dangerous after dark—turns into a distinctly "adult" playground. ⊠ *Western Paris* ☎ *01–53–64–53–80 Parc de Bagatelle, 01–40–67–90–85 Jardin d'Acclimatation* ⊕ *www.jardindacclimatation.fr* 🖾 *Parc de Bagatelle €2.50 (€6 during exhibitions, free Oct.–Mar.); Jardin Shakespeare free; Jardin d'Acclimatation €6.50 entry, €39 for 15-ride ticket book, €39 for entry and unlimited access to rides; Fondation Louis Vuitton €16* Ⓜ *Porte Dauphine for main entrance; Porte Maillot or Les Sablons for northern end; Porte d'Auteuil for southern end.*

Castel Béranger
HISTORIC HOME | It's a shame you can't go inside this house, which is considered the city's first Art Nouveau structure. Dreamed up in 1898 by Hector Guimard,

the wild combination of materials and the grimacing grillwork led neighbors to call it Castle *Dérangé* (Deranged). Yet the project catapulted the 27-year-old Guimard into the public eye, leading to his famous métro commission. After ogling the sea-inspired front entrance, go partway down the alley to admire the inventive treatment of the traditional Parisian courtyard, complete with a melting water fountain. A few blocks up the road at No. 60 is the Hotel Mezzara, designed by Guimard in 1911 for textile designer Paul Mezzara. You can trace Guimard's evolution by walking to the subtler Agar complex at the end of the block. Tucked beside the stone entrance at the corner of Rue Jean de la Fontaine and Rue Gros is a tiny café-bar with an Art Nouveau glass front and furnishings. ⊠ *14 rue Jean de la Fontaine, Western Paris* Ⓜ *Ranelagh; RER: Maison de Radio France.*

★ Fondation Le Corbusier

HISTORIC HOME | Maison La Roche is a must-see for architecture and design lovers. Built as a residence in 1923, it's a stellar example of Swiss architect Le Corbusier's innovative construction techniques based on geometric forms, recherché color schemes, and a visionary use of iron and concrete. The sloping ramp that replaces the traditional staircase is one of the most eye-catching features. Hour-long English tours are available (four-person minimum) by advance booking. ⊠ *8–10 sq. du Docteur Blanche, Western Paris* ☎ *01–42–88–75–72 Maison La Roche* ⊕ *www.fondationlecorbusier.fr* ⊠ *€10; €15 for guided tour or combined visit with Le Corbusier's studio-apartment* ⊗ *Closed Sun., Mon., and Wed.* Ⓜ *Jasmin, Michel-Ange–Auteuil.*

★ Fondation Louis Vuitton

ART MUSEUM | Rising up out of the Bois de Boulogne like a magnificent ship sporting billowing crystal sails, Frank Gehry's contemporary-art museum and cultural center is the most captivating addition to the Parisian skyline since the unveiling of the Centre Pompidou in 1977. Commissioned by Bernard Arnault (chairman and CEO of luxury-goods conglomerate LVMH), the museum, which opened in 2014, houses Arnault's substantial private collection, including pieces by Pierre Huyghe, Gerhard Richter, Thomas Schütte, Ellsworth Kelly, Bertrand Lavier, Taryn Simon, Sarah Morris, and Christian Boltanski, among others. La Fondation Louis Vuitton also hosts extensive temporary exhibitions, like the mesmerizing light installations of Danish-Icelandic artist Olafur Eliasson. Le Frank, the pricey on-site restaurant overseen by Michelin-starred chef Jean-Louis Nomicos, is noted for its sophisticated mix of French and international cuisine. The museum is a 12-minute walk from Les Sablons métro on Line 1; alternatively, you can catch the Fondation shuttle (€2 for a return ticket), which leaves every 10–15 minutes from Avenue de Friedland at Place de l'Étoile. ⊠ *8 av. du Mahatma Gandhi, Western Paris* ☎ *01–40–69–96–00* ⊕ *www.fondationlouisvuitton.fr* ⊠ *€10–€16, depending on the temporary exhibition* Ⓜ *Les Sablons.*

La Défense

NOTABLE BUILDING | FAMILY | First conceived in 1958, this Modernist suburb just west of Paris was inspired by Le Corbusier's dream of tall buildings, pedestrian walkways, and sunken vehicle circulation. Built as an experiment to keep high-rises out of the historic downtown, the Parisian business hub has survived economic uncertainty to become the city's prime financial district. Today, 20,000 people live in the suburb, but 180,000 people work here and many more come to shop in its enormous mall. Arriving via métro Line 1, you'll get a view of the Seine, then emerge at a pedestrian plaza studded with some great public art, including César's giant thumb, Joan Miró's colorful figures, and one of Calder's great red "stabiles." The Grande Arche de La Défense dominates the area. It was designed as a controversial closure to the

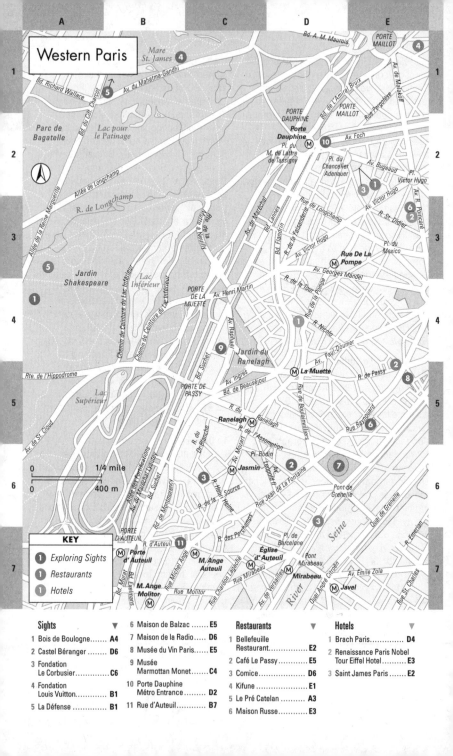

Western Paris

KEY

- **1** Exploring Sights
- **1** Restaurants
- **1** Hotels

Sights ▼

1 Bois de Boulogne........ **A4**
2 Castel Béranger **D6**
3 Fondation
Le Corbusier.............. **C6**
4 Fondation
Louis Vuitton............. **B1**
5 La Défense **B1**
6 Maison de Balzac **E5**
7 Maison de la Radio..... **D6**
8 Musée du Vin Paris..... **E5**
9 Musée
Marmottan Monet....**C4**
10 Porte Dauphine
Métro Entrance **D2**
11 Rue d'Auteuil............ **B7**

Restaurants ▼

1 Bellefeuille
Restaurant................ **E2**
2 Café Le Passy **E5**
3 Comice **D6**
4 Kifune **E1**
5 Le Pré Catelan **A3**
6 Maison Russe............. **E3**

Hotels ▼

1 Brach Paris.............. **D4**
2 Renaissance Paris Nobel
Tour Eiffel Hotel.......... **E3**
3 Saint James Paris **E2**

historic axis of Paris (an imaginary line that runs through the Arc de Triomphe, the Arc du Carrousel, and the Louvre Pyramide). Glass-bubble elevators in a metal-frame tower whisk you a heart-jolting 360 feet to the viewing platform. ⊠ *Parvis de La Défense, Western Paris* ☎ *01–40–90–52–20* ⊕ *www.lagrandearche.fr* 🎫 *Grande Arche €10* ⊙ *Closed Mon. in Feb. and Mar.* Ⓜ *Métro or RER: Grande Arche de La Défense.*

Maison de Balzac

HISTORIC HOME | The modest home of the great French 19th-century writer Honoré de Balzac (1799–1850) contains exhibits charting his tempestuous yet prolific career. Balzac penned nearly 100 novels and stories known collectively as *The Human Comedy,* many of them set in Paris. You can still feel his presence in his study and pay homage to his favorite coffeepot—his working hours were fueled by a tremendous consumption of the "black ink." He would escape his creditors by exiting the flat through a secret passage that led down to what is now the Musée du Vin. ⊠ *47 rue Raynouard, Western Paris* ☎ *01–55–74–41–80* ⊕ *www.maisondebalzac.paris.fr* 🎫 *Free; €8 during temporary exhibitions* ⊙ *Closed Mon.* Ⓜ *Passy, La Muette.*

Maison de la Radio

PERFORMANCE VENUE | Headquarters to France's state broadcasting company, this imposing, circular, 1963 building is more than 500 yards in circumference. It's said to have more floor space than any other building in the country and features a 200-foot tower that overlooks the Seine. Radio France sponsors 100-plus concerts a year, including performances by its own Orchestre Philharmonique de Radio France and the Orchestre National de France. Though the concerts take place at venues throughout the city, a great number are held here, and they're generally either free or inexpensive. French-only building tours are offered on various days at various times. Check the website for current information. ⊠ *116 av. du Président-Kennedy, Western Paris* ☎ *01–56–40–15–16 tour and concert information* ⊕ *www.maisondelaradioetdelamusique.fr* 🎫 *€10 for tours* ⊙ *Closed Sun.* Ⓜ *Ranelagh; RER: Maison de Radio France; Bus 22, 52, 72.*

Musée du Vin Paris

OTHER MUSEUM | Oenophiles with some spare time will enjoy this quirky museum housed in a 15th-century abbey, a reminder of Passy's roots as a pastoral village. Though hardly exhaustive and geared to beginners, the small collection contains old wine bottles, glassware, and ancient wine-related pottery excavated in Paris. Wine-making paraphernalia shares the grottolike space with hokey figures—including Napoléon appraising a glass of Burgundy—retired from the city's wax museum. But you can partake in a thoroughly nonhokey wine tasting, or bring home one of the 200-plus bottles for sale in the tiny gift shop. Check online for a calendar of tastings and classes offered in English. You can book ahead for a casual lunch, too (restaurant open Tuesday through Saturday, noon to 3 pm, reservations required). ⊠ *Rue des Eaux/5 sq. Charles Dickens, Western Paris* ☎ *01–45–25–70–89 reservations* ⊕ *www.museeduvinparis.com* 🎫 *From €12.50* ⊙ *Closed Sun. and Mon.* Ⓜ *Passy.*

★ Musée Marmottan Monet

ART MUSEUM | This underrated museum has the largest collection of Monet's work anywhere. More than 100 pieces, donated by his son Michel, occupy a specially built basement gallery in an elegant 19th-century mansion, which was once the hunting lodge of the Duke de Valmy. You can find such works as the *Cathédrale de Rouen* series (1892–96) and *Impression: Soleil Levant* (*Impression: Sunrise,* 1872), the painting that helped give the Impressionist movement its name. Other exhibits include letters exchanged by Impressionist painters Berthe Morisot and Mary Cassatt.

Upstairs, the mansion still feels like a graciously decorated residence. Empire furnishings fill the salons overlooking the Jardin du Ranelagh on one side and the private yard on the other. There's also a captivating room of illuminated medieval manuscripts. To best understand the collection's context, pick up an English-language audioguide (€4) on your way in. ⊠ 2 rue Louis-Boilly, Western Paris ☎ 01–44–96–50–33 ⊕ www.marmottan.fr ⊠ €12 ۞ Closed Mon. Ⓜ La Muette.

Porte Dauphine Métro Entrance

HISTORIC SIGHT | Visitors come here to snap pictures of the queen of subway entrances—one of the city's two remaining Art Nouveau canopied originals designed by Hector Guimard (the other is at the Abbesses stop on Line 12). A flamboyant scalloped "crown" of patina-painted panels and runaway metal struts adorns this whimsical 1900 creation. Porte Dauphine is the terminus of Line 2. The entrance is on the Bois de Boulogne side of Avenue Foch, so take the Boulevard de l'Amiral Bruix exit. ⊠ Av. Foch, Western Paris Ⓜ Porte Dauphine.

Rue d'Auteuil

NEIGHBORHOOD | This narrow shopping street escaped Haussmann's urban renovations and still retains the country feel of old Auteuil, a sedate bourgeois enclave. Molière once lived on the site of No. 2, and Racine was on nearby Rue du Buis. The pair met up to clink glasses and exchange drama notes at the Mouton Blanc Inn, now a traditional brasserie, at No. 40. Numbers 19–25 and 29 are an interesting combination of 17th- and 18th-century buildings. At the foot of the street, the scaly dome of the Église Notre-Dame d'Auteuil (built in the 1880s) is an unmistakable small-time cousin of Sacré-Coeur in Montmartre. Rue d'Auteuil is at its liveliest on Wednesday and Saturday mornings, when a much-loved street market crams onto Place Jean-Lorraine. ⊠ Western Paris Ⓜ Michel-Ange–Auteuil, Église d'Auteuil.

 Restaurants

★ Bellefeuille Restaurant

$$$$ | FRENCH | Set inside the gorgeously refurbished Saint James Hotel, one of the city's stand-out lodgings, the beautiful Bellefeuille has quickly become popular thanks to chef Julien Dumas's refined menu of inspired dishes with an emphasis on the freshest seafood and vegetables from the hotel's own gardens outside Paris (not to mention honey from the hives on-site). The eight-course tasting menu (with excellent desserts by pastry chef Sophie Bonnefond, paired with natural and biodynamic wines hand-picked by the restaurant's gifted sommelier) is highly recommended, but you'll be wowed no matter what you choose. **Known for:** lovely garden dining; Michelin star within nine months of opening; excellent variety of seafood. Ⓢ Average main: €45 ⊠ 5 Pl. du Chancelier Adenauer, 16e, Champs-Élysées ☎ 01-44-05-81-88 ⊕ www.saint-james-paris.com/en/the-chef.html ۞ Closed Sun. Ⓜ Porte Dauphine.

Café Le Passy

$$ | BRASSERIE | The plush chestnut-and-cream decor of this café is the work of one of Givenchy's nephews. Cocktails are classy, there's a good variety of beer on tap, and the food (brasserie fare such as steaks, fish, and frites) is tasty. **Known for:** glamorous candlelit space; cheese and charcuteries platters; extensive drink options. Ⓢ Average main: €18 ⊠ 2 rue de Passy, Western Paris ☎ 01–42–88–31–02 ⊕ www.lepassy.fr ۞ Closed Sun. Ⓜ Passy, Trocadéro.

★ Comice

$$$$ | FRENCH | The culinary experience here is a progression of delights, from your first luscious sip of carrot velouté to a light-as-air chocolate soufflé contrasted with a zesty yuzu macaron. In between, dishes like butter-poached lobster with beets, onions, and horseradish cream or foie gras en terrine with quince, walnuts, and dates—all meticulously sourced from the finest producers around France—surprise, comfort, and deeply satisfy. **Known for:** excellent selection of mostly natural wines; beautiful, serene setting; perfect service and presentation. [$] *Average main: €49* ✉ *31 av. de Versailles, 15e, Western Paris* ☎ *01–42–15–55–70* 🌐 *www.comice.paris* 🕒 *Closed weekends. No lunch* [M] *Mirabeau, Javel.*

Kifune

$$$$ | **JAPANESE** | Some Japanese expats say you won't find anything closer to authentic Japanese cooking in Paris than the kitchen in Kifune. Sit at the bar to admire the sushi chef's lightning-quick skills, or opt for a more intimate table for tasting the sublime crab-and-shrimp salad starter or a deeply comforting miso soup with clams. **Known for:** good-value lunch menu; top-notch service; small, intimate, and totally authentic. [$] *Average main: €35* ✉ *44 rue St-Ferdinand, 17e, Champs-Élysées* ☎ *01–45–72–11–19* 🌐 *kifune.fr* 🕒 *Closed Sun., Mon., 3 wks in Aug., and 1 wk in Dec.* [M] *Argentine.*

★ Le Pré Catelan

$$$$ | **MODERN FRENCH** | Live a Belle Époque fantasy as you dine beneath the chestnut trees on the terrace of this fanciful landmark *pavillon* in the Bois de Boulogne. Each of chef Frédéric Anton's dishes is a variation on a theme, such as *l'os à moelle*: bone marrow prepared two ways, one peppered and the other stuffed with porcini and cabbage, both braised in a concentrated meat jus. **Known for:** elegant service; "country" setting; three Michelin stars. [$] *Average main: €260* ✉ *Rte. de Suresnes, 16e, Western Paris* ☎ *01–44–14–41–14* 🌐 *www.restaurant-precatelan.com* 🕒 *Closed Sun.–Tues.; 2 wks in Feb.; 3 wks in Aug.; and 1 wk in late Oct.–early Nov.* 👔 *Jacket and tie* [M] *Porte Dauphine.*

★ Maison Russe

$$$$ | **FRENCH** | Oriental carpets, plush velvets, glossy wood, candlelight glinting off silver: this is a dream of Belle Époque Paris, where it's no stretch to imagine threadbare Russians once loading up on caviar to recoup something of the good life back home. Persian-French architect Laleh Amir Assef is to thank for this sumptuous fantasy of a restaurant, set in a 19th-century mansion where not a detail was overlooked, from the flawless service to the delicious food—a mix of Russian-French delicacies, like caviar, smoked salmon, and king crab, all washed down with champagne, vodka, or fine wine. **Known for:** gorgeous and over-the-top decor; Russian-themed cocktails and top vodkas; 10-minute evening entertainment that sets the festive mood. [$] *Average main: €55* ✉ *59 av. Raymond Poincaré, 16e, Eiffel Tower* ☎ *01–40–62–72–05* 🌐 *maisonrusse.com* [M] *Trocadéro, Victor Hugo.*

Hotels

★ Brach Paris

$$$$ | **HOTEL** | It may be a tad off the beaten path, but it's safe to say this is the only hotel in Paris where the eggs for your breakfast omelet come fresh from the rooftop chicken coop—just one of the things that sets this superchic Philippe Starck–designed hotel apart. **Pros:** dog- and family-friendly; lots of amenities; stunning classic contemporary decor. **Cons:** expensive for this neighborhood; staff still working out some kinks; out-of-the-way location. [$] *Rooms from: €570* ✉ *1–7 rue Jean Richepin, Eiffel Tower* ☎ *01–44–30–10–00* 🌐 *www.brachparis.com* 🛏 *52 rooms* 🍴 *No Meals* [M] *Rue de la Pompe.*

Renaissance Paris Nobel Tour Eiffel Hotel

$$$$ | **HOTEL** | **FAMILY** | Set in an upscale neighborhood, this spacious, historic urban retreat—now part of the Marriott brand—was once the home of Alfred Nobel (who would go on to establish the famous peace prize). **Pros:** near métro stations; quiet area; 24-hour fitness center and room service. **Cons:** service could be better; long walk from center of Paris; hosts large groups. $ *Rooms from: €446* ✉ *55–57 av. Raymond-Poincaré, Western Paris* ☎ *01–44–05–66–66* ⊕ *www.marriott.com* ↺ *122 rooms* ❑ *No Meals* Ⓜ *Trocadéro.*

Saint James Paris

$$$$ | **HOTEL** | This renovated, 19th-century mansion with a stone gateway and beautiful fountain feels like a countryside château nestled in the heart of the busy metropolis. **Pros:** beautiful decor and spacious rooms; fantastic wellness spa; extravagant breakfast served in-room or in the restaurant. **Cons:** far from all the major sights; residential area quiet at night; expensive rates. $ *Rooms from: €610* ✉ *43 av. Bugeaud, Western Paris* ☎ *01–44–05–81–81* ⊕ *www.saint-james-paris.com* ↺ *46 rooms* ❑ *No Meals* Ⓜ *Porte Dauphine, Victor Hugo, Rue de la Pompe.*

 Nightlife

★ Saint James Club Paris

BARS | Like a library room out of *Harry Potter,* the bar at the Saint James Club Paris—complete with 5,000 leather-bound volumes and a cozy fireplace—is studiously inviting. It's very French, and open to nonmembers only after 7 pm or during Sunday brunch. The owners are a venerable old Bordeaux family; accordingly, you'll find a respectable selection of Champagnes and wines. ✉ *5 pl du Chancelier Adenauer, 16e, Champs-Élysées* ☎ *01–44–05–81–81* ⊕ *www.saintjamesclub.com* Ⓜ *Porte Dauphine.*

⊕ Performing Arts

With the addition of the two state-of-the-art performance spaces at La Seine Musicale and the concert-hosting auditorium in the Fondation Louis Vuitton, Western Paris has become a go-to neighborhood for music lovers of all stripes.

La Seine Musicale

ARTS CENTERS | Rising up from the Seine like a futuristic ocean liner, Le Seine Musicale answers Paris's desire to compete as one of the world's prime music destinations. The structure's two state-of-the-art concert halls, the largest with a seating capacity of 6,000, feature a range of musical performances, from classical to the legends of jazz and rock (Bob Dylan played the inaugural concert). Behind the sleek mirrored facade—whose solar panels generate enough power to dramatically illuminate the building at night—lie a jazz club, three restaurants, art galleries, and outdoor gardens offering panoramic views of Paris. The 28-acre island on the Seine is technically in Boulogne-Billancourt, a suburb of Paris, but is easily reached by métro or bus. ✉ *Île Seguin, Boulogne-Billancourt, Western Paris* ☎ *01–74–34–54–00* ⊕ *www.laseinemusicale.com* Ⓜ *Pont de Sèvres, Brimborion, Musée de Sèvres.*

Les Folies Gruss

CIRCUSES | FAMILY | Formerly the Cirque National Alexis Gruss, Les Folies Gruss remains true to the *Cirque à l'Ancienne* philosophy, featuring a traditional circus with showy horseback riders, trapeze artists, and clowns. The large-scale production runs mid-October through early March, with performances twice daily at 3 pm and 9 pm. Tickets cost €20 to €75. ✉ *Carrefour des cascades, Porte de Passy, 16e, Western Paris* ☎ *01–45–01–71–26* ⊕ *www.folies-gruss.com* Ⓜ *Ranelagh.*

Chapter 15

SIDE TRIPS FROM PARIS

Updated by
Jennifer Ladonne

⊙ Sights	🍴 Restaurants	🛏 Hotels	🛍 Shopping	🍸 Nightlife
★★★★☆	★★★☆☆	★★★☆☆	★★☆☆☆	★☆☆☆☆

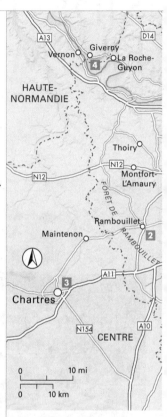

WELCOME TO SIDE TRIPS FROM PARIS

TOP REASONS TO GO

★ **Louis XIV's Versailles:** Famed as glorious testimony to the Sun King's megalomania, this is the world's most over-the-top palace and nature-tamed park.

★ **Gorgeous Chantilly:** Stately château and gardens, a stellar art collection, a fabulous forest, palatial stables all within the same square mile.

★ **Van Gogh in Auvers:** The artist spent his last, manically productive three months here—you can see where he painted, where he got drunk, where he shot himself, and where he rests today.

★ **Chartres Cathedral:** A pinnacle of Gothic achievement, this recently restored 13th-century masterpiece has peerless stained glass and a hilltop silhouette visible for miles around.

★ **Monet's water lilies:** Come to Giverny to see his lily pond—a half-acre 3-D "Monet"—then peek around his charming home and stroll the time-warped streets to the exceptional Musée des Impressionnismes.

1 Versailles. A famed palace and beloved icon.

2 Rambouillet. An upscale town with a historic château.

3 Chartres. One of the most famous cathedrals in the world.

4 Giverny. Monet's home and inspiration for *Water Lilies*.

5 St-Germain-en-Laye. A suburb with a château inspired by *The Count of Monte Cristo*.

6 Rueil-Malmaison. Once home to Napoléon and Joséphine, then Joséphine alone.

7 Auvers-Sur-Oise. Where Van Gogh spent the last months of his life.

8 Chantilly. A fabulous château and art collection, and a popular Paris day trip.

9 Senlis. A medieval town offering a charming glimpse into the past.

10 Compiègne. Town history includes Joan of Arc and World War I.

11 Disneyland Paris. For the young and the young at heart.

12 Chateau de Vaux-le-Vicomte. The inspiration for Versailles, with splendid gardens.

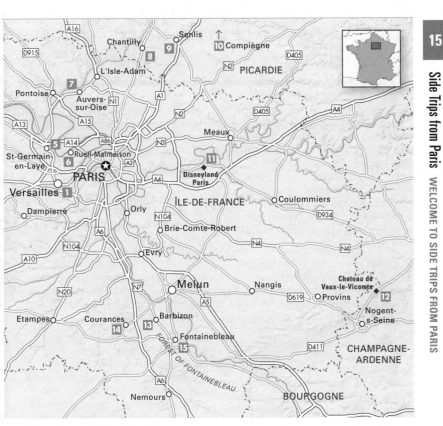

13 Barbizon. A charming town that attracts artists.

14 Courances. A lavish château and water garden.

15 Fontainebleau. Another glorious competitor to Versailles.

Just what is it that makes the Île-de-France so attractive, so comfortingly familiar? Is it its proximity to the great city of Paris—or perhaps that it's so far removed?

Had there not been the world-class cultural hub of Paris nearby, would Monet have retreated to his Japanese gardens at Giverny? Or Paul Cézanne and Van Gogh to bucolic Auvers? Kings and courtiers to the game-rich forests of Rambouillet? Would Napoléon have truly settled at Malmaison and then abdicated at the palace of Fontainebleau? Would abbeys and cathedrals have sprung skyward in Chartres and Senlis?

If you had asked Louis XIV, he wouldn't have minced his words: the city of Paris—yawn—was simply *démodée*—out of fashion. In the 17th century the new power base was going to be Versailles, once a tiny village in the heart of the Île-de-France, now the site of a gigantic château from which the Sun King's rays could radiate, unfettered by rebellious rabble and European arrivistes. Of course, later heirs kept the lines open and restored the grandiose palace as the governmental hub it was meant to be— and commuted to Paris, well before the high-speed RER.

That, indeed, is the dream of most Parisians today: to have a foot in both worlds. Paris may be small as capital cities go, with slightly fewer than 2¼ million inhabitants, but the Île-de-France, the region around Paris, contains more than 12 million people—a sixth of France's entire population. That's why on closer inspection the once-rustic villages of the Île-de-France reveal cosseted gardens, stylishly gentrified cottages, and extraordinary country restaurants no peasant farmer could afford to frequent.

The nation's heartland isn't really an *île* (island), of course. The green-forested buffer zone that enfolds Paris is only vaguely surrounded by the three rivers that meander through its periphery. But it nevertheless offers a rich and varied sampling of everything you expect from France—grand cathedrals, painters' villages, lavish palaces, plus the bubble-gum-pink turrets of Disneyland Paris—all delightfully located within easy shooting distance of the capital.

MAJOR REGIONS
Western Île-de-France. If you want to dig into the past, the Île-de-France's richest frontier is the western half of the 60-km (37-mile) circle that rings Paris. The towns are charming and the sylvan woods are full of châteaux—including the world's grandest one, Château de Versailles. Haunt of Louis XIV, Madame de Pompadour, and Marie-Antoinette, it is a monument to splendidly wretched excess and once home to 20,000 courtiers and servants. More spiritual concerns are embodied in Chartres Cathedral, a soaring pinnacle of Gothic architecture. Northwest of Paris are landscapes of lasting impressions: Giverny and Auvers-sur-Oise, immortalized by Monet and Van Gogh, respectively.

Eastern Île-de-France. By traveling an eastward arc through the remainder of the Île, you can savor the icing on the cake. Begin with Chantilly, an opulent château noted for its royal stables, stunning gardens, and a top-notch art collection rivaled only by the Louvre's. Northward lies medieval Senlis, and heading east, you'll hit Disneyland Paris, where Mickey Mouse and his animated friends get a French makeover. Continuing south, two more magnificent châteaux—Vaux-le-Vicomte and Fontainebleau—were built for some of France's most pampered monarchs and ministers.

Planning

When to Go

Spring and fall are the optimal times to come. The Île's renowned gardens look their best in the former, and its extensive forests are particularly beautiful in the latter. From May through June or September through early October, you can still take advantage of memorable warm-weather offerings—such as a candlelight visit to Vaux-le-Vicomte or an evening of music, dancing, and fireworks at Versailles—without having to contend with the high summer heat or the crowds that pack places like Disneyland Paris or Monet's Giverny, especially on weekends.

Be aware when making your travel plans that some places are closed one or two days a week, and many places also close for three weeks in August. The château of Versailles is closed Monday (the gardens remain open), and the château of Fontainebleau is closed Tuesday. In fact, as a rule, even well-touristed towns make their *fermeture hebdomadaire* (weekly closing) on Monday or Tuesday. At these times museums, shops, and

markets may be shuttered—check the website if in doubt. During the winter months, some spots shut completely (Vaux-le-Vicomte, for one, is closed from mid-November to early April, but reopens for the month of December through the New Year for their festive Christmas celebrations). So it's always best to check websites or phone ahead before venturing out in the off-season.

Planning Your Time

A great advantage to exploring this region is that all its major monuments are within a half-day's drive from Paris, or less if you take the trains that run to many of the towns. The catch is that most of those rail lines connect Île communities with Paris—not, in general, with neighboring towns of the region. Thus, it may be easier to plan on "touring" the Île in a series of side trips from Paris, rather than expecting to travel through it in clockwise fashion (which, of course, can be easily done if you have a car).

Threading the western half of the Île, the first tour heads southwest from Paris to Versailles and Chartres, turns northwest along the Seine to Monet's Giverny, and returns to Paris after visiting Vincent van Gogh's Auvers. Exploring the eastern half of the Île, the second tour picks up east of the Oise Valley in glamorous Chantilly, then detours east to Senlis, and finishes up southward by heading to Disneyland Paris, Vaux-le-Vicomte, and Fontainebleau.

For a stimulating mix of pomp, nature, and spirituality, your three priorities should be Versailles, Giverny, and Chartres. If you're allergic to crowds, swap out Fontainebleau for Versailles, a glorious mix of Renaissance architecture, gardens, and woods.

Experiencing Impressionism

Paris's Musée d'Orsay may have some of the most fabled Monet and Van Gogh paintings in the world, but the Île-de-France has something (almost) better—the actual landscapes that were rendered into masterpieces by the brushes of many great Impressionist and Postimpressionist artists. At Giverny, Claude Monet's house and garden are a moving visual link to his finest daubs—its famous lily-pond garden gave rise to his legendary *Water Lilies* series (some historians feel it was the other way around). Here, too, is the impressive Musée des Impressionnismes.

In Auvers-sur-Oise, Vincent van Gogh had a final burst of creativity before ending his life; the famous wheat field where he was attacked by crows and painted his last work is just outside town. Back then, they called him Fou-Roux (mad redhead) and derided his art; now the townspeople here love to pay tribute to the man who helped make their village famous. André Derain lived in Chambourcy, Camille Pissarro in Pontoise, and Alfred Sisley in Moret-sur-Loing: all were inspired by the silvery sunlight that tumbles over these hills and towns.

Earlier, Rousseau, Millet, and Corot paved the way for Impressionism with their penchant for outdoor landscape painting in the village of Barbizon, still surrounded by its romantic, quietly dramatic woodlands, as well as the untamed forest of Fontainebleau. A trip to any of these towns will provide lasting impressions.

Getting Here and Around

AIR
Proximity to Paris means that the Île-de-France is well served by both international and intracontinental flights. Charles de Gaulle Airport, commonly known as Roissy, is 26 km (16 miles) northeast of the capital; Orly Airport is 16 km (10 miles) south. Beauvais Airport, which services budget airlines, is 80 km (55 miles) north and is serviced by a frequently running bus.

BUS
Although many of the major sights—including Disneyland, Chartres, and Versailles—have rail lines connecting them directly to Paris, the lesser destinations pose more of a problem and require taking a local bus run by the SNCF or a taxi from the nearest train station (*gare*). Some larger towns are served by Uber, but not all. This will be the case if you're going onward to Senlis from the Chantilly Gare, to Fontainebleau and Barbizon from the Avon Gare, to Vaux-le-Vicomte (there is a limited "château shuttle" to and from Vaux-le-Vicomte) from the Verneuil l'Etang Gare, or to Giverny from the Vernon Gare.

CAR
A13 links Paris (from the Porte d'Auteuil) to Versailles. You can get to Chartres on A10 from Paris (Porte d'Orléans). For Fontainebleau take A6 from Paris (Porte d'Orléans). For a slower, more scenic route through the Forest of Sénart and the northern part of the Forest of Fontainebleau, take N6 from Paris (Porte de Charenton) via Melun. A4 runs from Paris (Porte de Bercy) to Disneyland. Although a comprehensive rail network ensures that most towns in the Île-de-France qualify as comfortable day trips from Paris, the only way to crisscross the region without returning to the capital is by car. There's no shortage of expressways or fast highways. However, you should be prepared for delays close to Paris, especially during the morning and evening rush hours and on Sunday evenings when everyone is returning from the countryside.

TRAIN

Departing from Paris, it's easy to reach key locales in this region by rail because you can take advantage of the SNCF's main-line and Transilien networks, as well as RER routes, which are part of Paris's comprehensive RATP public transit system. Chartres and Chantilly, for example, are served by both main-line and Transilien trains; those bound for Chartres leave from Gare Montparnasse (50–70 minutes), while those going to Chantilly leave from Gare du Nord (25–30 minutes). Versailles is best accessed via the RER-C line, which gets you within a five-minute walk of the château (45 minutes, and the RER-A line deposits you 100 yards from the entrance to Disneyland (40 minutes). Note that the Parisian station you start from is typically determined by the direction you're heading in.

TRAIN INFORMATION RATP. ⊕ *www. ratp.fr.* **SNCF.** ☎ *3635* ⊕ *www.sncf.com.* **Transilien.** ☎ *01–53–25–60–00* ⊕ *www. transilien.com.*

Restaurants

The Île-de-France's fanciest restaurants can be just as pricey as their Parisian counterparts. Close to the Channel for fresh fish, lush Normandy for beef and dairy products, and the rich agricultural regions of Picardy and the Beauce, Île-de-France chefs have all the ingredients they could wish for and shop for the freshest produce early each morning at the huge food market at Rungis, 18 km (10 miles) south of the capital. Traditional "local delicacies"—lamb stew, *pâté de Pantin* (pastry filled with meat), or pig's trotters—tend to be rare, although creamy Brie, made locally in Meaux and Coulommiers, remains a queen of the cheese board.

Hotels

In summer, hotel rooms are at a premium, and making reservations is essential; almost all accommodations in the swankier towns—Versailles, Rambouillet, and Fontainebleau—can be on the costly side. Take nothing for granted; picturesque Senlis, for instance, has only one hotel in its historic downtown area and its charming guesthouses fill up quickly.

Restaurant and hotel reviews have been shortened. For full information, visit Fodors.com. Restaurant prices are the average cost of a main course at dinner or, if dinner is not served, at lunch. Hotel prices are the lowest cost of a standard double room in high season.

What It Costs in Euros			
$	$$	$$$	$$$$
RESTAURANTS			
under €16	€16–€24	€25–€32	over €32
HOTELS			
under €125	€125–€225	€226–€350	over €350

Visitor Information

Special *forfait* tickets, combining travel and admission, are available for several regional tourist destinations (including Versailles, Fontainebleau, and Auvers-sur-Oise). For general information on the area, check the website of Espace du Tourisme Île-de-France (www.parisinfo. com), or visit one of its kiosks; you'll find them at the Charles de Gaulle airport, Orly airport, Versailles, and Disneyland. Further information on Disneyland can be obtained from the Disneyland Paris reservations office.

Tours

Euroscope

BUS TOURS | You can sign on for half-day or full-day minibus trips from Paris to Versailles, Giverny, and Fontainebleau. Check the Euroscope website for all the options and prices. ✉ *46 rue de Provence, Paris* ☎ *01–56–03–56–81* ⊕ *www.euroscope.fr* ✆ *From €120.*

★ Fat Tire Tours

BICYCLE TOURS | This company offers a wide range of tours in and around Paris by bicycle, Segway, or on foot. Tours are always led by cheerful, knowledgeable guides, and some include refreshments or a picnic lunch. Skip-the-line tours are an excellent way to save time, especially at the Eiffel Tower and Versailles. Prices are reasonable, and all tours can be booked online. ✉ *24 Rue Edgar Faure, Eiffel Tower* ☎ *01–82–88–80–97* ⊕ *www. fattiretours.com* ✆ *From €80.*

My Daily Driver

DRIVING TOURS | There's nothing quite so luxurious as touring around Paris, or anywhere in the Île de France and beyond, with your own personal driver. This service offers personable, knowledgeable drivers who will tailor an itinerary to your personal needs and desires. You can even choose your conveyance from a fleet of luxury cars. ✉ *Paris* ☎ *01–86–90–22–70* ⊕ *www.mydailydriver.fr* ✆ *From €180.*

Pariscityvision

BUS TOURS | Guided coach excursions to Giverny, Versailles, Vaux le Vicomte, and Fontainebleau—plus multiple destination combinations—can be booked through Pariscityvision. Some are offered year-round, but most run April through October. Half- and full-day minibus excursions for up to eight people are also available for a bit more. ✉ *2 rue des Pyramides, Paris* ☎ *01–44–55–60–00* ⊕ *www.pariscityvision.com* ✆ *From €55.*

Versailles

16 km (10 miles) west of Paris.

It's hard to tell which is larger at Château de Versailles—the world-famous château that housed Louis XIV and 20,000 of his courtiers, or the mass of tour buses and visitors standing in front of it. The grandest palace in France remains one of the marvels of the world. But this edifice was not just home to the Sun King; it was also the new headquarters of the French government (from 1682 to 1789 and again from 1871 to 1879). To accompany the palace, a new city—in fact, a new capital—had to be built from scratch. Tough-thinking town planners took no prisoners, dreaming up vast mansions and avenues broader than the Champs-Élysées.

GETTING HERE AND AROUND

Versailles has three train stations, but its Rive Gauche gare—on the RER-C line from Paris, with trains departing from Austerlitz, St-Michel, Invalides, and Champ-de-Mars—provides the easiest access and puts you within a five-minute walk of the château (45 minutes, €3.65).

VISITOR INFORMATION Versailles Tourist Office. ✉ *2 av. de Paris* ☎ *01–39–24–88–88* ⊕ *www.versailles-tourisme.com.*

Sights

Avenue de Paris

STREET | Not far from the palace, a breadth of 120 yards makes Avenue de Paris wider than the Champs-Élysées, and its buildings are just as grand and even more historic. The avenue leads down to Place d'Armes, a vast sloping plaza usually filled with tour buses. Facing the château are the Trojan-size royal stables. Recently added bike lanes along the length of the avenue allow for a scenic cycling tour that leads to the historic neighborhoods that flank Versailles:

the Quartier Saint-Louis to the south (to the left when facing the château) and the Quartier Notre-Dame to the north (to the right when facing the château). ⊠ *Av. de Paris.*

Cathédrale St-Louis

CHURCH | Not far from the Grandes Écuries stables, on a lovely square at the heart of the town's old center, the Cathédrale Saint-Louis (also known as the Cathédrale de Versailles) dates to the reign of Louis XV. Outside, the 18th-century seat of the Bishop of Versailles is notable for its dome and twin-tower facade; inside, the sanctuary is enriched with a fine organ and paintings. On Thursday and Saturday mornings, the square in front of the cathedral hosts a classic farmers' market. ⊠ *Pl. Saint-Louis* ☎ *01–39–50–40–65* ⊕ *www.cathe-drale-versailles.org.*

★ Château de Versailles

CASTLE/PALACE | A two-century spree of indulgence by the consecutive reigns of three French kings produced two of the world's most historic landmarks: gloriously, the Palace of Versailles and, momentously, the French Revolution. Less a monument than a world unto itself, Versailles is the king of palaces. The end result of countless francs, 40 years, and 36,000 laborers, it was Louis XIV's monument to himself—the Sun King. Construction of the sprawling palace and gardens, which Louis personally and meticulously oversaw, started in 1661 and took 40 years to complete. Today the château seems monstrously big, but it wasn't large enough for the army of 20,000 noblemen, servants, and hangers-on who moved in with Louis. A new city—a new capital, in fact—had to be constructed from scratch to accommodate them.

One of the palace highlights is the dazzling **Galerie des Glaces** (Hall of Mirrors). Lavish balls were once held here, as was a later event with much greater

world impact: the signing of the Treaty of Versailles, which put an end to World War I on June 28, 1919. The **Grands Apparte-ments** (State Apartments) are whipped into a lather of decoration, with painted ceilings, marble walls, parquet floors, and canopy beds topped with ostrich plumes. The **Petits Appartements** (Private Apartments), where the royal family and friends lived, are on a more human scale, lined with 18th-century gold and white rococo boiseries. The **Opéra Royal**, the first oval hall in France, was designed for Louis XV and inaugurated in 1770 for the marriage of 15-year-old Louis XVI to 14-year-old Austrian archduchess Marie-Antoinette. Considered the finest 18th-century opera house in Europe at the time (with acoustics to match), it is now a major venue for world-class performers. Completed in 1701 in the Louis XIV style, the **Appartements du Roi** (King's Apartments) comprise a suite of 15 rooms set in a "U" around the east facade's Marble Court. The **Chambre de la Reine** (Queen's Bed Chamber)—once among the world's most opulent—was updated for Marie-Antoinette in the chicest style of the late 18th century. The superb **Salon du Grand Couvert**, ante-chamber to the Queen's Apartments, is the place where Louis XIV took his supper every evening at 10 o'clock. The sumptuously painted walls and ceilings, tapestries, woodwork, and even the fur-niture have been returned to their original splendor, making this the only one of the queen's private rooms that can be seen exactly as it was first decorated in the 1670s. The park and gardens are a great place to stretch your legs while taking in details of André Le Nôtre's formal landscaping.

Versailles's royal getaways are as impres-sive in their own right as the main palace. A charmer with the ladies (as Louis's many royal mistresses would attest), the Sun King enjoyed a more relaxed atmos-phere in which to conduct his dalliances

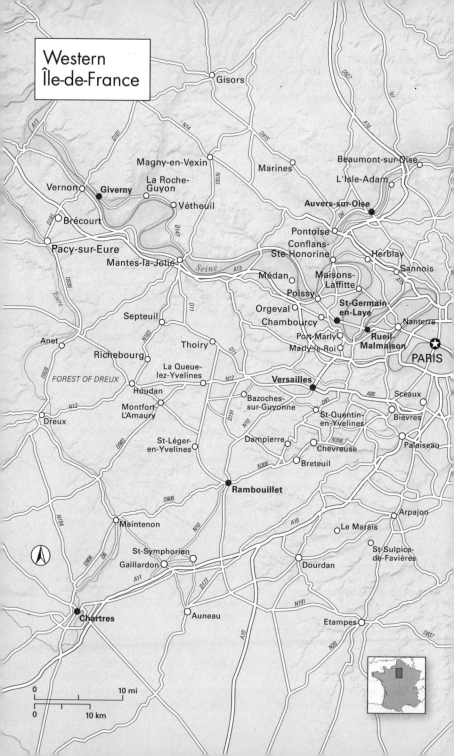

Western Île-de-France

Gisors

Magny-en-Vexin
Marines
Beaumont-sur-Oise
L'Isle-Adam
La Roche-
Guyon
Vernon
Giverny
Auvers-sur-Oise
Vétheuil
Brécourt
Pontoise
Conflans-
Ste-Honorine
Herblay
Pacy-sur-Eure
Sannois
Mantes-la-Jolie
Seine
Médan
Maisons-
Laffitte
Poissy
Orgeval
St-Germain-
en-Laye
Septeuil
Chambourcy
Nanterre
Port-Marly
Rueil-
Malmaison
Anet
Thoiry
Marly-le-Roi
PARIS
Richebourg
La Queue-
lez-Yvelines
Versailles
FOREST OF DREUX
Sceaux
Houdan
Bazoches-
sur-Guyonne
Montfort-
L'Amaury
St-Quentin-
en-Yvelines
Bièvres
Dreux
St-Léger-
en-Yvelines
Dampierre
Chevreuse
Palaiseau
Breteuil
Rambouillet
Arpajon
Maintenon
Le Marais
St-Symphorien
St-Sulpice-
de-Favières
Gaillardon
Dourdan
Chartres
Auneau
Etampes

0   10 mi
0   10 km

away from the prying eyes of the court at the **Grand Trianon.** But Versailles's most famous getaway, the **Hameau de la Reine,** was added under the reign of Louis XVI at the request of his relentlessly scrutinized wife, Marie-Antoinette. Seeking to create a simpler "country" life away from the court's endless intrigues, between 1783 and 1787, the queen had her own rustic hamlet built in the image of a charming Normandy village, complete with a mill and dairy, roving livestock, and delightfully natural gardens. One of the most visited monuments in the world, Versailles is almost always teeming, especially in the summer; try to beat the crowds by arriving at 9 am, and buying your ticket online. ⊠ *Pl. d'Armes* ☎ *01–30–83–78–00* ⊕ *www.chateauversailles.fr* ⊠ *€18, all-attractions pass €20, Marie-Antoinette's Domain €12, park free (weekend fountain show €9.50, Apr.–Oct.)* ⊗ *Closed Mon.*

Notre-Dame

CHURCH | If you have any energy left after exploring Louis XIV's palace and park, a tour of Versailles—a textbook 18th-century town—offers a telling contrast between the majestic and the domestic. From the front gate of Versailles's palace, turn left onto Rue de l'Independence-Américaine and walk over to Rue Carnot past the stately Écuries de la Reine—once the queen's stables, now the regional law courts—to octagonal place Hoche. Down Rue Hoche to the left is the powerful Baroque facade of Notre-Dame, built from 1684 to 1686 by Jules Hardouin-Mansart as the parish church for Louis XIV's new town. ⊠ *Versailles* ⊕ *notredameversailles.org.*

Place du Marché-Notre-Dame

PLAZA/SQUARE | This lively square in the heart of the Notre-Dame neighborhood is home to the largest market in the region, far outstripping anything in Paris. Outdoors, stalls offer a veritable cornucopia of fresh fruits, vegetables, herbs,

and spices; meanwhile, the four historic halls (dating to the reign of Louis XV and rebuilt in 1841) brim with every gourmet delight—foie gras, fine wines, seafood, game, prepared delicacies, cheese from every corner of France—providing a sensory experience that will overwhelm even the most jaded foodie. The open-air market runs three half days a week (Tuesday, Friday, and Sunday 7–2), but the covered food halls are open every day except Monday, from early morning until 7:30 pm (closing is at 2 on Sunday). If you're in the mood for more shopping, the town's marvelous antiques district begins at the northwest corner of the market square and extends along the cobbled streets to the charming Passage de la Geôle. ⊠ *Versailles.*

★ Potager du Roi

GARDEN | The King's Potager—a 6-acre, split-level fruit-and-vegetable garden—was created in 1683 by Jean-Baptiste de La Quintinye. Many rare heirloom species are painstakingly cultivated here by a team of gardeners and students studying at the famous École Nationale Supérieure d'Horticulture. You can sample their wares (which are used in some of the finest Parisian restaurants) or pick up a bottle of fruit juice or jam made from the king's produce. Perfumed "Potager du Roi" candles, sold at the delightful boutique, make a nice souvenir. ⊠ *10 rue du Maréchal Joffre* ☎ *01–39–24–62–62* ⊕ *www.potager-du-roi.fr* ⊠ *Weekends €8, weekdays €5* ⊗ *Closed Mon. year-round, weekends Jan.–Mar., and Sun. Nov.–Dec.*

Salle du Jeu de Paume

PUBLIC ART | On June 20, 1789, members of the Third Estate—the commoner's section of the three-part Estates General, which included nobles (First Estate) and clergy (Second Estate)—found themselves locked out of their regular meeting place by palace guards, so they

Continued on page 360

VERSAILLES

By Robert I.C. Fisher

Louis XIV's Hall of Mirrors

A two-century spree of indulgence in the finest riches of the age by the consecutive reigns of three French kings produced two of the world's most historic artifacts: gloriously, the Palace of Versailles and, momentously, the French Revolution.

Less a monument than an entire world unto itself, Versailles is the king of palaces. The end result of 380 million francs, 36,000 laborers, and enough paintings, if laid end to end, to equal 7 miles of canvas, it was conceived as the ne plus ultra expression of monarchy by Louis XIV. As a child, the king had developed a hatred for Paris (where he had been imprisoned by a group of nobles known as the Frondeurs), so, when barely out of his teens, he cast his cantankerous royal eye in search of a new power base. Marshy, inhospitable Versailles was the stuff of his dreams. Down came dad's modest royal hunting lodge and up, up, and along went the minion-crushing, Baroque palace we see today.

Between 1661 and 1710, architects Louis Le Vau and Jules Hardouin Mansart designed everything his royal acquisitiveness could want, including a throne room devoted to Apollo, god of the sun (Louis was known as *le roi soleil*). Convinced that his might depended upon dominating French nobility, Louis XIV summoned thousands of grandees from their own far-flung châteaux to reside at his new seat of government. In doing so, however, he unwittingly triggered the downfall of the monarchy. Like an 18th-century Disneyland, Versailles kept its courtiers so richly entertained they all but forgot the murmurs of discontent brewing back home.

As Louis XV chillingly foretold, "After me, the deluge." The royal commune was therefore shocked—shocked!—by the appearance, on October 5, 1789, of a revolutionary mob from Paris ready to sack Versailles and imprison Louis XVI. So as you walk through this awesome monument to splendor and excess, give a thought to its historic companion: the French Revolution. A tour of Versailles's grand salons inextricably mixes pathos with glory.

CROWNING GLORIES: TOP SIGHTS OF VERSAILLES

Seducing their court with their self-assured approach to 17th- and 18th-century art and decoration, a trinity of French kings made Versailles into the most vainglorious of châteaux.

Versailles from the outside

Galerie des Glaces (Hall of Mirrors). Of all the rooms at Versailles, none matches the magnificence of the Galerie des Glaces (Hall of Mirrors). Begun by Mansart in 1678, this represents the acme of the Louis Quatorze (Louis-XIV) style. Measuring 240 feet long, 33 feet wide, and 40 feet high, it is ornamented with gilded candlesticks, crystal chandeliers, and a coved ceiling painted with Charles Le Brun's homage to Louis XIV's reign.

Detail of the ceiling

In Louis's day, the Galerie was laid with priceless carpets and filled with orange trees in silver pots. Nighttime galas were illuminated by 3,000 candles, their blaze doubled in the 17 gigantic mirrors that precisely echo the banner of windows along the west front. Lavish balls were once held here, and you can still get the full royal treatment at the Serenade Royale. This reenacts one of Louis XIV's grand soirées with dancers in period costumes. The 40-minute spectacle is held every Saturday from mid-June to late September at 6:30, 6:50, 7:10, 7:30, and 7:50 pm (✉ €21-€42) ⊕ www.chateauversailles-spectacles.fr ☎ 01–30–83–78–98).

Hall of Mirrors

The Grands Appartements (State Apartments). Virtual stages for ceremonies of court ritual and etiquette, Louis XIV's first-floor state salons were designed in the Baroque style on a biceps-flexing scale meant to one-up the lavish Vaux-le-Vicomte château recently built for Nicolas Fouquet, the king's finance minister.

Inside the Apollo Chamber

Flanking the Hall of Mirrors and retaining most of their bombastic Italianate Baroque decoration, the Salon de la Guerre (Salon of War) and the Salon de la Paix (Salon of Peace) are ornately decorated with gilt stucco, painted ceilings, and marble sculpture. Perhaps the most extravagant is the Salon d'Apollon (Apollo Chamber), the former throne room.

Hall of Battles

Appartements du Roi (King's Apartments). Completed in 1701 in the Louis-XIV style, the king's state and private chambers comprise a suite of 15 rooms set in a "U" around the east facade's Marble Court. Dead center across the sprawling cobbled forecourt is Louis XIV's bedchamber—he would awake and rise (just as the sun did, from the east) attended by members of his court and the public. Holding the king's chemise when he dressed soon became a more definitive reflection of status than the possession of an entire province. Nearby is Louis XV's magnificent Cabinet Intérieur (Office of the King), shining with gold and white boiseries; in the center is the most famous piece of furniture at Versailles, Louis XV's roll-top desk, crafted by Oeben and Riesener in 1769.

Louis XIV

Versailles ceiling art

Chambre de la Reine (Queen's Bedchamber). Probably the most opulent bedroom in the world, this was initially created for Marie Thérèse, first wife of Louis XIV, to be part of the Queen's Apartments. For Marie Antoinette, however, the entire room was glammed up with silk wall-hangings covered with Rococo motifs that reflect her love of flowers. Legend has it that the gardens directly beyond these windows were replanted daily so that the queen could enjoy a fresh assortment of blossoms each morning. The bed, decked out with white ostrich plumes *en panache*, was also redone for Louis XVI's queen. Nineteen royal children were born in this room.

VINTAGE BOURBON

Versailles was built by three great kings of the Bourbon dynasty. Louis XIV (1638–1715) began its construction in 1661. After ruling for 72 years, Louis Quatorze was succeeded by his great grandson, Louis XV (1710–74), who added the Royal Opera and the Petit Trianon to the palace. Louis XVI (1754–93) came to the throne in 1774 and was forced out of Versailles in 1789, along with Marie Antoinette, both guillotined three years later.

Queen's Bedchamber

Petits Appartements (Small Apartments). As styles of decor changed, Louis XIV's successors felt out of sync with their architectural inheritance. Louis XV exchanged the heavy red-and-gilt of Italianate Baroque for lighter, pastel-hued Rococo. On the top floor of the palace, on the right side of the central portion, are the apartments Louis XV commissioned to escape the wearisome pomp of the first-floor rooms. Here, Madame de Pompadour, mistress of Louis XV and famous patroness of the Rococo style, introduced grace notes of intimacy and refinement. In so doing, she transformed the daunting royal apartments into places to live rather than pose.

Parc de Versailles. Even Bourbon kings needed respite from Versailles's endless maze, hence the creation of one of Europe's largest parks. The sublime 250-acre grounds (☏ *01–30–83–77–88 for guided tour*) is the masterpiece of André Le Nôtre, presiding genius of 17th-century classical French landscaping. Le Nôtre was famous for his "green geometries": ordered fantasies of clipped yew trees, multicolored flower beds (called *parterres*), and perspectival *allées* cleverly punctuated with statuary, laid out between 1661 and 1668. The spatial effect is best admired from inside the palace, views about which Le Nôtre said, "Flowers can only be walked on by the eyes."

Ultimately, at the royal command, rivers were diverted—to flow into more than 600 fountains—and entire forests were imported to ornament the park, which is centered around the mile-long Grand Canal. As for the great fountains, their operation costs a fortune in these democratic days, and so they perform only on weekends (9–7) from April through October; admission to the park during this time is €8. The park is open daily 7 am–8:30 pm in summer and 8-6 in winter.

LIGHTING UP THE SKY

The largest fountain at Versailles, the Bassin de Neptune, becomes a spectacle of rare grandeur during the Grandes Eaux Nocturnes, a light show to the strains of Baroque music, held Saturdays from mid-June through September at 8:30 pm, with fireworks at 11. Tickets start at €24 ⊕ *www.chateauversailles-spectacles.fr* ☏ *01–30–83–78–98.*

Dauphin's Apartments

Bassin de Neptune

Chapel and Opéra Royal: In the north wing of the château are three showpieces of the palace. The solemn white-and-gold Chapelle was completed in 1710—the king and queen attended daily mass here seated in gilt boxes. The Opéra Royal (Opera House), entirely constructed of wood painted to look like marble, was designed by Jacques-Ange Gabriel for Louis XV in 1770. Connecting the two, the 17th-century Galeries have exhibits retracing the château's history.

Opéra Royal

VERSAILLES: FIRST FLOOR, GARDENS & ADJACENT PARK

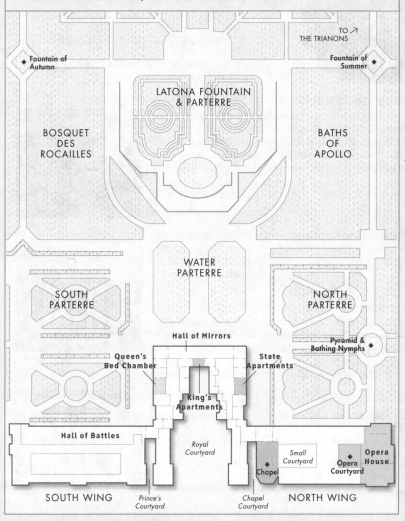

TO ↗
THE TRIANONS

Fountain of Autumn

Fountain of Summer

LATONA FOUNTAIN & PARTERRE

BOSQUET DES ROCAILLES

BATHS OF APOLLO

WATER PARTERRE

SOUTH PARTERRE

NORTH PARTERRE

Hall of Mirrors

Queen's Bed Chamber

State Apartments

Pyramid & Bathing Nymphs

King's Apartments

Hall of Battles

Royal Courtyard

Small Courtyard

Opera Courtyard

Opera House

Chapel

SOUTH WING

Prince's Courtyard

Chapel Courtyard

NORTH WING

MARIE ANTOINETTE'S ROYAL LAIR

Was Marie Antoinette a luxury-mad butterfly flitting from ball to costume ball? Or was she a misunderstood queen who suffered a loveless marriage and became a prisoner of court etiquette at Versailles? Historians now believe the answer was the latter and point to her private retreats at Versailles as proof.

R.F.D. VERSAILLES?

Here, in the northwest part of the royal park, Marie Antoinette (1755–93) created a tiny universe of her own: her comparatively dainty mansion called Petit Trianon and its adjacent "farm," the relentlessly picturesque Hameau ("hamlet"). In a life that took her from royal cradle to throne of France to guillotine, her happiest days were spent at Trianon. For here she could live a life in the "simplest" possible way; here the queen could enter a salon and the game of cards would not stop; here women could wear simple gowns of muslin without a single jewel. Toinette only wanted to be queen of Trianon, not queen of France. And considering the horrible, chamber-pot-pungent, gossip-infested corridors of Versailles, you can almost understand why.

TEEN QUEEN

From the first, Maria-Antonia (her actual name) was ostracized as an outsider. Upon arriving in France in 1770—at a mere 14 years of age—she was married to the Dauphin, the future King Louis XVI. But shamed by her initial failure to deliver a royal heir, she grew to hate overcrowded Versailles and escaped to the Petit Trianon. Built between 1763 and 1768 by Jacques-Ange Gabriel for Madame de Pompadour, this bijou palace was a radical statement: a royal residence designed to be casual and unassuming. Toinette refashioned the Trianon's interior in the sober Neoclassical style.

Hameau

Queen's House

Temple of Love

Petit Trianon

"THE SIMPLE LIFE"

Just beyond Petit Trianon lay the storybook Hameau, a mock-Norman village inspired by the peasant-luxe, simple-life daydreams caught by Boucher on canvas and by Rousseau in literature. With its water mill, thatched-roof houses, pigeon loft, and vegetable plots, this make-believe farm village was run by Monsieur Valy-Busard, a farmer, and his wife, who often helped the queen—outfitted as a Dresden shepherdess with a Sèvres porcelain crook—tend her flock of perfumed sheep.

As if to destroy any last link with reality, the queen built nearby a jewel-box theater (open by appointment). Here she acted in little plays, sometimes essaying the role of a servant girl. Only the immediate royal family, about seven or so friends, and her personal servants were permitted entry; disastrously, the entire officialdom of Versailles society was shut out—a move that only served to infuriate courtiers. This is how fate and destiny close the circle. For it was here at Trianon that a page sent by Monsieur de Saint-Priest found Marie-Antoinette on October 5, 1789, to tell her that Paris was marching on an already half-deserted Versailles.

Was Marie Antoinette a political traitor to France whose execution was well merited? Or was she the ultimate fashion victim? For those who feel that this tragic queen spent—and shopped—her way into a revolution, a visit to her relatively modest Petit Trianon and Hameau should prove a revelation.

Marie Antoinette

LES BEAUX TRIANONS

A mile from the château, the Grand Trianon was created by Hardouin Mansart in 1687 as a retreat for Louis XIV; it was restored in the early 19th century, with Empire-style salons. It's a memorable spot often missed by foot-weary tourists exhausted by the château, but well worth the effort. A special treat is Marie Antoinette's hideaway nearby, the Petit Trianon, presumably restored to how she left it before being forced to Paris by an angry mob of soon-to-be revolutionaries.

convened in this tennis court instead to discuss their demands. The resulting Tennis Court Oath stated that the sovereignty of the people did not reside with the king but with the people themselves. It became the first draft of the French Constitution (based closely on the American Declaration of Independence) and was a major first step in the Revolution and subsequent abolition of the monarchy. The members are depicted in a monumental painting on the court's far wall. A fascinating guided visit in English is available through the Versailles tourist office. ✉ *Rue du Jeu de Paume, Quartier Saint-Louis* ☎ *01–30–83–78–00* 🎟 *Free.*

🍴 Restaurants

Bleue, Blanche, Rouge
$$ | BISTRO | An unapologetic carnivore, chef Alix Guiet bucks the trend for veggie-conscious cuisine in his handsome new restaurant a quick walk from the palace, The seasonal menu offers all the tried-and-true French classics—sautéed duck hearts, bone marrow on toast, veal liver, steak tartare—from the famous meat-producing regions of France, served with your choice of delicious, artery clogging sauce: green peppercorn, béarnaise, *beurre Roquefort,* etc. There's also a choice of fish dishes. **Known for:** quality products; historic 17th-century town house; carnivores' delight. [$] *Average main: €22* ✉ *27 av. de Saint-Cloud* ☎ *01–30–84–98–85* 🌐 *www.bleue-blanche-rouge.fr* 🕘 *Closed Sun. and Mon.*

★ Gordon Ramsay au Trianon
$$$$ | MODERN FRENCH | Worldwide chef sensation Gordon Ramsay brings his conversation-worthy cuisine to this Versailles berth. Picture exemplary entrées like ravioli of langoustines and lobster cooked in a Riesling bisque with Petrossian caviar and lime consommé, or Périgord foie gras done "2 ways," roasted with a beetroot tart and pressed with green apple and Sauternes, all available on an expensive five-course tasting menu at dinner. **Known for:** one Michelin star; more casual Véranda outpost next door; stellar cuisine from a star chef. [$] *Average main: €78* ✉ *1 bd. de la Reine* ☎ *01–30–84–50–18* 🌐 *www.waldorfastoriaversailles.fr/restaurants-et-bar/gordon-ramsay-au-trianon* 🕘 *Closed Sun. and Mon. No lunch* 👔 *Jacket required.*

★ La Table du 11
$$$$ | MODERN FRENCH | With a Michelin star in his pocket, rising chef Jean-Baptiste Lavergne-Morazzani has answered the city's dire need for top-quality and well-priced dining at La Table du 11. A small menu features the freshest market dishes: maybe line-caught daurade with candied citrus, Argentine beef with roasted pumpkin and velvety buratina cheese, and a spectacular cheese plate for dessert. **Known for:** charming ambience; affordable prix-fixe menus; excellent traditional French cuisine. [$] *Average main: €44* ✉ *8 rue de la Chancellerie* ☎ *09–83–34–76–00* 🌐 *www.latabledu11.com* 🕘 *Closed Sun. and Mon.*

★ Le Corot
$$$$ | FRENCH | Chef Rémi Chambard's Michelin-starred dining room at the charming "countryside" luxury hotel Les Étangs de Corot is a favorite hideaway for Paris gastronomes not only for the lovely setting, between Paris and Versailles, but for his flawless cuisine made from top-notch ingredients (veggies are from the Versailles gardens). In warm weather, the famous Sunday brunch, served in the beautiful patio garden, is an experience to remember. **Known for:** superb cuisine; in a luxury hotel for a perfect weekend getaway between Paris and Versailles; beautiful lakeside setting with outdoor garden seating. [$] *Average main: €55* ✉ *55 rue de Versailles, Quartier Saint-Louis* ☎ *01–41–15–37–00* 🌐 *www.etangs-corot.com/en/* 🕘 *No lunch Mon., Tues., and Wed. No dinner Sun.*

Le Sept
$$ | FRENCH | The 15-minute walk from the palace gates to this cozy, well-priced

bistro is rewarded by an enticing daily menu of French classics all listed on a blackboard that's brought to your table. Dishes like homemade foie gras, roasted cod, and ham with parsley sauce are made with ingredients fresh from local suppliers. **Known for:** gets busy, so reservations necessary; excellent natural wine list; good-value prix-fixe menus. [$] *Average main: €19 ✉ 7 rue de Montreuil, Quartier Montreuil ☎ 01–39–49–55–27 🌐 www.lesept-versailles.com/restaurant ⏲ Closed Sun. and Mon.*

★ Ore

$$$ | FRENCH | There's no doubt that dining in the world's most famous palace at a restaurant conceived by the world's most famous chef is an experience worth having. Although Alain Ducasse is not actually cooking here, you can enjoy a gourmet version of breakfast, lunch, or teatime in splendid surroundings with views of the palace from the first-floor restaurant's floor-to-ceiling windows. **Known for:** serene atmosphere away from the crowds (just be sure to reserve in advance); elegant surroundings and linen-clad tables; on-site Versailles dining (with some prix-fixe menus that include admission). [$] *Average main: €28 ✉ Pl. d'Armes Château de Versailles, Quartier Saint-Louis ☎ 01–30–84–12–96 🌐 www.ducasse-chateauversailles.com ⏲ Closed Mon. No dinner.*

Hotels

Hôtel La Residence du Berry

$$ | HOTEL | On a quiet main street in the picturesque Saint-Louis district, this 18th-century hotel with wood-beam ceilings, antique engravings, and cozy rooms melds old-world charm with modern amenities. **Pros:** convenient yet quiet location; reasonable prices; charming bar. **Cons:** no air-conditioning; some rooms need a spruce-up; lovely breakfast not included in the price. [$] *Rooms from: €151 ✉ 14 rue Anjou ☎ 01–39–49–07–07 🌐 www.hotel-berry.com 🛏 38 rooms 🍴 No Meals.*

Le Cheval Rouge

$ | HOTEL | Built in 1676, this unpretentious option is in a corner of the market square, close to the château and strongly recommended if you plan to explore the town on foot. **Pros:** great setting in town center; original touches; good value for Versailles. **Cons:** style dated; some rooms need renovating; bland public areas. [$] *Rooms from: €114 ✉ 18 rue André-Chénier ☎ 01–39–50–03–03 🌐 www.chevalrougeversailles.fr 🛏 40 rooms 🍴 No Meals.*

★ Le Grand Contrôle Versailles

$$$$ | HOTEL | Set in the 17th-century quarters of Louis XIV's finance minister, this exquisite hotel—which actually abuts the château grounds—faithfully recreates the "palace" experience, from bathing (your personal butler will draw your bath for you) to dining (with Alain Ducasse–designed menus) to the staff (dressed like footmen). **Pros:** truly a royal experience; excellent restaurant and spa; before- and after-hours visits to Versailles and free rein of the palace gardens. **Cons:** incredibly expensive; the servant thing is not for everyone; minimum two-night stay. [$] *Rooms from: €1700 ✉ 12 rue de l'Indépendance Américaine, Quartier Saint-Louis ☎ 01–85–36–05–50 🌐 www.airelles.com/fr/destination/chateau-de-versailles-hotel ⏲ Closed Aug. 🛏 14 rooms 🍴 No Meals.*

Les Etangs de Corot

$$$ | HOTEL | Enjoy the pleasures of both village and countryside at this charming hotel a pleasant 20-minute walk from Versailles. **Pros:** spacious, full-service spa; just across the Seine from Paris; bucolic leafy setting on a lake. **Cons:** decor varies widely; some rooms overlook a busy road; restaurant service slow. [$] *Rooms from: €280 ✉ 55 rue de Versailles ☎ 01–41–15–37–00 🌐 www.etangs-corot.com 🛏 42 rooms 🍴 No Meals.*

L'Orangerie White-Palacio
$$ | **B&B/INN** | Across a charming garden from the main house, this pretty cottage offers two quiet and comfortable suites with private bathrooms, a common kitchen, and full garden access for meals or relaxation. **Pros:** friendly, helpful host; off-the-beaten tourist path; very close to main sights. **Cons:** don't expect hotel-style services; handheld shower in bath; cold breakfast. [$] *Rooms from: €175* ✉ *37 av. de Paris, Quartier Saint-Louis* ☎ *09–53–61–07–57* 🌐 *www.l-orangerie-versailles.fr* 🛏 *2 rooms* 🍴 *Free Breakfast.*

Waldorf Astoria Versailles-Trianon Palace
$$$$ | **HOTEL** | Like a modern-day Versailles, this deluxe turn-of-the-20th-century hotel is a creamy white creation of imposing size, filled with soaring rooms (including the historic Salle Clemenceau, site of the 1919 Versailles Peace Conference). **Pros:** palatial glamour; Gordon Ramsay's on-site restaurant; wonderful setting right by château park. **Cons:** newer rooms not as glitzy; glamorous setting not for everyone; lacks a personal touch. [$] *Rooms from: €450* ✉ *1 bd. de la Reine* ☎ *01–30–84–50–00* 🌐 *www.waldorfastoriaversailles.fr/en/trianon-palace/* 🛏 *199 rooms* 🍴 *No Meals.*

Performing Arts

Académie Equestre de Versailles
CIRCUSES | On most weekends (and on certain weekdays during school holidays), you can watch 28 elegant white horses and their expert riders perform balletic feats to music in a dazzling hour-long show directed by the great equine choreographer Bartabas. Located opposite the palace, the structure was built for Louis XIV's royal cavalry. ✉ *Av. Rockefeller* ☎ *01–39–02–62–75* 🌐 *www.bartabas.fr* 🎟 *Shows €28, includes stables visit.*

Centre de Musique Baroque
CONCERTS | An accomplished dancer, Louis XIV was also a great music lover who bankrolled the finest musicians and composers of the day—Lully, Charpentier, Rameau, Marais. So it's only fitting that France's foremost institute for the study and performance of French Baroque music should be based at Versailles. An excellent program of concerts is presented in the château's Opéra Royal and chapel; the latter are free of charge. ✉ *Versailles* ☎ *01–39–20–78–10* 🌐 *www.cmbv.fr.*

Mois Molière
ARTS CENTERS | In June, Mois Molière (Molière Month) heralds a program of concerts, dramatic productions, and exhibits inspired by the famous playwright. ✉ *Pl. du Marché Notre-Dame* ☎ *01–30–21–51–39* 🌐 *www.moismoliere.com.*

★ **Opéra Royal du Château de Versailles**
OPERA | One of the most beautiful opera houses in Europe was built for 14-year-old Marie-Antoinette on the occasion of her marriage to Louis XVI, and entering this extravagantly gilded performance hall from the hewn-stone passageway can literally take your breath away. But the beauty is not just skin-deep—the intimate 700-seat venue is blessed with rich acoustics. Home to the Royal Opera, it hosts a world-class roster of orchestral and chamber concerts, as well as modern dance and ballet performances. For arts lovers, this spot alone will justify the quick trip from Paris. ✉ *Château de Versailles* ☎ *01–30–83–78–89* 🌐 *www.chateauversailles-spectacles.fr.*

Théâtre Montansier
MUSIC | The calendar here features a full program of plays in French, music, dance, and children's entertainment. ✉ *13 rue des Réservoirs* ☎ *01–39–20–16–00* 🌐 *www.theatremontansier.com.*

🛍 Shopping

Aux Colonnes
FOOD | This charming, highly rated *confiserie* (candy shop) offers a cornucopia of chocolates and traditional French sweets. ✉ *14 rue Hoche* ⊕ *www.auxcolonnes.com.*

★ Costumes & Châteaux
OTHER SPECIALTY STORE | Anyone harboring a royal-for-a-day fantasy should head straight over to this charming costume boutique, where women, men, and kids can dress up in the high style of the Sun King's day. You can then have your picture taken or take the made-in-Versailles costume home as a memento. ✉ *1 pl. Saint Louis, Quartier Saint-Louis* ☎ *01–71–41–07–95* ⊕ *www.costumes-et-chateaux.com.*

Les Délices du Palais
FOOD | Everyone heads here to pick up homemade pâté, cold cuts, cheese, salad, and other picnic essentials. ✉ *4 rue du Maréchal-Foch* ⊕ *www.facebook.com/LesDelicesduPalaisVersailles.*

★ Quartier des Antiquaires
ANTIQUES & COLLECTIBLES | In the heart of the Notre-Dame neighborhood, a few steps from the fabulous market, the Quartier des Antiquaires is a warren of streets, passages, and squares beginning at the northwest corner of the market square and extending along the cobbled streets to the charming Passage de la Geôle. You'll find scores of elegant antiques shops brimming with eye-popping objects, paintings, furniture, china, and bibelots from every epoch. ✉ *14 bis, rue Baillet-Reviron* ☎ *01–30–21–15–13* ⊕ *www.antiques-versailles.com/le-quartier.*

Rambouillet

32 km (20 miles) southwest of Versailles, 42 km (26 miles) southwest of Paris.

Haughty Rambouillet, once favored by kings and dukes, is now home to affluent gentry and, occasionally, the French president.

GETTING HERE AND AROUND
Frequent daily trains from Paris's Gare Montparnasse arrive at Gare de Rambouillet on Place Prud'homme (35 minutes, €9.30).

VISITOR INFORMATION Rambouillet Tourist Office. ✉ *1 rue du Général de Gaulle* ☎ *01–34–83–21–21* ⊕ *www.rambouillet-tourisme.fr.*

👁 Sights

Bergerie Nationale
FARM/RANCH | **FAMILY** | Located within Parc du Château, the Bergerie Nationale (National Sheepfold) is the site of a more serious agricultural venture: the famous Rambouillet Merinos raised here, prized for the quality and yield of their wool, are descendants of sheep imported from Spain by Louis XVI in 1786. A museum alongside tells the tale and evokes shepherd life. Don't miss the wonderful boutique—it features products from the farm, including *fromage de brebis* (sheep's milk cheese), produce, potted pâtés, jams, honey, and, of course, wool. ✉ *Parc du Chateau* ☎ *01–61–08–68–00* ⊕ *www.bergerie-nationale.educagri.fr* 🎟 *€7* 🕐 *Closed Thurs., Fri., Mon., and Tues.*

Château de Rambouillet
CASTLE/PALACE | Surrounded by a magnificent 36,000-acre forest, this elegant château is a popular spot for biking and walking. Most of the structure dates to the early 18th century, but the brawny Tour François Ier (Francis I Tower), named

for the king who died here in 1547, was part of a fortified castle that earlier stood on this site. Highlights include the wood-paneled apartments, especially the Boudoir de la Comtesse (Countess's Dressing Room); the marble-sheathed Salle de Marbre (Marble Hall), dating to the Renaissance; and the Salle de Bains de Napoléon (Napoléon's Bathroom), adorned with Pompeii-style frescoes. Compared with the muscular forecourt, the château's lakeside facade is a scene of unexpected serenity and, as flowers spill from its balconies, cheerful informality. Guided visits in English are available on the hour (10–5) by reservation. ✉ *Rambouillet* ☎ *01–34–83–00–25* 🌐 *www.chateau-rambouillet.fr* 🎫 *€9.50* 🕓 *Closed Tues.*

Parc du Château

GARDEN | An extensive park—complete with island-dotted lake—stretches behind the château. Within it is the **Laiterie de la Reine** (Queen's Dairy), built for Marie-Antoinette: inspired by the writings of Jean-Jacques Rousseau, she came here to escape from the pressures of court life, pretending to be a simple milkmaid. It has a small marble temple and grotto and, nearby, the shell-lined Chaumière des Coquillages (Shell Pavilion). ✉ *Rambouillet* 🌐 *www.chateau-rambouillet.fr* 🎫 *Included in château ticket.*

🍴 Restaurants

Auberge du Louvetier

$$$ | **BISTRO** | With a roaring fire in winter and an outdoor terrace in summer, this quaint, country-style restaurant specializes in the fruits of the sea. Traditional dishes—like brioche-enrobed escargot with Roquefort sauce, plump seafood sausage, a hearty *soupe de poisson* (fish soup), and a heaping seafood platter—are served in a wood-beamed dining room. **Known for:** friendly service; homemade French specialties; charming setting. [$] *Average main: €25* ✉ *19 rue de l'Etang de la Tour* ☎ *01–34–85–61–00* 🌐 *aubergedulouvetier.com* 🕓 *Closed Mon. No lunch Sat. No dinner Sun.*

★ **Villa Marinette**

$$$$ | **FRENCH** | Three km (2 miles) from Rambouillet near the small town of Gazeran, this ivy-clad 18th-century home is a romantic setting for an elegant gastronomic meal. Dishes like roasted cod in beef reduction with black-truffle risotto or fillet of venison with parsnip mousse are made with the freshest ingredients—many from the kitchen garden—and can be followed by a copious cheese plate or tempting seasonal desserts. **Known for:** seasonal menu; romantic and refined atmosphere; garden terrace. [$] *Average main: €34* ✉ *20 av. du Général de Gaulle, Gazeran* 🌐 *www.villamarinette.fr* 🕓 *Closed Mon. and Tues. No dinner Sun.*

Chartres

39 km (24 miles) southwest of Rambouillet, 88 km (55 miles) southwest of Paris.

If Versailles is the climax of French secular architecture, Chartres is its religious apogee. All the descriptive prose and poetry that have been lavished on this supreme cathedral can only begin to suggest the glory of its 12th- and 13th-century statuary and stained glass, somehow suffused with burning mysticism and a strange sense of the numinous. Chartres is more than a church—it's a nondenominational spiritual experience. If you arrive in summer from Maintenon across the edge of the Beauce, the richest agrarian plain in France, you can see Chartres's spires rising up from oceans of wheat. The whole town, however, is worth a leisurely exploration. Ancient streets tumble down from the cathedral to the river, lined most weekends with *bouquinistes* selling old books and prints. The streets are especially busy each year on August 15, when pilgrims and tourists flock in

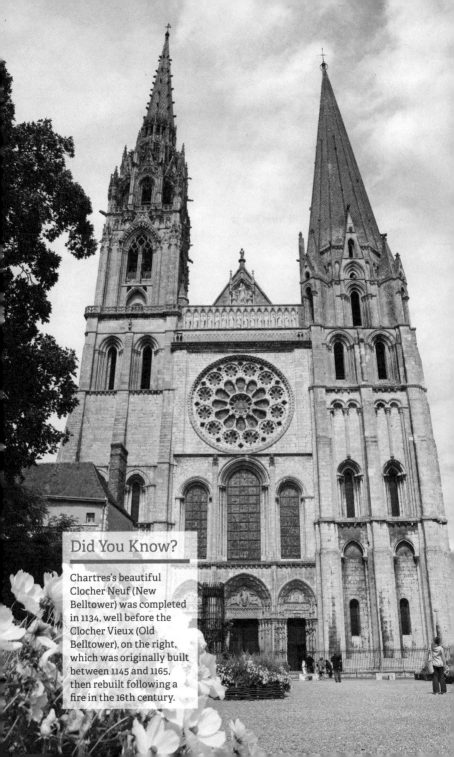

Did You Know?

Chartres's beautiful
Clocher Neuf (New
Belltower) was completed
in 1134, well before the
Clocher Vieux (Old
Belltower), on the right,
which was originally built
between 1145 and 1165,
then rebuilt following a
fire in the 16th century.

for the Procession du Vœu de Louis XIII commemorating the French monarchy's vow to serve the Virgin Mary.

GETTING HERE AND AROUND

Both Transilien and main-line (Le Mans–bound) trains leave Paris's Gare Montparnasse for Chartres (50–70 minutes, €10–€18.40 depending on time of day). The train station on Place Pierre-Sémard puts you within walking distance of the cathedral.

VISITOR INFORMATION Chartres Tourist Office. ⊠ *8 rue de la Poissonnerie,* ☎ *02–37–18–26–26* ⊕ *www.chartres-tourisme. com.*

 Sights

★ **Cathédrale Notre-Dame** (*Chartres Cathedral*)

CHURCH | Worship on the site of the Cathédrale Notre-Dame, better known as Chartres Cathedral, goes back to before the Gallo-Roman period—the crypt contains a well that was the focus of druid ceremonies. In the late 9th century Charles II (aka "the Bald") presented Chartres with what was believed to be the tunic of the Virgin Mary, a precious relic that went on to attract hordes of pilgrims. The current cathedral, the sixth church on the spot, dates mainly to the 12th and 13th centuries and was erected after most of the previous building, dating to the 11th century, burned down in 1194. A well-chronicled outburst of religious fervor followed the discovery that the Virgin Mary's relic had miraculously survived unsinged. Motivated by this "miracle," princes and paupers, barons and bourgeoisie gave their money and their labor to build the new cathedral. Ladies of the manor came to help monks and peasants on the scaffolding in a tremendous resurgence of religious faith that followed the Second Crusade. Just 25 years were needed for Chartres Cathedral to rise again, and although it

remained substantially unchanged for centuries, a 12-year, €20 million renovation that was completed in 2018 restored the cathedral's famously gloomy interiors to their "original" creamy white, sparking a major controversy among those who embraced the dark interiors. As spiritual as Chartres is, the cathedral also had its more earthbound uses. Look closely and you can see that the main nave floor has a subtle slant. It was designed to provide drainage because this part of the church was often used as a "hostel" by thousands of overnighting pilgrims in medieval times. Those who couldn't afford the entire pilgrimage could walk the cathedral's labyrinth, one of the most beautiful and famous in the world; today it's open for visitors every Friday and for a month during Lent (on other days it is covered with chairs).

Though the windows no longer pop from the previously dark interiors, the gemlike richness of the cleaned and restored stained glass, with the famous deep Chartres blue predominating, is still a thrilling experience. The restoration also uncovered some surprising illustrations of rose windows painted high up in the north and south narthex, just inside the cathedral entrance. The Royal Portal is richly sculpted with scenes from the life of Christ—these sculpted figures are among the greatest created during the Middle Ages. The rose window above the main portal dates from the 13th century, and the three windows below it contain some of the finest examples of 12th-century stained-glass artistry in France. The oldest window is arguably the most beautiful: Notre-Dame de la Belle Verrière (Our Lady of the Lovely Window), in the south choir.

A special tour of the cathedral crypt by candlelight is given every Saturday at 9:30 pm (in French; book on the Chartres Tourism site). For a bird's-eye view, book a tour of the towers. Guided tours of the Crypte start from the Maison de la Crypte opposite the south porch; tickets can be purchased at the gift store. ✉ *16 cloître Notre-Dame, Chartres* ☎ *02–37–21–75–02* 🌐 *www.cathedrale-chartres.org* 🎫 *Crypt €4.*

Chartres en Lumières

PUBLIC ART | If you need an incentive to linger here until dusk, "Chartres en Lumières" (Chartres's festival of lights) provides it: 28 of the city's most revered monuments, including the glorious Notre-Dame Cathedral, are transformed into vivid light canvases. Thematically based on the history and purpose of each specific site, the animated projections are organized into a city walk that covers a wide swath of the Old Town's cobbled streets and bridges. The spectacle is free and occurs nightly from sunset to 1 am from late April through mid-January. A train tour of the illuminated city operates several times a night from May through September. ✉ *10 pl. de l'Étape au Vin, Chartres* 🌐 *www.chartresenlumieres.com.*

Galerie du Vitrail

ART MUSEUM | Since *vitrail* (stained glass) is the key to Chartres's fame, you may want to visit the Galerie du Vitrail, which specializes in the noble art. Pieces range from small plaques to entire windows, and there are books on the subject in English and French. ✉ *17 cloître Notre-Dame, Chartres* ☎ *02–37–36–10–03 Closed Sun. and Mon. Oct.–Apr.* 🌐 *www.galerie-du-vitrail.com.*

Musée des Beaux-Arts

ART MUSEUM | Just behind the famed cathedral, the town art museum is housed in a handsome 18th-century building that once served as the bishop's palace. Its varied collection includes Renaissance enamels, a portrait of Erasmus by Holbein, tapestries, armor, and some fine (mainly French) paintings from the 17th, 18th, and 19th centuries. There's also a room devoted to the forceful 20th-century landscapes of Maurice de Vlaminck, who lived in the region. ✉ *29 cloître Notre-Dame, Chartres* ☎ *02–37–90–45–80* 🌐 *www.chartres.fr/musee-beaux-arts/horaires-et-animations* 🎫 *€6* ⏰ *Closed Mon. and Tues.*

St-Aignan

CHURCH | Exquisite 17th-century stained glass can be admired at the church of St-Aignan, around the corner from St-Pierre. ✉ *Rue des Grenets, Chartres.*

★ St-Pierre

CHURCH | Like Chartres Cathedral, the church of St-Pierre, near the Eure River, is considered a masterpiece of Gothic architecture, and its magnificent 13th- and 14th-century windows are from a medieval period not represented at the cathedral. The oldest stained glass here, portraying Old Testament worthies, is to the right of the choir and dates to the late 13th century. ✉ *Rue St-Pierre, Chartres.*

🍴 Restaurants

Crêperie La Picoterie

$ | **FRENCH** | **FAMILY** | If you're looking for a quick, traditional meal a few steps from the cathedral, look no further than this crêperie, a favorite in Chartres. You'll find a full list of savory (made with buckwheat flour) delights—ham, egg, smoked salmon, veggies, potatoes, and cheese—or sweet (made with white flour)—caramel *au beurre salé,* crêpes suzette, Grand Marnier, and ice cream—all washed down with a delicious Normandy cider. **Known for:** quick and cheap meals; lovely outdoor dining; family-friendly atmosphere. [$] *Average main: €12* ✉ *36 rue des Changes, Rambouillet* ☎ *02–37–36–14–54* 🌐 *www.picoterie.com/fr/accueil,2.html.*

★ Esprit Gourmand

$$ | **FRENCH** | **FAMILY** | On a picturesque street close to the cathedral, this quaint bistro is a lifesaver in a town sorely lacking in quality dining. The traditional

French favorites it serves—like roast *poulet* with buttery potatoes, sautéed fillet of daurade with grilled vegetables, and braised pork that's crisp on the outside and meltingly tender inside—are perennial crowd-pleasers. **Known for:** small space, so reservations recommended; garden terrace for outdoor dining; classic French bistro dishes. $ *Average main: €19* ⊠ *6 rue du Cheval-Blanc, Chartres* ☎ *02–37–36–97–84* ⊕ *espritgourmand. eatbu.com* ⏱ *Closed Mon. and Tues. No dinner Sun.*

★ **La Table de Julie**

$$ | FRENCH | This cozy bistro's namesake studied at the prestigious Ferrandi school and cut her teeth at Joël Robuchon in Paris before returning to her hometown to open her own "bistronomique" restaurant (meaning gastronomic bistro). The refined menu offers seasonal dishes made with ingredients from sustainable farms when possible, and all the wines are organic. **Known for:** close to the cathedral; food that's a cut above most other local restaurants; cozy atmsophere and terrace. $ *Average main: €19* ⊠ *7–11 rue Saint-Michel, Chartres* ☎ *02–37–32–57–60* ⊕ *www.latabledejulie.fr* ⏱ *Closed Sun. and Mon.*

★ **Le Georges Hôtel Le Grand Monarque**

$$$$ | FRENCH | If you want to make your visit or stay in Chartres a memorable one, this stellar hotel restaurant is the place to go. Excellent by any standards, the elegant dining room, impeccable service, and refined gastronomic menu from chef Thomas Parnaud, who breathed new life into the restaurant when he took the helm in mid-2018, make this dining room a standout in Chartres and the entire region. **Known for:** impeccable service; creative young chef; imaginative dishes. $ *Average main: €48* ⊠ *22 pl. des Epars* ☎ *02–37–18–15–15* ⊕ *www. grand-monarque.com/en/restaurant-bar/ restaurant-le-georges.html* ⏱ *Closed Sun. and Mon.*

★ **Les Feuillantines**

$$ | FRENCH | The adventurous cuisine served at Les Feuillantines (one of Chartres's few gastronomic restaurants) rarely falters and very often soars. Try the superb house-made terrine with tangy cornichons to start, followed by duck risotto topped with caramelized shallots or beef ravioli perfumed with lemongrass and smoked tea. **Known for:** great prices; outdoor garden; unique gastronomic dishes. $ *Average main: €21* ⊠ *4 rue du Bourg, Chartres* ☎ *02–37–30–22–21* ⊕ *www.restaurantlesfeuillantines.eatbu. com* ⏱ *Closed Sun. and Mon.*

Hotels

Best Western Le Grand Monarque

$$ | HOTEL | On Chartres's main square, not far from the cathedral, this Best Western Premier hotel in a converted coaching inn warmly evokes the 19th century; many guest rooms are outfitted with brick walls, attractive antiques, lush drapes, and modern bathrooms (the best are in a separate turn-of-the-20th-century building overlooking a garden, while the most atmospheric are tucked away in the attic). **Pros:** old-fashioned charm; Michelin-starred restaurant on-site; spa and fitness center offering beauty treatments and massage. **Cons:** some decor is worn; uphill walk to cathedral; best rooms are in an annex. $ *Rooms from: €175* ⊠ *22 pl. des Épars, Île de Nantes* ☎ *02–37–18–15–15* ⊕ *www.grand-monarque.com/en* ⥭ *55 rooms* ⏲ *No Meals.*

Giverny

70 km (44 miles) northwest of Paris.

The small village of Giverny (pronounced "jee-vair-knee"), just beyond the Epte River, which marks the boundary of the Île-de-France, has become a place of . pilgrimage for art lovers. It was here that Claude Monet lived for 43 years, until his

Entrancing views, like this one of a Japanese footbridge, are plentiful in Monet's Garden.

death at the age of 86 in 1926. Although his house is now prized by connoisseurs of 19th-century interior decoration, it's his garden, with its Japanese-inspired water-lily pond and bridge, that remains the high point for many—a 5-acre, three-dimensional Impressionist painting you can stroll around at leisure. Most make this a day trip, but Giverny has some lovely lodgings, so you could also overnight here.

GETTING HERE AND AROUND

Frequent main-line TER trains connect Paris's Gare St-Lazare with Vernon (50 minutes, between €9–€24 depending on the time and class); you can then cover the remaining 10 km (6 miles) to Giverny by taxi, bus, or bike (the last of these can be rented at the café opposite Vernon station). April through October, the SNgo shuttle bus meets trains daily and whisks passengers to Giverny (20 minutes) and back for €10.

Sights

★ Maison et Jardin Claude Monet (*Monet's House and Garden*)

GARDEN | After several years living north of Paris, Monet moved downriver to Giverny in 1883. With its pretty pink walls and green shutters, his house has a warm feeling that's a welcome change after the stateliness of the French châteaux. Rooms have been restored to Monet's original designs: the kitchen with its blue tiles, the buttercup-yellow dining room, and Monet's bedroom on the second floor. Reproductions of the painter's works, and some of the Japanese prints he avidly collected, crowd its walls. The garden *à la japonaise,* with flowers spilling out across the paths, contains the famous "tea-garden" bridge and water-lily pond. Looking across the pond, it's easy to conjure up the grizzled, bearded painter dabbing at his canvases—capturing changes in light and pioneering a breakdown in form that was to have a major influence on 20th-century art.

The garden—planted with nearly 100,000 annuals and even more perennials—is a place of wonder. No matter that about 500,000 visitors troop through each year; they seem to fade in the presence of beautiful roses, carnations, lady's slipper, tulips, irises, hollyhocks, poppies, daisies, nasturtiums, larkspur, azaleas, and more. With that said, it still helps to visit midweek when crowds are thinner. If you want to pay your respects to the original gardener, Monet is buried in the family vault in Giverny's village church.

■ **TIP→ Although the gardens overall are most beautiful in spring, the water lilies bloom during the latter part of July and the first two weeks of August.** ✉ *84 rue Claude Monet, Giverny* ☎ *02–32–51–28–21* 🌐 *www.fondation-monet.com* 🎟 *€11* 🕒 *Closed Nov.–late Mar.*

★ Musée des Impressionnismes

ART MUSEUM | After touring the painterly grounds of Monet's house, you may wish to see some real paintings at the Musée des Impressionnismes. Originally endowed by the late Chicago art patrons Daniel and Judith Terra, it featured a few works by the American Impressionists, including Willard Metcalf, Louis Ritter, Theodore Wendel, and John Leslie Breck, who flocked to Giverny to study at the hand of the master. But in recent years the museum has extended its scope with an exciting array of exhibitions that explore the origins, geographical diversity, and wide-ranging influences of Impressionism—in the process highlighting the importance of Giverny and the Seine Valley in the history of the movement. There's an on-site restaurant and *salon de thé* (tearoom) with a fine outdoor terrace, as well as a garden "quoting" some of Monet's plant compositions. Farther down the road, you can visit Giverny's landmark Hôtel Baudy, a restaurant that was once the preferred watering hole of many 19th-century artists. ✉ *99 rue Claude Monet, Giverny* ☎ *02–32–51–94–65* 🌐 *www.mdig.fr* 🎟 *€9* 🕒 *Closed early Nov.–mid-Mar.*

🍴 Restaurants

★ Le Jardin des Plumes

$$$$ | **FRENCH** | Owner and chef Eric Guérin brings all his considerable expertise to bear in the beautiful dining room at this hotel restaurant, where the menu focuses on the bounty of the Norman seaside. A destination unto itself, the restaurant and hotel are favorites of Giverny visitors seeking a dining "experience," so be sure to reserve in advance for both lunch and dinner. **Known for:** Michelin star; dining on the beautiful outdoor terrace; seasonal local products. [$] *Average main: €37* ✉ *1 rue du Milieu, Giverny* ☎ *02–32–54–26–35* 🌐 *www.jardindesplumes.fr/restaurant* 🕒 *Closed Mon. and Tues.*

★ Restaurant Baudy

$$ | **BRASSERIE** | Back in Monet's day, this pretty-in-pink villa was the favorite hotel of the American painters' colony. Today it remains one of the most charming spots in the Île-de-France (despite the tourists), although the surroundings retain more historic charm than the simple cuisine (mainly salads large enough to count as a main course in their own right, or straightforward, if unremarkable, dishes like an omelet or *gigot d'agneau* [lamb and mutton]). **Known for:** rustic atmosphere; crowd magnet; lovely rose garden. [$] *Average main: €22* ✉ *81 rue Claude-Monet, Giverny* ☎ *02–32–21–10–03* 🌐 *www.restaurantbaudy.com* 🕒 *Closed Mon. and Nov.–Mar. No dinner Sun.*

🛏 Hotels

La Musardière

$$ | **B&B/INN** | Just a short stroll from chez Monet, this beautifully refurbished 1880 manor house (the name means "Place to Idle") has a cozy lobby, guest rooms with views overlooking a leafy garden, and its own restaurant and crêperie. **Pros:** charming old building with beautifully refurbished interiors; great value; easy walk to Monet's house and gardens. **Cons:** restaurant could be better; staff could be friendlier; mediocre eatery attracts tourist crowds in peak season. [$] *Rooms from: €160* ✉ *123 rue Claude Monet, Giverny* ☎ *02–32–21–03–18* 🌐 *www.lamusardiere.fr* ⏲ *Closed Nov.–Mar.* 🛏 *11 rooms* 🍴 *No Meals.*

Le Clos Fleuri

$ | **B&B/INN** | Giverny's hotel shortage is offset by several stylish and affordable bed-and-breakfasts—this one, located just 600 yards from Monet's estate, is among the best. **Pros:** co-owner Danielle Fouché speaks fluent English thanks to years spent in Australia and will happily give advice about touring the area; each room has private patio; colorful oasis in the heart of the village. **Cons:** decor not for everyone; books up quickly; no air-conditioning. [$] *Rooms from: €120* ✉ *5 rue de la Dîme, Giverny* ☎ *02–32–21–36–51* 🌐 *www.giverny-leclosfleuri.fr* ⏲ *Closed Oct.–Mar.* 🛏 *3 rooms* 🍴 *Free Breakfast.*

Le Jardin des Plumes

$$$ | **B&B/INN** | This Norman-style half-timbered inn with its stylish contemporary interiors, lovely gardens, and Michelin-starred restaurant make this a destination unto itself. **Pros:** location, location, location; top-notch service; excellent restaurant. **Cons:** can feel oddly deserted on Monday and Tuesday (when restaurant is closed); extra cost for breakfast; dinner on the pricey side. [$] *Rooms from: €240* ✉ *1 rue du Milieu, Giverny* ☎ *02–32–54–26–35* 🌐 *www.lejardindesplumes.fr* ⏲ *Closed mid-Nov.–mid-Dec.* 🛏 *8 rooms* 🍴 *No Meals.*

★ Ô Plum'Art

$$$ | **HOTEL** | Top Chef and owner of Jardin des Plumes hotel and restaurant David Gallienne now runs this ultra-contemporary six-room B&B in a 19th-century milkman's cottage set in the countryside overlooking the Seine River. **Pros:** breakfast included in price; delightful spa and tearoom on the premises; walking distance to Monet's gardens. **Cons:** must book well ahead; pricey; better for couples than families. [$] *Rooms from: €250* ✉ *12 rue Claude Monet, Giverny* ☎ *02–32–54–26–35* 🌐 *www.jardindesplumes.fr* ⏲ *Restaurant closed Mon. and Tues.* 🛏 *6 rooms* 🍴 *Free Breakfast.*

St-Germain-en-Laye

29 km (18 miles) southwest of L'Isle-Adam, 17 km (11 miles) west of Paris.

Encircled by forest and perched behind Le Nôtre's Grande Terrace overlooking the Seine, this idyllic town has lost little of its original cachet—despite the invasion of wealthy former Parisians who commute to work from here.

GETTING HERE AND AROUND

Being on the RER-A line, St-Germain-en-Laye's station handles frequent trains to and from Paris (€4.45).

VISITOR INFORMATION St-Germain-en-Laye Tourist Office. ✉ *3 rue Henri IV* ☎ *01–30–87–20–63* 🌐 *www.ot-saintgermainenlaye.fr.*

Sights

Château de Monte-Cristo (*Monte Cristo Castle*)

HISTORIC HOME | If you're fond of the swashbuckling novels of Alexandre Dumas, you'll enjoy the Château de Monte-Cristo at Port-Marly on the southern fringe of St-Germain. Dumas built the château after the surging popularity of books like *The Count of Monte Cristo* made him rich in the 1840s. Construction costs and lavish partying meant he went broke just as quickly, and he skedaddled into a Belgian exile in 1849. You may find the fanciful exterior, where pilasters, cupolas, and stone carvings compete for attention, crosses the line from opulence to tastelessness, but—as in Dumas's fiction—swagger, not subtlety, is what counts. Dumas's mementos aside, the highlight of the interior is the luxurious Moorish Chamber, with spellbinding, interlacing plasterwork executed by Arab craftsmen (lent by the Bey of Tunis) and restored thanks to a donation from the late Moroccan king Hassan II. ✉ *1 av. du Président-Kennedy* ☎ *01–39–16–49–49* 🌐 *www.chateau-monte-cristo.com* 🎫 *€8* 🕒 *Closed Mon., and weekdays Nov.–Mar.*

Château de St-Germain-en-Laye
CASTLE/PALACE | Next to the St-Germain RER train station, this stone-and-brick château, with its dry moat, intimidating circular towers, and La Grande Terrasse, is one of the most spectacular of all French garden set pieces. The château itself, gleaming after a five-year renovation, dates to the 16th and 17th centuries, but a royal palace has stood here since the early 12th century, when Louis VI—known as Le Gros (the Plump)—exploited St-Germain's defensive potential in his bid to pacify the Île-de-France. A hundred years later, Louis IX (St. Louis) added the elegant Sainte-Chapelle, the château's oldest remaining section. Note the square-top, not pointed, side windows and the filled-in rose window on the back wall. Charles V (1364–80) built a powerful defensive keep in the mid-14th century, but from the 1540s François I and his successors transformed St-Germain into a palace with an appearance more domestic than warlike. Louis XIV was born here, and it was here that his father, Louis XIII, died. Until 1682, when the court moved to Versailles, it remained the country's foremost royal residence outside Paris, and several Molière plays were premiered in the main hall. Since 1867 the château has housed the impressive **Musée des Antiquités Nationales** (Museum of National Antiquities), holding a trove of artifacts, figurines, brooches, and weapons, from the Stone Age to the 8th century. Behind the château is André Le Nôtre's Grande Terrasse, a terraced promenade lined by lime trees. Directly overlooking the Seine, it was completed in 1673 and has rarely been outdone for grandeur or length. ✉ *Pl. Charles-de-Gaulle* ☎ *01–39–10–13–00* 🌐 *www.musee-archeologienationale.fr* 🎫 *€6* 🕒 *Closed Tues.*

Musée Maurice Denis (*Priory Museum*)
ART MUSEUM | This appealing museum in a historic priory is devoted to the work of artist Maurice Denis (1870–1943), his fellow Symbolists, and the Nabis—painters opposed to the naturalism of their 19th-century Impressionist contemporaries. Denis found the calm of the former Jesuit building, set above tiered gardens with statues and rosebushes, ideally suited to his spiritual themes, which he expressed in stained glass, ceramics, and frescoes as well as oils. ✉ *2 bis, rue Maurice-Denis* ☎ *01–39–73–77–87* 🌐 *www.musee-mauricedenis.fr* 🎫 *€6* 🕒 *Closed Mon.*

🍴 Restaurants

★ Lilla Krogen
$$ | **SWEDISH** | In the center of town just a few minutes from the Musée Maurice Denis, this contemporary French-style bistro is popular for its bright decor and healthy Swedish-inflected recipes. Appetizers like toasts Skagen—tiny shrimps in homemade dilled mayonnaise on toast—and salmon gravlax or marinated herring are fresh, healthy, and delicious. **Known for:** warm and welcoming service; healthy meals; freshest top-quality fish. [$] *Average main: €20* ✉ *1 pl. de Mareil* ☎ *09–81–89–89–56* 🌐 *www.lilla-krogen.com* 🕒 *No dinner Sun.*

Hotels

★ Cazaudehore La Forestière

$$ | **HOTEL** | St-Germain's only Relais & Château hotel is a quintessential Île-de-France country retreat: surrounded by forest, it's rambling and solid, with shuttered windows and 18th-century-style furnishings. **Pros:** cozy, classy hotel; good restaurant; run by a third-generation hotelier. **Cons:** breakfast not included; rooms lack air-conditioning, and some need a touch up; service can range from indifferent to terrible. ⓈＳ *Rooms from: €220* ⊠ *1 av. du Président Kennedy* ☎ *01–30–61–64–64* ⊕ *www.cazaudehore. fr* ⟿ *30 rooms* ⦵ *No Meals.*

Pavillon Henri IV

$$$ | **HOTEL** | This elegant hotel, in a historic 18th-century mansion a few steps from the château, restaurants, and shopping, offers lovely period decor and expansive views of Paris from some of the rooms and a gastronomic restaurant. **Pros:** big bathrooms; top-notch restaurant with stellar views; all-in-one getaway with easy access to Paris. **Cons:** dinner is expensive; service can be spotty; could use some updating. Ⓢ *Rooms from: €300* ⊠ *19 rue Thiers* ☎ *01–39–10–15–15* ⊕ *www.pavillonhenri4.fr* ⟿ *42 rooms* ⦵ *No Meals.*

Performing Arts

Fête des Loges (*Loges Festival*)

FESTIVALS | A giant fair and carnival is held in the Forest of St-Germain from late June to mid-August. Fans of cotton candy, roller coasters, and Ferris wheels turn up in droves every year. ⊠ *Camp des Loges* ⊕ *www.fetedesloges.org.*

Rueil-Malmaison

8 km (5 miles) southeast of St-Germain-en-Laye, 8 km (5 miles) west of Paris.

Rueil-Malmaison is a slightly dreary western suburb of Paris, but the memory of Napoléon and Joséphine still haunts its neoclassical château.

GETTING HERE AND AROUND

From Paris, take RER-A (direction St-Germain-en-Laye) directly to Rueil-Malmaison (40 minutes, €3.90).

ESSENTIALS

VISITOR INFORMATION Rueil-Malmaison Tourist Office. ⊠ *33 rue Jean Le Coz* ☎ *01–47–32–35–75* ⊕ *www.rueil-tourisme.com/en.*

⦿ Sights

★ Château de Malmaison

CASTLE/PALACE | Built in 1622, La Malmaison was bought by the future empress Joséphine in 1799 as a love nest for Napoléon and herself, three years after their marriage. Theirs is one of Europe's most dramatic love stories, replete with affairs, scandal, and hatred—the emperor's family often disparaged Joséphine, a name bestowed on her by Napoléon (her real name was Rose), as "the Creole." After the childless Joséphine was divorced by the heir-hungry emperor in 1809, she retired to La Malmaison and died here on May 29, 1814. The château has 24 rooms furnished with exquisite tables, chairs, and sofas of the Napoleonic period; of special note are the library, game room, and dining room. The walls are adorned with works by artists of the day, such as Jacques-Louis David, Pierre-Paul Prud'hon, and Baron Gérard. Take time to admire the clothes and hats that belonged to Napoléon and Joséphine, particularly the empress's gowns. Their carriage can be seen in one of the garden pavilions; another contains a unique collection of snuffboxes donated by Prince George of Greece. The gardens are delightful, reflecting Joséphine's love of roses and exotic plants (her collection was one of the most important in France), and especially beautiful when the regimented rows of tulips are blooming in spring. ⊠ *15 av. du Château* ☎ *01–41–29–05–55* ⊕ *musees-nationaux-malmaison.fr/chateau-malmaison* ⊠ *€6.50* ⊙ *Closed Tues.*

Auvers-sur-Oise

62 km (39 miles) east of Giverny, 33 km (21 miles) northwest of Paris.

The tranquil Oise River valley retains much of the charm that attracted Camille Pissarro, Paul Cézanne, Camille Corot, Charles-François Daubigny, and Berthe Morisot to Auvers-sur-Oise in the second half of the 19th century. Despite this lofty company, though, it's the spirit of Vincent Van Gogh—who spent the last months of his life painting no fewer than 70 works here—that haunts every nook and cranny of this pretty riverside village. On July 27, 1890, the tormented artist laid his easel against a haystack, walked behind the Château d'Auvers, shot himself, then stumbled to the Auberge Ravoux. He died on July 29. The next day, using a hearse from neighboring Méry (because the priest of Auvers refused to provide his for a suicide victim), Van Gogh's body was borne up the hill to the village cemetery. His heartbroken brother Theo died the following year and, in 1914, was reburied alongside him in a simple ivy-covered grave. Today many visitors make a pilgrimage to town sites associated with Van Gogh (the tourist office has information). Short hikes outside the center will lead you to lovely rural landscapes, including the one that inspired Van Gogh's last painting, *Wheat Fields with Crows.*

GETTING HERE AND AROUND

Take the RER-C line from Paris (direction Pontoise) to St-Ouen l'Aumone, and then a second train (direction Creil) onward to Auvers; the total travel is 45–55 minutes, the total cost €6.35. There is no connecting public transportation from the area around Vernon.

VISITOR INFORMATION Auvers-sur-Oise Tourist Office. ⊠ *38 rue du Général de Gaulle* ☎ *01–30–36–71–81* ⊕ *tourisme-auverssuroise.fr.*

 Sights

Maison-Atelier de Daubigny

HISTORIC HOME | The landscape artist Charles-François Daubigny, a precursor of the Impressionists, lived in Auvers from 1861 until his death in 1878. You can visit his studio, the Maison-Atelier de Daubigny, and admire the mural and roof paintings by Daubigny and fellow artists Camille Corot and Honoré Daumier. ⊠ *61 rue Daubigny* ☎ *01–34–48–03–03* ⊕ *www.atelier-daubigny.com* ⊠ *€6* ⊙ *Closed Nov.–late Mar. and Mon.–Wed.*

Maison de Van Gogh (*Van Gogh House*)
HISTORIC HOME | Opposite the town hall, the Auberge Ravoux—where Van Gogh lived and died—is now the Maison de Van Gogh. The inn opened in 1876 and owes its name to Arthur Ravoux, the landlord from 1889 to 1891. He had seven lodgers in all, who paid 3.50 francs for room and board (that was cheaper than the other inns in Auvers, where 6 francs was the going rate). A dingy staircase leads up to the tiny attic where Van Gogh stored some of modern art's most iconic paintings under his bed. A short film retraces the artist's time at Auvers, and there's a well-stocked souvenir shop. Stop for a drink or lunch in the ground-floor restaurant. ⊠ *8 rue de la Sansonne* ☎ *01–30–36–60–60* ⊕ *www.maisondevangogh.fr* ⊠ *€6* ⊙ *Closed Mon. and Tues.*

Maison du Dr. Gachet

HISTORIC HOME | The former home of Van Gogh's closest friend in Auvers, Dr. Paul Gachet, is a local landmark. Documents and mementos evoke both Van Gogh's stay and Gachet's passion for the avant-garde art of his era. The good doctor was himself the subject of one of the artist's most famous portraits (and the world's second most expensive painting when it sold for $82 million in the late 1980s); the actual creation of it was reenacted in the 1956 biopic, *Lust for Life*, starring Kirk Douglas. Even his house was immortalized on canvas, courtesy of Cézanne. A friend and patron to many of the artists who settled in and visited Auvers in the 1880s, Gachet also contributed to their artistic education by teaching them about engraving processes. Don't overlook the garden—it provided the ivy that covers Van Gogh's grave in the cemetery across town. ⊠ *78 rue du Dr-Gachet* ☎ *01–30–36–81–27* ⊕ *www.facebook.com/MaisonDuDocteurGachet* 🎫 *Free* 🕐 *Closed Mon. and Tues.*

Musée Daubigny

ART MUSEUM | You may want to visit the modest Musée Daubigny to admire the drawings, lithographs, and occasional oils by local 19th-century artists, some of which were collected by Daubigny himself. The museum is opposite the Maison de Van Gogh, above the tourist office, which shows a 15-minute film (in English on request) about life in Auvers, *From Daubigny to Van Gogh*. ⊠ *Manoir des Colombières, Rue de la Sansonne* ☎ *01–30–36–80–20* ⊕ *www.museedaubigny.com* 🎫 *€5* 🕐 *Closed Mon.*

Voyage au Temps des Impressionnistes

(*Journey Through the Impressionist Era*)
ART MUSEUM | FAMILY | Set above split-level gardens, this 17th-century village château (also depicted by Van Gogh) now houses the Voyage au Temps des Impressionnistes. You'll receive a set of headphones (English available),

with commentary that guides you past various tableaux illustrating life during the Impressionist years. Although there are no Impressionist originals—500 reproductions pop up on screens interspersed between the tableaux—this is one of France's most imaginative, enjoyable, and innovative museums. Some of the special effects, including talking mirrors, computerized cabaret dancing girls, and a simulated train ride past Impressionist landscapes, are worthy of Disney. ⊠ *Rue de Léry* ☎ *01–34–48–48–48* ⊕ *www.chateau-auvers.fr* 🎫 *€12* 🕐 *Closed Mon.*

🍴 Restaurants

Auberge Ravoux

$$$ | BISTRO | For total Van Gogh immersion, have lunch—or dinner on Friday and Saturday—in the restaurant he patronized regularly more than 100 years ago, in the building where he actually died. A three-course prix-fixe menu is available, and saddle of lamb and homemade terrine are among Loran Gattufo's specialties. **Known for:** rustic authenticity; historic

---

A Van Gogh Self-Tour

Auvers-sur-Oise is peppered with plaques marking the spots that inspired Van Gogh. They bear reproductions of his paintings, enabling you to compare his final works with the scenes as they are today. His last abode—the Auberge Ravoux—has been turned into a shrine. You can also visit the medieval village church, subject of one of Van Gogh's most famous pieces, *L'Église d'Auvers*; admire Osip Zadkine's powerful statue of Van Gogh in the village park; and visit the restored house of Dr. Gachet, his best friend.

backstory; good traditional, regional dishes. $ *Average main: €26* ✉ *52 rue Général-de-Gaulle* ☎ *01–30–36–60–63* ⊕ *www.maisondevangogh.fr* ⏱ *Closed Mon., Tues., and Nov.–Mar. No dinner.*

 Hotels

Hotel des Iris

$ | **HOTEL** | The old Auvers-sur-Oise post office is the setting for this charming, functional hotel a two-minute walk from the Maison Van Gogh and other sites in town. **Pros:** two step from the Maison Van Gogh and other sites; exceptional prices; charming rooms and service. **Cons:** only eight rooms; no dinner served; unreliable air-conditioning. $ *Rooms from: €99* ✉ *21 Rue du Général de Gaulle* ☎ *01–30–37–79–18* ⊕ *www.hoteldesiris. com* 🛏 *8 rooms* ⏸ *No Meals.*

Chantilly

37 km (23 miles) north of Paris.

Celebrated for lace, cream, and the most beautiful medieval manuscript in the world—*Les Très Riches Heures du Duc de Berry*—romantic Chantilly has a host of other attractions. Most notable among them are a faux Renaissance château with an eye-popping art collection second only to the Louvre's, a classy racecourse, and 18th-century stables that are called *grandes* for good reason.

GETTING HERE AND AROUND

Chantilly can be reached on both Transilien and main-line trains from Paris's Gare du Nord (25–30 minutes, €8.70).

VISITOR INFORMATION Chantilly Tourist Office. ✉ *73 rue du Connétable,* ☎ *03–44–67–37–37* ⊕ *www.chantilly-senlis-tourisme.com/en.*

 Sights

★ **Château de Chantilly**

ART MUSEUM | Although its lavish exterior may be 19th-century Renaissance pastiche, the Château de Chantilly, sitting snugly behind an artificial lake, houses the outstanding **Musée Condé**, with illuminated medieval manuscripts, tapestries, furniture, and paintings. The most famous room, the Santuario (sanctuary), contains two celebrated works by Italian painter Raphael (1483–1520)—the *Three Graces* and the *Orleans Virgin*—plus an exquisite ensemble of 15th-century miniatures by the most illustrious French painter of his time, Jean Fouquet (1420–81). Farther on, in the Cabinet des Livres (library), is the world-famous Book of Hours, whose title translates as *The Very Rich Hours of the Duc de Berry*. It was illuminated by the Brothers Limbourg with magical pictures of early-15th-century life as lived by one of Burgundy's richest lords; unfortunately, due to their fragility, painted facsimiles of the celebrated calendar illuminations are on display, not the actual pages of the book. Other highlights of this unusual museum are the Galerie de Psyché (Psyche Gallery), with 16th-century stained glass and portrait drawings by Flemish artist Jean Clouet II; the Chapelle, with sculptures by Jean Goujon and Jacques Sarrazin; and the extensive collection of paintings by 19th-century French artists, headed by Jean-Auguste-Dominique Ingres. In addition, there are grand and smaller salons, all stuffed with palace furniture, family portraits, and Sèvres porcelains, making this a must for lovers of the decorative and applied arts. ✉ *Domaine de Chantilly, Chantilly* ☎ *03–44–27–31–80* ⊕ *www. chateaudechantilly.fr/en* 🎫 *€17, includes Grandes Écuries and park* ⏱ *Closed Tues. in Nov.–Mar.*

★ **Grandes Écuries** (*Grand Stables*)

FARM/RANCH | **FAMILY** | The grandest stables in France were built by Jean Aubert in 1719 to accommodate 240 horses and 500 hounds used for stag and boar hunting in the forests nearby. Now with 30 breeds of horses and ponies living here in straw-lined comfort, the palatial stables function as the **Musée Vivant du Cheval** (Living Horse Museum). Equine history is explored through an array of artifacts, prints, paintings, textiles, sculptures, equipment, and weaponry. Visitors can also enjoy the elaborate horse shows and dressage demonstrations year-round; check the website for dates and times. ✉ *7 rue du Connétable, Chantilly* ☎ *03–44–27–31–80* 🌐 *www.chateaudechantilly.fr/en/great-stables* 🎟 *Included in château ticket; horse shows €22.*

Hippodrome des Princes de Condé

SPORTS VENUE | Chantilly, France's equestrian epicenter, is home to the fabled Hippodrome racetrack. Established in 1834, it comes into its own each June with two of Europe's most prestigious events: the Prix du Jockey-Club (French Derby) on the first Sunday of the month, and the Prix de Diane for three-year-old fillies the Sunday after. On main race days, a free shuttle bus runs between Chantilly's train station and the track. ✉ *Rte. de la Plaine-des-Aigles, Chantilly* ☎ *03–44–62–44–00* 🌐 *www.france-galop.com.*

Parc du Château de Chantilly

CITY PARK | Le Nôtre's park is based on that familiar French royal combination of formality and romantic eccentricity. The former is represented in the neatly planned parterres and a mighty, straight-banked canal; the latter comes to the fore in the waterfall and the Hameau, a mock-Norman village that inspired Marie-Antoinette's version at Versailles. You can explore on foot or on an electric train, and, in the warmer months, take a **rowboat** for a meander down the Grand Canal. ✉ *Chantilly* ☎ *03–44–27–31–80* 🌐 *www.chateaudechantilly.fr/en/grounds* 🎟 *€8 park only, €17 park and château* 🕒 *Closed Tues. Nov.–Mar.*

🍴 Restaurants

La Capitainerie

$$ | **FRENCH** | Housed in the stone-vaulted kitchens of the Château de Chantilly's legendary 17th-century chef Vorace Vatel, this quaint restaurant has an open-hearth fireplace big enough for whole lambs or oxen to sizzle on the spit. Reflect at leisure on your cultural peregrinations over mouthfuls of grilled turbot or roast quail, and don't forget to add a good dollop of homemade crème de Chantilly to your dessert. **Known for:** reasonable prices; quick dining; family-friendly vibe. [$] *Average main: €23* ✉ *Château de Chantilly, Chantilly* ☎ *03–44–57–15–89* 🌐 *www.domainedechantilly.com/fr/capitainerie* 🕒 *Closed Mon. and Tues. No dinner.*

🛏 Hotels

★ Auberge du Jeu de Paume

$$$ | **HOTEL** | Set within the Domaine de Chantilly, the largest princely estate in France, Auberge du Jeu de Paume combines its stunning setting with old-world elegance and modern comforts to create a deluxe country retreat. **Pros:** proximity to all the sights; luxe amenities; pretty setting abutting the palace grounds. **Cons:** garden-view rooms expensive; some common areas feel corporate; dining room could be more intimate. [$] *Rooms from: €350* ✉ *4 rue du Connétable, Chantilly* ☎ *03–44–65–50–00* 🌐 *www.aubergedujeudepaumechantilly.fr* 🔑 *92 rooms* 🍴 *No Meals.*

★ Hôtel le Chantilly

$$ | **HOTEL** | Expect a warm welcome and loads of charm at this recently refurbished boutique hotel set in Chantilly's old coach house, an excellent alternative to the pricier offerings in town. **Pros:** delicious homemade breakfast with organic products; reasonably priced; a short walk to the château and royal stables. **Cons:** breakfast not always included in price; no bar or restaurant; not all rooms

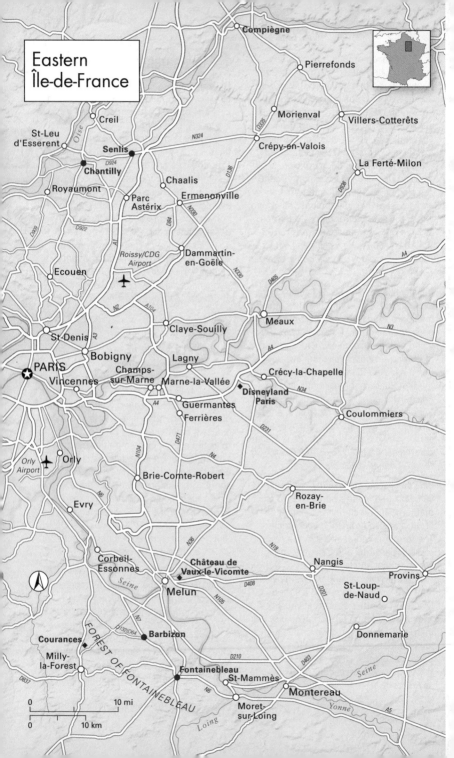

have air-conditioning, be sure to request. ⓢ *Rooms from: €167* ⊠ *9 pl. Omer Vallon, Chantilly* ☎ *03–44–21–42–84* ⊕ *www. hotel-lechantilly.com* ⥌ *20 rooms* ⦿ *No Meals.*

Senlis

10 km (6 miles) east of Chantilly, 40 km (26 miles) north of Paris.

Senlis is an exceptionally well-preserved medieval town with a crooked maze of streets dominated by the svelte, soaring spire of its Gothic cathedral. For a glimpse into the more distant past, be sure to also inspect the superb Musée d'Art et d'Archéologie.

GETTING HERE AND AROUND
Take either the Transilien or main-line trains from Paris's Gare du Nord to Chantilly (25–30 minutes, €8.70), then a bus onward to Senlis.

VISITOR INFORMATION Senlis Tourist Office. ⊠ *Pl. du Parvis Notre-Dame,* ☎ *03–44–53–06–40* ⊕ *www.chantilly-senlis-tourisme.com/en.*

 Sights

Cathédrale Notre-Dame
CHURCH | The breathtaking Cathédrale Notre-Dame, one of the country's oldest and narrowest cathedrals, dates to the second half of the 12th century. The superb spire—arguably the most elegant in France—was added around 1240, and the majestic transept, with its ornate rose windows, in the 16th century. ⊠ *Pl. du Parvis, Senlis.*

★ Musée d'Art et d'Archéologie
HISTORY MUSEUM | The excellent Musée d'Art et d'Archéologie displays finds ranging from Gallo-Roman votive objects unearthed in the neighboring Halatte Forest to the building's own excavated foundations (visible in the basement); note the superb stone heads bathed in half

light. Upstairs, paintings include works by Manet's teacher, Thomas Couture (who lived in Senlis), and charming naïve florals by the town's own Séraphine de Senlis. ⊠ *Palais Épiscopal, Pl. du Parvis Notre-Dame, Senlis* ☎ *03–44–24–86–72* ⊕ *musees.ville-senlis.fr* ⊡ *€6* ⊗ *Closed Mon. and Tues.*

Parc Astérix
AMUSEMENT PARK/CARNIVAL | **FAMILY** | A great alternative to Disneyland, and a wonderful day out for young and old, this Gallic theme park takes its cue from a French comic-book figure whose adventures are set during the Roman invasion of France 2,000 years ago. Among the 30 rides and six shows that attract thundering herds of families each year are a mock Gallo-Roman village, costumed druids, performing dolphins, splash-happy waterslides, and a giant roller coaster. ⊠ *Plailly* ✛ *10 km (6 miles) south of Senlis via A1* ☎ *03–44–62–34–04* ⊕ *www. parcasterix.fr* ⊡ *€55* ⊗ *Closed early Jan.–early Apr.*

 Restaurants

Le Scaramouche
$$ | **MODERN FRENCH** | This well-priced bistro, in an enviable spot facing the cathedral, provides a pleasant setting in which to enjoy some good French classics thanks to a menu that covers all the bases: a warm casserole of escargots with parsley butter, hand-chopped steak tartare with crispy frites, buttery scallops with lentils and a garlicky mayonnaise, and an array of salads and desserts. On a warm day, diners can enjoy the outdoor terrace with excellent views of the cathedral. **Known for:** attentive service; Italian specialties; nice views of the cathedral. ⓢ *Average main: €17* ⊠ *4 pl. Notre Dame, Senlis* ☎ *03–44–53–01–26* ⊕ *www.le-scaramouche.fr* ⊗ *Closed Sun. and Mon.*

Hotels

L'Hostellerie de la Porte Bellon
$ | **HOTEL** | This old stone house, near the bus station and five minutes by foot from the cathedral, is the closest you can get to spending a night in the historic center of Senlis; prettiest is Room 14, which overlooks the garden and has sloping walls and exposed beams. **Pros:** only hotel close to historic center; super quiet; attractive old building. **Cons:** no minibar or coffeemaker in rooms; some rooms need renovating; modest facilities. [$] *Rooms from: €89* ✉ *51 rue Bellon, Senlis* ☎ *03–44–53–03–05* 🌐 *www.portebellon.fr* ⏲ *Closed 1st 2 wks of Jan.* 🛏 *18 rooms* 🍴 *No Meals.*

Compiègne

32 km (20 miles) northeast of Senlis.

This bustling town of some 40,000 people sits at the northern limit of the Forêt de Compiègne (Compiègne Forest). The former royal hunting lodge here enjoyed its heyday in the mid-19th century under upstart emperor Napoléon III. But the town's history stretches further back—to Joan of Arc, who was captured in battle and held prisoner here, and to its 15th-century Hôtel de Ville (Town Hall), with its jubilant Flamboyant Gothic facade; and further forward—to the World War I armistice, signed in Compiègne Forest on November 11, 1918.

GETTING HERE AND AROUND

Frequent trains connect Compiègne with Paris's Gare du Nord (45 minutes, €15.40).

VISITOR INFORMATION Compiègne Tourist Office. ✉ *28 pl. de l'Hôtel-de-Ville,* ☎ *03–44–40–01–00* 🌐 *www.compiegne-tourisme.fr.*

Sights

★ **Château de Compiègne**
CASTLE/PALACE | **FAMILY** | The 18th-century Château de Compiègne, where the future Louis XVI first met Marie-Antoinette in 1770, was restored by Napoléon I and favored for wild weekends by his nephew Napoléon III. The first Napoléon's legacy is more keenly felt: his state apartments have been refurbished using the original designs for hangings and upholstery, and bright silks and damasks adorn every room. Much of the mahogany furniture gleams with ormolu, and the chairs sparkle with gold leaf. Napoléon III's furniture looks ponderous by comparison. Behind the palace is a gently rising 4-km (2½-mile) vista, inspired by the park at Schönbrunn, in Vienna, where Napoléon I's second wife, Empress Marie-Louise, grew up. Also here is the **Musée du Second Empire**, a collection of decorative arts from the Napoléon III era: its showstopper is Franz-Xaver Winterhalter's *Empress Eugénie Surrounded by Her Ladies in Waiting,* a famed homage to the over-the-top hedonism of the Napoléon Trois era. Make time for the Musée de la Voiture (Vehicle Museum) and its display of carriages, coaches, and old cars—including the *Jamais Contente* (*Never Satisfied*), the first car to reach 100 kph (62 mph). ✉ *Pl. du Général de Gaulle, Compiègne* ☎ *03–44–38–47–02* 🌐 *chateaudecompiegne.fr* 🎟 *€7.50* ⏲ *Closed Tues.*

Musée de la Figurine Historique (*Toy Soldier Museum*)
OTHER MUSEUM | **FAMILY** | A collection of 85,000 miniature soldiers—fashioned of lead, cardboard, and other materials—depicting military uniforms through the ages is on display in the Musée de la Figurine Historique. ✉ *28 pl. de l'Hôtel de Ville, Compiègne* ☎ *03–44–20–26–04* 🌐 *www.musees-compiegne.fr* 🎟 *€4* ⏲ *Closed Mon.*

The Alice in Wonderland Labyrinth delights children—and intrigues guests of all ages—at Disneyland Paris.

Wagon de l'Armistice (*Armistice Railcar*)
HISTORY MUSEUM | Off the road to Rethondes, the Wagon de l'Armistice is a replica of the one in which the World War I armistice was signed in 1918. In 1940 the Nazis turned the tables and made the French sign their own surrender in the same place, then tugged the original car off to Germany, where it was later destroyed. The replica is part of a small museum in a leafy clearing. *✉ Carrefour de l'Armistice, 7 km (4 miles) east of Compiègne via N31 and D546, Compiègne ☎ 03–44–85–14–18 🌐 www.musee-armistice-14-18.fr 🎟 €7 🕒 Closed Jan. and Feb.*

🍴 Restaurants

★ Les Ferlempins
$$$ | **FRENCH** | Don't be fooled by the casual interior: this popular "gastrobistro," helmed by two brothers passionate about food and wine, is where local foodies go for a special lunch or evening out. Products fresh from Compiègne's wonderful farmers' market are transformed into only a few sophisticated dishes each day that change with the season and are as beautiful to look at as they are delicious. **Known for:** excellent wine pairings; English-speaking owners who love to talk about their food; ethically sourced products. [$] *Average main: €26 ✉ 13 Cours Guynemer, Compiègne ☎ 03–44–83–53–31 🌐 www.lesferlempins.fr 🕒 Closed Sun. and Mon. No dinner Thurs.*

🛏 Hotels

Hôtel de Harlay
$ | **HOTEL** | A family-run hotel in a foursquare stone building, the Harlay is conveniently situated by the bridge linking the train station and downtown. **Pros:** close to the station; reasonable prices; rooms are quiet. **Cons:** breakfast extra; smallish rooms; bland interiors. [$] *Rooms from: €91 ✉ 3 rue de Harlay, Compiègne ☎ 03–44–23–01–50 🌐 www.hotel-compiegne.net 🛏 19 rooms 🍽 No Meals.*

Disneyland Paris

62 km (38 miles) south of Senlis, 38 km (24 miles) east of Paris.

Disneyland Paris is probably not what you've traveled to France for. But if you have a child in tow, the promise of a day with Mickey might get you through an afternoon at Versailles or Fontainebleau. If you're a dyed-in-the-wool Disney fan, you'll also want to make a beeline here to see how the park has been molded to suit European tastes (Disney's "Imagineers" call it their most lovingly detailed one, and it simultaneously feels both decidedly foreign and eerily familiar). And if you've never experienced this particular form of Disney showmanship before, you may want to put in an appearance simply to find out what all the fuss is about.

GETTING HERE AND AROUND

Take the RER-A from central Paris (stations at Étoile, Auber, Les Halles, Gare de Lyon, and Nation) to Marne-la-Vallée–Chessy—the gare there is 100 yards from the Disneyland entrance; trains operate every 10–30 minutes, depending on the time of day (40 minutes, €8). High-speed TGV train service links Disneyland to Lille, Lyon, Brussels, and London (via Lille and the Channel Tunnel). Disneyland's hotel complex also offers a shuttle bus service connecting it with the Orly and Charles de Gaulle airports; in each case, the trip takes about 45 minutes and tickets cost €23.

VISITOR INFORMATION Disneyland Paris Reservations Office. ☏ *08–25–30–05–00, 1–60–30–60–53 from outside of France* ⊕ *www.disneylandparis.com.*

Sights

★ Disneyland Paris

AMUSEMENT PARK/CARNIVAL | FAMILY | A slightly downsized version of its United States counterpart, Disneyland Paris is nevertheless a spectacular sight, created with an acute attention to detail. Disneyland Park, as the original theme park is styled, consists of five "lands": Main Street U.S.A., Frontierland, Adventureland, Fantasyland, and Discoveryland. The central theme of each land is relentlessly echoed in every detail, from attractions to restaurant menus to souvenirs. In Main Street U.S.A., tots adore Alice's Curious Labyrinth, Peter Pan's Flight, and especially the whirling Mad Hatter's Teacups, while everyone loves the afternoon parades, with huge floats swarming with all of Disney's most beloved characters—just make sure to stake your place along Main Street in advance for a good spot.

Top attractions at Frontierland are the chilling Phantom Manor, haunted by holographic ghosts, and the thrilling runaway mine train of Big Thunder Mountain, a roller coaster that plunges wildly through floods and avalanches in a setting meant to evoke Utah's Monument Valley. Whiffs of Arabia, Africa, and the Caribbean give Adventureland its exotic cachet; the spicy meals and snacks served here rank among the best food in the park. Don't miss Pirates of the Caribbean, an exciting mise-en-scène populated by lifelike animatronic figures, or Indiana Jones and the Temple of Doom, a rapid-fire ride that recreates some of this hapless hero's most exciting moments.

Fantasyland charms the youngest parkgoers with familiar cartoon characters from such classic Disney films as *Snow White, Pinocchio, Dumbo, Alice in Wonderland,* and *Peter Pan.* The focal point of Fantasyland, and indeed Disneyland Paris, is Le Château de la Belle au Bois Dormant (Sleeping Beauty's Castle), a 140-foot, bubble-gum-pink structure topped with 16 blue- and gold-tipped turrets.

Discoveryland is a high-tech, futuristic eye-popper. Robots on roller skates welcome you on your way to Star Tours,

Louis XIV was so jealous of the splendor of Vaux-le-Vicomte that he promptly went out and built Versailles.

a pitching, plunging, sense-confounding ride based on the *Star Wars* films; and another robot, the staggeringly realistic 9-Eye, hosts a simulated space journey in Le Visionarium.

The older the child, the more they will enjoy Walt Disney Studios, a cinematically driven area next to the Disneyland Park, where many of the newer Disney character–themed rides can be found. It's divided into four "production zones," giving visitors insight into different parts of the production process, including Animation Courtyard, where Disney artists demonstrate the various phases of character animation, and Production Courtyard, where you can go on a behind-the-scenes Studio Tram tour of location sites, movie props, studio interiors, and costumes, ending with a visit to Catastrophe Canyon in the heart of a film shoot.

A brand-new Avengers Campus, focused on the movies and characters in the Marvel Cinematic Universe, is expected to open in summer 2022. ✉ *Marne-la-Vallée* ☎ *08–25–30–05–00* ⊕ *www.disneyland-paris.com* 🎫 *€99, 3-day Passport €185; includes admission to all individual attractions within Disneyland or Walt Disney Studios; tickets for Walt Disney Studios are also valid for admission to Disneyland during last 3 opening hrs of same day.*

Hotels

Newport Bay Club

$$$$ | **HOTEL** | Set at the far end of Disneyland Paris's lake, the nautical-themed Newport Bay Club is the biggest four-star hotel in France—with the largest capacity in Europe—so don't expect intimacy, but hallways are bright and spacious and rooms are quiet and light-filled (especially those with lake views) and some offer balconies. **Pros:** three restaurant choices; nice views from lake-facing terraces; easy walk to the park. **Cons:** expect a lot of other people; no tea and coffee in rooms; very expensive. 💲 *Rooms from:*

€500 ✉ Av. Robert Schuman, Marne-la-Vallée ☎ 08–25–30–05–00 ⊕ www.disneylandparis.com/en-gb/hotels/disneys-newport-bay-club ⇌ 1,093 rooms ⦿ No Meals Ⓜ RER A to Disneyland Paris.

Sequoia Lodge

$$$ | HOTEL | Ranging from super-luxe to just barely affordable, Disneyland Paris has 5,000 rooms throughout several hotels, but your best bet on all counts may be the Sequoia Lodge—a grand re-creation of an American mountain lodge, just a few minutes' walk from the theme park. **Pros:** package deals include admission to theme park; great pools; cozy, secluded feel. **Cons:** prices can flutuate; many rooms do not have lake views; restaurants a bit ho-hum. Ⓢ *Rooms from: €300 ✉ Av. Robert Schuman, Marne-la-Vallée ☎ 08–25–30–05–00 within France, 1–60–30–60–53 from outside of France ⊕ www.disneylandparis.com ⇌ 1,020 rooms ⦿ No Meals.*

 Nightlife

Disney Village

GATHERING PLACES | Nocturnal entertainment outside the park centers on Disney Village, a vast pleasure mall designed by American architect Frank Gehry. Homesick kids who've had enough croque monsieurs will be happy to hear that vintage American-style restaurants—a diner, a deli, and a steak house among them—dominate the food scene here, as well as U.S. brands like Five Guys, McDonald's, and Planet Hollywood. ✉ *Marne-la-Vallée ☎ 01–60–45–71–00 ⊕ www.disneyland-paris.com.*

Château de Vaux-le-Vicomte

48 km (30 miles) south of Disneyland Paris, 5 km (3 miles) northeast of Melun, 56 km (35 miles) southeast of Paris.

A manifesto for French 17th-century splendor, the Château de Vaux-le-Vicomte was built between 1656 and 1661 by finance minister Nicolas Fouquet. The construction program was monstrous. Entire villages were razed; 18,000 workmen were called in; and architect Louis Le Vau, painter Charles Le Brun, and landscape architect André Le Nôtre were recruited at vast expense to prove that Fouquet's taste was as refined as his business acumen. The housewarming party was so lavish, it had star guest Louis XIV, testy at the best of times, spitting jealous curses. He hurled Fouquet in the slammer and set about building Versailles (for which he ransacked Vaux le Vicomte) to prove just who was top banana. Poor Fouquet may be gone, but his home, still privately owned, has survived to astonish and delight centuries of travelers.

GETTING HERE AND AROUND

Take a train from Paris's Gare de Lyon to Melun (25 minutes, €9.30), then a taxi for the 7-km (4-mile) trip to the château (about €20). April through mid-November, a special Châteaubus shuttle runs from the Melun train station (€7 round-trip).

 Sights

★ Château de Vaux-le-Vicomte

CASTLE/PALACE | The high-roof Château de Vaux-le-Vicomte, partially surrounded by a moat, is set well back from the road behind iron railings topped with sculpted heads. A cobbled avenue stretches up to the entrance, and stone steps lead to the vestibule, which seems small given the noble scale of the exterior. Charles

Le Brun's captivating decoration includes the ceiling of the Chambre du Roi (Royal Bedchamber), depicting *Time Bearing Truth Heavenward,* framed by stuccowork by sculptors François Girardon and André Legendre. Along the frieze you can make out small squirrels, the Fouquet family's emblem—squirrels are known as *fouquets* in local dialect. But Le Brun's masterpiece is the ceiling in the **Salon des Muses** (Hall of Muses), a brilliant allegorical composition painted in glowing, sensuous colors that some feel even surpasses his work at Versailles. On the ground floor the impressive **Grand Salon** (Great Hall), with its unusual oval form and 16 caryatid pillars symbolizing the months and seasons, has harmony and style even though the ceiling decoration was never finished.

The state salons are redolent of *le style Louis Quatorze,* thanks to the grand state beds, Mazarin desks, and Baroque marble busts—gathered together by the current owners of the château, the Comte et Comtesse de Vogüé—that replace the original pieces, which Louis XIV trundled off as booty to Versailles. In the basement, where cool, dim rooms were once used to store food and wine and house the château's kitchens, you can find rotating exhibits about the château's past and life-size wax figures illustrating its history, including the notorious 19th-century murder-suicide of two erstwhile owners, the Duc and Duchess de Choiseul-Praslin.

Le Nôtre's carefully restored **gardens**, considered by many to be the designer's masterwork, are at their best when the fountains—which function via gravity, exactly as they did in the 17th century—are turned on (the second and last Saturdays of each month from April through October, 4–6 pm). The popular illuminated evenings, when the château is dazzlingly lighted by 2,000 candles, are held every Saturday from early May to early October. Open for dinner during this event only, the formal Les Charmilles restaurant serves a refined candlelight dinner outdoors, complete with crystal and white linens, on the lovely Parterre de Diane facing the château (reservations essential). There's also a delightful Champagne bar with lounge chairs and music on these special evenings. At other times, L'Ecureuil (a more casual eatery) is a good choice for lunch or snacks, and you are always welcome to bring along a picnic to enjoy in the extensive gardens. ⊠ *Vaux-le-Vicomte* ☎ *01–64–14–41–90* ⊕ *www.vaux-le-vicomte.com* 🖾 *€16.90, candlelight château visits €19.90* ◷ *Closed early Jan.–Mar.*

Barbizon

17 km (11 miles) southwest of Vaux-le-Vicomte, 52 km (33 miles) southeast of Paris.

On the western edge of the 62,000-acre Forest of Fontainebleau, the village of Barbizon retains its time-stained allure despite the intrusion of art galleries, souvenir shops, and busloads of tourists. The group of landscape painters known as the Barbizon School—Camille Corot, Jean-François Millet, Narcisse Diaz de la Peña, and Théodore Rousseau, among others—lived here from the 1830s on. They paved the way for the Impressionists by their willingness to accept nature on its own terms, rather than using it as an idealized base for carefully structured compositions. Sealed to one of the famous sandstone rocks in the forest—which starts, literally, at the far end of the main street—is a bronze medallion by sculptor Henri Chapu, paying homage to Millet and Rousseau. Threading the village is a Painters Trail (marked in yellow), which links main village landmarks to natural splendors such as the rocky waterfall once painted by Corot.

GETTING HERE AND AROUND

Take a Transilien train from Gare de Lyon to Melun (25 minutes, €8.70) or Avon (38 minutes, €8.90); you can pick up a taxi to Barbizon in either town (around €30).

VISITOR INFORMATION Barbizon Tourist Office. ✉ *Pl. Marc Jacquet* ☎ *01–60–66–41–87* 🌐 *www.fontainebleau-tourisme.com.*

Sights

Atelier Jean-François Millet (*Musée Millet*)

HISTORY MUSEUM | Though there are no actual Millet works, the Atelier Jean-François Millet is cluttered with photographs and mementos evoking his career. It was here that the painter produced some of his most renowned pieces, including *The Gleaners.* ✉ *27 Grande rue* ☎ *01–60–66–21–55* 🌐 *www.musee-millet.com* 🎟 *€5* 🕒 *Closed Tues. year-round and Wed. Nov.–Mar.*

Musée Départemental des Peintres de Barbizon (*Barbizon School Museum*)

ART MUSEUM | Corot and company would often repair to the Auberge Ganne after painting to brush up on their social life; the inn is now the Musée de Peintres de Barbizon. Here you can find documents detailing village life in the 19th century, as well as a few original works. The Barbizon artists painted on every available surface, and even now you can see some of their creations on the upstairs walls. Two of the ground-floor rooms have been reconstituted as they were in Ganne's time—note the trompe l'oeil paintings on the buffet doors. There's also a video about the Barbizon School. ✉ *92 Grande rue* ☎ *01–60–66–22–27* 🌐 *www.musee-peintres-barbizon.fr* 🎟 *€6* 🕒 *Closed Tues.*

Restaurants

Le Relais de Barbizon

$$$ | **FRENCH** | French country specialties and fish are served at this rustic restaurant—one of Barbizon's very best—with a big open fire and a large terrace shaded by lime and chestnut trees. The three-course weekday menu is a good value, but wine here is expensive and cannot be ordered by the *pichet* (pitcher). **Known for:** top-quality French classic dishes; local favorite; lovely leafy terrace. [$] *Average main: €26* ✉ *2 av. Charles de Gaulle* ☎ *01–60–66–40–28* 🌐 *www.lerelaisbarbizon.fr* 🕒 *Closed Tues., Wed., part of Aug., and part of Dec.*

★ **L'Ermitage**

$$ | **FRENCH** | Beamed ceilings, tiled floors, and charming accents are just the beginning of a thoroughly enjoyable dining experience at this traditional bistro in the heart of Barbizon. All the beloved French classics—*chevre chaud,* leeks vinaigrette, *entrecôte de boeuf, noix de Saint-Jacques,* steak tartare—are served just as they're meant to be for lunch and dinner. **Known for:** excellent price-to-quality ratio; open seven days a week; lovely glassed-in terrace for all seasons. [$] *Average main: €20* ✉ *51 Grande rue* ☎ *01–64–81–96–96* 🌐 *www.lermitage-saintantoine.com.*

Hotels

Les Pléiades

$$ | **HOTEL** | **FAMILY** | Barbizon's best hotel offers unusually spacious rooms (all tastefully decorated in a contemporary style), a wellness area (with an extensive menu of spa treatments), and an indoor-outdoor pool, making it a good choice for couples or families. **Pros:** very good on-site dining; enormous rooms; smack in the center of town. **Cons:** parts of hotel could use an update; service is spotty; lacks old-world charm. [$] *Rooms* *from: €175* ✉ *21 Grande rue* ☎ *01–60–66–40–25* ⊕ *www.hotel-les-pleiades.com/en* 🛏 *22 rooms* 🍽 *No Meals.*

Courances

11 km (7 miles) west of Barbizon.

Set within one of the most lavish water gardens in Europe, the Château de Courances is a byword for beauty and style.

GETTING HERE AND AROUND
Take the train from Paris's Gare de Lyon to Fontainebleau-Avon, then La Patache shuttle bus to Courances.

Sights

★ Château de Courances
CASTLE/PALACE | Framed by majestic avenues of centuries-old plane trees, Château de Courances's style is Louis Treize, although its finishing touch—a horseshoe staircase (mirroring the one at nearby Fontainebleau)—was an opulent 19th-century statement made by Baron Samuel de Haber, a banker who bought the estate and whose daughter then married into the regal family of the de Behagués. Their descendants, the Marquises de Ganay, have made the house uniquely and famously *chez soi*, letting charming personal taste trump conventional *bon goût,* thanks to a delightful mixture of 19th-century knickknacks and grand antiques. Outside, the vast French Renaissance water gardens create stunning vistas of stonework, grand canals, and rushing cascades. The house can be seen only on a 40-minute tour. ✉ *13 rue de Chateau* ☎ *01–64–98–07–36* ⊕ *www.domainedecourances.com* 🎟 *€12, €9 park only* ⊘ *Park and château closed Nov.–Mar. and weekdays. Château closed July and Aug.*

Hotels

★ Hameau et Régie de Courances
$$$ | B&B/INN | FAMILY | You'll feel positively to the manor born in these three charming cottages and elegant manor house set in several 17-century outbuildings of the Château de Courances in the chateau's splendid gardens. **Pros:** free rein of the château's immense and beautiful gardens; breakfast delivered to your door every morning; bike furnished for touring the countryside and nearby Fôret de Fontainebleau. **Cons:** car essential; two-night minimum (you wouldn't want less); self-service, but there is a housekeeper. 💲 *Rooms from: €265* ✉ *13 rue du Château* ☎ *01–84–83–04–00* ⊕ *www.pierresdhistoire.com/en/adresse/la-regie-de-courances* 🛏 *5 rooms* 🍽 *Free Breakfast.*

Fontainebleau

9 km (6 miles) southeast of Barbizon, 61 km (38 miles) southeast of Paris.

Like Chambord in the Loire Valley or Compiègne to the north, Fontainebleau was a favorite spot for royal hunting parties long before the construction of one of France's grandest residences. Although not as celebrated as Versailles, this palace is almost as spectacular.

GETTING HERE AND AROUND
Fontainebleau—or rather, neighboring Avon—is a 38-minute train ride from Paris's Gare de Lyon (€8.90); from here take one of the frequent shuttle buses to the château, 2 km (1½ miles) away (€4.20 round-trip).

VISITOR INFORMATION Fontainebleau Tourist Office. ✉ *4 bis Pl. de la République* ☎ *01–60–74–99–99* ⊕ *www.fontainebleau-tourisme.com.*

Sights

★ Château de Fontainebleau

CASTLE/PALACE | The glorious Château de Fontainebleau was a pinnacle of elegance and grandeur more than 100 years before the rise of Versailles. The château began life in the 12th century as a royal residence and hunting lodge and still retains vestiges of its medieval past, though much of it dates to the 16th century. Additions made by various royal incumbents—including 30 kings of France—through the next 300 years add up to the fascinating and opulent edifice we see today. Fontainebleau was begun under the flamboyant Renaissance king François I, the French contemporary of England's Henry VIII, who hired Italian artists Il Rosso (a pupil of Michelangelo) and Primaticcio to embellish his château. In fact, they did much more: by introducing the pagan allegories and elegant lines of Mannerism to France, they revolutionized French decorative art. Their virtuoso frescoes and stuccowork can be admired in the Galerie François-Ier (Francis I Gallery) and in the jewel of the interior, the 100-foot-long Salle de Bal (Ballroom), with its luxuriant wood paneling and its gleaming parquet floor that reflects the patterns on the ceiling. Like the château as a whole, the room exudes a sense of elegance and style, but on a more intimate, human scale than at Versailles—this is Renaissance, not Baroque. Napoléon's apartments occupied the first floor. You can see a lock of his hair, his Légion d'Honneur medal, his imperial uniform, the hat he wore on his return from Elba in 1815, and one bed in which he definitely did spend a night (almost every town in France boasts a bed in which the emperor supposedly snoozed). Joséphine's Salon Jaune (Yellow Room) is one of the best examples of the Empire style—the austere neoclassical style promoted by the emperor. There's also a throne room—Napoléon spurned the one at Versailles, a palace he disliked, establishing his imperial seat in the former King's Bedchamber here—and the Queen's Boudoir, also known as the Room of the Six Maries (occupants included ill-fated Marie-Antoinette and Napoléon's second wife, Marie-Louise).

Although Louis XIV's architectural fancy was concentrated on Versailles, he commissioned Mansart to design new pavilions and had André Le Nôtre replant the gardens at Fontainebleau, where he and his court returned faithfully in fall for the hunting season. But it was Napoléon who spent lavishly to make a Versailles, as it were, out of Fontainebleau.

Created during the reign of Napoléon III for the Empress Eugénie, the exquisite Théâtre Impérial was "redisovered" in the early 2000s after being closed up in 1941. Though the theater's sumptuous golden upholstery, lighting, carpets, and gilded boiserie remained surprisingly intact, a restoration was completed in 2020. Visitors can see this jewel on one of the château's marvelous tours. ✉ *Pl. du Général de Gaulle* ☎ *01–60–71–50–70* 🌐 *www.chateaudefontainebleau.fr* 🎫 *Napoléon's Apartments and Museum €12; gardens free* 🕒 *Closed Tues.*

Restaurants

★ Frédéric Cassel

$ | **MODERN FRENCH** | **FAMILY** | A mandatory stop for pastry and chocolate lovers alike, this master pâtissier excels in classic French confections with all the bells and whistles. Light as air and made with the best ingredients, Cassel's award-winning creations are as beautiful as they are scrumptious. **Known for:** classic French tea salon; chocolates, caramels, and other French specialty sweets that make great gifts; to-die-for mille-feuille. [$] *Average main: €9* ✉ *21 rue des Sablons* ☎ *01–60–71–00–64* 🌐 *www.frederic-cassel.com* 🕒 *Closed Mon. No dinner.*

L'Axel

$$$$ | **FRENCH** | Young Japanese chef Kunihisa Goto has finally brought Fontainebleau's dining scene a Michelin star. The sleek contemporary dining room is the perfect setting for his refined cuisine that draws from the natural bounty of the lush Fontainebleau region, both wild and cultivated. **Known for:** stellar wine list; Japanese-inflected dishes; seasonal cuisine. $ *Average main: €55 ⊠ 43 rue de France* ☎ *01-64-22-01-57* ⊕ *laxel-restaurant.com* ⊘ *Closed Mon. and Tues. No lunch Wed.*

Les Prémices

$$$$ | **MODERN FRENCH** | Adjoining the property of the stately 17th-century Château de Bourron, in the heart of the Forest of Fontainebleau, this lovely restaurant is well worth the short trip out of town. Bright and airy, with an open terrace in warm weather, the elegant dining room shows meticulous attention to detail—from the crisp table linens to the stylish flower arrangements—all the better to highlight chef Dominique Maès's sophisticated French fare. **Known for:** romantic atmosphere; one of the town's few gastronomic tables; excellent location. $ *Average main: €38 ⊠ 12 bis rue Blaise de Montesquiou, 8 km (5 miles) south of Fontainebleau via D607, Bourron-Marlotte* ☎ *01-64-78-33-00* ⊕ *www.restaurant-les-premices.com* ⊘ *Closed Mon., Tues., and late Dec.–early Jan. No dinner Sun.*

🛏 Hotels

Aigle Noir

$$$ | **HOTEL** | This may be Fontainebleau's costliest hotel, but it does promise old-world elegance, graceful service, and oodles of atmosphere. **Pros:** period ambience; emphasis on service; great location opposite château. **Cons:** some rooms could use a spruce-up; breakfast somewhat lackluster; no restaurant. $ *Rooms from: €280 ⊠ 27 pl. Napoléon Bonaparte* ☎ *01-60-74-60-00* ⊕ *www.*

aiglenoirhotel.com/en ⇨ *53 rooms* ⊚| *No Meals.*

★ Hôtel de Londres

$$ | **HOTEL** | Established in 1850, the superbly located Londres has been run with pride by the same family for three generations, and guests are treated to a warm welcome by owners who go out of their way to make your stay pleasant. **Pros:** excellent value; two-minute walk to the Fontainebleau 18-hole golf course; château views from some rooms. **Cons:** breakfast not included in price; limited parking; not all rooms have air-conditioning. $ *Rooms from: €190 ⊠ 1 pl. du Général de Gaulle* ☎ *01-64-22-20-21* ⊕ *www.hoteldelondres.com* ⊘ *Closed 1 wk in Aug. and Christmas–early Jan.* ⇨ *16 rooms* ⊚| *No Meals.*

La Demeure du Parc

$$ | **HOTEL** | This beautiful design hotel and gourmet restaurant adds a welcome dose of chic to the Fontainebleau lodging and dining scene. **Pros:** quality in-hotel dining and bar; set in the center of town close to château and all amenities; beautiful contemporary decor. **Cons:** restaurant closed three nights at dinnertime; service is still working out kinks; some rooms are very small. $ *Rooms from: €210 ⊠ 36 rue Paul Séramy* ☎ *01-60-70-20-00* ⊕ *www.lademeureduparc.fr* ⇨ *27 rooms* ⊚| *No Meals.*

🏃 Activities

Club Alpin Français

BIKING | The Forest of Fontainebleau is laced with hiking trails; the *Guide des Sentiers* (trail guide), available at the tourist office, has details. The forest is also famed for its quirky rock formations, where many a novice alpinist first caught the climbing bug; for more information, contact the Club Alpin Français. Bikes can be rented at La Petite Reine (⊠ *14 rue de la Paroisse 01-60-74-57-57*). ⊠ *6 rue du Mont Ussy* ☎ *06-10-46-71-61* ⊕ *www.ffcam.fr.*

Index

Photo Credits

Front Cover: Jerome Labouyrie/ Alamy Stock Photo [Description: Paris, France: A back alley in Paris showcasing the architecture of the buildings with the Eiffel Tower in the background]. **Back cover, from left to right:** Britus/iStockphoto, Luciano Mortula - LGM/ Shutterstock, Viviane Teles/ vivianeteles.com. **Spine:** ProductionPerig/Dreamstime. **Interior, from left to right:** Anyaivanova/iStockphoto (1). KavalenkavaVolha/iStockphoto (2-3). Heracles Kritikos/ Shutterstock (5). **Chapter 1: Experience Paris:** Bennymarty/iStockphoto (6-7). Aliaksandrkazlou/Dreamstime (8-9). Danbreckwoldt/Dreamstime (9). Johnjqueenan/Dreamstime (9). Jacky D/shutterstock (10). Freephoton/ Dreamstime (10). Gianni triggiani/Shutterstock (10). Kiev.Victor/Shutterstock (10). Kovalenkov Petr/Dreamstime (11). Nightman1965/Shutterstock (11). DavidWebb/Shutterstock (12). Stephannie Kate Mozawa/Dreamstime (12). Scott Norsworthy/Shutterstock (12). Maxal Tamor/ Shutterstock (12). Minacarson/Dreamstime (13). Takashi Images/Shutterstock (13). Jakub Buza/Shutterstock (13). EQRoy/Shutterstock (13). Davidmartyn/Dreamstime (14). Manamana/Shutterstock (14). Sarah Sergent/Paris Tourist Office (15). TorriPhoto/istockphoto (20). Margouillatphotos/istockphoto (21). ChamilleWhite/istockphoto (22). Laulhère (23). Culturespaces / Sophie Lloyd (24). Paris Tourist Office - Photographer : Fabian Charaffi - Architect : Renzo Piano and Richard Roger (24). Paris Tourist Office- Photographer: Marc Bertrand (24). Musée du Louvre / Stéphane Olivier (25). Paris Tourist Office- Photographer: Sarah Sergent (25). P.Lemaitre/Centre des monuments nationaux (26). DanielThierry/ ParisTouristOffice (26). Centre des monuments nationaux (26). Daniel Vorndran CC-BY-SA (2014) (27). Saint Germain-des-Prés (27). Paris Tourist Office - Amelie Dupont (28). Paris Tourist Office- Photographer: Sarah Sergent (28). Paris Tourist Office- Photographer: Marc Bertrand (28). Paris Tourist Office- Photographer: Sarah Sergent (28). Sénat/Sonia Kerlidou (29). Paris Tourist Office- Photographer: Marc Bertrand (29). Manuel Cohen (29). Paris Tourist Office- Photographer: Marc Bertrand (29). Eric Bergoend/École de CuisineAlain Ducasse (30). Mbzt (31). 59Rivoli (32). Sophie Boegly Musée d'Orsay (33). **Chapter 3: Île de la Cité and Île St-Louis:** Luciano Mortula/iStockphoto (69). Nicolas Herrbach/iStockphoto (75). Manel Subirats/iStockphoto (76). **Chapter 4: Around the Eiffel Tower:** John Kellerman/ Alamy (81). Directphoto.org / Alamy (85). Tkachuk/Shutterstock (91). **Chapter 5: The Champs-Élysées:** Art Kowalsky / Alamy (103). Chrisdorney/ Dreamstime (111). UlyssePixel/Dreamstime (113). **Chapter 6: Around the Louvre:** Blickwinkel / Alamy (129). Mistervlad/Dreamstime (137). Fischer/Bilderberg (140-141). Public Domain (141). Sisterspro/Dreamstime (142). Nikmd/Dreamstime (143). Public Domain (143). Pseudolongino/Shutterstock (143). Interfoto Pressebildagentur / Alamy (143). PCL / Alamy (144). The Bridgeman Art Library (145). Jjkroese/ Dreamstime (145). Legge / Alamy (145). Musee Du Louvre (145). Heracles Kritikos/Shutterstock(146). Public Domain (147). Public Domain (147). Sforzza1/ Dreamstime(147). Public Domain (147). **Chapter 7: Les Grands Boulevards:** Kevin George / Alamy (169). Botond Horvath/ Shutterstock (175). Gilmanshin/Shutterstock (187). **Chapter 8: Montmartre:** Velishchuk/iStockphoto (197). Tatiana Diuvbanova/Shutterstock (200). Horizon Images/Motion / Alamy Stock Photo (207). Rfx/SHutterstock (210). **Chapter 9: The Marais:** PicsFactory/iStockphoto (213). Claude Valette/Flickr, [CC BY-ND 2.0] (223). Look / Alamy Stock Photo (225). **Chapter 10: Eastern Paris:** LENS-68/Shutterstock (243). Emile lombard/Flickr, [CC BY-ND 2.0] (256). Antoine2k/Dreamstime (263). **Chapter 11: The Latin Quarter:** Derek Croucher / Alamy (277). Aschaf/Flickr (281). **Chapter 12: St-Germain-des-Prés:** Robert Harding Picture Library Ltd / Alamy (293). Ekaterinabelova/Dreamstime (296). Vanbeets/ Dreamstime (301). **Chapter 13: Montparnasse:** Idealink Photography / Alamy Stock Photo (319). Jens_Lambert_Photography/iStockphoto (322). **Chapter 14: Western Paris:** Iwan Baan for Fondation Louis Vuitton ©Iwan Baan 2014 ©Gehry partners LLP (331). Georgios Alexandris/ iStockphoto (334). **Chapter 15: Side Trips from Paris:** Alvydas Kucas/Shutterstock (341). Mister_Knight/ Shutterstock (352-353). Elias H. Debbas II/Shutterstock (354). Jason Cosburn/Shutterstock (354). Public Domain (354). Michael Booth / Alamy (354). Infomods/ Dreamstime (354). Public Domain (355). Vincentho/Dreamstime (355). Walter_g/Shutterstock (355). Michel mory/iStockphoto (356). Mike Booth / Alamy (356). JByard/ iStockphoto (356). Gaspardwalterphoto/Dreamstime (357). Public Domain (358). Jason Cosburn/ Shutterstock (358). Laszlo Konya (358). Guillohmz/Dreamstime (359). Mistervlad/Shutterstock (359). Public Domain (359). Jose Ignacio Soto/ Shutterstock (365). ShutterbugBill, Fodors.com member (369). Bobyfume/wikipedia.org (381). Dan Breckwoldt/Shutterstock (383). **About Our Writers:** All photos are courtesy of the writers.

*Every effort has been made to trace the copyright holders, and we apologize in advance for any accidental errors. We would be happy to apply the corrections in the following edition of this publication.

Fodor's PARIS 2023

Publisher: Stephen Horowitz, *General Manager*

Editorial: Douglas Stallings, *Editorial Director;* Jill Fergus, Amanda Sadlowski, *Senior Editors;* Kayla Becker, Brian Eschrich, Alexis Kelly, *Editors;* Angelique Kennedy-Chavannes, *Assistant Editor*

Design: Tina Malaney, *Director of Design and Production;* Jessica Gonzalez, *Graphic Designer;* Erin Caceres, *Graphic Design Associate*

Production: Jennifer DePrima, *Editorial Production Manager;* Elyse Rozelle, *Senior Production Editor;* Monica White, *Production Editor*

Maps: Rebecca Baer, *Senior Map Editor;* Mark Stroud, Henry Colomb (Moon Street Cartography), David Lindroth, *Cartographers*

Photography: Viviane Teles, *Senior Photo Editor;* Namrata Aggarwal, Neha Gupta, Payal Gupta, Ashok Kumar, *Photo Editors;* Eddie Aldrete, *Photo Production Intern;* Kadeem McPherson, *Photo Production Associate Intern*

Business and Operations: Chuck Hoover, *Chief Marketing Officer;* Robert Ames, *Group General Manager;* Devin Duckworth, *Director of Print Publishing*

Public Relations and Marketing: Joe Ewaskiw, *Senior Director of Communications and Public Relations*

Fodors.com: Jeremy Tarr, *Editorial Director;* Rachael Levitt, *Managing Editor*

Technology: Jon Atkinson, *Director of Technology;* Rudresh Teotia, *Lead Developer*

Writers: Nancy Heslin, Jennifer Ladonne, Emily Monaco, Virginia Power Jestin, Jack Vermee

Editors: Amanda Sadlowski, Andrew Collins

Production Editor: Jennifer DePrima

36th Edition

ISBN 978-1-64097-533-0

ISSN 0149-1288

All details in this book are based on information supplied to us at press time. Always confirm information when it matters, especially if you're making a detour to visit a specific place. Fodor's expressly disclaims any liability, loss, or risk, personal or otherwise, that is incurred as a consequence of the use of any of the contents of this book.

SPECIAL SALES
This book is available at special discounts for bulk purchases for sales promotions or premiums. For more information, e-mail SpecialMarkets@fodors.com.

PRINTED IN CANADA

10 9 8 7 6 5 4 3 2 1

About Our Writers

 Since swapping Canada for the Côte d'Azur in 2001, **Nancy Heslin** is a go-to authority in the region, whether it's taking the TGV with Tom Cruise to Marseille, dining with Prince Albert in Monaco, or sipping Champagne with Paris Hilton in St-Tropez. The Editor-in-Chief of *Forbes Monaco* and *Good News, Monaco*, Nancy became a French citizen in 2010. She works her baguette butt off swimming and running along the French Riviera and writing for ÖTILLÖ Swimrun Life. She updated the Experience and Travel Smart chapters for this edition.

 Emily Monaco is an American writer based in Paris. Her work has appeared in *Food & Wine*, *Saveur*, the BBC, Atlas Obscura, and more. She updated the Around the Louvre chapter.

 When writer/editor **Jennifer Ladonne** decided it was time to leave her longtime home of Manhattan, there was only one place to go: Paris. Her insatiable curiosity—which earned her a reputation in New York for knowing just the right place to go for just the right anything—has found the perfect home in the inexhaustible streets of Paris. An avid cook and wine lover, she's a frequent contributor on food, culture, and travel and a monthly columnist for the magazine *France Today*. Whether you're looking for the best neighborhood bistros or the perfect little black dress, she's the person to ask, as we did for our Les Grands Boulevards, The Marais, Eastern Paris, Around the Eiffel Tower, Champs-Élysées, and Side Trips From Paris chapters.

 A lifelong urban explorer, journalist and photo editor **Virginia Power Jestin** has been strolling the streets of Paris for over 25 years. She has written and reported on a variety of subjects—culture, politics, sports, social issues—for *Newsweek*, *Paris* magazine, and other publications. Writing for Fodor's has brought her back to doing what she does best: wandering, discovering, and enjoying what Paris has to offer. This edition, she updated the Montparnasse and St-Germain-des-Prés chapters.

 Jack Vermee is a Canadian university lecturer, film critic, screenwriter, film festival programmer, and freelance writer/editor who happily exchanged nature for culture by moving from Vancouver to Paris several years ago. Starting in the pre-video days of the early 1980s, when he first visited the city to watch classic films at the old Cinémathèque Française, he has carried on a shameless love affair with *la ville-lumière* and its innumerable charms. He suspects the love affair will never run its course—with 6,100 city streets to explore and new adventures just around the next corner, how could it? Jack brought his knowledge to the following chapters: Ile St-Louis and Ile de la Cité, Montmartre, the Latin Quarter, and Western Paris. You can reach him at *jvermee@gmail.com*.

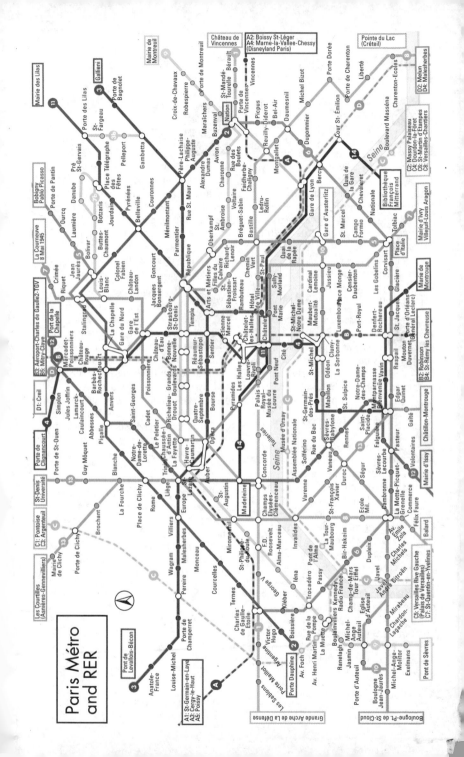

Paris Métro and RER